Vision, Brain, and Cooperative Computation

Computational Models of Cognition and Perception

Editors

Jerome A. Feldman
Patrick J. Hayes
David E. Rumelhart

Parallel Distributed Processing: Explorations in the Microstructure of Cognition. Volume 1: Foundation, by David E. Rumelhart, James L. McClelland, and the PDP Research Group

Parallel Distributed Processing: Explorations in the Microstructure of Cognition. Volume 2: Psychological and Biological Models, by James L. McClelland, David E. Rumelhart, and the PDP Research Group

Neurophilosophy: Toward a Unified Science of the Mind-Brain, by Patricia Smith Churchland

Qualitative Reasoning about Physical Systems, edited by Daniel G. Bobrow

Induction: Processes of Inference, Learning, and Memory, by John H. Holland, Keith J. Holyoak, Richard E. Nisbett, and Paul R. Thagard

Production System Models of Learning and Development, edited by David Klahr, Pat Langley, and Robert T. Neches

Minimal Rationality, by Christopher Cherniak

Vision, Brain, and Cooperative Computation, edited by Michael A. Arbib and Allen R. Hanson

Vision, Brain, and Cooperative Computation

edited by
Michael A. Arbib and
Allen R. Hanson

A Bradford Book
The MIT Press
Cambridge, Massachusetts
London, England

Third printing, 1988

© 1987 by The Massachusetts Institute of Technology

This book was set in Palatino by Asco Trade Typesetting Ltd., Hong Kong, and printed
and bound by Halliday Lithograph in the United States of America.

Library of Congress Cataloging-in-Publication Data

Vision, brain, and cooperative computation.

  (Computational models of cognition and perception)
  Based in part on papers presented at the Vision, Brain, and Cooperative Computation
Workshop, held at the University of Massachusetts at Amherst in May 1983 and
supported in part by the Alfred P. Sloan Foundation and the National Institutes of Health.
  "A Bradford book."
  Includes index.
  1. Vision—Congresses.   2. Computer vision—Congresses.   3. Artificial intelligence
—Congresses.   4. Psychophysics—Congresses.   I. Arbib, Michael A.   II. Hanson,
Allen R., 1942–.   III. Vision, Brain, and Cooperative Computation Workshop (1983:
University of Massachusetts at Amherst)   IV. Alfred P. Sloan Foundation.   V. National
Institutes of Health (U.S.)   VI. Series.
  [DNLM: 1. Artificial Intelligence.   2. Automation.   3. Psychophysics.   4. Visual
Perception—physiology. WW 105 V831]
  QP474.V46   1987   612'.84   86-19994
  ISBN 0-262-01094-1

Contents

III Machine Vision and Robotics

IV Connectionism and Cooperative Computation

Preface

For two decades, much of artificial intelligence was dominated by the serial computer and many problem-solving techniques were structured as if they were inherently serial. However, the field of character recognition, and the field of machine vision, which arose from it, have always been confronted with the fact that the primary input is structured as a vast array representing the stimulus. The analysis of the data in this array is a task of enormous computational complexity. Consequently, many algorithms in machine vision have been logically structured, if not always implemented, in terms of parallel computation. Perhaps for this reason, it is in the field of vision that the interchange between workers in artificial intelligence and those studying the brain has been most fruitful.

The aim of this volume is to look at the current state of vision research, stressing contributions from neurophysiology, psychophysics, and computer science. Through it all runs the theme of how best to structure the computations for visual systems. We have adopted the term *cooperative computation* to designate two different styles of computation. In low-level vision, the cooperation is in the form of vast arrays of intercommunicating identical processes carrying out such tasks as depth mapping, computing the optic flow, recovering local surface structure, and segmenting the image. At the higher level, processes can no longer be arranged retinotopically (in spatial arrays in correspondence with the two dimensions of the retina or input image) but instead exist in some logical space built on symbolic and relational structures relating to the semantic content of the stimulus. Here the cooperation between knowledge sources, or schemas, is exploited to bring a diversity of knowledge to bear on the interpretation of the various portions of an image, both in terms of the context they provide for each other and in terms of the evolving context of the activity of the organism or machine.

This book is an outgrowth of the Vision, Brain, and Cooperative Computation Workshop organized by the two editors and held at the University of Massachusetts at Amherst in May 1983. The workshop, which attracted thirty scientists, was supported in part by the Alfred P. Sloan Foundation and the National Institutes of Health. A number of the papers published in this volume were prepared for the workshop; others were commissioned in order to round out the volume's coverage of the cooperative-computation approach to vision. The first drafts were reviewed by the editors in light of the discussion that took place at the workshop and in view of the desirability of making them suitable for an interdisciplinary audience.

The overview introduces the themes developed in the subsequent chapters. Part I stresses data on vision that can be related to brain structures, treats both theoretical and experimental approaches to the study of the brain, and gives a first taste of the "many visual systems"—the brain's specialized subsystems for a number of different visual tasks (including motion mapping, depth perception, the control of eye movement, and the control of other forms of behavior). Part II is an introduction to the way in which the structure of the human visual system can be probed by the techniques of psychophysics. Of particular interest here is the way in which specific computational theories are playing an increasingly important role in shaping the design of psychophysical experiments, and the results of these experiments are leading to the refinement of computational models which were at first little more than machine-vision systems mapped arbitrarily onto the human brain in a superficial way. However, both for the worker in artificial intelligence and for the student of animal or human vision concerned with finding fresh ideas, it is important that work also progress on machine-vision systems not directly related to current hypotheses on the structure of the mind/brain. In part III, papers on the problems involved in interpreting a static scene are complemented by consideration of the challenges for knowledge interpretation and representation posed by dynamic visual input. This leads naturally to a consideration of robotics, and here we temporarily expand our focus on vision by looking at touch as another perceptual modality that is useful for real-time robot control. Finally, part IV introduces a very lively area of AI theory in which the brain provides concepts for distributed computation but the resultant models are thought of as parallel networks to be implemented in machine form rather than as models to be tested against the actual structure of animal or human brains. Much of the work being done in this area goes under the label of *connectionism*. The contributions presented here vary in their faithfulness to the data of neuroscience. Some of the models seem in danger of a combinatorial explosion, but they yield many new insights into what parallelism can achieve, as well as introducing the theme of how learning may play a role in the function and design of visual systems.

We thank our colleagues in the Department of Computer and Information Science at the University of Massachusetts at Amherst who have cooperatively computed with us in developing a group in which work in brain mechanisms of vision, in computer vision, and in robotics can proceed in a spirit of mutual enlightenment. We also thank the chapter authors; without their original contributions, their responsiveness, and their good will this volume would not have been possible. Finally, we thank Judy Rose, Nancy Stewart, and Laurie Waskiewicz for their help with the manuscript, and Darlene Friedman for her excellent editorial assistance.

Vision, Brain, and Cooperative Computation

Vision, Brain, and Cooperative Computation: An Overview

Michael A. Arbib and Allen R. Hanson

Vision in Perspective

The Tasks of Vision for Brains and Machines

The task of vision is to extract useful information from light, but this definition would include as simple a mechanism as the use of a photoelectric cell to trigger the opening of a door when the light falling upon it is momentarily interrupted. The subject of this volume is a more structured problem: Given a pattern of light falling upon a surface (the retina of an animal, or a video camera attached to a machine), infer relevant properties of the objects in the environment whose reflectances helped create that pattern.

Some authors have suggested that the job of the visual system is to provide a veridical representation of the external world; visual perception is then to invert the imaging process that transforms the pattern of light reflected off objects in the world into the pattern of ganglion-cell activation that is transmitted to the brain. However, the viewpoint developed here is that the job of the visual system is not to provide the animal with a representation of the world *in abstracto* but to provide the animal with the information it needs to interact with the world about it.

One can identify in the brains of various creatures structures specialized for the detection of prey and predators in the environment, as well as more generalized processes for extracting information about the structure of the world in which a particular animal lives. The spatial locations of objects, and the characteristics relevant to interaction with them, must be recognized and represented in the animal's brain in such forms that they can be used in the planning of actions. These representations must be responsive to the animal's goals and the context in which the animal finds itself.

As we turn to machine vision, we find an array of systems built for special purposes, ranging from character recognition and chromosome classification to the extraction of useful information about natural resources from satellite images of the earth, the recognition of the objects in a natural scene, and the extraction of information relevant to the movement of a robot. In artificial-intelligence terms, the tasks of a brain or the controller of a robot might be separated into three phases: the perceptual phase, which forms an abstract representation of the external environment; the formation of a plan that will guide the activity of the organism; and the execution of that plan, which will result in actions in the environment. Now, it is clear that in much of visually guided behavior there is no conscious planning, and it may be debatable to what extent it would be possible or appropriate to seek specific subsystems or processes that can be labeled as planning. The point we wish to make here is that, whether or not one sees the three phases of perception, planning, and action as separable, one must resist the temptation to think of them as executed in strict temporal order. Rather, the activity of an animal is to be seen as embedded within an action-perception cycle: The animal perceives to gain the knowledge it needs to act (in AI terms, it updates a representation to update a plan), and that representation of its world includes a structure of anticipations.

As we seek to draw insights into the design of visual systems from neural studies, we must continually return to these questions: What is vision for? What is it about the behavioral repertoire of an animal, or the uses to which a machine-vision system is to be put, that will place particular demands on the preprocessing of the visual system and on the high-level representations? To what extent will the dynamic performance of the overall system require continual updating of the visual representations? How is this visual updating to be integrated with planning and action? To what extent do the answers to these questions feed back to modify every aspect of the visual system?

Low-Level and High-Level Vision

In the 1950s and the 1960s, neurophysiologists began to chart the way in which the retinas of various animals could enhance the contrast of an image and extract certain features useful for the particular animal. (See Barlow 1953; Lettvin et al. 1959; Hubel and Wiesel 1962.) Further work has led to a greater understanding of the pathways involved in visuo-motor coordination, as in providing the information that will enable an animal to reach toward a moving target (Jeannerod and Biguer 1982) or to move its eyes so as to keep a moving object constantly in view (Robinson 1976, 1981).

Other research has brought a greater understanding of the "many visual systems" (that is, the parceling of the brain into many different regions, which extract diverse parameters of vision, such as shape, motion, and depth). There is an overall concern with "what" as well as "where," and a concern with the way in which eye and head movements are taken into account as visual data are integrated into a framework for the control of action. In many mammals, and especially in humans, the retina is not uniform; there is a fovea, which provides particularly detailed information about the visual scene. Thus, it is of great interest how the successive fixations are integrated, and how the information acquired with the eyes in one position is remapped as the eyes move (Didday and Arbib 1975). There are also other sensory modalities, such as audition and touch, that can provide an organism or a machine with information about its world; thus, sensory integration across modalities (Arbib et al. 1984) is an important research issue. As a brief introduction to this problem, two of the papers in this volume are devoted of the integration of vision and touch, (in one case in human hand movements, in the other case for a robot conducting an assembly task).

As one examines the diversity of visual systems in the biological world, one is struck by both the divergence and the convergence of visual systems. The vast majority of organisms with well-developed visual systems have either the multifaceted compound eye typical of the insects or the simple eye of the kind possessed by man. Here the terms *simplicity* and *complexity* have nothing to do with the information-processing capability of the visual system; they simply distinguish the simple eye in which a single lens focuses the light for a large population of retinal cells from the compound eye composed of many components (ommatidia), each with its own lens and receptive cells. This volume focuses almost exclusively on vertebrate visual systems based on the simple eye. Relevant work on invertebrate visual systems includes work on lateral inhibition by Hartline (1949), Ratliff (1969), and Knight (1973), work on motion detectors in the fly visual system by Riechardt and Poggio (1981), and work on visually guided navigation in the hover fly by Collett and Land (1978).

As is well known, the basic plan of the vertebrate retina is that of layers of cells. Furthest from the lens and from the brain are the receptors: the rods and the cones. Layered on top of the receptors are various intermediate cells: the horizontal cells, the bipolar cells, and the amacrine cells; these provide the input to the ganglion cells of the retina, whose fibers cross the surface of the retina to meet in the blind spot and there traverse the optic nerve back to the brain. As we shall discuss in more detail below, the ganglion cells are of diverse kinds, and their output feeds many different areas of the brain. Many, but by no means all, of these visual regions of the brain share with the retina the fact that they may be analyzed in terms of layers of interacting neurons. For each such cell, neurophysiologists determine what patterns of visual stimulation in the external world correlate with increased firing of the neuron. The pattern of activity that best activates such a visual neuron is called its *trigger feature* (a somewhat controversial notion). The area of the visual field in which this pattern best elicits the neural response is called the *receptive field* of the neuron.

It has been found that in the retina (not surprisingly), in the lateral geniculate nucleus (the mammalian thalamic "relay" en route to the visual cortex), in areas 17, 18, and 19 of visual cortex, and in the mid-brain visual system (the superior colliculus) there are layers of cells for which a relatively precise ascription of both trigger feature and receptive field can be made, although the receptive fields in the superior colliculus may subtend $20°$ of visual angle or even more. Nearby cells may have quite distinctive trigger features and yet have broadly overlapping receptive fields. The two-dimensional map of the retina projects in a continuous fashion, though not preserving metric relationships, onto the neural layers. Thus, such projections (connectivity patterns) are said to be *retinotopic* (from the Greek word *topos*, for place). However, a transition from retinotopy to abstract representation has been observed. There are regions, such as inferotemporal cortex, in which there seem to be mechanisms for pattern recognition that are not tied to the locus in visual space of the object being recognized. It is difficult to determine the trigger features for cells in these areas, and they do not seem to have specific receptive fields.

The distinction between the retinotopic representations in certain parts of the brain and the more abstract representations that seem to be associated with object recognition is reflected in the distinction between low-level and high-level machine vision. The visual system must go from a representation in terms of arrays of light intensity to a representation that is more symbolic in character, perhaps representing the positions of objects together with information about each object's relevant action. An important question, then, is: Where in this process must the system apply specific *a priori* knowledge about the type of objects it can recognize? It is becoming accepted wisdom that processing can be done to recode the information prior to the application of this knowledge; thus, we refer to *low-level vision* as comprising these prior processes, reserving the term *high-level vision* to denote the "knowledge-intensive processes." For example, one task for low-level vision is segmentation, the process of extracting information about areas of the image (called *regions* or *segments*) that are visually distinct from one another and are each continuous in some feature, such as color, motion, or depth. Regions, in turn, may be considered as candidates for parts of the distinguishable surfaces of objects in the environment. Another process of low-level vision is the formation of a depth map combining information from two eyes to provide information about distance in each spatial direction. Yet further low-level representations can be based on the information obtained over a period of time from one eye or through a sequence of frames input to a machine. It was Gibson (1955, 1966, 1977) who observed that the resultant pattern of "optic flow"— the movement of features across the retina from moment to moment— contained valuable information that could be used to guide navigation through the environment without prior recognition of objects. Thus, it appears that the biologically useful process of navigation, at least, can be accomplished with visual information extracted by low-level processes without involving any high-level vision in the sense of object recognition.

All these different representations delivered by low-level processes— providing the positions of surfaces in the environment, their depths, and how they are moving—can be fed into high-level processes that use knowledge of the world to postulate what objects there could be that have surfaces positioned, shaped, or moving in the observed ways. The problem is complicated by the fact that near objects project onto the retina on a larger scale than far objects, by the fact that objects can be moving in various directions, and by the fact that objects can partially occlude one another. Thus, a visual system working in complex environments must be able to solve the problems of perspective, noise, and occlusion. Once a preliminary interpretation of an image has been made, the vision system then has context and expectations, which can be used to guide further processing.

Styles of Computation

The comparative study of vision in brains and machines requires a rethinking of the concepts of computation. Since the mid 1940s, computer science has been dominated by the von Neumann concept of serial computation, in which programs are executed one instruction at a time in a fetch-and-execute cycle. By contrast, workers in machine vision have always been aware of the highly parallel nature of the computations underlying low-level processes. Similarly, in the brain, billions of components are active at the same time, passing messages to one another to modify their processing. Only now, with the techniques of very-large-scale integration (VLSI) and the increasing practice of distributing computation over networks containing many separate computers, is the technology of computers beginning to catch up with the concepts of parallel and distributed processing in both biological and machine visual systems.

Recalling the distinction between low-level vision and high-level vision, one can see the low-level parts of the visual system as composed of vast arrays in each of which local processors carry out the same operations in parallel. The processes of segmentation, stereopsis, and optic flow can each be carried out by algorithms involving the repetition of the same local process all over an image, and can thus be characterized as parallel computation. The resulting low-level representations of the visual scene are then provided to a network of more specialized processors, which are responsible for the more abstract, or high-level, tasks of vision. These processors must also be organized to allow messages to be passed back and forth to one another. Specialized *schemas* (concurrently activatable programs) for recognizing different objects or controlling various tasks will be looking at the distinctive shapes or other characteristics of different portions of the image as represented in the low-level data, and will have to pass messages to one another to settle on a coherent interpretation. In this case, we prefer to speak of distributed rather than parallel computation. We use *cooperative computation* as an umbrella term for both types of process for which communication between multiple processes is required. For the highly parallel processes, the use of the term *cooperative* is based on the analogy of the interactions within an array of neurons to the way in which the atomic magnets of a ferromagnet interact locally to organize themselves into a global state of magnetization. This cooperative analogy was introduced into brain theory by Cragg and Temperley (1954) and was specifically introduced into the study of vision by Julesz (1971), who used an analogy to an array of magnets coupled by springs to provide a possible explanation of depth-perception phenomena he had studied. In talk about high-level vision or about problem-solving processes in which a number of quite distinct schemas or computational processes interact to form a global interpretation, the use of the term *cooperative computation* is based on a social or organizational analogy to the way in which humans in a groups may cooperate to produce a global solution to a problem.

Having settled on what we shall call *computation*—the cooperative activity of arrays of identical processes, and the distributed cooperation of somewhat complex high-level processes—we can now note some of the other issues in computing for vision. An important question is: To what extent is visual processing "bottom-up" or "data-driven," and to what extent is it "top-down" or "knowledge-driven"? In the first case, one imagines that the low-level processes proceed to completion without any input from high-level processes, and that this is followed by successively higher levels of increasing abstraction. Moreover, within the low-level processes, one might posit that there is a strict hierarchy. For example, in their early studies of cat and monkey cortices, Hubel and Wiesel (1962, 1977) postulated that visual information in the brain is processed hierarchically from the retina to the lateral geniculate nucleus to area 17, then to area 18, then to area 19, and then to the so-called association areas. However, subsequent work has shown that this is not the case. Stone et al. (1979) have shown that the responses in areas 18 and 19 to visual stimulation are so fast that they must depend on direct pathways from the lateral geniculate nucleus rather than pathways routed through area 17, and other workers (e.g. Singer [1980]) have observed that there is a massive pathway from the visual cortex descending to the lateral geniculate nucleus.

There have been similar developments in machine vision. Marr (1978, 1982) used "the primal sketch" as his term for the representation of the results of "very low-level" processing, primarily the intensity changes and their geometrical organization in the image. He postulated that the primal sketch then feeds the depth-perception processes that form what he called "the $2\frac{1}{2}$D sketch," which makes explicit the orientation and the rough depth of the visible surfaces in the original scene; that this drives object-recognition processes which use the bas-relief information and simple surface and volumetric primitives (generalized cylinders) to build up three-dimensional shapes and their spatial distributions (Marr and Nishihara 1978); and that these shapes and distributions are used to access three-dimensional models of objects, resulting in an interpretation of the original scene. It is clear that this account of object recognition is at best hypothetical, and that it is one among many. What is more to the point here is that depth information is only one of many important outputs from low-level vision, and that the acquisition of low-level information can be under high-level control. This is dramatically demonstrated in human behavior by the dependence of eye movements on the spatial structure of the scene being viewed. However, the fact remains that most visual systems have a bottom-up hierarchical architecture meant to deliver a crisp representation of a scene when there is no noise or occlusion, while return pathways are there to incorporate context and to call upon further low-level processing when the ongoing process of interpretation runs into difficulty. It is also clear that the terms *low-level* and *high-level*, which imply a two-part decoupled strategy related to the data organization (iconic vs. symbolic), are somewhat misleading. Most researchers now tentatively agree that an interpretation is built up in stages through many levels of increasingly more abstract representations; in this view, the division into low-level and high-level processes is murky indeed.

Architectures for Machine Vision

This subsection is devoted to showing how the computational resources for low-level machine vision can be obtained by exploiting the two-dimensional structure of images and the local nature of many processing algorithms through the use of unconventional architectures exhibiting some form of parallelism (Preston and Uhr 1982; Fu and Ichikawa 1982; Uhr 1983). Recent advances in VLSI design and fabrication technology have made it feasible to consider increasingly powerful architectures that can be implemented in a cost-effective way. In general, parallel multiprocessor systems can be characterized by the nature of the instruction and data streams, by the geometry and flexibility of the connection network between processors (Siegel 1979), and by the capabilities of the individual processors in the network. Flynn (1975) proposed a classification of serial and parallel computing strategies into four general categories:

SISD (single instruction, single data stream),

MISD (multiple instruction, single data stream),

SIMD (single instruction, multiple data stream), and

MIMD (multiple instruction, multiple data stream).

The SISD category includes conventional serial computers, whose inherent limitations with regard to vision tasks are well known. The MISD category includes pipelined machines.

The SIMD category includes synchonous parallel processors in which all the processors simultaneously execute the same instruction on different data. In an SIMD machine, a centralized controller broadcasts instructions to a set of processing elements; each active processor then executes the instruction on a set of data local to the processor. SIMD architectures can take several forms, depending on the type of interconnection structure used. A common choice is a fixed two-dimensional interconnect strategy in which each processor can communicate directly with four (or eight) neighbors. This type of interconnect strategy is common in image-processing machines, since the resulting structure closely matches the geometry of the image data. These parallel arrays of processors are excellent candidates for VLSI implementations because of the regular arrangement of the processing elements. In most implementations the processing elements are relatively simple; in many cases they are restricted to performing arithmetic or Boolean operations on the data. Typically, a processing element may be active (i.e., execute the current instruction) or inactive. More complex local control decisions are usually not provided, because of the expense. MPP (Batcher 1980; Potter 1982) is an SIMD machine organized as a 128 × 128 array. Each processor is capable of performing bit serial arithmetic and logical operations. Gray-level images are viewed as bit planes stored in a shift-register stack. CAAPP (Weems 1985; Moldovan et al. 1985) is an interesting example of an SIMD machine designed as a 512 × 512 content-addressable-array parallel processor.

By stacking cellular logic arrays and extending each processor's interconnections to include parent and sibling connections in the stack, one can create a hierarchical architecture. If the interconnection structure for each processor is restricted to its four (or eight) immediate neighbors at one level (say L) in the stack, a small local neighborhood at level $L + 1$, and a unique parent at level $L - 1$, then a tapering "pyramid" or "cone" structure is created (Tanimoto and Klinger 1980; Burt et al. 1981).

Several hardware implementations of pyramid machines have been proposed. Dyer (1982) has described a VLSI pyramid implementation in which descendant pixel neighborhoods have a considerable degree of overlap. This represents a slightly more constrained version of the pyramid structure, proposed by Burt et al. (1981), in which parent-sibling connections are determined dynamically within a 4 × 4 block of pixels at the level below the processor and a 2 × 2 block of pixels at the level above.

MIMD machines are composed of multiple processors executing different instruction streams on different data streams. The FLIP processor (Luetjen et al. 1980) represents a MIMD architecture with a flexible interconnect structure. Each of sixteen identical processors performs arithmetic and logical operations on eight-bit data words. Each processor has two independent input ports and one output port and can communicate synchronously with any of the others. An internal high-speed bus system connects each processing unit with all the other processors. A separate bus connects each processor to a high-speed data buffer which provides the interface to the image memory, which in turn provides the interface to a host computer. System control via a data-flow model permits a wide variety of parallel interconnect strategies to be realized, making it possible to configure a network of processors that best matches the structure of the algorithm being implemented.

Pipelined architectures are composed of multiple processors on a common bus; processor modules execute operations according to their position. The Cytocomputer (Sternberg 1982) is a serial-array processor that uses programmable processors, each of which computes a transformed pixel from a neighborhood of pixels; algorithms are implemented as cascaded neighborhood operations. The Cytocomputer is composed of over 100 processors on a long pipeline; each processor executes 3×3 arithmetic and logical neighborhood operations. In general, the processors themselves exhibit substantial degrees of parallelism. Images are decomposed into neighborhoods and "pipelined" through the successive neighborhood computations, and the results are reassembled into an image. An entire $1,024 \times 1,024$ image can be processed in one video-frame time.

In general, the utility of a particular architecture for computer vision depends on its impact on the structure of the algorithms mapped onto the hardware. Point or local-neighborhood algorithms are useful for computing local image properties where the output pixel(s) is a function of only a single pixel or a small neighborhood containing the pixel. Examples include gray-scale transformations, blurring and sharpening, local thresholding, edge detection, and convolution. Algorithms such as these map directly onto the structure of cellular logic machines, since each processor executes the same instruction set using lockstep computations.

The algorithms in a second class, which includes transform computations (e.g., Fourier, Hadamard), image resampling, geometric correction, and histogram and co-occurrence matrix computations, either require larger neighborhoods of pixels in order to compute their results or have output pixels that vary in spatial relation to their input pixels. For example, although image resampling can be viewed as a convolution, it is unlikely that the computed pixels have the same position as corresponding pixels in the original image. Algorithms for computing these and similar image-processing algorithms on cellular machines have appeared in the literature; see, e.g., Preston and Uhr 1982. Operations that require larger but regular neighborhoods can be implemented in single-level arrays by using the interconnection network to shift the input image. Each processor computes partial results as the neighborhood pixels are shifted past; the number of shifts required is proportional to the neighborhood diameter, and hence implementations of these algorithms exhibit aspects of both serial and parallel processing.

Hierarchical architectures are natural structures for a large class of algorithms that can be represented by successive (i.e., serial) applications of parallel operations; see Rosenfeld 1983. Examples are algorithms that utilize some form of planning (Kelly 1971), those that depend on global values to guide local processes (e.g. context-guided thresholding), as well as property measurement over windows of varying sizes, hierarchical relaxation algorithms, and the like.

As we have already noted, vision tasks at the "cognitive" level appear to be more symbolic and hence to require, perhaps, fewer processors with larger granularity and variable interconnect structures. As the degree of image abstraction increases (i.e., regions, boundaries, local relations, symbolic representations, and so on), parallel cellular architectures become less natural representations, and their efficiency decreases because of their fixed interconnect structure. There has been little research on advanced architectures for addressing vision tasks beyond the initial image-processing algorithms, whose results map nicely onto the architectures discussed. Several large-scale systems have been discussed from the design viewpoint; these discussions (see, e.g., Hanson and Riseman 1978a) attempt to define conceptual system structures for vision and are usually far removed from hardware considerations.

Learning

The current concern with the recognition of complex scenes (and with the attendant problems of noise, occlusion, and the disambiguation of differing perspectives) grew out of an earlier concern with the recognition of isolated patterns, such as a single letter or a single face. Although current research is dominated by issues of representation and control structures for vision, much of the work in character recognition was dominated by issues of learning.

The idea of learning in pattern recognition took two basic forms.

In one view, the goal was to learn the parameters of a parameterized conditional density function. In this case, observing additional samples drawn from the pattern classes has the effect of sharpening the estimates of the parameters. The conditional density function provides the basis for a classification rule typically taken to be Bayes's rule; hence, this form of learning is called Bayesian learning. (See Duda and Hart 1973.) In general, there are two distinguishable cases. In the first, the number of distinct pattern classes is known, the class label for each sample is known, and the form of the conditional density is known. In the second and more difficult case, the class labels for the samples are not known. The first case is commonly referred to as *supervised learning* or *learning with a teacher* (who provides the class labels), the second as *unsupervised learning* or *learning without a teacher*.

In the other view of learning, the general idea was that the retina drove a network of "neurons," with connections which could be varied on the basis of experience. In the 1950s and the 1960s there flourished a whole field of study of *self-organizing systems*, one of the best known of which is the perceptron (Rosenblatt 1962). These networks could be trained to recognize certain classes of simple patterns, but they were limited by their inability to use sophisticated low-level representations and then call upon interacting high-level "specialists." This type of learning is the same as supervised learning, except that the form of the discriminant functions, rather than the class of conditional density functions, is assumed known and the goal is to learn the parameters of the discriminant functions. The Perceptron, for example, implemented a linear discriminant function represented by the weights. The recent rise of parallel computer hardware has stimulated increasing interest in these parallel-network models of learning, and the whole 1960s field of self-organizing systems now finds itself reborn under the title *connectionism* but now influenced by the concepts of artificial intelligence. In this area, brain models provide ideas rather than hard data which models must be constructed to explain. Part IV of this volume provides a sampler of connectionist models.

In line with our dichotomy between low-level and high-level vision, it might be suggested that learning in vision might also be analyzed at these levels in terms of acquiring useful features for building low-level representations, and in terms of recognizing new types of objects or new types of relations between objects. Clearly, there might also be questions about learning new types of control structures or new types of strategies. There has not been significant research addressing the question of learning in computer vision. The results from pattern recognition do not extend easily, and one could question the efficacy of the approach. Part of the problem appears to be the infant status of computer vision and the lack of general agreement about what constitutes an adequate model for vision. Learning is a difficult problem in its own right; when it is not clear what must be learned, the difficulty is even greater.

The biological research seems to have been done at the lower level. Hubel and Wiesel (1965), moving beyond their discovery of cells in cat visual cortex tuned for orientation specificity, asked whether or not these orientations were genetically specified. They found that a cat raised with one eye closed lost the orientation specificity. This led initially to the hypothesis that the brain was genetically precoded but that signals could lose their effectiveness through disuse. However, Hirsch and Spinelli (1970, 1971) showed that animals given special training could acquire features distinct from those of the normal repertoire. For example, a cat that had been able to see only a pattern of three bars through one eye and a bullseye pattern through the other had a large number of visual-cortex cells tuned for just these two patterns and could recognize each of these patterns only through the eye to which it had been presented. Subsequent research by Fregnac and Imbert (1978) and by others showed that the story is in some sense a mixture of the original view based on the Hubel-Wiesel study and the view advanced by Hirsch and Spinelli. It appears that there are populations of cells that are genetically pretuned, populations of cells that are somewhat modifiable, and other cells that are totally plastic in their wiring. In further research, Spinelli and Jensen (1979) discovered context-dependent somatotopy, with the amount of cortex allocated to a function dependent on experience. There have been related studies by Merzenich and Kaas (1983). A number of models of the formation of cortical feature detectors and of the formation of retinotopy between different regions of the visual system, all within the paradigm of cooperative computation at the low level, have been developed by von der Malsburg (1973, 1979). Bienenstock et al. (1982) have developed models that address the range of data synthesized by Imbert and Fregnac, and Amari (1980) has developed models related to the issue of context-dependent somatotopy.

Low-Level Vision

Representing the Image

As was mentioned above, the task of low-level vision is to map from the original pattern of light intensities to intermediate abstract representations. In the earliest stages of visual processing, receptors extract local information about the quantity of light reflected from surfaces in the world being viewed. The information may be from one spectral band or from multiple spectral bands (e.g., color). Low-level vision is not intrinsically restricted to spectral information; in a machine-vision system, direct depth measurements (perhaps from a laser rangefinder) are possible, as are measurements from radar, acoustic signals, and multiple sensors (e.g., stereo) and direct motion measurements. All subsequent processes then collate information from some neighborhood to come up with useful image descriptors. Early in the process, this information may be quite local (e.g., small neighborhoods about a point). For example, Lettvin et al. (1959) explored how frog retinal cells may signal back to the brain information about small moving objects in a small visual field, whereas other cells signal the presence of large moving objects in a somewhat larger visual field. Kuffler (1953) showed that cat and monkey retinal ganglion cells can signal information about local contrasts. Stone et al. (1979) and others showed that X, Y, and W cells can send information about transient and sustained movement. Different regions of the brain (and thus, presumably, different specialized subsystems of machine-vision systems) can take appropriate samples of this local information to build up more global information. In segmentation processes, local information of the Hubel-Wiesel type may be aggregated to yield strong hypotheses about edges separating one region from another, and grouping processes may determine regions on the basis of continuity of depth and structure. These processes of edge finding and region growing may then cooperate to build a segmented image.

Depth-mapping systems in animals can rely on stereo cues (matching features from the two eyes) and on accomodation cues (the focal length of the lens required to bring a feature into focus). Machine systems can use other senses to get depth information, such as sonar, radar, and laser rangefinders. Cooperative computation, both in terms of highly parallel algorithms using the cue from one source and in terms of the use of different types of information to complement one another in the development of a more accurate global representation, is again a basic issue. Depth information can also be obtained by inferring shape from shading.

Different animals seem to have retinas specialized for different purposes, sending different local features to brains which have regions specialized for different low-level representations. As Spinelli suggests in paper 4, it is an exciting problem in neuroethology to try to relate these specialized brain structures to the ecological niche of the animal. In the same way, we expect developments in machine vision not to lead to a single optimal machine-vision system, but rather to yield a set of techniques that will make it possible to efficiently tailor low-level and high-level machine-vision systems to specific applications.

Features and Frequencies

As mentioned above, the early stages of a visual system provide information about some specific local feature of the visual input, such as a local estimate of edge orientation. The Cambridge School of psychophysics, led by Fergus Campbell (1974), has developed psychophysical data (represented in this volume by the work of Burr and Ross) showing that the brain has cells whose features can be well described in terms of spatial frequency—they respond not so much to edges as to bars of a particular width or gratings of a certain spatial frequency. The demonstration that the spatial-frequency cells of the visual cortex could be seen as falling into different channels depending on the rough degree of their spatial tuning led Marr and Poggio (1979) to devise a stereo model in which coarse spatial-frequency channels were used to provide a preliminary depth map, which could then be quickly refined on the basis of data provided by the finely tuned spatial-frequency channels. These psychophysical observations, and a model based upon them, were developed further by Frisby and Mayhew (1980). More will be said about this below; here, we want to make a broader computational point, exemplified in low-level vision systems in what have been variously called pyramids and processing cones. Often, a coarse image of low resolution can very quickly yield a useful first approximation to a low-level representation of the image, which can then be refined where necessary by the incorporation of more refined visual data. It has proved computationally efficient to use such multiresolution algorithms rather than to proceed directly to use all the data at the finest level of resolution available (Glazer 1982; Rosenfeld 1983; Glazer et al. 1983).

However, another suggested inference from the finding of spatial-frequency-tuned channels in the visual system does not seem appropriate for models of biological vision—namely, that the brain extracts a spatial Fourier transform of the visual image and then uses this for holographic storage or for position-independent recognition (Pribram 1974). There is no evidence that the neural system has either the fine discrimination of spatial frequencies or the preservation of spatial phase information that would allow such Fourier transforms to be computed with sufficient accuracy for biological use of such processes. However, optical computing techniques and holographic techniques may have an important role to play in machine vision. At the present there is relatively little integration of optical and electronic computing, but the future may see machine architectures that conduct a number of low-level visual processes through optical computing while using electronic computers for the distributed computing involved in high-level vision.

Different animals make use of different visual features; the retinal "trigger features" of a frog, a rabbit, and a cat, for example, are quite different. In the frog, cells are well suited to provide input to a visual system that must detect small moving objects as prey and large moving objects as predators. In the rabbit visual system, the retina contains movement-detecting cells specifically tuned for movement along the ground plane. The cat's retina is more like those of primates (including humans), which seem to be concerned with "cleaning up the image" for contrast enhancement and motion detection. The cells in the retina provide overlapping receptive fields, so that information about any small locus in visual space affects the activity of a number of nearby cells. In the same way, information about the environment is to be sought not at one point in a low-level visual representation but throughout the population. The activity of one cell is inherently ambiguous. Take, for example, a cat visual-cortex cell of the kind studied by Hubel and Weisel. It is specific for position in the visual field and for orientation of the stimulus; however, the level of firing depends on many features, and thus a cell may fire at the same rate in response to an edge at exactly the right orientation but somewhat off center, or to an edge that is on center but of a somewhat different orientation, or even to an edge that is in the canonical position and orientation but is somewhat blurred. The task of the "intermediate" level of vision is thus to aggregate these local feature estimates to provide descriptors of depth, motion, and image structure expressed in relatively economical representations of edges, regions, and surface patches that can be used efficiently to guide the processes of navigation or high-level vision.

Lateral Inhibition and Relaxation Algorithms

The first successful chapter in the theory of parallel computation for low-level vision is probably that of lateral inhibition (see Ratliff 1969), which begins with the phenomenon of Mach bands. If one looks at a sheet of paper half of which is white and half of which is black, one will see parallel to the border a brighter band on the white side and a darker band on the black side—even though each half is of uniform intensity. These Mach bands can be explained by assuming that nearby cells have recurrent inhibition. Cells receiving stimulation on the light side but near the boundary will receive less inhibition than cells on the light side far from the boundary, and thus will be "lighter than light," while cells receiving signals from just within the boundary on the dark side will receive more inhibition than their neighbors well within the dark side, and thus will be "darker than dark." Von Békesy (1967) studied similar processes in the sense of touch. By assuming a peak of excitatory connections between nearby cells but a trough of inhibition between cells somewhat further apart, von Békesy explained why two pinpricks placed close together could be sensed as a single point whereas two stimuli placed further apart could be clearly distinguished. Such analysis at the psychophysical level has been followed by many studies in both visual systems and somato-sensory systems, which confirmed that lateral inhibition is indeed a pervasive feature of the wiring of arrays of neurons. Hartline and his colleagues provided a substantial amount of detail about lateral inhibition through their studies of the lateral eye of the limulus (the horseshoe crab). Lateral inhibition is clearly the process at work in the circuits for contrast enhancement in the mammalian retina, studied by Kuffler. Henn and Grüsser (1968) saw that the typical connection pattern for lateral inhibition—excitation close, inhibition further away—could be modeled as the difference of two Gaussian curves, with the positive curve for excitation having a higher, narrower peak than the negative curve for inhibition. In his theory of low-level vision, Marr (1982) adopted this difference of Gaussians (DOG) as the basic filter before all other processes of low-level vision (although his book does not cite any of the earlier work on lateral inhibition).

Workers in low-level vision influenced by the paradigm of brain modeling came up with other ways in which significant information could be computed through the cooperative activity of neurons on the basis of local interactions. Sperling (1970), Arbib et al. (1974), Nelson (1975), Dev (1975), and Marr and Poggio (1976) all used local interactions in building a cooperative stereo algorithm. This algorithm had cells coding for nearby direction and nearby disparity exciting one another and had cells of nearby direction and grossly different disparity inhibiting one another; thus, it embodied the environmental fact that much of the world is made up of surfaces, so that nearby directions are more likely than not to lie on the same surface and thus are more likely than not to have similar disparities.

Meanwhile, the notion of propagating local information was also developing within the machine-vision community, at a somewhat intermediate level of representation. Guzman (1969) noted that there were many interpretations for a single vertex in a line drawing viewed in isolation and asked: Do different faces around a vertex belong to the same or different objects? Do they face into or out of the image plane? He showed that an interpretation of a vertex was constrained by the interpretation of other vertices to which it was connected. This work, which was similar to work by Clowes (1971) and Huffman (1971), was extended by Waltz (1975), who showed how to apply this process of constraint satisfaction to a line drawing including shadows as well as objects. Rosenfeld et al. (1976) then provided a unified theory of all this, under the general title "relaxation algorithms." They recognized that this process of propagating local constraints was analogous to the relaxation methods used in numerical analysis to solve linear equations. These methods were developed in the 1930s by Southwell (1940) as a generalization of techniques for discovering the shape of a beam. (Imagine an estimate for the displacement of different points of a beam "relaxing" as each estimate is adjusted by a continuity criterion which says that the beam must be displaced continuously, without any abrupt dislocations.)

The relaxation algorithms of numerical analysis were initially developed for hand computation, and then for serial computers. In the same way, many of the relaxation algorithms for machine vision run on serial computers, perhaps with the speedups available through vector or array processing. A relaxation algorithm may be developed either to represent the interactions of neurons in the brain or to provide an efficient low-level process for machine vision, where the criterion of efficiency need not imply biological realism. The connectionists argue that even in the latter case, a relaxation algorithm should be represented explicitly through the interactions of a parallel network, with one cell to represent each hypothesis and with connections between cells to represent the constraints between the hypotheses they represent. This work is feeding the development of specialized computer architectures—the connection machines—which may have tens or even hundreds of thousands of connections that can be set variably to represent appropriate constraints (Hillis 1985).

Segmentation

As we suggested above, there are available in an image of a scene a variety of sources of low-level information that can be used to form an initial description of the syntactic structure of the image. The extraction of this description, in terms of important image and/or environmental "events," is an important precursor to the construction of a high-level, more abstract, description at the semantic level. Historically, computer-vision researchers have focused on regions and lines (or boundaries) as the initial primitive descriptions, although Marr (1982), Tenenbaum and Barrow (1976), Brady (1982), and others have suggested that direct extraction of three-dimensional elements (such as local surface patches) is more appropriate. In this case the descriptive elements are surface patches that directly capture aspects of the three-dimensional world from which the image was obtained. The implication is that the interpretation task will be far simpler when the surface description is used, since it is a representation of the actual physical world that is to be interpreted and therefore a broader spectrum of domain constraints can be brought to bear on the information. Although such a representation is useful in certain applications, reliable extraction of surface range, reflectance, and orientation information from monocular image data has yet to be demonstrated except in highly constrained domains or under very unrealistic constraints on the type of surfaces making up the objects in the scene. Since other cues may be more reliable, important work has been done on high-level vision processes which do not rely on a depth map.

As we have seen, *region segmentation* refers to processes that partition the two-dimensional image into connected areas (called *regions*) composed of groups of pixels that are uniform in some property, such as gray level (intensity, brightness), color, or texture. There are three basic approaches to region segmentation. In *region merging*, the image is divided into primitive regions (initially, perhaps, individual pixels), which are then merged according to some criteria until no further merges take place (Brice and Fennema 1970). In *region splitting*, a region (initially, perhaps, the entire image) is split into two sets of regions based on properties until no further splits are possible (Kohler 1981; Ohlander et al. 1979). In the *split and merge* approach, a region is split (usually in an arbitrary way, using a fixed geometric pattern) if there are detectable differences in its properties; the resulting regions are then candidates for merging with their neighbors (Horowitz and Pavlidis 1974).

In the recursive region-splitting algorithm of Ohlander et al. (1979), the segmentation was based on coherence of regions with respect to multiple features. Their algorithm used a one-dimensional histogram for each of nine multiple features to determine the best threshold value to be used to partition the image. The threshold was determined by a peak/valley analysis of the histograms; the feature having the most sharply defined peak surrounded by the deepest valley was chosen. Two thresholds were chosen (one on either side of the peak); these were used to generate a set of connected regions covering the original image. The process was applied recursively to the regions until all the histograms were unimodal. Nagin (1979) and Nagin et al. (1981a,b, 1982) used a similar approach in which histograms of a single image feature were computed independently over small areas (e.g., 16 × 16 or 32 × 32 subareas) of the image. After segmenting each subarea, the artificial boundaries created by the subdivision were removed by merging regions across the boundaries on the basis of both global region properties and properties extracted from a narrow strip on both sides of the boundary. Kohler (1984) extended this idea to include the "sharing" of information about peaks and valleys among adjacent subdivisions, in an attempt to minimize the effect of coincidental alignment of subdivision boundaries and actual region boundaries. He also developed a more sophisticated set of merging criteria, and was able to eliminate the relaxation component of Nagin's algorithm.

Region segmentation results in a two-dimensional region map in registration with the original image in which each region is uniquely identified by a region label. Regions have closed boundaries, by construction, and from the pixels making up the region (and their boundaries) a variety of primitive descriptions of the region may be measured. Typical region features include spectral properties (e.g., intensity, color, and texture), shape properties (e.g., area, eccentricity, and compactness), and boundary properties (e.g., curvature and contrast). The image map and associated features can be translated into a semantic network structure (Hanson and Riseman 1978c) in which each region is identified as a node via the region label, region properties are associated with the node, and the arcs connecting region nodes capture relationships between the regions (e.g., above, adjacent to, contained in). This structure may form the basis for higher-level interpretation processes, which may further group the regions into alternate structural hypotheses based on expectations, context, and object models.

Region extraction depends upon locating areas of the image that are somewhat homogeneous in one or more properties. A complementary approach is to locate discontinuities in image properties and to treat these discontinuities as edges or boundaries. Boundaries are known to be important psychologically (Attneave 1954), and their extraction is an important topic of research in computer vision. The locating of boundaries in images is often viewed as a two-step process, with the extraction of local-edge elements (usually associated with a pixel) followed by the aggregation of the local edges into more global elements such as straight lines or curves.

Local-edge extraction can be accomplished by a variety of operators (Rosenfeld and Kak 1976; Ballard and Brown 1982), which usually fall into one of two broad classes: approximations to the first or the second derivative of the image intensity surface (Roberts 1965; Macleod 1970; Marr and Hildreth 1980; Canny 1983); and estimation of the parameters of an assumed edge model (Hueckel 1971; Haralick 1980).

Local edges can be described by their image location (usually related to a pixel), their direction (usually aligned with the direction of maximum change in the image feature being used), and their magnitude (which measures the amount of change in the feature). The goal of these operators is to enhance those areas of the image where local edges exist. Since edges are a high-frequency phenomenon, most edge operators are sensitive to noise; since edges in an image deviate substantially from ideal step discontinuities, some form of postprocessing is required to eliminate the edges caused by noise and other effects. Such postprocessing steps range from simple global thresholding (not very effective, in general) to more complex methods that attempt to take into account the local context of an edge (Zucker et al. 1977; Prager 1980; Glazer et al. 1980).

The output from a local-edge detector applied to an image is a set of local-edge elements in registration with the original feature image. Additional processes must be applied to group the local edges into more global elements such as straight lines and curves. The criteria used for grouping may depend upon local properties of groups of edge elements, on global properties of the distribution of edge elements, or on constraints derived from the properties of assumed models. Methods for performing the grouping range from simple contour following via the application of traditional search techniques (with the directed edges represented as nodes in a graph) to dynamic programming methods (with the grouping criteria expressed in the optimization function). The result of the grouping process may be the set of local-edge elements satisfying the criteria, or it may be a more abstract representation obtained by fitting a curve or a straight line to the group of local edges.

A method that has been widely used when the desired line structure can be parametrized (e.g., as a straight line or a conic section) is the Hough transform (Duda and Hart 1972). In this technique, the line or curve parameters are quantized into some appropriate range, forming an n-dimensional parameter space. Each edge element contributes one "vote" to each set of parameters it satisfies through the parameter transform. Points in parameter space with large numbers of "votes" are assumed to correspond to global structural elements. The process may be generalized to match arbitrary shapes (Ballard 1981). The exponential increase in the size of the parameter space with the number of parameters can be overcome in some cases by partitioning the parameter space and constructing several independent transforms of lower dimensionality.

An alternative approach to the extraction of global lines is represented in the work of Burns et al. (1984), in which the goal is the extraction of straight lines in an image. Rather than compute local-edge elements, Burns estimates the local orientation of the intensity surface at each pixel and then groups pixels into regions for which the local orientations are similar. From these "line support regions" a straight line is extracted, and this is characterized by various attributes (length, contrast, orientation, etc). Subsequent filtering operations can then be applied to extract lines of interest, such as short high-contrast lines and long straight lines. This method can also be extended to the extraction of conic sections.

In some cases, it is possible to realize substantial computational savings in region and line algorithms by employing multiresolution images (Rosenfeld 1983; Tanimoto and Klinger 1980) obtained by successively reducing the resolution of the original image by a constant factor until a pyramid (Uhr 1983) or a cone (Hanson and Riseman 1980) of images is obtained. The savings are realized because the number of operations that must be applied and the amount of confusing or irrelevant detail in the original image is often reduced at the lower resolution. Strategies for employing multiresolution pyramids often involve finding rough structures in low-resolution data and then making successive refinements as the higher-resolution images are considered. Kelly (1971) used such an approach in an edge-detection process that found lines in a reduced-resolution image, projected them to the next finer level, and analyzed the areas between adjacent line endings in order to extend them. Similar techniques have been proposed by Levine (1978), Hanson and Riseman (1974, 1980), Dyer (1982), Burt (1980), Burt et al. (1981), and Rosenfeld (1983).

Reynolds et al. (1984) describe an effective method for hierarchical model-directed segmentation of high-resolution aerial images by combining the Nagin-Kohler region-segmentation algorithm with a multi-resolution representation of the image. By segmenting the image at a low resolution, roughly identifying areas of interest (such as airports, roads, and residential areas), and resegmenting at the next finer levels under the masks developed from the partial interpretation, they achieved substantial economies for segmentation as well as for model matching (since the object models were also hierarchical and organized to reflect the features expected at the various resolution levels).

Multiresolution structures have also been used for the extraction of depth and motion information. Various multiresolution representations have also been proposed and used for image structures (Rosenfeld 1983). The best-known of these is the quadtree (Samet 1980), a hierarchical encoding of the image array. Weiss et al. (1985) describe a hierarchical perceptual grouping process for extracting straight lines from an image starting from the zero-crossing points of the Laplacian. The local edges are grouped using a hierarchical linking and merging algorithm that uses both intrinsic and geometric properties of the edges to link them and a merging process that merges linked sets if they can be approximated sufficiently well by a straight line. The method has an advantage in that it can link and merge collinear segments even if they are separated by gaps. The hierarchical description of lines and their associated properties is very general and can form the basis for more sophisticated perceptual organization strategies.

Recovering Depth Information

Clearly, the location of objects in space is a crucial parameter for an animal interacting with its world. From a single eye, one can determine the direction in space of various features of the world. Further techniques are required to locate where the feature is along the given direction. As already mentioned, this can be done by stereopsis (using cues provided by correlating the visual input to two spatially separated eyes), or by optic flow (using the information provided to the eye at moments separated in time), or by accommodation (determining what focal length will best bring an object into focus). A machine-vision system can use all these methods and can also make use of direct measurements, such as the use of laser or sonar rangefinders. However, in this subsection we will concentrate on stereopsis. The recovery of surface information will be discussed briefly.

It is a familiar experience from using stereo viewers that the view of a three-dimensional scene presented to the left eye differs from that presented to the right eye, and that the disparity or displacement between the two images of a point provides the crucial cue to the depth of the point in the original scene. A key concern in the nineteenth century was whether depth perception comes before or after pattern recognition. Is it that the brain takes the image from each eye separately to recognize a house (for example) and then uses the disparity between the two house images to recognize the depth of the house in space, or is it that the visual system matches local stimuli presented to both eyes and thus builds up a depth map of surfaces and small objects in space which provides the input for perceptual recognition? To test the hypothesis that depth computation precedes recognition, Julesz (1971) developed a method based on random-dot stereograms—stereo pairs each of which contains only visual noise but which are so designed that the visual noise is correlated between the two images. Patches of random light and dark presented to one retina were identical to, but at varying disparities from, patches of light and dark presented to the other retina. Julesz found that human subjects were in fact able to carry out the appropriate matching to see surfaces stippled with random patterning at varying depths in space. In other words, without precluding that some depth perception could follow pattern recognition,

Julesz established that the formation of a depth map of space could precede the recognition of a pattern. He offered a model of this process in terms of cooperative computation involving an array of magentic dipoles connected by springs.

For the brain theorist, the following issue was thus raised: On the basis of the data on what constituted realistic neurons provided by Barlow et al. (1967), could a depth map be computed by a cooperative process involving such realistic neurons? Among the first to address this issue were Arbib et al. (1974), who built a neural-net cooperative-computation model for building the depth map "guided by the plausible hypothesis that our visual world is made up of relatively few connected regions." The neural manifold of this model had cells whose firing level represented a degree of confidence that a point was located at a corresponding position in three-dimensional space. The neurons were so connected via inhibitory inter-neurons as to embody the principle that cells that coded for nearby direction in space and similar depth should excite one another whereas cells that corresponded to nearby direction in space and dissimilar depth should inhibit one another. (See Sperling 1970 and Nelson 1975 for related models.) It was shown by computer simulation (Dev 1975), and later established by mathematical analysis (Amari and Arbib 1977), that this system did indeed yield a segmentation of the visual input into connected regions. Later, a variant of this model was published by Marr and Poggio (1976), and in subsequent writings Marr took the "plausible hypothesis that our visual world is made up of relatively few connected regions" and showed how it could be developed into an elegant mathematical theorem relating the structure of a depth-perception algorithm to the nature of surfaces in the physical world.

With this work, it was established that the perception of depth maps could be constructed by a method of computation that was guided by the hypothesis that the world was made up of surfaces, and that the algorithm could involve some form of cooperative computation. However, the co-operative-computation algorithms discussed above exhibited false minima. Consider, for example, a picket fence. Suppose that, by pure chance, a system starts by matching a number of fenceposts presented to one eye with the images of their neighbors one to the left presented to the other eye. In the cooperative-computation model, this initial mismatch could co-opt the possible choices of neighbors, and the result would then be a high-confidence estimate that the fence was at a different depth from that at which it actually occurred. This provides a local "energy minimum" for the algorithm. The question then arises of how one could come up with an algorithm that would avoid at least some of these false minima. The answer provided by Marr and Poggio (1979) can be seen as rooted in two contributions, one from machine vision and one from psychophysics: the idea of pyramids or processing cones and the idea of spatial-frequency channels, respectively. These ideas led Marr and Poggio to develop a system in which, with hardly any cooperative computation, a fairly confident rough depth estimate for different surfaces could be made using the low-spatial-frequency channel. This rough model was then used to control vergence eye movements, which led to the sculpting of a more detailed spatial map on the first approximation through the disparity information provided via channels of higher spatial frequency.

On the basis of psychophysical evidence showing that figural neighborhood interactions are involved in human stereopsis, Mayhew and Frisby (1980) conjectured that the matching processes are integrated with the construction of a primitive binocular-based description of changes in image intensity. They then offered an algorithm, STEREOEDGE, whose initial stages used local piecewise binocular grouping of adjacent, similar zero crossings or peak matches and whose later stages used a Waltz-type relaxation process (Waltz 1975; for a review of similar models see Davis and Rosenfeld 1981). The earlier stages were much influenced by the work of Marr and Poggio; the later stages exhibited the cooperative processing that Marr and Poggio (1979) sought to exclude. As noted in Mayhew and Frisby 1981, both Marr-Poggio algorithms seek to select matches according to depth continuity rather than figural continuity, and they thus differ considerably from STEREOEDGE.

Prazdny (in press) offered an explicit critique of the Marr-Poggio (1979) proposal that false matches may be avoided by trading off resolution for disparity range using a coarse-to-fine matching strategy. He noted that low and high spatial frequencies are often informationally orthogonal. For example, if grass is viewed through a picket fence, there is no reason why the disparities of the fence should be related in any way to the disparities of the grass surface. He offered a specific laboratory test using a random-dot stereogram in which the background plane is transparent and two depths, one from low and one from high spatial frequencies, can be observed simultaneously. He concluded that patches of the visual field may be fused and then held "locked" by some form of hysteresis, as proposed by Julesz (1971). An algorithm offered in Prazdny 1985 successfully detects disparities generated by opaque as well as transparent surfaces. An interesting feature of Prazdny's model is the absence of the explicit inhibitory connections employed by Sperling (1970), Dev (1975), and Nelson (1975).

The principal disambiguation mechanism is facilitation due to disparity similarity. Prazdny argues that dissimilar disparities should not inhibit one another because, when there are transparent surfaces, a disparity may be surrounded by a set of features corresponding to other surfaces.

Even if a specific brain mechanism is employed by the brain of one animal, this need not be the mechanism used by a distinct species. It is known that both frogs and toads can snap with moderate accuracy at prey located in the monocular visual field, and this led Ingle (1976) to hypothesize that for the frog it was accommodation (focal-length information for the lens) that subserved depth perception. More detailed experiments (Collett 1977) in which toads were fitted with spectacles showed that the story was more complex. Collett was able to show that a monocular animal did indeed use accommodation as the depth cue, but that in an animal with prey in the binocular field the major depth cue was disparity, with accommodation cues exerting a bias of perhaps 6 percent on the disparity-based depth judgment. This led House (1982) to suggest that another route to solving the problem of false minima was to use accommodation cues to disambiguate disparity. Consider, for example, the depth maps corresponding to two "worms" presented as visual targets to a simulated toad. In the accommodation map, the level of activity at a particular position and depth corresponds to the sharpness of the image obtained at that position when the lens was focused at the given depth. This activity has one peak for each worm, but the peak is rather broad and gives poor localization information. The disparity map of depth gained by pairing stimuli on the two eyes gives precise localization of the two worms, but it also gives precise localization of the "ghost worms" obtained by matching a stimulus on one eye with the wrong stimulus on the other eye. The key observation here is that the two sources of depth information provide complementary information. House's model uses a variant of Dev's model to refine the depth estimates within each depth field, but adds mutual coupling between the models so that activity localized within one map helps increase activity at the corresponding focus on the other map. This interaction can yield both a sharpening of the peaks in the accommodation map and a suppression of the "ghost peaks" in the disparity map, finally converging on a state in which both maps agree and present a sharp, accurate localization of the targets.

In mammals, the disparity information seems to be precise over only a very small depth range. Disparity cues must be augmented by vergence information. Whitman Richards, working in human psychophysics, and Gian Poggio, working in monkey neurophysiology, have suggested that primates use three broad classes of depth detectors: those tuned for fine depth disparities, those tuned for stimuli nearer than the coarse fixation distance (near cells), and those tuned for stimuli further than the coarse distance (far cells). The hypothesis is that near and far neurons help initiate vergence, while tuned excitatory neurons guide completion and maintenance of vergence. These approaches to stereopsis are reviewed in Poggio and Poggio 1984.

Turning to machine vision, we find that the computation of depth from stereo imagery usually proceeds in two steps: first, the establishment of a correspondence between selected points in the two images to provide a disparity map, followed by the computation of the depth at the points; second, the application of some interpolation process that extends the depth map to all points in the images, followed by the discovery, extraction, and description of the surfaces in the three-dimensional scene.

Common methods for solving the correspondence problem are either intensity-based approaches, which rely on the similarity of the light intensity reflected from a scene point in the two images, or token-based approaches, which identify stable image structures in the two images which are subsequently matched. It is also possible to impose a multifrequency, multiresolution framework on top of either of these methods, as discussed above. See Anandan 1985 and Barnard and Fischler 1982 for reviews.

An example of the intensity-based method is the correlation approach used by Anandan (1984), Anandan and Weiss (1985), and Gennery (1980). Here, "interesting" points in one of the images are identified through the use of an interest operator (Moravec 1980), and an area around this point is chosen as the sample window. A target area in the second image is identified as a search area, and the sample window is correlated with an identical window around each point in the search area; the value of the correlation function represents how well the sample window matches the point in the search area, and the best match is chosen as the corresponding point in the second image. The correlation method depends on the behavior of the correlation function over the search area, which depends on the underlying structure of the intensity surface. Generally, these methods tend to break down when the images have large featureless areas, when the textural structure is repetitive, or when there are many surface discontinuities.

Token-based methods extract easily identifiable structures in one image and match them with corresponding structures in the second image. Structures commonly used include interesting points, corners (Kitchen and Rosenfeld 1980), high-curvature points along a contour, and local edges. The stereo system developed by Ohta and Kanade (1985) is an edge-based system that uses the intensity information in the intervals between edges on an image scanline as the match data. The order of edge matches is preserved using an optimization technique (dynamic programming) embedded in a parallel, iterative scheme for searching for the optimal set of matches. The Ohta-Kanade method is an extension of one developed by Baker (1982). Lim and Binford (1985) extended Baker's approach to include junctions, edge elements, curved segments, and regions, and the relationships between them. The 3D Mosaic system of Herman and Kanade (1984) uses similar types of structural features to incrementally reconstruct complex scenes (such as cityscapes) from multiple aerial images.

Once global matches have been achieved and the depth has been obtained for the matched points, two questions remain: How is the depth at *all* the image points obtained? How are surface patches constructed from the depth data? These two questions may be only one: How are surfaces obtained from the *sparse* depth data? In either event, they remain open research issues. The most obvious approach is to treat the points at which the depth is known as samples from a continuous depth function and to approximate the function using conventional approximation methods. One would not expect this method to work where there are sharp depth discontinuities. Grimson (1984) used a surface-consistency constraint which assumed that the absence of zero crossings between points of known depths constrains the surface to vary smoothly and slowly in depth. A third approach is to attempt to fit object models to the depth map and to use the model constraints to interpolate (in the appropriate way) between the points (Besl and Jain 1985a).

Stereo is not the only way to obtain depth information. Motion is similar to stereo, both in the methods used and the results of the analysis (e.g., a depth map). In some cases it is also possible to generate depth maps directly from monocular color or intensity images. These methods are known as shape-from-X, where X may be shading (Horn 1975, 1977; Woodham 1978, 1984), texture (Kender 1980; Stevens 1980; Witkin 1980), or contour (Brady and Yuille 1984). The general idea behind shape-from-shading, for example, is to assume a model of the image-formation process that describes how the intensity of a point in the image is related to the geometry of the imaging process and the surface properties of the object(s) being imaged. In a restricted set of cases, which depend on assumptions of the reflectivity functions of the objects, this model can be used with two constraints on the underlying surface to recover the shape (e.g., surface normals) of the surface. The first constraint states that each image point corresponds to at most one surface orientation (the uniqueness constraint);

the second constraint states that the orientations of the underlying surface vary smoothly almost everywhere (the smoothness constraint). Ikeuchi (1980) added contour information as the boundary conditions in an iterative (cooperative) relaxation algorithm to recover shape from scanning-electron-microscope images.

There is no unique algorithm for solving a given problem, in part because many different sources of information can be employed. The important elements of a stereo matching system are the choice of features to be matched, the constraint relations assumed to hold (e.g., features are invariant or change slowly as the point of view changes), and the structure of the strategies for local and global matching. In general, any one source of information will be incomplete, and the skillful deployment of several sources of information—whether it be disparity information at several levels of resolution, motion cues, occlusion cues, or disparity and accommodation information in conjunction—will often yield a far better estimate than could be gained by using one source alone.

Images in Motion

For an organism or a robot interacting with its environment, it is often not enough to know what an object is and where it is; it is often necessary to determine its pattern of movement as well. An animal seeking to escape a predator should know whether the predator is approaching or going away; a robot on an assembly line needs to judge the rate at which objects are moving along a conveyor belt if it is to direct a gripper appropriately to grasp one of them. This raises the two issues of detecting and representing motion. As was mentioned above, Gibson made a vital contribution by observing that one could associate with a sequence of images an optic flow field—low-level vision information—from which one could extract parameters suitable for navigation. (See also Lee and Lishman 1977.) In the present volume, Tsotsos and Burt address the issue of the temporal domain. Burt discusses moving memories, which can update the location of objects in the retinotopic representation even when the fovea is not providing information about that object.

Motion information can be derived from a sequence of images obtained over time. Such a sequence may be obtained from a stationary sensor observing scenes with moving objects, from a moving sensor observing a static world, or from a combination of both. The goal of the analysis of motion includes the determination, in the general case, of the three-dimensional structure of the environment and the objects in it (which, as in the case of stereo, includes depth information) and the relative motions of the sensor and all independently moving objects. With respect to an arbitrary coordinate system, the motion of any rigid body (e.g., the sensor) can be decomposed into a translational component and a rotational component. In the absence of independently moving objects, information about the depth of a scene point along the optical axis of the moving sensor is contained in the translational component of the sensor motion; points that are closer to the sensor will exhibit larger displacements than points that are further away. (This is called *motion parallax.*) Thus, much of the work in motion is concerned with determining the frame-to-frame displacements of such points (which involves the decomposition of the sensor motion into its rotational and translational components) and the detection of independently moving objects and the determination of their motion parameters.

Approaches to the extraction of motion information are varied (see Barron 1984 for a comprehensive survey), but most involve the computation of "optic flow (or velocity) fields" from instantaneous changes in displacement of selected image points in the two-dimensional image plane. Lawton et al. summarize much of this work in their chapter; here we will give only a brief overview. Continuous motion through a three-dimensional world gives rise to the motion of points on the two-dimensional retina of the sensor. If the sensor is translating, then the motion seems to "flow" from a single point at infinity, called the *focus of expansion* (FOE), and the motion of points in the scene is constrained to move along the line from the FOE through the point. Each independently moving object in the scene also has a focus of expansion related to the direction of its motion. Determining the focus of expansion, which relates the two-dimensional motion exhibited by image points to the motion of the corresponding points in the three-dimensional world, is thus one of the central issues.

Optic flow fields can be generated by measuring the displacement of image points from frame to frame (e.g., computing a disparity image, as in stereo) or by measuring the instantaneous velocity of the points and creating a two-dimensional velocity field. Methods for computing the disparity image include differencing operations, such as simple frame-to-frame subtraction (Jayaramumurthy and Jain 1983; Tang et al. 1981; Nagel and Rekers 1981); token matching, as in stereo (Barnard and Thompson 1980; Ullman 1979; Dreschler and Nagel 1982; Roach and Aggarwal 1980; Tsai and Huang 1984); and gradient techniques which simultaneously make use of the temporal and spatial gradients of image features such as intensity (Horn and Schunk 1981; Fennema and Thompson 1979; Cornelius and

Kanade 1983; Thompson and Barnard 1981; Nagel 1983; Marr and Ullman 1981). Many of the approaches based on gradient methods make use of the smoothness constraint, which assumes that the local velocity field (or disparity) varies smoothly everywhere, which is necessary because of the aperture problem (i.e., the fact that only velocity normal to a gradient discontinuity can be measured locally). Reliance on the smoothness constraint causes problems at occlusion boundaries, where there are discontinuities in the disparity field.

The computational burden of computing dense displacement fields has led to the development of multiresolution techniques, which typically utilize a coarse-to-fine control strategy for refining the motion estimates obtained at a coarser level of resolution (Glazer 1981, 1982).Glazer et al. (1983) and Burt et al. (1983) used band-pass-filtered images in a multiresolution structure. Burt utilized an independent search at each level of resolution to obtain a structure in which the coarser levels (low frequency) were matched to detect large displacements with low resolution while the finer levels were used to detect smaller displacements with higher resolution. Glazer et al. used the results from lower-frequency, coarser-resolution searches to constrain the search at the next higher resolution. Anandan (1984) addressed the poor performance of matching algorithms around occlusion boundaries by extending the Glazer algorithm to include a confidence measure associated with each displacement or flow vector. The confidence values were used to restrict the projection of coarse estimates to those with high confidence, and thus the accuracy of the flow field was improved. The confidence measure was based on a characterization of the behavior of the autocorrelation and cross-correlation functions around candidate matches. Adiv (1985) used the same confidence measure in his matching algorithms.

Regardless of the technique used to generate the optic flow fields from an image sequence, the next major step toward understanding the environmental and egomotion involved is the interpretation of the flow field. The goals of this interpretation step often include figure-ground separation, the recovery of three-dimensional shape, object recognition, and the extraction of information about the sensor's motion relative to the environment. When the scene contains independently moving objects, detection and description of these objects are also important goals.

Most of the 3D reconstruction approaches make use of the relationship between 3D motion and 2D optic flow fields as constrained by the projective transformation mapping 3D to 2D. The two types of projection used are orthogonal and perspective transforms. Orthogonal, or parallel, projections are valid only for points at infinity; in real situations this is valid only for distant points in the scene, and for this reason we consider only those methods assuming a perspective projection.

There are three common approaches to the reconstruction problem. The first of these does not require the prior computation of an optic flow field and usually applies only to restricted cases of camera motion (Lawton 1982, 1983a,b, 1984; Lawton and Rieger 1983). This approach is described in some detail in the chapter by Lawton et al., and consequently it will not be discussed here. Often, the optic flow field can be recovered simultaneously with the recovery of 3D motion parameters. The second approach requires knowledge of the frame-to-frame correspondences for a few points in the image and usually excludes independently moving objects. The third method assumes a prior computation of the optic flow field.

The approaches that make use of the correspondences between a few points depend on the rigidity assumption (Ullman 1979), which states that any set of points undergoing a 2D transformation between images that has a unique interpretation as a rigid object moving in space should be interpreted as such a body in motion. Ullman also showed that three distinct views of five non-coplanar points in a rigid configuration are sufficient to uniquely determine the structure and motion of the points (the structure-from-motion theorem). Since some psychophysical results indicate that the assumption of a perspective transformation is not required because humans apparently do not make such an assumption, Ullman proposes a polar-parallel projection method. (A locally orthographic transform is used.)

Roach and Aggarwal (1980), Webb and Aggarwal (1981), Prazdny (1980), Tsai and Huang (1982), Dreschler and Nagel (1982), Prager and Arbib (1983), and others developed methods for extracting 3D motion information that involve the iterative solution of a number of nonlinear equations (the Tsai-Huang method uses linear equations) for which closed-form solutions are not known. Many of these approaches are sensitive to noise and require considerable computational resources. They also require the ability to accurately match image points from frame to frame, which (as was mentioned above) is still largely an unsolved problem. It is also not clear in many cases how the methods deal with independently moving objects.

A number of researchers have assumed the prior computation of a fairly dense flow field, rather than knowing optic flow at only a few points, and have developed methods for recovering the 3D structure and motion using local or global methods. Prazdny (1980) suggested that using these denser fields might be a reasonable way to overcome the need for very accurate computations at a few points (in order to account for errors in the field). Some of the advantage may be lost with local techniques, since they usually require first and second derivatives of the flow at a point. Spatial differentiation enhances noise, so these methods are also sensitive to inaccuracies in the local field. The global methods have the disadvantage that the entire flow field must be processed, which results in large computational requirements.

Prager and Arbib (1983) developed a cooperative (relaxation-type) algorithm to match two arrays of feature points (edges, corners, and high-contrast points) extracted from successive frames. They extended the algorithm to multiple frames by introducing the idea of "moving memories" (Burt 1975) that shift the frames using a diffusion process, resulting in a stabilized view of the world.

Koenderink and Van Doorn (1975, 1976a,b) advocate the extraction of local invariant properties of the flow field: curl, divergence, deformation, and others. There is some psychophysical evidence that the human visual system has channels that are sensitive to invariant properties derived from those measures (Regan and Beverley 1979). Koenderink and Van Doorn among others (Longuet-Higgins and Prazdny [1980]; Waxman and Ullman [1983]; Bruss and Horn [1983]; Rieger and Lawton [1983]) are concerned with the separation of the flow field into two separate components (the translational field and the rotational field) and with the detection of independently moving bodies. Waxman and Ullman (1983) propose the use of twelve flow deformation parameters (the two components of image velocity, three independent strain rates, the spin, and the six independent derivatives of the strain rate and spin) measured in a coordinate system attached to the image projection of a point on a rigid surface moving through space relative to an observer; these twelve parameters are used to compute motion and structure.

One of the few attempts to deal explicitly with the problem of extracting motion information from scenes containing multiple, independently moving objects has been that of Adiv (1985). Assuming a dense flow field, Adiv uses a two-stage approach. In the first stage, the flow field is segmented into regions which are roughly consistent with the motion of planar patches (an affine transformation). In the second step, adjacent regions which are consistent with the same 3D motion are merged using an error-minimization approach in which the error is expressed as the difference between the motion predicted from the first stage and the actual flow vectors weighted by a confidence measure associated with the flow

vectors (Anandan 1984). The individual motion parameters are determined from the merged regions.

Although many of these techniques are promising, they all rely on accurate computation of the optic flow field at a few judiciously chosen points or on the computation of a (possibly less accurate) dense flow field. Neither of these problems has been solved as yet, and it may be that the future of motion research lies in extracting more quantitative descriptions of motion rather than in extending the highly qualitative approaches so prevalent in the literature. It may also be that the motion descriptors necessary for the interaction of an organism with its environment, such as looming detection and time until collision, are obtained from separate processes or channels rather than from a single monolithic motion system. In addition, most approaches to date have relied on the information from only two frames, yet motion is a continuous process in which detection and prediction over multiple frames could be used to refine early, rough estimates of the motion decomposition. Indeed, Prager and Arbib (1983) and Bharwhani et al. (1985) have shown that prediction can be used to reduce computational costs and to refine initial motion estimates.

There has also been little work done on combining stereopsis with motion. (See Jenkin 1984.) Exactly how motion and depth information is integrated into a more complete image-understanding system and merged with interpretation processes and object models is still a largely unexplored area. However, Arbib (1981b) has noted that occlusion/disocclusion can cooperate with the detection of discontinuities in the optic flow to provide cues for segmentation, and that information about putative boundaries can be used to loosen the coupling of neighbors in a relaxation process while optic flow is being computed. This volume's papers by Tsotsos and Burt are relevant; Tsotsos discusses the integration problem in detail and offers a preliminary design of a system for accomplishing it, while Burt discusses aspects of the interdependence of temporal and spatial information in vision. Much work remains to be done.

High-Level Vision

High-Level Issues and the Need for Knowledge

Following in the tradition of Gibson, but with a stress on mechanism (be it neural or computational), we have seen that low-level vision can deliver important information about noteworthy regions in the environment (shape, color, depth, and texture) as well as about the positions and the relative motions of objects in the environment. Clearly, however, the utility of a machine-vision system, or the behavior or survival of an animal, depends not only on its knowing the locations or the motions of objects but also on its abilities to discern their identities and to react appropriately. A robot must be able to tell whether an object is something to be grasped at the end of a trajectory or something to avoid. An animal must, at the very minimum, be able to distinguish prey from predators. The task of high-level vision is to take advantage of whatever information can be provided by lower-level processes to interpret objects in the environment. Different low-level systems can, at times, deliver discordant (distorted, incomplete, and sometimes meaningless) information, since each is based on a different sample of the environment. Segmentation of an image into regions, each of which is composed of a spatially contiguous set of pixels, is a very difficult and ill-formed problem (Hanson and Riseman 1978c; Nagin et al. 1982). The inherent noisiness and ambiguity of the sensory data leads to segmentations that are unreliable and vary in uncontrollable ways; for example, regions and lines are often fragmented or merged. Occlusion leads to the difficult problem of partial model matching, where a strong match with part of the model rather than a weak match of the whole model is desired. One must also expect that many region and line samples will not belong to any of the model classes because they may be parts of shadow regions, portions of occluded objects that cannot be identified, objects that have not been included in the set of object classes in the knowledge base, or object parts that are identifiable only in the context of the object hypothesis.

In some cases, as in House's depth-perception system, interaction of low-level systems can remove some of this confusion. Nonetheless, high-level systems will in many cases "break the tie" by coming up with the best interpretation. A famous example from pattern recognition involves a broken letter that can be interpreted as either an A or an H. Clearly, for a system that is interpreting English text, the preferred interpretation would be A in the context C_T but H in the context T_E. In interpreting natural scenes, where objects can be at different distances and at different orientations and where one object can occlude another, the mobilization of world constraints and expectations can play the decisive role in translating fragmented surface cues into confident interpretations of the environment. Scene interpretation requires processes that construct complex descriptions. During the processing, many hypotheses are put forth before a subset that can be verified and which satisfies a consistent set of relational constraints is accepted. AI systems are often faced with fitting a set of very weak but consistent hypotheses into a more reliable whole. This usually is a complex process that requires a great reliance on stored knowledge of the object classes. This knowledge takes the form of object attributes and relations between objects, particularly relations between parts of objects. The expression of such relationships requires a hierarchical decomposition of the knowledge base.

The role of context is to send expectations about regions of the environment which are related in space or in time. In the case of time, we may talk of anticipations. (Compare Neisser's [1976] anticipatory schemas.) As was discussed above, the processing of images in a new situation must start bottom-up, but in general a process will be occurring in a context that will allow some top-down biased processing. When two conflicting hypotheses are available, knowledge can also be used in deciding what type of image information might resolve the conflict, and thus directing the focus of attention. Through such a network of context, expectations, and predictions, we can see high-level vision proceeding in terms of cooperative computation in the high-level sense. Another aspect of high-level knowledge is that the way one looks at an object—and, correspondingly, the way a machine-vision system should represent an object—can depend strongly on the intentions of the organism or the robot. If the goal of perception for an active organism or robot is to pass action parameters to a planning or action-guiding process, then different representations are required for different purposes. For example, the representation of a chair is very different when the task is "painting" than when the task is "sitting."

A crucial question in both the analysis of biological systems and the design of machine-vision systems is to what extent low-level processes are under the control of high-level processes. Certainly, the biological data on the different structures of retinal cells in different species suggest that the style of representation to be delivered by the low-level system is task dependent. But this does not address the question of whether the actual processing in the low-level system is dependent on the current state of high-level representation of the environment. Weisstein's matching studies have at least shown overall bias of high-level or low-level, in that there are definite timing effects and the identification of barely perceptible briefly flashed line segments shows an object superiority. In this volume, Weisstein and Wong suggest that low-level processing proceeds differently when the portion of the image has been classified as figure than when it has been classified as ground. All these distinctions make sense in the vocabulary of the low-level vision system without requiring the vocabulary of specific objects in the world. It is thus perhaps a reasonable working hypothesis that future machine-vision systems will have their low-level components tailored to the particular application domain, but that the communication pathway from high-level to low-level processes will be in terms of a "low-level vocabulary" rather than in terms of the recognition of specific objects (Kohl 1986).

At the other end of the spectrum is the problem of representing the complexity of the 3D physical world in a form useful to the interpretation process. The 3D shape, color, texture, and size in an object class, as well as the spatial and functional relations to other objects, often have a great deal of natural variation from object to object and from scene to scene. This problem is compounded by the fact that the 2D appearance of these objects in the image is affected by variations in lighting, perspective distortion, point of view, occlusion, highlights, and shadows. These difficulties ensure that the transformation processes for grouping intermediate symbols and matching them to knowledge structures will produce highly unreliable results. The interpretation processes will require general mechanisms for dealing with this uncertainty, detecting errors, and verifying hypotheses.

The goal of many general computer-vision systems is the construction of a symbolic description of the three-dimensional world (an "interpretation") portrayed in an image or an image sequence, including the naming of the objects that are present, their sizes and distances from the observer, their motion attributes, their functional and relational properties, and the like. Image interpretation involves the recovery of the structure of the three-dimensional world lost during the projection of a scene onto a two-dimensional image or image sequence. The 3D-to-2D projection is not uniquely invertible, and hence inference processes must be employed during the recovery process; the ambiguous nature of the image data can be resolved somewhat by using general knowledge of the physical properties of the world to constrain the alternative hypotheses that arise during the reconstruction process. For this reason, the process of image interpretation is often viewed as an incremental mapping from the initial syntactic description of the image (e.g., pixels, edges and lines, regions, surfaces, and their associated properties) to a cognitive (semantic or structural) representation of the sensory data.

The mapping is dependent on assumptions about the scene domain and the scene-to-image projections, about the descriptive primitives that can be extracted from the image data, about the relationships between the primitives and the objects in the domain the system is attempting to recognize, and about the goals of the system. The mapping can be thought of as operating over a multilevel representation of partially constructed interpretations, in which the more image-oriented information is at the lower levels and the more abstract, symbolic descriptions are at the higher levels (hence the terms *low-* and *high-level* vision). World knowledge may also be represented hierarchically in a manner that facilitates the application of the constraints during the construction of a more abstract representation of the image from less abstract hypotheses. The world knowledge may exist in a variety of forms and may include expected contexts (e.g., "a house scene"), knowledge of both specific and general objects (part/subpart decomposition, shape, relational and functional properties, class membership, etc.), assumptions concerning the properties of elementary descriptors such as surfaces (e.g., continuous almost everywhere), and externally imposed goals (e.g., "find the road"). In effect, the collection of constraints and the processes of obtaining evidence for which of the constraints are relevant form a model of the world within the system. An interpretation can thus be viewed as an association between explicit image structures and events (including temporal changes) and their implicit characterization in world knowledge, via a sequence of intermediate, incrementally constructed descriptions.

A vision system must be capable of constructing and maintaining the belief structure captured in the interpretation. These functions are mitigated by the control processes responsible for deciding which hypotheses to expand next (focus of attention), how to expand them, what knowledge and constraints are appropriate and how they are to be applied, when a hypothesis is sufficiently believable that it may be instantiated, how to detect and resolve conflicting hypotheses, how to achieve specific goals, and so on. Control strategies are often categorized as "bottom-up" (data-directed), "top-down" (goal-directed), or a combination of the two. In bottom-up control, an interpretation is constructed from the image toward descriptions, as opposed to the matching of expectations or predictions from internal models (world knowledge) to less abstract data that occurs in top-down methods. Combined, these two control strategies can be used to generate very powerful control mechanisms incorporating sophisticated focus of attention and ambiguity-resolving mechanisms, such as those used in the Hearsay speech-understanding system (Erman et al. 1980), the VISIONS image-understanding system (Hanson and Riseman 1978b, 1983; Weymouth 1986), the ACRONYM system (Brooks 1981a,b, 1983), and Ballard's (1976, 1978) system for detecting tumors in chest radiographs. In this volume, many of the papers in parts II, III, and IV touch on various issues of control.

To a large extent, research in computer vision is concerned with the discovery of the most appropriate representations and associated processes for constructing an interpretation. There is much disagreement and healthy debate. A variety of issues must be addressed and resolved before substantial progress in computer vision can be achieved:

• Effective intermediate symbolic representations must be obtained to serve as the interface between the sensory data and the knowledge base.

• Knowledge representations capable of capturing the tremendous variability and complexity in the appearance of natural objects and scenes, particularly 3D shape representations, must be defined.

• Techniques must be developed for flexibly organizing the intermediate symbols under the guidance of the knowledge base.

• Mechanisms for integrating information and data from multiple sources must be developed.

• Inference mechanisms must be available for assessing the indirect implications of the direct evidence.

• Mechanisms must be developed for coping with the great degree of uncertainty in every stage of data transformation that is part of the interpretation process.

Representing World Knowledge

A central problem in image understanding is the representation and use of all available sources of knowledge during the interpretation process. This problem is compounded by the diversity of the forms of knowledge available and the need to structure the knowledge in such a way that the relevant knowledge is accessible at the appropriate time. In some cases, the knowledge is declarative in form ("The sky is blue"). Vision systems must have access to knowledge of the attributes of objects and their parts: color, texture, shape. In other cases the knowledge is relational in form: the decomposition of objects into parts, the relationships between objects, and the contextual properties of larger collections of objects. Other knowledge is more procedural in form, such as knowledge of the perspective transformations in mapping from 3D to 2D.

There is a large conceptual gap between the initial sensory data (pixels and their properties) and the high-level symbolic descriptions that constitute an interpretation. Consequently, the idea of hierarchical representations of knowledge, in which the levels correspond roughly to the vocabulary of the intermediate representation of an interpretation, has gained acceptance among vision researchers. Marr (1982) identified three very general levels of representation: the primal sketch (the low-level representation of lines and edges), the $2\frac{1}{2}$D sketch (the intermediate representation of surfaces), and the symbolic (high-level) representation of objects, their parts, their shape properties, and their spatial relations. Hanson and Riseman (1978b), Brooks (1981a,b), Barrow and Tenenbaum (1981), and others have suggested similar multilevel representations starting with pixels at the lowest level and progressing through vertices, line segments, regions, surfaces, volumes, objects, and schemas. In general, however, intermediate representations need not form a strict hierarchy, as can be seen from such pairs as depth/motion or, at a finer grain, disparity/accomodation. Although such hierarchies provide the possibility of rich descriptive capabilities, it is necessary to distinguish between the representation of a specific instance of a visual entity and the general class to which it belongs. For example, a particular object labeled TREE (however the labeling is achieved and represented) is an image-specific instance of the image-independent class of "TREE" at the object level and should inherit the basic properties of TREE from its class association, modified by the properties and attributes of the particular TREE in the image. These values should be associated with each particular instance of a tree, since there may be several in the image. This suggests that the interpretation should be constructed in a structure parallel to the representation of world knowledge, but in the same form so that associations can be made between each image instance and its corresponding representation in the knowledge structure.

There are many different kinds of knowledge that may be relevant at various points in the interpretation process, and each imposes different kinds of constraints on the underlying representation. Most knowledge representations currently in use can be viewed as combinations of data structures and interpretative procedures encoding knowledge of objects (individual instances, classes, and descriptions), of events (actions, situations, cause and effect), of performance (how-to, skills), and metaknowledge (knowledge about what is known: extent, origins, reliability, etc.) Characteristics of knowledge that are independent of the choice of the representation include scope (what portion of world knowledge is represented), grain size (how detailed is the knowledge), modularity, and accessibility (e.g., explicit representation in a declarative data structure or implicit representation in a procedure).

The problem of developing adequate representations of knowledge has a long history in artificial intelligence (Barr and Feigenbaum 1981). Among the most common representations are logic-based representations (e.g., predicate calculus), special-purpose analogical representations, semantic networks, procedural representations, production systems, frames, scripts, and schemas. In logic-based representations, world knowledge is captured in a set of logical propositions resident in a knowledge base, and inference is accomplished via proof procedures based on classical resolution techniques (Robinson 1965). The disadvantages of these representations include difficulties in representing procedural and heuristic knowledge and some evidence that first-order logics are insufficient to support the deductive processes used by humans. In addition, the structure of the knowledge (e.g., relations) is not explicit, and sometimes the axioms needed to represent rather common concepts are not at all obvious. First-order logic has not found widespread use as a knowledge representation in computer vision. PROLOG, a relatively new programming language intended for use in artificial intelligence, was developed from predicate logic (Warren et al. 1977). Analogical representations are representations that directly capture the physical aspects of the knowledge in the structure of the representation, such as maps and three-dimensional models of objects. Some of the knowledge needed in vision (such as the image itself, derived images, shape information, and maps) can profitably be represented in analogical form. The disadvantages of these representations are that they may be clumsy to manipulate for some operations and that they may not generalize easily.

A semantic network is a representation of knowledge in the form of a graph structure consisting of nodes (representing objects and their properties) and directed arcs (representing relationships and their properties). Semantic networks provide a natural representation of taxonomies and property-inheritance hierarchies by including special relations (such as IS-A and SUBSET) in the relation set (Lowrance 1978; Lowrance and Corkill 1979; Williams and Lowrance 1977). Associations between objects are explicit, and relevant facts can be inferred directly from closely linked nodes; directed search processes can be used for nodes that are relatively far apart. The disadvantages of semantic networks include the lack of formal inferencing mechanisms and the lack of a formal semantics of the primitives from which the net is constructed; the meaning of the net structures depends entirely on the programs that manipulate it.

Procedural representations encode knowledge in small programs, or procedures, in a manner similar to the classical style of programming. This idea first appeared in artificial intelligence in the programming language PLANNER (Hewitt 1972); however, any program that does not specifically encode the knowledge in an explicit representation can be viewed as using a procedural representation. Procedural representations are most appropriate for knowledge about how to accomplish a goal or how to perform some transformation (i.e., process descriptions). In PLANNER, for instance, procedures are activated via a "pattern directed" invocation mechanism; in this model, procedures are stored in the knowledge base with an associated pattern that, when satisfied, causes the procedure to be invoked with parameters bound to values obtained during pattern matching. The major disadvantage of this representation is that the knowledge and the control process are encapsulated in the same structure, so that it difficult to modify either. Knowledge is not represented explicitly, and thus it is difficult to understand the knowledge and its structure.

Production systems are rule-based inference systems in which knowledge (either declarative or procedural) is represented in the form of a loose collection of IF condition THEN action (antecedent-consequent) rules which are activated if the pattern specified in the IF condition is satisfied. The "action" component of all activated rules is then executed; the resulting action usually updates a global data base (a "blackboard"), which represents the partial interpretation being constructed. A rule interpreter provides the system-control function (e.g., deciding which rules to activate and updating the global data base). Production rules, a very popular knowledge representation in the area of expert systems (Barr and Feigenbaum 1981), have been used in vision to provide both the knowledge representation and the control and inferencing functions. Production systems are highly modular; rules behave as independent "chunks" of knowledge and can be modified easily. The rules impose a uniform structure on the knowledge, and the inferencing mechanisms easily support both bottom-up and top-down control (forward and backward chaining). The disadvantages of production systems are that the consistency of the knowledge is difficult to maintain in large systems, the flow of control is somewhat opaque because it is distributed, and large systems are often inefficient. The major difference between procedural systems (such as PLANNER) and production systems is in the communication pathways between the procedures or rules. In procedural systems, procedures can usually communicate directly with one another; in production systems, communication is usually limited to changes in the global blackboard.

It is clear that all these representations can be generalized to the hierarchical structures we argued for earlier, and that additional structure can be added by partitioning the stored knowledge in various ways so that only portions of the knowledge need be active at any given time. Although the hierarchical representations directly incorporate relationships between objects in the representation, there are larger complexes of related elements whose organization will be of importance to the visual processes. (By this we mean the expected and familiar structures of the visual world, such as an office scene, one's house and neighborhood, the activities at a birthday party, and known methods for achieving a goal.) Minsky (1975), Neisser (1976), Piaget (1971), and Arbib (1972, 1975) have all argued that knowledge carries with it a substantial predictive capability, that appropriate structuring of the knowledge allows quick access to related "chunks" of knowledge and to important aspects of a situation, and that this structuring will involve a combination of various types of knowledge and local control information represented in different ways. According to Minsky's description, a frame is a complex data structure for representing stereotyped objects, events, and situations. Central to the frame is the idea of a slot, which describes the objects and the relations between them that are relevant to the situation described by the frame. Slots initially contain descriptions of the objects or values that may fill them, and are bound to objects or values when a frame is instantiated. A frame also contains local control information about how to use the frame, what to do if unexpected situations arise, what procedures may be applicable, and default values for slots. Schank's scripts (Schank and Abelson 1977) are framelike structures for representing stereotypical sequences of events, such as eating in a restaurant. Schank has used scripts as the knowledge structures in a system for understanding natural language.

Arbib (1981a) developed the idea of a schema as the basic unit of knowledge mediating between perception and action in his theory of perceptual structures and distributed motor control. (See papers 13 and 14 in this volume.) In this theory, an organism's internal representation of the world is viewed as an assemblage of general schemas each corresponding to some object or domain of interaction in the environment. Schemas may be in various states of activation depending upon how well a schema's structure matches events in the environment or how much the schema is implied by other active schemas. Related schema parameters represent properties of the hypothesized object, such as size, location, and motion. Activation of perceptual schemas provides access to related motor schemas without causing the system to activate those schemas. Motor schemas are viewed as control systems in the classical biological sense, and are the basic structures manipulated by a planning system to construct a plan of action as a coordinated control program of such schemas. In a system that works with dynamic images, such as a robot (Arbib et al. 1984), the motor schemas should contain anticipatory schemas to monitor task satisfaction and to determine errors that require modification of action, or even modification of plan, via dynamic high-level planning.

In general, the representations currently used in vision are hybrid structures combining many different kinds and types of knowledge in a suitably organized structure. The representations must be sensitive enough to capture subtle differences and variations in object classes yet robust enough to capture broadly applicable "sketches" of objects and expected scenarios. Schemas may be viewed as defining (possibly overlapping) partitions of the knowledge base related to the situations of interest in the task domain. Knowledge of individual objects and of their parts and their relations may also be represented in a schema system, a semantic network structure, or a production system. Procedural knowledge embedded within the structure provides local control information; global control may be supplied by inferencing mechanisms defined over the knowledge structure. Knowledge invocation may be accomplished locally via pattern-directed invocation of nodes, schemas, or rules or via top-down activation as a function of context, expectations, and goals. Pattern-matching procedures must be capable of achieving partial matches (e.g., part of an object may be occluded), and the system as a whole must be capable of distinguishing between good partial matches and poor complete matches. This implies that a system must contain mechanisms for dealing with possibly ambiguous and erroneous hypotheses and assessing the most likely interpretation on the basis of evidence accumulated in many different ways and with varying credibilities. Existing vision systems address these issues in very different ways.

The question of what knowledge to represent, rather than how to represent it, is a function of the task domain and the goals of the system. A system for interpreting satellite photographs will use very different kinds of knowledge than one designed to recognize objects from ground level, and detailed knowledge of three-dimensional shape may be important in the latter case but not in the former. A mobile autonomous robot requires knowledge of spatial organization, object motion, and its own capabilities in order to navigate; an industrial inspection robot may not require the same knowledge.

Shape, an extremely important attribute of objects, plays a major role in recognition and discrimination tasks; it also presents one of the most severe representational problems in computer vision. An adequate description of shape should permit an object to be recognized from partial views and varying points of view and orientations; this implies that internal models should be described in a view-independent manner. Paradoxically, such a representation might take the form of an exhaustive set of "typical" views. Not only should a representation permit recognition; it should also allow comparison of shape in order to determine similarities and differences. The representation should be equally valid for rigid, piecewise-rigid (i.e., jointed), and nonrigid objects, and should describe properties of the surfaces and contours of the object in a language that permits computationally effective procedures for matching to primitives extracted from the image. No existing representation even comes close to this ideal representation, and the representation and use of shape in general is an open research issue in computer vision.

Three-dimensional shape descriptions are generally thought of as two-part descriptions, with one part capturing the structural and relational decomposition of an object into its parts and the other capturing aspects of the surface or volumetric description of the parts. Three-dimensional object recognition, then, generally involves matching the internal model of an object to the (processed) sensory data. The matching process may involve transforming both the model and the sensory data into a common intermediate representation in which primitives computable from the sensory data and predictions computable from the model share a set of descriptive primitives. The matching process should be relatively insensitive to modest amounts of noise in the sensor data and should be capable of handling partial matches. (objects are often partially occluded.)

The structural and relational aspects of shape are usually represented in a relational structure similar to those discussed earlier. Solid modeling in computer graphics is similar in philosophy to the representation of shape in computer vision, and shares with it many organizational principles (Foley and Van Dam 1982) and the need to capture the realistic form of an object. However, in graphics visual rendering of the object model is the desired result, while in vision the requirement of object recognition (matching the model to a given image) places additional constraints on the representation. In graphics the rendering is usually one of a specific instance of the object; in vision the representation must be broad enough to capture variations in the collection of specific instances making up a class of objects. For these reasons, the shape representations that have been used in vision have tended to be somewhat simpler than those used in graphics, and (with a few exceptions) computer vision has not dealt with sophisticated shape representations.

The representations for rigid objects encountered in vision fall into three general categories: boundary, surface, and volume representations. (Tsotsos, in paper 11, discusses the case of nonrigid bodies exemplified by a heart model.) Each of these representations captures some aspects of shape explicitly while others are implicit and must be computed. The computation of implicit information may be difficult and expensive. For example, volume representations are often in the form of discrete three-dimensional "occupancy" arrays in which cells intersecting the object are marked in some way. Surface properties are not explicitly represented and must be computed from the array. Besl and Jain (1985b) and Ballard and Brown (1982) have provided thorough discussions of current methods of shape representation in computer vision; in the following paragraphs we are concerned with two methods, one of which (generalized cones) is encountered quite frequently in the vision literature.

A generalized cone (Binford 1971) is a volumetric model of shape in which a volume is generalized by sweeping an arbitrarily shaped bounded planar surface (called a *cross section*) along an arbitrary three-dimensional space curve (called the *axis*). The axis passes through the centroid of the cross section and is normal to it. The size and shape of the cross section may change as it is swept along the axis; the changes are specified by a sweeping rule. Complex objects are modeled by decomposing them into simpler shapes, each represented by a generalized cone, and linking them through a common coordinate system via a relational structure. Marr (1982) argued that a shape representation does not have to reproduce the surface characteristics of an object in order to be useful, and proposed a shape representation in which the axes of generalized cones are associated with the "natural" axes of a shape. Although generalized cones are adequate for many shapes, particularly those having elongated parts, they are not particularly useful for descriptions of shapes not having elongated parts (Nevatia 1982). Another shortcoming of this kind of description is that it does not easily describe local variations (distortions) of the volume because a description of the variations must be defined as a function along the length of the axis. Nevatia also surveys methods for computing generalized cones from image data. (The ACRONYM model-based vision system described below uses generalized cones as its underlying shape representation.)

The shape of a three-dimensional object should be defined unambiguously by the three-dimensional surfaces that bound the object. In the case of polyhedral objects, the surfaces are planar and descriptions are expressed in terms of planar surfaces and vertices. If polygons are used as the primitive representation, curved surfaces may be approximated to arbitrary fidelity; this is a common method in computer graphics. These methods may be generalized to use curved surface patches as the underlying primitives. The patches may be defined in various ways as bounded parameterized quadric or cubic surfaces; higher-order surfaces are rarely used because of computational complexities. York et al. (1980, 1981) described a volumetric representation called the *quilted solid* made up of Coons (1974) surface patches with B-splines as the defining polynomials. In this representation, the four boundaries of a surface patch are defined by parameterized spline functions. Blending functions, which are also splines, are used to interpolate interior surface points. The advantage of using splines is that local deformations can be isolated to closed intervals on the spline without affecting neighboring intervals. Two adjacent surface patches can be smoothly joined by equating the first and second derivatives of the blending functions across the common boundary. Each surface patch can be locally deformed by appropriate choices of the parameters of the blending functions associated with the patch without distorting adjacent patches and without disturbing the smooth join of the patches. Six or fewer surface patches define the shape of a volume around an axis (the quilted solid) which is used to relate the spatial orientation of such volumes to other patches via a relational structure. Three-dimensional objects defined in terms of the quilted-solid representation may be projected to two dimensions using standard techniques, and the resulting contours are also spline curves. The general approach to matching involved characterizing two-dimensional contours extracted from the images by a variety of features and then using these features to index into plausible models; each possible model was then used to drive a process that attempted to instantiate the correct one. The matching and recognition processes for this kind of representation have not been convincingly demonstrated for systems with a large number of complex objects; the projection and matching processes are extremely expensive, particularly if there are no prior constraints on the orientations of objects. However, it is theoretically possible to generate those constraints in a manner analogous to that proposed by Marr for the generalized cylinder models: A rough characterization is obtained by ignoring surface details and matching only the stick figures defined by the axes. Again, this has never been adequately demonstrated in the general case.

One potential solution to the difficulties in matching caused by the multiplicity of views generated by the unconstrained orientations of a 3D object is through the use of characteristic 2D views. Here, an object is described by a set of two-dimensional views as seen from a set of predetermined viewpoints, representing the salient aspects of the two-dimensional projections. Recognition then involves matching all the 2D views to find the best match; this would provide not only recognition data but also the object-viewer geometry up to the resolution of the original representation. There are several objections to this brute-force approach, the most obvious of which concerns the computational costs (in both time and space). In cases where the object-viewer geometry is sufficiently constrained such as the case of an airplane against the sky (Wallace and Wintz 1980), the computational costs may be quite reasonable. Callahan and Weiss 1985, building on the work of Koenderink and Van Doorn (1976b, 1979), have proposed a model for describing surface shape that represents the canonical ("generic") two-dimensional projections of an object onto a viewing sphere. The sphere is tesselated into closed areas as a function of the geometry of the object; transitions between areas represent changes in viewing position for which the projections of the object undergo topological changes. Thus, only a fixed known number of views must be represented. Although this idea has not been implemented in any significant way, it does appear promising.

Representing and organizing knowledge as it is relevant to vision remains a challenge. The nature of vision is apparently such that many different types and forms of knowledge are necessary and, consequently, monolithic representations are probably too limited. Rather, multiple representations are probably necessary, each selected according to the representational and application requirements of the knowledge. Partitioned semantic networks composed of schemas or frames, with embedded procedures, have been used with some success to structure knowledge in vision systems.

Since three-dimensional shape is such a pervasive visual and tactile experience, it is somewhat surprising that so little is known about its representation and use in vision. The use of depth and range information derived from images or special sensors is just beginning to be studied seriously; the representation of nonrigid temporally varying objects has hardly been studied at all. It is clear that a significant amount of effort will be required before sophisticated shape descriptions, in a form that minimizes the matching effort, will be available to computer-vision systems.

Mapping between Images and Symbols

In the preceding subsection we discussed the idea of hierarchical knowledge representations partitioned along several different dimensions: generalization and specialization (IS-A links in semantic networks), part/whole decomposition (PART-OF links), and expectations (schema or frame structures). Specialization provides inheritance of general object attributes by more specialized instances of the object, part/whole decomposition expresses complex objects in terms of more primitive parts and their relationships as part of the whole, and expectations provide an organization of objects into common scenarios and describe the role assumed by an object within a scenario. The knowledge representation, regardless of the form it takes, contains the general world knowledge available to the system and constitutes the world model. As Tsotsos argues in this volume, perception takes place in a spatio-temporal context, and time represents another dimension across which the representation should be partitioned.

We have also argued that the role of knowledge in vision is not only to represent symbolic names that can be attached to objects in an image but also to overcome the ambiguities inherent in the construction of the two-dimensional image from the three-dimensional scene. World knowledge must capture the constraints necessary to finally arrive at an unambiguous result from the ambiguous image, to the degree that this is possible. Some images are inherently ambiguous and may support multiple legitimate interpretations (the Necker cube and Wittgenstein's duck-rabbit image, for example); in these cases, a vision system should support all the interpretations.

While the knowledge provides general world models and constraints, it is the image or the image sequence that provides the window into a specific world, and it is from the image that the descriptive properties of the image events corresponding to world events must be derived. Thus, there is a tight coupling between the derived image descriptions and world knowledge through the primitives used to describe them. It must be possible to match image properties to world properties in a way that relates the image to world models. This implies a commonality of representation and places the matching processes briefly discussed above in clearer perspective: They form the links between the image and the knowledge. Although in some cases it is possible that two fully instantiated models will explain (or fit) the same data, these cases are probably rare. The real problem arises in matching and hypothesis formation: As the number and the complexity of the world models increase, the potential correspondences between models and a primitive image event increase excessively. (How many models does a single straight line relate to?) Any particular image event gives rise to multiple world models. Consequently, much of the work in vision is concerned with the extraction of image descriptions at a level far removed from individual pixels and with identification of generally applicable constraints that can be used to group the primitives into more abstract stable descriptions that better match the primitives used in the knowledge representation. The grouping processes may be bottom-up processes relying on object-independent principles, or they may be task-dependent processes applied in a top-down manner in a specific context. In paper 6 Weisstein and Wong discuss some of the ways in which knowledge affects grouping processes in human vision, and in paper 7 Zucker discusses the diversity of perceptual processes for grouping. The techniques for region and line extraction described above may be considered to be generalized grouping processes based on a principle of similarity applied to pixels/attributes and edge orientations, respectively. Adiv's motion algorithm, which recovers the motion of an observer and of independently moving objects, is a grouping process based on similarity of motion, a rather high-level concept.

The general notion of grouping has been of interest in cognitive psychology for some time. Cognitive psychologists (notably Wertheimer and Rubin) have identified various factors that determine grouping behavior in human perception, particularly figure perception. The factors identified are generally taken to include the following:

Nearness or proximity in the field of view. Objects relatively close together are readily seen as a group.

Sameness or similarity. Objects with similar attributes, such as color or shape, have a tendency to be viewed as a group.

Common fate. Objects that move together or in a consistent manner relative to one another are seen as a group.

Good continuation or good figure. Objects with featural continuity (such as direction), with closed contours, or with symmetry or balance are preferred.

Conformity with momentary "set." The observer can define a grouping and hence resist the factors of proximity and similarity.

Experience or custom. Familiar objects are seen as a group.

The term *object* was used here in a loose sense, to include entities such as points and lines as well as more familiar objects such as cars and trees. The purpose of these principles was to help explain why the visual system prefers certain organizations over others—particularly the grouping of all the proximal stimuli related to one object in that object rather than grouping stimuli across objects. As Rock (1983) pointed out, very little progress has been made in explicating the processes that give rise to the global grouping behavior in perception. On the other hand, the cognitive psychologists have lacked a computational theory that would permit more than a qualitative description of grouping principles. Each of the principles is applicable to many different features of the objects involved, and at many different levels of description. Consequently, there has been a resurgence of interest in grouping phenomena in computer vision, but from the viewpoint of generating more abstract (higher-level) descriptions of collections of primitive elements in terms of relations that are likely to be nonaccidental within an object. (See, e.g., Witkin and Tenenbaum 1982.) These descriptions are typically more compact than those in terms of the individual elements in the grasp, but the grouped collection is also more than the sum of the parts, since the grouping criterion also represents a relation that holds between the entities in the group. One result of grouping into larger units is a reduction in the size of the search space when the units are matched to world knowledge. Hence, the emphasis in computer vision is on the discovery of process-oriented grouping mechanisms based on general principles that are applicable without recourse to specific object knowledge.

A system that produces multiple consistent interpretations can be thought of as being uncertain about what it "sees," because there remains ambiguity about which is the "correct" interpretation. A major factor contributing to this ambiguity is the incomplete and inaccurate information obtained from the feature-extraction processes and/or the grouping mechanisms. Erman et al. (1980), Hanson and Riseman (1978b), Parma et al. (1980), and Waltz (1975) have shown that ambiguity arising from a lack of perfect information can be reduced considerably if partially redundant information is obtained from a variety of different sources. A major problem has been to develop machanisms that can take such information and interpret it within the context of some representation of knowledge.

In the visual world, partial occlusion, shadowing, and accidental alignment conspire to produce ambiguous, imperfect, and possibly incorrect descriptions. Grouping mechanisms employing general object-independent and context-independent mechanisms may be viewed as forming hypotheses about possible structures with associated confidence values that indicate the degree to which the relationship expressed by the grouping mechanism is satisfied. Subsequent use of these hypotheses—for example, by further grouping mechanisms or by data-to-object-model or object-model-to-data matching processes—must take into account these confidence values in a way that tends to reduce the inherent ambiguities in the resulting descriptions. Treating the hypotheses as evidence for a set of models and the confidence values as belief in the evidence leads to the general idea of inferencing mechanisms operating over the knowledge base. The inference mechanisms must be capable of pooling (combining) evidence from multiple sources of direct evidence (image features) or indirect evidence (inferred features) in a consistent manner and propagating this pooled information over the knowledge representation, subject to the constraints captured in the knowledge.

Some highly successful knowledge-based expert systems use a Bayesian-based model for reasoning about their tasks. (See Adams 1976; Duda et al. 1976; Buchanan et al. 1969.) However, such systems require a complete specification of all conditional dependencies between the occurrence of environmental events and hypotheses about the state of their respective environments. It is well known that this type of specification is extremely difficult if not impossible to obtain; Lowrance (1982), Shortliffe (1976), and Buchanan et al. (1969) have shown that this difficulty places a severe restriction on the environmental inferences that can be made. One approach to this problem is to estimate the conditional-dependence information that is needed by the system but is unobtainable. The accuracy of these estimates depends on the system's assumption(s) about how missing information can be pooled. For example, Prospector (Duda et al. 1977) is a Bayesian-based system that assumes that some unobtainable information can be combined with existing data in an independent manner. Lowrance (1982) has shown that such assumptions can result in violation of Bayes's Law or cause inference mechanisms to diverge. Solutions to these problems, like that employed in the Prospector system, are typically ad hoc or heuristic. The complexity of many ad hoc and heuristic solutions make it difficult to understand the dependence between the interpretation(s) produced by a system and the operation of its inference mechanism.

Confirmation theory (Carnap 1950; Hempel 1965), as a foundation for a confirmation-based model of reasoning, has been used successfully in such systems as MYCIN (Shortliffe 1976). In one respect, such models are less restrictive than Bayesian-based models: They do not require a complete specification of the information needed to complete some task. However, there remain some requirements that are extremely difficult to satisfy. For example, as Shortliffe (1976) states, "... (unless the requisite conditional probabilities are known), we must insist that dependent pieces of evidence be grouped into single rather than multiple rules." Grouping dependent evidence, a strategy similar to that described by Edwards (1972), makes it easier for MYCIN-like systems and experts to approximate the aggregate conditional dependence. However, this freedom forces the researcher to combine, into a "unit" representation (e.g., a single rule), some knowledge that might have to be reasoned about by separate rules. In addition, the

researcher must devise some intuitive, usually heuristic, mechanism constrained by confirmation theory (Tornebohm 1966) for incrementally combining new and existing environmental information.

Some of the limitations of a standard Bayesian approach (Wesley and
Hanson 1982) are overcome by the use of the Dempster-Shafer formalism
for evidential reasoning, in which an explicit representation of partial
ignorance, uncertainty, and conflict is provided (Dempster 1968; Shafer
1976). The inferencing model allows "belief" or "confidence" in a proposition to be represented as a range within the [0, 1] interval. The lower and
upper bounds represent the support and the plausibility, respectively, of a
proposition, while the width of the interval can be interpreted as ignorance.
The effect of applying Dempster's rule to mass functions involving different partially restricted subsets is to focus that mass or belief onto the
consistent subsets of possibilities. Used this way, the ideas of Shafer and
Dempster become a process of *possibilistic* rather than *probabilistic* reasoning. The mass attributed to impossible situations is viewed as conflict
or mass assigned to an "unknown" object and monitored to evaluate the
correctness of the knowledge sources and the knowledge base (frame of
discernment). In this approach, evidential information enters the inference
engine in the form of "mass" (or belief) distributions defined over sets of
propositions common to both them and the model. These mass distributions are combined according to the structure imposed by the world knowledge through Dempster's (1967) rule of combination. The result is a new
mass distribution representing the consensus of the information combined.
This information is converted to the interval representation, and the model
allows "inference" from those propositions upon which it bears directly to
those upon which it bears indirectly. The *a priori* probabilities (which are
often difficult or impossible to collect in artificial-intelligence domains, but
which are required by many other systems of inexact reasoning) are not
needed. This form of evidential reasoning is more general than either a
Boolean or a Bayesian approach, yet it reduces to Boolean or Bayesian
inferencing when the appropriate information is available.

There are many reasons why the evidential model is attractive. It provides a simple mechanism for representing uncertain information and for
pooling partial evidence. The evidential inference engine is a plausible
connection between data-directed and goal-directed hypothesis formation
and instantiation. It separates the mechanisms for combining evidence from
the mechanisms for making environmental inferences, allowing experimentation with many mechanisms for combining data independent of the
representation of domain knowledge. The model does not require perfect

information; however, if perfect information is available it can easily be integrated with existing information. The model can perform both data-directed and goal-directed inferences over a single knowledge network. The theoretical foundation of the evidential model makes it easier to understand the relationship between the manipulation of environmental information and knowledge and the performance of the system. The model's formality makes it easier to prove, if necessary, why the system performed the way it did, given some body of evidence and domain knowledge.

The Status of Machine-Vision Systems

There have been several extensive efforts to build functional computer-vision systems that will be complete in the sense that they will incorporate low-level processes, world knowledge, interpretation strategies, inferencing mechanisms, and so on and will attempt to build interpretations of reasonably complex images. Existing systems differ in their emphases on selected aspects of vision at the expense of others. Some, such as ACRONYM and 3D Mosaic, emphasize three-dimensional geometrical structures; others, including VISIONS and Ohta's system, rely more heavily on image-based knowledge and structures. Not one of the systems discussed in this section approaches the sophistication of human vision; each, either explicitly or implicitly, functions in a restricted domain. A good review of existing systems can be found in Binford 1982.

Early work in computer vision was focused on highly constrained domains, most notably the blocks world. Roberts (1965), observing that techniques being developed in pattern classification and their attendant theories were contributing very little to theories of machine perception, explored the transition from the 2D world of images to the 3D model world, and the knowledge required for this transition, in the microworld of polyhedra (cubes, rectangular wedges, and hexagonal prisms) on a flat surface. Using knowledge of the geometry of the imaging process (position, orientation, and focal length of the camera), Roberts's system assumed a gray-level image as input and tried to work from the image to a description. The approach embedded knowledge of polyhedra in a collection of projective transformations and 3D models derived from geometrical considerations and topological invariants of the objects known to be in the scene. The system worked from the image toward a description by looking for cues in the line representation of the image and using those cues to select a possible model; it then asked whether a possible transformation allowed by the rules could have produced the picture (or some part of it) from an actual instance of one or more of the abstract models. The best interpretation, as determined by the degree of match between the picture and the prediction, was then selected.

The major failings of Roberts's system were the relatively limited and static nature of the knowledge employed, the very simple strategies used for recognition, and the difficulty of extending the system to more unconstrained domains. (Roberts worked with many blocks on a table top, and controlled the lighting and the contrast carefully in order to minimize the problem of extracting line boundaries of the blocks.)

The research triggered by Roberts's work is still very much in evidence in the careful investigation of the semantics of a microworld, the representation of these semantics in a form applicable to the image-understanding task, and the development of methods for applying this knowledge to achieve a goal. Often the goal is stated explicitly, but it may be implicit in the system's structure.

Instead of attempting to recognize known polyhedra, Guzman's (1969) SEE system attempted to partition a scene (a line drawing) into polyhedral bodies by assigning the regions in the image to individual bodies. Guzman focused on the semantics of polyhedral vertices and categorized them into eight classes of vertex types. Using these types in conjunction with permissible patterns of relations between them, the SEE system was able to infer a set of regions from a line description of the image (provided to the system) and to assign these regions to a set of bodies, without knowing *a priori* what the permissible bodies were (other than that they were polyhedra). The approach was notable for the systematic attempt at exploring the semantics of the domain; its failure lay in the heuristics used to infer the overall structure of the bodies and in the incomplete representation of the semantics of the domain. The rules for linking vertices (i.e., the allowable patterns of relationships between them) were derived not on the basis of a 2D/3D representational theory taking into account the overall geometry of polyhedral bodies, but rather in an intuitive way based on Guzman's observations about blocks. What was needed was a way to link the semantics of lines connecting vertices to the vertex semantics defined by Guzman.

Huffman (1971) and Clowes (1971) noted two essential points lacking in the previous work: A line or a vertex in isolation could represent one of several states in the physical world, but neighboring isolated fragments could be interpreted coherently if the physical constraints of the 3D world were taken into account. Huffman pointed out that a line can depict either a concave or a convex edge with both "attached" bodies visible, or it can depict an occluding edge that "hides" part of a surface to one side or the other. Furthermore, a line cannot be labeled differently at different points; thus, Huffman's line semantics integrate naturally into Guzman's vertex semantics and induce subclasses on his original classes as a function of line labels. Clowes's approach was very similar, but was slightly more complete since it could deal with multiply occluded bodies (which Huffman had not addressed). Mackworth (1973, 1974) extended this work by considering vertices in which more than three lines met; he was thus able to exploit information about skewed surfaces and the relative "tilt" of surfaces, so that the tilt of other surfaces could be immediately inferred. Mackworth's system concentrated on line and *surface* semantics, and thus the knowledge employed was more general (i.e., the class of "understandable" images was wider).

None of the systems described thus far was capable of dealing with shadows; indeed, shadows were considered a nuisance and a hindrance. Lighting was carefully arranged to eliminate them, or the system assumed a shadowless abstract description of the lines making up the polyhedral bodies. However, shadows provide another source of information about the 2D projection of the 3D world. Waltz (1975) examined the role of shadows in scenes of polyhedral bodies and incorporated a set of additional constraints into a system for analyzing scenes with shadows. He found that lines in images could represent not only object boundaries but also shadow boundaries, and thus the Huffman-Clowes label sets had to be enlarged to include them. The descriptions inferred by Waltz's program were in terms of concepts such as "behind," "in front of," "leans on," "rests against," "is supported by," "is shadowed by," "is turned away from the light source," and "can support."

The major problem confronted by Waltz derived from the fact that as the label set size increased, the number of possible labelings for a scene was subject to a combinatorial increase. For example, Waltz increased the number of edge types to 57, thus increasing the total number of logically possible vertex labels to 57^L, where L was the number of lines visible at the vertex. If a coherent interpretation could be obtained only by considering all possibilities at each location in the scene, then an exhaustive search was necessary. In this case, Waltz showed, there was an efficient way of obtaining the interpretation other than a brute-force search through the space of possible labels. The first observation was that exploiting the constraints of the physical world could reduce the number of physically possible labelings drastically. Thus, despite the very large set of candidate labelings, typically only one was a coherent labeling given the set of physical constraints between connected vertices; at most there were only a few. The second observation was that a technique existed (known variously as constraint satisfaction, relaxation, consistency filtering, or label propagation) that exploited local consistencies to generate global consistencies. It was, essentially, a parallel iterative technique by which local constraints (in this case, constraints known to hold at a given vertex) were propagated to adjacent local areas in an effort to find a mutually satisfactory labeling. As the process iterated, the local constraints propagated further and further, mutually affecting each local area, until a global optimum was reached. The constraints were thus propagated throughout the network without the need for an explosive exhaustive search.

In Waltz's system, the use of knowledge of geometry and illumination for determining the choice of cues, the distinction between meaningless and sensible local interpretations, the constraint-satisfaction filtering operation, and a plausible initial labeling strategy were combined to provide a set of interpretive constraints without which the computational requirements of his program would have been intractable. Waltz's system underscores the need for a deep understanding of the semantics of the domain, a choice of representations within which to embed these semantics, a method of expressing the relationships between the components of the scene and their mutual effect on each other, and a way of efficiently utilizing this knowledge at the right place and the right time.

Kanade (1979, 1980) extended the microworld of trihedral objects to what he termed the origami world, in which objects were composed of planar surfaces (rather than solids), no more than three of which met at a vertex. Vertices could be labeled in a manner similar to the Huffman-Clowes labeling, but the dictionary was larger, admitting a larger number of interpretations consistent with the label set. In order to eliminate physically unrealizable labelings, Kanade augmented the junction dictionary with surface-gradient constraints. A Waltz-type filtering operator on the vertex labels was performed using the augmented set of constraints. In order to extract quantitative shape descriptions, Kanade introduced two regularity heuristics: a parallel-line heuristic and a skewed-symmetry heuristic, which were used to further filter the multiple "realizable" interpretations remaining after constraint filtering.

Although much was learned from the polyhedral world, it was a fairly heavily constrained domain, and the techniques developed there do not extend naturally to more complex domains, such as the outdoors world. Recent approaches to machine vision have been directed toward more comprehensive representations of objects and world knowledge, more gen-

eral inferencing techniques, and more sophisticated image-data abstraction mechanisms, for the reasons cited above. Owing to the magnitude of
the system-development task (Kohler and Hanson 1982) and the research
effort required, only a few such systems have actually been built.

One system that does make use of trihedral object models is the 3D
MOSAIC system being developed by Herman and Kanade (1984). A direct
outgrowth of earlier work on junction labeling, 3D MOSAIC is a system
designed to incrementally reconstruct complex 3D scenes from multiple
images—specifically, aerial photographs of urban scenes. The initial interpretation, a three-dimensional wire-frame description of the scene in terms
of lines and vertices, is transformed into a surface-based model. The model
is successively refined and updated as more views of the scene are obtained. In that it extends from images to interpretations, 3D MOSAIC is a
complete system.

The input to 3D MOSAIC is an image of the scene, either a stereo pair
or a monocular image. Although different low-level analyses are applied
in the two cases, in both cases the initial image description is composed
of portions of surfaces, edges, and corners (vertices). Partial linear connected structures composed of vertices and (possibly hypothesized) lines
are formed from the primitive description. The two-dimensional structures
are converted to a three-dimensional wire-frame description by the application of a perspective analysis to the "vertical" and "horizontal" lines
emanating from the vertices. The three-dimensional structure is determined
relative to some arbitrarily assigned height above the ground plane; if
points on the ground plane can be found, relative heights can be related to
a single parameter associated with the ground plane. Next, the three-
dimensional wire-frame description is converted to a surface-based scene
model by the use of new vertices, edges, and faces hypothesized on the
basis of task-specific knowledge. Buildings are assumed to be composed of
regular polygonal planar surfaces, and heuristic rules are used to hypothesize the faces. If a partial scene model already exists from analysis of
previous views, the scene model is updated by matching the current wire-
frame model to the scene model using the vertices and edges, merging the
two descriptions, and completing partial structures using the set of wire-
frame-to-surface heuristics used earlier. The 3D MOSAIC system has generated partial interpretations of several urban scenes. One of the interesting
characteristics of 3D MOSAIC is that it does not use explicit models of
buildings; rather, the construction of the scene model proceeds by applying
a set of very general constraints to the primitive description, guided by the
observation that buildings are block-shaped objects that can be adequately

modeled by planar surfaces and limited geometric information (e.g., that roofs are parallel to the ground plane and that sides of buildings are vertical to the ground plane).

Another system that emphasizes object geometry and interobject relations is ACRONYM (Brooks 1981a,b), although in a significantly different representation than 3D MOSAIC. ACRONYM is intended to generate three-dimensional interpretations of scenes in a viewpoint-independent manner, using geometric models of objects. The primitive three-dimensional modeling construct in ACRONYM is the generalized cylinder. Objects are built up from primitive parts through part/whole graphs and class/subclass graphs describing both generic objects (e.g., an airplane) and specific instances of the generic objects (e.g., a 747). Spatial, part/subpart, and class/subclass relations between nodes in the graphs are parameterized and defined in a restriction graph that contains sets of constraints on the relations. These networks constitute the geometric knowledge employed by the system. The matching of object models to an image is facilitated by a prediction graph constructed by a geometric reasoning process. The prediction graph contains a representation of those object features and relations among them that are expected to be invariant and observable over a (possibly constrained) range of viewing parameters. The predictions are used for hypothesizing image-to-object matches and, given a match, determining how three-dimensional constraints can be generated from measurements on the image feature. Construction of the prediction graph does not require any image data and can be viewed as compilation of the three-dimensional-model data into a representation that can be matched more directly. From a specific image, a picture graph is constructed by representing the image as a collection of lines and line segments. The primitive shapes predicted by the prediction graph are extracted from the line representation, but no explicit matches are made. Interpretation then consists of matching portions of the prediction graph to portions of the picture graph. During the matching process, the "back" constraints generated from local feature matches must be both internally consistent and consistent with those stored in the prediction graph. Consistency is checked by a very general algebraic constraint-manipulation system that instantiates values or ranges of values to the model parameters. ACRONYM has been applied primarily to aerial images of airports and has successfully extracted instances of specific airplanes from the data. It has also been applied to low-angle views of collections of industrial parts.

Both 3D MOSAIC and ACRONYM use monocular available-light images as the starting point. In some cases other sensor technologies (see above) can be employed to generate representations with depth data as an integral part. In other cases, special lighting (Albus 1982) can be used to simplify the extraction of three-dimensional data from the monocular image. Several systems for inspecting industrial parts use a form of light striping to simplify depth extraction.

Several vision systems (Glicksman 1982; Nagao and Matsuyama 1980; McKeown et al. 1984) have been designed to interpret aerial or satellite images, in which the need for three-dimensional object models is reduced because of the constraints on the viewpoint. These systems rely on other visual characteristics, such as color, texture, two-dimensional shape, expected relations, and context, to arrive at a consistent interpretation.

Nagao, Matsuyama, and Ikeda developed a system for interpreting multispectral aerial photographs that used two-dimensional object models composed of object names, sets of object features, associated interpretation strategies, and relationships between objects. The interpretation strategies (procedures) of this system describe how to use the features to locate instances of the object in the image. The image is first segmented into primitive regions that are homogeneous in their spectral attributes. Each of these elementary regions is then labeled as one of a number of different types of characteristic regions (e.g., large homogeneous regions, elongated regions, high-contrast regions, shadow regions, shadow-making regions), and a set of descriptors for the regions (color, texture, size, etc.) is extracted and stored with the region. The characteristic regions are used to estimate the approximate domains of objects (a focus-of-attention mechanism). Object-detection subsystems examine the appropriate characteristic regions and use object-specific knowledge to confirm or reject the initial hypothesis. These subsystems may apply specialized feature-extraction processes to the candidate regions and may rely on previous interpretations of spatially or functionally related characteristic regions. The control structure is a production system with a global blackboard that provides a uniform interface to the object models. All communication between the object subsystems is via the blackboard. When an object module creates a hypothesis, a node is created on the blackboard and linked to the object node, the characteristic region(s), and other object-hypothesis nodes whose interpretation depends on the current hypothesis. The system is quite effective in locating and identifying cropfields, lakes, roads, rivers, railroads, buildings, and residential areas in aerial imagery. The use of characteristic regions to trigger plausible object models is a bottom-up approach to interpretation that switches to a top-down (or combined) strategy as hypotheses are formed. Both Glicksman and McKeown also consider the use of maps and other high-level knowledge about the image in order to further constrain the interpretation processes.

Several systems have been developed to interpret monocular ground-level outdoor scenes in color. Ohta (1985) views his system as a "region analyzer" in that it matches world models to the set of regions produced from a segmentation process. Knowledge is represented in a semantic network containing production rules associated with each node. Rules are triggered by region features (such as color, texture, simple two-dimensional shape, and two-dimensional spatial relations to other regions) and, when activated, attempt to instantiate the object label as the region descriptor. Object-specific procedural knowledge is activated either as part of the pattern-matching procedure or as part of the action to condition in the production role. The control strategy is both bottom-up and top-down, and world knowledge is partitioned into two sets corresponding to these alternate control strategies. The set of top-down rules is further partitioned by the object models as described above. Bottom-up rules are responsible for forming a rough plan of the image from the region segmentation, while the top-down rules generate a detailed semantic description. Rule activation is controlled by an "agenda"; each potentially active rule is given a priority rating (which may be a function of applicable knowledge and the state of the interpretation) and placed on the agenda. Rules are activated according to their priority rating and executed. All communication between rules is via the common interpretation database (blackboard). Ohta's system performed quite well on several color outdoor scenes of the Kyoto University campus that contained sky, trees, buildings, and roads.

The VISIONS image-understanding system is a knowledge-based system designed as a test bed for the development of computer-vision systems (Belknap et al. 1985; Hanson and Riseman 1978b,c, 1983, 1985, and in this volume; Weymouth et al. 1983; Weymouth 1986; Parma et al. 1980). In the VISIONS system, scene-independent knowledge is represented in a hierarchical schema structure organized as a semantic network. The hierarchy is structured so as to capture the decomposition of visual knowledge into successively more primitive entities, which are eventually expressed in symbolic terms similar to those used to represent the intermediate-level description of a specific image obtained from region, line, and surface segmentations. Each schema defines a highly structured collection of elements in a scene or an object and has both a declarative component (describing the relations between the parts of the schema) and a procedural component (describing image-recognition methods as a set of hypothesis and verification strategies called *interpretation strategies*). The schema system provides a hierarchy of memory structures, from vertices (or even pixels) at the bottom level through semantic objects at the top. A further division of knowledge into long-term memory (LTM) and short-term memory (STM) across the levels of hierarchy provides a convenient way of differentiating the system's permanent *a priori* knowledge base from the knowledge it has received or derived from a specific image. The goal of the system is an interpretation: a collection of objects within STM that is consistent with both the image data and the system's *a priori* knowledge of the world as represented in LTM.

The general strategy by which the VISIONS system operates is to build an intermediate symbolic representation of the image data using processes that initially do not make use of any knowledge of specific objects in the domain. The result is a representation of the image in terms of intermediate primitives such as regions, lines, and local surface patches with associated feature descriptors. These primitives may be directly associated with an object label (using bottom-up object-hypothesis generators) or they may be grouped into more abstract descriptions. The grouping processes may be guided by high-level contextual constraints (e.g. top-down), which effectively select certain groupings related to the interpretation goals; they may be guided by very general object-independent constraints (e.g. bottom-up); or they may be guided by both, changing their form depending on the constraints available. Once a schema is activated, local and global control information is provided by the interpretation strategies, which guide the application of knowledge in the local context defined by the schema and the (partial) interpretation in STM. The VISIONS system has been applied to a variety of complex monocular color scenes, including house and road scenes, aerial images, and industrial scenes, with good results.

Tsotsos has developed a system called ALVEN for generating a descriptive network (interpretation) of multiframe motion data from the medical domain (Tsotsos et al. 1984; Tsotsos, in this volume). Knowledge is represented in framelike structures called *classes*, which provide a generalized definition of the components of world knowledge, attributes, and relationships organized along four representational hierarchies: IS-A, PART-OF, SIMILARITY, and temporal precedence. The temporal-precedence hierarchy assists in the discrimination of proper temporal order, and is necessary for temporal grouping and for the construction of high-order temporal events from lower-order ones. The basic recognition paradigm in ALVEN is hypothesize-and-test, in which currently active hypotheses are expanded simultaneously through the four hierarchies. Hypothesis activation is a cyclic process; initially it is data driven via a matching process between the image and knowledge structures, but then it cycles among goal-driven, model-driven, temporally directed, and failure-directed activations. SIMI-LARITY links are used in the selection of additional relevant hypotheses, and are used when hypothesis instantiation fails. They relate classes which, taken together, are a discriminator set in the sense that only one of them can be active at a time. Global hypothesis consistency and the valuation of the most reasonable hypotheses are accomplished by means of a coopera-tive relaxation process that incorporates the conceptual adjacency relations between hypotheses across the various representational levels as compati-bility factors in the update equation. ALVEN has been used to evaluate the performance of the left ventricle of the human heart from a series of x-ray images, with good results. Its contributions are the mechanism by which temporal knowledge is incorporated into the system and distributed, co-operative mechanisms for hypothesis ranking and focus of attention.

The Many Visual Systems

Having discussed a number of man-made vision systems, we conclude our review with a brief look at the diversity of vertebrate visual systems.

Different animals live in different environments, have different behaviors (e.g., prey behavior versus predator behavior), and have different capabili-ties for motor behavior. As a result, the information that they need about their world varies greatly. On this basis, we may hope to better understand the problem of vision if we can come to see why it is that there are convergences in certain aspects of visual-system "design" while at the same time there are many differences, which we can attempt to correlate with differing behavioral needs. As we have already observed, the retinal "trigger features" in the frog, the rabbit, and the cat are quite distinct. An important question is: How are the utilities of these different modes of visual preprocessing related to the different visuomotor skills that these animals must possess? Again, as we study "the many visual systems," we find that areas which are anatomically similar in different animals may have similar general functions but quite distinctive specific modes of operation. Yet there are also distinctive convergences in the biological "design" of visual systems. Perhaps the best known of these is the convergent evolu-tion, from disparate backgrounds, of octopus and vertebrate retinas. (The octopus has a simple eye that is essentially like a vertebrate eye, but the receptors lie on the surface of the retina, while the ganglion cells lie—as one would have expected—furthest from the lens.) A dramatic story of convergent evolution is unfolding at the hands of Pettigrew, Konishi, and their colleagues in comparative studies of stereopsis in the owl and the cat. (See, e.g., Cooper and Pettigrew 1979.) Like the cat, the owl has keen stereopsis based on forward-facing eyes. It had been thought that the visual systems of birds and mammals were quite disparate in gross structure until Karten et al. (1973) showed that the owl had a visual relay nucleus that could be treated as the homologue of the mammalian lateral geniculate nucleus and that the visual Wulst (situated at the front of the owl's brain) could be treated as the homologue of the visual cortex (located at the back of the mammalian brain). However, whereas in the cat the optic chiasm before the thalamus brings together optical input from the two eyes in the lateral geniculate (though the lateral geniculate is separated in layers) en route to visual cortex, in the owl each half of the LGN receives input from only one eye. There is now known to be a decussation in the owl *after* the thalamus, so that the Wulst does indeed receive binocular input. Pettigrew and Konishi (1976) found that in the owl Wulst, as in the cat cortex, orientation and binocularity are critical parameters for activating the cortical neurons. The understanding of this convergent evolution may yield fresh insights into the computational problems posed by stereopsis.

The early work of Hubel and Wiesel gave a simple hierarchical view of the mammalian visual system: The retina extracted local information about contrast, successive levels of visual cortex (areas 17, 18, and 19) extracted successively refined features running from the simple to the complex to the hypercomplex cells, and some further processing (unspecified as to anatomical localization or putative mechanism) was then required to recognize objects. However, it has since been shown that the story is more complicated, since the latencies of cells in areas 18 and 19 are such that they must be able to respond to input from the lateral geniculate directly, without waiting for preprocessing by area 17 (Stone et al. 1979).

Another move to a more subtle understanding of brain mechanisms in vision came with the symposium on "Locating and Identifying," at which it was suggested that vision be thought of not in terms of a single pathway running through the lateral geniculate nucleus to visual cortex but rather in terms of the interaction of two pathways: the geniculo-striate system, for identifying, and a mid-brain system, the superior colliculus or tectum, for locating (Ingle et al. 1967). It thus became fashionable to talk about the "two visual systems."

However, analysis of the frog (to take just one example) showed that there could be more than two visual systems, with different parts of the brain serving different visual mechanisms. For example, prey catching by the frog seems to rely on the tectum for the processing of visual cues. The tectum also seems to be involved in the avoidance of visual threat. Optokinetic responses are mediated by the basal optic system, and phototactic behavior by the rostral thalamus.

Similar studies in monkeys also led to the conclusion that there are many visual systems. Allman (1977) conducted a comparative study of different primates in an attempt to suggest how the visual subsystems in the brains of different primate species could reflect the ecological niches into which the species had evolved. He suggested that the early primates lived in an ecological niche that favored frontally directed eyes with high activity relating to the functions of tracking and identifying appropriate prey and to head-eye coordination. An early system to evolve (in nocturnal creatures) was poor in orientation selectivity but well suited to discriminate relative brightness. Color perception evolved as primates adopted a diurnal form of life. Area MT of cortex was found to compute the velocities of objects relative to ground, rather than the local velocities normal to contour observed more peripherally in the visual system.

With this, we can turn to a brief tour of the many visual systems (based in large part on Cowey 1981). The analysis starts with V1 (visual area 1), which is the same as the striate cortex (Brodmann's area 17). Daniel and Whitteridge (1963) showed that the contralateral half of the visual field is represented in V1 of the opposite hemisphere with a magnification factor that declines monotonically from the cortical representation of the fovea to that of the periphery. Adjacent to V1 is a region called V2 in which the retina is also represented, but the map there is roughly a mirror image of that in V1. There are, in fact, at least eight "pure" visual areas in the monkey (see Allman 1977 and Kaas 1978 for the owl monkey and Zeki 1978a for the rhesus monkey), and many more that integrate visual information with other modalities, such as the frontal eye fields, areas 5 and 7 of the parietal lobes, and parts of the anterior temporal lobe, where cells may also have tactile or auditory receptive fields. Cowey (1981) argued that such monkey data also apply to the human visual system. Retinal fibers reach the superior colliculus, the suprachiasmatic nucleus, the pretectal nuclei, the accessory optic nuclei, the nucleus of the optic tract, the ventral lateral geniculate nucleus, and the dorsal lateral geniculate nucleus. Only the dorsal lateral geniculate nucleus projects directly to the cerebral cortex, where in primates the fibers terminate solely in the striate cortex (V1).

Zeki (1978b) suggested that Brodmann's area 18 may be divided into V2 and the functionally distinct areas V3, V3A, V4, and LSTS (lateral superior temporal sulcus), and checked the projections between these regions

(Cowey 1979). It appears that different cell populations, at least in V1, may provide the source for different projections. In V3A and LSTS, the retina is topologically represented but the input is not from V1. Berson and Graybiel (1983) used thalamic as well as transcortical projections to delineate subsystems within the visual-association cortex. Secondary visual areas receive projections from the pulvinar nucleus of thalamus. Since monkeys in which V1 has been totally removed can still discriminate many patterned and colored stimuli (Butter et al. 1982), such pathways presumably play an important role. Gross et al. (1972) found cells in inferotemporal cortex that were responsive to monkey hands as the preferred stimulus. More generally, they found that cells in inferotemporal cortex have large receptive fields that always include the fovea and often are bilateral, and that many of these require a very specific complex shape for maximal response but are insensitive to substantial changes in its position.

Hubel and Wiesel (1968, 1977) classified the receptive fields of V1 cells into nonoriented, simple, complex, and hypercomplex, and found (1970) that about half the cells in V2, and probably half those in V3, code for retinal disparity, whereas in V1 this property is absent (or, according to other workers, disparity tuning is much smaller).

Zeki (1978c) reported that orientation specificity is much commoner in V2, V3, and V3A than in V4 or STS, that opponent color coding is common only in V4 and LSTS, and that in MSTS (referred to above as MT) almost all cells show directional selectivity combined with little sensitivity to size or shape.

The above-discussed notion of an optic-flow algorithm in which the simple relaxation algorithm could provide information about the presence of edges in the image, and the idea that the original algorithm could then be made more effective by the use of these edge hypotheses to decouple the local processes corresponding to different regions of the image (Arbib 1981b), are parts of a general evolutionary view of the brain that goes back to the nineteenth-century neurologist Hughlings Jackson, who hypothesized that the brain evolves not simply by adding new systems in isolation or by replacing old systems but rather by adding to and modifying old systems. We thus see the evolutionary refinement of extant subsystems in interaction with "new" systems.

All this has implications for the evolutionary development of computer-vision systems, which can be expected to be designed as networks of subsystems, with the development of new tasks for a vision system adding new nodes to the network but also leading to the redesign of other systems to provide appropriate interfacing information. Just as the superior colliculus receives far more cortical input in more highly evolved animals, so can we expect low-level visual systems to receive more complex control signals from a variety of high-level systems. The control of these to yield cooperative computation, rather than a chaos of conflicting signals, poses a major challenge for vision research. We expect that for many years to come there will be an exciting interchange of ideas about cooperative computation between workers in machine vision and workers studying brain mechanisms of vision. This will continue to be the case even though developments in machine vision will see the application of technological tricks that are far indeed from whatever biological mechanisms motivated the search for them.

Acknowledgments

The preparation of this introduction was supported in part by the National Institutes of Health under NINCDS grant 14971, by the Defense Advanced Research Projects Agency under contract N00014-82-K-0464, and by the Air Force Office of Scientific Research under grant AFOSR-86-0021.

References

Adams, J. B. 1976. A probability model of medical reasoning and the MYCIN model. *Mathematical Biosciences* 32: 177–186.

Adiv, G. 1985. Interpreting Optical Flow. Ph.D. dissertation, University of Massachusetts, Amherst.

Albus, J., E. Kent, M. Nashman, P. Mansback, and L. Palombo. 1982. A 6-D vision system. In Proceedings of the International Society for Optical Engineering (SPIE), Arlington, Virginia.

Allman, J. M. 1977. Evolution of the visual system in the early primates. *Progress in Psychobiology and Physiological Psychology* 7: 1–53.

Amari, S. 1980. Topographic organization of nerve fields. *Bulletin of Mathematical Biology* 42: 339–364.

Amari, S., and M. A. Arbib. 1977. Competition and cooperation in neural nets. In *Systems Neuroscience*, ed. J. Metzler (Academic).

Anandan, P. 1984. Computing dense displacement fields with confidence measures in scenes containing occlusion. In Proceedings of the SPIE Intelligent Robots and Computer Vision Conference. Also available as COINS Technical Report 84-32 from University of Massachusetts, Amherst.

Anandan, P. 1985. Motion and Stereopsis. COINS Technical Report 85-52, University of Massachusetts, Amherst.

Anandan, P., and R. Weiss. 1985. Introducing a smoothness constraint in a matching approach for the computation of optical flow fields. In Proceedings of the Third Workshop on Computer Vision, Bellaire, Michigan.

Arbib, M. A. 1972. *The Metaphorical Brain: An Introduction to Cybernetics as Artificial Intelligence and Brain Theory*. Interscience.

Arbib, M. A. 1975. Artificial intelligence and brain theory: Unities and diversities. *Annals of Biomedical Engineering* 3: 238–274.

Arbib, M. A. 1981a. Perceptual structures and distributed motor control. In *Handbook of Physiology: The Nervous System. II. Motor Control*, ed. V. B. Brooks (American Physiological Society).

Arbib, M. A. 1981b. Visuomotor coordination: From neural nets to schema theory. *Cognition and Brain Theory* 4: 23–29.

Arbib, M. A., C. C. Boylls, and P. Dev. 1974. Neural models of spatial perception and the control of movement. In *Cybernetics and Bionics*, ed. W. D. Keidel et al. (Oldenbourg).

Arbib, M. A., K. J. Overton, and D. T. Lawton. 1984. Perceptual systems for robots. *Interdisciplinary Science Reviews* 9, no. 1: 31–46.

Attneave, F. 1954. Some informational aspects of visual perception. *Psychological Review* 61: 183–193.

Baker, H. H. 1982. Depth from Edge and Intensity Based Stereo. Report STAN-CS-82-930, Department of Computer Science, Stanford University.

Ballard, D. H. 1976. *Hierarchic Recognition of Tumors in Chest Radiographs*. Birkhauser.

Ballard, D. H. 1978. Model-directed detection of ribs in chest radiographs. In Proceedings of the Fourth International Joint Conference on Pattern Recognition, Kyoto.

Ballard, D. H. 1981. Generalizing the Hough transform to detect arbitrary shapes. *Pattern Recognition* 13, no. 2: 111–122.

Ballard, D. H., and C. M. Brown. 1982. *Computer Vision*. Prentice-Hall.

Barlow, H. 1953. Summation and inhibition in the frog's retina. *Journal of Physiology (London)* 119: 69–88.

Barlow, H. B., C. Blakemore, and J. D. Pettigrew. 1967. The neural mechanism of binocular depth discrimination. *Journal of Physiology* 193: 347–342.

Barnard, S. T., and M. A. Fischler. 1982. Computational stereo. *Computing Surveys* 14, no. 4: 553–572.

Barnard, S. T., and W. B. Thompson. 1980. Disparity analysis of images. *Pattern Analysis and Machine Intelligence* 2, no. 4: 333–340.

Barr, A., and E. A. Feigenbaum. 1981. *Handbook of Artificial Intelligence*, vol. 1. Kaufmann.

Barron, J. 1984. A Survey of Approaches for Determining Optic Flow, Environmental Layout, and Optic Flow. Technical Report RBCV-TR-84-5, Department of Computer Science, University of Toronto.

Barrow, H. G., and J. M. Tenenbaum. 1981. Computational vision. *IEEE Proceedings* 69: 572–595.

Batcher, K. E. 1980. Design of a massively parallel processor. *IEEE Transactions on Computers* 29: 836–840.

Belknap, R., E. Riseman, and A. Hanson. 1985. The information fusion problem and rule-based hypotheses applied to complex aggregations of image events. In Proceedings of the DARPA Image Understanding Workshop.

Berson, D. M., and A. M. Graybiel. 1983. Subsystems within the visual association cortex as delineated by their thalamic and transcortical affiliations. *Progress in Brain Research* 58: 229–238.

Besl, P. J., and R. C. Jain. 1985a. Range image understanding. In Proceedings of the IEEE Computer Vision and Pattern Recognition Conference.

Besl, P. J., and R. C. Jain. 1985b. Three dimensional object recognition. *Computing Surveys* 17, no. 1: 75–145.

Bharwani, S., E. M. Riseman, and A. R. Hanson. 1985. Refinement of environmental depth maps over multiple frames. In Proceedings of the DARPA Image Understanding Workshop.

Bienenstock, E. L., L. N. Cooper, and P. N. Munro. 1982. Theory for the development of neuron selectivity, orientation specificity, and binocular interaction in visual cortex. *Biological Cybernetics* 2: 32–48.

Binford, T. 1971. Visual perception by a computer. In Proceedings of the IEEE Conference on Systems and Controls, Miami.

Binford, T. 1982. Survey of model based image analysis systems. *International Journal of Robotics Research* 1: 18–64.

Brady, M. 1982. Computational approaches to image understanding. *ACM Computing Surveys* 14, no. 1: 3–71.

Brady, M., and A. Yuille. 1984. An extremum principle for shape from contour. *IEEE Transactions on Pattern Analysis and Machine Intelligence* 6, no. 3: 288–301. Paper 10 in the present volume.

Brice, C., and C. Fennema. 1970. Scene analysis using regions. *Artificial Intelligence* 1, no. 3: 205–226.

Brooks, R. A. 1981a. *Model-Based Computer Vision.* UMI Research Press.

Brooks, R. A. 1981b. Symbolic Reasoning among 3-D Models and 2-D Images. Report 343, Department of Compter Science, Stanford University.

Brooks, R. A. 1983. Model-based three-dimensional interpretations of two-dimensional images. *IEEE Transactions on Pattern Analysis and Machine Intelligence* 5, no. 2: 140–150.

Bruss, A. R., and B. K. P. Horn. 1983. Passive navigation. *Computer Vision, Graphics, and Image Processing* 21: 3–20.

Buchanan, B. G., G. L. Sutherland, and E. A. Feigenbaum. 1969. Heuristic DENDRAL: A program for generating explanatory hypotheses in organic chemistry. In *Machine Intelligence 4,* ed. B. Meltzer and D. Michie (Edinburgh University Press).

Burns, J. B., A. Hanson, and E. Riseman. 1984. Extracting straight lines. In Proceedings of the Seventh International Conference on Pattern Recognition, Montreal. Also available as COINS Technical Report 84-29 from University of Massachusetts, Amherst.

Burt, P. J. 1975. Computer simulation of a dynamic visual perception model. *International Journal of Man-Machine Studies* 7: 529–546.

Burt, P. J. 1980. Tree and pyramid structures for coding hexagonally sampled binary images. *Computer Graphics and Image Processing* 14: 271–280.

Burt, P. J., T. H. Hong, and A. Rosenfeld. 1981. Segmentation and estimation of image region properties through cooperative hierarchical computation. *IEEE Transactions on Systems, Man, and Cybernetics* 11: 802–809.

Burt, P. J., C. Yen, and X. Xu. 1983. Multi-resolution flow-through motion analysis. In Proceedings of the Computer Vision and Pattern Recognition Conference.

Butter, C. M., D. Kurtz, C. C. Leiby III, and A. Campbell, Jr. 1982. Contrasting behavioral methods in the analysis of vision in monkeys with lesions of the striate cortex or the superior colliculus. In *Analysis of Visual Behavior,* ed. D. Ingle et al. (MIT Press).

Callahan, J., and R. Weiss. 1985. A model for describing surface shape. In Proceedings of the Computer Vision and Pattern Recognition Conference, San Francisco.

Campbell, F. W. 1974. The transmission of spatial information throught the visual system. In *The Neurosciences: Third Study Program,* ed. F. O. Schmitt and F. G. Worden (MIT Press).

Canny, J. F. 1983. Finding Edges and Lines in Images. Technical Report 720, AI Lab, Massachusetts Institute of Technology.

Carnap, R. 1950. The two concepts of probability. In *Logical Foundations of Probability* (University of Chicago Press).

Clowes, M. B. 1971. On seeing things. *Artificial Intelligence* 1: 79–116.

Collett, T. Stereopsis in toads. *Nature* 267: 349–351.

Collett, T. S., and M. F. Land. 1978. How hoverflies compute interception courses. *Journal of Comparative Physiology* 125: 191–204.

Coons, S. A. 1974. Surface patches and B-spline curves. In *Computer Aided Geometric Design*, ed. R. E. Barnhill and R. F. Riesenfeld (Academic).

Cooper, M. L., and J. D. Pettigrew. 1979. A neurophysical determination of the vertical horopter in the cat and the owl. *Journal of Comparative Neurology* 184: 1–26.

Cornelius, N., and T. Kanade. 1983. Adapting optical flow to measure object motion in reflectance and x-ray image sequences. In Proceedings of the ACM Siggraph/Sigart Interdisciplinary Workshop on Motion, Toronto.

Cowey, A. 1979. Cortical maps and visual perception. *Quarterly Journal of Experimental Psychology* 31: 1–17.

Cowey, A. 1981. Why are there so many visual areas? In *The Organization of the Cerebral Cortex*, ed. F. O. Schmitt et al. (MIT Press).

Cragg, B. G., and H. N. V. Temperley. 1954. The organization of neurones: A cooperative analogy. *EEG Clinical Neurophysiology* 6: 85–92.

Daniel, P. M., and D. Whitteridge. 1963. The representation of the visual field on the cerebral cortex in monkeys. *Journal of Physiology* 159: 203–221.

Davis, L. S., and A. L. Rosenfeld. 1981. Cooperating processes for low-level vision. *Artificial Intelligence* 17: 245–263.

Dempster, A. P. 1967. Upper and lower probabilities induced by a multivalued mapping. *Annals of Mathematical Statistics* 38: 325–339.

Dempster, A. P. 1968. A generalization of Bayesian inference. *Journal of the Royal Statistical Society* B 30: 205–247.

Dev, P. 1975. Perception of depth surfaces in random-dot stereograms: A neural model. *Journal of Man-Machine Studies* 7: 511–528.

Didday, R. L., and M. A. Arbib. 1975. Eye movements and visual perception: "Two visual systems" model. *International Journal of Man-Machine Studies* 7: 547–569.

Dreschler, L. S., and H. H. Nagel. 1982. Volumetric model and 3-D trajectory of a moving car derived from monocular TV-frame sequences of a street scene. *Computer Graphics and Image Processing* 20: 199–208.

Duda, R. O., and P. E. Hart. 1972. Use of the Hough transform to detect lines and curves in pictures. *Communications of the ACM* 15, no. 1: 11–15.

Duda, R. O., and P. E. Hart. 1973. *Pattern Classification and Scene Analysis.* Wiley.

Duda, R. O., P. Hart, and N. Nilsson. 1976. Subjective Bayesian methods for rule-based inference systems. *AFIPS Conference Proceedings* 45: 1075–1082.

Duda, R. O., P. Hart, N. Nilsson, R. Reboh, J. Slocum, and G. Sutherland. 1977. Development of a Computer-Based Consultant for Mineral Exploration. Annual Report on SRI Projects 5821 and 6145, SRI International, Menlo Park, Calif.

Dyer, C. R. 1982. Pyramid algorithms and machines. In *Multicomputers and Image Processing*, ed. K. Preston and L. Uhr (Academic).

Edwards, W. 1972. $N = 1$: Diagnosis in unique cases. In *Computer Diagnosis and Diagnostic Methods*, ed. J. A. Jacques (Thomas).

Erman, L., and V. Lesser. 1980. The Hearsay-II speech-understanding system: Integrating knowledge to resolve uncertainty. *Computing Surveys* 12, no. 2: 213–253.

Fennema, C. L., and W. B. Thompson. 1979. Velocity determination in scenes containing several moving objects. *Computer Graphics and Image Processing* 9: 301–315.

Flynn, M. J. 1975. Interpretation, microprogramming, and control of a computer. In *Introduction to Computer Architecture*, ed. H. S. Stone (Science Research Associates).

Foley, J. D., and A. Van Dam. 1982. *Fundamentals of Interactive Computer Graphics.* Addison-Wesley.

Fregnac, Y., and M. Imbert. 1978. Early development of visual cortical cells in normal and dark-reared kittens: Relationship between orientation selectivity and ocular dominance. *Journal of Physiology (London)* 278: 27–44.

Frisby, J. P., and J. E. W. Mayhew. 1980. Spatial frequency tuned channels: Implications for structure and function from psychophysical and computational studies of stereopsis. *Philosophical Transactions of the Royal Society (London)* B 290: 95–116.

Fu, K. S., and T. Ichikawa. 1982. *Special Computer Architectures for Pattern Processing.* CRC.

Gennery, D. B. 1980. Modelling the Environment of an Exploring Vehicle by Stereo Vision. Ph.D. dissertation, Stanford University.

Gibson, J. J. 1955. The optical expansion-pattern in aerial location. *American Journal of Psychology* 68: 480–484.

Gibson, J. J. 1966. *The Senses Considered as Perceptual Systems.* Allen and Unwin.

Gibson, J. J. 1977. The theory of affordances. In *Perceiving, Acting, and Knowing*, ed. R. E. Shaw and J. Bransford (Erlbaum).

Glazer, F. 1981. Computing optic flow. In Proceedings of the Seventh International Joint Conference on Artificial Intelligence.

Glazer, F. 1982. Multilevel Relaxation in Low Level Computer Vision. Technical Report 82-30 Department of Computer and Information Science, University of Massachusetts, Amherst. Also in Rosenfeld 1983.

Glazer, F., A. Hanson, and E. Riseman. 1980. Edge Relaxation and Boundary Continuity. Technical Report 80-11, Computer and Information Science Department, University of Massachusetts, Amherst.

Glazer, F., G. Reynolds, and P. Anandan. 1983. Scene matching by hierarchical correlation. In Proceedings of the IEEE Computer Vision and Pattern Recognition Conference.

Glicksman, J. 1982. A Cooperative Scheme for Image Understanding Using Multiple Sources of Information. Ph.D. dissertation, University of British Columbia.

Grimson, W. E. L. 1984. On the reconstruction of visible surfaces. In *Image Understanding 1984*, ed. S. Ullman and W. Richards (Ablex).

Gross, C. G., C. E. Rocha-Miranda, and D. B. Bender. 1972. Visual properties of neurons in inferotemporal cortex of the macaque. *Journal of Neurophysiology* 35: 96–111.

Guzman, A. 1969. Decomposition of a visual scene into three dimensional bodies. In *Automatic Interpretation and Classification of Images*, ed. A. Grasselli (Academic).

Hanson, A. R., and E. M. Riseman. 1974. Processing Cones: A Computational Structure for Scene Analysis. COINS Technical Report 74C-7, University of Massachusetts, Amherst.

Hanson, A. R., and E. M. Riseman, eds. 1978a. *Computer Vision Systems*. Academic.

Hanson, A. R., and E. M. Riseman. 1978b. VISIONS: A computer system for interpreting scenes. In *Computer Vision Systems*, ed. A. R. Hanson and E. M. Riseman (Academic).

Hanson, A. R., and E. M. Riseman. 1978c. Segmentation of natural scenes. In *Computer Vision Systems*, ed. A. R. Hanson and E. M. Riseman (Academic).

Hanson, A. R., and E. M. Riseman. 1980. Processing comes: A computational structure for image analysis. In *Structured Computer Vision*, ed. S. Tanimoto (Academic). Also available on COINS Technical Report 81-38 from University of Massachusetts, Amherst.

Hanson, A., and E. Riseman. 1983. A summary of image understanding research at the University of Massachusetts. In Proceedings of the DARPA Image Understanding Workshop.

Haralick, R. M. 1980. Edge and region analysis for digital image data. *Computer Graphics and Image Processing* 12: 60–73.

Hartline, H. K. 1949. Inhibition of activity of visual receptors by illuminating nearby retinal elements in the Limulus eye. *Federation Proceedings* 8: 69.

Hempel, C. G. 1965. Studies in the logic of confirmation. In *Aspects of Scientific Explanation ₁ ₁d Other Essays in the Philosophy of Science* (Free Press).

Henn, V., and O. J. Grüsser. 1968. The summation of excitation in the receptive field of movement sensitive neurons of the frog's retina. *Vision Research* 9: 57–69.

Herman, M., and T. Kanade. 1984. The 3D MOSAIC scene understanding system: Incremental reconstruction of 3D scenes from complex images. In Proceedings of the DARPA Image Understanding Workshop.

Hewitt, C. 1972. Description and Theoretical Analysis (Using Schemata) of PLANNER, a Language for Proving Theorems and Manipulating Models in a Robot. Report TR-258, AI Laboratory, Massachusetts Institute of Technology.

Hillis, W. D. 1985. *The Connection Machine*. MIT Press.

Hirsch, H. V. B., and D. N. Spinelli. 1970. Visual experience modifies distribution of horizontally and vertically oriented receptive fields in cats. *Science* 168: 869–871.

Hirsch, H. V. B., and D. N. Spinelli. 1971. Modification of the distribution of receptive field orientation in cats by selective visual exposure during development. *Experimental Brain Research* 12: 502–527.

Horn, B. K. P. 1975. Obtaining shape from shading information. In *The Psychology of Computer Vision*, ed. P. H. Winston (McGraw-Hill).

Horn, B. K. P. 1977. Understanding image intensities. *Artificial Intelligence* 8: 201–231.

Horn, B. K. P., and B. G. Schunk. 1981. Determining optical flow. *Artificial Intelligence* 17: 185–203.

Horowitz, S. L., and T. Pavlidis. 1974. Picture segmentation by a directed split and merge procedure. In Proceedings of the Second International Joint Conference on Pattern Recognition.

House, D. H. 1982. The frog/toad depth perception system—a cooperative/competitive model. In Proceedings of the Workshop on Visuomotor Coordination in Frog and Toad: Models and Experiments, Technical Report 82-16, Department of Computer and Information Science, University of Massachusetts, Amherst.

Hubel, D. H., and T. N. Wiesel. 1962. Receptive fields, binocular interaction, and functional architecture in the cat's visual cortex. *Journal of Physiology* 160: 106–154.

Hubel, D. H., and T. N. Wiesel. 1965. Binocular interaction in striate cortex of kittens reared with artificial squint. *Journal of Neurophysiology* 28: 1041–1059.

Hubel, D. H., and T. N. Wiesel. 1968. Receptive fields and functional architecture of monkey striate cortex. *Journal of Physiology* 195: 215–243.

Hubel, D. H., and T. N. Wiesel. 1970. Cells sensitive to binocular depth in area 18 of the macaque monkey cortex. *Nature* 225: 41–42.

Hubel, D. H., and T. N. Wiesel. 1977. Functional architecture of macaque monkey cortex. *Proceedings of the Royal Society (London)* B 198: 1–59.

Hueckel, M. H. 1971. An operator which locates edges in digitized pictures. *Journal of the Association for Computing Machinery* 18, no. 1: 113–125.

Huffman, D. A. 1971. Impossible objects as nonsense sentences. In *Machine Intelligence 6*, ed. B. Meltzer and D. Michie (Edinburgh University Press).

Ikeuchi, K. 1980. Numerical Shape from Shading and Occluding Contours in a Single View. AI Memo 566, Massachusetts Institute of Technology.

Ingle, D. 1976. Spatial vision in anurans. In *The Amphibian Visual System*, ed. K. Fite (Academic).

Ingle, D., G. E. Schneider, C. B. Trevarthen, and R. Held. 1967. Location and identifying: Two modes of visual processing. *Psychologische Forschung* 31, nos. 1 and 4.

Jayaramumurthy, S. N., and R. Jain. 1983. An approach to the segmentation of textured dynamic scenes. *Computer Graphics and Image Processing* 21: 239–261.

Jeannerod, M., and B. Biguer. 1982. Visuomotor mechanisms in reaching within extrapersonal space. In *Analysis of Visual Behavior*, ed. D. Ingle et al. (MIT Press).

Jenkin, M. 1984. The Stereopsis of Time Varying Imagery. Technical Report RBVC-TR-84-3, Department of Computer Science, University of Toronto.

Julesz, B. 1971. *Foundations of Cyclopean Perception.* University of Chicago Press.

Kaas, J. H. 1978. The organization of the visual cortex in primates. In *Sensory Systems of Primates*, ed. C. R. Noback (Plenum).

Kanade, T. 1979. Recovery of the Three-Dimensional Shape of an Object from a Single View. Report CMU-CS-79-153, Computer Science Department, Carnegie-Mellon University. Also in *Artificial Intelligence* 17 (1981): 409–460.

Kanade, T. 1980. A theory of origami world. *Artificial Intelligence* 13: 279–311.

Karten, H. J., W. Hodos, W. J. H. Nauta, and A. M. Revzin. 1973. Neural connections of the "visual Wulst" of the avian telencephalon: Experimental studies in the pigeon (Columbia livia) and owl (Speotyto curicularia). *Journal of Comparative Neurology* 150: 253–278.

Kelly, M. D. 1971. Edge detection in pictures by computer using planning. In *Machine Vision 6*, ed. B. Meltzer and D. Michie (Edinburgh University Press).

Kender, J. R. 1980. Shape from Texture. Ph.D. dissertation, Carnegie-Mellon University.

Kitchen, L., and A. Rosenfeld. 1980. Grey Level Corner Detection. Technical Report 887, Computer Science Center, University of Maryland, College Park.

Knight, B. W. 1973. The horseshoe crab eye: A little nervous system that is solvable. In *Lectures on Mathematics in the Life Sciences*, vol. 5 (American Mathematical Society).

Koenderink, J. J., and A. J. Van Doorn. 1975. Invariant properties of the motion parallax field due to the movement of rigid bodies relative to an observer. *Optica Acta* 22, no. 9: 773–791.

Koenderink, J. J., and A. J. Van Doorn. 1967a. Local structure of motion parallax of the plane. *Journal of the Optical Society of America* 66: 717–723.

Koenderink, J. J., and A. J. Van Doorn. 1976b. The singularities of the visual mapping. *Biological Cybernetics* 24, no. 1: 51–59.

Koenderink, J. J., and A. J. Van Doorn. 1979. Internal representation of solid shape with respect to vision. *Biological Cybernetics* 32, no. 4: 211–216.

Kohl, C. 1986. Knowledge Based Image Segmentation. Ph.D. dissertation in preparation, University of Massachusetts, Amherst.

Kohler, R. 1981. A segmentation system based on thresholding. *Computer Graphics and Image Processing* 15: 319–338.

Kohler, R. 1984. Integrating Non-Semantic Knowledge into Image Segmentation Processes. Ph.D. dissertation (COINS Technical Report 84-04), University of Massachusetts, Amherst.

Kohler, R., and A. Hanson. 1982. The VISIONS image operating system. In Proceedings of the Sixth International Conference on Pattern Recognition, Munich.

Kuffler, S. W. 1953. Discharge patterns and functional organization of mammalian retina. *Journal of Neurophysiology* 16: 37–68.

Lawton, D. 1982. Motion analysis via local translational processing. In Proceedings of the IEEE Workshop on Computer Vision; Representation and Control, Rindge, N.H.

Lawton, D. 1983a. Processing restricted motion. In Proceedings of the DARPA Image Understanding Workshop, Arlington, Va.

Lawton, D. 1983b. Processing translational motion sequences. *Computer Vision, Graphics, and Image Processing* 22: 116–144.

Lawton, D. 1984. Processing Dynamic Image Sequences from a Moving Sensor. Ph.D. dissertation (COINS Technical Report 84-05), University of Massachusetts, Amherst.

Lawton, D., and J. Rieger. 1983. The use of difference fields in processing sensor motion. In Proceedings of the DARPA Image Understanding Workshop, Arlington, Va.

Lee, D. N., and J. R. Lishman. 1977. Visual control of locomotion. *Scandinavian Journal of Psychology* 18: 224–230.

Lettvin, J. Y., H. Maturana, W. S. McCulloch, and W. H. Pitts. 1959. What the frog's eye tells the frog's brain. *Proceedings of the Institute of Radio Engineers* 47: 1940–1951.

Levine, M. D. 1978. A knowledge-based computer system. In *Computer Vision Systems*, ed. A. R. Hanson and E. M. Riseman (Academic).

Lim, H. S., and T. Binford. 1985. Stereo correspondence: Features and constraints. In Proceedings of the 1985 DARPA Image Understanding Workshop.

Longuet-Higgins, H. C., and K. Prazdny. 1980. The interpretation of a moving image. *Proceedings of the Royal Society of London* B 208: 385–397.

Lowrance, J. 1978. GRASPER 1.0 Reference Manual. COINS Technical Report 78-20, University of Massachusetts, Amherst.

Lowrance, J. D. 1982. Dependency-Graph Model of Evidential Support. Ph.D. dissertation (COINS Technical Report 82-26), University of Massachusetts, Amherst.

Lowrance, J., and D. Corkill. 1979. The Design of GRASPER 1.0: A Graph Processing Programming Language Extension. COINS Technical Report 79-6, University of Massachusetts, Amherst.

Luetjen, K., P. Gummar, and H. Ischen. 1980. FLIP: A flexible multiprocessor system for image processing. In Proceedings of the Fifth International Joint Conference on Pattern Recognition.

Mackworth, A. 1973. Interpreting pictures of polyhedral scenes. *Artificial Intelligence* 8: 121–137.

Mackworth, A. 1974. On the Interpretation of Drawings as Three-Dimensional Scenes. Ph.D. dissertation, University of Sussex.

MacLeod, I. D. G. 1970. On finding structures in pictures. In *Picture Language Machines*, ed. S. Kanelf (Academic).

Marr, D. 1978. Representing visual information. In *Computer Vision Systems*, ed. A. Hanson and E. Riseman (Academic).

Marr, D. 1982. *Vision: A Computational Investigation into the Human Representation and Processing of Visual Material.* Freeman.

Marr, D., and E. Hildreth. 1980. Theory of edge detection. *Proceedings of the Royal Society (London)* B 211: 187–217.

Marr, D., and H. K. Nishihara. 1978. Representation and recognition of the spatial organization of three-dimensional shapes. *Proceedings of the Royal Society (London)* B 200: 269–294.

Marr, D., and T. Poggio. 1976. Cooperative computation of stereo disparity. *Science* 194: 283–287.

Marr, D., and T. Poggio. 1979. A computational theory of human stereopsis. *Proceedings of the Royal Society (London)* B 204: 301–328.

Marr, D., and S. Ullman. 1981. Directional selectivity and its use in early visual processing. *Proceedings of the Royal Society (London)* B 211: 151–180.

Mayhew, J. E. W., and J. P. Frisby. 1980. The computation of binocular edges. *Perception* 9: 69–86.

Mayhew, J. E. W., and J. P. Frisby. 1981. Towards a computation and psychophysical theory of stereopsis. *Artificial Intelligence* 17: 349–385.

McKeown, D., W. Harvey, and J. McDermott. 1984. Rule-based interpretation of aerial imagery. In Proceedings of IEEE Workshop on Principles of Knowledge-Based Systems.

Merzenich, M. M., and J. H. Kaas. 1983. Reorganization of somatosensory cortex in mammals following peripheral nerve injury. *Trends in Neuroscience* 5: 434–436.

Minsky, M. 1975. A framework for representing knowledge. In *The Psychology of Computer Vision*, ed. P. H. Winston (McGraw-Hill).

Moldovan, D. I., C. I. Wu, J. G. Nash, S. Levitan, and C. Weems. 1985. Parallel processing of iconic to symbolic transformation of images. In Proceedings of the Computer Vision and Pattern Recognition Conference.

Moravec, H. P. 1980. Obstacle Avoidance and Navigation in the Real World by a Seeing Robot Rover. Ph.D. dissertation, Stanford University.

Nagao, M., and T. Matsuyama. 1980. *A Structural Analysis of Complex Aerial Photographs*. Plenum.

Nagel, H. H., and G. Rekers. 1981. Moving object masks based on an improved likelihood test. In Proceedings of the International Joint Conference on Artificial Intelligence.

Nagin, P. 1979. Studies in Image Segmantation Algorithms Based on Histogram Clustering and Relaxation. Ph.D. dissertation (COINS Technical Report 79-15), University of Massachusetts, Amherst.

Nagin, P., A. Hanson, and E. Riseman. 1981a. Region relaxation in a parallel hierarchical architecture. In *Real-Time Parallel Computing Image Analysis*, ed. M. Onoe et al. (Plenum).

Nagin, P., A. Hanson, and E. Riseman. 1981b. Variations in relaxation labelling techniques. *Computer Graphics and Image Processing* 17: 33–51.

Nagin, P., A. Hanson, and E. Riseman. 1982. Studies in global and local histogram-guided relaxation algorithms. *IEEE Transactions on Pattern Analysis and Machine Intelligence* 4: 263–277.

Neisser, U. 1976. *Cognition and Reality: Principles and Implications of Cognitive Psychology.* Freeman.

Nelson, J. I. 1975. Globality and stereoscopic fusion in binocular vision. *Journal of Theoretical Biology* 49: 1–88.

Nevatia, R. 1982. *Machine Perception.* Prentice-Hall.

Ohlander, R., K. Price, and R. Reddy. 1979. Picture segmentation using a recursive region-splitting method. *Computer Graphics and Image Processing* 8, no. 3: 313–333.

Ohta, Y. 1985. *Knowledge-Based Interpretation of Outdoor Natural Color Scenes.* Pitman.

Ohta, Y., and T. Kanade. 1985. Stereo by intra- and inter-scanline search using dynamic programming. *IEEE Transactions on Pattern Analysis and Machine Intelligence* 7, no. 2: 139–154.

Parma, C. C., A. R. Hanson, and E. M. Riseman. 1980. Experiments in Schema-Driven Interpretation of a Natural Scene. COINS Technical Report 80-10, University of Massachusetts, Amherst.

Pettigrew, J. D., and M. Konishi. 1976. Neurons selective for orientation and binocular disparity in the visual wulst of the barn owl (*Tyto alba*). *Science* 193: 675–678.

Piaget, J. 1971. *Biology and Knowledge.* Edinburgh University Press.

Poggio, G. F., and T. Poggio. 1984. The analysis of stereopsis. *Annual Review of Neuroscience* 7: 379–412.

Potter, J. L. 1982. MPP architecture and planning. In *Multicomputers and Image Processing,* ed. K. Preston and L. Uhr (Academic).

Prager, J. M. 1980. Extracting and labeling boundary segments in natural scenes. *IEEE Transactions on Pattern Analysis and Machine Intelligence* 2, no. 1: 16–27.

Prager, J. M., and M. Arbib. 1983. Computing the optic flow: The MATCH algorithm and prediction. *Computer Vision and Image Processing* 24: 271–304.

Prazdny, K. 1980. Egomotion and relative depth map from optical flow. *Biological Cybernetics* 36: 87–102.

Prazdny, K. 1985. Detection of binocular disparities. *Biological Cybernetics* 52: 93–99.

Prazdny, K. Human binocular vision may not use a coarse-to-fine stereomatching strategy. In press.

Preston, K., and L. Uhr, eds. 1982. *Multicomputers and Image Processing.* Academic.

Pribram, K. H. 1974. How is it that sensing so much we can do so little? In *The Neurosciences: Third Study Program,* ed. F. O. Schmitt and F. G. Worden (MIT Press).

Ratliff, F. 1969. *Mach Bands*. Holden-Day.

Regan, D., and K. I. Beverley. 1979. Binocular and monocular stimuli for motion in depth: Changing-disparity and changing-size feed the same motion-in-depth stage. *Vision Research* 19: 1331−1342.

Reichardt, W. E., and T. Poggio, eds. 1981. *Theoretical Approaches in Neurobiology*. MIT Press.

Reynolds, G., N. Irwin, A. Hanson, and E. Riseman. 1984. Hierarchical knowledge-directed object extraction using a combined region and line representation. In Proceedings of the Workshop on Computer Vision: Representation and Control, Annapolis.

Rieger, J. H., and D. T. Lawton. 1983. Determining the instantaneous axis of translation from optic flow generated by arbitrary sensor motion. In Proceedings of the ADM Siggraph/Sigart Interdisciplinary Workshop on Motion, Toronto.

Roach, J. W., and J. K. Aggarwal. 1980. Determining the movement of objects from a sequence of images. *IEEE Transactions on Pattern Analysis and Machine Intelligence* 2: 554−562.

Roberts, L. G. 1965. Machine perception of three-dimensional solids. In *Optical and Electro-Optical Information Processing*, ed. J. T. Tippett et al. (MIT Press).

Robinson, D. A. 1965. A machine-oriented logic based on the resolution principle. *Journal of the Association for Computing Machinery* 12, no. 1: 23−41.

Robinson, D. A. 1976. Adaptive gain control of vestibulo-ocular reflex by the cerebellum. *Journal of Neurophysiology* 39: 954−969.

Robinson, D. A. 1981. The use of control systems analysis in the neurophysiology of eye movements. *Annual Review of Neuroscience* 4: 463−503.

Rock, I. 1983. *The Logic of Perception*. MIT Press.

Rosenblatt, F. 1962. *Principle of Neurodynamics*. Spartan.

Rosenfeld, A., ed. 1983. *Multiresolution Image Processing*. Springer-Verlag.

Rosenfeld, A., and A. C. Kak. 1976. *Digital Picture Processing*. Academic.

Rosenfeld, A., R. A. Hummel, and S. W. Zucker. 1976. Scene labeling by relaxation operations. *IEEE Transactions on Systems, Man, and Cybernetics* 6: 420−433.

Samet, H. 1980. Region representation: Quad trees from boundary codes. *Communications of ACON* 23, no. 3: 163−170.

Schank, R. C., and R. P. Abelson. 1977. *Scripts, Plans, Goals, and Understanding*. Erlbaum.

Shafer, G. 1976. *A Mathematical Theory of Evidence*. Princeton University Press.

Shortliffe, E. H. 1976. *Computer-Based Medical Consultations: MYCIN*. Elsevier.

Siegel, H. J. 1979. A model of SIMD machines and a comparison of various interconnection strategies. *IEEE Transactions on Computers* 28, no. 12: 207.

Singer, P. 1980. *Marx*. Oxford University Press.

Southwell, R. V. 1940. *Relaxation Methods in Engineering Science*. Oxford University Press.

Sperling, G. 1970. Binocular vision: A physical and neural theory. *American Journal of Psychology* 83: 463–534.

Spinelli, D. N., and F. E. Jensen. 1979. Plasticity: The mirror of experience. *Science* 203, no. 4375 75–78.

Sternberg, S. R. 1982. Pipeline architectures for image processing. In *Multicomputers and Image Processing*, ed. K. Preston and L. Uhr (Academic).

Stevens, K. 1980. Surface Perception by Local Analysis of Texture and Contour. AI Memo 512, Massachusetts Institute of Technology.

Stone, J., B. Dreher, and A. Leventhal. 1979. Hierarchical and parallel mechanisms in the organization of visual cortex. *Brain Research Reviews* 1: 345–394.

Tang, I. S., W. F. Snyder, and S. A. Rajala. 1981. Extractions of moving objects in dynamic scenes. In Proceedings of the International Joint Conference on Artificial Intelligence.

Tanimoto, S., and A. Klinger. 1980. *Structured Computer Vision*. Academic.

Tenenbaum, J. M., and H. Barrow. 1976. Experiments in Interpretation-Guided Segmentation. Technical Note 123, AI Center, Stanford University.

Thompson, W. B., and S. T. Barnard. 1981. Lower-level estimation and interpretation of visual motion. *IEEE Computer* 14, no. 8: 20–28.

Tornebohm, H. 1966. Two measures of evidential strength. In *Aspects of Inductive Logic*, ed. J. Hintikka and P. Suppes (North-Holland).

Tsai, R. Y., and T. S. Huang. 1982. Uniqueness and estimation of three-dimensional motion parameters of rigid objects with curved surfaces. In Proceedings of the conference on Pattern Recognition and Image Processing.

Tsai, R. Y., and T. S. Huang. 1984. Uniqueness and estimation of three-dimensional motion parameters of rigid objects with curved surfaces. *IEEE Transactions on Pattern Analysis and Machine Intelligence* 6, no. 1: 13–27.

Tsotsos, J. K., D. Covey, J. Mylopoulos, and P. McLaughlin. 1984. The role of symbolic reasoning in left ventricular performance assessment. The ALVEN system. In *Ventricular Wall Motion*, ed. R. U. Sigwart et al. (Thieme-Stratton).

Uhr, L. 1983. *Algorithm-Structured Computer Arrays and Networks*. Academic.

Ullman, S. 1979. *The Interpretation of Visual Motion*. MIT Press.

von Bekesy, G. 1967 *Sensory Inhibition*. Princeton University Press.

von der Malsburg, C. 1973. Self-organization of orientation-sensitive cells in the striate cortex. *Kybernetik* 14: 85–100.

von der Malsburg, C. 1979. Development of ocularity domains and growth behavior of axon terminals. *Biological Cybernetics* 32: 49–62.

Wallace, T. P., and P. A. Wintz. 1980. An efficient three-dimensional aircraft recognition algorithm using normalized Fourier descriptors. *Computer Graphics and Image Processing* 13: 96–126.

Waltz, D. L. 1975. Generating semantic descriptions from drawings of scenes with shadows. In *The Psychology of Computer Vision*, ed. P. H. Winston (McGraw-Hill).

Waltz, D. L. 1978. A parallel model for low-level vision. In *Computer Vision Systems*, ed. A. Hanson and E. Riseman (Academic).

Warren, H. D., L. Pereira, and F. Pereira. 1977. PROLOG: The language and its implementation compared with LISP. In Proceedings of the Sigplan/Sigart Symposium on Artificial Intelligence and Programming Languages (Sigplan Notices 12, 8).

Waxman, A. M., and S. Ullman. 1983. Surface Structure and 3-D Motion from Image Flow: A Kinematic Analysis. Report CAR-TR-24, Center for Automation Research, University of Maryland.

Webb, J. A., and J. K. Aggarwal. 1981. Visually interpreting the motion of objects in space. *IEEE Transactions on Computers*.

Weems, C., D. Lawton, S. Levitan, E. Riseman, A. Hanson, and M. Callahan. 1985. Iconic and symbolic processing using a content addressable array parallel processor. In Proceedings of the IEEE Conference on Computer Vision and Pattern Recognition, San Francisco.

Weiss, R., A. Hanson, and E. Riseman. 1985. Geometric grouping of straight lines. In Proceedings of the DARPA Image Understanding Workshop.

Wesley, L., and A. Hanson. 1982. The use of an evidential-based model for representing knowledge and reasoning about images in the VISIONS system. In Proceedings of the Workshop on Computer Vision, Rindge, N.H.

Weymouth, T. E. 1986. Using Object Descriptions in a Schema Network for Machine Vision. Technical Report 86-24, Department of Computer and Information Science, University of Massachusetts, Amherst.

Weymouth, T. E., J. Griffith, A. Hanson, and E. Riseman. 1983. Rule-based strategies for image interpretation. In Proceedings of the DARPA Image Understanding Workshop, Arlington, Va.

Williams, T., and J. Lowrance. 1977. Model-Building in the VISIONS High-Level System. COINS Technical Report 77-1, University of Massachusetts, Amherst.

Witkin, A. P. 1980. A statistical technique for recovering surface orientation from texture in natural imagery. In Proceedings of the first annual meeting of the American Association of Artificial Intelligence.

Witkin, A. P., and J. M. Tenenbaum. 1982. On the role of structure in vision. In *Human and Machine Vision*, ed. J. Beck et al. (Academic).

Woodham, R. J. 1978. Photometric stereo: A reflectance map technique for determining surface orientation from image intensity. In Proceedings of the 22nd Annual Society of Photo-Optical Instrumentation Engineers Conference, San Francisco.

Woodham, R. J. 1984. Photometric method for determining shape from shading. In *Image Understanding 1984*, ed. S. Ullman and W. Richards (Ablex).

York, B. W., A. R. Hanson, and E. M. Riseman. 1980. A surface representation for computer vision. In Proceedings of the Fifth International Conference on Pattern Recognition, Miami.

York, B. W., A. R. Hanson, and E. M. Riseman. 1981. 3D object representation and matching with B-splines and surface patches. In Proceedings of the Seventh International Joint Conference on Artificial Intelligence, Vancouver.

Zeki, S. M. 1978a. Functional specialization in the cortex of the rhesus monkey. *Nature* 274: 423–428.

Zeki, S. M. 1978b. The cortical projections of foveal striate cortex in the rhesus monkey. *Journal of Physiology* 277: 227–244.

Zeki, S. M. 1978c. Uniformity and diversity of structure and function in rhesus monkey prestriate visual cortex. *Journal of Physiology* 277: 273–290.

Zucker, S., R. Hummel, and A. Rosenfeld. 1977. An application of relaxation labeling to line and curve enhancement. *IEEE Transactions on Computers* 26, no. 4: 394–403.

I

Visual Neurophysiology

This part of the book stresses data on vision that can be related to brain structures. But it also places vision in the context of its use, and strikes a good balance between experimental and theoretical analysis of brain function. Robinson analyzes oculomotor tracking systems, both the saccadic and smooth pursuit patterns. He shows that a continuation of positive feedback and parameter adaptation can account for the absence of the instabilities that would attend a pure negative-feedback system with the large delays observed in oculomotor tracking. Robinson concludes his study by spelling out the implications of his work for the neural control of limb movements. (For a phenomenological account of this, see paper 13.)

The next two papers focus on the mid-brain visual system. Sparks and Jay analyze the role of primate superior colliculus in sensorimotor integration, while Arbib and House study the role of the tectum (the homologous structure in the brains of frogs and toads) in interaction with other brain regions in subserving depth perception and detour behavior. There is a paradox at the heart of the study of the primate superior colliculus: Its upper layers provide a sensory map (the loci of neural-activity correlates with the position of stimuli in the usual field), while its deep layers provide a motor map (the locus of neural-activity correlates with the direction of the ensuing eye movement). Moreover, the two maps are in register. The paradox is that no direct pathway has been found within superior colliculus to subserve the integrated functioning of the two maps. By contrast, the tectum of a frog or a toad is an integrated structure with direct coupling between its layers.

Sparks and Jay offer convincing evidence that it is motor error, the difference between current eye position and desired eye position, that provides the coordinates for collicular deep layers. When a monkey is shown two visual targets to be fixated in succession, but these two lights are switched off once the monkey starts to move its eyes to the first target, the representation of the second target in the deep layers corresponds not to where the target was seen but to its position relative to the first target—the motor-error coordinate for the second fixation. They also show that the response of collicular neurons to auditory stimuli is arranged in motor-error coordinates, depending jointly upon the position of the target in space and the position of the eye in the orbit.

Arbib and House also look at a two-target problem, but in their paper the problem is that of a toad that must detour around a barrier to reach its prey. The two targets are the edge of the barrier and a worm. The paper first presents models for depth perception by frog and toad. These are cooperative-computation models in that they involve cooperative activity of different systems. One model, for barrier depth perception, involves cooperation between a system using disparity depth cues and one using accommodation depth cues. The prey-selection model involves the co-operative activity of the tectum on the two sides of the brain (coupled by the nuclei isthmi with the control system for lens accommodation). The authors then discuss models for how this depth information might be used by the animal's brain in guiding detour behavior.

The comparative note struck by papers 2 and 3 is extended by Spinelli, who provides an evolutionary perspective on the visual system. There are two main points. First, both the gross structure and the detailed neural features of the retina differ from animal to animal. Spinelli argues that each retina in some sense provides an environmental frame for the animal, freeing the visual system to concentrate on the particularities of the current scene. Second, however good the genetically programmed structures may be, they must adapt both to environmental changes and to the animal's changing body geometry. Spinelli presents studies from his own laboratory showing how early experience can affect the formation of "feature de-tectors" in cat cortex, and how the gross allocation of neurons in the body map in somatosensory cortex may be reallocated. He also outlines a model for the coordinated growth of pyramidal cells in cortex, suggesting an im-portant role for the consequent dendritic bundling in learning and memory.

1

Why Visuomotor Systems Don't Like Negative Feedback and How They Avoid It

D. A. Robinson

Delays Cause Oscillations; How to Avoid Them

When one designs a control system with negative feedback, a large delay in the loop, and a large forward gain, one is headed for trouble, for the system will probably be unstable. Figure 1A is an example; its forward path contains a pure delay τ, a central controller with a transfer function $G(s)$ in Laplace transform notation, and a plant transfer function $P(s)$. Assume that the steady-state gain of the plant $P(0)$ (the gain at zero frequency) is 1.0, so that the significant gain is in $G(s)$. If the response R is to resemble the command C accurately in steady state, the steady-state gain $G(0)$ must be reasonably large in comparison with 1.0, since R/C equals $G(0)/[1 + G(0)]$. If $G(0)$ were 9.0, for example, R would be only 90% of C in steady state. Accuracy would deteriorate further if $G(0)$ were any smaller. As the gain increases, the risk of oscillation increases because if, at some frequency, the accumulated phase lag of the forward path reaches $180°$ while the gain is still 1.0 or larger, an oscillation at that frequency can sustain itself by supplying its own input through the feedback pathway. Most devices such as those described by $G(s)$ and $P(s)$ have gains that decrease rapidly at high frequencies where the phase shift approaches $180°$. The problem with the delay is that its gain is 1.0 at all frequencies and its phase lag increases linearly with frequency so it contributes severely to phase shift without affecting gain. The critical thing in figure 1A is whether the delay τ is small in comparison with the response times of $G(s)$ and $P(s)$. If not, the system will be unstable. Put in its simplest terms, if a system is to be accurate (large gain) and fast (small response time) it cannot afford to have significant delays.

All this poses problems in biological control, where significant delays are the rule. They can be tolerated in such control systems as respiratory and cardiovascular regulation because the response times of those systems

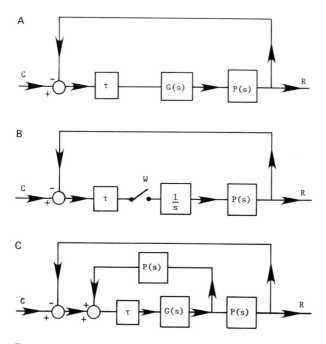

Figure 1
Three types of negative-feedback systems with significant delays τ. C is the command,
R is the response, $P(s)$ is the transfer function of the physical plant (eye or limb), and $G(s)$
is the central nervous system. A: Conventional feedback. If $G(s)$ had a gain large enough
to achieve much accuracy, the delay would cause instability. B: A sample-data model that
can tolerate the delay and still be stable. C: Another method of achieving stability by the
use of internal positive feedback.

are large. In visuo-motor control such is not the case. In oculomotor control
it is definitely not the case; the systems that move the eyes have response
times equal to or less than the delays, which are in the range 0.13–0.2 sec.
Yet they have built-in negative feedback; the retina detects the error
between target motion and eye motion, and that error leads in turn to
another eye motion, thus forming a negative feedback with a gain of
1.0. So visually induced eye movements are fast, accurate, have negative
feedback, and a large delay. Why don't they oscillate? Two solutions have
been suggested; one for saccades and one for pursuit.

Saccadic System

Saccades are the rapid shifts in eye position we make in looking around.
The movements are very fast; velocities are typically 200°–400° per

second, with durations of 50–100 msec. If one tests the system by asking a subject to track a jumping target, the saccade occurs about 200 msec after the target jumps. About 50 msec of this delay is in the retina, and another 30 msec is in motor circuits, so that 120 msec represents the computation time of the nervous system. It is clear here that the delay in this system is even larger than the response time of 50–100 msec, and that any attempt to model it along the lines of figure 1A would not work.

Following an observation of Westheimer (1954), Young and Stark (1963) modeled the saccadic system as a sampled-data system (figure 1B). The switch samples the error every W sec, and the integrator ($1/s$) holds the sample. The gain of the plant (the eyeball and muscles), $P(0)$, is 1.0, so that a $10°$ error leads to a $10°$ saccade. The system is stable because it is refractory; after each saccade the system will not respond to target behavior until another sample is taken W sec later. This also can be put another way: Most of the time the feedback loop is open, because the switch closes only momentarily every W sec, and this prevents oscillations of the type that can occur in figure 1A. Sampled-data systems can become unstable. It is important in figure 1B that the response of $P(s)$ be so fast that the movement is over before the next sample. If not, the next sampled error would be wrongly attributed to a new target movement and a new, inappropriate eye movement would occur, which could lead to instability. Consequently, if T_p is the time for $P(s)$ to complete the movement then W must be greater than $(\tau + T_p)$. In general, then, this method of achieving stability works only for very rapid movements, such as occur in saccades. For systems that are not so rapid (such as limb movements), this scheme could again lead to oscillations unless some novel features were added.

Pursuit System

The pursuit system is a good example of the other solution. Smooth pursuit movements are used to keep the image of a moving target on the fovea. It covers the range 0–100°/sec. When a stationary target suddenly begins to move at a constant velocity, the eyes do nothing for 130 msec and then accelerate over the next 120 msec to achieve a steady-state velocity that is about 90% of target velocity. If one subtracts 80 msec for peripheral delays, the central computation for pursuit is only 50 msec, versus 120 msec for the saccadic system. This reflects the fact that pursuit is more reflexive and automatic than are saccades. It has also been demonstrated experimentally (Robinson 1965) that the pursuit system is not sampled but is a continuous system. If one tries to use the model in figure 1A, $G(0)$ should be 9 so that the closed-loop, steady-state gain, $G(0)/[1 + G(0)]$, will be 0.9. The change in velocity is roughly exponential, so that 120 msec may be taken as three time constants. This makes the closed-loop time constant 40 msec, so that the open-loop time constant, which is $[1 + G(0)]$ larger, becomes 400 msec. Also, in figure 1A, C and R would be interpreted as target and eye *velocity*, since—unlike the saccadic system, which is concerned with eye position—the pursuit system is mainly concerned with eye velocity.

Consequently, in figure 1A one should choose 1.0 for $P(s)$ and $9/(0.4s + 1)$ for $G(s)$ to fit these physiological observations. If one did, however, the system would be hopelessly unstable, given that τ is 0.13 sec. Young et al. (1968) (see also Young 1971) solved this problem in a bold, imaginative way: If the feedback gives you trouble, take it away. Since the feedback is buit in for oculomotor systems, this means canceling the external negative feedback by internal positive feedback, as in figure 1C. Since $P(s)$ (the plant) must lie outside the inner feedback loop, it is necessary to simulate it in that loop, since the inner and outer loops must appear identical for one to cancel the other. Since there is now no effective feedback and the system is absolutely stable, $G(s)$ can be anything, and the delay causes no problems. For pursuit, since R is $0.9C$ in steady state, $G(0)$ should be 0.9.

In each of these examples a way around the problem of stability was found—in one case by sampling the error, in the other by getting rid of the negative feedback. I would like to consider the case that the saccadic system also gets rid of its negative feedback.

The Saccadic System Revisited

There is a big argument about whether the saccadic system directs the eye to move in a certain direction by a certain distance, regardless of initial position, to reduce retinal error (called retinotopic coding), or whether it is directed to go to a certain position in the orbit, in head coordinates. The former idea is favored by many (see e.g. Henn et al. 1982) and is the one used in figure 1B, but evidence for the latter has been accumulating steadily (van Gisbergen et al. 1981a; Mays and Sparks 1980a). The idea, first proposed by Zee et al. (1976), is illustrated in figure 2A. (Only major features appear here; details and reviews of evidence for and against may be found in van Gisbergen et al. 1981a, Zee and Robinson 1979, and Robinson 1981.) The basic premise is that the central nervous system adds an internal copy E' of eye position to retinal error, e, to reconstruct an internal copy of target position, T'. This measure is then taken to be

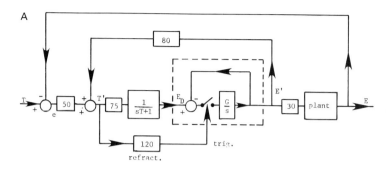

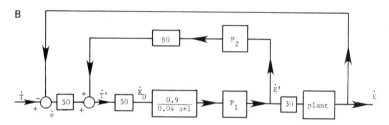

Figure 2

Two models of eye-movement control using internal positive feedback. A: The saccadic system. B: The pursuit system. T and $\dot{T}$ are target position and velocity, E and $\dot{E}$ are eye position and velocity, e and ė are retinal error and its velocity, T' and $\dot{T}'$ are reconstructed target position and velocity, E_D and $\dot{E}_D$ are desired eye position and velocity, and E' and $\dot{E}'$ are motor commands for E and $\dot{E}$. Delays are distributed and are indicated by numbers in boxes (msec). Saccades in diagram A (adapted from Zee et al. 1976) are triggered (trig.) by a system that exhibits refractoriness (refract.) Pursuit in diagram B is continuous and shows no refractoriness. Elements P_1 and P_2 are gains that are normally 1.0 but are under parametric control.

desired eye position, E_D. The peripheral delays, 50 and 30 msec, are shown explicitly to point out that if the signals E' and e are to be combined to form T' they must arrive at the same time. Since the journey around the outer loop has a delay of 80 msec, a similar delay should be added to the inner loop. Only in this way can the two loops cancel each other.

A major hypothesis of the model is that a low-level brain-stem circuit (enclosed in dashed lines) compares E' with E_D and drives the difference (the motor error) rapidly to zero. An important virtue of this scheme is that one saturating nonlinearity in the forward path, G/s (not shown), can account for the shape, duration, and peak velocity of all saccades over a size range of 3 minutes of arc to 90°. This ability to explain a large amount of data by a minimal assumption is the main strength of the hypothesis. The discharge rates of medium-lead burst neurons in the pontine reticular formation form a neurophysiological substrate for this hypothesis (van Gisbergen et al. 1981a). These cells discharge at high rates during saccades and are silent otherwise. Their rate may be interpreted as an eye velocity command that is quantitatively compatible with this hypothesis.

In order to generate the high velocity of saccades, G is very large—so large that, with an inevitable neuronal delay of 10–20 msec around this inner loop, it is itself unstable. This problem seems to have been solved by turning the system on when a saccade is wanted and off otherwise. The neurons that appear to do this are called pause cells. They fire at a constant rate at all times but stop while a saccade is in progress. Behavioral and anatomical evidence indicate that pause cells inhibit burst cells turning the system off most of the time. When a saccade is wanted, pause cells are inhibited and burst neurons are released to execute the saccade. At the end of the saccade, pause neurons are released from inhibition by burst neurons and the system is turned off. This activity is represented by a triggered switch in figure 2A. This may seem a bizarre way of doing things, but it is one way to utilize the virtues of negative feedback and make saccades very fast while not having to worry about oscillations. Not only is this scheme compatible with neural behavior, it also explains a great variety of saccadic behaviors. There exist a variety of situations, normal and pathological, in which saccadic oscillations occur, and these are easily explained by this model (Zee and Robinson 1979).

What is important for the present discussion, however, is that the system is made time-discrete by the trigger signal, so that saccades occur intermittently. Also, despite some exceptions and modifications, the saccadic system does resemble a sampled-data system to the extent that there is a refractory period (usually 200 msec) after one saccade before another will be made. In figure 2A this attribute is assigned to the trigger pathway, since there is evidence that processing between T' and E_D is continuous (see e.g. van Gisbergen et al. 1981b). Thus, there is clearly a difference between the saccadic system and the pursuit system in this regard; it is generally agreed that the latter is a continuous system showing no intermittency or refractoriness. One can argue that because the pursuit system is continuous and does not use sampling to achieve stability, internal positive feedback becomes a simple, very probable solution to the stability problem; however, one cannot argue this way for the saccadic system, since refractoriness (sampling in figure 1B, triggering in figure 2A) also achieves stability. One can only argue that sampling an internal reconstruction of target position (figure 2A) is equally successful; there is nothing incompatible with internal positive feedback *and* sampling. Only the accumulating evidence in favor of the scheme in figure 2A can be used to support the notion that, like the pursuit system, the saccadic system has divested itself of its negative feedback.

There are two fairly compelling bits of evidence that support figure 2A over figure 1B. The first comes from a study of patients who—probably because of a loss of burst neurons in the pons, which would decrease the gain G in figure 2A—make slow saccades (Zee et al. 1976). Saccadic velocities can be 80°/sec or lower (400 is normal), so that saccade durations are extended beyond 200 msec. If the target jumped to the right but jumped back again after about 200 msec, the patient would start a slow saccade to the right but would stop in mid-saccade and, with no delay, return her eyes to the starting point. This showed that saccades are not actually ballistic; they only appear so because they are normally of such short duration. It also showed that the patient could continue to process visual information during a saccade. What is especially interesting is that the model in figure 1B could not simulate this behavior. In fact, it would become unstable; that scheme works only if the response time of $P(s)$ is very short. The scheme in figure 2A has no such problems and simulates slow saccades quite well.

The second bit of evidence is simpler. If a subject fixates a target at point A and it suddenly jumps to point B, stays there for about 100 msec, then jumps in a different direction to point C, and then disappears, the subject will, in total darkness, make a saccade from A to B and then, after a pause, a saccade from B to C (see e.g. Mays and Sparks 1980b). Note that the retinal error appropriate for the $B-C$ saccade never existed. The system obviously takes the retinal error $A-C$ and corrects it for the movement $A-B$ to obtain the coordinates of C with respect to B. The system in figure 1B could not simulate this simple behavior. Because of the E' pathway in the system in figure 2A, it can. These are examples of the evidence that favors a scheme employing an internal, eye-position, feedback path (in other words, a system that has divested itself of negative feedback).

Smooth Pursuit Revisited

The scheme in figure 1C is unrealistic because the positive loop cannot encompass the entire delay τ of 0.13 sec. Since 50 msec of this delay is in the retina and 30 msec is in the plant and premotor circuits, only 50 msec can be put under the loop. If $P(s)$ were 1.0, $G(s)$ were $0.9/(0.04s + 1)$, and the delays were distributed as described, simulation shows that the scheme in figure 1C would be marginally stable at best. The basic reason is that a signal from the output of $G(s)$ would return to its input around the outer loop in 130 msec but in only 50 msec around the inner loop. The·problem is solved simply by, as shown in figure 2B, adding an 80-msec delay in the positive loop so that $\dot{E}'$ (a form of efference copy) and $\dot{e}$ (a form of reafference) may be added in the same time frame. This delay is the same as that in figure 2A and is there for the same reasons, with the additional reason that the system will be unstable if it is not there. To remove the negative feedback, the delays in the inner loop must equal those of the outer loop. Once this is done, the system is effectively without feedback and is, of course, perfectly stable. The scheme in figure 2B has been left in a rather simplified form; important nonlinearities have not been included because the main concerns here are internal positive feedback and stability. Given all the experimental data, one is almost driven to the scheme in figure 2B, in the sense that it is difficult to think of a simpler way to keep the system stable.

Loss of Negative Feedback Requires Parametric-Adaptive Control

If we throw away negative feedback in figure 2, its virtues as well as its problems are gone. A main virtue is maintaining accuracy despite large changes in system parameters (lesions). The steady-state, closed-loop gain in figure 1A, if it were stable, would be $G(0)/[1 + G(0)]$. If $G(0) \gg 1$, this number would be close to 1.0 even though $G(0)$ should undergo large changes. Without the protection of feedback, both systems would be totally at the mercy of parameter variations. The solution is the use of what is called parametric-adaptive feedback. In such a scheme, part of the system compares the input and the output and determines if the latter was the desired output. If not, it changes the *parameters* of the main system in a direction that causes the output to change in the desired way. This system does not correct errors immediately, as does conventional negative feedback (figure 1A); rather, it corrects them on a trial-by-trial basis. This method has been studied extensively in the vestibulo-ocular reflex, a system inherently lacking the type of on-line feedback shown in figure 1. The function of this reflex is to prevent images from moving on the retina during head movements; this is achieved by sensing head velocity with the semicircular canals and using this signal to drive the eyes at the same velocity in the opposite direction so that the visual axes in space do not move. An important parameter of this reflex is its gain (eye velocity/head velocity), which is normally close to 1.0. If the gain is disturbed (known clinically as dysmetria), the central nervous system detects the simultaneous occurrence of retinal-image motion and head velocity as reported by canal stimulation and slowly (over the course of about 3 days for large retinal slip velocities) returns the gain to near 1.0 (Robinson 1976) so that dysmetria is eliminated. This type of motor repair has been found in eight forms in the oculomotor system (Robinson and Optican 1981) and has recently been discovered in pursuit (Optican et al. 1982). The cerebellum is involved in all these forms of plasticity, whenever tested, and it has been proposed that it is responsible for such motor learning (Ito 1982). The interesting thing in the present considerations is that this slow, parametric-adaptive repair is found in systems with or without negative feedback, as though systems with built-in negative feedback had gotten rid of it and sought protection instead with parametric-adaptive feedback. Again, oculomotor systems can act as examples.

Pursuit

To simulate plasticity, a gain element P_1 has been added in the forward path (figure 2B) that is under parametric-adaptive control. Its normal value is 1.0. Its plasticity can be demonstrated by a patient with an eye-muscle palsy (Optican et al. 1982). Assume that the left lateral rectus has a weakness so that when the patient looks to the left, the left eye only goes half as far or half as fast as the right eye. If the patient wears a patch over the normal eye and views only with the weak eye, pursuit in the direction of the weak muscle's action will be too slow. One can simulate this by dropping the gain of the plant from 1.0 to 0.5 in figure 2B. The central nervous system learns in a few days to counter this problem by raising the innervation for pursuit in that direction until pursuit is almost restored to normal. This means P_1 has been raised to 2.0 to compensate. Of course $\dot{E}'$ no longer is a copy of $\dot{E}$ because of the smaller plant gain. To compensate, a plastic gain change from 1.0 to 0.5 must occur in the positive feedback loop (P_2) so that it continues to simulate (and cancel) the negative loop. These plastic changes are seen rather dramatically when the patch is switched and the good eye now pursues in the direction of the weakened muscle. Since the viewing eye now has a plant gain of 1.0 but P_1 and P_2 are still 2.0 and 0.5 respectively, the good eye will now take off after the target at twice the target's speed because the net forward gain (P_1 plus plant) is now 2.0. This overcorrection will, not surprisingly, lead to ringing and oscillations because the net gain around the inner loop is still 1.0 (2 × 0.5) while that around the outer loop is now 2.0 (2 × 1). Negative feedback is no longer correctly canceled, and stability therefore becomes a problem. This is what actually happens experimentally (Optican et al. 1982).

Computer simulation of figure 2B confirms that this predicted instability does occur, as shown in figure 3. Technically, the system is just barely stable; the oscillations do die out, but the overshoot and the ringing render the system essentially useless for tracking.

The demonstration of plasticity in the pursuit system indicates that it is protected from dysmetria by parametric-adaptive control and therefore does not rely on conventional negative feedback. This is strong additional support that it has gotten rid of its negative feedback.

Saccades

The same case cannot be made so easily for saccades. They too are under parametric control (Optican and Robinson 1980), but that is required in any case by their rapid, intermittent nature. In figure 1B, if some lesion changed the gain of, say, $P(0)$, a compensatory gain change would be required elsewhere to eliminate this form of dysmetria. A movement that is over within 50 msec can hardly be helped by visual feedback with a delay of 200 msec. Thus, the saccadic system requires parametric control whether or not it has positive feedback. This fact speaks neither for nor against the elimination of negative feedback by positive feedback.

Other Oculomotor Systems

The evidence is strong that the pursuit system has gotten rid of its negative feedback, and much evidence points in the same direction for the saccadic system. Is this true of all oculomotor systems? The vestibulo-

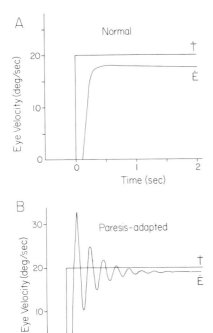

Figure 3
The model of figure 2B is simulated and tested by asking it to pursue a target velocity $\dot{T}$
of 20°/sec. A: The normal case. The gains of P_1, P_2, and the plant equal 1.0. B: The case of
a patient with a weak muscle in the direction of target motion after adaptation to viewing
with the weak eye and a sudden switch to viewing with the normal eye. P_1 has a gain of
2.0, P_2 a gain of 0.5, and the plant a gain of 1.0.

ocular reflex obviously has no on-line feedback, and its companion the optokinetic system is so slow (time constants of 3 sec) that it is not in danger of oscillating because of negative feedback. Models have been proposed for positive feedback in the optokinetic system (Robinson 1977), but the reasons have nothing to do with stability. The vergence system (that system that converges the eyes to look at near objects) has a delay of 0.16 sec and a total time of response of about 0.6 sec (Rashbass and Westheimer 1961). The latter is just slow enough to make the system stable but not comfortably so. It has never been considered whether the vergence system, which is continuous (i.e., there is no refractory period), might make use of positive feedback. The safest conclusion at the moment is that negative feedback is removed not simply because a system is oculomotor but because it can respond rapidly in comparison with delays in the system.

Visuo-Motor Limb Control

A number of limb movements can be made with speeds comparable to those of the pursuit system, if not to those of the saccadic system. They include movements of the head, the hands, and the fingers, all of which have a low inertia/force ratio. Such movements begin about 0.13 sec after their visual initiation. For the next 0.13 sec no visual feedback will be available to guide the movement. If most of the movement is completed by then, most of the movement occurred in an open-loop manner without benefit of negative feedback.

Ballistic and Preprogrammed: Words with Equivocal Connotations

It is tempting to call various eye and limb movements ballistic or preprogrammed, but these words have connotations that may be incorrect. The pursuit system (figure 2B) is a case in point. During the 130 msec after the eye starts to move, it accelerates to near target velocity without any visual feedback; but could one claim that the simple gain and lag in that system represents anything ballistic or preprogrammed? Clearly not. Subsequent target behavior modifies central processing as soon as it reaches it. This is what is meant by calling it a continuous control system; the output follows the input with a delay of only 0.13 sec (Robinson 1965). In particular, the pursuit system does not have a refractory period. This makes it an interesting counterexample of the generally accepted notion that all visuo-motor tracking systems have such a period (Poulton 1981). As pointed out above, when saccades are slowed down by a disease process, one discovers that they, too, are not ballistic or preprogrammed; they can be modified in flight, and they only appear so because of their normal speed. Consequently, the terms *ballistic* and *preprogrammed*—terms usually not defined in any strict sense—will not be used here, since they connote methods of operation that have not really been demonstrated. In the sense in which these words are usually used, none of the models in this discussion are ballistic or preprogrammed.

Limb Tracking

It is suggested instead, in figure 4, that the central nervous system, having calculated the position of the target, T', simply uses it to drive the limb position, L, to equal target position. In this figure the oculomotor systems are at the top, and, for simplicity, they represent a combination of saccadic and pursuit tracking in the fashion of figure 2; the main points are that negative feedback has been gotten rid of and that the target position T' (or the velocity, or both) has been recreated centrally. The target position is also independent of the eye position, because of positive feedback. If the eye should move for some reason, the fed-back signals E and E' will cancel each other, so that T' will be (as it should be) invariant with respect to eye movements. The main course of events then is that T' will be considered the desired limb position L and that fast premotor circuits (fast PMC) will be allowed to achieve this goal. Visual feedback is not required and would not be in time anyway. The circuits are driven by T', and their operation is not considered to be either ballistic or preprogrammed.

It is generally recognized that rapid limb movements achieve only 90 percent of their goal and are usually followed by a slower, visually guided movement. This dual nature of control is illustrated by a comparison between hammering a nail and threading a needle. Many movements are a combination of the two. The rapid part saves time but falls short since an overshoot in tasks such as reaching would knock the object away or painfully stub the finger. The slow part is an accurate, final adjustment. It uses visual feedback, but, since it is much slower, it does not run the risk of instability caused by the delays. Such a system, using slow premotor circuits (slow PMC), is illustrated at the bottom of figure 4. It may or may not be error-driven as shown. This circuit is not of interest here; it is included only to avoid the implication that visual feedback is not utilized at all in movement control.

Since the rapid circuits are open-loop circuits, they must be protected by parametric, adaptive feedback (Adapt. cntl. in figure 4). This mechanism can

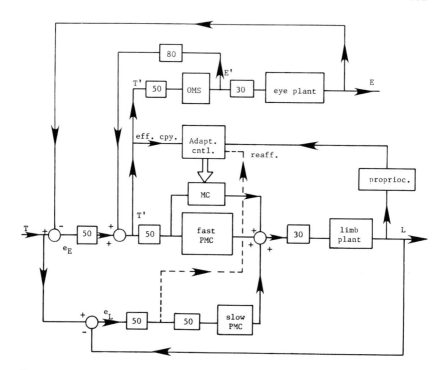

Figure 4

A proposal for open-loop, rapid control of limb position L in a visuo-motor task. The oculomotor system (OMS), at the top, combines those of figure 2 for simplicity. At the bottom is a possible error-driven system for slow, visually guided limb control by slow premotor circuits (slow PMC). The main system is in the middle. The reconstructed target position, T', is translated into end-point specifications for limb position by fast premotor circuits (fast PMC). This behavior is not considered to be ballistic or preprogrammed, just fast and driven by T'. It may or may not show refractoriness. Its accuracy is under parametric adaptive control (Adapt. cntl.), which compares efference copy against visual (e_L) and proprioceptive (proprioc.) feedback to detect dysmetria. If dysmetria is detected, modifiable circuits (MC), in parallel with more or less fixed circuits, are altered until movements are correct. This process is slow (hours or days) and works on a trial-by-trial basis. Retinal error between eye and target is represented by e_E, retinal error between target and limb by e_L.

regard T' as the efference copy or desired limb behavior, and it utilizes reafference from proprioception and vision (dashed line) to measure actual limb behavior. In the vestibulo-ocular reflex and the saccadic system, loss of the cerebellum does not abolish these movements, only the ability to modify them; this suggests that modifiable circuits (MC) involve a trans-cerebellar path in parallel with more or less fixed premotor circuits, as shown. When dysmetria (inaccurate limb behavior) is detected for a fast movement, the adaptive controller changes parameters in the plastic circuits of MC (presumably through altered synaptic strengths) until the movement is again correct. Similar protection for the oculomotor systems is not illustrated.

It goes without saying that the limb commands are complex vectors representing commands to several muscles operating about several joints, and that the coordinate systems of these signals are largely unknown.

The main thrust of the proposal in figure 3 is not new. It suggests that T' is translated into desired limb position. This presumably specifies a list of muscle lengths, joint angles, and associated forces. These can be translated into firing levels of motoneuron pools which are established and which cause the limb to assume the desired position regardless of its initial position. This could be done by negative feedback, as in figure 2A, and there is much to commend that idea. In figure 2A, an inner negative-feedback loop is used to drive the eye, E', to its desired position, E_D. A nonlinearity here can account for all the nonlinear behavior of saccades. Since the motor error $(E_D - E')$ is different for different initial positions, the circuit can produce the correct dynamic signal to get the eye from any initial position to the final one. The same is the case for figure 2B, as determined in unpublished studies by the author. The element $0.9/(0.4s + 1)$ may be replaced by a negative-feedback system similar to that in figure 2A (but without the switch), and a single nonlinearity in its forward path can again account for the major nonlinearity of pursuit movements, which is an acceleration saturation (Lisberger et al. 1981). The success of such a scheme in modeling two visuo-oculomotor systems is a good recommendation for suggesting it in the control of rapid limb movements as well, but this lies beyond the scope of the present discussion.

The idea that a movement is driven by its end-point specifications and not by the error has been proposed by Bizzi et al. (1976) and Kelso and Holt (1980), who have provided experimental evidence to support it. Thus, the main contributions of figure 3 are that end-point specifications require a knowledge of T' and that T' can be provided (in a manner independent of eye position) only if internal feedback is used. The proposal also looks at the problem from the standpoint of stability, which is often overlooked since most proposals of visuo-motor tracking are not specific enough to simulate on a computer to see if they are stable (as is often done for oculomotor models). It is important to realize that internal positive feedback (efference copy) can eliminate stability problems for limb as well as eye tracking.

Refractoriness

There remains the question of refractoriness in figure 3. The general belief among psychologists interested in movement control is that the central nervous system cannot solve two problems at once, so that in dealing with the response to one target jump it must defer calculations concerning subsequent target behavior until the response to the first jump has been made (Poulton 1981). When I first demonstrated a lack of refractoriness in the pursuit system (Robinson 1965), and when Zuber and Stark (1968) did the same in the vergence system, we did not fully appreciate how unusual this was for a visuo-motor system. Conversely, psychologists who study motor control have apparently been unaware for 20 years of these exceptions to the rule. The saccadic system, on the other hand, does exhibit refractoriness. Perhaps the pursuit and vergence systems are such simple reflex-like movements that few or no calculations by the central nervous system are needed (a dubious idea). An explanation cannot relate to position control versus velocity control, since pursuit controls velocity whereas vergence controls position. Perhaps we should turn the question around and ask whether refractoriness should be so unquestioningly accepted in all of limb control. The only reason the issue is important in this context is that sampling (with its refractoriness) is a possible way to achieve stability in an error-driven system. It is obviously not the solution for all oculomotor systems, but if all visuo-motor, limb-control systems could be shown to be refractory it could be argued that sampling is all one needs to achieve stability (although this needs to be proved by model simulation). Recent evidence (Georgopoulos et al. 1981) challenges the inevitability of a fixed refractory period in eye-hand tracking and indicates that such a period may be small to negligible in tasks in which the transformation between stimulus and response is relatively simple (as in making hand or eye position or velocity equal to target position or velocity). At any rate, the accumulating evidence in oculomotor systems and that for end-point control in limb movements argues strongly in favor of the use of internal positive feedback, whether or not refractoriness is also included.

Summary

We in oculomotor physiology are acutely aware of the many simplifying features we enjoy, in contrast to the physiology of motor control in general—simplifications that have permitted us to penetrate much deeper into central processing than is possible in spinal systems. But we are also aware that, because of these features, what we learn about oculomotor control may have little bearing on the general principles of motor control. This review suggests that achieving stability and accuracy in rapid visuomotor systems with large delays is a problem common to eye and limb control, and that this problem is exacerbated by negative feedback. Recent theoretical and experimental results in oculomotor physiology indicate that negative feedback is gotten rid of by internal positive feedback (called, by some, efference copy). This certainly achieves stability, and protection against dysmetria is provided by parametric-adaptive control (a method that is common to all motor control). The application of these concepts to the control of the movements of a limb fits in perfectly with the evolving notion that limb movements are driven by commands that specify the desired final position of that limb.

Acknowledgments

I thank A. McCracken for typing the manuscript, and C. Bridges for the art work. I thank J. L. Gordon for computer programming, and L. M. Optican and H. P. Goldstein for creating the simulation system. This research was supported by the National Eye Institute under grants EY00598 and EY01765.

References

Bizzi, E., A. Polit, and P. Morasso. 1976. Mechanisms underlying achievement of final head position. *J. Neurophysiol.* 39: 435–444.

Georgopoulos, A. P., J. F. Kalaska, and J. T. Massey. 1981. Spatial trajectories and reaction times of aimed movements: Effects of practice, uncertainty, and change in target location. *J. Neurophysiol.* 46: 725–743.

Henn, V., K. Hepp, and J. A. Büttner-Ennever. 1982. The primate oculomotor system. II. Premotor system. *Human Neurobiol.* 1: 87–95.

Ito, M. 1982. Cerebellar control of the vestibulo-ocular reflex—around the flocculus hypothesis. *Ann. Rev. Neurosci.* 5: 275–296.

Kelso, J. A. S., and K. G. Holt. 1980. Exploring a vibratory systems analysis of human movement production. *J. Neurophysiol.* 43: 1183–1196.

Lisberger, S. G., C. Evinger, G. W. Johanson, and A. F. Fuchs. 1981. Relationship between eye acceleration and retinal image velocity during foveal smooth pursuit in man and monkey. *J. Neurophysiol.* 46: 229–249.

Mays, L. E., and D. L. Sparks. 1980a. Saccades are spatially, not retinocentrically coded. *Science* 208: 1163–1165.

Mays, L. E., and D. L. Sparks. 1980b. Dissociation of visual and saccade-related responses in superior colliculus neurons. *J. Neurophysiol.* 43: 207–232.

Optican, L. M., and D. A. Robinson. 1980. Cerebellar-dependent adaptive control of the primate saccadic system. *J. Neurophysiol.* 44: 1058–1076.

Optican, L. M., F. C. Chu, A. V. Hays, D. B. Reingold, and D. S. Zee. 1982. Adaptive changes of oculomotor performance in abducens nerve palsy. *Soc. Neurosci. Abstr.* 8: 418.

Poulton, E. C. 1981. Human manual control. In *Handbook of Physiology*, section 1, volume II, part 2, ed. V. B. Brooks (American Physiological Society).

Rashbass, C., and G. Westheimer. 1961. Disjunctive eye movements. *J. Physiol.* 159: 339–360.

Robinson, D. A. 1965. The mechanics of human smooth pursuit eye movement. *J. Physiol.* 180: 569–591.

Robinson, D. A. 1976. Adaptive gain control of vestibuloocular reflex by the cerebellum. *J. Neurophysiol.* 39: 954–969.

Robinson, D. A. 1977. Linear addition of optokinetic and vestibular signals in the vestibular nucleus. *Exp. Brain Res.* 30: 447–450.

Robinson, D. A. 1981. The use of control systems analysis in the neurophysiology of eye movements. *Ann. Rev. Neurosci.* 4: 463–503.

Robinson, D. A., and L. M. Optican. 1981. Adaptive plasticity in the oculomotor system. In *Lesion-Induced Neuronal Plasticity in Sensorimotor Systems*, ed. H. Flohr and W. Precht (Springer-Verlag).

van Gisbergen, J. A. M., D. A. Robinson, and S. Gielen. 1981a. A quantitative analysis of generation of saccadic eye movements by burst neurons. *J. Neurophysiol.* 45: 417–442.

van Gisbergen, J., S. Gielen, H. Cox, J. Bruijns, and H. K. Schaars. 1981b. Relation between metrics of saccades and stimulus trajectory in visual target tracking; implications to models of the saccadic system. In *Progress in Oculomotor Research*, ed. A. F. Fuchs and W. Becker (Elsevier).

Westheimer, G. 1954. Eye movement responses to a horizontally moving visual stimulus. *AMA Arch. Ophthalmol.* 52: 932–941.

Young, L. R. 1971. Pursuit eye tracking movements. In *Control of Eye Movements*, ed. P. Bach-y-Rita, C. C. Collins, and J. E. Hyde (Academic).

Young, L. R., and L. Stark. 1963. Variable feedback experiments testing a sampled data model for eye tracking movements. *IEEE Trans. Professional Tech. Grp. on Human Factors in Electronics* 4: 38–51.

Young, L. R., J. D. Forster, and N. van Houtte. 1968. A revised stochastic sampled data model for eye tracking movements. In proceedings of Fourth Annual NASA–University Conference on Manual Control, University of Michigan, Ann. Arbor.

Zee, D. S., and D. A. Robinson. 1979. An hypothetical explanation of saccadic oscillations. *Ann. Neurol.* 5: 405–414.

Zuber, B. L., and L. Stark. 1968. Dynamical characteristics of the fusional vergence eye-movement system. *IEEE Trans. Sys. Sci. and Cyb.* 4: 72–79.

Zee, D. S., L. M. Optican, J. D. Cook, D. A. Robinson, and W. K. Engel. 1976. Slow saccades in spinocerebellar degeneration. *Arch. Neurol.* 33: 243–251.

2

The Role of the Primate Superior Colliculus in Sensorimotor Integration

David L. Sparks and Martha Jay

For many years, the superior colliculus was thought to be primarily involved in processing visual information, since this midbrain structure receives input directly from the retina as well as signals from the visual cortex. (See figure 1.) Now it is known that visual, auditory, and somatosensory signals converge in the superior colliculus, and that some collicular neurons have motor properties. On the basis of these findings, a number of investigators interested in the general problem of sensorimotor integration have turned their attention to the superior colliculus, a brain region that may be involved in translating sensory signals into motor commands.

General Organization of the Superior Colliculus

In mammals, the superior colliculus is composed of seven alternating fibrous and cellular layers. On the basis of functional considerations (Casagrande et al. 1972; Casagrande and Diamond 1974; Harting et al. 1973) and the pattern of anatomical connections (Lund 1964), comparative neuroanatomists have divided the colliculus into two major divisions: superficial and deep. The superficial layers (comprising the stratum zonale, the stratum griseum superficiale, and the stratum opticum) receive inputs devoted almost exclusively to vision. The outputs of the superficial layers are primarily ascending and terminate for the most part in various regions of the thalamus, including the pulvinar. (See figure 2.) In contrast, the deeper layers (the stratum griesum intermedium, the stratum album intermedium, the stratum griseum profundum, and the stratum album profundum) receive inputs from several modalities (visual, auditory, and somatosensory), contain neurons with motor properties, and have both ascending and descending efferent projections. (For reviews, see Sprague 1975; Sparks and Pollack 1977; Goldberg and Robinson 1978; Wurtz and Albano 1980.) Whether or not there is significant *direct* communication between the superficial and deep divisions is an unresolved issue (Edwards 1980).

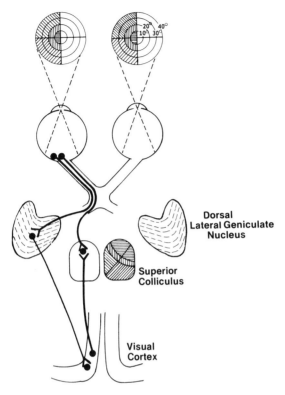

Figure 1

Simplified diagram of visual pathways and retinotopic projection to the superior colliculus. Note that the superficial layers of the superior colliculus receive visual inputs directly from the retina and from the visual cortex. Note, too, that neurons in the right colliculus are activated by stimuli in the contralateral visual field, that approximately one-third of the superior colliculus is devoted to the central 10° of the visual field, and that the upper visual field is represented medially and the lower visual field laterally.

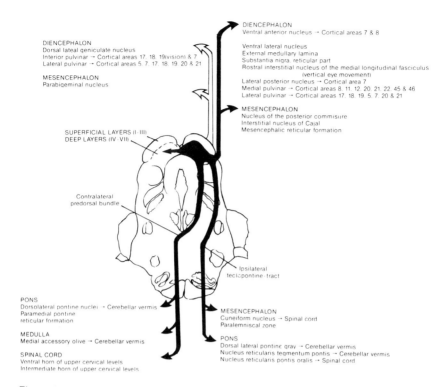

Figure 2

Efferent projections of the superficial and deep divisions of the superior colliculus. Major nuclei receiving axonal projectons from the superficial (open arrows) and deep (filled arrows) layers of the superior colliculus of the rhesus monkey are indicated. Major projection sites of some areas receiving input from the superior colliculus are indicated by the small arrows. (Figure adapted from Huerta and Harting 1984.)

Superficial Division

A well-defined retinotopic map (figure 1) in which over one-third of the collicular surface is devoted to the central 10° of the visual field is found in the superficial division (Cynader and Berman 1972). Neurons in the superficial layers of each colliculus are responsive to visual stimuli presented in the contralateral visual field. Cells with receptive fields in the upper visual field are located medially; those with receptive fields in the lower visual field are located laterally. Units with receptive fields near the center of the visual field are anterior in the colliculus; those with peripheral receptive fields are posterior. The representation of the horizontal meridian runs from anteriolateral to posteriomedial. Visual inputs to the superficial layers arise both directly from the retina and from the visual cortex (see Sparks and Pollack 1977 for references), and these inputs are maintained in register (that is, a region of the superior colliculus that receives input from a specific retinal region will also receive input from an area of the visual cortex that processes information about the same retinal locus). Efferent projections of neurons in the superficial layers ascend and terminate in various diencephalic and mesencephalic nuclei (figure 2).

Deep Division

Organization of Sensory Inputs

The deeper division of the superior colliculus contains neurons with sensory responses, neurons with saccade-related activity, and neurons with both sensory and motor properties. The receptive fields of visually responsive neurons in the deeper division are larger than those of neurons found in the superficial layers (Updyke 1974; Goldberg and Wurtz 1972). However, the deeper division contains a topographic map of the visual field that, in the anesthetized animal, is in register with the retinotopic map observed in the overlying superficial layers. Neurons responsive to auditory and tactile stimuli have been observed (Goldberg and Wurtz 1972; Updyke 1974), but the nonvisual afferents to the superior colliculus have not received careful attention in the monkey. In the cat, the deeper division of the superior colliculus receives proprioceptive inputs from extraocular muscles, neck, and limbs (Abrahams and Rose 1975), as well as somatosensory, auditory, and visual inputs (see Stein et al. 1976 for references). Bimodal and trimodal neurons are found in the deeper division. Gordon (1973) reported that if a cell in the superior colliculus of the cat responded to both auditory and visual stimuli, the auditory and visual receptive fields were overlapping—that is, both auditory and visual stimuli were effective only when moving through a particular region of space. Stein et al. (1976) described a stratified organization of visual, somatic, and acoustic modalities within the cat superior colliculus. The magnified representation of central visual fields overlaps the magnified tactile representation of the face, and, as visual receptive fields move temporally in the visual field, the underlying tactile receptive fields are displaced posteriorly and distally on the body surface. Similar stratified arrangements of visual, somatosensory, and auditory modalities have been reported in other species (Drager and Hubel 1975; Chalupa and Rhoades 1977).

Motor Organization

Microstimulation of a discrete point in the deeper division of the superior colliculus produces a contralateral saccade with a particular direction and a particular amplitude (Robinson 1972; Schiller and Stryker 1972). The current required to evoke a saccade is low (5–20 μA), and the latency of the saccade is short (20–30 msec). The direction and the amplitude of the saccade are functions of the site of collicular stimulation and are largely independent of both stimulation parameters and original eye position. An extensive "motor" map of the amplitude and the direction of stimulation-evoked saccades was developed by Robinson (1972). This "motor" map corresponds to the map of the visual field formed by the retinotopic projection to the overlying superficial layers. Given the lack of evidence for direct connections between the superficial and deep divisions (see above), the correspondence between the retinotopic map of the superficial layers and the motor map of the deeper division is puzzling. This issue is likely to resolved soon; a number of investigators are using intracellular methods that permit the axonal and dendritic processes of individual collicular neurons to be traced and reconstructed.

Chronic single-unit studies have revealed the neural basis of the stimulation motor map. Many neurons in the deeper layers of the superior colliculus discharge before saccadic eye movements (Wurtz and Goldberg 1972; Schiller and Stryker 1972; Sparks 1975). Each of these neurons discharges before saccades that are within a specific range of directions and amplitudes (the movement field), and there is a topographic arrangement of neurons with movement fields. Neurons that discharge before small saccades are located in the anterior colliculus; neurons that fire before large saccades are found caudally. Neurons near the midline discharge before saccades with up components, and neurons located laterally fire before saccades with down components. Some neurons that discharge before saccades also have visual receptive fields; other neurons have only movement fields. Neurons that discharge in response to visual stimuli *and* before eye movements have overlapping but not necessarily coextensive movement and receptive fields (Wurtz and Goldberg 1972).

One type of collicular neuron, the saccade-related (SR) burst neuron, generates a pulse of spike activity beginning approximately 20 msec before the onset of saccades to the center of their movement field. These neurons meet two criteria for participation in the initiation of visually elicited saccades: First, the pulse of spike activity is tightly coupled to saccade onset (Sparks et al. 1976); second, under conditions in which a visual stimulus sometimes elicits a saccade and sometimes fails to do so, the spike pulse is present only if a saccade occurs (Sparks 1978).

Neurons in the deeper layers have both ascending and descending projections (figure 2). Though it is known that collicular neurons with saccade-related activity have axons that project to other brain-stem nuclei involved in the control of saccadic eye movements (Harting 1977; Keller 1979; Raybourn and Keller 1977), it is not known how information concerning saccade amplitude and direction, contained as a spatial code in the superior colliculus, is transmitted to subsequent oculomotor brain regions. The pattern of spike activity originating from a single SR burst neuron does not encode saccade direction or amplitude (Sparks and Mays 1980). Identical discharges may precede a wide range of saccades. Neither the magnitude, the configuration, nor the timing of the discharge is related in any unique way to the duration of the saccade alone or to the amplitude of the saccade alone. Furthermore, for different neurons there is no consistent relationship between the parameters of the burst and the optimal saccade amplitude or direction. Thus, the information needed to generate signals concerning saccade amplitude or direction is not contained within the spike discharges of individual collicular neurons but must be extracted from the spatial distribution of activity within the superior colliculus.

Models of the Saccadic System

Early models of the saccadic-eye-movement system (Young and Stark 1963; Robinson 1973) suggested that saccades were directed by retinal information alone. Retinal error (the distance and the direction of the target image relative to the fovea) was thought to be computed by the visual system and used by the oculomotor system to produce a ballistic saccade. The superior colliculus was suggested as the site of this simple sensory-motor transformation (Schiller and Koerner 1971; Robinson 1972). According to this view, the appearance of a visual target 20° to the right of fixation would elicit a discharge of visual neurons in a particular region of the superficial layers of the left superior colliculus. In this manner, retinal error was represented by the site of visually triggered activity in the colliculus. The visually triggered discharge was assumed to activate subjacent regions of the superior colliculus containing neurons that discharge before saccadic eye movements. Since the sensory and motor maps were aligned, the resulting saccade would bring the foveal projection onto the region of the visual field containing the target. This simple model of the saccadic system and the corresponding view of collicular function have failed to receive experimental support (Sparks and Mays 1981). Moreover, recent data provide strong support for alternative models of the saccadic system in which it is assumed that saccade targets are localized in spatial (head or body) coordinates.

In a model proposed by Robinson and colleagues (Robinson 1975; Zee et al. 1976), the trajectory of a saccade to a visual target is computed as follows (see figure 3A): First, the image of a visual target on the retina creates a retinal-error signal (RE); second, the retinal-error signal is added to an eye-position signal to produce a neural representation of the target's location with respect to the head (T/H); third, motor error (ME) is computed by continuously subtracting the current position of the eye in the orbit (E/H) from the location of the target with respect to the head. Thus, the motor-error signal indicates, at any time, the distance and the direction required of a saccade to direct the eyes toward the target. If there is no change in eye position between the time the target appears and the saccade to it, then retinal error and motor error are identical. If the position of the eye changes between the appearance of a target and its acquisition, then motor error (not retinal error) will be the appropriate signal for the saccadic controller.

We (Mays and Sparks 1980a; Sparks and Mays 1983) conducted an experiment that strongly supports the view that saccade targets are localized in a nonretinocentric frame of reference. The experimental paradigm for this study is shown in figure 4A. Monkeys were trained to look at small light-emitting-diode targets in an otherwise darkened room. On a typical trial, the fixation target (represented by the intersection of the axes) was extinguished and an eccentric target (T) was illuminated for 100 msec. The monkey usually looked to the position of target T with a latency of 160–200 msec. Randomly, on 30 percent of the trials, after target T was extinguished but before the animal could begin a saccade, the eyes were

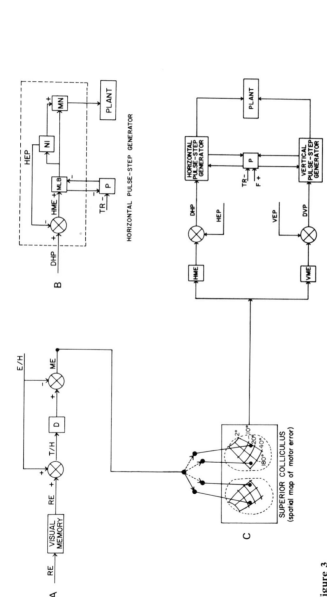

Figure 3

A: Simplified version of spatial models of the saccadic system. (See text, Robinson 1975, and Zee et al. 1976 for more detail.) E/H: Position of the eyes in the head. ME: Motor error. RE: Retinal error (distance and direction of target image from fovea). T/H: Target position with respect to head. **B:** Robinson's model of the horizontal pulse-step generator. DHP: Desired horizontal position of eye in orbit. HEP: Current horizontal eye position. HME: Horizontal motor error (difference between DHP and HEP). NI: Neural integrator. MN: Motoneuron. MB: Medium-lead burst neuron. P: Pause neuron. TR: Trigger signal. **C:** The deep layers of the superior colliculus contain an anatomical map of motor error. The switches indicate that inputs to this area must address different populations of collicular neurons if (with the head stationary) either the target moves or the eyes move. Each collicular burst neuron discharges maximally before saccades with a particular direction and a particular amplitude. Since separate pulse-step generators for horizontal and vertical components of saccades have been isolated, the magnitude of the horizontal and vertical saccade components must be extracted from the anatomical map of motor error.

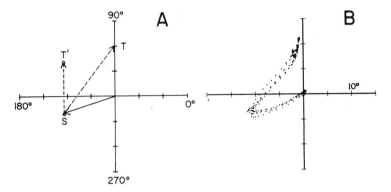

Figure 4
Compensation for stimulation-induced perturbations in eye position. **A:** The experimental paradigm. In complete darkness, while monkeys were fixating a center target represented by the intersection of the axes, an eccentric target *T* was flashed for 60–100 msec. After the offset of *T* but before the animal initiated a saccade, electrical stimulation of the superior colliculus drove the eyes to another position in the orbit (*S*). Retinocentric models predict that the animal will look to position *T'*; spatial models predict that the animal will look to *T*. **B:** Typical results. The trajectories of the eye movements occurring on four stimulation trials are superimposed. Each dot represents the horizontal and vertical position of the eye sampled at 2-msec intervals. The target was flashed 20° above the fixation point. Stimulation drove the eyes downward and leftward. After a brief delay, the animal compensated for the stimulation-induced movement by making a saccade that directed gaze to the approximate position of the target in space. See text and Sparks and Mays 1983 for more detail.

driven to another position (*S*) in the orbit by electrical stimulation of the superior colliculus. Under these circumstances, if the monkey attempts to look to the position where target *T* appeared, where will it actually look? Retinocentric models require that the saccade be based entirely upon a retinal-error signal, and predict that the animal will produce a saccade with a predetermined distance and direction. Thus, the animal should look from *S* to *T'*. Spatial models assume that the retinal-error signal is combined with information about the change in eye position produced by collicular stimulation and predict that the animal will look to the position of the target in space—that is, to position *T*.

Two important features of the experimental design should be emphasized. First, except for the fixation target and the briefly flashed target, the task was performed in total darkness. Thus, the targets could not be localized through the use of visual background cues as an external frame of reference. Second, the target at position *T* was extinguished before the stimulation-induced saccade. A saccade to the position of the target could not be based on a visual update of target position.

Representative data obtained in this experiment are plotted in figure 4B. The animal was able to compensate for the stimulation-induced perturbation in eye position by generating a saccadic eye movement to the position of the target in space. These findings support a spatial rather than a retinocentric model, since on stimulation trials saccades to the actual target locations could not be directed by retinal error alone. Furthermore, since the occurrence of the stimulation trials was completely unpredictable, compensation for the stimulation-induced perturbation could not have been predetermined; rather, the target must have been localized through the use of both retinal information and information about the stimulation-induced change in eye position.

Results of recent electrophysiological experiments also support spatial models of the saccadic system. Spatial models imply that there are at least three stages in the translation of sensory signals into motor (saccade) commands. Visual signals are first coded retinotopically. Later, information about eye, head, and body position is combined with retinal signals to constitute a neural representation of the target position in spatial coordinates. Finally, signals are translated into motor-error coordinates. We (Sparks et al. 1977; Mays and Sparks 1980b) found that collicular neurons discharged before saccades to a visual target localized in nonretinocentric coordinates. These experiments included trials in which an intervening saccade changed the position of the eyes after the target had been extinguished but before the acquisition saccade. On these trials, the trajectory of the acquisition saccade must be computed using information about the site of retinal stimulation and the eye position (the direction and the amplitude of the intervening saccade). Most SR burst neurons discharged before the saccades required by this task. Thus, their discharge must have occurred after the retinal-error and the eye-position signals had been combined. We also discovered a type of neuron (the quasi-visual or QV cell) that was visually responsive but appeared to encode motor error (the difference between current and desired eye position) and to hold this information in spatial register until a saccade occurred or was canceled. If a target was displaced or if the eyes moved after a brief target had disappeared, the site of QV-cell activity shifted to a location that represented the new motor error. We tested this hypothesis in a separate experiment (Sparks and Porter 1983) by recording the activity of QV and SR burst neurons during trials in which the monkey compensated for stimulation-induced perturbations in eye position. The neural command for the compensatory saccade must be based on information about the stimulation-induced change in eye position and on stored information about the site of retinal stimulation. We found that almost all neurons in the superior colliculus that discharged before visually triggered saccades also discharged before saccades made to compensate for stimulation-induced perturbations in eye position; this confirmed the motor-error hypothesis.

Hypotheses of Superior-Colliculus Function

Our current working hypotheses concerning the functional organization of the superior colliculus and its role in the control of saccadic eye movements, which are based on the above and on other findings, are summarized here.

Sensory Signals

The signals relayed to the superior colliculus from cortical and subcortical "sensory" areas may be organized in motor coordinates rather than in sensory coordinates. The deeper layers of the superior colliculus contain a spatial map of motor error. Motor error specifies the *change* in eye position required to move the eyes to a certain position in the orbit. Motor-error signals are created by the sudden appearance of an eccentric visual target or by a change in eye position after a brief target disappears. Similarly, the site of activity in the deep colliculus encodes the *change* in eye position required to move to a particular orbital position. Collicular neurons discharge before saccades when motor error is produced by the appearance of a new visual target and when motor error results from changes in eye position (Mays and Sparks 1980b; Sparks and Porter 1983). Thus, collicular burst neurons may be viewed as "vector generators," since the activity of these neurons, through subsequent synaptic connections, initiates saccades with particular directions and amplitudes. Since the collicular "motor map" is fixed, inputs to the intermediate layers must be in motor-error coordinates in order to activate the particular subset of collicular neurons that will initiate a saccade of the desired direction and amplitude.

The computation of a motor-error signal is based on a combination of eye-position and retinal-error information. But we have never observed neurons in the superior colliculus that encode the position of the target in head or body coordinates, nor have we observed activity precisely related to the position of the eye in the orbit. Thus, we assume that the translation of sensory signals into motor coordinates occurs outside the superior colliculus and that the inputs to the intermediate layers of the colliculus are already in motor coordinates.

On the assumption that the superior colliculus is organized in motor coordinates rather than retinal coordinates, we also assume that the superior colliculus represents a site where signals from different sensory modalities converge to become translated into a command signal in motor coordinates. The convergence of inputs from many brain areas representing a variety of sensory modalities is a striking feature of collicular organization.

Motor Commands

Two supranuclear neural networks controlling saccadic eye movements have been isolated: the paramedian pontine reticular formation (PPRF), which is thought to control horizontal movements, and a network in the midbrain reticular formation, which is presumed to control vertical saccades. A model of the PPRF circuitry generating the signals required for horizontal saccades is illustrated in figure 3B. (See Robinson 1975 for details.) An important feature of this model is that the input to the circuit is a signal specifying the desired position of the eye in the orbit. Once triggered, the circuit drives the eye at a high velocity until the actual eye position matches the desired eye position and the eye automatically stops on target.

How are the motor-command signals observed in the superior colliculus related to those observed in the other brain-stem circuits? The direction and the amplitude of saccades produced by microstimulation of the superior colliculus are functions of the site of stimulation and are largely independent of both stimulation parameters and original eye position. Similarly, the discharge of collicular neurons is not related to movement of the eye to an absolute position in the orbit; it is related to a change in eye position—that is, to saccades with a particular direction and amplitude. As emphasized above, the input needed by the horizontal and vertical brain-stem networks is the desired position of the eye in the orbit. Thus, collicular signals specifying a change in eye position must be transformed into signals specifying the absolute desired orbital position.

Our current speculations concerning how this translation might occur are represented by figure 3C. On the left is a schematic representation of the superior colliculus, containing a spatial map of motor error. We suggest that, as a first stage, the motor-error signal is separated into two components: horizontal motor error (the difference between the current horizontal eye position and the desired horizontal eye position) and vertical motor error (the difference between the current vertical eye position and the desired vertical eye position). Later, a signal representing current horizontal eye position is combined with the horizontal motor error to provide a representation of the desired horizontal position of the eye in the orbit. A signal of the desired vertical position of the eye in the orbit (DVP) is constructed in a similar fashion. In this scheme, the advantages of the pontine-local-feedback model are preserved; saccades of all sizes are produced that have the correct velocity and duration. Whether or not the discharge of brain-stem neurons receiving collicular inputs shows evidence of extracting the horizontal or the vertical components of the motor-error signal is currently under investigation.

Recent Experiments

In recent experiments (Jay and Sparks 1982, 1983), we trained monkeys to look to either visual or auditory targets in a completely darkened room. The apparatus was similar to that used by Knudsen and Konishi (1978) to study the auditory and visual systems of the barn owl. A hoop 6 feet in diameter surrounded the monkey, which was seated inside magnetic fields used to measure eye position. A computer-controlled stepping motor could be activated to rotate the hoop and to change the elevation of the speaker. Another stepping motor controlled the movement of a miniature speaker around the hoop to change target azimuth. A small light-emitting diode (LED) was attached to the center of the speaker, so that both visual and auditory stimuli could be presented. Mounted slightly closer to the monkey were three LEDs used to control initial fixation position. The center LED was straight in front of the monkey; the others were 24° to the left or the right of center.

A delayed-saccade task was used to temporally separate sensory and motor activity. One of the three fixation lights was activated at the beginning of each trial, and after a variable time an auditory or visual target was presented. In order to receive a liquid reward, the monkey had to maintain fixation of the initial light until it was extinguished and then look to the peripheral target. The fixation light and target overlapped for 500–700 msec, but the saccade target remained on for another 700 msec or until the monkey completed a saccade to it. The auditory stimulus was a broad-band noise burst (20–20,000 Hz); the visual stimulus was a green LED subtending a visual angle of 12 minutes. Eye position was monitored with the scleral search coil technique (Fuchs and Robinson 1966). Extracellular unit recordings were made with tungsten microelectrodes.

There were two basic questions we wanted to answer in these experiments:

(1) At what point do the auditory and visual systems begin to share the same motor circuitry for producing saccadic eye movements? Since localization of auditory targets uses different cues (binaural time, intensity, and phase differences) than the visual system, it is possible that the auditory and visual systems use different premotor pathways. However, since all eye movements are mediated by the same motoneurons, at some point the auditory and visual signals must be converted into the same coordinate system in order to share a final common pathway. Do superior-colliculus neurons that burst before visually guided saccades also burst before saccades to auditory targets? If the answer is yes, this indicates that auditory and visual signals have already been converted into the same coordinates and are sharing collicular circuitry. If some neurons in the superior colliculus burst before visually triggered saccades and others burst before saccades to auditory targets, this indicates that, at the level of the superior colliculus, separate motor circuits are employed.

(2) Are the receptive fields of auditory cells in the superior colliculus organized in head coordinates, or in motor coordinates? If the receptive fields are organized in head coordinates, then in these experiments (in which the head is fixed) the response of collicular neurons should depend entirely upon the azimuth and the elevation of the speaker. If the hypothesis that the superior colliculus is organized in motor-error coordinates is correct, then the responses of auditory cells in the superior colliculus should depend not only on the position of the speaker in auditory space but also on the position of the eyes in the orbit.

We found that neurons in the superior colliculus that burst before saccades to visual targets also burst before saccades to auditory targets. This is illustrated in figure 5. With the gaze directed at the center fixation target, saccades to visual targets to the left (16°) and up (10°) were preceded by a vigorous burst of activity (top left). The neuron responded equally vigorously before saccades of the same trajectory (up and left) made in response to auditory targets (bottom left). As expected, the neuron did not produce a consistent response before saccades to the same target location when the initial fixation was 24° left, since this required an up and rightward saccade rather than an upward and leftward saccade (figure 5, right).

Figure 6 illustrates, under four different conditions, the response of a superior-colliculus neuron that was responsive to auditory stimuli. On the trial illustrated in the top left panel, the animal was fixating the center

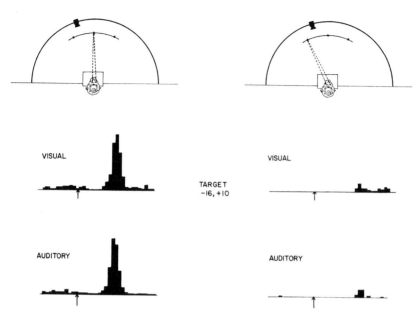

Figure 5
Saccade-related burst neurons discharge before saccades to visual and auditory targets.
With gaze directed at the center fixation target, a vigorous burst of activity preceded
saccades to visual (top left) or auditory (bottom left) targets presented 16° to the left and
elevated 10°. A comparable burst failed to occur before saccades to either auditory or
visual targets in the same spatial location if initial fixation was 24° to the left (right, top
and bottom). Each histogram sums the spike activity occurring on five trials. The arrows
indicate target onset.

fixation light and a noise burst was presented with the speaker 10° to the
left of center and 8° above horizontal. A vigorous response occurred, as is
indicated by the instantaneous-frequency histogram. On the trial illustrated
at top right, the speaker remained in the same location but the animal was
fixating a target 24° to the left of center when an identical noise burst was
delivered. The neural response was either absent or markedly attentuated.
When the animal was fixating the center LED and the speaker was located
10° to the right of center and 8° above horizontal, noise bursts produced
no consistent neural response (bottom left). However, a vigorous response
to the noise burst occurred with the speaker in the same location if the
initial fixation was such that an upward and leftward saccade was required
to look to the location of the noise burst (bottom right).

Thus, consistent with the hypothesis that the superior colliculus is organized in motor-error coordinates, the response of auditory neurons de-

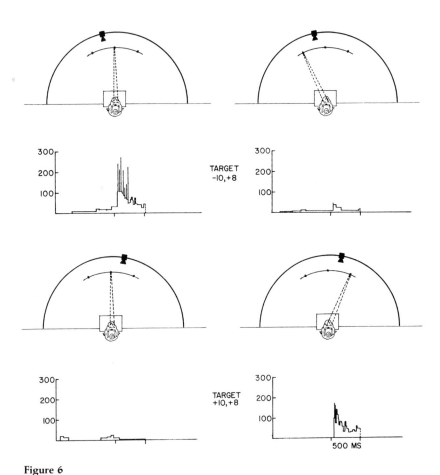

Figure 6

Instantaneous frequency plots of the activity of a collicular neuron responsive to auditory stimuli. In the top two panels, the noise burst was presented while the speaker was 10° to the left of center and 8° above horizontal. When the animal was fixating the center LED, a vigorous response was observed. When the monkey was fixating the LED 24° to the left of center, only spontaneous levels of activity were observed even though the speaker was in the same location and a physically identical noise burst was delivered. The bottom panels illustrate trials in which the target was 10° to the right of center and elevated 8°. The neuron was unresponsive to auditory stimuli presented while the animal was fixating the center LED. A vigorous response occurred (bottom right) to the same auditory stimulus with the speaker in the same location if the animal was fixating a target 24° to the right of center.

pends jointly on the position of the target in space and the position of the eye in the orbit. Stated differently, it is motor error (the difference between current eye position and desired eye position) that is important, not the position of the target in space.

In summary: Visual-saccade targets are localized in spatial (head or body) coordinates using a combination of retinal and eye-position signals. Existing data are consistent with the hypothesis that the primate superior colliculus contains a spatial map of motor error and is organized in motor, rather than sensory, coordinates. Moreover, in the deeper layers of the colliculus, the activity of neurons responsive to visual and/or auditory stimuli has already been converted into motor coordinates. Thus, the superior colliculus represents a site where signals from different sensory modalities are translated into common motor command signals.

Acknowledgments

The auditory experiment was conducted by Martha Jay in partial fulfillment of the requirements for a Ph.D. in Physiology and Biophysics at the University of Alabama in Birmingham. We thank Robert Deich, Ken Hammrick, Isabel Ragland, Kathy Pearson, and Haw-Tsang Chiu for technical assistance. This research was supported by the National Institutes of Health under grants R01 EY01189 and P30 EY03039.

References

Abrahams, V. C., and P. K. Rose. 1975. Projections of extraocular, neck muscle and retinal afferents to superior colliculus in the cat: Their connections to cells of origin of tectospinal tract. *J. Neurophysiol.* 38: 10–18.

Casagrande, V. A., and I. T. Diamond. Ablation study of the superior colliculus in the tree shrew (*Tupaia glis*). *J. Comp. Neurol.* 156: 207–238.

Casagrande, V. A., J. J. Harting, W. C. Hall, and I. T. Diamond. 1972. Superior colliculus of the tree shrew: A structural and functional subdivision into superficial and deep layers. *Science* 177: 444–447.

Chalupa, L. M., and R. W. Rhoades. 1977. Responses of visual, somatosensory, and auditory neurones in the golden hamster's superior colliculus. *J. Physiol.* 270: 595–626.

Cynader, M., and N. Berman. 1972. Reception field organization of monkey superior colliculus. *J. Neurophysiol.* 35: 187–219.

Drager, U. C., and D. H. Hubel. 1975. Responses to visual stimulation and relationship between visual, auditory, and somatosensory inputs in mouse superior colliculus. *J. Neurophysiol.* 38: 690–713.

Edwards, S. B. 1980. The deep cell layers of the superior colliculus: Their reticular characteristics and structural organization. In *The Reticular Formation Revisited: Specifying Functions for a Non-specific System*, ed. J. A. Hobson and M. A. Brazier (Raven).

Fuchs, A. F., and D. A. Robinson. 1966. A method for measuring horizontal and vertical eye movement chronically in the monkey. *J. Appl. Physiol.* 21: 1068–1070.

Goldberg, M. E., and D. L. Robinson. 1978. Visual system: Superior colliculus. In *Handbook of Behavioral Neurobiology*, ed. R. B. Masterton (Plenum).

Goldberg, M. E., and R. H. Wurtz. 1972. Activity of superior colliculus in behaving monkey. I. Visual receptive fields of single neurons. *J. Neurophysiol.* 35: 639–656.

Gordon, B. 1973. Receptive fields in deep layers of cat superior colliculus. *J. Neurophysiol.* 36: 157–178.

Harting, J. K. 1977. Descending pathways from the superior colliculus: An autoradiographic analysis in the rhesus monkey (*Macaca mulatta*). *J. Comp. Neurol.* 73: 583–612.

Harting, J. K., W. C. Hall, I. T. Diamond, and G. F. Martin. 1973. Anterograde degeneration study of the superior colliculus in *Tupaia glis*: Evidence for a subdivision between superficial and deep layers. *J. Comp. Neurol.* 148: 361–386.

Huerta, M. F., and J. K. Harting. 1984. Connectional organization of the superior colliculus. *Trends in Neuroscience* 7: 286–289.

Jay, M. F., and D. L. Sparks. 1982. Auditory and saccade-related activity in the superior colliculus of the monkey. *Soc. Neurosci. Abstr.* 12: 951.

Jay, M. F., and D. L. Sparks. 1983. The spatial coding of auditory-visual cells in the primate superior colliculus. *Inv. Ophthal. Vis. Sci.* 22: 82.

Keller, E. L. 1979. Colliculoreticular organization in the oculomotor system. In *Progress in Brain Research*, ed. R. Granit and O. Ponpeiano (Elsevier/North Holland).

Knudsen, E., and M. Konishi. 1978. A neural map of auditory space in the owl. *Science* 200: 795–797.

Lund, R. D. 1964. Terminal distribution in the superior colliculus of fibres originating in the visual cortex. *Nature* 204: 1283–1285.

Mays, L. E., and D. L. Sparks. 1980a. Saccades are spatially, not retinocentrically, coded. *Science* 208: 1163–1165.

Mays, L. E., & Sparks, D. L. 1980b. Dissociation of visual and saccade-related responses in superior colliculus neurons. *J. Neurophysiol.* 43: 207–231.

Raybourn, M. S., and E. L. Keller. 1977. Colliculoreticular organization in primate oculomotor system. *J. Neurophysiol.* 40: 861–878.

Robinson, D. A. 1972. Eye movements evoked by collicular stimulation in the alert monkey. *Vision Res.* 12: 1795–1808.

Robinson, D. A. 1973. Models of the saccadic eye movement control system. *Kybernetik* 14: 71–83.

Robinson, D. A. 1975. Oculomotor control signals. In *Basic Mechanisms of Ocular Motility and Their Clinical Implications*, ed. G. Lennerstrand and P. Bach-y-Rita (Pergamon).

Schiller, P. H., and F. Koerner. 1971. Discharge characteristics of single units in superior colliculus of the alert rhesus monkey. *J. Neurophysiol.* 34: 920–936.

Schiller, P. H., and M. Stryker. 1972. Single-unit recording and stimulation in superior colliculus in the alert rhesus monkey. *J. Neurophysiol.* 35: 915–924.

Sparks, D. L. 1975. Response properties of eye movement–related neurons in the monkey superior colliculus. *Brain Res.* 90: 147–152.

Sparks, D. L. 1978. Functional properties of neurons in the monkey superior colliculus: Coupling of neuronal activity and saccade onset. *Brain Res.* 156: 1–16.

Sparks, D. L., and L. E. Mays. 1980. Movement fields of saccade-related burst neurons in the monkey superior colliculus. *Brain Res.* 190: 39–50.

Sparks, D. L., and L. E. Mays. 1981. The role of the monkey superior colliculus in the control of saccidic eye movements: A current perspective. In *Progress in Oculomotor Research*, ed. A. Fuchs and W. Becker (Elsevier/North Holland).

Sparks, D. L., and L. E. Mays. 1983. The spatial localization of saccade targets. I. Compensation for stimulation-induced perturbations in eye position. *J. Neurophysiol.* 49: 45–63.

Sparks, D. L., and J. G. Pollack. 1977. The neural control of saccadic eye movements: The role of the superior colliculus. In *Eye Movements*, ed. Brooks and Bajandas (Plenum).

Sparks, D. L., and J. D. Porter. 1983. The spatial localization of saccade targets. II. Activity of superior colliculus neurons preceding compensatory saccades. *J. Neurophysiol.* 49: 64–74.

Sparks, D. L., R. Holland, and B. L. Guthrie. 1976. Size and distribution of movement fields in the monkey superior colliculus. *Brain Res.* 113: 21–34.

Sparks, D. L., L. Mays, and J. G. Pollack. 1977. Saccade-related unit activity in the monkey superior colliculus. In *Control of Gaze by Brain Stem Neurons*, ed. Baker and Berthoz (Elsevier).

Sprague, J. M. 1975. Mammalian tectum: intrinsic organization, afferent inputs, and integrative mechanisms. Anatomical substrate. *Neurosci. Res. Prog. Bull.* 13: 204–213.

Stein, B. E., B. Magalhaes-Castro, and L. Kruger. 1976. Relationship between visual and tactile representations in cat superior colliculus. *J. Neurophysiol.* 39: 401–419.

Updyke, B. V. 1974. Characteristics of unit responses in superior colliculus of the cebus monkey. *J. Neurophysiol.* 37: 896–909.

Wurtz, R. H., and J. E. Albano. 1980. Visual-motor function of the primate superior colliculus. *Ann. Rev. Neurosci.* 3: 189–226.

Wurtz, R. H., and M. E. Goldberg. 1972. Activity of superior colliculus in behaving monkey. III. Cells discharging before eye movements. *J. Neurophysiol.* 35: 575–586.

Young, L. R., and L. Stark. 1963. Variable feedback experiments testing a sampled data model for eye tracking movements. *IEEE Trans. Hum. Factors Electron.* 2: 32–37.

Zee, D. S., L. M. Optican, J. D. Cook, D. A. Robinson, and W. K. Engel. 1976. Slow saccades in spinocerebellar degeneration. *Arch. Neurol.* 33: 243–251.

3

Depth and Detours: An Essay on Visually Guided Behavior

Michael A. Arbib and Donald H. House

This paper is one of a series in which we build neural models of visuomotor coordination in the frog and the toad in order to exemplify the style of neural processing that involves dynamic parallel interaction between layers of neurons, rather than a simple stimulus-response chain or a control action which can be adequately represented in terms of lumped models. Among the earlier studies in this series are those of pattern recognition, which indicate how a neural network can use a spatial array of stimulation to tell prey from predators (Lara et al. 1982; Cervantes et al. 1985), and a model of prey selection that offers possible mechanisms for how an animal confronted with a spatially structured environment containing several prey objects will come to snap at only one of them (Didday 1976; Lara and Arbib 1982). In the present paper we move beyond models of the recognition of visual patterns that serve to trigger stereotyped (though appropriately spatially directed) responses and consider situations in which an animal exhibits behavior that takes account of a complex spatial context. We shall start from data on a toad viewing a vertical paling fence behind which is a worm. It has been shown that the animal may either snap directly at the worm or detour around the barrier, but that it will not go around the barrier if there is no worm behind it. Thus, we may still see the worm as triggering the animal's response, but we no longer see only the stereotyped snap directly at the worm; rather, we see a complex trajectory that depends on the relative spatial positions of the worm and the barrier.

A first view of the data is given in figure 1. The row of dots indicates a paling fence. The two circles indicate two alternative placements of worms, which are to attract a toad's attention; the "T" indicates an opaque barrier that prevents the toad from seeing the worms after it has moved from the start position. The position of the toad is represented by a dot for its head and a line for its orientation. The sequence of such "arrows" on the right side of the figure indicates successive positions taken by the toad in a

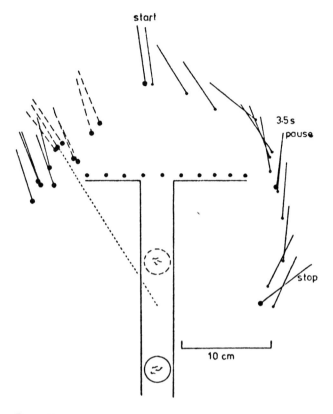

Figure 1

Results of several experiments involving a toad's approach to prey behind an occluding barrier. Solid lines at right indicate orientation of toad's body axis and snout position (dots) at intervals along path toward prey. For this case, prey objects are shown enclosed in solid circle. After the toad begins its movement, the T-shaped opaque barrier prevents it from seeing the prey. Solid lines at left show orientation of toad's body axis, for several trials, during its pause at the end of the fence. Dashed lines are similar, but are for prey positioned within dashed circle. These data make clear the toad's ability to extract depth information from its visual world, to maintain a short-term memory of this depth information, and to integrate this memory with some notion of its own body movement. Reprinted, with permission, from Collett 1982a,b.

single approach to the prey. The animal sidesteps around the barrier, pauses for several seconds, and then continues to a position at which it stops, pointing in approximately the direction of the worm (which, because of the opaque barrier, is no longer visible). On the left side of the figure, we indicate the position of the toad, on a number of different occasions, at the pause. The dashed arrows correspond to the nearer position for the worm, the solid arrows to the position of the pause for the further position. Even though the worms are no longer visible to the toad at the time of the pause, the orientation of the animal correlates well with the position of the target. Thus, not only must we explain how the animal chooses whether to proceed directly toward the prey or to sidestep around the barrier; we must also come to understand how the position of the target can be encoded in such a way as to be available to guide the animal's behavior even if the target does not continue to be visible.

We may note, with Ingle 1976 and Collett 1982b, that the full detour behavior exhibited here is quite complex—the animal does not simply orient toward the prey or the end of the barrier; rather, if it does not proceed directly toward the prey, it sidesteps around the barrier, orienting in a way that depends on the position of the target and the length of the sidestep. We postulate that each component of the behavior (sidestep, orient, snap, etc.) is governed by a specific control system called a *motor schema*. We then see detour behavior as an example of the coordination of motor schemas (Arbib 1981), where the sidestepping schema acts to modulate the orienting schema. The full analysis of such motor-schema coordination is beyond the scope of the present paper, but Ingle (1982a) has offered some clues as to the possible neural correlates of the various schemas. He finds that lesion of the crossed-tectofugal pathway will remove orienting, lesion of the crossed-pretectofugal pathway will block sidestepping, and lesion of the uncrossed-tectofugal pathway will block snapping.

The strategy of modeling in this paper will be to first develop a simple one-dimensional model of detour behavior in terms of determining the initial target for the animal (namely, directly to the prey, or to one end or the other of the barrier). Then, after reviewing further data and ways of modeling depth discrimination, we shall turn to a somewhat more sophisticated model in which the choice of the direction in which to turn is augmented by the formation of an appropriate depth map to represent how far away the first target is in the given direction. Then we shall look at a first model for generating the full spectrum of information that should be available for a variety of motor schemas not only to determine orientation and distance but to actually plan an initial sidestep around a barrier, the orienting movement at the end of this sidestep, and the final approach to the prey. It is our intention, by considering a variety of models, to create a space of alternatives in which the design of a rich set of neuroethological and neurophysiological experiments will be possible. Thus, the final section is devoted to a discussion of experiments suggested by the models and some of the open questions to be addressed by modelers.

1 The One-Dimensional Model

In the one-dimensional model, the retinal input is represented in terms of a map of neural firing rates indexed by the directions in which the animal could turn in a horizontal plane. One of the first models of this kind (Didday 1970, 1976) addressed the problem of the animal confronted with two or more fly-like stimuli and offered a distributed-neural-network model of how the animal could come, in general, to snap at just one of these targets. This model was given mathematical form by Amari and Arbib (1977), whose primitive competition model is illustrated in figure 2. Here the "tectum" is represented by an array of n cells, whose membrane potential at any time is u_i, with corresponding firing rate $f(u_i)$. The conversion of potential to firing rate is shown by the graph of f at bottom left in the figure. Each of these cells is driven by an input s_i, which indicates the output of a preprocessing element corresponding to the likelihood that a prey object is present in the corresponding portion of the visual field.

The cells are reexcited as shown, and also drive an inhibitory cell whose membrane potential v is converted into a firing rate $g(v)$ which provides inhibition distributed to all the cells. Basically, with appropriately adjusted synaptic weights, we have that a cell will be able to continue its firing, owing to its recurrent self-excitation, so long as its initial stimulation is high enough to allow it to win out over the pooled inhibition of the other cells. Typical results of the mathematical analysis are that the synaptic weights can be set so that at most one element can be excited in an equilibrium, and that, if all the u_i's are initially the same and an element remains excited in the equilibrium, it is the one receiving the maximum stimulus. However, once the model has responded to one pattern of stimulation, the buildup of inhibition will be such that the system exhibits hysteresis—it will not necessarily respond to the new maximal stimulus. However, a temporary change of threshold of all the units can be used to "release" a "blocked" response to a new maximal stimulus. It has been posited that this function is carried out in tectum by cells whose firing

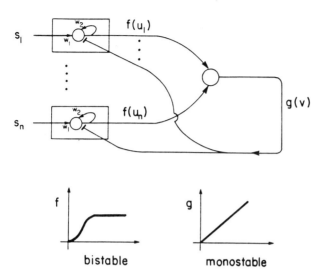

Figure 2

Amari-Arbib primitive competition model. This model selects the maximum stimulus from an input vector s by a nonlinear, distributed, competitive process. Circles represent simulated neurons, arrow-headed connections to neurons are excitatory, and flat-ended connections are inhibitory. Input to the system is supplied by the vector s; w_1 and w_2 are excitatory weights; u is the vector of excitation levels in the input array of cells; v is the excitation level in a cell that provides a global inhibitory feedback to the input cells. Functions f and g convert internal excitation to external firing rate. When properly tuned, the model will converge with only the element i, corresponding with the maximal input element s_i, above its firing threshold.

indicates a change in visual stimulation in their receptive fields, and which are thus called *newness cells*.

Our first detour model (Epstein 1979) is simply the Amari-Arbib model with a different input for prey and barrier stimuli. In figure 3a each prey-like stimulus is represented as a tectal input with a sharp peak at the tectal location corresponding to the position of the stimulus in the visual field, and with an exponential decay away from the peak. (Epstein used a gerbil responding to sunflower seeds rather than a frog responding to flies or a toad responding to worms in his computer graphics.) Note also that the size of the peak decreases with eccentricity. On the other hand, as shown in figure 3b, each segment of fence is represented by one trough of inhibition whose tectal extent is just slightly greater than the extent of the fence in the visual field. The sum of this excitation and inhibition when the three prey stimuli and the two barriers are combined is shown in figure 3c, where the combined excitation of the two central stimuli is lowered greatly by the

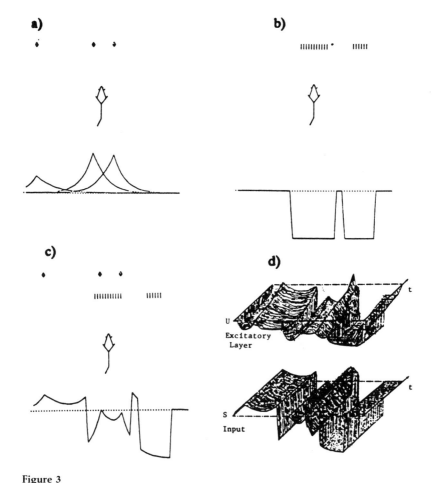

Figure 3

Epstein's prey-selection model. In diagrams a−c, the central object indicates the position and the orientation of a gerbil, the diamond shapes represent food pellets, and the vertically hatched regions represent barriers. The curves below the gerbil indicate spatially distributed patterns of excitation (above dotted line) and inhibition (below dotted line) elicited in the model by the configuration of pellets and barriers. In diagram a the presence of three prey objects results in an overlapping pattern of excitation, whereas in diagram b the barriers result in a trough of inhibition extending a small distance beyond each barrier end. The net effect of summing excitation due to pellets and inhibition due to barriers is shown in diagram c. The presence of inhibition leaves the maximally excited position to the right of the left fence. The curves traced in diagram d show the time course of the model in response to the stimulus pattern in diagram c. The time dimension t is drawn going into the paper; the horizontal axis represents the spatial dimension and the vertical axis the level of excitation. The curve of input vector S (bottom) simply shows the stimulus pattern of diagram c held constant as time advances. The curve of excitation level U (top) shows that the model eventually converges with all orientations suppressed except for the one corresponding with the initial maximal input. According to the assumptions of the model, this triggers a turn to the right edge of the left barrier.

trough of the left barrier but is still able to yield positive contributions at spatial locations just beyond the end of either barrier. Given the nature of the Amari-Arbib model of figure 2, it then comes as no surprise that a computer simulation of the effect of such an input yields the situation shown at the top of figure 3d, in which it is the cells corresponding to the rightmost end of that leftmost barrier that first attain a sufficiently high level of firing to command the overt response of the animal as a move toward that end of the barrier. We will refine this model in terms of the depth dimension in later sections of this paper; it seems worth exhibiting this sample run here because the logic of this model will constitute an essential subsystem of the model in section 3.

Ingle and Collett, in looking at the behavior of the animal confronted with prey and a barrier, do not find a single unequivocal direction but rather plot a histogram of directions of response over a number of trials. Collett (personal communication) reports that, except for a few animals that exhibit a strong directional preference, the histograms for multiple trials with single animals do not appear to differ significantly from those obtained across a population. Thus, a model should not yield a single unequivocal response; rather, it should be capable of yielding a histogram of preferred directions. The first strategy that suggests itself is to replace deterministic neurons by stochastic neurons whose output is driven by a noise term as well as by the other inputs. A second strategy, and an important one for many classes of nonlinear models, is to vary the initial conditions while keeping the elements of the models deterministic. However, a third strategy will be followed here, and that is to identify an explicit model parameter that is likely to be subject to significant variation due to the motivational state and the immediate experience of the animal and whose variation will readily affect the model's convergence characteristics. In section 3 we will show how such a variation in the spread of excitation due to prey-like stimuli can have significant effects on a model of orientation behavior.

2 Introducing the Depth Dimension

In this section we briefly review data indicating the need to take the depth dimension into account in any model of detour behavior in the toad, we sketch the general setting for our models of sections 3 and 4, and we briefly compare two recent models of depth discrimination.

Figure 4 illustrates a number of experiments on detour behavior. In each case the solid square with tail indicates the initial position of the toad, a row

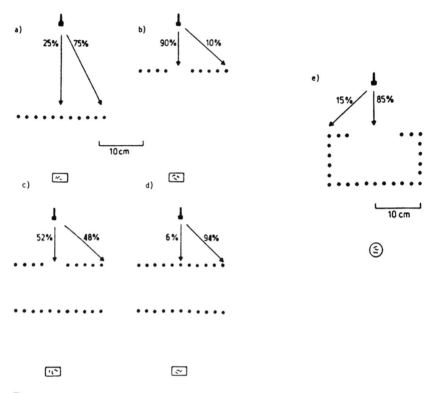

Figure 4

Histograms of the initial orientation response of a toad presented with various prey/barrier configurations (shown in top view). Rows of dots represent paling-fence barriers, boxes with worms indicate prey position, and inverted T's represent position and orientation of toad. Distances are to scale shown in diagram. Percentages indicate number of trials on which toads elected to head directly toward prey versus number of trials on which they elected to detour around either of fence ends. Reprinted, with permission, from Collett 1982a,b.

of dots indicates the position of a barrier, and the rectangle with squiggles represents the position of the worm. The arrows labeled with percentages show how frequently the indicated directions were chosen by the toad over a large number of trials. Figure 4a shows that the toad preferred to detour around an uninterrupted barrier; figure 4b shows that the toad preferred to go through a gap rather than detour. In figure 4c there is an uninterrupted fence at the same position relative to the toad and the worm as in 4a, but now there is the fence with a gap, as in figure 4b. In this case, the toad discounts the rear fence by choosing to go through the gap more than half the time, even though it would have detoured around the rear fence three-fourths of the time in the situation shown in figure 4a. Thus, it would seem that, to a first approximation, the response of the toad is a weighted sum of its responses to the individual fences, with the effectiveness of a fence in the sum declining with distance. Figure 4d shows that the toad's tendency to detour was strong when both the near and the far fence were uninterrupted; figure 4e shows that with a large gap in the front fence, the toad overwhelmingly chose to go through the gap even when, as in this case, there were side fences joining the front and rear fences so that the toad was in fact entering a cage. Such results lend weight to the search for a model that does take the depth dimension into account, but which is not highly cognitive in the sense that the animal would be posited to use representations of such high-level constructs as one fence vs. two, or a gap vs. a cage.

Figure 5 superimposes two possible coordinate systems for representing the ground plane in front of a frog or a toad. This figure also introduces the graphical notation to be used to describe the visual scenes that will form the input to the models of sections 3 and 4. The T-shaped object at the bottom of the figure represents the animal. The disks at the ends of the crossbar indicate the animal's eye positions. The small disks within the grid area represent fenceposts, and the solid rectangle a prey object. The 40×40-cm ground plane is divided into a Cartesian grid with an interval size of 10 cm. The radial coordinate system overlaid on this grid is centered on the midpoint between the two eyes. The radial lines of this system are placed at intervals of $7\frac{1}{2}°$. The curved lines are lines of constant visual disparity, spaced apart by a constant disparity increment.

We posit that neurons may be more appropriately indexed by the radial system than by the rectangular coordinates. The use of an angular measure is clearly motivated by the way in which an image is projected onto the retinal surface. Also, since disparity cues, like other depth cues, are more acute closer to the animal, the curves are longer and farther apart with

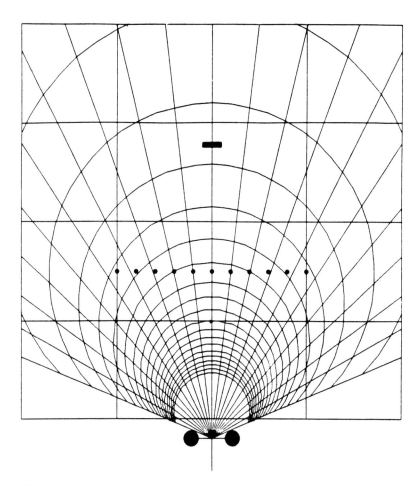

Figure 5
Cartesian and radial coordinate systems used in the models. The area shown represents a
40 × 40-cm square in top view. The cross-like icon at the bottom represents a toad, with
its eyes at the positions of the filled circles. The black rectangle in the upper-central part of
the grid represents a prey object, and the dots across the lower-central portion represent
the posts of a paling fence. The squares of the Cartesian grid are 10 cm on a side. In the
radial system, the radial lines are at equal angular increments from the toad's midline and
the arcs are lines of constant disparity spaced at equal increments of disparity. The spacing
of the equidisparity arcs illustrates the decrease of depth acuity with increasing distance
from the toad.

increasing radial distance from the animal. Thus, they have a general appeal
as a system for the representation of depth, and we would posit that they
represent regions that have approximately the same density of neural
representatives. However, figure 5 simply represents the ground plane of
the animal, and not the full visual field. One structure that could support
the full representation is a mapping of the whole ground plane onto a linear
strip of cells in the brain, with each small region in that strip corresponding
to a single angular direction, but a full range of depth, with the proportion
of cells representing nearer depths much greater than the proportion of
cells representing further depths. In summary: We represent the ground
plane by neurons indexed by an orientation coordinate θ and a discrete
depth zone coordinate d, but we do not posit that θ and d also function as
the coordinates for a two-dimensional array of neurons.

The general scheme of the detour model is then as shown in figure 6.
The visual input to the retinas provides two maps based on the θ coordinate, which can be further processed to yield depth mappings. We have
made the assumption that the barriers are recognized by one population of
cells and processed for depth separately from worm-like stimuli, which are
represented by a separate depth mapping. This assumption is supported by
the work of Ingle (1977) and of Ewert (1976), who demonstrated the likelihood that processing of prey stimuli is localized to the tectum whereas
contraindicative stimuli are processed in the pretectal region. On this
assumption, it is possible for these two mappings, indexed by the (θ, d)
coordinates, to be separately convolved—the barrier depth mapping B
being convolved with a kernel I that assigns inhibitory weight to barriers,
and the worm depth mapping W being convolved with a kernel E that
assigns an excitatory weight to the prey. The resulting sum $B * I + W * E$
then provides the input for the target selector, and the output of this target
selector can be combined with the barrier and worm depth maps to provide
the necessary input to coordinated motor schemas for the motor output for
snapping, sidestepping, orienting, jumping, etc. We shall provide two different instantiations of this general model scheme in sections 3 and 4. The
rest of this section briefly describes recent work on the modeling of depth
perception.

Recent Models of Depth Perception

It is well known (Julesz 1971) that the input to a single eye at a given time
does not, in and of itself, convey depth information. Among possible
mechanisms for extracting depth information are lens accommodation,

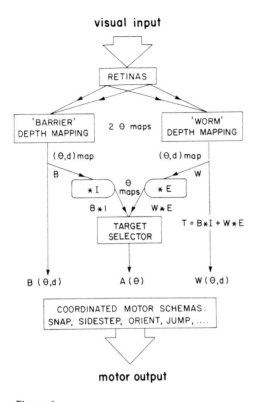

Figure 6
Conceptual schematic of our view of a general scheme by which visual input could
be processed to produce motor output. This scheme is based on the assumptions that
separate depth maps are maintained for prey and barrier stimuli, that the direction for an
orientation turn is obtained by combining information from these two maps, and that
information on preferred orientation and depth of prey and barriers is simultaneously
available to the various motor schemas. The motor schemas are, in turn, capable of
integrating this information with information about current body position to produce a
coordinated motor output.

binocular disparity matching, and optic flow from the change in input to a single eye over time. Recent evidence indicates that toads must integrate information from at least two of these sources when determining the depth of prey.

On the one hand, Ingle (1976) showed that monocularly blind frogs snapped accurately within the intact monocular field and in the ipsilateral portion of the normal binocular field. He suspected that lens accommodation was the source of these monocular depth estimates, since estimates were systematically distorted within the contralateral binocular field in a way that might have been predicted on the basis of the decreasing resolving power of the lens in its periphery. The conclusions from these observations are that monocular depth cues are sufficient for frogs to determine depth of prey and that lens accommodation is the probable cue source. These conclusions have since been confirmed by Collett (1977) and Jordan et al. (1980). On the other hand, by fitting toads with prisms and testing their prey-catching abilities, Collett (1977) was able to show that binocularity dominates the depth-discrimination process in normal binocular toads. His experimental data suggests a 94 percent contribution from binocular cues and only a 6 percent contribution from accommodation. These results, taken together, indicate that binocular cues dominate when they are available but that monocular cues are sufficient in the absence of binocular cues.

This evidence for the use of multiple depth cues led House (1982, 1984) to develop a model extending the earlier depth-perception models of Dev (1975) and Amari and Arbib (1977). We call this model the *cue-interaction model*. Its overall structure is depicted in figure 7. Both accommodative and disparity-matching cues are used to guide a cooperative-competitive process that segments a visual scene into depth regions. Further, it is possible to tune the model so that depth cues from binocularity dominate, while monocular accommodative cues remain sufficient to determine depth in the absence of binocular cues. The model produces a complete depth map of the visual field, and therefore it addresses the problem of collecting the kind of depth information that is necessary for barrier navigation. (This task is explored in the next two sections.) In computing the binocular disparities that are necessary to produce these maps, however, the model relies on binocular visual input to a single neural surface.

More recently, Collett and Udin (1983) used lesion experiments to demonstrate that, at least for the more limited problem of unobstructed prey catching, toads are able to make accurate binocularly based depth

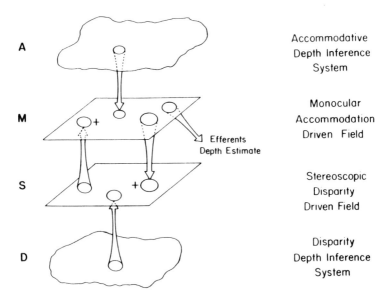

A — Accommodative Depth Inference System

M — Monocular Accommodation Driven Field

Efferents Depth Estimate

S — Stereoscopic Disparity Driven Field

D — Disparity Depth Inference System

Figure 7

Schematic view of the connectivity of the cue-interaction depth model. The various layers of the model and their interconnections are shown. Layer A represents an inference system that provides monocular depth cues from lens accommodation, and layer D represents an inference system that provides binocular cues from disparity matching. Layers M and S represent spatially organized fields over which two depth-mapping processes operate. Arrows from layers A and D to these fields indicate that field M receives only monocular depth cues and field S receives only binocular cues. The ovals and arrows between fields M and S indicate mutual excitatory interconnections that map each local region (oval) of one field onto the corresponding local region of the other field. By means of these interconnections, points of high excitation in one field provide additional excitation to corresponding points in the other field. Competition among depth estimates within each field ensures that points excited in only one field will have little chance to sustain this excitation when there are other points receiving stimulation in both fields.

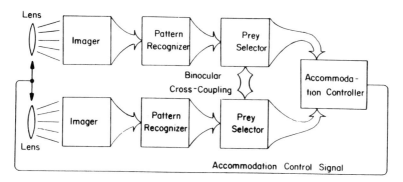

Figure 8

Schematic view of prey-localization model, showing the functional components of the model and their interconnections. Lenses are coupled so that they are accommodated to the same depth. Imagers produce visuotopically mapped output signals whose intensity is proportional to the crispness of focus at each image point. Pattern recognizers produce visuotopically mapped output signals that are strongest where the image most closely corresponds to the recognizer's matching criteria. Prey selectors take their input from the recognizers and from cross-coupled connections with each other. Their outputs are highly selective, giving a high weight to points receiving the maximum input stimulation and suppressing all others. Since the prey selectors take their input both from the pattern recognizers and from cross-coupling, they are biased in favor of points receiving strong stimulation on both sides of the binocular system. The accommodation controller converts the weighted image coordinates from both prey selectors into an estimate of depth. It then uses this calculated depth to adjust the lenses.

estimates even after the major cross-brain binocular relay (nucleus isthmi) has been severed. To explain their results, Collett and Udin postulated that the toad may use a neurally implemented triangulation process to localize prey, rather than a process based on disparity matching. This postulate suggests a depth-resolving system that does not attempt to produce a complete depth map but instead selects a single point (the position of a prey object) and locates that point in space.

Our most recent depth-modeling efforts have been directed at exploring the postulate of Collett and Udin while still incorporating the use of multiple depth cues. These efforts have led to the development of the *prey-localization model* (House 1984). This model, summarized in figure 8, uses pattern recognizers and prey selectors on each side of the brain to select and identify the position of a prey target on each eye. The right and left eye positions are used to compute a depth, which is used, in turn, to adjust lens focus. If the selected points on the two eyes correspond with the same point in space, then the depth estimate will be accurate and the object will be brought into clearer focus. This effectively locks the system onto the object. If the points do not correspond, then the computed depth will be incorrect, and the resulting lens adjustment will usually serve to bring one of the objects into better focus while simultaneously degrading the focus of the other object. Consequently, the system will tend to choose one of the objects over the other, and will eventually correctly locate this object.

Neither of our depth models can, by itself, fully explain the complete range of data on the depth-resolving system of toads. The cue-interaction model successfully integrates binocular and accommodation cues in a way that allows it to replicate behavioral data. However, it relies on a neural connectivity that does not appear to be necessary for binocular depth perception. The prey-localization model successfully addresses the lesion data and integrates both depth-cue sources. However, it is not capable of operating in a purely monocular mode. Further, this model does not allow us to address as broad a range of visual data as does the first model. In particular, it locates only a single point in space, and therefore it is not well suited to locating barrier-like objects. It may well be that, instead of a single general depth-perception mechanism, we have here a case of various neural strategies functioning either cooperatively or alternatively to cope with the vast array of visuo-motor tasks required of the freely functioning animal. One way in which both of the processes outlined in our models might be integrated in the brain of the toad is described in House 1984. Figure 9 illustrates our proposal for how these two processes may be distributed in the toad's brain. Caine and Gruberg (1985) provide support for the anatomical separation of figure 9, but their results are in flat contradiction to those of Collett and Udin, posing a clear challenge for both future theory and future experiment. They found that frogs with lesions of nucleus isthmi failed to respond to either threat or prey stimuli presented in the corresponding region of the visual field (contradicting Collett and Udin); however, the frogs exhibited normal barrier-avoidance and optokinetic nystagmus in all areas of the visual field (consistent with the scheme of figure 9). Caine and Gruberg conclude that the behavioral deficit seems to be "visual" and not "motor," and that it appears to be identical to that induced by unilateral tectal aspiration.

In developing the barrier-negotiation models outlined in the following two sections, we have thus assumed that toads are able to infer the depth of barriers and prey simultaneously, and that this information is determined by different neural substrates or is at least separable by object category.

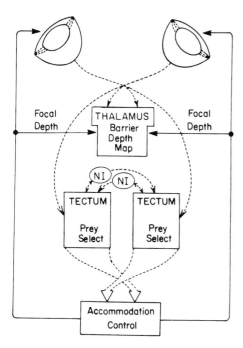

Figure 9

Possible anatomical distribution of the integrated depth-perception system. This diagram shows how both depth mapping of barrier surfaces and localization of prey may be distributed in the nervous system of frogs and toads. Eyes are represented at the top of the figure, and internal brain regions are indicated by labeled rectangles. Dashed arrows depict information inflow, and solid lines represent outflow. The thalamus receives overlapping projections from both eyes as well as signals indicating the current lens accommodative state. These inputs would allow the development of a depth map of visual space using a mechanism similar to that outlined in the "cue-interaction model." Each tectal lobe receives only a monocular projection from the contralateral eye, but ipsilateral information is available from tecto-tectal relays through the nucleus isthmi (NI). These inputs provide tectal prey selectors with the information necessary to localize a single prey. Prey-selector output projects to the accommodation controller.

3 A Model for Choosing Orientations

This section presents our first model of detour behavior to take depth into account, specializing the general scheme of figure 6 in the manner shown in figure 10a. Here, the depth map for prey is convolved with the excitatory mask shown in figure 10b and the depth map for the barrier is convolved with the inhibitory mask shown in 10c to yield two two-dimensional arrays, whose sum is shown as array E in figure 10a. The shapes of the two masks were chosen to take into account the way in which toads, when confronted with a "prey behind barrier" configuration, make the choice between turning around the barrier and proceeding directly toward the prey. Collett (1982b) reported that the path selection was governed by the distance of the worm from the fence and by the absolute length of the fence. Within a distance from the toad of 20−30 cm, neither the distance of the toad from the fence nor the visual angle subtended by the fence seemed to be important. Thus, the mask for barrier edges (fence posts) was chosen to project behind the edge at a constant maximum height after an initial rise to that maximum; i.e., there was a short distance behind the edge in which there was little inhibition, after which inhibition was equally strong at all distances. The mask for prey objects projected very broadly in a lateral direction and somewhat less broadly in the forward direction. The net result was that, with a prey object significantly far behind a barrier, the barrier projection substantially reduced the prey projection except beyond the barrier ends. For prey close to the barrier, the prey projection was not significantly reduced; thus, it was strongest directly in front of the prey. To approximate the "size constancy" exhibited by actual animals, the effects of the non-Cartesian coordinate system were partially counteracted by decreasing the spread effect of the masks by a linear factor with increasing distance from the toad.

The input depth maps D_b and D_p are assumed to be cleanly segmented as to depth, so that there is at most one computed depth for barrier and one computed depth for prey in each visual direction. This is not the case for E, which represents the superposition of the convolutions applied to these two arrays. We thus subject E to two independent processes in the present model. In the left path of figure 10a, we integrate the total excitation along each visual direction to provide a one-dimensional map, which is then fed to an orientation-selector model, which will extract the orientation θ of maximal total excitation. Thus, this portion of the model is an extension of the one-dimensional model presented in section 1. However, the present model also subjects the map E to a further process of depth seg-

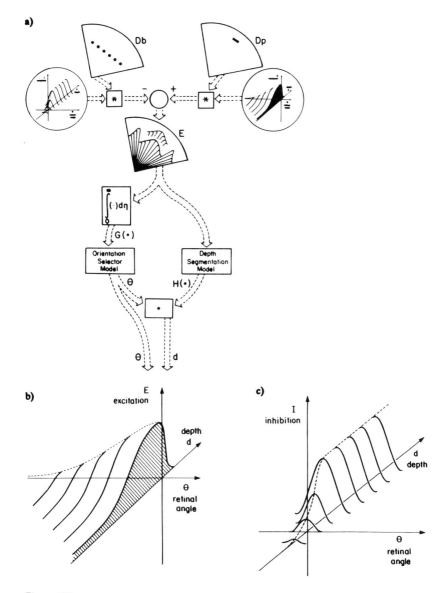

Figure 10

The general model of figure 6 is shown here in a specific implementation that is specialized to the barrier-negotiation problem. Diagram a shows the information flow and indicates the operations performed. D_b represents the barrier depth mapping, and D_p the prey depth mapping. Diagrams b and c show the details of the spread functions, which are convolved with the prey and barrier depth maps to produce the selection surface E. This surface may have multiple peaks at a given visual direction; thus, it is resegmented in depth in order to produce the vector, which encodes a single depth target for each angular orientation. The orientation of the selected target is provided by a primitive Amari-Arbib model, which takes as its input the vector G obtained by integrating, for each orientation angle, total excitation along the depth dimension in surface E. The selected orientation angle θ is then used to index H to yield depth d.

mentation. Thus, when the orientation selector returns an angle through which the animal is to turn, the motor schemas can also consult the depth-segmentation model to provide the depth at which the target at orientation θ is to be found. Note that the target being considered now may not correspond to the initial prey stimulus. Instead, it represents the point in space to which motor activity will be directed. If this point corresponds to the prey location, the object is achieved. Otherwise, we suggest that further processing will ensue when this target has been reached.

Figure 11 illustrates the operation of this model for the case of the single worm behind a single barrier configuration. The length of the arrow with orientation θ at the base of figure 11b corresponds to the total excitation $G(\theta)$ provided as input to the orientation-selector model for that θ. The array of squares and ovals represents the input E to the depth-segmentation model, with ovals corresponding to inhibition and squares corresponding to excitation. The level of intensity of either excitation or inhibition is encoded by the size of the corresponding symbol. As figure 11c shows, the direction chosen by the orientation-selector model in this case is that of the left end of the barrier, and the squares indicate that the depth returned by the depth-segmentation model does indeed correspond to the end of the barrier.

Figure 12 illustrates the ability of the model to replicate some of Collett's behavioral data. Figure 12a depicts a fence-and-worm configuration identical to that of figure 11 except for a gap in the center of the fence. To the left is the model input, and to the right is the converged state of the model. The preferred direction is now straight ahead, and depth information is provided for the edges of the gap and for the worm. Figure 12b shows data for the case of a solid fence moved back to a position near the worm. Here the preferred direction is also straight ahead. In figure 12c we have the net result of placing a fence containing a gap in front of a fence near the worm. Again, the directional preference is straight ahead towards the worm. The cage of figure 12d gives similar results.

The experiments illustrated in figure 13 address the variable orientation preference indicated by Collett's histograms (figure 4). These nine runs were made with three different distances of a solid fence from a single worm. For each fence distance, three choices of the prey spread function were made. The minimum spread necessary to cause selection of a fence end for the farthest fence distance was chosen as the base spread. Figure 13 illustrates model input, with the large circle centered on the direction and distance selected by the model when run against this input. The diagrams in the left column were made with a spread 33 percent greater than this

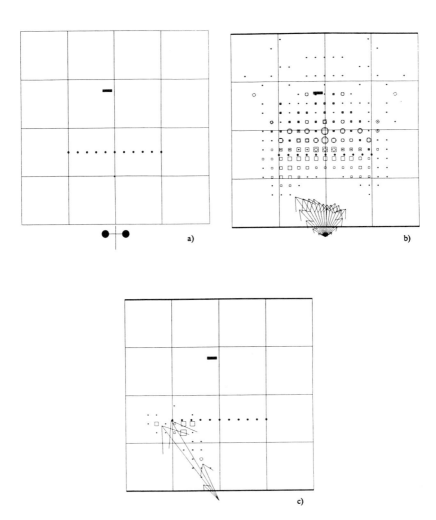

Figure 11
Orientation model, test case. (a) The scene used as input to the model, showing a single prey object behind an unbroken fence. (b) The selection surface E superimposed on the original scene. Square blocks indicate areas of excitation due to spread of the prey stimulus. Ovals indicate inhibition from fence posts. Strength of excitation or inhibition is indicated by size of corresponding symbol. Arrows indicate visual direction and strength of elements of vector, G, which provides input to orientation selector. (c) After nearing equilibrium, the model has selected a single orientation preference to the left end of the fence, and a localized set of preferred depths (indicated by squares near left fence end).

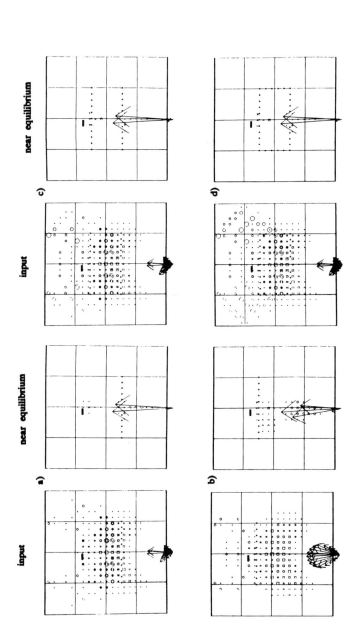

Figure 12
Orientation model, comparison with behavioral experiments. Selection surface and equilibrium state for several configurations used in behavioral studies. (a) Fence with gap. (b) Solid fence close to prey. (c) Fence with gap in front of solid fence. (d) Cage. The model results are consistent with behavioral results; compare with figure 4.

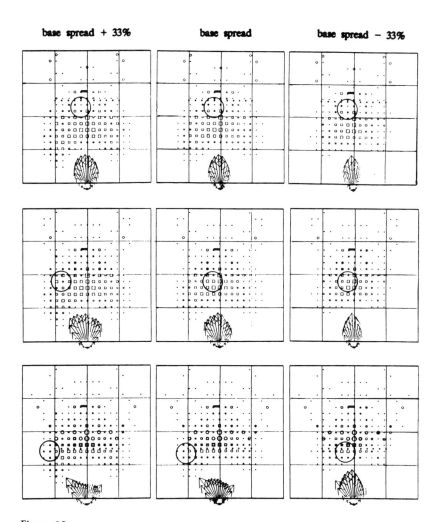

Figure 13

Model performance for various fence distances and spread parameters. The nine trials shown here were made with three distances of the fence from the prey and, for each distance, three settings of the prey attractant spread parameter. The images shown are the model input for each configuration, with the approximate spatial target selected by the model indicated by a large circle. The "base spread" used in the central images was that which just caused the model to select a fence end for the farthest fence distance. The model's choice of fence end vs. direct approach to prey is highly sensitive to this parameter, suggesting a way in which the variation in actual animal behavior might be explained.

amount, those in the central column with the base spread, and those in the right column with a spread 33 percent less than the base value. Here the model shifts preference between the fence ends and the fence middle, depending upon the extent of spread. In no case does the model converge on an orientation other than toward a fence end or directly toward the worm. The variation in the sensitivity of orientation preference as a function of the distance of the fence from the prey is qualitatively consistent with behavioral results previously demonstrated by Collett (1982b). However, further research needs to be done to test the quantitative adequacy of the model.

4 A Model for Planning Paths

The preliminary model of section 1 and the depth-based model of section 3 serve simply to choose the direction and, in the latter model, the depth of the target for the animal's first move. It is not clear from such a model how the animal would determine whether that target is the target for a sidestep (as in detouring around a barrier), or for a snap (as in direct approach to the prey), nor is it clear how such a model would explain how the animal has in its brain the information necessary to determine the orientation following a sidestep if that occurs first. In the present section, then, we turn from models that are based on the selection of a single target to models that suggest how the brain might go about planning overall paths of action that would require the coordination of several motor schemas. We present the two models of sections 3 and 4 side by side because we believe that at this preliminary stage of the search for the neural substrates of detour behavior it is premature to focus on a single model. It is hoped that the contrast between these models will serve to stimulate the design of new behavioral and physiological experiments. We also stress that the models are not tightly constrained, in that they do not attempt to specify what particular neurons are doing in the posited behaviors. Rather, they represent processing schemes that could plausibly be carried out in neural structures, and thus they represent postulates that there are populations of neurons that carry out the indicated operations. We pose it as an important challenge to lesion studies, in collaboration with studies in neuroethology, neurophysiology, and neuroanatomy, to determine whether indeed there are neural structures that perform these operations, and then to determine whether the posited functional interactions indeed take place between the layers thus identified. We expect that the refinement of our models will go hand in hand with the development of further data of this kind, and that theory and experiment will stimulate each other.

The depth-selection portion of the model in figure 10 had an excitatory field whose neurons were specified by two coordinates: one for angular direction and one for depth or disparity. We then postulated that the activity of the neuron with coordinates (θ, d) was to be seen as a measure of confidence that there was indeed a feature in the external world at the corresponding position in the visual field. The function of the model was to converge on a configuration in which only one depth was given a high confidence level for each visual direction. In the present model, we associate with each coordinate not a single number but a vector; this vector is to indicate the preferred direction of motion of the animal were it to follow a path through the corresponding point. For conceptual simplicity, and not because of any change in thinking about what internal representation is most likely, the coordinate system used in this model is the Cartesian (x, y) system. Our task with this model will be twofold: to specify how the vector field is generated and to specify how the vector field is processed to determine the appropriate parameters for the coordinated activation of motor schemas. In the technical jargon of differential geometry, then, the neural surface corresponds to a manifold representing space in some internal coordinate system, while the firing of a group of neurons associated with a particular coordinate is to represent the vectors of a tangent field or flow. The question is how those local vectors are to be integrated to determine the overall trajectory for the animal.

The model that follows is meant to indicate a style rather than to be seen as a fully articulated hypothesis about the nature of the vector fields that could be represented in the visuomotor system of the frog or the toad (or the gerbil). Our first choice is shown in figure 14. Figure 14a suggests that a single prey object will set up an attractant field in which from every point in the animal's representation of space there is an arrow suggesting a choice of movement toward the prey, with the length of the vector (the strength of choice for a movement in the given direction) being the greater the closer is the point to the prey. Figure 14b shows that we have associated a repellant field with a single fencepost, with the strength of the field contributing mostly to the determination of a lateral movement relative to the position of the fencepost from the viewpoint of the animal. Figure 14c illustrates the animal's representation of itself within the field. This representation consists of a set of vectors radiating out in all directions from the animal's current position, with a decay similar to that for the prey field. Figure 15 illustrates the various effects obtained by summing the vectors

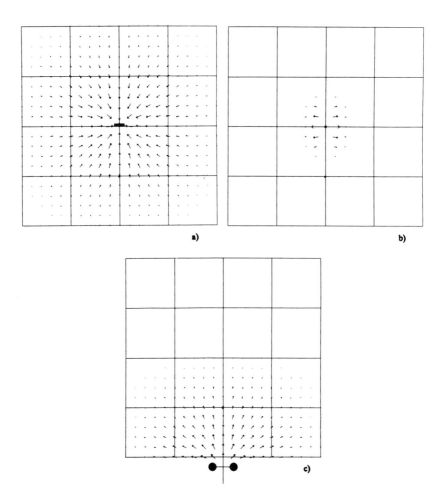

Figure 14
Vector field model, primitive fields. The vector field model envisions objects in the
animal's visual world as determining a space of potential motor activities. The fields
depicted here represent a first exploratory attempt at defining a set of primitive fields
that will interact in interpreting a more complex scene. (a) A single prey object sets up a
radially symmetric attractant field whose strength decays gradually with distance from the
prey. (b) A single barrier object sets up a repellant field whose effect is more localized to
its point of origin than is that of the prey field. The barrier field is not radially symmetric
but has a lateral component that is stronger but decays more rapidly with distance than
does its opposing component. (c) The vector field model also contains a representation of
the animal itself. This representation is simply the converse of the prey representation, i.e.,
it is radially symmetric but diverges from its point of origin.

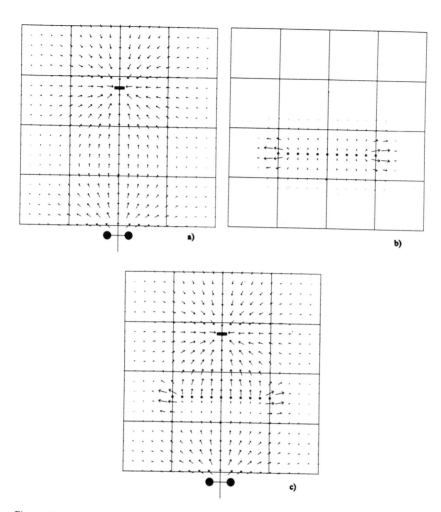

Figure 15

The three types of primitive field of figure 14 shown in interaction. (a) The prey attractant field in interaction with the animal's self-representation produces a field suggesting various curved paths terminating at the position of prey. (b) The effect of the interaction of the fields from several barrier objects arranged to form a fence is to provide a strong lateral thrust at the fence ends. The lateral components produced by the interior posts is effectively canceled by neighboring posts. (c) The net field produced by the interaction of all of the elements of the configuration can be thought of as tracing out a set of paths, most of which are diverted around the fence ends.

for each point of the manifold: the bug attractant field in interaction with the animal's self-representation (15a), the summed effect of the fenceposts corresponding to a field that repels from the fence as a whole but with especially strong lateral flow at the edges of the barrier (15b), and the overall net field set up by a scene containing a single worm behind a fence (15c).

The total field may be interpreted as representing the "net motor effect" of the scene on the animal, whether the animal is an essentially ballistic creature, like a frog or a toad, or a more "tracking" creature, like a gerbil. In the case of the gerbil (Ingle 1982b), we would postulate that the vector field is integrated to yield a variety of trajectories, with a weight factor for each trajectory. This field would have two "bundles" of trajectories receiving high weight: the trajectories that go around the left end of the barrier to approach the worm and those that go around the right end of the barrier to approach the worm. Thus, if we were to change "worm" to "sunflower seed" we would posit that the gerbil actually builds within its brain a representation of the entire path, that one of the paths is selected, and that this path regulates the pattern of footballs that will move the animal along this trajectory. In yet more sophisticated models, we could see the path not as being generated once and for all but rather as being dynamically updated on the basis of optic flow as the animal proceeds along a chosen direction.

In the toad, however, we would postulate not that the vector field is processed to yield a continuous trajectory or a bundle of continuous trajectories of which one is to be chosen, but rather that it serves to generate a map of motor targets, appropriately labeled as to type. The divergence operator is a likely candidate for this form of processing. Once a suitably constructed representation of a vector field is set up, the computation of divergence is a simple local process that may be carried out in the parallel distributed fashion associated with neural mechanisms. Further, the divergence of a vector field is a scalar field. The negative of the divergence will contain peaks where the flow lines in the field tend to converge and valleys where they tend to diverge. Figure 16 displays the negative of the divergence of the net field of figure 15c. This contour indicates a trough of high divergence in front of the fence, peaks of convergence corresponding to the two edges of the fence, and a third peak corresponding to the worm. We would postulate that a scalar field of this sort could be used by motor schemas so that one of the fence ends is chosen as the motor target for a sidestep. However, the relative position of the worm is simultaneously available to determine the coordinates for the

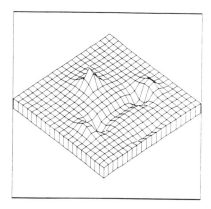

Figure 16
The negative of the divergence of the net field of figure 15c shown as a three-dimensional plot. Peaks on this plot represent regions of strong path convergence or bundling of paths; valleys represent a strong divergence. The two peaks separated from each other by a trough are centered on the two fence ends. The large rear peak is centered on the prey. There is a trough of divergence in front of the fence.

orienting schema and for the subsequent second leg of the motor sequence that we saw to follow the pause in the trajectory shown on the right side of figure 1.

In figure 17 we offer corresponding analyses for the following cases: a fence at the position of the fence in figure 15c but with a central gap (17a), a solid fence near to the prey (17b), a solid fence behind a fence with a gap (17c), and a cage (17d). Our research has not yet isolated the most suitable algorithm for extracting a path from data of this sort. However, these preliminary results are suggestive of a strong agreement with the behavioral data. The powerfully attractive quality of fence gaps noted by Collett (1982a,b) is especially apparent.

5 Discussion

The detour model of section 3 is successful in several ways in replicating data obtained from behavioral studies. First, in the prey-barrier configurations tested it always converged on an orientation to either a fence end or the prey. Since actual animals rarely choose any other orientation, this test is critical. Second, the selection made between a turn to a fence end and a movement toward the prey can be modulated for a variety of fence distances by a simple modification of a single model parameter: the extent of

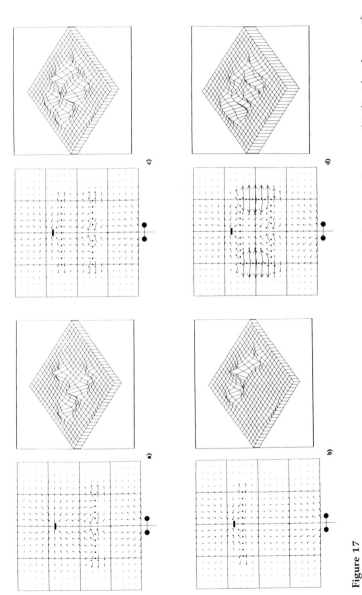

Figure 17
Vector model, comparison with behavioral experiments. Although an analysis has not yet been completed to identify a specific means for deriving motor activity from the vector fields, these figures indicate that the relevant information is efficiently encoded by the vector model. (a) Fence with gap. (b) Fence near to prey. (c) Fence with gap in front of a solid fence. (d) Cage. The model results are consistent with behavioral results; compare with figure 4.

the lateral spread of prey information. This is also critical, since it suggests a mechanism to explain the apparent discrepancy between the deterministic character of the computer model and the stochastic (or at least variable) character of the actual animal's response to a particular configuration.

The fact that the histogram results of the behavioral trials can be explained simply in terms of the prey-stimulus spread effect suggests the need for physiological studies of the susceptibility of tectal-cell receptive-field sizes to modulation based on motivational state and experience. If receptive-field sizes are prone to significant variation, then the difference between the behavior of animals and this style of model will have at least one plausible source.

Several tests showed that the orientation preference of the orientation model was extremely sensitive to the position of the prey behind the barrier. When the visual input was prefectly balanced (symmetrical about the midline), the model was unable to select a single preferred orientation. However, the slightest imbalance to either side resulted in an unequivocal selection of the more heavily weighted side. This suggests the need for a series of behavioral experiments to determine whether or not animals also exhibit this quality. What needs to be determined is whether histograms of turn preference show a marked shift in peak orientation preference or whether there is a smooth shift in preference when the visual scene is gradually shifted from a central bias to (for instance) a left bias. Our model predicts the marked shift. An example of this sort of behavior is the "snap zone" of frogs (Ingle 1982b). Here the animal snaps at prey within the zone, orients to or hops toward prey outside the zone, and exhibits ambiguous behavior within a narrow band between the zones.

Lara et al. (1984) have offered an alternative model in the spirit of figure 6. They posit the recognition of gaps as an explicit step in the computation underlying detour behavior. It is thus a challenge to experimentalists to design ways to discriminate between the hypotheses that "the brain 'recognizes' barriers as inhibitory" and that "the brain 'recognizes' gaps as excitatory" in the cooperative computation of behavior. Lara et al. (1984) also report models—at the level of interacting schemas, rather than layers of neuron-like elements—for prey acquisition in environments containing chasms as well as barriers, and for predator avoidance. Future research will test these models by developing their possible neural instantiations.

The vector model presented in section 4 differs significantly from the simple orientation model of section 3. The primary source of the difference is that here visual stimuli are not seen as setting up a simple decision surface that can be processed to select among several optional actions.

Rather, what is set up is a spatially encoded map of potential motor activity that, in some sense, is the net result of the interaction of all the pertinent visual stimuli. Although in the simple Cartesian representation used in this paper the vectors are described in terms of components of forward and lateral motion, there is no reason to expect that the nervous system would encode vector quantities in this way. What is more likely is that they would be encoded in terms of the various types of schematized motor patterns available to the animal. For instance, a particular vector could be envisioned as having components governing sidestepping, turning, and snapping. The coordinate system for such a vector field would, most appropriately, be body centered rather than eye centered.

Ingle (1982b) also suggests a model for detour behavior based on principles similar to those employed in our simple orientation model. In this model he envisions wide-field tectal neurons driven by retinal prey detectors as providing the kind of spread effect we hypothesized in our model. He proposes that if inhibition from pretectal cells driven by barrier detectors is sufficient to suppress excitation in narrow-field tectal neurons, the effect of the wide-field neurons will be to provide a lateral shift of the locus of tectal excitation. This shift in locus would then be translated into a corresponding shift in orientation turning angle. However, his model is quite different in character from either of the ones we propose. He has shown that pretectum governs sidestepping and tectum governs orientation turning and snapping. This has led him to suggest that the signals to the motor area from tectum and pretectum are of the nature of commands intended to be executed in a coordinated way by the motor area. In our models, however, we see these signals as describing a field of potential motor activity, which contains within it a spatial model of the animal's visual world. We would agree with Ingle's placement of the barrier-related field in pretectum and that associated with prey in tectum. Further, we agree that final processing and decision making based on this kind of scheme must take place in the motor area. However, we do not see it as the nature of this process to select among and coordinate independent motor commands. Rather, we see it as a process of deriving appropriate motor responses on the basis of a set of spatially distributed motor cues which already contain the results of an interaction among the various visual cues.

In apparent confirmation of the notion of the global interaction embodied (especially) in our vector model, Grobstein et al. (1982) have reported findings indicating that tectal locus cannot be the unique determiner of orientation preference. For instance, lesions to the tectum abolish visually guided orientation turning but leave orientation to tactile stimuli intact.

Conversely, lesions to the lateral torus semicircularis abolish tactile orientation but do not affect visual orientation. More dramatic, Grobstein et al. have shown that small lesions of the neuraxis do not produce orientation scotomas but, rather, result in inaccurate turning and undershooting throughout the disturbed hemifield. Their conclusion is that these small lesions do not destroy linkages between particular tectal loci and turn-generating circuits but produce a more global disturbance for all tectal regions ipsilateral to the lesion.

If the vector model is to adequately represent spatially directed activity, the vector field set up by the fence posts should probably be represented by a field that survives translation of the toad's position within the field. The present model does not account for this, since the fencepost field shape depends on the position of the toad (in contrast to the prey field, which is radially symmetric about the prey's position). Further studies with the model are needed to correct this.

Acknowledgment

The research reported in this paper was supported in part by the National Institutes of Health under grant NS14971-04.

References

Amari, S., and M. A. Arbib. 1977. Competition and cooperation in neural nets. In *Systems Neuroscience*, ed. J. Metzler (Academic).

Arbib, M. A. 1981. Perceptual structures and distributed motor control. In *Handbook of Physiology—The Nervous System II. Motor Control*, ed. V. B. Brooks (American Physiological Society).

Caine, H. S., and E. R. Gruberg. 1985. Ablation of nucleus isthmi leads to loss of specific visually elicited behaviors in the frog, *Rana pipiens. Neurosci. Lett.*

Cervantes, F., R. Lara, and M. A. Arbib. 1984. A neural model subserving prey-predator discrimination and size preference in anuran amphibia. *J. Theor. Biol.* 113: 117–152.

Collett, T. 1977. Stereopsis in toads. *Nature* 267: 349–351.

Collett, T. 1982a. Picking a route: Do toads follow rules or make plans? In Proceedings of the Workshop on Visuomotor Coordination in Frog and Toad: Models and Experiments, technical report 82-16, Computer and Information Science Department, University of Massachusetts, Amherst.

Collett, T. 1982b. Do toads plan routes? A study of the detour behavior of *Bufo viridis. J. Comp. Physiol.* 146: 261–271.

Collett, T., and S. Udin. 1983. The role of the toad's nucleus isthmi in prey-catching behavior. In Proceedings of the Second Workshop on Visuomotor Coordination in Frog and Toad: Models and Experiments, technical report 83-19, Computer and Information Science Department, University of Massachusetts, Amherst.

Dev, P. 1975. Perception of depth surfaces in random-dot stereograms: A neural model. *Int. J. Man-Machine Studies* 7: 511–528.

Didday, R. L. 1970. The Simulation and Modelling of Distributed Information Processing in the Frog Visual System. Ph.D. dissertation, Stanford University.

Didday, R. L. 1976. A model of visuomotor mechanisms in the frog optic tectum. *Math. Biosci.* 30: 169–180.

Epstein, S. 1979. Vermin Users Manual. Unpublished project report, Computer and Information Science Department, University of Massachusetts, Amherst.

Ewert, J.-P. 1976. The visual system of the toad: Behavioral and physiological studies on a pattern recognition system. In *The Amphibian Visual System: A Multidisciplinary Approach*, ed. K. Fite (Academic).

Grobstein, P., C. Comer, and S. K. Kostyk. 1982. Frog prey capture behavior: Between sensory maps and directed motor output. In Proceedings of the Workshop on Visuomotor Coordination in Frog and Toad: Models and Experiments, technical report 82-16, Computer and Information Science Department, University of Massachusetts, Amherst.

House, D. H. 1982. The frog/toad depth perception system—A cooperative/competitive model. In Proceedings of the Workshop on Visuomotor Coordination in Frog and Toad: Models and Experiments, technical report 82-16, Computer and Information Science Department, University of Massachusetts, Amherst.

House, D. H. 1984. Neural Models of Depth Perception in Frogs and Toads. Ph.D. dissertation, University of Massachusetts.

Ingle, D. 1976. Spatial visions in anurans. In *The Amphibian Visual System: A Multidisciplinary Approach*, ed. K. Fite (Academic).

Ingle, D. 1977. Detection of stationary objects by frogs (*Rana pipiens*) after ablation of the optic tectum. *J. Comp. Physiol. Psychol.* 391: 1359–1364.

Ingle, D. 1982a. Visual mechanisms of optic tectum and pretectum related to stimulus localization in frogs and toads. In *Advances in Vertebrate Neuroethology*, ed. J.-P. Ewert, R. R. Capranica, and D. J. Ingle (Plenum).

Ingle, D. 1982b. The organization of visuomotor behaviors in vertebrates. In *Analysis of Visual Behavior*, ed. D. Ingle, M. Goodale, and R. Mansfield (MIT Press).

Jordan, M., G. Luthardt, C. Meyer-Naujoks, and G. Roth. 1980. The role of eye accommodation in the depth perception of common toads. Z. Naturforsch. 35c: 851–852.

Julesz, B. 1971. Foundations of Cyclopean Perception. University of Chicago Press.

Lara, R., and M. A. Arbib. 1982. A neural model of interaction between tectum and pretectum in prey selection. Cognition and Brain Theory 5: 149–171.

Lara, R., F. Cervantes, and M. A. Arbib. 1982. Two-dimensional model of retinal-tectal-pretectal interactions for the control of prey-predator recognition and size preference in amphibia. In Competition and Cooperation in Neural Nets, ed. S. Amari and M. A. Arbib (Springer-Verlag).

Lara, R., M. Carmona, F. Daza, and A. Cruz, 1984. A global model of the neural mechanisms responsible for visuomotor coordination in toads. J. Th. Biol. 110: 587–618.

4

A Trace of Memory: An Evolutionary Perspective on the Visual System

D. N. Spinelli

Some Evolutionary Considerations

On the way to discussing some findings and ideas that concern the epigenetic development of vision in cats, I intend to detour into the phylogeny of vision. Such a step back might be useful for a number of reasons. My aim, however, is to apply a Darwinian approach to the selection and evolution of mechanisms pertaining to vision.

Neural mechanisms consist of populations of cells and are subject to selection. Let's attempt a recasting of Darwin's thinking as applied to mechanisms. From this point of view, homologous mechanisms acquire extra meaning.

At each branching point in the phylogenetic tree, some mechanisms (homologous) survive, some die, and some new ones appear. Thus, we could say that there is a struggle for existence among mechanisms. It follows that the more powerful mechanisms are those that are present in large numbers of species and have changed the least over time.

What I am attempting to do is reemphasize the following:

- When observing homologous mechanisms, we are dealing with various manifestations of what is fundamentally the same structure often performing similar functions. That this structure has survived selection simultaneously shows great structural stability and functional adaptability.

- "Fitter mechanisms" will displace less fit ones.

- If there is a phylogeny of mechainsms, then the concepts of homology and analogy can be used to great advantage in the analysis of function.

- The more powerful mechanisms must have left very large signposts at the crossroads of evolution.

In the following paragraphs I will point out a few of the signposts and attempt to argue that the most powerful mechanisms have been so effective and enduring because they have been selected along the principle of isomorphic complementarity. By this I mean that the simplest and most effective mechanisms are those that produce equal but opposite reactions to the environment, e.g., darkening of the skin as a reaction to light. I will further argue, from my own work and that of others, that this principle is still operative at higher levels of neural organization.

Let us turn to the input of animal vision systems. Eyes of almost any conceivable type and complexity, signposting evolutionary experiments, exist among invertebrates. But a curious phenomenon about the vertebrate eye is this: "Within the vertebrate phylum, the eye shows no progress of increasing differentiation and perfection as seen in the brain, the ear, the heart and most other organs. In its essentials, the eye of a fish is as complex as that of a bird or a man.... The vertebrate phylum is of enormous antiquity and stems from the primitive Agnatha which are 400 million years old, their descendants have become the lords of the earth.... In the extant representatives of this primitive stock, the lampreys, the eyes emerge as fully differentiated organs." (Duke-Elder 1958)

To be sure, there are minor variations between members of the series. They represent adaption to habitats rather than expressions of phylogenetic evolution. But in each vertebrates there is a three-layered retina, pigmented epithelium, the same dioptric apparatus. And, most important, the eyes of vertebrates arise from the neural ectoderm rather than from the surface ectoderm. Because of its origin, the vertebrate eye has been called "the cerebral eye."

If mechanisms face a struggle for existence, then for the last several hundred million years the vertebrate eye has emerged victorious. In fact, it has invaded the whole subphylum, while other "organs" (e.g., brains) have changed tremendously.

If this were a computer interface, we would say that everybody uses it becase nothing else can be the job better, faster, or cheaper.

It also brings to mind two important possibilities.

First, it seems unlikely, to say the least, that the functional substructure of the retina (i.e., the receptive fields of ganglion cells) was set up to be favorable for exotic computations to be performed by structures that would come into existence millions of years later. I am referring here to the geometrical or spatial frequency theories of vision which attempt to demonstrate that vision analysis proceeds from a set of "abstract primitives" capable of encoding any and all images. These theories are elegant and very popular, and deserve to be true. But computation, elegant or not, requires time even when done in parallel, and these theories, as we know from artificial intelligence, are computationally demanding. Arbib (1972) and Feldman and Ballard (1981) generated some cogent comments concerning time and structure in biological brains, which merit attention.

Second, the eye must deliver the "right" kind of information to the structure that can use it with the shortest delay, and that has to be memory. But what is the right kind of information? Some help might come from an interesting fact that Lashley (1950) used to exemplify the problem posed by what he called the transposability of inputs: Humans can recognize letters, or other patterns, drawn on the skin.

To my knowledge, no one has described edge and orientation sensitive neurons, simple or complex, or spatial frequency selective cells in somatosensory cortex. Rather, we know from the work of Mountcastle (1957) that in somatosensory cortex there are columns of cells responsive to pressure, light touch, and joint displacement. That is, the basic mechanisms are primarily set to identify the where and the what of what skin is interested in, because the where and the what are isomorphically encoded at the receptor and at the neural level. Astonishingly, this same system seems to have little problem deciphering patterns for which it has no practice and no edge or spatial frequency-sensitive cells.

If we were to design such a system, it would pay to encode some things directly for immediate action. Given a sufficient repertoire of such high-priority analyzers, lower-priority patterns could be computed a bit more leisurely. In this fashion, we can view input transposability not as a problem, but as inspiration to understanding sensory systems.

The same principle applies to the vertebrate eye. What should be directly encoded is what is most needed for immediate action, and the vertebrate eye's arena is the outdoors. As Gibson (1950) put it: "An out-of-doors world is one in which the lower portion of the visual field (corresponding to the upper portion of each retinal image) is invariably filled by a projection of the terrain. The upper portion of the visual field is usually filled with a projection of the sky. Between the upper and lower portions is the skyline, high or low as the observer looks down or up, but always cutting the normal visual field in a horizontal section. This is the kind of world in which our primitive ancestors lived. It was also the environment in which took place the evolution of visual perception in their ancestors. During the millions of years in which some unknown animal species evolved into our human species, land and sky were the constant visual stimuli to which the eyes and brain responded."

The outdoor world is not quite as reliably stereotyped as Gibson describes it, except for some animals that live on plains or water. The fundus of the eye of these animals shows images of remarkably evocative power. Casey Albert Wood's book *The Fundus Oculi of Birds* (1917) shows many fundi in which the receptor density is increased not only at the fovea but also where the horizon will image. Further, the dark-pigmented pecten is just where it should be to absorb the image of the sun (Barlow and Ostwald 1972). I am, of course, assuming, as do Barlow and Ostwald, that appropriate head and eye movements will bring about the above scenario in a large percentage of fixations, simply because these mechanisms seek activation.

The alternative could be atrophy from disuse, and Wood comments that large degenerative changes in the fundus take place when these animals are in captivity.

There are other examples of animals with the environment painted on the fundus, this time different colors or shapes of the tapetum. In the cat's retina, for example, the reflective tapetum is located where the dark ground will image, whereas the sky, which is brighter, will image below, where the dark pigmented epithelium will absorb scattered photons. Again there is a clear horizon line in between.

There are other interesting examples in Wood's book. Large numbers of birds have the lower quadrants of the retina colored in red, orange, or brown-red and the upper quadrants gray, as in the bald eagle. If we remember that the sky is blue, that grass and trees are green, and that the skyline is in the middle, we can see that these would be called "favorable variations."

But it seems to me that it is more than that. How many scenes are there in the life play of the Nubian ostrich? Just one, containing the vast plains, the sky, and the horizon—actually there are two, the other one being at night, but that doesn't count. When the Nubian ostrich wakes up in the morning, or at any other time of day, the smart money says that this scene will be the arena for action. It would be baroque to do a line, edge, or spatial frequency breakdown and recombination plus memory search. Quite a few milliseconds would certainly be gained by representing that knowledge directly at the retina. That way, anything that does not belong to "the scene" automatically belongs to "the object."

The bold claim, then, is that we are not simply looking at some retinal calluses, but at a macroscopic expression of the general mechanism at work in vision, namely an isomorphic complementary representation of the scene abstracted to its most reliable features. What this means is that the secrets of the thalamus can be revealed by looking at the eye, and that the secrets of the cortex will be revealed by understanding the thalamus.

A striking manifestation of the principle can be found in the tectum of the iguana. Gaither and Stein (1983) mapped the visual field and the body surface on the tectum of the iguana. They then remapped the tectum onto the visual field. "In general," they report, "the lateral tectum represents visual space and body sectors toward the front of the animal, while the medial tectum represents visual space and body regions toward the rear. The caudal tectum represents lower parts of both visual space and body, and the rostral tectum represents upper visual space and body.... Consequently stimuli of either modality can produce the same orientation movement via the same efferent circuits.... The sensory representations in the mammalian superior colliculus and the reptilian optic tectum have fundamental similarities."

This interpretation is undoubtedly correct. However, two critical details in the remap seem to demand a different or expanded interpretation: (1) The body map is, quite precisely, below the horizontal meridian, the only exception being (2) the face part, a small percentage of which is above the horizontal meridian.

As a generator of orienting reflexes, this representation seems far from perfect, in that activity above the horizontal meridian seems to find no body map—a terribly maladaptive situation if a hungry bird comes by. However, in a knowledge representation of the one scene where the life play of the iguana takes place, it makes eminent sense to have body below, head just a bit higher than body, a horizon, and an empty sky above so that any activity there would be noted instantly.

A somewhat counterintuitive prediction follows from the above: The precision of these representations should decrease in more visually sophisticated animals (even though upstage, downstage, etc. will always be present), simply because the handling of more scenes requires that they be represented dynamically.

Suddenly we need large memory spaces (i.e., cortex) with efferents downstream (Palmer et al. 1972) to set up the particular scene that is being played. Cajal (1903) called these "the fibers of immanent expectation."

Should we expect to find, in some fashion, isomorphic representations of visual-world scenes from the epigenetic life plays of particular animals? We can and we do.

What we have been observing has been brought about by what one could call megascenes in phylogenetic development. It is possible to generate large and visible signposts in the brains of individual animals by the use of compelling experiences.

Some Experiments in Visual Plasticity and Memory

If kittens are shown vertical lines to one eye and horizontal lines to the other as the only visual stimuli during development (Hirsch and Spinelli 1970), one finds on recording from single cells in the visual cortex that only two types of cells can be found: diffuse cells (i.e., cells that have very weak responses to visual stimuli, are nonselective for bars and/or edges of any orientation, and have no clear receptive field when mapped by the computer method that I described in 1966) and cells with elongated receptive fields. These were either vertical or horizontal. If vertical, they could be mapped only through the eye that had seen verticals through development; if horizontal, they could be mapped only through the eye that had seen horizontals.

The remarkable finding in some of the experiments was that some receptive fields looked like recognizable images of the bars seen by the kitten in its infancy (figure 1). We interpreted these results to mean that tremendous adaptation takes place in the visual mechanisms to conform with available image primitives. We also felt that some of the maps obtained, such as the one shown in figure 1, were in fact direct memory readouts (Spinelli et al. 1972). A large number of workers in the meantime became involved in what have become essentially visual-deprivation experiments, involving monocular closure and recovery under various conditions.

Our subsequent work concentrated on strengthening our interpretation of the results, (that is, that adaptation and isomorphic recording of scenes and features was at work rather than deprivation). We obtained many interesting results (Spinelli 1977), but it was only in 1978 that we succeeded in designing an instrumental conditioning paradigm that produced massive adaptive changes in the visual and sensory-motor cortex of normally reared kittens (Spinelli and Jensen 1979a). The critical ideas used in the design of the training procedure are that neural memory traces are probably isomorphic with the generating events, that within the above limits the primary function of memory is the recording of meaningful relations, and that only a relation "never" encountered in nature would produce a memory trace unequivocally identifiable in normal animals. The last requirement has also the purpose of avoiding the usual arguments about nature vs. nurture and cell-class ratios. We call this a "unique experience" because, without being abnormal, it compels the adaptive mechanism to do something unusual and thus easily recognizable in our evaluation of neural changes.

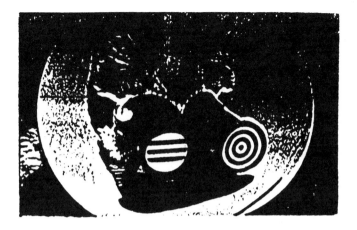

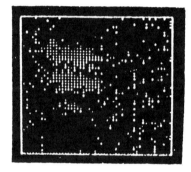

Figure 1
The bottom of the figure shows a computer map of the receptive field of a single cell in the visual cortex of a cat that had viewed the patterns in the goggles (top) during development. Notice the striking isomorphism between the computer map and the pattern, even though the map was done weeks after the viewing had ended. In fact, these "memory" readouts can be obtained up to a year and a half later.

We trained kittens to two visual stimuli presented separately to each eye: vertical bars to the left and horizontal bars to the right. Only one of the two stimuli was present at any one time. The meaning of one of the stimuli (say, the vertical bars) was danger; the kitten had to lift its right foreleg or receive a mild shock on it. Correct performance turned off the danger stimulus and turned on the safe one, i.e., horizontal bars for the right eye. About 8 minutes of training was given every day, and the kittens learned the task very easily. At all other times they were with mother and siblings doing the kinds of things kittens do in a normal environment. Although the elements of the experience are rather simple, their relationship is unique: In all their evolutionary history, cats have never (or I should say hardly ever) encountered a dangerous stimulus that is visible to one eye and invisible to the other, disappears when dealt with properly, and reappears as a safe signal of orthogonal orientation in the other eye. This is because animals with frontally located eyes see the same thing with both eyes. Thus the visual cortex cells, if binocular, have the same response properties for both eyes. (What this means is that if a cell responds to vertical bars when tested through one eye it will also respond to vertical bars when tested through the other eye.) To repeat: This is called a "unique experience" because its characteristics are such that it requires unique neural adaptations that will, as a consequence, be easily distinguishable and recognizable when functional properties of single cells are investigated.

Thus, we expected and obtained functional responses from adapted neurons not present in normal cats that have not received this training. These were a class of cells in visual cortex that were tuned for vertical bars in one eye and horizontal bars in the other (figure 2), polysensory cells in sensory-motor cortex responsive to the danger stimulus (visual) and to the foreleg skin (somatic) used during training, and a fourfold to sixfold enlargement of the cortical representation for the foreleg. Cells with this type of selectivity are simply not found in animals that have not received this training. Their response properties fulfill our requirements to be identified as memory traces; that is, they are isomorphic with the experience, they encode a meaningful relation, and that relation is not encountered in nature. The third requirement, of course, is necessary only to avoid the usual controversies about nature vs. nurture, percentages of cell classes, etc. In later work aimed at studying underlying anatomical structures, we showed that in the enlarged cortical representation of the trained forearm, as compared with the untrained one, dendritic trees are larger (Spinelli et al. 1980) and there is considerably more dendritic bundling (Spinelli and Jensen 1979b). In a further study (Spinelli and Jensen 1982) we confirmed the

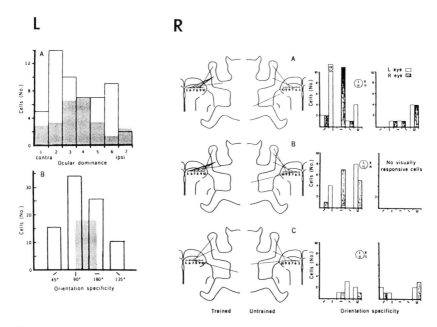

Figure 2
Left: (A) Ocular-dominance histograms, normalized, pooled from all cats trained from
4 and $5\frac{1}{2}$ weeks. Cells in group 1 were driven only by the contralateral eye, cells of group
4 were equally driven by either eye, and group 7 cells were driven only by the ipsilateral
eye. Other groups indicate intermediate eye dominance. (B) Orientation specificity
pooled from all cats trained from 4 and $5\frac{1}{2}$ weeks. The bars represent classes of cells that
were responsive to horizontal, vertical, and diagonal line orientations. The shaded area
corresponds to the population of binocular cells with different orientation sensitivites
for the two eyes. **Right:** On the left side are cortical representations of the trained and
untrained sides of the body for all cats. Electrode penetrations are marked (in millimeters
lateral to the midline) along the postcruciate cortex 1.5 mm posterior to the cruciate
sulcus. Lines are drawn from each penetration to the part of the body it represents on the
figurine. On the right side are histograms of orientation specificities of units in the
somatosensory cortex. Angle of oriented line stimulus to which the units were responsive
is indicated on the abscissa. Left and right histograms are from the hemispheres
corresponding to the trained and untrained body sides, respectively. (A) Cat 5, trained
from 4 weeks. (B) Cat 6, yoked condition, trained from 4 weeks. (C) Cat 1, trained from
11 weeks. The stimulus types used during training for each eye are indicated next to each
pair of histograms, and the stimulus that was concurrent with the foreleg shock is circled.
(Reprinted, with permission, from Spinelli and Jensen 1979a. Copyright 1978 AAAS.)

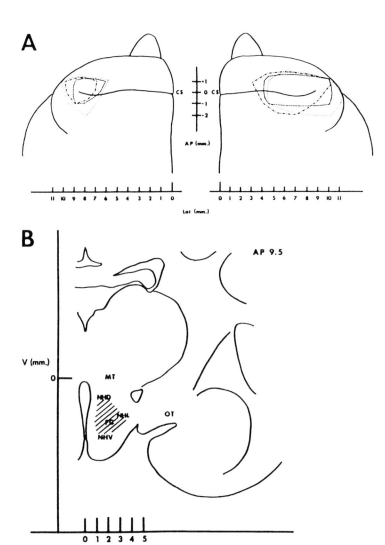

Figure 3
A: Varied line boundaries show the representational areas in motor cortex of three cats in which foreleg movement could be induced by cortical stimulation. Hemispheres contralateral to the untrained and the trained foreleg are shown. The area located to the control of movement in the trained foreleg was enlarged an average of 30 percent over that area concerned with movement of the untrained foreleg. **B:** Diagrammatic representation of a section taken through the cat's brain at AP: +9.5. Striped area represents regions where cells were marked after recording and verified histologically. Ventral, lateral, and dorsal hypothalamic nuclei are labeled NVL, NHL, and NDL, respectively. Lateral and ventral stereotaxic axes are also shown. (Reprinted, with permission, from Spinelli and Jensen 1982.)

PERFORMANCE ON PLACEMENT TEST

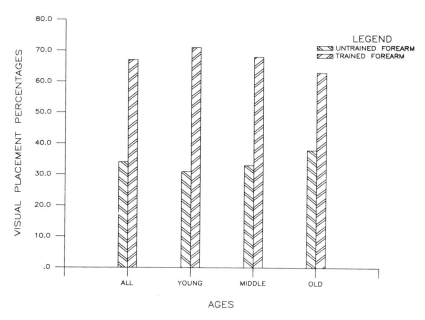

Figure 4

Results from visual placing test. The test consisted of simply holding the kitten in the air near a table edge and scoring which one of the forelegs touched the table first. The results clearly show that a kitten will make first contact with the trained leg in a statistically significant percentage of trials. In each pair of bars, the second bar represents the results for the trained leg.

above results and also showed that the motor cortex representation for the trained foreleg is 3–4 times larger than that for the untrained one (figure 3A). We also found that polysensory cells responsive to the danger stimulus could be found in the hypothalamus (figure 3B). In addition, we have completed a behavioral study aimed at determining whether these changes in cortical representation give the trained foreleg greater intelligence in other tasks (figure 4).

Much more needs to be done behaviorally to establish exactly what it means to have motor cortex dedicated to one foreleg, but we are beginning to see that tasks similar to the one learned in development are executed with a preference for the trained foreleg. To our knowledge this is the first instance of hemispheric specialization induced by a simple instrumental conditioning procedure. (Of course, parents who have trained left-handed children to use the right hand might have a few things to say on the subject.)

Relating the size and shape of cortical representations to behavior has been an ongoing process in neuroscience, but I want to reemphasize that I view these representations as representations of knowledge rather than simple topological maps of body surface.

If the visual system has the capability of representing scenes, parts of scenes, and parts of objects adaptively at various levels, then we need a mechanism capable of modifying connections. The results brought about by our training procedure in fact require not just the strengthening or weakening of preexisting synapses but also the capability to create new connections.

In a series of classic works, Penfield discovered that the sizes of cortical representations of different parts of the body relate not to their sizes but to their sensory and motor sophistication. As already stated, we have demonstrated experimentally in normally reared kittens that the amount of cortex allocated to a given part of the body (a foreleg) is not unalterably determined by the genone but can be increased if during development that leg is required to perform an action that is unusually important to the organism. The direction of change is important in that it excludes explanations based on atrophy of preexisting structures. The same reasoning applies even more to those cells in visual cortex that are responsive to verticals for one eye and horizontals for the other eye. In this enlarged cortical representation of the trained foreleg we have found greater dendritic branching than in the corresponding contralateral cortex for the untrained foreleg (Spinelli et al. 1980). The work of Sheibel and Sheibel (1971) on dendritic bundling and their suggestion that bundles could be implicated in motor sequences prompted us to investigate dendritic bundling in the cortical representations for the trained and the untrained foreleg to determine whether early experience (i.e., the training of one foreleg) had any effect.

The experimental results (figure 5) show that indeed more bundling occurs in the enlarged cortical representation of the trained foreleg (Spinelli and Jensen 1979b). Even though these results need to be extended to more precisely determine the elements at work, I want to speculate on a possible mechanism that could account for dendritic bundling as the foundation upon which novel neural circuitry, isomorphic with the visual world, can be built. The model I want to suggest is based on three experimental findings and one theoretical suggestion. The first experimental finding, already mentioned, is our demonstration that experience does indeed increase bundling. The second is that, if one eye is closed during development, then

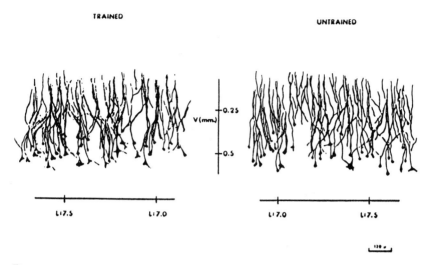

Figure 5
Camera lucida tracing of dendritic bundles from a Cajal-stained section taken through
the cortical representation for the trained and the untrained foreleg of a normally reared
kitten. Notice that the same number of cells is stained on both loci, but that dendrites
show considerably more bundling in the trained locus.

lateral geniculate cells in the layers connected to the normal eye show
normal or enhanced growth, whereas those in the layers connected to the
closed eye appear small and underdeveloped (Wiesel and Hubel 1963).
Thus, activity stimulates growth, and inactivity and inhibition (by the cells
from the normal eye) do the opposite. The third experimental finding is
that, if an electric field is present in a culture of nerve cells, it acts as a guide
or a beacon so that the neurites grow toward the cathode. In fact, "neurites
will turn through considerable angles to do so" (Jaffe and Poo 1979). The
theoretical suggestion, which comes from the hypothesis of Klopf (1972)
that neurons "seek depolarization," seems to receive literal verification
from the work just quoted, in that negativity (that is, cathodic potential)
applied to the outside of a positive nerve cell depolarizes it. We begin to
see here how dendritic buidling would take place in a population of neurons, some of which are firing and some of which are growing. The
growing dendrites would grow toward the active ones, because active cells
are negative on the outside. Indeed, full depolarization would be unnecessary, because even cells depolarized just a few millivolts (one EPSP depolarizes a cell by about 2 millivolts for about 2 milliseconds) behave as
current sinks; that is, cathodes and neurites grow toward cathodes. If this
happens, it has an interesting effect. Neurons are the basic elements re-

sponsible for adaptation in metazoans. There are many facets to the mechanisms that support successful adaptation. However, goal seeking and the detection of causality are of paramount importance. The Romans used to say "post hoc ergo propter hoc" ("after that, because of that.") Though not a sufficient condition to establish causality, this temporal sequence is a dictate of the physical world. Thus, in this model we want dendrites to bundle more if they belong to neurons that are firing in sequence. This seems to follow naturally from what has been said about activity stimulating growth; the only requirement is that growth be limited to a short time after activity.

The consequences of the above are straightforward: A neuron surrounded by other neurons firing at random will grow in a rather independent way, much as a tree in a well-lit area of a yard. However, if some neurons are firing in a time-linked way, their dendrites will grow toward one another and bundle (figure 6). A rather simple computer model shows that all this works, in fact, as expected.

The implications of this model are far-reaching. Much like a personal computer that has several character sets in ROM but can create unusual ones for the user in RAM, cats are born with a set of receptive fields pretuned for the circumstances that are prevalent during phylogeny. However, reprogramming is very easy. There are several cortical levels; visual cortex is represented three times in areas 17, 18, and 19. There is an additional representation in the Claire-Bishop area. Contrary to what has been believed for a long time, areas 17, 18, and 19 receive independent inputs from the lateral geniculate body, and so does the Claire-Bishop area. The receptive fields increase in size and complexity from area 17 to 18 to 19, and these areas are connected by intracortical fibers. U fibers also connect area 19 to the Claire-Bishop area, and there is good reason to suspect that all these connections are reciprocal (Hubel and Wiesel 1969).

What to me seems extremely important is that receptive-field shapes can be completely reprogrammed by the animal's individual experiences. I recently have begun some recordings from single cells in the Claire-Bishop area of animals trained to the instrumental conditioning procedure described above. The receptive fields are enormous; many are $30°$ of visual arc or more, as had been described by Hubel and Wiesel (1969). However, in this case, receptive fields are in the shape of giant double vertical bars or giant horizontal bars corresponding to the stimuli that were used during training (Spinelli 1983). There are efferent fibers going from areas 17, 18, and 19 to the lateral geniculate body, and from the Claire-Bishop area there are efferents going to the superior colliculus. Indeed, B. Wicklegreen re-

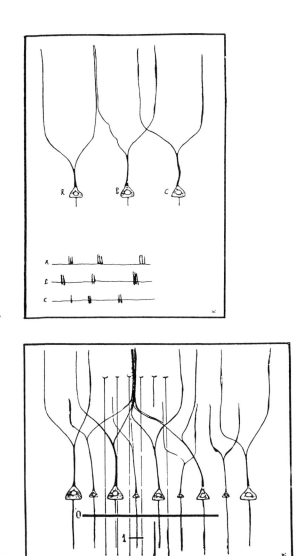

Figure 6
A: Firing in the B cell raises metabolism and accelerates growth toward cell A because of
the time link between growth in B and depolarization in A. Depolarizations in other cells
that are not time locked (C) will have no appreciable effect. The mechanism suggested
rejects noise while amplifying time-locked signals, much in the fashion of averaging
evoked potentials. **B:** Conceptual schema of how bundling of dendrites accretes more
processing power (0) to a small number of input lines (1). Potential connections are then
assumed to provide the structure for learning predisposition, i.e., a crystal of knowledge.
(Reproduced, with permission, from Spinelli and Jensen 1984.)

ports that areas 17, 18, and 19 also have efferents to the superior colliculus. What I want to suggest is that animals such as cats have the capability of projecting on the colliculus and the geniculate a knowledge representation of the present scene, and that scenes are contained in cortical areas (such as the Claire-Bishop) where the receptive fields of cells are large. For the cat, the iguana, and the Nubian ostrich, anything that is not scene is object. However, for the cat, the scene can be changed. Blurred representations of objects could be present in area 19, sharp representations of small parts of objects in area 17. Area 18 would be somewhat in the middle.

Conduction speeds measured on afferent fibers indicate that information from the geniculate arrives faster in areas in 18 and 19 than in area 17. Clearly, by the time information reaches areas 18 and 19 intracortically from area 17 the appropriate cells are already on, and since the Claire-Bishop area has an independent input from the geniculate (Hubel and Wiesel 1969), the same line of reasoning applies to this cortical area.

Thus, in this hypothesis the cat visual system avoids breaking down the image into lines and edges or spatial frequencies and never has to face the problem of recombining them into meaningful objects. Right or wrong, a decision has already been made as to what scene is being played and what objects are present by the time the precise details concerning objects arrive, rather slowly, from area 17.

Acknowledgments

I want to thank Michael Arbib for many stimulating discussions on these topics, and A. Harry Klopf for contributing some unorthodox but fruitful ideas on neural function.

This work was supported in part by the Air Force Office of Scientific Research under grant AFOSR-83-0207 and contract AFOSR F33615-80-C-1088.

References

Arbib, M. A. 1972. Toward an automata theory of brains. *Commun. ACM* 15: 521–527.

Barlow. H. B., and T. J. Ostwald. 1972. Pecten of the pigeon's eye as an inter-ocular eye shade. *Nature New Biol.* 236.

Cajal, R. S. 1903. Las fibras nerviosas de origen cerebral del tuberculo cuadrige-mino anterior y talamo optico. *Trab. Lab. Invest. Biol. Univ. Madrid* 2: 5–21.

Duke-Elder, S. 1958. *System of Ophthalmology: The Eye in Evolution,* Volume 1. Mosby.

Feldman, J. A., and D. H. Ballard. 1981. Computing with Connections. Technical report TR-72, University of Rochester.

Gaither, S. N., and B. E. Stein. 1983. Reptiles and mammals use similar sensory organizations in the midbrain. *Science* 205: 595–597.

Gibson, J. J. 1950. *The Perception of the Visual World.* Riverside.

Hirsch, H. V. B., and D. N. Spinelli. 1970. Visual experience modifies distribution of horizontally and vertically oriented receptive fields in cats. *Science* 168: 869–870.

Hubel, D. H., and T. N. Wiesel. 1969. The visual area of the lateral suprasylvan gyrus (Claire-Bishop area) of the cat. *J. Physiol.* 202: 251–260 [?].

Jaffe, L. B., and M.-M. Poo. Neurites grow faster towards the cathode than the anode in a steady field. *J. Exp. Zool.* 209: 115–128.

Klopf, A. H. 1972. Brain Function and Adaptive Systems—A Heterostatic Theory. Research report AFCRL-72-0164, Air Force Cambridge Research Laboratories, Bedford, Mass.

Lashley, K. S. 1950. In search of the engram. *Soc. Exp. Biol.*, symposium 4, pp. 454–482.

Mountcastle, V. B. 1957. Modality and topographic properties of single neurons of cat's somatic sensory cortex. *J. Neurophysiol.* 20: 408–434.

Palmer, L. A., A. C. Rosenquist, and J. M. Sprague. 1972. Corticotectal systems in the cat: Their structure and function. In *Corticothalamic Projections and Sensorimotor Activities,* ed. T. L. Frigyeri, E. Rinvik, and M. D. Yahr (Raven).

Sheibel, M. A., and A. B. Sheibel. 1971. Developmental relationship between spinal motoneuron dendrite bundles and patterned activity in the forelimb of cats. *Exp. Neurol.* 30: 367–373.

Spinelli, D. N. 1977. Texture viewing during development in kittens modifies the functional properties of single cells in visual cortex. *Soc. Neurosci Abstr.* 3: 378.

Spinelli, D. N. 1983. Claire-Bishop area as repository of visual experience in the cat.

Spinelli, D. N., and F. Jensen. 1979a. Plasticity: The mirror of experience. *Science* 203: 75–78.

Spinelli, D. N., and F. Jensen. 1979b. Early experience effect on dendritic bundles. *Soc. Neurosci. Abstr.* 5.

Spinelli, D. N., and F. Jensen. 1982. Plasticity, experience and resource allocation in motor cortex and hypothalamus. In *Conditioning,* ed. C. D. Woody (Plenum).

Spinelli, D. N., and F. Jensen. 1984. Brains, machines and crystals of knowledge. In *Machine Intelligence*, volume 10, ed. J. Hayes and D. Michie (Ellis Horwood).

Spinelli, D. N., J. Metzler, and R. W. Phelps. 1972. Neural correlates of visual experience as determinants of the response characteristics of cortical receptive fields in cats. *Exp. Brain Res.* 15: 289–304.

Spinelli, D. N., F. Jensen, and G. Viana Di Prisco. 1980. Early experience effect on dendritic branching in normally reared kittens. *Exp. Neurol.* 68: 1–11.

Wiesel, T. N., and D. H. Hubel. 1963. Single-cell responses in striate cortex of kittens deprived of vision in one eye. *J. Neurophysiol.* 28: 1062–1072.

Wood, C. A. 1917. *The Fundus Oculi of Birds.* Lake Side Press.

II

Visual Psychophysics

This part of the book stresses data on vision that can be obtained by the measurement of human response to precisely quantized visual stimuli. Burr and Ross address the issue of whether there are separate systems that give information about motion and form. Their evidence indicates, on the contrary, that there is a motion system that gives information about form as well as motion. They use the technique of mapping human contrast sensitivity to usual sine-wave gratings, which has given us much insight into the spatial-frequency-filtering properties of the visual system. The novelty is to add velocity as a variable. The main observation is that large objects (low-frequency gratings) can be seen at velocities (such as 3,000°/sec) that reduce smaller objects (higher frequencies) to a meaningless blur—their form is clearly discernible, but detail is lost. Further results suggest that the motor-sensitive system is switched off, fully or partially, during saccadic eye movements. They conclude with a discussion of spatio-temporal receptive fields.

Weisstein and Wong analyze how the early visual pattern analyses by spatial and temporal frequency channels contribute to our perception of objects and things in the world. In particular, they question the assumption, exemplified in Marr's models, that information flow is unidirectional from the sensory to the higher stages of processing. In fact, they offer psychophysical evidence for the effect of perceptual organization on early visual processing. Their observations include the following: The orientation of tilted lines is discriminated better in figural regions than in ground regions; sharp targets are detected better in figure and blurred targets are detected better in ground; figure was found to facilitate the discriminability of sharp tilted line segments but not blurred ones. They then argue that their data reintroduce the problem of figure and ground at a level of processing before surface properties are extracted, with figure analysis responsible for detailed examination of small areas while ground analysis extracts overall textural pattern and is a candidate for an "early warning system" when global information is picked up for later detailed analysis.

Zucker explicitly addresses the theme of perceptual grouping, the agglomeration of distinct local entities into more abstract and less local ones. He stresses, contrary to tradition, the diversity of grouping processes. His argument focuses on the distinction between type I patterns (which involve the inference of one-dimensional contours from a spatial distribution of dots) and type II patterns (which involve orientation information distributed across areas, as in flow patterns). He shows that these give rise to computational differences in the algorithms that accomplish orientation selection. These suggest certain psychophysical differences in detecting changes with these patterns.

Burt's paper continues the themes of the preceding papers: the interdependence of temporal and spatial information in early vision; the efferent projection from later stages of visual processing, which modify and control earlier stages; and the fruitful interaction between the study of computational mechanisms and psychophysical experiments. An analysis of the capacities of different schemes for representing moving objects suggests the utility of having two systems, one of which uses temporal subsampling to enhance object recognition while the other maintains full temporal sampling to obtain more precise measures of object position and velocity. The story is made more subtle by the finding that many aspects of perception obey scale independence; e.g., if a stereogram appears fused at one scale, it will still appear fused at a scale where the stereogram may exceed the classical Panum's fusional limit by manyfold. This suggests that the brain may encode and process images at many scales simultaneously, in a manner akin to the multiresolution approach now used extensively in computer vision. Finally, Burt relates all this to cooperative computation, and to the system's building of an internal model of its environment, with special stress on the possible role of neural patterns whose dynamics mimic the movement of objects in the environment.

5

Visual Analysis
during Motion

David Burr and John Ross

If one were to be faced with the task of designing a visual system to see objects in motion, one might well insist that the system give information about velocity and about form. Tolhurst (1973) and others have suggested that there are separate systems that give information and information about form, that they are distinct from one another, and that they are built, respectively, on transient and sustained units within the visual system. (See also Breitmeyer and Ganz 1976.) The motion system is supposed to give information only about motion, and not about form. The evidence we outline below indicates that, on the contrary, there is a motion system that gives information about form as well as about motion, although at the expense of some information about detail. This is not intended to be a complete review of the literature; it concentrates principally on our own work and on other work that is relevant to the points we wish to make.

Physical Limits

There is a limit to the temporal frequency at which visual mechanisms can respond, both in the retina (where limits are set by the photochemistry of the receptors) and in the visual pathways (Baylor and Hodgkin 1974; Brindley 1962). The contrast sensitivity functions found when temporal frequency is varied (Robson 1966) and the response curves for single units with variation in temporal frequency of the stimulus reflect these physical limitations of the units from which the visual system is composed.

The implication of temporal frequency limitation is not, as it has often been assumed to be, that there is a fixed upper limit to the velocities that we can see. Velocity is found by dividing temporal frequency by spatial frequency. For a fixed temporal frequency, spatial frequency decreases as velocity increases. If the motion system is limited by the temporal frequency at which it can follow, but in compensation is equipped with units with large receptive fields that are capable of responding to low spatial frequencies, the consequence is that it will be tuned to progressively lower spatial frequencies at progressively higher velocities.

Motion Sensitivity

We have measured sensitivity to moving sine-wave gratings and to objects consisting of one cycle of grating (Burr and Ross 1982). We went deeper into the low spatial-frequency range and worked with objects of larger size than is customary. Our criterion was always seeing motion clearly enough to be sure of its direction, not just seeing something. As figure 1 shows, we found that the shape of the contrast-sensitivity function for sine-wave gratings does not change with increasing velocity. The peak sensitivity remains the same, and so does the bandwidth. What does happen is that the function slides farther and farther down the spatial-frequency scale as velocity increases. At a velocity of 100°/sec, the peak of the function is to be found at about 0.1 cycle per degree—more than an order of magnitude below the peak for stationary gratings.

Another way of looking at the results is to say that motion makes low-spatial-frequency components more conspicuous. A sine-wave grating of spatial frequency 0.01 is visible only at high contrast (above about 0.3) when it is still. However, it can be seen, and seen to move, at contrasts well below 0.01 when it moves at a velocity of 800°/sec. The reason is that it is temporal frequency that determines visibility when gratings or objects move. In figure 2, where the data of figure 1 are replotted on a temporal-frequency axis, it is clear that temporal frequency is what counts.

The story for single objects is told by figure 3, in which contrast-sensitivity functions are plotted on a velocity axis for objects ranging in size from 1° to 80°. The bigger the object, the higher is the velocity at which it is best seen. Objects 80° in size are best seen at a velocity of almost 800°/sec, at which the temporal frequency of their fundamental is 10 Hz. If their contrast is sufficiently high, they can still be seen moving at a velocity of 10,000°/sec. It should be remembered that many of the objects with which we deal visually are big. A head at normal conversational distance subtends about 10°, and a body considerably more.

It is not just that the visual system responds at high velocities when spatial frequency is sufficiently low. More important, big sine-wave gratings and single objects are clearly visible as objects in motion at extreme velocities (e.g., 3,000°/sec). Their form is clearly discernible, and they do not appear to move at disconcerting speeds. If the visual system can handle

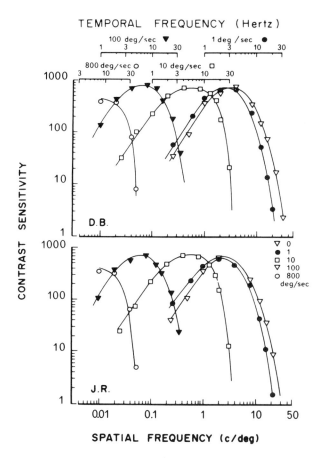

Figure 1
Contrast-sensitivity curves measured at five image speeds. Contrast sensitivity is
measured by asking observers to adjust grating contrast, defined conventionally as
$(L_{max} - L_{min})/(L_{max} + L_{min})$ until they can just discern motion, and tell reliably its direction
of drift. This contrast is termed *threshold*, and its inverse *contrast sensitivity*. For each image
speed, measurements are made over a range of spatial frequencies.

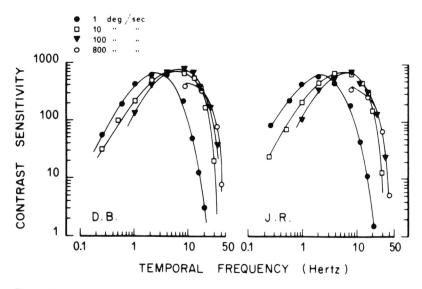

Figure 2

The data of figure 1 plotted against temporal frequency. Note the similarity of the curves at all image speeds.

the temporal frequencies caused by motion, it can follow at arbitrarily high velocities.

Clearly, detail will be lost about complex objects. Only those components whose temporal frequencies are within the temporal-frequency window will be visible, and at this page it is not clear to what extent spatial phase will be preserved by the motion system. What is clear is that the motion system does give information about the form of objects in motion.

Bandwidth Constancy

Any communication channel has a limited bandwidth. When objects are stationary (or as stationary as they can be in normal viewing), bandwidth limitations manifest themselves as limitations on the spatial frequencies that we can see, and the contrasts required to see them. When objects move, the bandwidth of the visual system is not diminished, but the visual channels that now report information about objects carry information about a different range of spatial frequencies. This is because the channel limitations for moving objects are set by the temporal limitations of the motion system.

We can imagine the bandwidth limitations of the motion system as being represented by a contrast-sensitivity function, plotted on a loga-

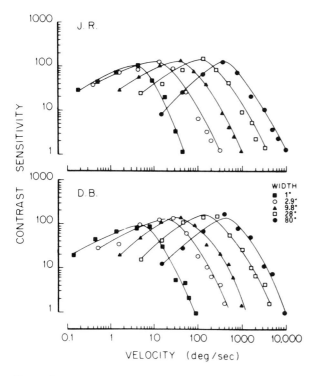

Figure 3
Contrast sensitivity for a single cycle of sine waves of five different widths, plotted as a
function of velocity.

rithmic abscissa, that is free to slide along the abscissa and which does so
in response to changes in velocity. The close similarity of the spatial and
temporal contrast-sensitivity functions, first remarked upon by Robson
(1966), is probably a safeguard to ensure that the bandwidth of the visual
system is fully utilized both when the images on our eyes are stationary (or
nearly so) and when they are moving. If this were not the case, there would
be serious mismatching between the low-pass and band-pass temporal
systems of vision. The low-frequency cut of the contrast-sensitivity function is due to active suppression of information. One possible reason for
the suppression is to limit bandwidth so as not to overload the visual
system.

Saccadic Vision

The fact that it is possible to see at very high velocities raises an immediate
problem for saccadic vision: Why do we not see motion during saccades,

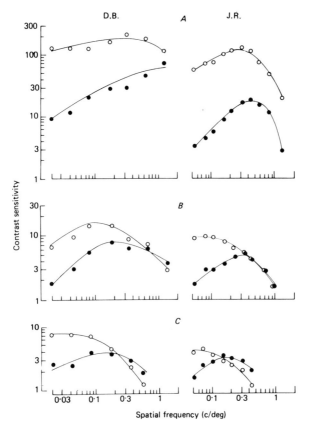

Figure 4
Contrast sensitivity for seeing a briefly presented sine-wave grating during normal viewing (open circles) and during saccades at three different luminances: 400 cd/m² (A), 0.04 cd/m² (B), and 0.0004 cd/m² (c).

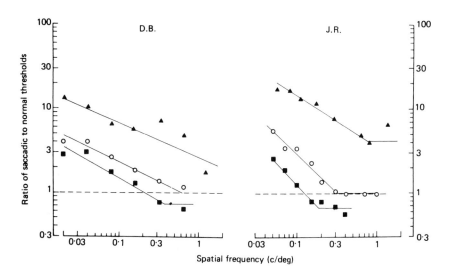

Figure 5

The data of figure 4 replotted as a ratio of saccadic to normal thresholds.

which typically cause image motion at about 200°/sec? We (Burr et al. 1982) investigated this question in some detail; the results (shown in figures 4—7) suggest that there is a motion-sensitive system which is switched off, fully or partially, during saccadic movements of the eyes.

Figure 4 plots sensitivity, at three luminance levels, to a horizontal grating, flashed for 20 msec when the eyes were at rest and when they were executing a saccade. The same data are replotted in figure 5 as the ratio of saccadic to normal thresholds. The important point is that, at each luminance level, the ratio increases linearly below a certain spatial frequency and is constant above it. In other words, there is a progressive loss of sensitivity during saccades as the bar size of the flashed grating increases.

The significance of this result is revealed by figure 6, which compares, at the three luminance levels, sensitivity to a stationary grating, to a grating drifting at 5 Hz, and to a grating flashed for 20 msec as in the experiment on saccades. The curves for the stationary condition exhibit a low-frequency cut; sensitivity declines at frequencies below a peak. The curves for the drifting and for the flashed conditions do not; sensitivity is maintained at all frequencies below the stationary peak, in both cases by mechanisms sensitive to motion. These mechanisms respond to the flashed grating because it has a wide spread of components in the temporal frequency domain. That sensitivity declines for the flashed grating during saccades indicates that mechanisms sensitive to motion are silenced during

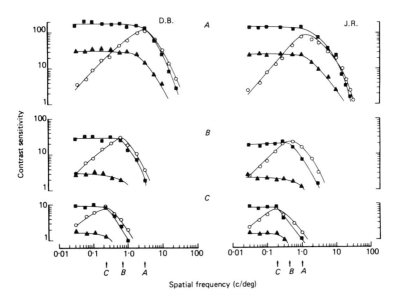

Figure 6
Contrast-sensitivity during normal viewing at three luminances (A: 400 cd/m²;
B: 0.04 cd/m²; C: 0.004 cd/m²) for stationary (open circles), briefly flashed (closed
triangles), and drifting (closed squares) gratings. Observe the spatial frequencies at which
the stationary curves peel away from the drifting curves for each luminance, and compare
these with the spatial frequency at which the curves of figure 5 flatten out.

saccades. This conclusion is reinforced by the fact that the loss of sensitivity evident in figure 5 begins to appear, at each luminance level, precisely at the spatial frequency at which the stationary and moving curves in figure 6 begin to diverge. Figure 7 shows that during saccades there is sharply diminished sensitivity to a hitch in the trajectory of a horizontal grating scrolling vertically. This is what would be expected if motion mechanisms were switched off during saccades. As a consequence, we are not disturbed by image motion during saccades.

Spatial and Temporal Tuning

At high spatial frequencies, the visual system has channels that are clearly identifiable by adaptation and masking techniques. The picture is less clear at spatial frequencies below 1 cycle per degree. A comprehensive study was carried out in our laboratory (Anderson and Burr 1985) in an attempt to clarify the tuning of mechanisms that sense moving gratings by measuring sensitivity to moving gratings in the presence of masks. Vertical test

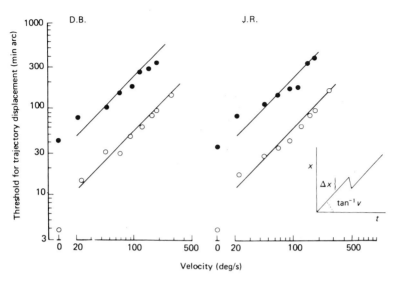

Figure 7
Threshold for detecting a momentary displacement of the trajectory of a grating moving
at various velocities in normal viewing (open circles) and during saccades (filled circles). At
all velocities, performance during saccades is more than half a log unit worse.

grating drifting at 5 Hz were observed in the clear and in the presence of
masks which jittered randomly to give them a flat temporal spectrum. The
spatial frequency of the masks was varied widely about the test frequency
to exhibit the shape of the masking function. The results (figure 8) show
that at every spatial frequency masking is maximal when test and mask
frequencies correspond, but that the tuning functions broaden progressively as spatial frequency decreases, especially below 1 cycle per degree.

A strikingly different picture emerges when the mask has a flat spatial
spectrum (a random grating) and is made to counterphase to give each
spatial component a constant temporal frequency. In this experiment, a
vertical sine-wave grating is made to drift at a fixed temporal frequency
and the rate of counterphase of the mask is varied over a wide range about
the drift frequency of the test. The most effective masking frequency is
independent of the drift frequency of the mask (figure 9), indicating the
absence of separate channels tuned to different rates of drift. This holds
true at each of the three test spatial frequencies. There is, however, a slight
increase in the temporal frequency that masks best at all rates of drift as the
spatial frequency of the test decreases.

Orientation tuning, like spatial-frequency tuning, broadens as spatial
frequency is decreased (figure 10). Vertical gratings drifting at 5 Hz were

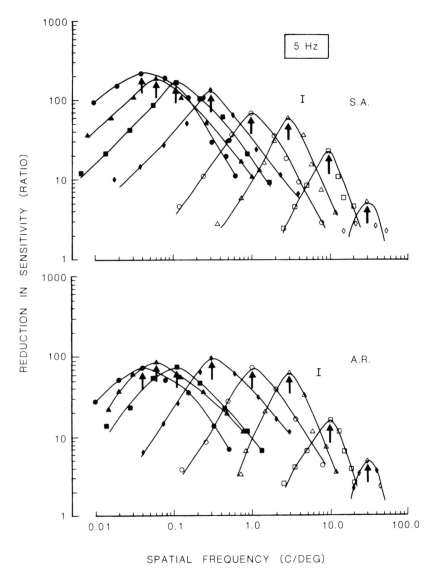

Figure 8

Masking of a sine-wave grating drifting at 5 Hz by a jittering sine-wave grating. The test was fixed at each of the eight spatial frequencies shown by the arrows, and the mask varied in spatial frequency. Masking was always maximal when the mask had the same spatial frequency as the test, indicating spatially tuned mechanisms at spatial frequencies. The degree of selectivity, however, was higher at high than at low spatial frequencies.

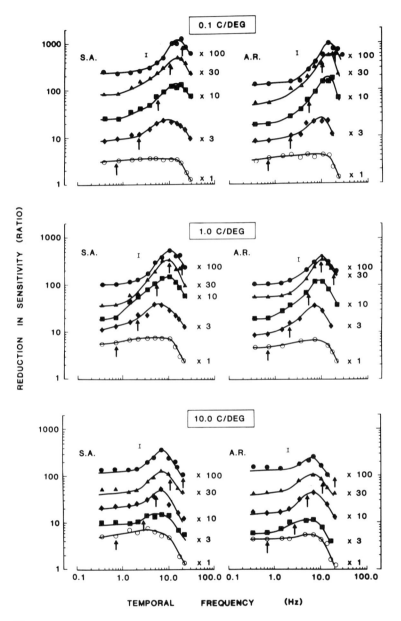

Figure 9

Masking of a drifting sine-wave grating by a random-noise grating caused to reverse in contrast sinusoidally. The test had three spatial frequencies—0.1 (A), 1.0 (B), and 10 (C) cycles per degree—and the temporal frequencies indicated by the arrows. The temporal frequency of the sinusoidal modulation of the mask varied. Here masking is independent of the temporal frequency of the test, but peaks at a constant value which decreases slightly as spatial frequency increases.

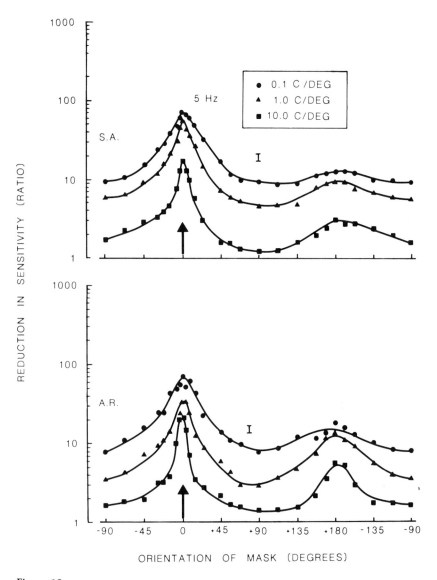

Figure 10

Masking of a vertical sinusoidal grating (three spatial frequencies) drifting at 5 Hz by a random-noise grating of various orientations. The curves each have two peaks, one corresponding to a mask of the same orientation and direction and one to a mask of the same orientation but the opposite direction. The results indicate the existence of orientation selectivity and direction selectivity at all spatial frequencies, with the orientation selectivity increasing at high spatial frequencies.

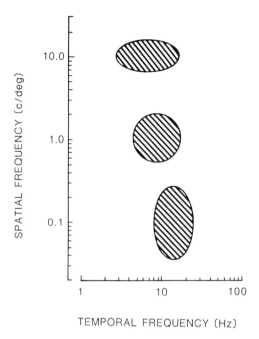

Figure 11

Summary tuning characteristics indicated by figures 8 and 9. The width of each region is temporal tuning at half height, and the height spatial tuning. Note that the regions cover a wide spatial-frequency range but are narrowly confined in temporal frequency. We depict here only three representative spatial filters, but there will in fact be a virtual continuum covering the visible spatial spectrum.

observed in the presence of random gratings drifting at four-fifths their speed. Orientation was defined by path of motion, so that a mask that was vertical like the test but moving in the opposite direction differed from it in orientation by 180°. Masking decreased as the difference in orientation increased from zero, then began to increase again, reaching a secondary peak at a lower level at 180°, where the undirected orientations correspond. The spread of masking is broader around both primary and secondary peaks at lower spatial frequencies. The existence of a secondary peak is consistent with the involvement of a direction-indifferent mechanism and with the existence of paired mechanisms tuned 180° apart in orientation and coupled so as to give information about directed temporal frequency.

What these results suggest about tuning is indicated schematically in figure 11. Each ovoid region indicates the joint spatial and temporal frequency requirements of a mechanism sensitive to motion. The higher the spatial frequency, the narrower the spatial bandwidth and the lower the temporal frequency at which the mechanism responds best, though this last change is slight. There is also a slight increase in width in the temporal-frequency domain (that is, a slight change in temporal bandwidth) with increasing spatial frequency.

By virtue of their joint spatial and temporal tuning requirements, each of the mechanisms captures components from a certain size range moving within a certain velocity range. It should be stressed that figure 11 is schematic, and is not meant to indicate the number of mechanisms that might exist; there are certainly more than three.

Summation and Blur

Burr (1981) investigated spatial and temporal summation for moving dots and gratings. For velocities of up to 16°/sec, temporal summation for moving dots is as strong as for stationary dots, proceeding for about 120 msec. During this time the dot has moved up to 2°, which shows that spatial summation can occur over this extended region if the target is in motion. Spatial summation for stationary targets, measured under comparable conditions, is less than half of this (Burr 1981).

In normal viewing, moving objects are seen without smear (Burr 1980). This is surprising, given the fact that energy from moving targets is summated for about 120 msec. A camera left open for 125 msec registers considerable smear (figure 12), yet when we view comparable targets we see virtually no smear. However, smear is absent only for objects that are in motion for sufficiently long; briefly moving dots are seen to be smeared, the length of the smear approximating the distance the dot traveled during viewing (figure 13). In formulating a model of motion mechanisms, we must reconcile summation over space and time with the absence of visual smear.

Interpolation and Motion

Motion also gives information about relative position, about form, and about depth that is not available when the motion system is not activated. Ross and Hogben (1975) showed that the classical Pulfrich effect (depth seen when a moving target is viewed with a filter in front of one eye) could be obtained when the motion was stroboscopic. Under conditions of stroboscopic motion, both eyes see the target in the same place, since it jumps

Figure 12

A photograph taken with a 125-msec shutter speed. If the temporal summation observed by Burr (1981) acted like a frame store, we would expect motion blur of this magnitude.

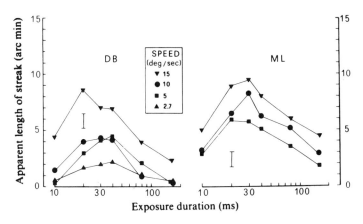

Figure 13

Apparent length of the streaks of a field of moving dots as a function of exposure duration. Whereas briefly exposed dots leave a considerable streak, an exposure of 100 msec causes them to be seen veridically, as dots.

from station to station, but the filter introduces a delay. The eyes see the target in the same place, but at different times. Burr and Ross (1979) and Burr (1979) investigated the effects of delay directly and found that, under conditions of stroboscopic motion, a delay of less than a millisecond was sufficient for stereopsis. This delay corresponds to a virtual, not an actual disparity of a few seconds of arc, roughly the same as stereo acuity for stationary targets. The results suggest that the visual system can convert temporal differences into spatial differences when the motion mechanisms come into play.

One possible explanation is that, because we track motion, stimuli at the same external position stimulate different retinal sites at different times. This is undoubtedly true, but Burr showed that time can give information about relative spatial position even when eye movements are eliminated. He moved two bars stroboscopically across seven stations, a top set and a bottom set, precisely aligned vertically. When there was a delay or a phase asynchrony between top and bottom, an observer saw two bars with a vernier offset between them, although they were precisely aligned at each station both in external space and on the retina. Retinal alignment was guaranteed by keeping the sequence brief (150 msec, which is too short for the tracking reflex to begin) and by randomizing the direction of movement. As a safeguard, eye movements were monitored electrically. Others, including Fahle and Poggio (1981) and Morgan and Watt (1983), have confirmed Burr's basic result and the fact that it obtains only when stroboscopic stimulation results in the perception of smooth motion. Burr found that his effect was abolished when only two rather than seven stations were used.

Metacontrast

Burr (1984) investigated the well-known phenomenon of "metacontrast" (the apparent attenuation of a flash of light when followed by two flanking flashes after an appropriate delay) to see if it may result from activation of the motion system (figure 14). In addition to measuring the amount of metacontrast "masking" for various delays, he measured the sensitivity for seeing the test stimulus and the flanking stimuli when presented together and when presented alone. Contrary to what may be expected were one stimulus to mask (that is, inhibit) the other, the two stimuli summate visually to yield a lower combined threshold. Furthermore, sensitivity peaks at precisely the delays at which metacontrast is greatest (that is, at

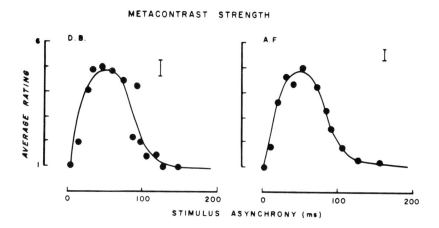

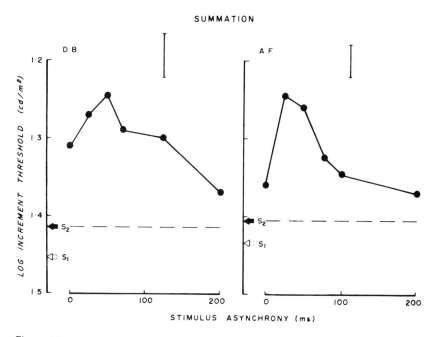

Figure 14

Metacontrast strength (above) and amount of positive summation between test and "mask" stimulus (below). The sensitivity for the test and the mask alone are indicated by the arrows marked S1 and S2. The summation between these two shows that the mask does not inhibit the test, as is classically thought, but adds with it. The stimulus asynchrony yielding maximum summation corresponds well with the stimulus asynchrony yielding maximum metacontrast.

which the masked component appears most invisible). This seems paradoxical, but not if metacontrast is a consequence of optimal stimulation of the motion-sensitive system. When it collects the information to which it is most sensitive, it reports motion, and nothing is seen in the position occupied by the first target. The motion system deduces a spatial structure which leaves a blank in the field.

Spatio-Temporal Receptive Fields

Conventional models of space and time, and concepts of frames and of buffers, tempt us to collapse over time or in space when we try to imagine what a motion system might do. This essentially amounts to an attempt to freeze motion into a perceptual moment (see, for example, Stroud 1955). We abandon the notion of the frame and urge that time and space be considered together. We know from the masking studies of Anderson and Burr (1985) and others that motion detectors are tuned in both spatial and temporal frequency (figure 11). By transforming the spatio-temporal-frequency tuning function into the space-time domain, we can gain some insight into the type of localization required of a motion detector to give it its tuning characteristics. One plausible result for a hypothetical unit (selected from the range of units shown in figure 11) is illustrated schematically in figure 15. This representation depicts the spatio-temporal receptive field of a candidate motion detector. Opposite hatching indicates excitatory and inhibitory regions. (The transform that yields receptive fields of the type shown in figure 15 is the Fourier transform, with the simplifying assumptions of linearity and linear phase. These assumptions are not strictly valid for the visual system, but nonlinearities and phase shifts should not alter significantly the line of argument pursued here.)

The receptive field is elongated and oriented in time-space in much the same way that two-dimensional receptive fields are oriented in two-dimensional space. The orientation gives the velocity tuning. Other motion detectors will have receptive fields of different slants, indicating different velocity preferences.

Just as a receptive field extended in space collects energy from an object appropriately oriented in space, so a motion detector will collect energy from an appropriate object moving at an appropriate velocity. It will therefore summate, responding more vigorously the longer motion continues, up to the limit of the detector's spatio-temporal field, thereby accounting for the extended temporal and spatial summation of moving objects (Burr 1981).

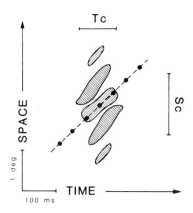

Figure 15

Hypothetical spatio-temporal receptive field of a motion detector. (Hatched areas indicate possible on-off configuration.) The orientation of this field in space-time gives its preferred velocity. An object moving at that velocity will be summated along the whole length of the field, but this summation need not cause smears. Tc: limit of temporal summation. Sc: spatial summation. The oriented fields will effectively rotate the spce-time axes and hence "cancel" the motion. As these fields are tuned to the trajectory of motion, alteration to the trajectory—be it a shift in time or in space—can be perceived as a spatial displacement.

Similarly, the elongated spatio-temporal receptive field of motion detectors explains the lack of motion smear despite summation over time. Such a detector would effectively track an object over time, rather than collect into frames as does a frame-based televideo camera. It would have the effect of aligning itself with the motion trajectory, thus rotating the axes of reference. The spatial characteristics of the moving object will then be specified by the receptive-field structure orthogonal to its axis. A range of detectors of different spatial preference could cooperate to provide a spatial analysis of moving objects in much the same way that motion-independent detectors analyze stationary scenes: By being tuned to a particular velocity, they cancel that velocity and allow spatial analysis to proceed as if the object were stationary. We do not at this stage wish to speculate on how this cooperative analysis may proceed; we merely observe that the same techniques used by motion-independent detectors for pattern analysis may also be used by motion detectors.

The notion of receptive fields in time-space also sheds some light on the problems of apparent motion (Wertheimer 1912) and on spatio-temporal interpolation (Burr 1979; Barlow 1979). An object in apparent motion will stimulate the receptive field at discrete positions along its axis, rather than the entire excitatory field. However, provided that the energy is matched and the strobe rate is sufficiently high, the unit will be unable to detect the difference between discrete and continuous motion, and will therefore report continuous motion.

These units will also exhibit spatio-temporal interpolation. Because they are orthogonal neither to the space axis nor to the time axis, spatial and temporal offsets should be treated equally. Thus a temporal vernier offset in a stroboscopically moving line is seen as a spatial offset, with almost the same precision as a real spatial offset (Burr 1979), provided the motion train is sufficiently long.

We have ignored one spatial dimension of the visual image to simplify the task of describing the spatio-temporal configuration of motion fields. Obviously, detectors must be tuned in both spatial dimensions, as well as in time. We have also ignored the problem of cooperation between different fields. Our results suggest that all motion fields have much the same stretch in time (about 90 msec) but a spatial extent that increases with velocity. The variety of motion detectors of different tuning will combine, just as do motion-independent detectors, to give a full description of objects in motion. The receptive fields of the visual system are structured so as to give resonance to image motion, and by the pattern of units which respond, to specify both form and velocity. They do not freeze motion, but record its passage.

Note Added in Proof

This manuscript was prepared for the conference in 1983. Since then, the ideas presented at that conference have been elaborated and expanded, both in our laboratory and by others. A more recent account of our work, including references to the work of Adelson and Bergen, von Santen and Sperling, Watson and Ahumada, and others, is available in Burr, Morrone, and Ross 1986.

References

Anderson, S., and D. Burr. 1985. Spatial and Temporal Selectivity of the Human Motion Detection System. *Vision Res.* 25: 1147–1154.

Barlow, H. B. 1979. Reconstructing the visual image in space and time. *Nature* 279: 189–190.

Baylor, D. A., and A. L. Hodgkin. 1974. Changes in the time peak and sensitivity in turtle photoreceptors. *J. Physiol.* 242: 729–758.

Breitmeyer, B. G., and L. Ganz. 1976. Implications of sustained and transient channels for theories of visual pattern masking, saccadic suppression and information processing. *Psychological Rev.* 83: 1–36.

Brindley, G. S. 1962. Beats produced by simultaneous stimulation of the human eye with intermittent light and intermittent alternating current. *J. Physiol.* 164: 157–167.

Burr, D. C. 1979. Acuity for apparent vernier offset. Vision Res. 19: 835–837.

Burr, D. C. 1980. Motion smear. *Nature* 284: 164–165.

Burr, D. C. 1981. Temporal summation of moving images by the human visual system. *Proc. Roy. Soc.* B 211: 321–339.

Burr, D. C. 1984. Summation of target and mask metacontrast stimuli. *Perception* 13: 183–192.

Burr, D. C., and J. Ross. 1979. How does binocular delay give information about depth? *Vision Res.* 19: 523–532.

Burr, D. C., and J. Ross. 1982. Contrast sensitivity at high velocities. *Vision Res.* 22: 479–484.

Burr, D. C., J. Holt, J. R. Johnstone, and J. Ross. 1982. Selective desensitization of motion mechanisms during saccades. *J. Physiol.* 333: 1–15.

Burr, D. C., M. C. Morrone, and J. Ross. 1986. Seeing objects in motion. *Proc. R. Soc.* B 227: 249–265.

Fahle, M., and T. Poggio. 1981. Visual hyperacuity: Spatiotemporal interpolation in human vision. *Proc. Roy. Soc.* B 213: 451–477.

Morgan, M. J., and R. J. Watt. 1983. On the failure of spatiotemporal interpolation: A filtering model. *Vision Res.* 23: 997–1004.

Robson, J. G. 1966. Spatial and temporal contrast sensitivity function of the visual system. *J. Optical Soc. of America* 56: 1141–1142.

Ross, J., and J. H. Hogben. 1975. The Pulfrich Effect and short-term memory in stereopsis. *Vision Res.* 15: 1289–1290.

Stroud, J. 1955. The structure of psychological time. In *Information theory in psychology*, ed. H. Quaster (Free Press).

Tolhurst, D. J. 1973. Separate channels for the analysis of the shape and the movements of a moving visual stimulus. *J. Physiol.* 231: 385–402.

Wertheimer, M. 1912. Experimentelle Studien über das Sehen von Bewegung. Z. *Psychol.* 61: 161–265.

6

Figure-Ground Organization Affects the Early Visual Processing of Information

Naomi Weisstein and
Eva Wong

Research into the question of how we make a representation of the physical world out of discrete image-intensity points has traditionally been split into two approaches: the sensory and the cognitive. Modern cognitive approaches model perception on thought processes such as hypothesis testing (Gregory 1980), problem solving (Rock 1983), and schema fitting (Hochberg 1968). Artificial-intelligence and computer-vision programs formulate rules of shape recognition and feature combination (Winston 1975; Waltz 1975; Barrow and Tenenbaum 1978; Pentland 1982; Pentland and Gazis 1984). While many of these theories have considered the contribution of sensory data, the emphasis has been on what happens *after* the sensory information have been encoded. Contemporary sensory approaches have paid little attention to what happens after the coding of sensory data. For instance, sensory approaches propose that the perception of orientation, motion, direction, and edges can be account for by the firing of a single cell (Barlow 1972) or a group of cells (Movshon et al. 1982). Spatial-frequency models of perception have suggested that many perceptual phenomena can be explained in terms of spatial-frequency filtering without any reference to higher-order processes (Ginsburg 1975, 1984).

In recent years, psychophysical research has emphasized responses to the spatial-frequency and temporal-frequency components of stimuli. A common assumption is that the visual system contains multiple channels, each sensitive to a relatively narrow range of spatial and temporal frequencies (Graham 1980, 1981; Wilson and Bergen 1979; Watson 1981). However, there has been little explicit attention to how the early visual pattern analyses by spatial-frequency and temporal-frequency channels contribute to our perception of objects and things in the world. The work of David Marr and his associates (Marr 1976, 1980, 1982; Marr and Nishihara 1978; Marr and Poggio 1979; Marr and Hildreth 1980; Marr and Ullman 1982; Ullman 1979) is one important exception to this slip between

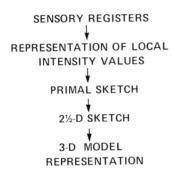

SENSORY REGISTERS
↓
REPRESENTATION OF LOCAL
INTENSITY VALUES
↓
PRIMAL SKETCH
↓
2½-D SKETCH
↓
3-D MODEL
REPRESENTATION

Figure 1
Marr's scheme of visual processing.

the sensory and cognitive emphases. Their work is specifically directed toward the investigation of the whole process of visual perception, from the extraction of the intensity array to the full representation of the visual world. Their theories have provided an elegant computational approach to obtaining representations of shapes and surfaces from initial registrations of sensory data. However, even in Marr's approach the contribution of quantitative sensory response to visual analysis is assumed to be limited to an early stage of processing, before the emergence of the "raw primal sketch" (Marr 1982). Once the sensory data have been synthesized and interpolated to form higher-order representational modules (this begins at the primal sketch), information available from the later stages cannot retroactively influence the information gathered by the sensory mechanisms.

If we examine Marr's model of visual processing, we find that the direction of information flow is from the sensory stage to the higher stages of processing. In other words, even in its consideration of the role of computation algorithms it is still a "bottom-up" approach. The database information (the algorithms and procedural rules stored in the database) does not figure in the construction of the representation, at least until a fairly advanced stage of visual processing (that is, until the $2\frac{1}{2}$-dimensional sketch and the final representation of the three-dimensional sketch). In addition, the kind of database information that influences the construction of the $2\frac{1}{2}$D sketch and the 3D sketch is primarily in the form of computational algorithms that determine how information from the earlier stages is interpolated and synthesized. In other words, the "top-down" influences, when they occur, generally do not contain information pointing to the structure or the content of the representation, such as perceptual organization. However, despite Marr's unwillingness to discuss "top-down" influ-

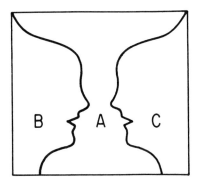

Figure 2
Rubin's faces-vase reversible picture. This was the stimulus used in our experiments on the effect of figure-ground organization on the detection and discrimination of sharp and blurred targets. Targets were flashed in locations A, B, and C.

ences, his approach included an attempt to examine visual processing from the early stages of sensory data registration to the emergence of higher-order representations of patterns. Thus, we have chosen to examine our psychophysical findings in the light of Marr's theory of visual processing. The exclusion of top-down influences in Marr's and others' models may be due to the general lack of psychophysical research on whether or not such influences exist. We would now like to introduce some visual phenomena and some psychophysical evidence that strongly suggest that perceptual organization can affect early visual processing (Wong and Weisstein 1983).

The Orientation of Tilted Lines Is Discriminated Better in Figural Regions Than in Ground Regions

Figure 2 can be seen as a vase or as two faces. If a vase is seen, the central region is the figure and the flanking regions are the background; if two faces are seen, the flanking regions are figures and the central area is the background. This type of reversible picture is ideal for studying the effects of perceptual organization, since organization can be manipulated without changing the physical aspect of the stimulus.

Using this figure, we conducted experiments examining the discrimination of tilted lines presented under threshold and suprathreshold conditions in figure regions and in ground regions. Observers were asked to look at the fixation point in the center of the display. In one session of the experiment they initiated a trial only if they perceived the central region as a vase; in another session they initiated a trial only if they perceived two

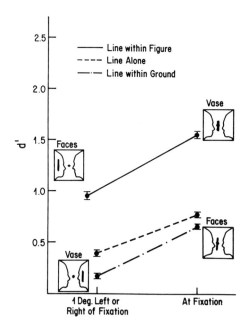

Figure 3

The discrimination of tilted lines in figure, ground, and contextless regions when the targets are at tilt threshold but above luminance threshold. Accuracy is measured in terms of d'. Reprinted from Wong and Weisstein 1982; copyright 1982 by American Association for the Advancement of Science.

faces. A line, tilted left or right randomly, was presented at one of the three locations in the picture (A, B, C). For example, in a session in which the observer monitored the central region as the figure and in which the target was presented in the central region, the line was imaged in a figural area. If the target appeared in the flanking regions, it would be imaged in the ground areas. Four observation conditions were generated by the design: The target was viewed at fixation in a figure region, off fixation in a figure region, at fixation in a ground region, and off fixation in a ground region. The observer's task was to identify whether the target line was tilted left or right. In each trial the target was flashed for a duration of 20 msec.

Figure 3 shows results from an experiment in which the target line was presented as tilt threshold but above luminance threshold. Responding "left" when the target was tilted to the left constituted a hit; responding "left" when the target was tilted to the right constituted a false alarm. The index of discriminability, d', was obtained by comparing the hit rate and the false-alarm rate. When the targets were presented in a figural region,

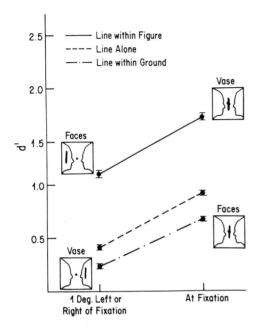

Figure 4
The discrimination of tilted lines in figure, ground, and contextless regions when the targets are at luminance threshold but above tilt threshold. Accuracy is measured in terms of d'. Reprinted from Wong and Weisstein 1982; copyright 1982 by American Association of the Advancement of Science.

orientation-discrimination accuracy was almost 3 times what it was when targets were flashed in the same region when it was perceived as ground. This facilitative effect of figure on the orientation discrimination of targets was also obtained when the targets were at luminance threshold but above tilt threshold. Figure 4 summarizes the findings from this condition. Again the discrimination of the tilted targets was more accurate when they were flashed in figure areas than when they were flashed in ground areas. Subsequently, we also found the same facilitative effect of figure on tilt discrimination in a suprathreshold condition where the target line was above both tilt and luminance thresholds (Wong and Weisstein 1984). However, in comparison with the data obtained under the threshold conditions, the facilitative effect of figure was slightly attenuated. These findings are shown in figure 5. The diminished facilitation of figure over ground in suprathreshold conditions might be due to the fact that the target's signal is already high to begin with, so that enhancement would only bring it to a maximum level. For instance, if the effect of a figure was to raise the

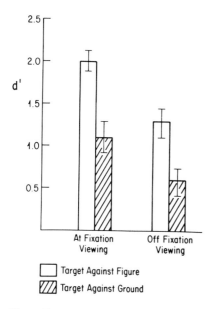

Figure 5
The discrimination of tilted lines in figure and ground regions when the targets are above both tilt and luminance thresholds. Accuracy is measured in terms of d'.

signal to a certain fixed level, then the relative gain in acuracy would be dependent on the target's baseline signal strength. The higher the initial level, the smaller the gain would be, since it would take less boost to bring it to the maximum level. At suprathreshold levels, the relative gain in the signal strength would be less, and as a result the facilitative effect of figure on discrimination would be diminished.

Sharp Targets Are Detected Better in Figure; Blurred Targets Are Detected Better in Ground (Wong and Weisstein 1983)

Figure has been shown to facilitate the discrimination of small tilted line segments. This facilitative effect of figure on perceptual-task performance has also been found under other performance conditions, such as detection of contour discontinuity (Weitzman 1963) and detection of retinal image displacement during eye movements (Bridgeman 1981).

One approach to accounting for the facilitative effect of figure proposes that the higher accuracy of task performance is due to the attention made toward figural regions. It is known that attending to certain regions of the visual field increases the accuracy of detection of targets presented in those regions (Posner et al. 1980). If figure was attended to more than ground, one would expect targets in figural regions to be resolved with higher accuracy.

An alternate approach to understanding the facilitative effect of figure originates from the idea that figure and ground involve different kinds of perceptual processes. The Gestalt theorists described figure as having a "thing-like" character (Rubin 1921) and being "more strongly structured, and more impressive" (Koffka 1935). Rather than emphasize the consistent dominance of figure over ground, the Gestalt theorists viewed the dichotomy of figure and ground in terms of a functional difference. Julesz (1978, 1982) has formulated a similar approach, proposing not only that different visual processes mediate the processing of figure and ground but also that figure perception and ground perception involve different specialized functions. Figure processing is concerned with high resolution of details; ground processing is concerned with the extraction of global background information. Given these differences in processing demands and requirements, one would expect that under certain conditions ground might facilitate perceptual performance and figure might not. Would there be a stimulus and task condition where ground would facilitate task performance? It has been hypothesized that different perceptual functions are associated with different bands of spatial and temporal frequencies (Breitmeyer and Ganz 1976; Kulikowski and Tolhurst 1973; Weisstein 1968; Weisstein et al. 1975). It is suggested that the high spatial frequencies are involved in resolution of edges, details, and phase, whereas the low spatial frequencies are insensitive to phase and primarily carry information concerning the global structure of the visual field (Henning et al. 1975; Broadbent 1977; Julesz 1978, 1982; Carpenter and Ganz 1972). A process sensitive to high spatial frequencies might then be a good candidate for figure analysis if it is assumed that such analysis is specialized in detail resolution and vernier signal processing (Julesz 1978, 1982). On the other hand, a process sensitive to low spatial frequencies might be appropriate for ground analysis if ground perception is concerned with the extraction of global information. If these inferences were correct, we might expect the visual system to be more sensitive to high spatial frequencies in a figure region and more sensitive to low spatial frequencies in a ground region.

At threshold, the most sensitive system mediates the detection of the stimulus. A theory that associated enhanced sensitivity of high spatial frequencies in figural regions and enhanced sensitivity of low spatial frequencies in ground regions would predict that targets with high spatial frequencies present would be detected more accurately in figure and that

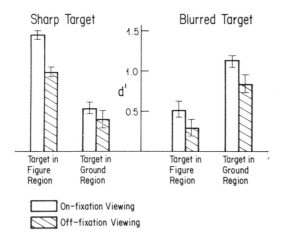

Figure 6
The detection of sharp and blurred targets in figure and in ground regions. Accuracy is measured in terms of d'. Reprinted from Wong and Weisstein 1983; copyright 1983 by American Psychological Association.

targets with only low spatial frequencies present would be detected more accurately in ground regions. In an experiment where sharp and blurred targets were flashed in figure and ground regions, it was found that the sharp targets were detected more accurately in figure regions and blurred targets were detected better in ground regions (Wong and Weisstein 1983). The sharp targets had high spatial frequencies present, whereas in the blurred target all frequencies above 16.67 cycles were absent. Figure 6 shows the results of this experiment. The sharp line segments were clearly more visible in figural regions than in ground regions. However, the converse was true for the blurred targets, which were detected with high accuracy when they were flashed in ground regions. These results are consistent with the idea that high spatial frequencies are associated with figure analysis and low spatial frequencies with ground analysis. Under the assumption that high spatial frequencies are needed for discrimination and resolution of details, as proposed earlier (Carpenter and Ganz 1972; Broadbent 1977), if the high spatial frequencies were to be removed from a small line segment tilted slightly left or right of vertical then the performance of an orientation-discrimination task should be degraded. Furthermore, if figure analysis facilitates the discrimination of details then removing the high spatial frequencies should attenuate or destroy the facilitatory effect of figure on the performance of discrimination tasks.

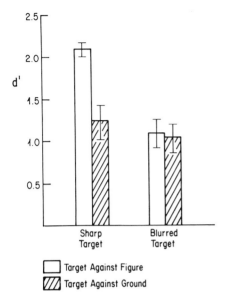

Figure 7
The discrimination of sharp and blurred targets in figure and in ground regions. Accuracy of discrimination is measured in terms of d'.

The Discrimination of Blurred (Low Spatial Frequencies) Lines Is Facilitated by Neither Figure nor Ground (Wong and Weisstein 1984a)

Ground analysis is thought to enhance background information extracted primarily from the low spatial frequencies. It is known that in a detection task ground analysis enhances low-spatial-frequency targets. Would ground analysis also help in the discrimination of targets if the targets contained only low spatial frequencies?

When blurred targets where no energy was present in the spectrum above 16 cycles per degree were flashed in figure regions, no facilitation in tilt discrimination was observed. Figure 7 shows results comparing discrimination of tilted targets, sharp or blurred, flashed in figure regions and in ground regions.

Sharp tilted line segments, as usual, were discriminated with higher accuracy in figure regions than in ground regions. However, neither figure nor ground facilitated the discrimination of blurred tilted line segments. These data are compatible with an approach that emphasizes the specialized processing function of figure analysis and ground analysis. It was proposed that figure analysis involves detailed scrutiny of a local part of the visual field. Tasks of orientation discrimination of minutely tilted target lines called for resolution of fine details. It was also suggested that high spatial frequency and edge information are necessary to these types of tasks. Removal of the high-spatial-frequency response would deprive the visual system data from extracting information. Thus, if figure analysis is specialized in the resolution of details and is selectively sensitive to the high spatial frequencies, removing the high-spatial-frequency response would diminish if not totally attenuate any facilitative effect of figure. This was what was found when the tilted line segments to be discriminated were blurred. Ground analysis, although more sensitive to the low spatial frequencies and therefore an aid in the detection of blurred targets, cannot enhance the discrimination of either sharp or blurred tilted lines because the information necessary to perform detail analysis was not available through ground analysis.

Perceived Figure and Ground Affect the Bandwidth of Orientation Channels (Wong and Weisstein 1984b)

Figure was found to facilitate the discriminability of sharp tilted line segments but not blurred ones. What underlying process might be responsible for this enhancement? There is much psychophysical evidence suggesting that the visual system picks up information with mechanisms akin to channels in a receiving system. This idea that the visual system contain "channels" has proved useful in conceptualizing how certain information in the visual world is picked up and used. Most models of early processing of visual information are tuned-channels models, which propose that information is picked up by channels tuned to certain orientations, spatial, and temporal frequencies. Channels are signal pathways sensitive to certain regions of a stimulus dimension. By "tuning" we refer to a pathway's maximum response for a given stimulus. Each pathway or channel has a response distribution. The peak of the distribution defines the stimulus to which the channel is maximally responsive. In most models, the shape of the response distribution is assumed to have a cosine sensitivity function, and the shapes of the response distributions of all the channels for a given type of stimulus (for example, orientation) are identical. This conception has been very useful in describing the characteristics of the visual system's ability to pick up information. For example, it has been shown that channels tuned to high spatial frequency are also maximally sensitive to low temporal frequency, and that channels tuned to low spatial frequency are also maximally sensitive to high temporal frequency (Robson 1966; Breitmeyer and Ganz 1977; Burbeck and Kelly 1981). The low-spatial/high-temporal-frequency channels have a faster response than the high-spatial/low-temporal-frequency channels (Breitmeyer 1975; Nachmias 1967; Vassilev and Mitov 1976). There is also evidence suggesting that direction of motion and velocity are processed through tuned channels (Sekuler et al. 1968; Pantle and Sekuler 1968; Pantle et al. 1978).

Tuned-channels models also assume that the channels have a certain bandwidth and that signals less than one bandwidth apart are processed in the same pathway. The likelihood of signal confusion in discriminability is higher for stimuli that are less than one bandwidth apart than for stimuli that are more than one bandwidth apart. In other words, discrimination of targets should be better for stimuli that are at least one bandwidth apart than for stimuli that are less than one bandwidth apart. Given the differences we found in the accuracies of tilt discrimination in figure and in ground regions, we might ask whether this accuracy difference is related to bandwidth behavior of the orientation channels in figure and in ground regions. The tuning and the bandwidth of orientation channels have been examined in terms of several psychophysical methods, including orientation-specific masking (Campbell and Kulikowski 1966; Wilson et al. 1983; Phillips and Wilson 1984); subthreshold summation (Kulikowski et al. 1973); adaptation (Blakemore and Campbell 1969; Blakemore and Nachmias 1971); and comparison of discrimination and detection performance at threshold, also known as the discrimination/detection ratio (Thomas and Gille 1979; Thomas et al. 1982).

Using the discrimination/detection ratio, we examined the bandwidth of orientation channels with tilted line segments flashed in figure and in ground regions. This method of bandwidth measurement compares the probability of discrimination (or identification) accuracy with the probability of detection at a number of detection levels. Some assumptions, however, have to be made concerning the number and the distribution of the channels. First, it is assumed that all the channels have symmetrical cosine sensitivity functions. Second, the channels must have equal bandwidth and peak sensitivity. Third, the sensitivity peaks of the channels must be at uniform intervals on the orientation dimension. One more characteristic of channels has to be considered if methods other than the discrimination/detection ratio are used: channel spacing. The discrimination/detection ratio is almost independent of channel spacing for orientation differences in stimulus pairs up to $10°$ (Thomas and Gille 1979).

Therefore, the assumption of channel spacing does not have to be made if one uses the discrimination/detection method in estimating bandwidth.

In a typical discrimination/detection experiment, a single trial consists of two stimulus-presentation intervals. The stimulus is presented randomly from trial to trial in one of the two intervals, and the task of the observer is to first judge in which interval the stimulus appeared. This constitutes the detection measure. Then the observer has to identify which of a given pair of stimuli has been presented. This constitutes the discrimination part of the task. Since the stimulus setting also varies from trial to trial, relationships of discrimination and detection at various detection probabilities are generated. From these relationships the discrimination/detection ratio emerges. Through the plotting of discrimination against detection at each detection probability, a regression line can be fitted to the data points. This is the discrimination (identification)/detection slope (I/D), and the greater the slope the better the discriminability of a pair of stimuli.

When we examined the bandwidth of orientation channels in figure and ground contexts using the discrimination/detection ratio, we found that the slopes of the same pair of stimuli of a given orientation difference were very different depending on whether they were presented in figure or in ground areas.

The most striking result is the big difference of I/D slopes for stimuli presented in figure and in ground contexts. Whereas the slopes for the ground conditions never exceeded 0.3, the slopes for the figure conditions approached unity (table 1). The discrimination/detection ratio is an indicator of whether a given pair of stimuli is at least one bandwidth apart. We assumed that the visual system picks up orientation information through

Table 1
I/D slopes of targets presented alone and in figure and ground contexts.

Orientation difference	I/D slope*		
	Figure	Ground	Line alone
3.2°	0.51	0.24	0.43
4.9°	0.86	0.22	0.33
9.8°	1.00	0.27	0.33
13.0°	0.91	0.46	0.54
19.5°	0.98	0.46	0.79
25.8°	0.98	0.78	0.96
31.8°	0.95	0.94	0.94

*The I/D slopes are calculated from the discrimination/detection ratios.

tuned channels—a reasonable assumption, since the existing psychophysical evidence is consistent with such conceptualization of visual processing. Consider the case where a pair of stimuli activate two sets of channels (in other words, the difference between the stimuli is greater than the bandwidth of the channel). In this case, the stimuli should be discriminated as accurately as detected, since the two signals are processed through two separate pathways. Confusion errors should be minimal. If the stimulus can be detected, it can also be identified. Here the discrimination/detection ratio (the I/D slope) should approach unity. However, if the stimulus pair were less than one bandwidth apart, they would not be activating separate receiving channels. In this case, identification-confusion errors will occur at a higher rate, since the two stimuli are not being processed through separate pathways. Thus, although the stimuli could be detected with accuracy, they could not be discriminated reliably. This discrepancy of discrimination and detection would yield a low discrimination/detection ratio, indicating that the stimuli are less than one bandwidth apart.

Returning to the I/D slopes for tilted lines presented in figure and ground regions, notice that although the I/D slope measured in figure areas approached unity for both stimulus pairs, the I/D slope obtained in the ground regions did not exceed 0.3. Where the stimuli are at least one bandwidth apart in figure regions, these same pairs of tilted lines are less than one bandwidth apart in ground regions. The orientation difference at which the I/D slope becomes unity is the lower limit for the channel bandwidth. From our data, at an orientation difference of 3.2° the I/D slope is 0.51 for targets flashed in figure regions, 0.24 for targets flashed in ground regions, and 0.43 for targets flashed in the absence of any surrounding context. At this orientation difference, stimuli are less than one bandwidth apart in all context conditions. At an orientation difference of 4.9°, the I/D slope is 0.86 for targets in figure regions, 0.22 for targets in ground regions, and 0.33 for targets in the absence of context. Table 1 gives the I/D slope for the various orientation differences used in the experiment for one observer. At an orientation difference of 9.8°, the I/D slope for targets presented in figure regions approaches unity. However, for targets presented in ground regions and targets presented in the absence of any context the I/D slopes are still substantially less than unity. These data show that when stimuli are at least one bandwidth apart in figure regions these same tilted line segments are less than one bandwidth apart in ground regions and in contextless fields. It is not until an orientation difference of 25.8° that the I/D slope for targets in contextless fields becomes unity. For ground regions, the orientation difference where the I/D slope approaches unity is at least 31.8°. These differences in I/D slopes for targets presented in figure and ground regions are consistent with the finding that discrimination of sharp tilted lines is better in figural regions, since stimuli 4.9° apart in orientation are being processed through different pathways in figure regions but not in ground regions. The likelihood of discriminability confusion in figure regions is thus much less than that in ground regions.

Metacontrast Masking of Targets by Figure and Ground

We have also been able to obtain metacontrast masking functions of targets presented in figure and in ground regions. In a metacontrast masking condition, a target is presented for a brief period and followed by the masking stimulus. In our experiment the target was a tilted line, 45° left or right of vertical, and the mask was the Rubin faces-vase outline picture. The target was flashed for 50 msec, and the masking stimulus was presented at various stimulus onset asynchronies (SOAs) before and after the target for 50 msec. The target was tilted left or right randomly, and the observer's task was to identify the orientation of the target and to report seeing either faces or a vase in that particular trial. Targets were always presented in the central region of the Rubin picture. Figure 8 shows the results obtained from one observer.

When the masking stimulus preceded the target by a large interval, no effect of mask on target was seen whether the masking area was perceived as figure or as ground. When the mask preceded the target by a short

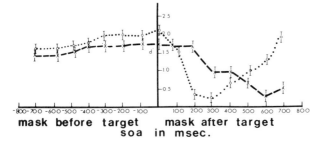

mask before target   mask after target
soa   in   msec.

o···o **figure mask**

x—x **ground mask**

Figure 8
Metacontrast masking functions of tilted lines by a figure mask and by a ground mask. Accuracy of target identification is measured in terms of d'.

interval (300—0 msec), an enhancement of the target's discriminability was observed if the masking area was perceived as figure.

When the condition was changed to backward (or metacontrast) masking (that is, target preceded mask), degradation of the target was observed whether the masking region was seen as figure or as ground. However, the masking functions were very different for a "figure" mask than for a "ground" mask. When the masking area was seen as ground, the degradation of the target occurred at much longer SOAs than when the masking region was seen as figure. The maximum masking by ground occurred at an SOA of 600 msec, whereas the maximum masking of figure occurred at an SOA of 300 msec. By an SOA of 700 msec, the masking effect of figure had disappeared but the masking effect of ground was still strong.

The metacontrast masking functions reveal further information about how perceptual organization affects early visual processing. In a masking situation, both the mask and the target appear for brief periods. In contrast with the designs of the experiments described earlier, in this design there is no opportunity for the observer to anchor onto a particular organization and be alerted to "look" for certain stimulus aspects. This is especially so for the backward masking conditions, where the masking stimulus is presented after the target. In this situation, one is looking at how perceptual organization interferes with the processing of orientation. In a metacontrast masking situation, it is assumed that masking (or degradation of target discriminability) occurs when the neural signal of the masking stimulus interferes with that of the target. Thus, metacontrast can inform us of the speed and timing of the mask and the target (Weisstein et al. 1975; Breitmeyer and Ganz 1976). Given a theory of metacontrast that postulates that fast and slow components of a signal are associated with response to a stimulus and that metacontrast is the interruption of the slow response to the target by the fast response (Weisstein et al. 1975; Breitmeyer and Ganz 1976), the faster the speed of processing of the mask, the longer the SOA must be in order for the responses to the mask and the target to coincide to produce masking. Therefore, if the longer SOAs are associated with the "ground" mask and shorter SOAs with the "figure" mask, the processing of ground must be faster than that of figure. This agrees with the conclusions of Calis and Leeuwenberg (1981). Backgrounds are processed faster before the figure. The metacontrast results and the data that establish an association between fast low spatial frequencies and ground processing support the idea that figure and ground have different functional and processing requirements (Julesz 1978). The functional differences are associated with particular and special tasks that the visual system is required to perform:

detail resolution in figure analysis, and global background-information extraction in ground processing.

Conclusions

We have introduced and discussed some psychophysical evidence for the influence of figure-ground organization on the processing of orientation and spatial frequency. In our experiments, the figure-ground organization was defined by contours marking the outlines of a reversible picture of a vase and the faces. That a picture context affects the spatial and orientation responses of the visual system shows that a high-order representation affects an elementary level of visual processing, suggesting some top-down influences on the early stages of processing.

We shall now consider our psychophysical findings in the light of David Marr's scheme of visual processing. (Recall figure 1.) We are going to examine each stage of processing formulated in Marr's scheme and consider whether our figure-ground effects could have taken place there. First, consider the most advanced level of processing, the stage where the three-dimensional sketch is constructed and where shapes of objects are interpolated and described. Our figure-ground influences on the processing of orientation and spatial frequency could not have occurred here, because the elementary primitives of orientation and zero crossings have already been synthesized and combined to yield more complex configurations of shape. For the same reason, our figure-ground effects also could not have occurred at the stage where the $2\frac{1}{2}$-dimensional sketch is constructed, since raw orientations have been combined to yield descriptions of surface textures. The nature of the interaction of figure-ground organization and spatial frequency and orientation processing is such that it must occur at a stage where orientation and termination of lines is represented before local surface texture is extrapolated from groups of lines. Moreover, because figure and ground selectively boost sensitivity to (respectively) high and low spatial frequencies, these effects must occur where the zero crossings are registered. In other words, they must occur before the emergence of the raw primal sketch, which contains the image descriptions arising from the raw zerocrossings.

Can we place our figure-ground effects at the level where intensity is registered? We think not. Our effects concern orientation and spatial frequency, which are at least "one step" removed from local intensities at each point in the image. Therefore we propose that the figure-ground organization effects are occurring just where orientation and zero crossings are registered. It seems that perceptual organization serves to selectively boost the outputs of fine-grain and coarse-grain analysis, so that figure enhances the outputs of the small filters and ground enhances the outputs of the large filters. In this case, organizational factors serve as boosters rather than filters. Their influences occur after the differential operators take effect, not before.

The effects of figure on the bandwidth behavior of orientation channels would also be occurring before the emergence of the primal sketch. This is because in the primal sketch elements are already grouped to form higher primitives. Resolution of orientation must occur before lines can be grouped and represented as a single unit. The bandwidth behavior of channels affects whether two signals can be discriminated or resolved reliably, and, depending on how the orientation of lines is resolved, a different representation arising from grouping may result. Therefore, any enhancement or degradation of resolution leading to different groupings of elements must be occurring before the emergence of the primal sketch.

Marr's approach to visual processing has had the advantages over early theories of image segmentation and pattern recognition. The early attempts in computer vision ran into difficulty in determining objects, shapes, and backgrounds; Marr's model of vision avoided such difficulties by having the system deal with surface properties of an image rather than segmenting the image into regions. The representation of the visual world is built up in stages by way of sketches where successive computational procedures would extract and make explicit more complex representations based on the information given in the previous stage of visual processing. Thus depth, distance, and surface textures are arrived at directly, without the need to segment the image into regions first. No attempt is required to segregate figure from background. However, Marr's approach would have difficulty in incorporating a number of visual phenomena associated with figure-ground perception.

In Marr's approach (and other related ones, the extraction of surface textures and contours is based on what is given in groupings made explicit in the primal sketch. If the flow of visual information is such that the transition from one representation to another is constrained only by the information made explicit in the representations, then there is no problem (at least logically) in arriving at surface properties given curvature, grouping, boundaries, edges, and blobs. However, in human visual processing, orientation resolution and discrimination are very different depending on whether line segments are lying in a figural or a ground region. This means that the grouping of lines, at least in the orientation dimension, would be different for elements in the two areas. Moreover, the detection of edge and contour continuation—in fact, even the detection of blobs—depends on figure and ground (Weitzman 1963; Wong and Weisstein 1983). This reintroduces the problem of figure and ground at a level of processing before surface properties are extracted. Although the difficulties of image segmentation and figure-ground segregation are avoided in the transition from the primal sketch to the emergence of surface structures and depth, the problem returns when the effects of figure-ground organization have to be contended with in an early stage of visual processing. Thus, if Marr's model provides an accurate approximation of human vision, figure-ground cannot be avoided.

Earlier on, we introduced the idea of a functional difference between figure analysis and ground analysis: that each process is responsible for performing a special kind of visual processing and is optimally sensitive to different input information. The top-down effects of figure and ground organization thus have a purpose other than being merely a structural characteristics of information processing in the visual system. Figure analysis has been suggested to be responsible for detailed scrutiny of small areas where edges, phase, are important dimensions to be picked up. Ground analysis has been suggested to be responsible for extracting overall textural pattern and global regional information about the visual field. Moreover, ground processing has been designated as a candidate for an "early warning system" that picks up global information for later detail analysis. In fact, it has been shown that the representation of background emerges before the representation of figure is built up (Calis and Leeuwenberg 1981). That the visual system is more sensitive to low spatial frequencies in ground regions is also consistent with the idea that ground analysis is a faster system, since the time constants of low spatial frequencies are faster than those of high spatial frequencies (Vassilev and Mitov 1976; Lupp et al. 1976; Watson and Nachmias 1977).

The separate functions of figure analysis and ground analysis allow the visual system to select aspects of the given information array to highlight and focus on while ignoring others. Details inside figures are scrutinized, whereas with backgrounds it is sufficient to register blobs or textures which might give depth and distance information. The top-down figure-ground effects on visual information processing thus serve to orient the visual system to points of interest in the visual field and to organize the incoming visual data so that plans of action may be made by an organism interacting with the environment.

References

Barlow, H. B. 1972. Single units and sensation: A neuron doctrine for perceptual psychology? *Perception* 1: 371–394.

Barrow, H. G., and J. M. Tenenbaum. 1978. Recovering intrinsic scene characteristics from images. In *Computer Vision Systems*, ed. A. R. Hanson and E. M. Riseman (Academic).

Blakemore, C., and F. W. Campbell. 1969. On the existence of neurons in the human visual system selectively sensitive to the orientation and size of retinal images. *J. Physiology* 203: 237–260.

Blakemore, C., and J. Nachmias. 1971. The orientation specificity of two visual after-effects. *J. Physiology* 213: 157–174.

Breitmeyer, B. 1975. Simple reaction time as a measure of the temporal response properties of transient and sustained channels. *Vision Res.* 15: 1411–1412.

Breitmeyer, B., and L. Ganz. 1976. Implications of sustained and transient channels for theories of visual pattern masking, saccadic suppression, and information processing. *Psychological Rev.* 83: 1–36.

Breitmeyer, B., and L. Ganz. 1977. Temporal studies with flashed gratings: Inferences about human transient and sustained channels. *Vision Res.* 17: 861–865.

Bridgeman, B. 1981. Cognitive factors in subjective stabilization of the visual world. *Acta Psychologica* 48: 111–121.

Broadbent, D. E. 1977. The hidden preattentive process. *Am. Psychologist* 32: 109–118.

Burbeck, C. A., and D. H. Kelly. 1981. Contrast gain measurement and the transient/sustained dichotomy. *J. Optical Soc. America* 71: 1335–1342.

Calis, G., and E. Leeuwenberg. 1981. Ground the figure. *J. Exp. Psychology: Human Perceptional and Performance* 7: 1386–1397.

Campbell, F. W., and J. J. Kulikowski. 1966. Orientational selectivity of the human visual system. *J. Physiology* 187: 437–445.

Carpenter, P. A., and L. Ganz. 1972. An attentional mechanism in the analysis of spatial frequency. *Perception and Psychophysics* 12: 57–60.

Ginsburg, A. P. 1975. Is the illusory triangle physical or imaginery? *Nature* 257: 219–220.

Ginsburg, A. P. 1984. The spatial bandwidth for the identification of geometric form. *Investigative Ophthalmology and Visual Science Suppl.* 25: 72.

Graham, N. 1980. Spatial-frequency channels in human vision: Detecting edges without edge detectors. In *Visual Coding and Adaptability*, ed. C. S. Harris (Erlbaum).

Graham, N. 1981. Psychophysics of spatial frequency channels. In *Perceptual organization*, ed. M. Kubovy and J. Pomerantz (Erlbaum).

Gregory, R. L. 1980. Perceptions as hypotheses. *Philos. Trans. Roy. Soc. Lond.* B 290: 181–197.

Henning, C. B., B. C. Hertz, and D. E. Broadbent. 1975. Some experiments bearing on the hypothesis that the visual system analyses spatial patterns in independent bands of spatial frequency. *Vision Res.* 15: 887–898.

Hochberg, J. 1968. In the mind's eye. In *Contemporary Theory and Research in Visual Perception*, ed. R. N. Haber (Holt, Rinehart, and Winston).

Julesz, B. 1978. Perceptual limits of texture discrimination and their implications to figure-ground separation. In *Formal Theories of Perception*, ed. E. Leeuwenberg and H. Buffart (Wiley).

Julesz, B. 1982. Figure and ground perception in briefly presented isodipole textures. In *Perceptual Organization*, ed. M. Kubovy and J. Pomerantz (Erlbaum).

Koffka, K. 1935. *Principles of Gestalt Psychology*. Harcourt, Brace.

Kulikowski, J. J., and R. Abadi, and P. E. King-Smith. 1973. Orientation and selectivity of grating and line detectors in human vision. *Vision Res.* 13: 1479–1486.

Lupp, U., G. Hauske, and W. Wolf. 1976. Perceptual latencies to sinusoidal gratings. *Vision Res.* 16: 969–972.

Marr, D. 1976. Early processing of visual information. *Philos. Trans. Roy. Soc. Lond.* B 275: 483–519.

Marr, D. 1980. Visual information processing: The structure and creation of visual representations. *Philos. Trans. Roy. Soc. Lond.* B 290: 199–218.

Marr, D. 1982. *Vision*. Freeman.

Marr, D., and E. Hildreth. 1980. Theory of edge detection. *Proc. Roy. Soc. Lond.* B 207: 187–217.

Marr, D., and H. K. Nishihara. 1978. Representation and recognition of the spatial organization of three-dimensional shapes. *Proc. Roy. Soc. Lond.* B 200: 269–284.

Marr, D., and T. Poggio. 1979. A computational theory of human stereo vision. *Proc. Roy. Soc. Lond.* B 204: 301–328.

Marr, D., and S. Ullman. 1982. Directional selectivity and its use in early visual representations. *Proc. Roy. Soc. Lond.* B 211: 151–180.

Movshon, J. A., D. J. Tolhurst, and A. F. Dean. 1982. How many neurons are involved in perceptual decisions? *Investigative Ophthalmology and Visual Science Suppl.* 22: 207.

Pantle, A., and R. Sekuler. 1968. Velocity-sensitive elements in human vision: Initial psychophysical evidence. *Vision Res.* 8: 445–450.

Pantle, A., S. Lehmkuhle, and M. Candill. 1978. On the capacity of directionally selective mechanisms to encode different dimensions of moving stimuli. *Perception* 7: 261–267.

Nachmias, J. 1967. Effect of exposure duration on visual contrast sensitivity with square-wave gratings. *J. Optical Soc. America* 57: 421–427.

Pentland, A. 1982. Perception of Shape from Shading. Paper presented at the 1982 annual meeting of the Optical Society of America.

Pentland, A., and L. Gazis. 1984. Perception of three-dimensional textures. *Investigative Ophthalmology and Visual Science* 25: 201.

Phillips, G. C., and H. R. Wilson. 1984. Orientation bandwidths of spatial mechanisms measured by masking. *J. Optical Soc. America: Optics and Image Science* 1: 226–232.

Posner, M. I., C. R. R. Snyder, and B. J. Davidson. 1980. Attention and the detection of signals. *J. Exp. Psychology: General* 109: 160–174.

Robson, J. G. 1966. Spatial and temporal contrast sensitivity functions of the visual system. *J. Optical Soc. America* 56: 1141–1142.

Rock, I. 1983. *The Logic of Perception*. MIT Press.

Rubin, E. 1921. Figure and ground. Reprinted in *Readings in Perception*, ed. D. C. Beardslee and M. Wertheimer (Van Nostrand, 1958).

Sekuler, R., E. L. Rubin, and W. H. Cushman. 1968. Selectivities of human visual mechanisms for direction of movement and contour orientation. *J. Optical Soc. America* 58: 1145–1150.

Thomas, J. P., and J. Gille. 1979. Bandwidths of orientation channels in human vision. *J. Optical Soc. America* 65: 652–660.

Thomas, J. P., J. Gille, and R. A. Barker. 1982. Simultaneous visual detection and identification and data. *J. Optical Soc. America* 72: 1642–1651.

Ullman, S. 1979. The interpretation of structure from motion, *Proc. Roy. Soc. Lond.* B 203: 405–426.

Vassilev, A., and D. Mitov. 1976. Perception time and spatial frequency. *Vision Res.* 16: 89–92.

Waltz, D. 1975. Understanding line drawings of scenes with shadows. In *The Psychology of Computer Vision*, ed. P. H. Winston (McGraw-Hill).

Watson, A. B. 1981. A single-channel model does not predict visibility of asynchronous gratings. *Vision Res.* 21: 1799–1800.

Watson, A. B., and J. Nachmias. 1977. Patterns of temporal interaction in the detection of gratings. *Vision Res.* 17: 893–902.

Weisstein, N. 1968. A Rashevsky-Landahl neural net: Simulations of metacontrast. *Psychological Rev.* 75: 494–521.

Weisstein, N., G. Ozog, and R. A. Szoc. 1975. A comparison and elaboration of two models of metacontrast. *Psychological Rev.* 82: 325–343.

Weitzman, B. 1963?. A threshold difference produced by figure-ground dichotomy. *J. Exp. Psychology* 66: 201–205.

Wilson, H. R., and J. R. Bergen. 1979. A four mechanism model for threshold and spatial vision. *Vision Res.* 19: 19–32.

Wilson, H. R., D. K. McFarlane, and G. Phillips. 1983. Spatial frequency tuning of orientation selective units estimated by oblique masking. *Vision Res.* 23: 873–882.

Winston, P. H. 1975. Machine vision. In *The Psychology of Computer Vision*, ed. P. H. Winston (McGraw-Hill).

Wong, E., and N. Weisstein. 1982. A new perceptual context-superiority effect: Line segments are more visible against a figure than against a ground. *Science* 218: 587–589.

Wong, E., and N. Weisstein. 1983. Sharp targets are detected better against a figure and blurred targets are detected better against a ground. *J. Exp. Psychology: Human Perception and Performance* 9: 194–202.

Wong, E., and N. Weisstein. 1984a. The effects of perceived figure and ground on the orientation discrimination of sharp and blurred targets. *Perception*.

Wong, E., and N. Weisstein. 1984b. Perceived figure and ground affect the bandwidth of orientation channels. In preparation.

7   The Diversity of Perceptual Grouping

Steven W. Zucker

The term *grouping* is usually taken to indicate those processes that organize and agglomerate different entities into increasingly more abstract ones. These entities necessarily derive from a wide range of phenomena, starting with early, sensory events and ending with more cognitive ones. Thus, any description of grouping capable of including all of these phenomena must be highly abstract, like the one above. But the danger in this much abstraction is that it usually leads to the further presupposition that grouping results from the recursive or repeated application of the same kind of process to the same kind of entity. Thus, a solution to one grouping problem is a solution to all. It is this latter conclusion with which we disagree most strongly, and which we argue against in this paper. We shall argue that the above form of theorizing is so abstract that it misses much of the diversity that is the key to understanding early vision.

The paper is organized into three main sections. In the first, I develop the tradition behind the homogeneity of grouping and argue for its diversity. To substantiate these arguments in detail, I develop in the next section a theory of early orientation selection, perhaps the earliest form of grouping. This forces a consideration of what one type of grouping must accomplish in some detail, as well as how it might actually be carried out in biologically plausible computations. Finally, I sketch several examples illustrating the different properties of other, higher-level grouping processes.

Tradition and the Homogeneity of Grouping

The homogeneity of perceptual grouping (i.e., the belief in the form of one basic grouping process) has a long tradition. In a modern sense it began with the Gestalt psychologists' striking figure/ground demonstrations. (See, e.g., Koffka 1935.) The key to these demonstrations was the manner in which certain elements in particular arrangements were organized to produce an emergent figure. The simplest examples were Wertheimer's (1923) original ones involving dots: "... one sees a series of discontinuous dots upon a homogeneous ground not as a sum of dots, but as figures" (pp. 72–73). We shall come back to dot grouping shortly; for now it is significant to note that the Gestalt psychologists went further than these observations and assumed that a homogeneous mechanism was responsible for them.

The motivation of the Gestalt psychologists came from physics, for it was here that they believed the foundations of mechanism were to be found. Köhler (1920, p. 250) observed: "In all processes which terminate in time independent states the distribution shifts toward a minimum of energy." The next step was stated by Koffka (1935, p. 108): "If nervous processes are physical processes, they must fulfil this condition." Given the belief in an energy-minimization mechanism for organizational processes, it is a small step to assume homogeneity across all the mechanisms for grouping. All the psychological phenomena of grouping were thus reduced to a single physical mechanism—an exciting possibility if true. Unfortunately, what began as a Gestalt metaphor at least in part has taken on the status of literal theorizing.

The Gestalt tradition of designing displays in which different local entities segregate continues to the present (Beck 1982; Kubovy and Pomerantz 1981). However, the Gestalt idea of how to reduce psychological events to physical ones has been overwhelmingly disproved in its literal form. Therefore, it is surprising that the assumption of homogeneity in mechanisms for grouping persists to the present. It is there, for example, in Marr's computational model; grouping is postulated to be that class of processes that write from the "primal sketch" (an explicit representation of the "important information about the two-dimensional image, primarily the intensity changes there and their geometrical organization" [Marr 1982, p. 37]) back into the "primal sketch" (ibid., p. 91). Mathematically this sounds like a single mapping. But the notions that the Gestalt psychologists used to characterize grouping, namely *organize* and *agglomerate*, are only suggestive metaphors; they do not take on substantive meaning until they are specified operationally. And the attempts at such specification have been failures. For example, Wertheimer's laws of perceptual organization have so far eluded operational specification (Uttal 1981). There is a sense in which the Gestalt laws are of the wrong granularity: They are an attempt to force too many diverse phenomena and processes into one category. They attempt to explain too much with too little. Such is the case for the concept of the "primal sketch" as well. This, too, is just a suggestive term which, upon closer examination, hides an enormously complex amount of processing within a single (and, to a large extent, still elusive) data structure.

Overview of the Argument

It is my thesis that the assumption of homogeneity hides the wonderful diversity of perceptual grouping. As each possible task for grouping, or each phenomenon of grouping, is analyzed in further detail, more structure will emerge for the processes required to implement it. What appears at first to be a single, simple conceptual stage will in reality turn out to be an elaborate complex of stages. The limit, in terms of detail, will probably be determined by the physiology. But it is just this diversity that reveals the detailed manner in which the early visual problem is solved.

The above claims are radical, and the bulk of this paper consists of arguments to support them. The attack is two-sided. First, to illustrate how the diversity of grouping is apparent only with deep and detailed investigation, we study the domain of dot grouping. This domain, which was first studied by Wertheimer and the Gestalt psychologists, was chosen because common sense suggests to nearly everyone that it is homogeneous. It turns out that it is not, however, as can be demonstrated mathematically, phenomenally, and computationally. Similar conclusions are possible from other grouping experiments, such as the figures used by Beck (1966), Julesz (1981), and others (see Beck 1982 for a review), although their specific interpretation is more complicated. The second prong of the attack consists of a survey of several other examples of grouping which are taken to be "higher-level." This survey is necessary to show that the evidence in favor of a diversity is typical; it is not an isolated special case.

The particular examples that I choose come from orientation selection, or the inference of abstract orientation information from discrete images of distinct entities. This is most likely the earliest form of processing that can be characterized as grouping. A simple example is the inference of a line connecting two nearby dots; the line has an orientation but the dots do not. My particular demonstrations are more subtle than this, however. One of them involves a distinction between what I refer to as type I and type II patterns. The numerals here give an indication of how orientation information is distributed across space. The first, one-dimensional case corresponds to the inference of one-dimensional contours from a spatial distribution of dots. The type II patterns involve orientation information that is densely distributed across areas rather than curves. It arises for orientation selection within flow patterns. These mathematical differences give rise to computational differences in the algorithms that accomplish orientation selection, which in turn implies certain psychophysical differences to detecting change within these patterns. Such differences are demonstrated.

The distinction between type I and type II patterns is not unrelated to the classical Gestalt notions of "figure" and "ground," although it is not identical. Type I grouping amounts to the precise inference of contours, such as those that arise when surfaces occlude one another. It is these contours that often delimit "figures" in the Gestalt sense, and it is to these figures that the contours belong. Of course, contour inferencing such as this is an application of the Gestalt law of good continuation. Type II inference is necessary in other image areas, namely those in which the scene consists of complex material structures, such as the hair on an animal's surface or the surface topography underlying a field of tall grass. Orientational information associated with the latter task is more difficult to infer, since the hairs are randomly and frequently going in and out of occlusion relationships with one another. The latter task cannot be accomplished as precisely as the former one. Rather, it gives rise to more of a smooth "flow" than a precise contour. And this flow covers a surface both in the direction of the flow and perpendicular to it; it has both length and width. Type I contours, on the other hand, have only length (along the contour); in the perpendicular direction they have insignificant width.

But this is just the beginning of the diversity of processes that group dots. Another distinction derives from computational (and putative physiological) implementation considerations. I call it a size/density constraint, because it dictates differences in the nature of the mechanisms that process dense as compared with sparse patterns. Consider just type I processing, or the inference of one-dimensional curves from collections of points. The nature of our proposed mechanisms for accomplishing such inferences opens the possibility that one takes place rather early in the visual process whereas the other must be later. It also raises a basic conceptual connection between the processes of grouping and the structure of the physical world. Many classes of events are dense in their spatial support, such as the points lying along an occluding contour that is completely in view. But imagine viewing this same contour through a picket fence. Now some lengths of contour will be dense in image support (namely those that project through the pickets), while other regions will be completely obscured by the pickets and will have no image support. As will be shown, the processing of dense image structure (e.g., the visible contour) is in many senses simpler than the processing of sparse structure (the same contour seen through the fence).

Several of these differences are revealed through the study of dot patterns, with the mechanistic requirements for sparse patterns much more sophisticated than those for dense ones. Thus, even a form of grouping as seemingly simple as inferring curves from dot patterns consists of several different processes, some of which occur very early in processing and others only later. And the putative early processes are appropriate for inferences involving the projection of one class of physical structures—those that result in dense image structures—whereas the later processes are appropriate for a different class.

Once figures begin to emerge, another class of grouping processes can begin to operate on selected aspects of them. For example, once orientation is explicitly represented, discontinuities in orientation can be located. These then provide new candidate objects (or, as Koffka [1935] would say, units), which can in turn be grouped. The precise criteria underlying these more abstract grouping processes still remain to be studied. (In order to ensure a kind of continuity between the results of grouping processes at different stages, one might conjecture that the smoothness and sensitivity constraints for the later processes will match those for the earlier ones.)

In Gestalt terms, the model for dot grouping that will be sketched below can be taken as an operational specification of the law of good continuation within dense dot patterns. Precisely how this law should be applied to orientation discontinuities, endpoints, inflection points, and so on is still an open question.

At a more abstract level, grouping processes begin to act on certain form cues to produce various subjective edges. These take place over a much wider range of distances and configurations, and can affect judgements about seemingly direct measurements such as the length of lines. Aside from interesting demonstrations of the phenomenology of such effects, little is known about them. Finally, at the most abstract levels, one is able to separate "cognitive" from "perceptual" grouping (Kanisza 1979).

Criteria for Differentiating between Grouping Processes

To summarize the preceeding overview: A number of criteria emerge by which the diversity of perceptual grouping can be formulated. Some of these criteria arise within different explanatory levels; some are interrelated. They include the following:

• abstract mathematical properties, such as orientation and dimensionality,

- the physical scene structure (and its image projection) to which they could be applicable,

- computational consequences of mathematical properties that must hold over algorithms for inferring them,

- emergent psychophysical properties, such as sensitivity to differences or subjective appearances, and

- how early in the visual process they could possibly be realized.

Early Orientation Selection

Wertheimer's original examples with dots provide a number of provocative questions: Why are the dots grouped into a contour? How, when, and where (in neurophysiological terms) does this grouping take place?

The why question is perhaps the most basic, and one answer, I believe, lies in the processes that are active in forming contours of intensity discontinuity (Zucker et al. 1983). Intensity discontinuities are fundamentally important, since they often delimit changes in surface orientation, reflectance, or lighting—in short, events of real physical significance. But the detection of such events begins locally (Leclerc and Zucker 1984)—in the limit, pointwise—so the question of how to infer the locus of discontinuities from these local signals arises. A similar, even more fundamental form of the argument holds for inferring contours through a locus of almost any intensity-based events, since by the nature of the sensing process they are "pointillist" in structure. That is, they consist of arrays of distinct values; think, for example, of the retina. Some process or other must be responsible for inferring contours through these distinct events. Dots allow us to study the geometry of such situations without the complication of explicit intensity interactions. They can be taken as indicating the locations at which intensity discontinuities (or, indeed, other local events) have taken place.

The problem, then, is how to group these points into contours, or how to infer a contour from a collection of points. The development that follows attempts to show that, while this would seem to be a single task, it actually is a quite complex one. What appears abstractly to require just a single process for implementation actually requires, upon analysis, several.

Before addressing the "how" question, however, we must first determine what our goal is; that is, we must determine what a contour is and how it can be specified. A contour is a locus of points that satisfies a given (but perhaps unknown) functional relationship. Smooth contours arise when the function is differentiable. In such cases we locally require that the tangent, or the direction in which the contour is going as it passes through each point, must be known as well. *Orientation selection,* the early form of dot grouping with which we shall be concerned for the present, is the process of inferring a representation of these tangents. The particular representation that we adopt is a vector field, a collection of unit-length vectors or "needles" arranged over a two-dimensional, planar region. Each of these unit vectors points in a direction that is tangent to the contour at that point. Of course, since there is no difference at this level between traversing a contour forward or backward, we shall not distinguish between the head and the tail of the vector; orientation, in other words, will span $180°$ and not $360°$.

A physical example often helps to motivate the idea of a vector field. Consider a particle of dust moving in a dust storm. Clearly, it sweeps out a curve through space such that, at every point, the velocity is given by a vector at that point. The length of this vector is proportional to the speed of the particle, and its orientation indicates the direction in which it is going just as it passes through that point. The velocity vector is always tangent to the path of the particle; the tangents at every point along a curve are an arrangement of vectors in $\Re^2$. Such an assignment of vectors to points in the plane is a vector field. The naturalness of this choice as a representation for contour inferencing will become clear shortly. Of course, for static images we are not concerned with the issue of whether the particle is moving forward or backward.

A Model for Orientation Selection

Our model for orientation selection consists of two distinct stages, the first one aimed at producing a local representation based on quantized measurements and the second one actually recovering a representation of the contour. The stages are as follows:

Stage 1 Estimate a vector field of tangents. This is a spatial arrangement of unit "needles" touching the contour at exactly one position and pointing in the direction in which the curve is going as it passes through that point. The tangent can thus be interpreted as the best linear approximation to the contour at a point, an interpretation that motivates our decomposition of this first stage of the model into two steps:

Step 1 Perform measurements on a representation of the dot patterns. These measurements will be modeled as convolutions of operators that are related to physiologically observed receptive fields against the dot image. But their interpretation is not unique, so we must perform step 2.

Step 2 Interpret the results of the measurements. This step is formulated both as a functional minimization problem (the response matching problem) and as a cooperative network that computes solutions to the problem. Physiologically, this amounts to interactions between the various receptive fields.

Stage 2 Find integral curves through the vector field. The second stage of the model is based on the fact that the tangent is the first derivative of the contour. This suggests that contours can be recovered by a process of integration, which for our model is primarily a matter of numerical analysis and will not be treated in this paper.

These ideas will now be developed intuitively in more detail. For a more formal development, see Zucker 1985a and Parent and Zucker 1985. We concentrate, in this paper, on the two steps that constitute the first stage.

Step 1: Orientation-Sensitive Measurements

Suppose that two arbitrarily close points along a curve are given. The line joining them will be an approximation to the tangent to the curve in a neighborhood of the first point. Since this is what we are after, the problem of estimating the tangent reduces to estimating the line joining nearby points. In actual vision applications, however, noise will be introduced by the sensors, by quantization, and so on. Therefore, the formulation that we seek should allow some degree of flexibility, as in the following re-statement of the problem: Given the trace of the curve (which can be defined as the collection of points through which the curve passes), match a template for a unit line segment (i.e., a unit tangent) with it; or find the unit line segment that agrees most closely with the trace samples in a neighborhood around each point.

This is a mathematical problem, and it can be solved in many ways. We seek a solution in an abstraction of early visual physiology—orientation-ally selective receptive fields—in order to introduce a sense of biological plausibility into our model. Recall that receptive fields of cells in the visual system are methodologically defined by the class of stimuli that influence them. *Orientation selectivity* is a property that requires nonisotropic stimulus patterns, such as bars and lines, and indicates that the response is a function of the orientation of the stimulus. The striate cortex, area V1, is the earliest

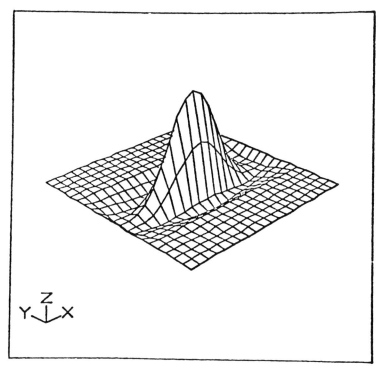

Figure 1
The orientation-sensitive operator used for initial measurements. It can be thought of as
an elongated difference of Gaussians, or as an approximation to the second directional
derivative. Convolutions are performed in n ($= 8$ in our implementation) discrete
orientations.

location in the primate visual system at which any orientation selectivity
can be evoked. When receptive fields here are mapped, some exhibit an
elongated structure with well-defined excitatory and inhibitory regions.
We shall be particularly interested in the subclass of these cells that Hubel
and Wiesel (1968) referred to as *simple cells*. These cells exhibit receptive
fields with a single, usually elongated center and antagonistic surrounds on
either side. We shall model these as an elongated difference of Gaussians
with the form shown in figure 1. Electrophysiologically it has been reported that these cells respond maximally to straight-line stimuli with a
given orientation and location; if either of these is varied, the response
drops.

The initial goal of our model is the inference of a vector field of tangents
whose orientations span 180° in quantized steps. We shall start by abstract-
ing the above receptive fields into mathematical operators that can be

convolved against the image. (This, too, is a gross simplification, since there is some preprocessing of the image into, say, positive and negative contrast versions. Since we are concerned primarily with the geometric properties of arrangements of dots, however, we shall ignore these preprocessing stages in this paper.) For pattern situations in which the points are densely arranged along implicit straight contours, and for which these contours are far enough apart so that they do not overlap within the image support, or receptive field, of the operators, image convolutions are sufficient to recover the underlying orientation. The technique is as follows: First quantize orientation into, say, n steps, and then, at each image location, convolve the image with each of these differently oriented operators. (The receptive fields that underly the operator convolutions can both store the values of the convolutions and represent the orientation to which a value corresponds.) Then, from all the measurements at each point, simply select the one with the strongest response; this will correspond to the operator whose orientation matches the underlying pattern most closely.

But the real situation is more complex than this. Lines are not necessarily straight within the spatial support of a receptive field. Positional and orientational quantization introduce noise, and the basic measurements themselves may be distorted by scene-domain object and light source occlusions. Thus, the strongest local measurement at each position does *not* necessarily signal the correct orientation (Zucker 1982). How, then, might the responses (convolution values) be interpreted?

Step 2: Interpreting the Convolution Values

Conceptually, the key to the interpretation problem lies in noticing that there is important information in the mediocre and low operators' responses as well as in the strong ones. In particular, there is a well-defined operator response profile that can be computed for every expected pattern or conjunction of patterns. These profiles give the response of the operator to a known pattern as a function of orientation. As long as the underlying pattern is straight, the operator's response drops off with orientation, as is typically measured for simple cells. But when the pattern is curved, the expected response varies rather differently with orientation. It is this information that is required to solve the response-interpretation problem.

The generalization now runs as follows. Consider a richer universe of contours, and let the expected response profiles to all local contour configurations be known. (This is straightforward, since we could precompute them.) Label these profiles with the contour over which they were evalu-

ated. The interpretation problem then becomes one of matching the observed response profiles, obtained from an unknown pattern, to these
expected response profiles. The labeling for the best match provides a best
estimate of what the underlying pattern was. In symbols, let $\lambda_i(x, y)$, where
$i = 0, 1, 2, \ldots, n$, be a set of labels indicating the orientation at position
(x, y), with λ_0 denoting a null label. (This label indicates that there is no
oriented entity at that position. It is necessary only to simplify the presentation.) The goal then is to find the labeling $\hat{\lambda}_i(x, y)$ at every position (x, y)
that minimizes the norm difference:

$$\| R_{\exp}(\hat{\lambda}_i; x, y) - R_{\mathrm{obs}}(\lambda_i; x, y) \| \tag{1}$$

For reasons to be described shortly, we refer to this minimization process
as a *type I process*. It can be solved by relaxation labeling techniques
(Hummel and Zucker 1983), and it results in an algorithm that essentially
amounts to lateral inhibition running among differently oriented operators
at neighboring positions. It is a terrific simplification of what is technically
required; for a more detailed description see Zucker 1985a and Parent and
Zucker 1985. It is this cooperative processing (or its equivalent) that is in
principle necessary to solve the general problem. The compatibilities are
proportional to the norm difference in equation 1, and may be viewed as a
sophisticated version of the boundary process sketched by Sejnowski and
Hinton in this volume.

Experiments with the Model on Noisy Contours

Explicit design choices must be made before the above model can be
programmed and tested, and details of the implementation can be found in
Parent and Zucker 1985. In this paper I shall only demonstrate that it
works. See figure 2. Note how the tangent field follows the individual
contours that make up the fingerprint, and how the only thickening results
from inadequate orientation quantization. Only 8 distinct orientations were
represented, perhaps one-third as many as occur in primates (Hubel and
Wiesel 1968). Even with these assumptions, however, it is clear that the
model works and gives just what we are after for type I patterns.

Type I and Type II Patterns

Well-defined, one-dimensional contours are one class of stimuli on which a
theory of orientation selection must work; are there others? Since contours
often arise from *between-surface* events, such as occlusions, it seems logical

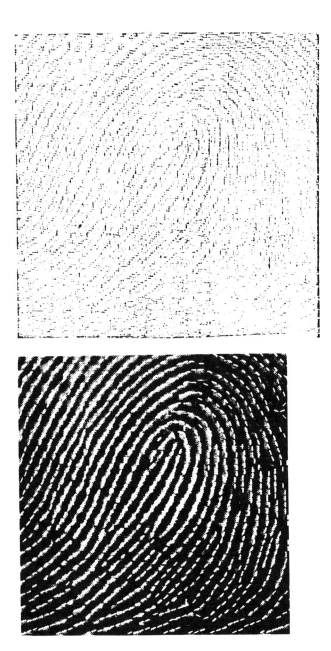

Figure 2
An image of a fingerprint and the computed tangent field.

to look for *within-surface* events that may differ. There is one important class of such events, the structure of which can be understood by considering the image of hair or fur on an animal's body (Stevens 1978). While the structure of the individual hairs is often obscured by occlusion or highlight, the overall flow of the pattern remains clear. The important structural feature of these patterns is that there are no well-defined contours running through them; rather, the flow is filled out from the partial information provided by each piece of visible hair. These flow patterns should be contrasted with the fingerprint pattern just analyzed. Fingerprints consist of packed (but not mathematically dense) arrangements of well-defined contours that cover a surface the same way pinstripes do; there is almost no occlusion or interaction between them. Flow patterns, on the other hand, cover a surface densely. There is no "space" between the "hairs," there are no complete contours (only fragments), and the interaction between them is significant. Flow patterns are, to be somewhat more mathematical, two-dimensional, while type I contours are one-dimensional. That is, if we consider an infinitesimal neighborhood covering part of either a contour or a flow pattern, then, upon close examination, the contour will cover only a one-dimensional subneighborhood running through it. Flow patterns, on the other hand, will occupy the entire neighborhood.

Glass (1969) discovered a way in which analogous patterns can be created artificially: Simply take a pattern of random dots, make a copy of it, transform the copy by a rotation or a translation, and then superimpose the transformed copy on the original. The result is not twice as many random dots, but rather a flow field of exactly the right structure. It, too, contains no well-defined contours running completely through it. Such patterns are referred to as random-dot Moiré patterns (RDMPs).

The model for orientation selection appears to be sufficient for noisy contours; however, as figure 4 shows, it does not work for these RDMPs. The reason follows from the difference in the structure of these patterns as compared with those from the previous section; the interpretation process is based on the expected responses to single, complete contours, not to random, short, and incomplete ones. Clearly, the model for matching must be altered so that additional assumptions related to this variation in the structure of the patterns can be incorporated. Two possibilities are open. First, we could simply acquire new expected response profiles for RDMPs. This would result in a process analogous to the original one, but the precise structural relationship between them would be obscure. The second alternative, which is in a certain sense equivalent, makes the relationship between the processes directly analogous to the relationship between the

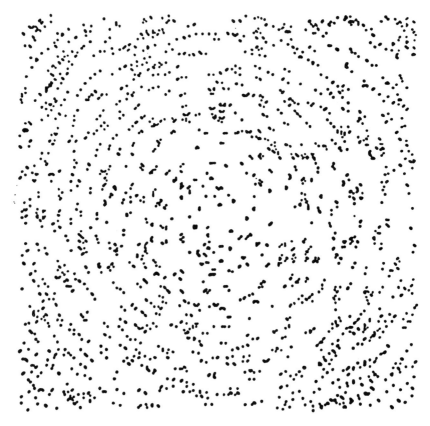

Figure 3

A random-dot Moiré pattern created by taking a pattern of 1,000 dots and superimposing it with a copy rotated about 2°. This is a circular *flow* pattern; there are no individual dotted contours running through.

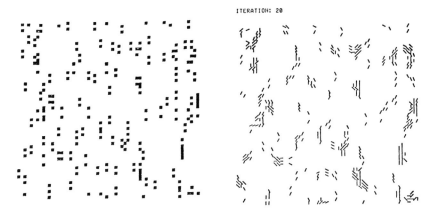

ITERATION: 20

Figure 4
A small section of a random-dot Moiré pattern for computational experiments in which the displacement is vertical. The tangent field computed by the type I process is sparse and inappropriately oriented; it does not resemble the dense field that we seek.

patterns. Since the random nature of RDMP generation can be shown to be equivalent to randomly skewing the positions of the dots perpendicular to their axis of orientation, within the matching process each response should be interpolated—or blurred—across several spatial positions perpendicular to the orientation of the operator. This will have the effect of spreading the orientation formerly associated with just one position to a small region of positions, so that "effective contours" could then be said to exist. It is these effective contours that give rise to the flow associated with this class of patterns. The success of such interpolation strategies is illustrated in figure 5. It is this second process, in which the perpendicular interpolation takes place concurrent with the response matching, that we call a type II process. In symbols, the match now becomes: Find the labeling $\hat{\lambda}_i(x, y)$ at every position (x, y) that minimizes the norm difference:

$$\|R_{\mathrm{exp}}(\hat{\lambda}_i; x, y) - R_{\mathrm{obs}}(\lambda_i; \alpha, \beta)\|, \tag{2}$$

where (α, β) is contained in a local neighborhood around (x, y).

The difference between the formulations of type I and type II processes above illustrates where the names come from. Since the type I matching process takes place only along the curve, it is essentially a one-dimensional process. The type II process, however, which incorporates interpolation in the other direction, is essentially a two-dimensional process. This difference is reflected in the formal matching problems when the specific coordinate (x, y) is replaced by a $\min_{\alpha, \beta}$; see figure 5.

ITERATION: 20

Figure 5
The tangent field computed for the small vertical RDMP in figure 4 with the extra lateral
interpolation, or spreading, included. Now it is dense, and the predominant orientation is
vertical.

Response Matching and Energy Minimization

The common thread through the two processes for orientation selection is
their organization into steps: operator convolution followed by response
interpretation. Since the latter step involves matching by minimization, it
would seem to recall the original Gestalt psychologists' notion that energy
minimization underlaid perceptual grouping. We can now appreciate how
they leaped too rapidly from the abstract study of mechanism to particulars. The key point to emphasize is that, although the abstract framework
was the same for type I and type II processing, the details differ in essential
ways. Conceptualizing them only abstractly in terms of the framework
makes them seem the same. It closes the door to differences. We have
already discussed several of these differences, such as dimensionality and

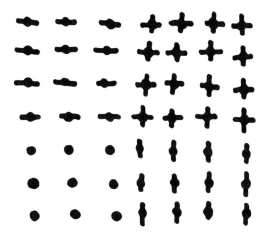

Figure 6
Lateral spreading of tangents. In the neighborhood of a discontinuity, the spreading will overlap, resulting in a "smoothed" field rather than a discontinuity.

their role in vision, and will now address perceptual consequences and possible differences in biological implementation.

Sensitivity Differences between Type I and Type II Processes

Since the essential difference between type I and type II processing is the lateral interpolation or spreading orthogonal to the direction in which tangents are pointing, discontinuities in orientation should be effected differently within type I and type II patterns. The reason is that the interpolation will smear across the discontinuity (figure 6). In particular, the extra interpolation ought to smooth over small differences in orientation. This is exactly what happens. Figure 7 contains two patterns made from identical distributions of dot pairs, with one small difference. In the top pattern, the dot pairs are all arranged along contours so that they form a distribution of type I contours. The small difference in orientation across

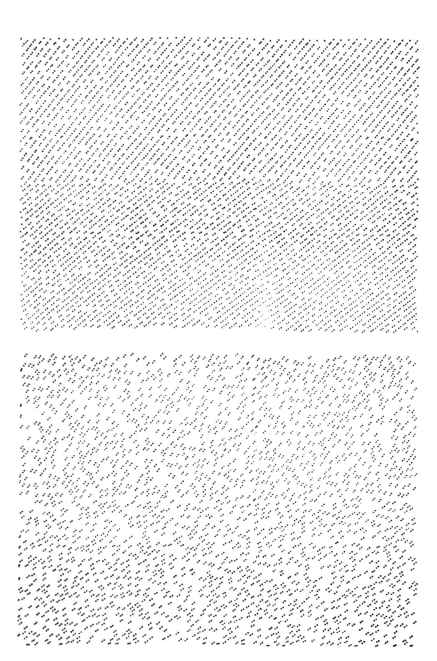

Figure 7

Illustration of the difference between type I and type II orientation selection. The difference in slope is apparent in the top figure, which is composed of "pinstripes," but not in the bottom (RDMP) one. The distribution of orientations of nearest-neighbor dot pairs is identical in the top and bottom illustrations.

the middle of the pattern is immediately obvious. The lower pattern contains the same dot pairs, but spatially arranged uniformly. Now the entire line of discontinuity has been smoothed away, and the entire pattern appears curved. In order to see such discontinuities in type II patterns, a much larger difference in orientation is required (figure 8).

The Physiological Realization of Orientation Selection

In highly simplified neurophysiological terms, the computational differences between type I and type II processes bear a striking resemblance to certain of the differences that have been described between simple and complex cells (Hubel and Wiesel 1968). In particular, simple cells respond to a particular orientation at a particular location; this is exactly the requirement for type I processes. Complex cells respond selectively to orientation, but over a range of positions; this is the requirement for type II processes. Thus, simple and complex cells provide some evidence that the above model is not completely implausible biologically, and this leads us to conjecture that simple cells are involved in type I contour inferencing, whereas complex cells are involved in type II. Actually, the difference is slightly more subtle, since the spatial insensitivity in complex cells results only from the way in which their receptive fields have been mapped. Other patterns, such as RDMPs, should be used as stimuli to reveal their interpolatory role. Whether this conjecture is true will probably also involve motion, a domain in which the type I/type II distinction also seems to hold (Zucker 1983).

Criteria for Grouping and Orientation Selection

The criteria by which the grouping processes could be organized fit together as follows:

Mathematical properties In early orientation selection there were (infinitesimally) one-dimensional and two-dimensional processes. These corresponded, in our terms, to type I and type II processes; their difference was shown mathematically within a functional minimization framework.

Physical scene structure One-dimensional contours arise from occlusions or, when arranged spatially, in fingerprint (and other pin-striped) patterns. Two-dimensional patterns arise from surface coverings, such as hair and fur.

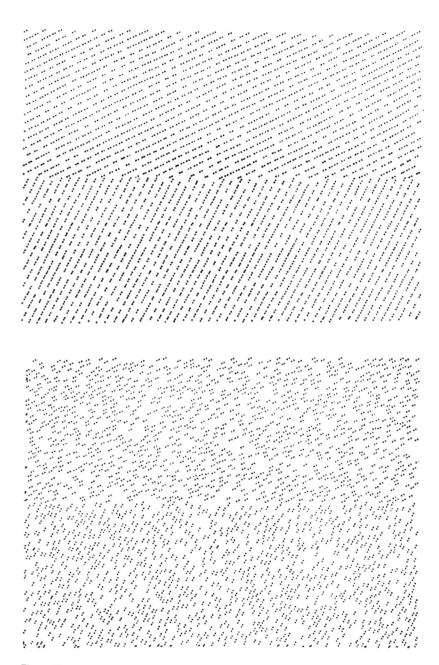

Figure 8
A figure similar to figure 7, but with a larger orientation difference across the discontinuity. Now it can be perceived in both the type I (top) and type II (bottom) patterns.

Computational consequences The difference between type I and type II processing was in the lateral interpolation, or the speading of orientation information orthogonal to the direction of flow.

Emergent psychophysical properties (the sensitivity difference between type I and type II processes).

Physiological implementations It was conjectured that type I processes are realized by simple cells, and type II processes by complex cells.

The Size/Density Constraint: Transition to Higher-Level Processes

The above model for orientation selection begins with local image measurements. Are such measurements likely to be veridical for all patterns of dots? No! For such measurements to succeed, the patterns must satisfy certain structural requirements. Enough dots must fall into appropriate portions of the receptive fields (or image operators) to supply proper initial information. For the case of dot patterns, this amounts to the dots' being fairly dense (with respect to their size). If the dots are not dense enough, the initial information will be spotty at best and wrong or random most of the time. In these latter, sparse situations, dot grouping must be realized by processes that differ in a basic way from the one we have developed for orientation selection. Thus, to echo the opening theme: Whereas curvilinear dot grouping would seem to be a single task abstractly, dense and sparse patterns have different implementation requirements.

Is there any evidence of this difference in processing for sparse as opposed to dense patterns? In a variety of tasks there is, and it is called a size/density constraint. Both size and density are involved because, in brief, the size of the dots selects the size (or scale) of the operators that are most active (the constraint is that they need to fill the central excitatory area but not the inhibitory surround), while the spacing between dots must not exceed their length. If the spacing becomes too great, and the density too low, the first stage of the model is ineffective (Zucker 1985). Such size/density constraints do in fact have psychophysical manifestations. A well-known Kanizsa (1979) pattern has been altered slightly in figure 9 by replacing the solid lines with dotted ones. Note how the subjective edge is clearly present, but that when the dots are made less dense it is no longer inferred. This apparent change occurs abruptly when the density of dots crosses a critical ratio of one dot per five spaces for dots ranging from less than 1 to more than about 15 minutes of visual angle. It almost seems as if the visual system is willing to take dense arrangements of dots as the

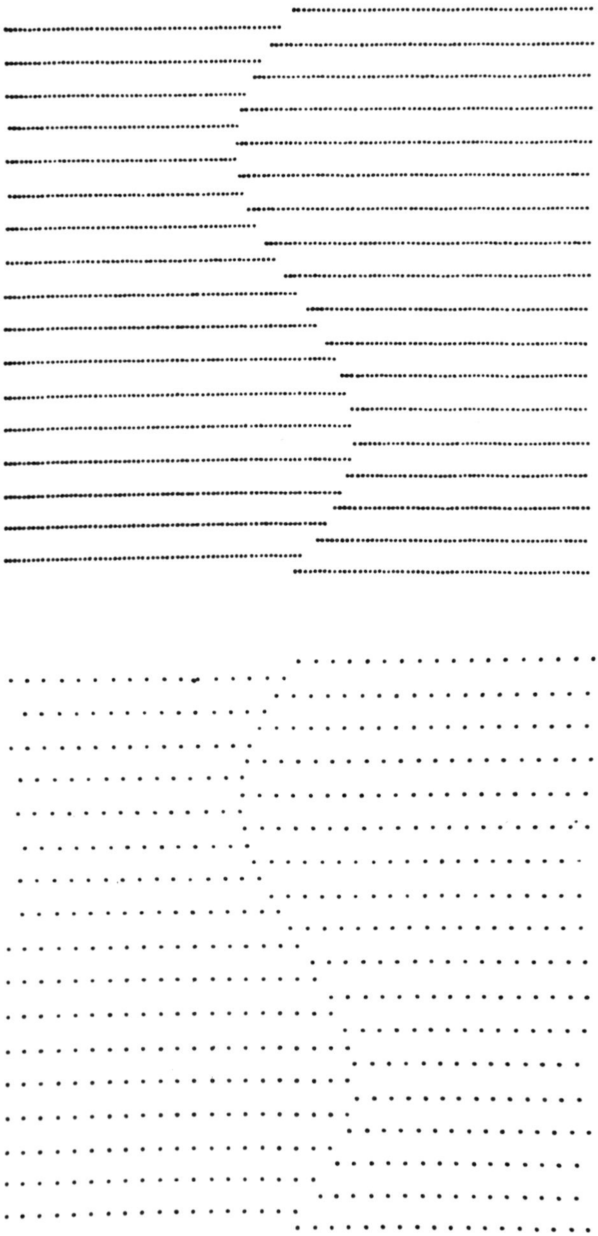

Figure 9
An illustration of the size/density constraint. Note the appearance of the subjective edge, i.e., the apparent difference in depth of the pattern on either side of the edge and the subjective brightness along it. When the dots are made less dense, the subjective effects disappear, although the geometry of the dots may still give rise to grouping effects.

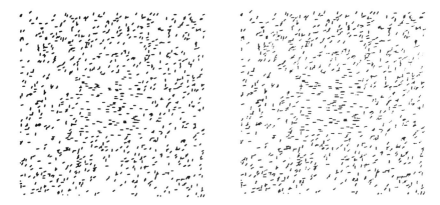

Figure 10
Demonstration that densely dotted contours behave identically to solid contours (with respect to orientation structure) in a texture configuration. The pattern consists of a central region containing only one orientation, while the surround is random. Discrimination is immediate. When the central region is composed of short (solid or dotted) segments of three different orientations, discrimination becomes impossible.

equivalent of solid image structures, so that occlusion processing still holds. When the density becomes sparse enough to require higher-level machinery, however, inferences about occlusion and surfaces must arise by other means.

Other Forms of Grouping

The study of dot grouping is important because it decomposes the geometry of grouping problems from other features, such as intensities or local features. Beck (1982) showed that for a large class of patterns the principal criteria by which items are grouped include orientation (or slope), intensity, color, and movement. This holds both for the grouping of entities into contours and for grouping into clusters. (See also Olson and Attneave 1970; Hochberg and Silverstein 1956; Beck 1966.) Grouping is, further, an integral part of whatever processing is responsible for so-called texture perception, and similar variables are implicated (Julesz 1981). For example, it can be shown that various texture-discrimination tasks with densely dotted contours are analogous to the same tasks with solid contours (figure 10), but that this is not the case for sparsely dotted contours (Zucker 1982).

Computational models for certain texture-grouping tasks can be formulated in abstract terms that will have some aspects in common with those formulated for orientation selection (e.g., the grouping of dots into clusters, a two-dimensional extension; see Zucker and Hummel 1979), although the initial measurement stage will certainly be more sophisticated. Such models may have to be extended to include certain phenomenal relationships as well (Rock and Brosgole 1964). It is not clear whether similar models hold for the types of test stimuli used by Beck and Julesz, which are (relatively sparse) arrangements of patterns.

Other significant differences begin to emerge when one considers further roles for grouping. In an interesting interpolation task, Morgan and Watt (1982) considered how densely an intensity function must be sampled before its reconstruction degrades. His finding was that, for certain intensity functions, a sampling of only one foveal receptor in ten is sufficient for acuity tasks indicating 100 times as much resolution. Such results become relevant to grouping tasks when one considers a view of the world through a picket fence. In this case a regular obstruction occludes the world behind it. Somehow the visual system must "group" the correct portions of the retinal image so that appropriate interpolation functions can be applied. If interpolation were carried out using all the data, or even some of the incorrect data, clear inconsistencies would emerge. Thus, such grouping processes amount to "selection" processes active in both intensity and disparity spaces. Another side of such selection processes is discussed in Binford 1981.

An impressive series of examples illustrating how other "selection" processes can trigger the inference of subjective edges was discovered by Kanizsa (1979); see figure 11, which shows a subjective triangle that is apparently interpreted as an invisible but occluding surface in front of three circles (Coren 1972). Many other related examples are possible; see Kanizsa 1979. These grouping processes are clearly much more complicated than those described in the previous section, although in both cases local, discrete events trigger the inference of subjective entities. Several authors have attempted theories of subjective contour construction (see, e.g., Ullman 1976), but no one has yet produced a selection theory of the "trigger features."

The preceding section of this paper was concerned with orientation selection as it is inferred from intensity patterns (arrangements of dots). Orientation structures arising from subjective figures can play a salient role in subjective patterns as well, as is shown by the texture-discrimination task illustrated in figure 12. Here the texture is either a regular structure—the Ehrenstein illusion—or it is a phase-shifted (control) version of it. When the Ehrenstein pattern is viewed as shown, it is barely discriminable

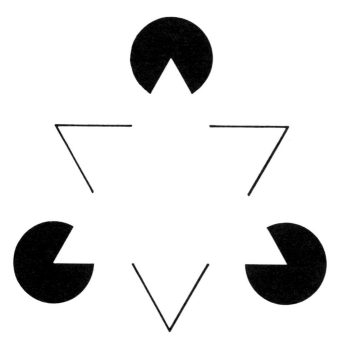

Figure 11
A Kanizsa subjective triangle (after Kanizsa 1979).

from the control pattern. When the two patterns are rotated 45°, however, there is a significant jump in discriminability (Zucker and Cavanagh 1985). The reason, it can be argued, is that at 45° the subjective "spots" form subjective "swaths" that are highly discriminable. Should these swaths be viewed as the result of grouping processes on the spots?

For a final example of an abstract form of grouping, let us return to dots through another demonstration by Kanizsa; see figure 13, in which the dots appear to be joined by what might be referred to as virtual lines (Stevens 1978). These vitual lines appear to arise in many long-distance grouping tasks, and the illustration shows that they can influence other perceptual judgments. The significant property of this configuration that I would like to emphasize is that it is primarily the geometry that matters; the same effect can be shown to take place even when the inducing dots are of different contrast (with respect to the background). Since grouping processes are usually associated with surface inferencing tasks, it is normally assumed that they operate on units that are likely to come from the same surface. Whereas surface orientation or light-source effects may make absolute intensities unreliable in this regard, most grouping tasks appear to require

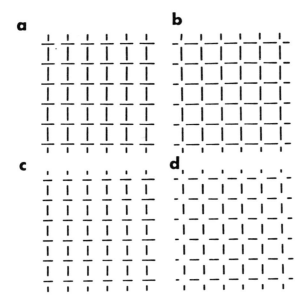

Figure 12
The Ehrenstein illusion (b and d) and a control (shifted) pattern. Subjective "spots" are present in both the Ehrenstein and the control; but when the page is rotated 45° the Ehrenstein "spots" form into "swaths," making discrimination between the patterns significantly better.

that the entities over which they operate have the same contrast sign. Early tasks can be shown to never group across contrast sign changes (Zucker et al. 1983), even ones on the sparse side of the size/density constraint. This last example does. Clearly, the mechanism responsible for these "higher-level" grouping processes must differ from those proposed for early orientation selection.

From Environmental Structure to Perceptual Function

Images are formed by a myriad of physical processes involving light, surface reflectance, transparency, and so on. The equations of photometry allow us to calculate the precise structure of an image given the structure of the physical scene, but, of course, not to go in the other direction. This is the task of vision. Or, stated in different terms, the process of image formation is what is known in mathematics as a forward problem; the process of vision is an inverse problem. The solution to this inverse problem is, of course, underdetermined; there are an infinite number of physical

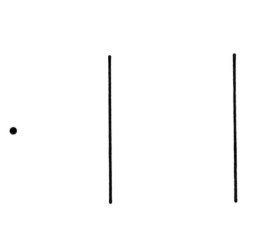

Figure 13
The Ponzo illusion (after Kanizsa 1979). It can be induced by three points, regardless of
their contrast sign, thus implying that it results from a much higher-level process than the
early grouping of dots.

scenes that would give rise to an identical image. How, then, can this
inverse problem be solved? Clearly, additional constraints are required,
perhaps in the form of high-level, "semantic" assumptions about particular
objects that define the class of scenes. The classical example is that if the
system "knows" it is looking for a "telephone," then assumptions about
color, size, shape, etc. can be made. This is possible in certain restricted
environments, such as industrial inspection (Dodd and Rossol 1979), but
there is no hope of finding such universal assumptions for general scene
domains. Rather, the solution is to be found in decomposition of the full
problem into a collection of many "smaller" problems. Here "smaller" has
many different meanings, all of which are related to locality; the problem
might be spatially localized, conceptually or semantically localized, or both.
For example, instead of trying to find an inverse mapping from images to
scenes, one should try to structure a collection of mappings from, say,
images to local contours, from local contours to longer ones, to closed
contours, to bounded surface patches (using the surface contours as boundary conditions to constrain stereo and shape-from-shading estimates), and
so on. This is exactly the kind of reasoning that is present in the Dewey
Decimal System; books are organized into a collection of categories, each

of which branches only a few times, rather than arbitrarily many. For a specific discussion relating grouping to indices into complex data bases, see Lowe 1984. (Another form of this argument can be related to pseudo-inverse theory; see Kimia et al. 1984.)

Given this overall model, we can now see how to add the additional assumptions necessary for the vision problem: Since few (if any) of the individual local inverse problems have unique solutions (that is, are one-to-one), assumptions will have to be made for each of them. For the first of these problems, the assumptions will be very general; i.e., they will hold over wide classes of image structure. (In fact, most of this paper was concerned with some of the earliest of these assumptions, namely those that deal with orientation selection.) It thus follows that, since the local problems are different, the assumptions required to solve them will be different. One special case of this conclusion is that, since some of these local problems will be grouping problems, they will all differ.

Conclusions

The study of a complex process, of which vision surely is an example, can proceed only if one decomposes it into smaller, more manageable "chunks." How, then, is one to decide on the size, or the granularity, of these chunks? Previous attempts to approach vision have tended to be rather coarse in the decomposition; consider, e.g., the preattentive/attentive distinction introduced by Neisser (1967) and now carried on by Triesman (1983) and Julesz, the serial/parallel distinction that has been popular in psychology, or the early-processing/later-processing distinction common today in computational vision. Though such "large-grain" or coarse decompositions have played a role in bringing us to the present understanding, it is now time to take a much more fine-grained look at vision. The particular decomposition that I have attacked is one that is widely accepted today; namely, that perceptual grouping is a distinct process recursively applied to increasingly more abstract entities. My position, in contrast, is that grouping consists of a diversity of processes, and that it is only by confronting this diversity that real progress will be made.

The process of imaging the physical world decomposes it into an array of discrete, disconnected intensities. Subsequent processing replaces these intensities with more abstract entities, each of which is local in some sense. It is the task of grouping processes to agglomerate these local entities into more global ones according to homogeneity criteria. But as these criteria become more specified, it is readily seen that they encompass much of the structure of the visual process. The result is that grouping is not one simple class of processes, but rather is a diverse collection of increasingly more complex ones.

The purpose of this paper was to begin to sketch this complexity. I began with the seemingly distinct task of orientation selection, and derived a (biologically feasible) model for accomplishing it. Two consequences were immediate from this model: that orientation selection must take place differently within different pattern classes (two of which were identified) and that very early processing stages, such as those that could be accomplished by simple and complex cells and their interactions, give rise to psychophysical differences from those that are of necessity more abstract. Some of these early consequences were summarized as a size/density constraint.

More abstract forms of grouping still appear to be connected with surface inferencing tasks, although the precise mechanisms governing them remain to be studied in most cases. Some are extremely well known, such as Kanizsa subjective edges, and are believed to involve constraints about surface occlusion. But no convincing models exist. One of these subjective effects even allows grouping to take place across contrast sign changes, which suggests that it is taking place at a rather high level. The models for the earlier forms of grouping certainly cannot account for it.

Acknowledgments

An earlier version of this paper was presented at the workshop on Vision, Brain, and Cooperative Computation at the University of Massachusetts. Amherst, in 1983. Research was supported by NSERC grant A4470. The simulation was developed with Pierre Parent, and the psychophysics were done with Norah Link. I thank them and Yvan Leclerc for comments on the manuscript.

References

Beck, J. 1966. Effect of orientation and shape similarity on perceptual grouping. *Perception and Psychophysics* 1: 300–302.

Beck, J. 1982. Textural segmentation. In *Organization and Representation in Perception*, ed. J. Beck (Erlbaum).

Binford, T. 1981. Inferring surfaces from images. *Artificial Intelligence* 17: 205–245.

Coren, S. 1972. Subjective contours and apparent depth. *Psych. Rev.* 79: 359–367.

Dodd, G., and L. Rossol. 1979. *Computer Vision and Sensor-Based Robots*. Plenum.

Glass, L. 1969. Moiré effect from random dots. *Nature* 243: 578–580.

Hochberg, J., and A. Silverstein. 1956. A quantitative index of similarity: Proximity versus difference in brightness. *Am. J. Psychology* 69: 456–468.

Hubel, D., and T. Wiesel. 1968. Receptive fields and functional architecture of monkey striate cortex. *J. Physiol. (Lond.)* 195: 215–243.

Hummel, R. A., and S. W. Zucker. 1983. On the foundations of relaxation labeling processes. *IEEE Trans. Pattern Analysis and Machine Intelligence* 5: 267–287.

Julesz, B. 1981. Textons, the elements of texture perception, and their interactions. *Nature* 290: 91–97.

Kanizsa G. 1979. *Organization in Vision*. Praeger.

Kimia, B., R. Hummel, and S. W. Zucker. 1984. Deblurring Gaussian Blur. Technical Report, Computer Vision and Robotics Lab, McGill University.

Koffka, K. 1935. *Principles of Gestalt Psychology*. Harcourt, Brace.

Köhler, W. 1920. *Die physischen Gestalten in Ruhe und im stationären Zustand*.

Kubovy, M., and J. Pomerantz. 1981. *Perceptual Organization*. Erlbaum.

Leclerc, Y., and S. W. Zucker. 1984. The local structure of intensity discontinuities in one dimension. In proceedings of Seventh International Conference on Pattern Recognition, Montreal.

Lowe, D. 1984. Perceptual Organization and Visual Recognition. Ph.D. thesis, Stanford University.

Marr, D. 1982. *Vision*. Freeman.

Morgan, M., and R. Watt. 1982. Mechanisms of interpolation in human spatial vision. *Nature* 299: 553–555.

Neisser, U. 1967. *Cognitive Psychology*. Appleton-Century-Crofts.

Olson, R. K., and F. Attneave. 1970. What variables produce similarity grouping? *Am. J. Psychology* 83: 1–21.

Parent, P., and S. W. Zucker. 1985. Co-Circularity and the Role of Curvature in Curve Detection. Technical report, Computer Vision and Robotics Lab, McGill University.

Rock, I., and L. Brosgole. 1964. Grouping based on phenomenal proximity. *J. Exp. Psychology* 67: 531–538.

Stevens, K. 1978. Computation of locally parallel structure. *Biol. Cyber.* 29: 19–26.

Triesman, A. 1983. The role of attention in object perception. In *Physical and Biological Processing of Images*, ed. O. Braddick and A. Sleigh (Springer).

Ullman, S. 1976. Filling in the gaps: The shape of subjective contours and a model for their generation. *Biol. Cyber.* 25: 1–6.

Uttal, W. 1981. *A Taxonomy of Visual Processes*. Erlbaum.

Wertheimer, M. 1923. Laws of organization in perceptual forms. *Psych. Forsch.* 4: 301–350. Reprinted in *A Source Book of Gestalt Psychology*, ed. W. Ellis (Routledge & Kegan Paul, 1938).

Zucker, S. 1982. Early Orientation Selection and Grouping: Evidence for Type I and Type II Processes. Technical Report 82–8, Department of Electrical Engineering, McGill University.

Zucker, S. W. 1983a. Cooperative grouping and early orientation selection. In *Physical and Biological Processing of Images*, ed. O. Braddick and A. Sleigh (Springer).

Zucker, S. W. 1983b. The Fox and the Forest: A Type I, Type II Constraint for Early Optical Flow. Technical Report 83–11, McGill University; presented at ACM Workshop on Motion: Representation and Control, Toronto.

Zucker, S. W. 1985. Early orientation selection and grouping. In *From Pixels to Predicates: Progress in Computer Vision*, ed. A. Pentland (Ablex).

Zucker, S. W., and P. Cavanaugh. 1985. Subjective Figures and Texture Perception. Technical report, Computer Vision and Robotics Lab, McGill University.

Zucker, S. W., and R. A. Hummel. 1979. Toward a low-level description of dot clusters: Labelling edge, interior, and noise points. *Computer Graphics and Image Processing* 9: 213–233.

Zucker, S. W., and P. Parent. 1982. Multiple size operators and optimal curve finding. In Proceedings of the International Conference on Pattern Recognition, Munich.

Zucker, S. W., K. Stevens, and P. Sander. 1983. The relation between brightness and proximity in dot patterns. *Perception and Psychophysics* 34: 513–522.

8

The Interdependence of Temporal and Spatial Information in Early Vision

Peter J. Burt

The visual system is limited in its computing power. There are limits to the complexity of objects and situations that can be perceived and to the speed at which these perceptions can be achieved. In the very first steps of visual information processing, in "early vision," there are limits to the rate at which new information from a changing scene can be sensed and encoded.

The factors limiting the visual system's capabilities may be analogous to those that limit processing in a computer, particularly a computer with a distributed, highly parallel architecture. These factors include the number and speed of computing elements, the complexity of their computations, the speed of communications between elements, and the overall organization of the system.

To turn this view around: An examination of the visual system's limitations may provide insight into its computational structure. This is particularly true for early vision, where computations are imagined to be relatively simple and information to be represented in a spatial rather than symbolic form. The system's ability to resolve image changes in space and in time then may be used as a measure of its information-processing capabilities. There are tradeoffs between spatial and temporal resolution when objects move. It may be presumed that these reflect an organization that makes optimal use of the available computing resources to extract useful information from the image and pass it to later stages of processing.

In the following discussion I will examine several relationships that may exist between resolution achieved in vision and the organization of the underlying computations. The development is not intended to be complete, and no attempt is made to review the considerable literature relating these issues. I will distinguish two types of processes in early vision. The first is concerned with the afferent flow of information from the receptors through early processing to higher-level vision. It is assumed that these computations are organized as sequences of filter-like operations within a set of parallel channels. Important characteristics of such processes may be stated in the language of linear systems and information theory. The second type of process is concerned with efferent projection, or feedback, from later stages of processing which modify and control earlier stages. A primary function of efferent processes is to segment the incoming flow of image information while it is still represented in a spatially and temporal organized fashion. Interactions between afferent and efferent processes may be regarded as a form of cooperative computation. It appears likely that these two processes will have quite different space/time characteristics. Much of the debate at the workshop at which this paper was presented concerned the importance, or even the existance, of processes of the second type.

Information Rates and Representations

How much information can be processed by the visual system per second? One estimate of the information rate in early vision is provided by Shannon's information theory under the assumption that the input signal (the image) is a random process that is band-limited in time and space. Such band limits include the inevitable effects of blur due to the optics of the eyes and spatial and temporal integration at each stage of neural processing. In fact, the Shannon estimate must be regarded as an upper bound on the actual information rate which is far less due to redundancy in the image. The input signal is not random but structured, since objects present characteristic, often familiar spatial patterns, which move coherently in time.

Computational efficiency is determined in large part by the way information is encoded. The visual system can take advantage of structure in the signal to reduce its computational burden and to improve its performance. However, it does so only to the extent that it extracts the structure as it encodes the signal. Strictly speaking, a perfect representation is one that removes all structure, leaving a completely random residue to be processed. However, the encoding process itself requires considerable computation, and an optimal balance between the cost of encoding and the cost of subsequent analysis is obtained when the representation removes some but not all of the image structure. In early vision, this might be a representation in which simple generic patterns, such as edges, constitute the code elements. The representation then becomes more complex in succeeding stages of processing as progressively more image structure is removed.

We may use Shannon's measure to specify the efficiency of an encoding scheme. Let the "effective information rate" at a given stage of vision be defined as the rate obtained under the assumption that all code elements at this stage are independent. Let the "actual information rate" be the rate that could be obtained if an optimal code were used in which the code elements were indeed independent. The ratio of actual to effective rates then gives the efficiency of the representation. The effective information rate decreases with each successive stage of processing as the efficiency and the complexity of the representation are increased.

The effective information rate may be used in turn to predict the functional relationship between temporal and spatial resolution in perception when objects move in the visual field. Consider a very early stage of vision in which processing is effectively just a low-pass filter. If the frequency limits are f_x, f_y, and f_t in the x, y, and time dimensions, respectively, then the signal can be exactly represented by discrete samples taken at the Nyquist rate, or $8f_xf_yf_t$ samples per unit solid angle per second. Suppose in addition that the system has sufficient computing power to process a fixed maximum number of samples, R, per second per unit of solid angle. Then we must have $8f_xf_yf_t \leq R$ at all times. If an object moving in the x direction at velocity v has a maximum resolvable spatial frequency in that direction of $\hat{f}_x$, then the maximum temporal frequency will be $\hat{f}_t = v\hat{f}_x$. Our constraint becomes $\hat{f}_x f_y \hat{f}_t = 8v\hat{f}_x^2 fy \leq R$, or

$$\hat{f}_x \propto \frac{1}{\sqrt{v}}. \tag{1}$$

It is predicted that spatial resolution in the direction of motion decreases with the square root of velocity. This estimate of the decrease in spatial resolution with velocity may be realistic for a computer system in which performance is limited by the rate at which a central processing element can handle data sample. However, it is probably an optimistic estimate for the human visual system. We often think of the latter as a highly parallel network of computing elements, each of which is dedicated to a particular type of data (e.g. a particular spatial frequency and position in the visual field). Performance is then limited by the inability of elements to change their functions (as in a general-purpose computer) and by limitations in the rate at which data can be communicated between elements. In this view, each processing element will have a maximum temporal frequency at which it may function. When an object moves with a velocity that exceeds the limit for a particular unit, the unit becomes idle. Thus, image motion results in a reduction in the overall information rate of the system.

An estimate of the relationship between temporal and spatial resolution for a distributed computing system may be obtained as follows. Suppose that computing elements form spatial-frequency-tuned channels, and that all channels have the same limiting temporal rate, T. Then $v\hat{f}_x = \hat{f}_t \le T$, and

$$\hat{f}_x \propto \frac{1}{v}. \tag{2}$$

It is predicted that spatial resolution decreases inversely with v, or more rapidly then when general-purpose computing elements are assumed. (See equation 1.) Evidence from psychophysical experiments suggests it is this simple inverse relationship that holds in human vision (Kelly 1979; Burr and Ross, in this volume).

Motion has almost no effect on the information content of an image, since the primary changes are in pattern position rather than pattern detail. (There may be a slight increase in available information with velocity as background patterns are uncovered when foreground objects move or new objects move into view.) The rapid degradation of spatial resolution with motion expressed in equations 1 and 2 indicates that the image representations are inefficient. This is due to our assumption that the system treats temporal and spatial changes as independent, whereas in the case of simple motion they are almost exactly correlated. The system could perform a great deal better if moving patterns were represented directly as code elements.

Snapshots and the What-Where Duality

The situation described in the preceding section presents a paradox: Object motion results in image blur and reduced system performance at the same time that it causes processing elements tuned to high spatial frequencies to become idle. The efficiency of such a system would be improved if the constraints imposed by motion could be removed. Suppose that "snapshots" of a changing scene were taken at regular intervals in time and then processed separately. Without temporal change, the full spatial resolution of the system would become available and its computing resources could be fully utilized. In this way the system's efficiency and spatial resolution would be improved, although at the cost of reduced resolution for image motion. This tradeoff is reminiscent of the Heisenberg uncertainty relationship in physics: Changes in temporal sampling which lead to increased accuracy of shape estimates result in reduced accuracy of position and motion estimates.

In signal-processing terms, improved spatial resolution is obtained by permitting temporal sampling to fall below the Nyquist rate. If the signal were properly filtered in time prior to sampling, the spatial resolution of moving patterns would be reduced. By omitting this temporal filter, the full spatial resolution is retained, but at the cost of introducing ambiguities in how patterns change from moment to moment. This would be completely unacceptable if the signal itself were a random process, but it may be acceptable with the highly structured images encountered in the real world. Because object motions result in coherent displacement of extended pattern, motion detected in unaliased low spatial frequencies may be used disambiguate motion in higher, aliased, frequencies.

What sampling should be adopted by a biological system in order to make the optimal use of its computing resources? An expedient strategy might be to divide these resources between two systems, one of which uses temporal subsampling to enhance object recognition while the other maintains full temporal sampling to obtain more precise measures of object position and velocity. The resulting dual system is suggestive of the "what" and "where" systems postulated in vision (Schneider 1969). The dual scheme may be expected to work reliably when moving objects are isolated from one another so that motions observed in the high-temporal-resolution system can be unambiguously associated with objects observed by the high-spatial-resolution system.

Sampling in Space and Time

Let us now adopt the relationship expressed in equation 2—that spatial resolution attained in perception decreases in inverse proportion to pattern velocity—as a working hypothesis. In a qualitative sense, this expresses a familiar experience. If one waves a hand in front of one's face, it is difficult to count the fingers. Performance in reading an eye-test chart would decrease markedly if the doctor insisted on moving the chart. Again the relationship is reasonable from a computational point of view, as it acknowledges a limit to the information-processing capabilities of the system.

Let us also suppose that motion analysis takes place within a set of spatial-frequency-tuned channels similar to the channels described by psychologists and postulated in various visual-perception functions. It follows from our hypothesis that motion analysis of rapidly moving images is carried out in low-frequency channels, whereas processing of low velocities is carried out in (or includes) high-frequency channels. Assume that the same temporal-frequency limit applies to all channels, so that their effective temporal sampling rates may also be identical. It may be further assumed,

without loss of generality, that pattern information in low-frequency channels is represented at reduced sample density, in accordance with the
Nyquist rate (as in the "pyramid" image representations used in computer
vision [Burt 1984]). It then follows that the range of image velocities
handled by each channel is exactly the same as all others when velocity is
expressed in terms of the channel sampling distance. In short, computations
are independent of channel. Only the resolution and spatial sample density
of image information changes from channel to channel.

Fixed Limits and Perceptual Scaling

The relationship between spatial resolution and velocity stated in our
hypothesis (equation 2) is not the simplest we might have considered.
Instead, it might have been supposed that there are essentially independent
limits to spatial resolution and velocity: When pattern velocity is less than
some fixed velocity limit (V_{max}), all pattern details that are larger than some
fixed spatial limit (d_{min}) can be perceived, whereas no details can be perceived when pattern velocity is significantly larger than the velocity limit.

The notion that fixed limits exist in spatial resolution and velocity may
be compared to the classical notion of a Panum's fusional limit in stereopsis
(about 7 minutes of arc in central vision), or to the idea of short-range
processes in apparent motion (15 minutes of arc [Braddick 1974]). The
existence of such limiting distances in perception has important implications for the computations underlying perception. It may be assumed that
such computations take place within a retinotopically organized neural
structure. A spatial limiting distance in perception may imply that lateral
interactions in this structure are restricted to a corresponding neural distance. In the present case this limit is imagined to be independent of the
image information being processed. By contrast, the limit implied by equation 2 is proportional to spatial wave lengths within the image. This also
becomes a fixed neural distance in spatial frequency channels if subsampling is assumed to follow the Nyquist rate.

In recent years it has been found that many aspects of perception obey
scale independence. That is, if a pattern is perceived in a certain way when
it occurs at one size, then it will be perceived in the same way if its size is
increased or decreased uniformly by some scaling factor. For example, if a
stereogram appears fused at one scale, it will still appear fused when its
scale is doubled or quadrupled, even though disparities within the new
stereogram may exceed the classical Panum's fusional limit by many times
(Tyler 1973; Burt and Julesz 1980). The same has been found to hold in

texture perception (Tyler and Chang 1977) and for certain types of motion (Lappin and Bell 1976; Burt and Sperling 1981). Scaling phenomena of this sort are generally inconsistent with the notion of image-independent fixed limits.

Equation 2 suggests that a similar scaling property should hold in the perception of detail in moving patterns. If an image containing motion is changed by some scale factor, both pattern detail and velocity are changed by the same factor. Thus, details visible before the scale change should still be visible after the change, even though the patterns may be moving many times faster.

Time-Space Asymmetry

Why should time not be considered simply as a third spatial dimension, equivalent to the two dimensions that define the image plane? Then the temporal dimension of perception would be functionally related to the spatial dimensions in the same way that spatial dimensions are related to one another. For example, just as we may apply edge operators in the spatial domain to determine the orientation of a contour, we can apply edge operators in time-space to determine the velocity of moving objects. Or, just as we may analyze stationary patterns in terms of their spatial frequency components, we may analyze moving patterns in terms of their spatial-temporal frequency components. In short, when considering the interdependence of time and space in perception, it may not be necessary to make any particular distinction between the temporal and spatial dimensions.

As one test of time-space equivalence, we may ask whether perceptual scaling applies in the temporal dimension as it does in the spatial dimension. Such a proportional relation between optimal spatial and temporal intervals for apparent motion was suggested by the Gestalt psychologists, and is expressed in Korte's "laws." However, recent experiments provide contrary evidence. For example, Burt and Sperling (1981) found scaling to hold in spatial dimensions while a fixed interval of about 20 msec was "optimal" in the temporal domain, regardless of spatial scale.

Perception Is an Organization Process

Implicit in the foregoing discussion is the notion that computations performed in early vision are filter-like. One imagines that the afferent flow of information divides into a set of more or less independent channels, in each of which it undergoes a sequence of relatively simple processing steps. These steps serve to enhance certain pattern elements, or to integrate previously enhanced elements into more complex property measures. Early vision may be regarded as a set of processes that compute image properties within local image regions. These properties become the basis of object perception in later stages of image analysis.

However, perception cannot be based on property measurements alone. In order to interpret complex scenes, the visual system must often draw on its own knowledge of physical objects and its environment. In effect, the system attempts to construct an "internal model" of the three-dimensional world it is viewing that is consistent with the information available in the two-dimensional images and that satisfies constraints on how objects may interact in the physical world.

Active model-building processes play an essential role even in early vision. Such processes are required to segment, or parse, the image into regions which may correspond to separate physical objects. These segmenting processes may be said to organize the stimulus through efferent control of the property-measuring processes considered above. For example, efferent control may place constraints on processes that measure local texture statistics, so that measures are not computed within regions that cross segment boundaries. Such measures would confound properties of different objects and obscure the boundaries between these objects. In broad terms, the early-stimulus-organizing processes enforce a "use once" constraint, to ensure that a given image point is not interpreted as part of more than one object.

The afferent-property-estimating processes and the efferent-organizing processes interact with one another in cooperative computation. Even as organizing processes constrain the image segments in which properties are measured, these measures are used to determine the locations of segment boundaries. The iterative computation might begin with unconstrained property measures which serve to determine the rough locations of prominent segments boundaries. The properties are then reestimated subject to the constraint that they not be computed in windows that cross the initial boundary locations. The resulting improved property measures can be used to refine estimates of boundary positions and to detect less prominent boundaries.

Evidence

Cooperative computation has been studied extensively in the context of stereopsis (Julesz 1971; Dev 1975; Marr and Poggio 1976). Motion-

Figure 1
In this well-known ambiguous figure it seems impossible to see both the faces and the vase at the same time.

analysis procedures that involve relaxation or minimization through distributed interative computation may also be considered instances of cooperative computation (Barnard and Thompson 1980; Prager and Arbib 1983; Horn and Schunck 1981). Processes that segment images may involve cooperative computation, as suggested above. I will use examples of this latter sort to motivate further discussion.

To begin, consider the familiar figure-ground problem illustrated in figure 1. One explanation of why the faces and the vase cannot be perceived simultaneously goes as follows: If the visual system interprets a particular line within an image as part of the outline of an object, then it treats that line as an occluding contour. Points on such a contour are perceptually associated with just one of the regions the contour separates, in this case the region to the right or the left. At the same time, the region on the other side is perceived to be occluded and hence to have no visible boundary. Thus, when the contours in the figure are perceptually associated with the face regions, the vase is left without defining contours and cannot be seen. However, if the contour lines are doubled (figure 2), enough contours exist to define both the faces and the vase, so all can be seen simultaneously.

The important point to be made here is that an association or link must be established between each local feature and a global region. These links enforce the "use once" constraint, preventing any single edge point from being associated with two regions at once. The set of links define what I shall refer to as an *organization map*.

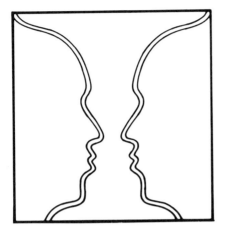

Figure 2
Both the faces and the vase can be seen simultaneously if the contour lines are doubled.
Thus, the mechanism that prevents simultaneous perception in figure 1 must operate
locally between line elements (low-level description) rather than globally between face
and vase percepts (high-level description).

A second, somewhat more subtle example of perceptual organization is
illustrated by figure 3. This ambiguous drawing may be interpreted as a
duck (looking left) or a rabbit (looking right), but apparently it is never seen
as both at once. To account for mutual exclusion of the global percepts, we
may postulate an organization map between one global percept (duck or
rabbit) and the individual image points. Thus, when the map links the duck
and the image points, these points are no longer available for the rabbit.

Resolution of the Organization Map in Space and Time

The organization map outlined above must be spatially precise if each
resolvable image point is to be mapped to just one global interpretation
(organization). This raises an interesting question: Just how can such a
highly articulated map be represented within a neural structure, particularly
if it exists between a spatially amorphous construct (such as the perceived
"duck") and a spatially precise structure (the image)?

One answer might be that the map is not as precise as has been suggested here. Rather mutual exclusion is enforced by a map of rather low
resolution. A link might indicate, in effect, that all contour points within
such-and-such general region of the image are assigned to the duck percept
and so are not available for any other percept, including the rabbit. How-

Figure 3
This figure may be seen as a rabbit looking right or a duck looking left. However, the duck and the rabbit cannot be seen simultaneously.

ever, the suggestion that the map has limited resolution is not altogether satisfactory. For example, it implies that separate duck and rabbit images that happen to occur sufficiently close to one another, within the resolution limit of the organization map, could not both be perceived at the same time (figure 4).

The case for high resolution in the map can also be made with the face-vase figure. When contours are doubled (figure 2), these nearby contours are somehow mapped to separate percepts. It is probably safe to assume that a process that uses feedback to modify earlier processes will take appreciably longer to complete its computation than a process that measures image properties directly. Thus, efferent-organizing processes are expected to have comparable spatial resolution and reduced temporal resolution in relation to the afferent property measures.

Time-Space Interdependence and "Moving Memories"

What happens to the organization map when objects within an image are moving, or when the image as a whole is displaced because of the observer's motion? Suppose that the resolution distance of the organization map is d and the time to generate the map after the presentation of a new image is t. Must a new map be generated every time the image is displaced a distance d, when it is no longer in register with the current map? If so, there should be a maximum velocity, $v = d/t$, at which perceptual organization can be maintained. Our observations that d is small and t is large suggest that this limiting velocity must be quite small. It is likely that the spatial resolution of the organization map decreases inversely with image velocity, just as was suggested for image-property measurements in equation 2. Then d should increase in proportion to v.

Another possibility is that the organization map can itself be moved

Figure 4
If the mutual exclusion of the duck and rabbit percepts in figure 3 is due to competition at a high level of image description, where position information is represented with low spatial resolution, then it should be impossible to see both a duck and a rabbit if they stand too close to one another.

within its supporting neural structure in coincidence with and in anticipation of image motion. In this way, high resolution could be maintained at velocities considerably greater than would be suggested by the ratio d/t. However, a question remains: How can we model a neural structure that supports a pattern of activity (representing the organization map) that is spatially articulated and yet can move?

To use a computer analogy; Suppose that the image is available in an array $I(x, y)$ and that the organization map is represented in an array $M(x, y)$. Then as the image shifts within I the contents of M should shift as well. This is possible if M is structured as a shift-register memory, so that the contents of each memory cell can be passed to neighboring cells at a rate appropriate for the given image velocity.

A possible neural network realization of the shifting property was suggested in Burt 1975. Certain local interactions are postulated which cause the network to act like an elastic medium on which patterns of neural activity ("moving memories") may propagate like waves on water. The velocity of propagation is determined by the elastic "constant" of the network. This is controlled by the output of a second network, where the level of neural activity represents perceived object velocity. The organization map and the image information are represented in separate but interacting structures. Thus, it is possible for the image to change significantly without any change in the organization map; such is the case with dynamic random-dot stereograms.

Summary

Visual performance is limited, inevitably, by the computational resources available to the visual system. In early vision, these limitations are manifested as an inability to perceive spatial details that are smaller than a critical size or events that occur in less than a critical time. Thus, an important measure of the system's performance is its resolution in space and time. Given that limitations are inevitable, how should the system be organized to take best advantage of the computing resources it does have? What relationship may then be expected to hold between its spatial and temporal characteristics?

I have suggested a number of factors that may bear on resource allocation. The system is limited, ultimately, by the rate at which it can process independent data samples. If the resolution achieved by a system is known, then a first approximation to its data rate is given by the product of the spatial and temporal sampling rates required to obtain that resolution. The temporal rate of change is increased when objects move in the image. This means the overall data rate can remain constant in the presence of motion only if spatial resolution in the direction of motion decreases with the square root of the velocity (equation 1). However, a different relationship is predicted if computations are performed by specialized elements, such as elements tuned to particular spatial frequencies. Then the data rate itself will be reduced when objects move, and spatial resolution will decrease in inverse proportion to velocity (equation 2).

These predictions ignore the fact that images are highly structured. Because the physical world is made up of objects, images tend to be mosaics of compact regions in which pattern properties are fairly uniform, and which move as units when objects move. The efficiency of image analysis depends in large part on how well these types of image structure are captured in the code the system uses to represent image data. An ideal representation is one that removes all structure from the data, leaving a much reduced and completely random residual to be processed. A curious consequence of image structure, and of pattern coherence as objects move, is that sampling may be well below the Nyquist rate. In particular, a dual "what/where" system may achieve spatial and temporal resolution in excess of that expected from the sampling theorem.

Another characteristic property of object images is that they occur over a range of scales as objects are viewed from different distances. Since the scale of salient features is generally not known *a priori*, it is often most efficient to encode and process images at many scales simultaneously. This multiresolution approach to analysis is now used extensively in computer vision. Spatial-frequency-tuned channels in natural vision systems may play a related role.

Finally, to perform certain perceptual tasks the system must build an internal model of its environment. Model building is required even in early vision, where it serves to organize and segment image data and thereby to ensure that no single image feature is associated with more than one perceived object. The processes that generate this "organization map" interact with other processes responsible for computing image properties through cooperative computation. The importance and complexity of organizing processes is indicated in part by the spatial and temporal resolution of the organization map they generate. These considerations raise a question: How can an organizational state be represented within a neural structure in such a way that it is spatially articulated and does not have to be regenerated every time image patterns move a distance comparable to its spatial resolution? This may require the organization to be represented by a pattern of neural activity that can move within a supporting neural structure as object move.

Acknowledgment

The preparation of this paper was supported by the National Science Foundation under grant ECS-8205321.

References

Barnard, S. T., and W. B. Thompson. 1980. Disparity analysis of images. *IEEE Trans. Pattern Anal. and Mach. Intelligence* 2: 333−340.

Braddick, O. J. 1974. A short-range process in apparent motion. *Vision Res.* 14: 519−527.

Burt, P. J. 1975. Computer simulations of a dynamic visual perception model. *Int. J. Man-Machine Studies* 7: 529−546.

Burt, P. J. 1984. The pyramid as a structure for efficient computation. In *Multiresolution Image Processing and Analysis*, ed. A. Rosenfeld (Springer-Verlag).

Burt, P. J., and B. Julesz. 1980. A disparity gradient limit for binocular fusion. *Science* 208: 615−617.

Burt, P. J., and G. Sperling. 1981. Time, distance, and feature trade-offs in visual apparent motion. *Psychological Rev.* 88: 171–195.

Dev, P. 1975. Perception of depth surfaces in random-dot stereograms: A neural model. *Int. J. Man-Machine Studies* 7: 511–528.

Horn, B. K. P., and B. G. Schunck. 1981. Determining optical flow. In Proceedings of the DARPA Image Understanding Workshop.

Julesz, B. 1971. *Foundations of Cyclopean Perception.* University of Chicago Press.

Kelly, D. H. 1979. Motion and vision. II. Stabilized spatio-temporal threshold surface. *J. Opt. Soc. Am.* 69: 1340–1349.

Lappin, J. S., and H. H. Bell. 1976. The detection of coherence in moving random-dot patterns. *Vision Res.* 16: 161–168.

Marr, D., and T. Poggio. 1976. Cooperative computation of stereo disparity. *Science* 194: 283–287.

Prager, J. M., and M. A. Arbib. 1983. Computing the optic flow: The MATCH algorithm and prediction. *Computer Vision and Image Processing* 24: 271–304.

Schneider, G. E. 1969. Two visual systems. *Science* 163: 895–902.

Tyler, C. W. 1973. Stereoscopic vision: Cortical limitation and a disparity scaling effect. *Science* 181: 276–278.

Tyler, C. W., and J. J. Chang. 1977. Visual echoes: The perception of repetition in quasi-random patterns. *Vision Res.* 17: 109–116.

III

Machine Vision and Robotics

Whereas parts I and II of the book were concerned with brain function and structure and the response of the visual system to stimuli, this part is concerned with the construction of artificial sensory processing systems. The goal of these systems is typically the transformation of a stimulus (say visual or tactile) into a symbolic internal model of the structure of the external world in a form that can be used to achieve a set of goals usually related to some form of manipulation of the environment (e.g. navigation). Progress in these kinds of systems, particularly computer-vision systems, has been hampered by a number of problems, including a lack of precise understanding of what constitutes an adequate primitive internal description of the stimulus, of the kinds of grouping processes operating over these descriptions, of how internal world models and *a priori* knowledge affect the transformation, of shape and its role in perception, of the structure of processes creating the transformation, and of how the ambiguities inherent in the sensory data may be resolved.

Riseman and Hanson discuss some of these issues in the context of an evolving system for understanding static color images of outdoor scenes. They argue that the inherent ambiguities in the visual data (and consequently in the image abstractions that form the basis of subsequent interpretations) can be resolved only through the use of higher-level knowledge, including the contextual relations expected among the components. They conjecture that image interpretation begins with the forming of an abstract representation of important visual events in the image without knowledge of its contents. The primitive elements forming this representation are collected, grouped, and refined to bring their collective description into consistency with high-level semantic structures representing the observer's knowledge about the world and the constraints that can be obtained from it. The grouping and refinement processes are controlled in a top-down fashion via active knowledge structures which are accessed bottom-up by object hypothesis and focusing rules operating on the intermediate-level image abstractions. The focus of the paper is on the object hypothesis rules. Examples of top-down interpretations are given.

Brady and Yuille consider the problem of recovering three-dimensional surface orientation from a contour representing the two-dimensional projection of a surface. Their approach is an example of a class of bottom-up interpretation strategies that includes stereopsis, structure from motion, shape from texture gradients, and shape from shading. Their method is based on general knowledge of primitive shapes and their projections, utilizing an extremum principle that maximizes a measure of the compactness or symmetry of an oriented surface. It is shown that the extremum principle interprets regular figures and real symmetries correctly. In the concluding section of their paper, Brady and Yuille suggest a method whereby the extremum principle could be used to interpret contours as oriented curved surfaces and to recover interior surface curvature. Their proposed method is similar to suggestions appearing the psychophysical literature—particularly the "economy principles" of the Gestalt psychologists, which can be viewed as minimization problems in which local differences are minimized.

Tsotsos notes that static images are a most unnatural kind of input to artificial visual systems because they represent the state of the world over a single time slice. The real world is normally changing in time, and integration of the temporal aspects of world dynamics into a vision system requires substantially different abstractions, representational structures, and interpretation processes than those proposed for static image understanding. Tsotsos is concerned with the representation and organization of temporal concepts, leading to an iterative hypothesize-and-test reasoning structure that proceeds sequentially through time. Tsotsos develops a knowledge representation involving four organizational axes: the three axes commonly found in the artificial-intelligence literature (IS-A, PART-OF, and similarity) and time. The interpretation strategies utilized extend over the temporal axis. The ALVEN system, a perceptual system designed to interpret x-ray image sequences of the left ventricle of the human heart, is an implementation of the concepts developed in Tsotsos's paper. Such a system is required for real-world tasks that extend over finite intervals, such as navigation and robot planning and manipulation.

The paper by Lawton, Rieger, and Steenstrup is concerned with techniques for extracting motion information and descriptors (of the type assumed by Tsotsos) from an image sequence. Noting that the inference of environmental information from displacement or flow fields may be an inherently unstable problem due to the discrepancy between the precision and reliability of the extracted flow and the sensitivity of the inference procedures to noise and resolution errors (see also paper 1), they describe several computationally feasible approaches that rely on processing restricted cases of motion (such as only translation). They then extend these methods to practical situations and discuss a straighforward implementation of three-dimensional inference based on the decomposition of an optic flow field into its rotational and translational components on a content-addressable array parallel processor. Finally, they show how differential image motion can be processed at occlusion boundaries to determine motion parameters, noting that this has direct relevance to animal perception.

The last two papers in this part deal with the processing of sensory data in robotics, the role of sensory data in planning and control systems for robot arms, and methods for integrating the information obtained from tactile and visible-light sensors into coordinated control systems. The paper by Overton is concerned with tactile sensing and methods by which information derived from multimodal perceptual systems and feedback from motor activity may be integrated with planning and control mechanisms to produce a smoothly functioning robot. A tactile sensor developed by the author at the Laboratory for Perceptual Robotics at the University of Massachusetts is described and its use demonstrated in a series of tactile sensing experiments. The experimental data are analyzed using simple techniques similar to those used in processing visible light images. In the second half of the paper Overton proposes a schema-based control mechanism based on the Action/Perception cycle originally proposed by Neisser. The schema control mechanism embodies the idea that robots exist in a world of actions, which in turn produce new sensory information, perhaps leading to new actions. Two classes of schemas are proposed: motor schemas, which capture local control activity related to actions and classes of actions, and perceptual schemas, which represent an internal model of the environment related to the possible actions the robot can take. Overton concludes the paper with a walkthrough of the actions required to lift a coffee mug and discusses a number of control issues within this context. In a related paper, Arbib, Iberall, and Lyons further develop the concept of schema coordinated control The goal is the specification of a schema formalism with sufficient expressive power to describe primate hand control as well as form the basis of a schema language to be used to control robot hands. Using the task of "grasping a mug" as the backdrop, the authors propose a hierarchical motor-schema organization whose function is to map high-level task descriptions such as "grasp the mug" into detailed patterns of motor activity sufficient to accomplish the task. Embedded within each motor schema, perceptual schemas provide visual and tactile descriptions of the task domain at the appropriate level of detail. Using a set of schemas developed with the aid of psychomotor observations on humans, the authors discuss the schema interaction strategies and the control mechanisms involved in "grasping a mug." A computer simulation demonstrates the preshaping and grasping behaviors of the schema descriptions. The paper concludes with a discussion of possible neural and behavioral correlates of the schema mechanisms.

9 A Methodology for the Development of General Knowledge-Based Vision Systems

Edward M. Riseman and
Allen R. Hanson

Expert system technology, especially techniques for rule-based knowledge engineering, has been successfully applied to many practical problems. Although there are inherent limitations on the complexity and power that can be achieved with traditional expert system approaches [1], particularly when the number of rules is not constrained, there has been little evidence of application to image interpretation. Typically, vision systems [e.g. 2–17] are highly system- or application-dependent, and consequently it has been difficult to transfer them to different task domains. This paper will discuss some of the problems that are specific to computer vision and describe one general methodology for the development of knowledge-based vision systems. The focus of the paper is on the initial iconic-to-symbolic mapping, which associates portions of the image with hypothesized semantic labels. The proposed approach addresses the start-up problem of interpretation by creating tentative "islands of reliability" from which context-directed processing can be initiated. Since the initial processes are somewhat independent and are usually associated with separate parts of the images, they can be executed independently and in parallel; multiple processes can also compete in order to arrive at the best interpretation among a set of alternatives. The relations and expected consistencies between local interpretations form the basis for a cooperative/competitive style of processing among the possible interpretations as the system attempts to extend the islands to uninterpreted parts of the image.

The complexity of visual tasks can be made explicit by examining almost any complex image. Although this initial discussion is qualitative, we believe the conjectures are intuitive and reasonable even though it is very difficult to be introspective of one's own visual processing. Humans are rarely aware of any significant degree of ambiguity in local portions of the sensory data, nor are they aware of the degree to which they are employing a more global context and stored expectations derived from experience. However, if the visual field is restricted so that only local information is available about an object or an object part, interpretation is often difficult or impossible. Increasing the contextual information so that spatial relations to other objects and object parts are present makes the perceptual task seem natural and simple. Consider the scenes in figure 1 and the closeup images in figure 2. In each case we have selected subimages of objects showing the following:

- "primitive" visual elements—image events that convey limited information about the identity of the objects or of their decomposition into parts (this is at least partly a function of resolution)

- absence of context—there is limited information about other objects which might relate to the given object in expected ways.

In figure 2, as some of the surrounding context of the shoes and the head are supplied, the perceptual ambiguity disappears and the related set of visual elements are easily recognized. In each of the above cases the purely local hypothesis is inherently unreliable and uncertain and there may be little surface information to be derived in a bottom-up manner. It appears that human vision is fundamentally organized to exploit the use of contextual knowledge and expectations in the organization of the visual primitives. However, it may be impossible to associate object labels with these ambiguous primitives until they are grouped into larger entities and collectively interpreted as a related set of object or scene parts. Thus, the inclusion of knowledge-driven processes at some level in the image-interpretation task, where there is still a great degree of ambiguity in the organization of the visual primitives, appears inevitable.

We conjecture that image interpretation initially proceeds by forming an abstract representation of important visual events in the image without knowledge of its contents. The primitive elements forming this representation are then collected, grouped, and refined to bring their collective description into consistency with high-level semantic structures that represent the observer's knowledge about the world.

Issues Facing Knowledge-Based Vision Systems

The development of knowledge-based vision systems has been hampered by several factors: the lack of agreement on what constitutes an adequate representation of image events, the lack of low-level processes that can

a

b

c

Figure 1

Original images. These images are representative samples from a larger data base. All are digitized to 512 × 512 spatial resolution, with eight bits in the red, green, and blue components.

Figure 2
Closeups from original images. In many cases, the identity or function of an object or object part cannot be determined from a small local view. Only when the surrounding context becomes available can the objects be recognized.

reliably extract relevant image features, the lack of satisfactory three-dimensional representations that can capture the inherent variability in the structure of physical objects and scenes, the lack of adequate mechanisms for utilizing knowledge during the interpretation process, and the necessity of a tremendous investment in software development before the capability for even simple interpretation experiments can be achieved. Most of the systems in the current literature address only some of these issues. Perhaps even more discouraging, there do not appear to be ways in which these systems can be easily generalized. This paper does not attempt to carefully survey the literature in knowledge-based vision systems. However, a partial review of image interpretation research can be found in [5, 18, 31], and descriptions of several individual research efforts are found in [2–17].

Early attempts to interface stored knowledge to image data at the pixel level met with only limited success and little possibility generalization [15]. For example, blue pixels could immediately be hypothesized to have "sky" labels, and appropriate constraints could be propagated, but such an approach to interfacing visual knowledge seems rather futile in the face of increasing numbers of objects and increasing complexity of the task domain. In an image of reasonable resolution there are $512 \times 512 \cong \frac{1}{4}$ million pixels; hence, vision systems must confront the problem of dynamically forming from the large number of individual pixels more useful entities to which propositions will be attached. Transforming the data into a much smaller set of image events is the goal of segmentation processes. For the reasons discussed above, algorithms for extracting primitives (such as 2D regions of homogeneous color and texture, straight lines, simple geometric shapes, and/or local surface patches) have proved to be complex and quite unreliable, suggesting that substantial further processing is required before one can expect this intermediate representation to support a globally consistent interpretation.

Overview of the VISIONS System Approach to These Issues

Since the mid 1970s, the VISIONS group at the University of Massachusetts has been evolving a general system for knowledge-based interpretation of natural scenes, such as house, road, and urban scenes [8, 25, 33–36]. The goal of this effort is the construction of a system capable of interpreting natural images of significant complexity by exploiting the redundancies and general constraints expected between and within scene elements.

The general strategy by which VISIONS system operates is to build an intermediate symbolic representation of the image data using segmen-

Image Interpretation

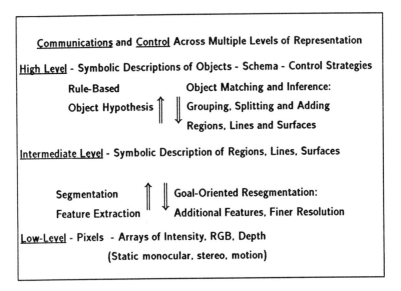

Figure 3
Multiple levels of representation and processing in VISIONS.

tation processes which initially do not make use of any knowledge of specific objects in the domain. From the intermediate-level data, a partial interpretation is constructed by associating an object label with selected groups of the intermediate primitives. The object labels are used to activate portions of the knowledge network related to the hypothesized object. Once activated, the procedural components of the knowledge network direct further grouping, splitting, and labeling processes at the intermediate level to construct aggregated and refined intermediate events which are in closer agreement with the stored symbolic object description. Figure 3 is an abstraction of the multiple levels of representation and processing in the VISIONS system. Communication between these levels is by no means unidirectional; in most cases, recognition of an object or part of a scene at the high level establishes a strategy for further manipulating the intermediate-level primitives within the context provided by the partial interpretation, and for feedback for goal-directed resegmentation. Although the following discussion is based primarily on 2D abstractions of the image data (such as regions and lines), it should be clear that the general ideas extend naturally to 3D abstractions such as surfaces as well as to attributes such as motion and depth.

Let us consider some of the stages of processing in a bit more detail.

1. Segmentation processes [20−22] are applied to the sensory data to form a symbolic representation of regions and lines and their attributes, such as color, texture, location, size, shape, orientation, and length. Figures 4 and 5 show sample results from two segmentation processes applied to the images in figure 1. The region and line representations are integrated so that spatially related entities in either can be easily accessed [23]. Two-dimensional motion attributes can also be associated with these entities.

2. Object hypothesis rules are applied to the region and line representation to rank-order candidate object hypotheses [24]. This initial iconic-to-symbolic mapping, which provides an effective *focus-of-attention* mechanism to initiate semantic processing, is described in more detail below. A simple rule is defined as a range over any scalar feature of the lines or regions. If the attribute of the line/region has a value in the range, it will be considered as a "vote" for a particular object label. More complex rules are formed via a logical or arithmetic combining function over several simple rules. The rules can also be viewed as sets of partially redundant features, each of which defines an area of feature space which represents a vote for an object. The region features could include color, texture, size, location in image, simple shape, and motion; the line features could include location, length, width, contrast, and motion. To the degree that surface patches have been formed, rules can be applied to surface features such as depth, size, location, orientation, reflectance, curvature, and motion.

3. More complex object-dependent interpretation strategies are represented in a procedural form in knowledge structures called schemas [8, 25, 28]. These strategies represent control local to a schema node and top-down control over the interpretation process. One interpretation strategy that utilizes the output of the rule set involves the selection of reliable hypotheses as image-specific object exemplars. They are extended to other regions and lines through an object-dependent similarity matching strategy [24]. Thus, as in the HEARSAY paradigm, partial interpretations begin to extend from "islands of reliability" [26]. At this point in the development of the VISIONS system, we are concentrating on the identification and implementation of intermediate grouping strategies for merging and modifying region and line elements to match expected object structures [28]. For this purpose, general knowledge of objects and scenes is organized around the relationships that would be found in standard 2D views of 3D objects. Verification strategies exploit particular spatial relationships between the hypothesized object and other specific expected object labels or image

a

b

c

Figure 4
Region segmentations. Regions partition the image into areas which are relatively uniform in some feature (in this case, intensity). Mapped into a symbolic structure with a rich set of descriptors, they provide one form of link between the image data and the interpretation system.

Figure 5
Extraction of straight lines. The straight-line algorithm uses a local estimate of gradient orientation to group pixels into regions. A straight line and an associated set of features are extracted from each region. The resulting line image (which contains many lines not shown here) can be filtered in various ways. The two images on the left show all lines whose gradient magnitude exceeds ten gray levels per pixel; the right images represent a second filtering on the basis of length. The short, high-contrast lines in the images in the left images are used as the basis of a texture measure.

features. In cases of simple 3D shapes, such as the planar surfaces forming a "house" volume, 3D models and associated processing strategies are employed. We hope to evolve similar intermediate grouping strategies for complex 3D shape representations in the future.

4. Feedback to the lower-level processes for more detailed segmentation can be requested in cases when interpretation of an area fails, when an expected image feature is not found, or when conflicting interpretations occur. Both the region and line algorithms have parameters for varying the sensitivity and amount of detail in their segmentation output. However, the control of such strategies and the integration of their results is an open problem that is under examination.

5. Because of the inherent ambiguities in both the raw image data and the extracted intermediate representations, a method for handling uncertainty is required if there is to be any possibility of combining this information into a coherent view of the world [29–31]. Some of the limitations of inferencing using Bayesian probability models are overcome using the Dempster-Shafer formalism for evidential reasoning, in which an explicit representation of partial ignorance is provided [32]. The inferencing model allows "belief" or "confidence" in a proposition to be represented as a range within the [0, 1] interval. The lower and upper bounds represent support and plausibility, respectively, of a proposition; the width of the interval can be interpreted as ignorance.

Rule-Based Object Hypothesis Strategies

The interpretation task of concern in this paper is that of labeling an initial region segmentation of an image with object (and object part) labels, when the image is known to be a member of a restricted class of scenes (e.g., outdoor scenes). An important aspect of this task is the mechanisms for focusing attention on selected areas of the image for which plausible hypothesis of object identities can be generated and for merging regions with a common semantic label. This latter task can occur simultaneously with the labeling process or can be delayed until a later phase of the interpretation process.

We propose a simple approach to object hypothesis formation, relying on convergent evidence from a variety of measurements and expectations. In the early interpretation phase, when little is known about the scene or its contents, the approach is primarily bottom-up and involves the generation of a few reliable hypotheses about prominent image events. The object hypothesis system provides the first link between the image data and the knowledge structures. Control can then shift to a more top-down orientation as context and expectations allow the use of further knowledge-dependent processing to validate and extend the initial hypotheses.

Our goal, therefore, is to develop methods for selecting specific image events that are likely candidates for particular object labels, rather than to select the best object label for each region and line. For example, given a set of regions in an outdoor scene (and assuming a standard camera position), one might choose to select a few bright blue areas, with a low degree of texture, near the top of the image, which are likely to be "sky." Similarly, in an outdoor scene one could select grass regions by using the expectation that they would be of medium brightness, have a significant green component, be located somewhere in the lower portion of the image, and so on. (A camera model and access to a 3D representation of the environment could dynamically modify the value of these location limits in the image; thus, the use of rules on relative or absolute environmental location in a fully general system would involve modification of expectations about image location as the system orients the camera up or down relative to the ground plane.) For each object, these expectations can be translated into a "rule" combining the results of many measurements into a confidence level that a region (or a small group of regions) represents that object.

Knowledge as Rules

Simple rules are defined as the ranges over a scalar-valued feature which will map into a vote for an object label. Typically a feature will be the mean or variance of a property of the pixels or edges composing the regions or lines, respectively. Complex rules involve a combination of simple rules, and they allow fusion of information from a variety of different types of measurements.

We will now develop a simple rule which captures the expectation that grass is green using a feature which is a coarse approximation to a green-magenta opponent color feature by computing the mean of $2G-R-B$ for all pixels in this region (where R, G, and B refer to the red, green, and blue components of the color image, respectively). In order to demonstrate the actual basis and form of knowledge embodied in the rule, in figure 6 we compare histograms of the green-magneta feature distribution of grass pixels to the distribution of the same feature for all pixels. The data were

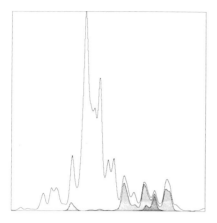

Figure 6
Image histogram of a "green-magenta" feature (2G−R−B). The unshaded histogram represents the global distribution of the feature across all pixels in eight hand-labeled images. The intermediate diagonal shading represents the feature distribution of all grass regions in the eight images. The darkest cross-hatched histogram is the feature distribution of grass regions in a single image.

obtained by hand-labeling segmentations from eight sample images of outdoor house scenes.

The basic idea is to construct a mapping from a measured value of the feature obtained from an image region, say f_1, into a vote for the object. One approach is to define this mapping as a function of distance in feature space between the measured value and a stored prototype feature vector which captures the feature properties of the object. Let $d = d(f_p, f) = f − f_p$ be the distance between the measured feature value f and the prototype feature point f_p, and let $\theta_1 \leq \theta_2 \leq \cdots \leq \theta_6$ be thresholds on d (see figure 7). The response R of the rule is then

$$R(f) = 1 \qquad \text{if } -\theta_3 < d \leq \theta_4$$

$$= \frac{d + \theta_2}{\theta_2 - \theta_3} \quad \text{if } -\theta_2 < d \leq -\theta_3$$

$$= \frac{d - \theta_5}{\theta_4 - \theta_5} \quad \text{if } \theta_4 < d \leq \theta_5$$

$$= 0 \qquad \text{if } (-\theta_1 < d \leq -\theta_2) \text{ or } (\theta_5 < d \leq \theta_6)$$

$$= -\infty \qquad \text{otherwise.}$$

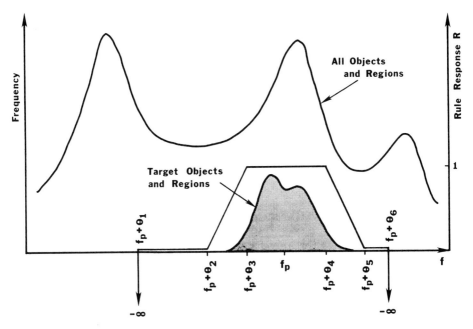

Figure 7
Structure of a simple rule for mapping an image feature measurement f into support for a
label hypothesis on the basis of a prototype feature value obtained from the combined
histograms of labeled regions across image samples. The object-specific mapping is
parametrized by seven values, f_p, θ_1, ..., θ_6, and stored in the knowledge network.

The thresholds θ_i ($i = 1, ..., 6$) represent a coarse interpretation of the
distance measurements in feature space. When the measured and expected
values are sufficiently similar, the object label associated with the rule
receives a maximum vote of 1. Since small changes in a feature measurement should not dramatically alter the system response, the voting function
is linearly ramped to 0 as the distance in feature space increases.

A "veto" vote is allowed by θ_1 and θ_6 if the measured feature value
indicates that the object label associated with the prototype point cannot
be correct. For example, a certain range of the green-magenta opponent
color feature implies a magenta, red, or blue color, which should veto the
grass label. Thus, certain measurements can exclude object labels. This
proves to be a very effective mechanism for filtering the summation of
several spurious weak responses. Of course there is the danger of excluding
the proper label owing to a single feature value, even in the face of strong
support from many other features. A natural extension of the mechanisms
presented here would generalize the rule form to be parametrically varied

from the fixed form that we have defined. Thus, the ranges could be dynamically varied so that fewer or more regions are in the positive voting range of a particular rule. If there are multiple peaks in the histogram, then a simple rule can be defined for each peak independently. Their results can be combined using a simple function, such as the maximum of the responses.

A simple rule is a specification of a constraint on the value of a feature that should be satisfied if the object is present. A complex rule is defined as a (partially redundant) set of simple features that is assembled into a composite rule via a combining function which can take any logical or arithmetic form; this is an extension of the functional form of hypothesis rules in [12]. The premise is that by combining many partially redundant rules, the effect of any single unreliable rule is reduced.

It is useful to provide a hierarchical semantic structure on the set of simple rules. In this paper the rule for each object is organized into a composite rule of five components which provide a match of color, texture, location, shape, and size of the object. This allows some flexibility in combining several highly redundant features (e.g., several color features) into a composite rule which is somewhat more independent of the other composite rules (e.g., color vs. location). However, this is only one alternative for imposing a hierarchical structure on the set of simple rules. Many other combination functions are possible, and the choice of the function determines how the features "cooperate" to provide an initial hypothesis.

Each of the five composite rules is in turn joined into a composite rule. Any rule might have a weight of 0, which means that the rule will have no effect on the weighted response of the composite rule except that the veto range of the rule can reject a region as a candidate for the object in question. The structure of the composite rule for grass is shown in figure 8 with two levels of hierarchy; it consists of a normalized weighted average of the five components C_j:

$$\text{Grass score} = \frac{1}{N} \sum_{j=1}^{5} W_j C_j,$$

where the W_j are the weights and where $N = \sum_{j=1}^{5} W_j$. Each of the components is in turn a weighted sum of a set of individual rules:

$$C_j = \frac{1}{M} \sum_k V_k R(f_k),$$

where $R(f_k)$ is the response from an individual feature rule based on feature

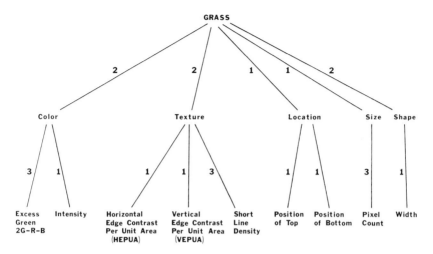

Figure 8
Structure of the grass rule. The rule response is the normalized weighted sum of the
responses of five component rules, each of which is in turn a normalized weighted sum
of the responses from simple rules associated with a single feature. A weight could be 0,
thereby allowing the veto range for that feature to be propagated.

f_k and where the V_k are the weights ($M = \sum_k V_k$). Similar rules were
developed for sky and foliage.

The weights shown in figure 8 capture the heuristic importance of each
of the contributions to the rule. The weights are integers from 0 to 5 and
reflect a belief that only a few levels of relative importance are needed
("weak" $\equiv 1$, "medium" $\equiv 3$, "strong" $\equiv 5$ in importance). The intention is
to avoid twiddling of numbers, but to allow obvious relative weightings to
be expressed. Since the composite rule response is used only to order the
regions on the basis of their similarity to the stored feature templates,
rather than classifying them as instances of a specific class, the expectation
is that the rule response is relatively insensitive to small changes in the
weights. The rules extend easily and naturally to include other features and
attributes, such as depth and motion.

Relationship to Bayesian Theory Classification

One of the most familiar problems in the pattern-recognition literature is
that of character recognition, where the identities of a sequence of unknown
characters are to be determined. The jth character R_j is to be classified as
one of a fixed set of classes C_i ($i = 1, \ldots, N$) on the basis of a feature vector

$\overline{X}_j$ extracted via measurements on character R_j. One can view the region-labeling problem to be equivalent, in that a set of feature measurements can be extracted from all regions and then can each be classified according to a maximum-likelihood decision process.

A training set of characters is usually provided *a priori*, from which statistical estimates of feature distributions can be extracted; it is necessary that the training set be large enough to capture the expected variations in the domain. The optimal decision process for a given character R_j involves the computation of the *a posteriori* Bayesian probability for each class given the feature vector $\overline{X}_j$, followed by the selection of the maximum-likelihood class as the output decision. Thus, using the Bayes rule, character R_j is classified as C_i, where

$$\max_i P(C_i|\overline{X}_j) = \max_i \frac{P(\overline{X}_j|C_i)P(C_i)}{P(\overline{X}_j)}.$$

Since $P(\overline{X}_j)$ is constant across the N classes, it cannot affect the decision and may be ignored. Thus, the decision rule is now simplified to

$$\max_i P(\overline{X}_j|C_i)P(C_i),$$

with $P(\overline{X}_j|C_i)$ estimated from the training set and $P(C_i)$ obtained via statistical analysis of the task domain. (There are a number of variations to the basic paradigm, which we note here but do not wish to explore in this treatment. Some samples could be rejected if the maximum likelihood is sufficiently low; by avoiding classification of a difficult subset of characters the error rate might be reduced, but more important there is the possibility of focusing attention on samples where additional information would be valuable. Another extension involves the dependencies between characters that are a function of the characteristics of the language; contextual analysis via conditional probabilities of letter sequences could be used to improve the estimates of the likelihoods [37–39].)

In the pattern recognition/classification case, the set of classes is known, fixed, and usually not large. Also, $P(\overline{X}_j)$ could be factored out of the computation of the posterior class likelihoods, because the set of feature measurements was the same for each class; i.e., one set of measurements were performed and these results were used to determine all the $P(\overline{X}_j|C_i)$. However, the *a priori* class probability $P(C_i)$ does vary in the computation of each class likelihood. Finally, the intent of this classification process is the classification of every character sample.

The region-labeling problem is far more difficult than the typical pattern-recognition problem. For a variety of reasons, one must expect the data at the level of representation of this stage of processing to be distorted, incomplete, and sometimes meaningless. Segmentation of an image into regions, each of which is composed of a spatially contiguous set of pixels, is a very difficult and ill-formed problem [31]. As we have pointed out, the sensory data are inherently noisy and ambiguous, and this leads to segmentations that are unreliable and vary in uncontrollable ways; regions and lines will be fragmented and merged, and thus the decision processes often will be fed region and line samples only some of which are meaningful. In the character-recognition problem this would be akin to being given joined letters and split letters at a very high frequency. In fact, this is one of the major problems in cursive-script recognition that makes it much harder than recognition of printed or typed characters. The system is repeatedly faced with the difficulty of organizing the input data into appropriate segments.

The classical pattern-recognition approaches are not powerful enough by themselves to produce effective classification in the domains we wish to consider. Scene interpretation involves processes that construct complex descriptions, where many hypotheses are put forth and a subset that can be verified and satisfy a set of relational constraints are accepted. AI systems are often faced with fitting a set of very weak but consistent hypotheses into a more reliable whole. This usually is a complex process that requires a great reliance on stored knowledge of the object classes. This knowledge takes the form of object attributes and relations between objects (particularly relations between parts of objects, which leads to a part-of hierarchy in the knowledge base).

In contrast, we have modified the classification strategy to become a "focus-of-attention" process, since it is not feasible to initially classify all image events. The organization of the input data is not sufficiently well defined to pose the classical pattern-recognition goals in our domain. Thus, rather than the selection of the best object label for each region and line, we are looking for good region and line candidates for a particular object label.

Now, instead of the measurement vector $P(\overline{X}_j)$ being held constant across samples, the *a priori* class probability $P(C_i)$ is constant across regions to be classified. While there is a common set of features measured on each region, the measurement vector $\overline{X}_j$ may be different for each (i.e. a different set of feature values). This changes the optimal decision rule via a Bayes formulation to

$$\max_{j} \frac{P(\bar{X}_j | C_i)}{P(\bar{X}_j)},$$

which will decompose into the product of individual feature terms under an assumption of independence.

It should now be clear that our simple piecewise-linear rule form is more than just an approximation to $P(X_j | C_i)$, where $j = 1, \ldots, K$. What it also must balance is the relation to $P(X_j)$, which appears in the denominator of the Bayesian focus-of-attention ratio. This term is important because it brings in the degree of *discrimination* of each feature measurement X_j for class C_i. For example, there would be little value in a feature that exhibited a very tight range (i.e., very low variance) for some object class if in fact it also exhibited the same distribution for all classes. In actual practice, the vision system designer/knowledge engineer is reponsible for the selection of the features used in the object rules. To the degree that a rule developed by this expert covered $P(X_j | C_i)$ and excluded $P(X_j | C_k)$, for all $k \neq i$, that rule would be effective. Of course there is still the problem of the usually invalid assumption of feature independence, and therefore our heuristic hierarchical combination of features may be just as reasonable. In fact the use of the veto range for individual features has the same effect as a ratio of 0 in the product of probabilities under the assumption of independence.

Results of Rule Application

Figure 9 shows the results of applying selected simple rules for grass to the region segmentation from figure 4c. For each rule there are two images. The left image of each pair is a composite feature histogram showing the feature distribution across all pixels (the unshaded curve) in a set of images and the distribution for grass pixels (the cross-hatched curve) across the same set of images. The histograms were computed from a set of eight hand-labeled images and were smoothed. The right image of each pair shows the strength of the rule response for each region coded as a brightness level; bright regions correspond to high rule output.

The rule that was developed interactively by the user is superimposed on the histograms in piecewise linear form. In the upper left "Target" refers to the object associated with the rule, in this case grass, while "Other" refers to all objects other than the target object. The first row of numbers shows the weighted average response of grass regions and other regions to the rule function (100 is maximum), while the lower numbers tabulate the percentage of target regions and other regions vetoed. Thus, the ideal rule is one that responds maximally with a value of 100 to the target regions while vetoing 100% of all other regions. In practice, there is almost always a tradeoff and optimal settings are not at all obvious. In some cases rules for the target object were set to exclude regions associated with other objects; in other cases the goal was to maximize the response for the target-object regions. There is no intent here to put forth these specific rules as a significant contribution or even as a satisfactory set; in fact some of these rules probably need modification.

Figure 10 shows the response for three of the five rule components and the final result for the composite rule. For each rule the region response is shown superimposed over the image in two complementary formats. The left image of each pair shows the strength of the rule response coded in the intensity level of each region; bright regions correspond to good matches. The right image shows the vetoed regions in black (with all others uniformly gray). Figure 11 shows the final results for the foliage, grass, and sky rules in the house image in figure 1b (vetoed regions not shown).

The effectiveness of the rules can be seen by examining the rank order-ings of the regions on the basis of the composite rule responses. For the grass results shown in figure 10, for example, the two top ranked regions are actually grass. For the grass results shown in figure 11, the top six regions are grass and eight of the top ten regions are grass; the two nongrass regions were actually sidewalk and driveway. For the foliage responses shown in figure 11b, the top 21 regions were some form of foliage (tree, bush, or undergrowth); of the 30 regions not vetoed, there were only seven nonfoliage regions. These seven regions were actually grass and were among the lowest-ranked of the nonvetoed regions (seven of the last nine). For the sky results in figure 11c, only four regions were not vetoed and the top three were sky. The fourth region, with a signifi-cantly lower rule response, was actually foliage with some sky showing through. Figure 12 shows the highest-ranked regions for each of the three object hypothesis rules when applied to the three example images. How these initial object hypothesis results may be used as the basis of a strategy to produce a more complete interpretation will be discussed below.

A Language Interface for Knowledge Engineering

Knowledge engineering of rules is facilitated by an interactive environment for rule construction. A user can get an immediate sense of their effective-ness by displaying the rating of each symbolic candidate inintensity or color. Thus, rule development is a dynamic process with a natural display medium for user feedback.

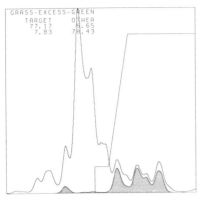

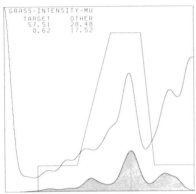

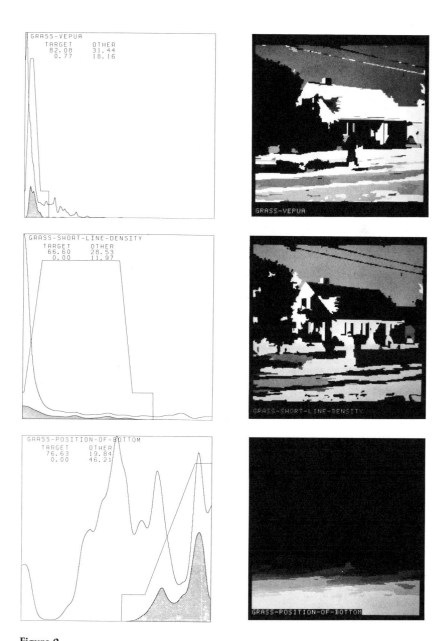

Figure 9

Results from the simple grass rules. In each image pair, the left image is a composite feature histogram showing the feature distribution across all pixels in a set of images, the distribution of grass pixels in the same set, and the rule. The right image shows the brightness-encoded strength of the rule response when applied to all regions in the segmentation of figure 4c; bright regions correspond to a high rule response. See text for a discussion of the four numbers in the upper left corner of the histograms.

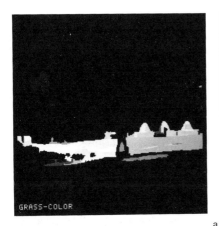

a

b

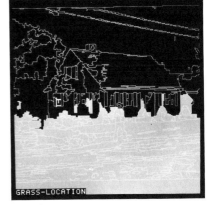

c

d

Figure 10
Rule responses for the grass component rules and the final composite rule. In each pair of
images, the left image shows the brightness-encoded (bright ≡ high) rule response. The
right image shows regions vetoed by the rule in black; all others (nonvetoed regions) are
uniformly gray. (a) Color component rule. (b) Texture component rule. (c) Location
component rule. (d) Final result from grass composite rule.

In addition to receiving an immediate visual response to a proposed rule
or rule set, the knowledge engineer must not be forced into a "parameter twiddling" mode. The rules should be robust enough so that a fairly
crude specification of the rule parameters generates reasonable results. The
specification can then be interactively refined, if necessary. As a first step
toward an interactive specification facility, a simple language interface has
been constructed so that rules can be specified on any feature in terms
of five intervals of the dynamic range of a feature: "very low," "low,"
"medium," "high," and "very high" [24, 36]. These labels induce a partition
on the range of the feature; for each interval, the user specifies whether the
rule response is "ON," "OFF," or "VETO."

The results obtained from the coarsely quantized rules are quite good
and are comparable to the results obtained in the preceding section using
the more carefully defined rules. Typical results from this rule set are shown
in figure 13 using the foliage hypothesis rule on the three test images
(figure 1); these results are comparable to those shown in figure 10. For the
segmentation of the house image of figure 1a, a total of 24 regions were
not vetoed by the rule. Of these, only two were incorrect (window and
grass). For the image in figure 1b, 16 regions were not vetoed and all of
them were some form of foliage (tree, bush, tall grass, or undergrowth);

a   b

c

Figure 11
Composite rule responses applied to figure 1b for grass, foliage, and sky rules, encoded in brightness. (a) Grass. (b) Foliage. (c) Sky.

Figure 12
Highest-ranked object hypothesis for the three example images.

Figure 13
Foliage results from the coarsely quantized rules applied to the segmentations of figure 4.

only one grass region was included. Twenty-eight regions remained after running the rule on the regions making up the house scene in figure 1c. Of these, twenty were bush or tree, two were grass, and the remainder were rocks, house windows, or shadowed areas. All the incorrect regions were rated fairly low by the rule. In all cases, the most highly rated regions were foliage.

Similar results were obtained for the sky and grass rules. For the image in figure 1b, for example, nine regions were not vetoed; of these, five were sky, two were a mixture of sky and the telephone or power wire (see figure 4b), and two were a mixture of tree and sky. Applying the grass rule to the segmentation of figure 1a results in 41 regions, 17 of which are grass and are among the 18 top-rated regions (the other region is bush). The remaining 23 regions, all rated very low, are bushes, trees, windows, house steps, and shutters.

Coarse quantization of the feature range offers the knowledge engineer the opportunity to quickly develop and assess a rule set without detailed examination of feature statistics. It may be possible, in some cases, to completely develop the rule base using semantic terms that are intuitive to the user, including the structure of the composite rules and the relative weights, as well as the setting of the individual rule values.

The rule system, as described in this section and above, has been applied to a number of outdoor images of several different types (including road scenes). Although quantitive data are not yet available, qualitatively the results presented here are typical. The rules for grass, foliage, and sky appear to be effective in extracting a set of regions that includes actual grass, foliage, and sky regions ranked at or near the top of the list. Similar results have been obtained for road and sidewalk (concrete and macadam) and, to a somewhat lesser extent, for house roof. The rules appear to be loosely enough defined that normalization of the features has not been necessary. Additional experimental results are being generated for these and other rules; the results will be reported in the future.

Schemas and Their Interpretation Strategies

In the VISIONS system, scene-independent knowledge is represented in a hierarchical schema structure organized as a semantic network [8, 24, 25, 33]. The hierarchy is structured to capture the decomposition of visual knowledge into successively more primitive entities, eventually expressed in symbolic terms similar to those used to represent the intermediate-level description of a specific image obtained from the region line, and surface segmentations. Each schema defines a highly structured collection of elements in a scene or object; each object in the scene schema, or each part in the object schema, can have an associated schema which will further describe it. For example, a house (in a house scene hierarchy) has roof and house wall as object parts, and the house-wall object has windows, shutters, and doors as object parts. Each schema node (e.g. house, house wall, and roof) has both a declarative component appropriate to the level of detail, describing the relations between the parts of the schema, and a procedural component describing image-recognition methods as a set of hypothesis and verification strategies called *interpretation strategies.*

The contextual verification of hypotheses via consistency with stored knowledge leads to a variety of interpretation strategies that are referred to as data-directed (or bottom-up), knowledge-directed (or top-down), or both. In addition, these strategies can be domain-dependent and object-dependent or uniform across domains. A rich set of possibilities open up, which unfortunately have not been sufficiently explored by the research community carrying out knowledge-directed vision processing. The first type of interpretation strategy discussed uses the rule system to select "exemplar" regions as object candidates, extending the labels to similar regions. A second class of strategies use geometric information to direct the grouping of intermediate events to better match the expected model. A third strategy involves the detection and correction of errors in the interpretation process.

Exemplar Selection and Extension

The most reliable object hypotheses obtained by applying the object hypothesis rules to the intermediate-level data (e.g. regions, lines, and surfaces) can be considered object "exemplars" which capture image-specific characteristics of the object. The set of exemplars can be viewed as a largely incomplete kernel interpretation. There are a variety of ways by which the exemplar regions can be used to extend and refine the kernel interpretation [24, 28]; we will briefly present one specific implementation for an exemplar-extension strategy.

For those objects with spectral characteristics that are reasonably uniform over the image, the similarity of region color and texture can be used to extend an object label to other regions. The image-specific variation of a feature of an object is expected to be much less than the inter-image variation of that feature for the same object. In many situations, another instance can be expected to have a similar color, size, or shape, and this expectation can be used to detect similar objects.

There are a variety of ways by which the exemplar regions can be used and by which the selection of similar regions can be made, depending on the data and the knowledge available as well as on the complexity of the object [23, 29]. For those objects for which the spectral characteristics can be expected to be reasonably uniform over the image, the similarity of region color and texture can be used to extend an object label to other regions, perhaps using the expected spatial location and relative spatial information in various ways to restrict the set of candidate regions examined. The similarity criteria might also vary as a function of the object, so that regions would be compared with the exemplar in terms of a particular set of features associated with that object. Thus, a sky exemplar region would be restricted to comparisons with regions that are above the horizon and that look similar (in terms of color and texture) to the largest, bluest region located near the top of the picture. A house wall showing through foliage can be matched to the unoccluded visible portion on the basis of color similarity and spatial constraints derived from inferences from house-wall geometry.

The shape and/or size of a region can be used to detect other instances of multiple objects, as in the case when one shutter or window of a house has been found [27], or when one tire of a car has been found, or when one car on a road has been found. In many situations another instance can be expected to have a similar size and shape. This, together with constraints on the image location, permits reliable hypotheses to be formed even with high degrees of partial occlusion. If one is viewing a house from a view-point approximately perpendicular to the front wall, other shutters can be found via the presence of a single shutter since the single shutter provides strong spatial constraints on the location of other shutters. If two shutters are found, then perspective distortion can be taken into account when looking for the other shutters, even without a camera model, under an assumption that the tops and bottoms of the set of shutters lie on a straight line on the face of the house. There are many alternatives by which features of an object could be used to determine the full set of regions representing the object. In the current version of the VISIONS systems, these alternatives are represented in the interpretation strategies associated with the object schema.

We have made a basic assumption that exemplar extension will in fact involve a knowledge-engineering process that will use different strategies for each object. In some cases, color and texture may be more reliable than shape and size (as in a sky exemplar region); in other situations, shape and size might be very important (as in the shutters). Spatial constraints may be used very differently in each case. One possibility is to utilize the object-specific set of simple features that were associated with the object hypothesis rules. In fact, the same rule system presented earlier can be used to weight the feature differences to form the similarity rating. Similarity extension rules can be implementations of distance metrics or functions, with values of feature differences used to determine the rule response for each. It might be appropriate in one case to employ a piecewise-linear distance function, with high values for small differences and low values for large differences; in another case, a rule might provide a uniformly high response within some threshold. If is also easy to use the veto region for large differences, or for spatial constraints to restrict the spatial area over which region candidates for exemplar extension will be considered.

For the similarity results shown in figures 14 and 15, the full object hypothesis rules discussed earlier were used to measure the similarity between the exemplar region and each candidate region. The rule response was converted into a distance metric, and bright regions correspond to small differences. Each of the rules contained location and size components, which enter into the final distance measurement, but in general there are more intelligent ways of using these features in the interpretation strategy responsible for grouping regions. Our goal here was simply to rank order the regions that were candidates for extension; again, the specific results shown in the figures are not as important as the overall philosophy.

Figure 14 shows the similarity rating of regions obtained by comparing the features of the grass rule (figure 8) with the exemplar region (figure 11). In addition to the final grass similarity response, the similarities obtained from the color component rule and two of its constituent simple rules (green-magenta and intensity) are also shown. Figure 15 shows similar results for foliage.

It is interesting to compare the region rankings produced by the image-independent initial grass rule and the rankings obtained from the exemplar matching strategy. The original grass rule applied to the same image as figure 14 (these results are shown in figure 11) vetoed all but 27 regions; of these, 15 were grass and the six highest-ranked regions were grass. By way of comparison, of the 27 regions most similar to the grass exemplar region, 18 were actually grass, and the eight highest-ranked regions were grass. Of the 16 regions most similar to the exemplar, all but two were grass. Again, the confusion was between grass, sidewalk, and driveway.

a

b

c

d

Figure 14
Similarity of grass exemplar region and all other regions for figure 4b. (a) Similarities from
the composite object-hypothesis rule. (b) Similarities from only the color component of
the composite rule. (c,d) Similarities from the simple rules associated with excess green
and intensity. In all cases, similarity is encoded as brightness.

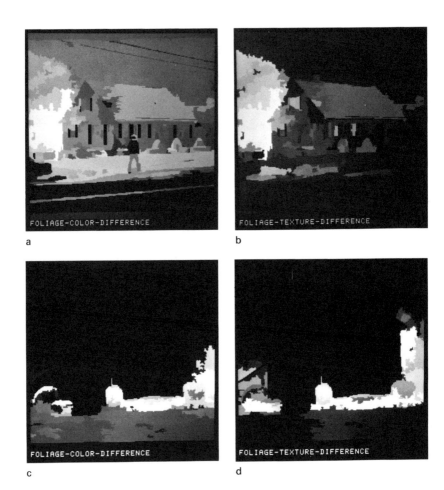

a   b

c   d

Figure 15

Foliage exemplar matches. (a,b) Foliage matches using the largest region in the tree area on the left side of the image (region 69 in figure 4c). (c,d) Foliage matches using the large region in the low bushes in front of the house (region 128 in figure 4a).

The exemplar matching strategy produces more reliable results than the initial hypothesis rule, since it takes into account image-dependent characteristics of the object's appearance.

Interpretation Strategies for Intermediate Grouping

In this section we briefly motivate the types of additional top-down strategies that will be necessary for properly interpreting the primitives of the intermediate respresentation in terms of the hypothesized higher-level context. The work presented here is taken from Weymouth [28], and is the subject of active exploration within the vision group at the University of Massachusetts.

We sketch the basic idea using as an example the problem of grouping and interpreting a house roof from a fragmented intermediate representation. Figure 16 shows a number of intermediate stages in the application of a house-roof interpretation strategy associated with the house-roof schema. Figures 16a and 16b portray a pair of region and line segmentations that exhibit difficulties expected in the output of low-level algorithms; figure 16a also shows the initial roof hypothesis. In this example the region-segmentation algorithm was set to extract more detail from the image by producing more regions; the result, which is typical of a class of segmentation problems, was the fragmentation of the roof, so that the shadowed left portion was broken into several regions separate from the main roof region. (The segmentation in this example as different from the segmentation used to present the interpretation results in other sections.) When examined carefully, the line-extraction results show line segments that are fragmented into pieces, multiple parallel lines, and gaps in lines.

The goal is to use typical segmentation results to produce the trapezoidal region (which is almost a parallelogram) representing the perspective projection of a rectangular roof surface, as well as the orientation in 3D space of that surface. The top-down grouping strategy that we employ here is organized around evidence of the almost parallel lines forming the two sets of sides of the trapezoid. There are alternate strategies for other typical situations where some of this information is missing. Thus, this roof grouping strategy expects some evidence for each of the four sides, and, in particular, uses the long lines bounding the putative roof region. Figure 16c shows the long lines along the region boundary. "Long" is determined as a relative function of the image area of the roof region, here $\frac{1}{3}$ of the square root of the roof region area. Figure 16d illustrates the result of merging similar regions which are partially bounded by the long lines.

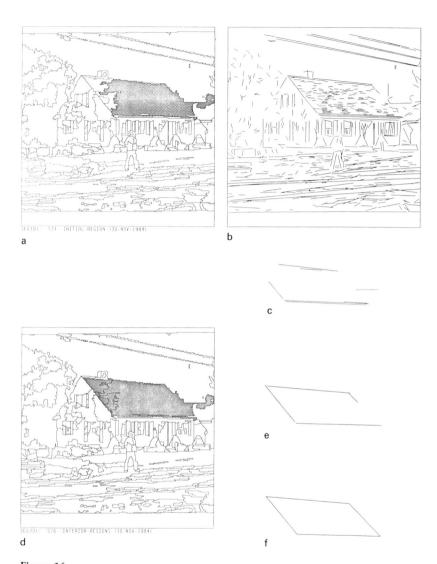

Figure 16

Steps in the schema-directed interpretation of a roof. (a,b) Region and line representations; the initial roof hypothesis region is cross-hatched. (c) Long lines bordering the roof-hypothesis-region boundary. (d) New roof hypothesis after merging regions partially bounded by the long lines in the previous image. (e) After joining collinear, nearby segments and fitting a straight line to the joined boundaries. (f) Completed hypothesized roof trapezoid.

Figure 16e shows the lines bounding the extended roof region, after removing shorter, parallel, almost adjacent lines, joining co-linear nearby segments, and then fitting straight lines to the boundaries to form a partial trapezoid. Figure 16f shows the complete hypothesized roof trapezoid. The three-dimensional geometry of the roof can then be computed (up to some possibly nontrivial degree of error) on the basis of either the location of the pair of vanishing points of the two sets of image lines that are parallel in the physical world, or one pair of parallel lines and an assumption of perpendicular angles to a third line [37].

The point of this discussion is that the interpretation process required a flexible strategy for grouping and reorganizing the lines and regions obtained from imperfect segmentation processes. At this point in our understanding, we are developing each strategy independently; however, we hope to begin to define some standard intermediate grouping primitives that would form the basis of a variety of general top-down strategies.

Results of Rule-Based Image Interpretation

Interpretation experiments are being conducted on a large set of "house scene" images. Thus far, we have been able to extract sky, grass, and foliage (trees and bushes) from many of these images with reasonable effectiveness, and we have been successful in identifying shutters (or windows), wall, and roof in some of them. Object-hypothesis and exemplar-extension rules as described above were employed. Additional object-verification rules requiring consistent spatial relationships with other object labels are being developed. The features and knowledge utilized vary across color and texture attributes, shape, size, location in the image, location relative to identified objects, and similarity in color and texture to identified objects. In the following figures, we show isolated intermediate and final results from the overall system.

The interpretation results shown were obtained from a version of the VISIONS system that used different (somewhat coarser-grained) initial segmentations than those presented earlier and a set of object-hypothesis and exemplar-extension strategies that differed in structure (but not in principle) from those presented earlier. Figure 17 shows selected results from the object-hypothesis rules after exemplar extension and region merging. Figure 18 illustrates typical interpretations obtained from a house-scene schema-interpretation strategy that utilizes a set of object-hypothesis rules for exemplar selection, extends the partial model from the most reliable of these hypotheses, and employs relational information

a

b

c

d

Figure 17
Results from schema interpretation strategies. (a) Roof rule, based on roof features and spatial relation to house wall. (b,c) Grass and sky, based on exemplar selection and similarity extension. (d) Shutter rule, based on shape and spatial relationships to each other and house wall.

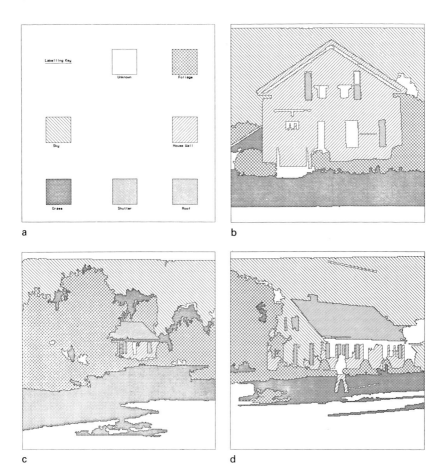

Figure 18

Final interpretations. These images show the final results obtained by combining the results of the interpretation strategies under the constraints generated from the knowledge base. (a) Interpretation key. (b–d) Interpretation results. In (d), the missing boundary between sky and wall results in a labeling conflict; the identification shown is sky, but a second interpretation has this region labeled house wall.

for verifying hypotheses and predicting image location of object parts and related objects. The image areas shown in white in figure 18 are uninterpreted either because the object did not exist in the knowledge network (and hence no label could be assigned) or because the object varied in some way from the rather constrained set of alternate descriptions of the object stored in the knowledge base.

The interpretation shown in figure 18d illustrates a problem that may be expected to occur quite frequently. The original interpretation was produced using a fairly coarse segmentation, which is desirable from the standpoint of computational efficiency since fewer regions are involved. However, the sky and the house wall are merged into one region (as is shown more clearly in figure 19a), because the difference between the two areas was below the resolution of the segmentation process. This is the disadvantage of using a coarse segmentation. Parameters of the segmentation processes can be set to produce a finer-grained segmentation, but many more regions are produced. On the other hand, the smaller regions can be expected to find more of the desired boundaries, and sometimes to better match the object descriptions in the knowledge base, at the risk of overfragmentation. Because of these conflicting constraints, we believe it is extremely important to closely couple the lower-level processes responsible for constructing the intermediate representation and the interpretation processes which operate on the intermediate- and higher-level representations. The interpretation processes should have focus-of-attention mechanisms for correction of segmentation errors, extraction of finer image detail, and verification of semantic hypotheses. The advantage of top-down application of these processes rests in the focused nature of the processing. Since the processes do not have to be applied everywhere in the image, they can be more computationally expensive and make heavier use of knowledge specific to the particular problem.

An example of the effectiveness of semantically directed feedback to the segmentation processes is shown in figure 19. The missing boundary between the house wall and the sky led to competing object hypotheses (sky and house wall) based on local interpretation strategies. The region is hypothesized to be sky by the sky strategy, whereas application of the house-wall strategy (using the roof and shutters as spatial constraints on the location of house wall) leads to a wall hypothesis. There is evidence available that some form of error has occurred in this example: Conflicting labels are produced for the same region by local interpretation strategies; the house-wall label is associated with regions above the roof (note that, although there are houses with a wall above a lower roof, the geometric

a   b

c

Figure 19
Resegmentation of house/sky region from figure 18d. (a) The original segmentation,
showing the region to be resegmented. (b) The regions resulting from the resegmentation
of the selected region. (c) Final interpretation of the house scene in figure 1c, after
inserting resegmented house/sky regions and reinterpreting the image.

consistency of the object shape is not satisfied in this example); and the sky extends down close to the approximate horizon line in only a portion of the image (which is possible, but worthy of closer inspection).

In this case, resegmentation of the sky—house wall region, with segmentation parameters set to extract finer detail, produces a reasonable segmentation of this region (figure 19b). It should be pointed out that in this image there is a barely discernible boundary between the sky and house wall. However, once the merged region is resegmented with an intent of overfragmentation, this boundary can be detected. Now, the same interpretation strategy used earlier produces the quite acceptable results shown in figure 19c. (This capability of detecting labeling conflicts and resegmentation is not automatic in the current version of the system.)

Future work is directed toward refinement of the segmentation algorithms, object-hypothesis rules, object-verification rules, and interpretation strategies. System development is aimed toward more robust methods of control: automatic schema and strategy selection, interpretation of images under more than one general class of schemata, and automatic focus-of-attention merchanisms and error-correcting strategies for resolving interpretation errors.

Principles to Guide Knowledge-Based Vision Research

In summary, we list some of the principles of our work on knowledge-based vision systems that might provide guidance to other researches. In no way are we asserting that this is the "only" or "correct" or "complete" approach to high-level vision. Rather, the problem domain has been so difficult that there has been little work of any generality. Thus our statements at this time are distilled from the experience of a partially successful approach to general knowledge-based vision that is continuously evolving as we understand the visual domain more thoroughly.

• An integrated symbolic representation of 2D image events (such as regions and lines) and 3D world events (such as surface patches) should be used as the symbolic interface between sensory data and world knowledge. In particular, it is the attributes of these elements, potentially including depth (3D) and motion (2D and 3D) information (see papers 5 and 8 in this volume), that provides linkages to stored knowledge and higher-level processing strategies.

• In the initial stages of bottom-up hypothesis formation, focus-of-attention mechanisms should be used to selectively group elements of the intermediate representation and to construct tentative object hypotheses (see paper 7 in this volume). The interpretation should be extended from such "islands of reliability." The choice of object classes for initial consideration can be controlled (top down) via context or expectation (see paper 6 in this volume).

• A simple initial interface to knowledge can be obtained via rules defined over a range of the expected values of the attributes of the symbolic events that have been extracted. These rules can be organized around the most likely events or the easiest events to extract when highly structured situations are expected.

• Knowledge of the physical world should be organized around a scene schema and an object schema that can be represented as a structured collection of parts. This allows the contextual relationships to guide the further processing of partial interpretations. In places where 3D shape and spatial relations are complex, the general relationships between image events in typical 2D views can be used to interface to the bottom-up 2D symbolic representation (see paper 10 in this volume). However, long-range progress is dependent on more effective 3D shape representations.

• More complex strategies will be needed for matching salient aspects of the ambiguous, incomplete, and sometimes incorrect intermediate data representation to the object models stored in the knowledge base. They involve a diverse collection of goals, and, given our understanding at this time, it may be easier to represent them as procedural knowledge. These strategies include knowledge-directed grouping, deletion, and manipulation of intermediate symbolic entities, as well as goal-oriented feedback to low-level processes. Several papers in this volume (e.g. paper 11) touch on this aspect of vision; others address it in the context of robot control (papers 13 and 14).

• Inference mechanisms for utilizing distributed fine-grained and weak hypotheses will be needed. These inference mechanisms must deal with the issues of high degrees of uncertainty and of pooling a variety of sources of information in order to control processes for extending partial interpretations.

• Highly interactive user-friendly environments for visually displaying results of knowledge application are very important. The vision domain provides a natural medium for user feedback and interaction.

Acknowledgments

This work has been supported by the Air Force Office of Scientific Research under contract AFOSR-85-0005 and the Defense Mapping Agency under contract 800-85-C-0012. The authors wish to acknowledge the many members of the VISIONS research community, particularly Robert Belknap, Joey Griffith, and Terry Weymouth, who have contributed to the technical ideas developed in this paper and the software that produced the results. Our thanks also to Janet Turnbull and Laurie Waskiewicz for their patience and perseverance in producing the manuscript.

References

1. R. Davis. Expert systems: Where are we? And where do we go from here? *AI Magazine* 3 (spring 1982): 3–22.

2. R. Bajcsy and M. Tavakoli. Computer recognition of roads from satellite pictures. *IEEE Transactions on Systems, Man, and Cybernetics* 6 (1976): 623–637.

3. D. Ballard, C. Brown, and J. Feldman. An approach to knowledge-directed image analysis. In *Computer Vision Systems*, ed. A. Hanson and E. Riseman (Academic, 1978).

4. H. Barrow and J. Tenenbaum. MSYS: A System for Reasoning about Scenes. Technical Note 121, AI Center Stanford Research Institute, 1976.

5. T. Binford. Survey of model based image analysis systems. *International Journal of Robotics Research* 1 (1982): 18–64.

6. R. Brooks. Symbolic Reasoning among 3-D Models and 2-D Images. Report STAN-CS-81-861/AIM-343, Department of Computer Science, Stanford University, 1981.

7. O. Faugeras and K. Price. Semantic descriptions of aerial images using stochastic labeling. *IEEE Transactions on Pattern Analysis and Machine Intelligence* 3 (1981): 638–642.

8. A. Hanson and E. Riseman. VISIONS: A computer system for interpreting scenes. In *Computer Vision Systems*, ed. A. Hanson and E. Riseman (Academic, 1978).

9. T. Kanade. Model representation and control structures in image understanding. In Proceedings of the Fifth International Joint Conference on Artificial Intelligence, 1977.

10. M. Levine and S. Shaheen. A modular computer vision system for picture segmentation and interpretation. *IEEE Transactions on Pattern Analysis and Machine Intelligence* 3 (1981): 540–556.

11. A. Mackworth. Vision research strategy: Black magic, metaphors, mechanisms, miniworlds, and maps. In *Computer Vision Systems*, ed. A. Hanson and E. Riseman (Academic, 1978).

12. M. Nagao and T. Matsuyama. *A Structural Analysis of Complex Aerial Photographs.* Plenum, 1980.

13. Y. Ohta. A Region-Oriented Image-Analysis System by Computer. Ph.D. thesis, Kyoto University, 1980.

14. K. E. Price and R. Reddy. Matching segments of images. *IEEE Transactions on Pattern Analysis and Machine Intelligence* 1 (1979): 110–116.

15. J. M. Tenenbaum and H. Barrow. Experiments in Interpretation-Guided Segmentation. Technical Note 123, AI Center, Stanford Research Institute, 1976.

16. J. Tsotsos. Knowledge of the visual process: Content, form, and use. In Proceedings of the Sixth International Conference on Pattern Recognition, Munich, 1982.

17. Y. Yakimovsky and J. Feldman. A semantics-based decision theory region analyzer. In Proceedings of the Third International Joint Conference on Artificial Intelligence, 1973.

18. D. Marr. *Vision.* Freeman, 1982.

19. M. Brady. Computational approaches to image understanding. *Computing Surveys* 14 (March 1982): 3–71.

20. P. A. Nagin, A. R. Hanson, and E. M. Riseman. Studies in global and local histogram-guided relaxation algorithms. *IEEE Transactions on Pattern Analysis and Machine Intelligence* 4 (May 1982): 263–277.

21. R. Kohler. Integrating Non-Semantic Knowledge into Image Segmentation Processes. COINS Technical Report 84-04, University of Massachusetts, Amherst, 1984.

22. J. B. Burns, A. R. Hanson, and E. M. Riseman. Extracting linear features. In Proceedings of the Seventh International Conference on Pattern Recognition, Montreal, 1984.

23. G. Reynolds et al. Hierarchical knowledge-directed object extraction using a combined region and line representation. In Proceedings of the Workshop on Computer Vision: Representation and Control, Annapolis, 1984.

24. T. Weymouth, J. S. Griffith, A. R. Hanson, and E. M. Riseman. Rule based strategies for image interpretation. In Proceedings of AAAI, Washington, D.C., 1983. A longer version of this paper appears in the Proceedings of the DARPA Image Understanding Workshop, Arlington, Va., 1983.

25. C. C. Parma, A. R. Hanson, and E. M. Riseman. Experiments in Schema-Driven Interpretation of a Natural Scene. COINS Technical Report 80–10, University of Massachusetts, Amherst, 1980.

26. V. R. Lesser and L. D. Erman. A retrospective view of the Hearsay-II architecture. In Proceedings of the Fifth International Joint Conference on Artificial Intelligence, Cambridge, Mass., 1977.

27. L. Erman et al. The Hearsay-II speech-understanding system: Integrating knowledge to resolve uncertainty. Computing Surveys 12, no. 2 (1980): 213-253.

28. T. E. Weymouth. Using Object Descriptions in a Schema Network for Machine Vision. Ph.D. dissertation in preparation, Computer and Information Science Department, University of Massachusetts, Amherst.

29. J. D. Lowrance. Dependency-Graph Models of Evidential Support. COINS Technical Report 82-26, University of Massachusetts, Amherst, 1982.

30. L. Wesley and A. Hanson. The use of an evidential-based model for representing knowledge and reasoning about images in the VISIONS system. In Proceedings of the Workshop on Computer Vision, Rindge, N.H., 1982.

31. A. Hanson and E. Riseman. Computer Vision Systems. Academic, 1978.

32. G. Shafer. A Mathematical Theory of Evidence. Princeton University Press, 1976.

33. A. Hanson and E. Riseman. A Summary of Image Understanding Research at the University of Massachusetts. COINS Technical Report 83-35, University of Massachusetts, Amherst, 1983.

34. A. Hanson and E. Riseman. Segmentation of natural scenes. In Computer Vision Systems, ed. A. Hanson and E. Riseman (Academic, 1978).

35. E. Riseman and A. Hanson. The Design of a Semantically Directed Vision Processor. COINS Technical Report TR 71C-1, University of Massachusetts, 1975. Revised version: COINS Technical Report 75C-1.

36. E. Riseman and A. Hanson. A methodology for the development of general knowledge-based vision systems. In Proceedings of the IEEE Workshop on Principles of Knowledge-Based Systems, Denver, 1984.

37. H. Nakatani, R. Weiss, and E. Riseman. Application of vanishing points to 3D measurements. In Proceedings of the 28th International Technical Symposium on Optics and Electro-Optics, 1984.

38. A. Hanson, E. Riseman, and E. Fisher. Context in word recognition. Pattern Recognition 8, no. 1 (1976): 35–45.

39. E. Fisher. The Use of Context in Character Recognition. COINS Technical Report 76-12, University of Massachusetts, Amherst. 1976.

40. E. Riseman and A. Hanson. A contextual post processing system for error corrections using binary n-grams. IEEE Transactions on Computers 23 (1974): 480–493.

10

An Extremum Principle
for Shape from Contour

Michael Brady and
Alan Yuille

1 Introduction

An important goal of early vision is the computation of a representation of the visible surfaces in an image, in particular the determination of the orientation of those surfaces as defined by their local surface normals [9, 30]. Many processes contribute to achieving this goal, stereopsis and structure from motion being currently the most studied in image understanding. Three other important contributing processes are shape-from-contour, shape-from-texture-gradients, and shape-from-shading. Several psychophysical demonstrations show that shape-from-contour is significantly more powerful than shape-from-texture-gradients [13, 14, 25]. Similarly, Barrow and Tenenbaum [7, fig. 1.3 ff.] suggest that shape-from-contour is a more effective clue to shape than shape-from-shading.

In this paper we consider the computation of shape-from-contour. Figure 1 shows a number of shapes that are typically perceived as images of surfaces which are oriented out of the picture plane. The corresponding (sets of) surface normals (up to tilt reversal) are shown to the right. It may be supposed [21, pp. 168 ff.]) that the slant judgments in figure 1 are largely determined by familiarity with regular shapes such as circles and squares. Figure 2 strains that hypothesis (although Gregory proposes that we are familiar with the shape of puddles) and suggests that the computation is based on more general knowledge of shapes and surfaces. The method we propose is based on such general knowledge, namely a preference for symmetric, or at least compact, surfaces. Note that the contour does not need to be closed in order to be interpreted as oriented our of the image plane. Figure 3 shows that, in general, contours are interpreted as curved three-dimensional surfaces.

We develop a extremum principle for determining three-dimensional surface orientation from a two-dimensional contour. Initially, we work out

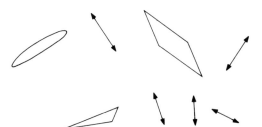

Figure 1
Two-dimensional contours that are often interpreted as planes oriented with respect to the image plane. The commonly judged slant is shown next to each shape.

Figure 2
Some unfamiliar shapes that are also interpreted as planes oriented with respect to the image plane. The shape on the far left is from reference 21; the others are from reference 39.

Figure 3
Some shapes that are interpreted as curved three-dimensional surfaces.

the extremum principle for the cases illustrated in figures 1 and 2, that is, assuming *a priori* that the contour is closed and that the interpreted surface is planar. Later, we discuss how to extend our approach to open contours and how to interpret contours as curved surfaces as shown in figure 3.

The extremum principle maximizes a familiar measure of the compactness or symmetry of an oriented surface, namely the ratio of the area to the square of the perimeter. It is shown that this measure is at the heart of the maximum-likelihood approach to shape-from-contour developed by Witkin [39] and Davis et al. [15]. The maximum-likelihood approach has had some success interpreting irregularly shaped objects. The method is ineffective, however, when the distribution of image tangents is not random, as is the case when the image is a regular shape, such as an ellipse or a parallelogram. Our extremum principle interprets regular figures correctly. We show that maximum-likelihood method approximates the extremum principle for irregular figures but does not compute the correct slant for an ellipse. Witkin [39, figure 5] provides empirical evidence that the maximum-likelihood method computes a good approximation to the perceived tilt but underestimates the slant. We prove in appendix A that the maximum-likelihood method consistently overestimates the slant of an ellipse. A more thorough investigation of the difference between the extremum principle and the maximum-likelihood method is needed.

One class of figures that are readily perceived as lying in a plane other than the image plane are skew symmetries, which are two-dimensional linear (affine) transformations of real symmetries. Kanade [29, p. 424] has suggested a method for determining the three-dimensional orientation of skew-symmetric figures, under the "heuristic assumption" that such figures are interpreted as oriented real symmetries. We prove that our extremum principle necessarily interprets skew symmetries as oriented real symmetries, thus dispensing with the need for any heuristic assumption to that effect. Kanade shows that there is a one-parameter family of possible orientations of a skew-symmetric figure, forming a hyperbola in gradient space. He suggests that the minimum-slant member of the one-parameter family is perceived. In the special case of a real symmetry, Kanade's suggestion implies that symmetric shapes are perceived as lying in the image plane (that is, having zero slant). It is clear from the ellipse in figure 1 that this is not correct. Our method interprets real symmetries correctly.

First, we review the maximum-likelihood method. In section 3 we discuss several previous extremum principles and justify our choice of the compactness measure. In section 4 we derive the mathematics necessary to extremize the compactness measure, and relate the extremum principle to the maximum-likelihood method. In section 5 we investigate Kanade's work on skew symmetry. One approach to extending the extremum principle to interpret curved surfaces, such as that shown in figure 3, is sketched in section 7. In the final section, we relate this work to the psychophysical literature on slant estimation and the image-understanding work on shape-from-texture.

2 The Sampling Approach

Witkin [39] treated the determination of shape-from-contour as a problem of signal detection. Davis et al. [15] corrected some of Witkin's mathematics and proposed two efficient algorithms to compute the orientation of a planar surface from an image contour. Witkin's approach uses a geometric model of (orthographic) projection and a statistical model of the distribution of surfaces in space (statistics of the universe) and of the distribution of tangents to the image contour. We shall adopt the geometric model, but dispense with the statistical model in favor of an extremum principle.

First, the geometric model. Assume that the image plane is horizontal with coordinates (x, y) (figure 4). To obtain a plane with slant σ and tilt τ, we rotate (x, y) by τ in the image plane and then rotate the image plane by σ about the new y axis. Assume that the coordinate frame in the plane (σ, τ) is chosen so that it projects into (x, y). (In section 4 we describe this transformation more precisely; see also [15, p. 3].)

Now suppose that a curve is drawn in the plane (σ, τ), and denote by β the angle that the tangent makes at a typical point on the curve. Let α be the tangent angle in the image plane at the point corresponding to β. Then α and β are related by equation 2.1.

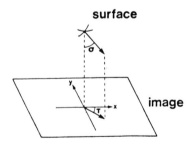

Figure 4
The geometry of orthographic projection. Details of notation are described in text.

$$\tan(\alpha - \tau) = \frac{\tan\beta}{\cos\sigma}. \tag{2.1}$$

We now turn to the statistical model, which consists of two assumptions called *isotropy* and *independence*. Isotropy reasonably supposes that all surface orientations are equally likely to occur in nature and that tangents to surface curves are equally likely in all directions. Most succinctly, it is assumed that the quantities (β, σ, τ) are randomly distributed and that their joint probability density function ("density") $D(\beta, \sigma, \tau)$ is given by [15]

$$D(\beta, \sigma, \tau) = \frac{1}{\pi^2} \sin\sigma. \tag{2.2}$$

We assume that the ranges of the angles are $0 \le \sigma \le \pi/2$, $0 \le \tau \le \pi$, and $0 \le \beta \le \pi$. Similarly, the density of (σ, τ) is given by

$$D(\sigma, \tau) = \frac{1}{\pi} \sin\sigma. \tag{2.3}$$

The independence assumption requires that the image tangents α_i $(1 \le i \le n)$ are statistically independent. That is, it is assumed that the tangent directions at different points on the image curve are independent. This is true only if the contour is highly irregularly shaped, or if the number of samples is small. In any case, the assumption of independence is an inherent weakness of the sampling approach [39, p. 36].

Witkin [39, pp. 25–26] shows that the joint density function $D(\alpha, \sigma, \tau)$ is given by

$$D(\alpha, \sigma, \tau) = \frac{1}{\pi^2} \frac{\sin\sigma \cos\sigma}{\cos^2(\alpha - \tau) + \cos^2\sigma \sin^2(\alpha - \tau)}. \tag{2.4}$$

For the conditional density $D(\alpha|\sigma, \tau)$ we find

$$D(\alpha|\sigma, \tau) = \frac{1}{\pi} \frac{\cos\sigma}{\cos^2(\alpha - \tau) + \cos^2\sigma \sin^2(\alpha - \tau)}. \tag{2.5}$$

Denote the sample $(\alpha_1, \alpha_2, \ldots, \alpha_n)$ by A. (The sample is independent by assumption.) It has conditional density

$$D(A|\sigma, \tau) = \prod_{i=1}^{n} D(\alpha_i|\sigma, \tau). \tag{2.6}$$

By Bayes's formula we obtain

$$D(\sigma, \tau|A) = \frac{D(A|\sigma, \tau)D(\sigma, \tau)}{\iint D(A|\sigma, \tau)D(\sigma, \tau)\, d\sigma\, d\tau}. \tag{2.7}$$

The numerator is independent of σ and τ. The sampling approach takes a random sample A and defines the most likely orientation of the plane (σ, τ) to be that which extremizes $D(\sigma, \tau | A)$. Witkin [39] quantizes σ and τ, and describes an algorithm to find the maximizing (σ_j, τ_k). Davis et al. [15] develop a more efficient algorithm that first estimates σ and τ and then uses those estimates in a Newton iterative process. They provide evidence that their method is more accurate than Witkin's. Curiously, however, they state [15, p. 24] that "the iterative algorithm was not used [in the experiments they report] because the initial estimates (whose computation is trivial) are very accurate and the iterative scheme often failed to converge to the solution."

3 Extremum Principles

Brady and Horn [12] survey the use of extremum principles in image understanding. The choice of performance index or measure to extremized, and the class of functions over which the extremization takes place, are justified by appealing to a model of the geometry or photometry of image forming and constraints such as smoothness. For example, the use of extremum principles in surface reconstruction is based on surface consistency theorems [22−24, 40] and a thin plate model of visual surfaces [12, 36].

There are several plausible measures of a curve that might be extremized in order to compute shape-from-contour. First, $\oint \kappa^2 \, ds$, where κ is the curvature of the contour, has been investigated as a curve of least energy for interpolating across gaps in plane curves [27]. Here we seek a measure of a curve that is extremized when the plane containing the curve is slanted and tilted appropriately. Contrary to what appears to be a popular belief, given an ellipse in the image plane, $\oint \kappa^2 \, ds$ is not extremized in the plane that transforms the ellipse into a circle. Appendix B contains a proof of this assertion. Since ellipses are normally perceived as slanted circles, we reject the square curvature as a suitable measure.

Another possible measure is proposed by Barrow and Tenenbaum [7, p. 89]. Assuming planarity (the torsion τ is zero), it reduces to

$$\oint \left(\frac{d\kappa}{ds} \right)^2 ds.$$

One objection to this measure is that it involves high-order derivatives of the curve. This means it is overly dependent on small scale behavior. Consider, for example, a curve which is circular except for a small kink. The circular part of the curve will contribute a tiny proportion to the integral even when the plane containing the curve is rotated. The kink, on the other hand, will contribute an arbitrarily large proportion and so will dominate the integral no matter how small it is compared with the rest of the curve. This is clearly undesirable. For example, it suggests that the measure will be highly sensitive to noise in the position and orientation of the points forming the contour.

A second objection to the measure proposed by Barrow and Tenenbaum is that it is minimized by, and hence has an intrinsic preference for, straight lines, for which $d\kappa/ds = 0$. This means that the measure has a bias toward planes that correspond to the (nongeneral) side on viewing position. These planes are perpendicular to the image plane and have slant $\pi/2$.

• Contours that are the projection of curves in planes with large slant are most effective for eliciting a three-dimensional interpretation.

• A curve is foreshortened by projection by the cosine of the slant angle in the tilt direction, and not at all in the orthogonal direction.

We conclude that three-dimensional interpretations are most readily elicited for shapes that are highly elongated in one direction. Another way to express this idea is that the image contour has large aspect ratio or is radially asymmetric. The measure we suggest will pick out the plane orientation for which the curve is most compact and most radially symmetric. Specifically, our measure is

$$M = \frac{(area)}{(perimeter)^2}. \tag{3.1}$$

This is a scale-invariant number characterizing the curve. For all possible curves it is maximized by the most compact one, a circle. By most compact, we mean most radially symmetric. This gives the measure an upper bound of $1/4\pi$. Its lower bound is clearly zero, and it is achieved for a straight line. It follows that our measure has a built-in prejudice against side-on views for which the slant is $\pi/2$.

In general, given a contour, our extremum principle will choose the orientation in which the deprojected contour maximizes M. For example, an ellipse is interpreted as a slanted circle. The tilt angle is given by the minor axis of the ellipse. It is also straightforward to show that a parallelogram corresponds to a rotated square. Appendix C discusses the interpretation of several simple shapes. In particular, an ellipse is interpreted as a slanted circle, a parallelogram as a slanted square, and a triangle as a slanted equilateral triangle. In section 5 we extend the parallelogram result to the more general case of skewed symmetry.

The quantity M is commonly used in pattern recognition and industrial vision systems [1, 5, 33] as a feature that measures the compactness of an object. Furthermore, it can be shown that the measure M defined in equation 3.1 is at the heart of the geometric model in the maximum-likelihood approach.

From section 2, we see that the maximum-likelihood approach maximizes the product of a number of terms of form

$$f(\alpha) = \frac{\cos\sigma}{\cos^2(\alpha - \tau) + \cos^2\sigma \sin^2(\alpha - \tau)}. \tag{3.2}$$

Differentiating equation 2.1 with respect to the arc length s_I along the image curve and s_R along the rotated curve, respectively, we obtain

$$\frac{\kappa_I \, ds_I}{\kappa_R \, ds_R} = \frac{1}{f(\alpha)}, \tag{3.3}$$

where κ_I and κ_R are the curvature at corresponding points of the image contour and its deprojection in the rotated plane, respectively. In fact, $\kappa_I = d\alpha/ds_I$ and $\kappa_R = d\beta/ds_R$. There is no σ or τ dependence in the numerator of equation 3.3. We can write each term $\kappa \, ds$ as $(ds \, ds)/(\rho \, ds)$, where ρ is the radius of curvature. Now $(\rho \, ds)/(ds \, ds)$ is just a local computation of area divided by perimeter squared. Hence, maximizing each $f(\alpha)$ in the maximum-likelihood approach is equivalent to locally maximizing area over perimeter squared. In section 4 we will examine this connection more rigorously.

The area, as well as the perimeter, can be obtained by an integral round the contour. If $\mathbf{n}$ is the nomal to the curve, then it is a straightforward application of Stokes's theorem to show that

$$(\text{area})\mathbf{n} = \tfrac{1}{2} \oint \mathbf{r} \times d\mathbf{r}, \tag{3.5}$$

where (area) is a scalar quantity and $\mathbf{r}$ is a vector coordinate system in the plane of the figure. This formula simplifies the calculations and means that the perimeter and the area can be computed simultaneously.

4 Extremizing the Measure

We now write down the measure for a curve with arbitrary orientation and then extremize with respect to the orientation. Let the unit normals to the image plane and the rotated plane be $\mathbf{k}$ and $\mathbf{n}$, respectively. The slant σ of the rotated plane is given by the scalar product

$$\cos\sigma = k \cdot n. \tag{4.1}$$

Let Γ_R and Γ_I be the contour in the rotated and image planes. A vector $\mathbf{r}$ in the image plane satisfies $\mathbf{r} \cdot \mathbf{k} = 0$ and is the projection of a vector $\mathbf{v}$ in the rotated plane that satisfies $\mathbf{v} \cdot \mathbf{n} = 0$. The projection relationship between $\mathbf{v}$ and its image $\mathbf{r}$ is defined by

$$\mathbf{r} = \mathbf{k} \times (\mathbf{v} \times \mathbf{k}) = \mathbf{v} - (\mathbf{v} \cdot \mathbf{k})\mathbf{k}, \tag{4.2}$$

$$\mathbf{v} = \frac{\mathbf{n} \times (\mathbf{r} \times \mathbf{k})}{(\mathbf{n} \cdot \mathbf{k})} = \frac{(\mathbf{n} \cdot \mathbf{k})\mathbf{r} - (\mathbf{n} \cdot \mathbf{r})\mathbf{k}}{(\mathbf{n} \cdot \mathbf{k})}, \tag{4.3}$$

where $\times$ denotes vector product. Now Γ_R and Γ_I have (vector) areas $\mathbf{A}_R$ and $\mathbf{A}_I$ given by

$$\mathbf{A}_R = \tfrac{1}{2} \oint_{\Gamma_R} \mathbf{v} \times d\mathbf{v} \tag{4.4}$$

and

$$\mathbf{A}_I = \tfrac{1}{2} \oint_{\Gamma_I} \mathbf{r} \times d\mathbf{r}. \tag{4.5}$$

The area vectors have the same direction as the normal to the plane containing the area. In particular, $\mathbf{A}_R$ is in direction $\mathbf{n}$ and $\mathbf{A}_I$ is in direction $\mathbf{k}$. Substituting 4.3 into 4.4 and using 4.1, we find

$$\mathbf{A}_R = \mathbf{A}_I + \frac{\mathbf{k} \times (\mathbf{n} \times \mathbf{A}_I)}{(\mathbf{n} \cdot \mathbf{k})}$$

$$= \frac{(\mathbf{k} \cdot \mathbf{A}_I)}{\cos\sigma}\mathbf{n}. \tag{4.6}$$

It follows that

$$\|\mathbf{A}_R\| = \frac{\|\mathbf{A}_I\|}{\cos\sigma}. \tag{4.7}$$

(The range of σ guarantees that $\cos\sigma$ is positive.) The perimeter lengths P_R and P_I are given by

$$P_R = \oint_{\Gamma_R} \|d\mathbf{v}\| \tag{4.8}$$

and

$$P_I = \oint_{\Gamma_R} \|d\mathbf{r}\|. \tag{4.9}$$

Substituting 4.3 into 4.8 gives

$$P_R = \oint_{\Gamma_R} \left((d\mathbf{r})^2 + \frac{(\mathbf{n} \cdot d\mathbf{r})^2}{(\mathbf{n} \cdot \mathbf{k})^2} \right)^{1/2}. \tag{4.10}$$

In general there is no simple relationship between the perimeters analogous to 4.6 between the areas. Nevertheless, by 4.7,

$$\frac{\|A_R\|}{P_R{}^2} = \frac{\|A_I\|}{P_R{}^2 \cos\sigma}, \tag{4.11}$$

and so our extremum principle is equivalent to extremizing $\cos^{1/2}\sigma\, P_R$, which we write as

$$I = \oint_{\Gamma_R} \left((\mathbf{n} \cdot \mathbf{k})\, d\mathbf{r}^2 + \frac{(\mathbf{n} \cdot d\mathbf{r})^2}{(\mathbf{n} \cdot \mathbf{k})} \right)^{1/2}. \tag{4.12}$$

We extremize this with respect to the orientation $\mathbf{n}$ of the rotated plane, maintaining the constraint that $\mathbf{n}$ is a unit vector by a Lagrange multiplier $\Lambda/4$. This gives

$$\mathbf{k} \oint \left((\mathbf{n} \cdot \mathbf{k})\, d\mathbf{r}^2 + \frac{(\mathbf{n} \cdot d\mathbf{r})^2}{(\mathbf{n} \cdot \mathbf{k})} \right)^{-1/2} \frac{(\mathbf{n} \cdot \mathbf{k})^2\, d\mathbf{r}^2 - (\mathbf{n} \cdot d\mathbf{r})^2}{(\mathbf{n} \cdot \mathbf{k})^2}$$

$$+ 2 \oint \left((\mathbf{n} \cdot \mathbf{k})\, d\mathbf{r}^2 + \frac{(\mathbf{n} \cdot d\mathbf{r})^2}{(\mathbf{n} \cdot \mathbf{k})} \right)^{-1/2} \frac{(\mathbf{n} \cdot \mathbf{k})(\mathbf{n} \cdot d\mathbf{r})\, d\mathbf{r}}{(\mathbf{n} \cdot \mathbf{k})^2}$$

$$+ \Lambda\mathbf{n} = 0. \tag{4.13}$$

Taking scalar products of equation 4.13 with $\mathbf{k}$ and $\mathbf{n}$, respectively, gives

$$0 = (\mathbf{n} \cdot \mathbf{k})\Lambda$$

$$+ \oint \left((\mathbf{n} \cdot \mathbf{k})\, d\mathbf{r}^2 + \frac{(\mathbf{n} \cdot d\mathbf{r})^2}{(\mathbf{n} \cdot \mathbf{k})} \right)^{-1/2} \frac{(\mathbf{n} \cdot \mathbf{k})^2\, d\mathbf{r}^2 - (\mathbf{n} \cdot d\mathbf{r})^2}{(\mathbf{n} \cdot \mathbf{k})^2} \tag{4.14}$$

and

$$0 = \Lambda + (\mathbf{n} \cdot \mathbf{k}) \oint \left((\mathbf{n} \cdot \mathbf{k})\, d\mathbf{r}^2 + \frac{(\mathbf{n} \cdot d\mathbf{r})^2}{(\mathbf{n} \cdot \mathbf{k})} \right)^{-1/2}$$

$$\times \frac{(\mathbf{n} \cdot \mathbf{k})^2\, d\mathbf{r}^2 + (\mathbf{n} \cdot d\mathbf{r})^2}{(\mathbf{n} \cdot \mathbf{k})^2}. \tag{4.15}$$

We use equation 4.14 to remove the integral coefficient of $\mathbf{k}$ in 4.13, allowing us to express 4.13 as a sum of the second integral and $\mathbf{k} \times (\mathbf{k} \times \mathbf{n})$ times Λ. We now use 4.15 to eliminate Λ from this new form of 4.13. We recall that the unit tangent $\mathbf{t}$ is defined by

$$\mathbf{t} = \frac{d\mathbf{r}}{ds},$$

where s is arc length along the contour. It follows that

$d\mathbf{r} = \mathbf{t}\,ds.$

Recalling that $(\mathbf{n} \cdot \mathbf{k}) = \cos\sigma$, we find

$$2 \oint [\cos^2\sigma + (\mathbf{n} \cdot \mathbf{t})^2]^{-1/2} (\mathbf{t} \cdot \mathbf{n})\, d\mathbf{r}$$

$$= -\mathbf{k} \times (\mathbf{k} \times \mathbf{n}) \oint [\cos^2\sigma + (\mathbf{n} \cdot \mathbf{t})^2]^{1/2}\, ds, \tag{4.16}$$

where $\mathbf{t} = d\mathbf{r}/\|d\mathbf{r}\|$ is the unit tangent to the image contour.

Let the unit vectors in the x and y directions in the image plane be $\mathbf{i}$ and $\mathbf{j}$ and the normal to the image plane $\mathbf{k}$. By definition, $\cos\sigma = \mathbf{k} \cdot \mathbf{n}$. The tilt τ is defined by

$$\cos\tau = \frac{\mathbf{i} \cdot \mathbf{n}}{\sin\sigma}, \tag{4.17}$$

$$\sin\tau = \frac{\mathbf{j} \cdot \mathbf{n}}{\sin\sigma}. \tag{4.18}$$

The tangent vector $\mathbf{t}$ and the normal $\mathbf{n}$ can be written as

$$\mathbf{t} = \cos\alpha\,\mathbf{i} + \sin\alpha\,\mathbf{j} \tag{4.19}$$

and

$$\mathbf{n} = \sin\sigma\,\cos\tau\,\mathbf{i} + \sin\sigma\,\sin\tau\,\mathbf{j} + \cos\sigma\,\mathbf{k}, \tag{4.20}$$

where α is the tangent angle in the image. We now form the scalar products of equation 4.16 with $\mathbf{i}$ and $\mathbf{j}$ to obtain (with appropriate canceling)

$$2 \oint [\cos^2\sigma + \sin^2\sigma\,\cos^2(\alpha - \tau)]^{-1/2} \cos(\alpha - \tau) \cos\alpha\, ds$$

$$= \cos\tau \oint [\cos^2\sigma + \sin^2\sigma\,\cos^2(\alpha - \tau)]^{1/2}\, ds \tag{4.21}$$

and

$$2 \oint [\cos^2\sigma + \sin^2\sigma \cos^2(\alpha - \tau)]^{-1/2} \cos(\alpha - \tau) \sin\alpha \, ds$$

$$= \sin\tau \oint [\cos^2\sigma + \sin^2\sigma \cos^2(\alpha - \tau)]^{1/2} \, ds \tag{4.22}$$

We can rewrite there equations, after multiplying by factors of $\pm \cos\tau$ and $\pm \sin\tau$, as

$$2 \oint [\cos^2\sigma + \sin^2\sigma \cos^2(\alpha - \tau)]^{-1/2} \cos^2(\alpha - \tau) \, ds$$

$$= \oint [\cos^2\sigma + \sin^2\sigma \cos^2(\alpha - \tau)]^{1/2} \, ds \tag{4.23}$$

and

$$2 \oint [\cos^2\sigma + \sin^2\sigma \cos^2(\alpha - \tau)]^{-1/2} \cos(\alpha - \tau) \, ds = 0. \tag{4.24}$$

We use equations 4.23 and 4.24 in appendix D to determine the extremizing orientation for a skew symmetry. We can rewrite these equations in the form

$$\frac{\partial}{\partial\sigma} \left(\frac{1}{\cos^{1/2}\sigma} \oint [\cos^2\sigma + \sin^2\sigma \cos^2(\alpha - \tau)]^{1/2} \, ds \right) = 0, \tag{4.25}$$

$$\frac{\partial}{\partial\tau} \left(\frac{1}{\cos^{1/2}\sigma} \oint [\cos^2\sigma + \sin^2\sigma \cos^2(\alpha - \tau)]^{1/2} \, ds \right) = 0 \tag{4.26}$$

to emphasize that they correspond to extremizing with respect to σ and τ.

We can implement the extremum method directly from equations 4.25 and 4.26 by quantizing the tangent angle α_i, the slant σ_j, and the tilt τ_k, replacing the integral by a sum. This gives good results, even though we use fixed-point integers in our edge finder. A multilevel search speeds the algorithm by a factor of 10. For large slant, the ratio of the greatest to the least value of the expression is large, and the result is numerically well conditioned. For smaller slants (less than about 45° in the case of an ellipse), the ratio is small and the result poorly conditioned, so roundoff errors can be significant.

These equations are similar, although not identical, to those obtained by the maximum-likelihood method in the limit as the number of sampled tangents tends to infinity. To see this, recall from equation 2.7 that this method involves extremizing $D(A|\sigma, \tau)$ with respect to σ and τ. Since the denominator is independent of σ and τ, this amounts to extremizing $D(A|\sigma, \tau)D(\sigma, \tau)$. This is the same as extemizing $\log D(A|\sigma, \tau)D(\sigma, \tau)$. Using equations 2.3, 2.5, and 2.6, we obtain

$$E = n \log \cos\sigma + \log \sin\sigma$$

$$- \sum_{i=1}^{n} \log(\cos^2(\alpha_i - \tau) + \cos^2\sigma \sin^2(\alpha_i - \tau)), \tag{4.27}$$

where we have ignored factors of π which will vanish on differentiation. Dividing E by n and taking the limit as n tends to infinity gives

$$F = \log \cos\sigma \oint dr$$

$$- \oint \log(\cos^2(\alpha - \tau) + \cos^2\sigma \sin^2(\alpha - \tau)) \, dr. \tag{4.28}$$

Using the identity

$$\cos^2(\alpha - \tau) + \cos^2\sigma \sin^2(\alpha - \tau) = \cos^2\sigma + \sin^2\sigma \cos^2(\alpha - \tau) \tag{4.29}$$

gives

$$F = \log \cos\sigma \oint dr - \oint \log(\cos^2\sigma + \sin^2\sigma \cos^2(\alpha - \tau)) \, dr. \tag{4.30}$$

This formula is similar to equations 4.25 and 4.26. Thus, we expect the extremum method to give similar results to the sampling method when the contour is sufficiently irregular. However, we can show formally that the sampling method and the extremum method are not equivalent. In appendix A we show that the sampling method overestimates the slant of an ellipse. The precise discrepancy between the methods, and its practical consequence for computing shape from contour, are under investigation.

5 Skew Symmetry

We now consider a more general class of shapes for which the maximum-likelihood approach is not effective. Kanade [29, section 6.2] has introduced *skew symmetries*, which are two-dimensional linear (affine) transformations of real symmetries. There is a bijective correspondence between skew symmetries and images of symmetric shapes that lie in planes oriented to the image plane. Kanade proposes the heuristic assumption that a skew symmetry is interpreted as an oriented real symmetry, and he considers the problem of computing the slant and tilt of the oriented plane.

Denote the angle between the x axis of the image and the images of the symmetry and an axis orthogonal to it (the skewed transverse axis) by α and β, respectively. The orthogonality of the symmetry and transverse axes make it possible to derive one constraint on the orientation of the plane. Kanade uses gradient space (p, q) to represent surface orientations [9, 26]. He shows [29, p. 425] that the heuristic assumption is equivalent to requiring the gradient (p, q) of the oriented plane to lie on the hyperbola

$$p_1{}^2 \cos^2 \frac{\alpha - \beta}{2} - q_1{}^2 \sin^2 \frac{\alpha - \beta}{2} = -\cos(\alpha - \beta), \tag{5.1}$$

where

$$p_1 = p \cos\left(\frac{\alpha + \beta}{2}\right) + q \sin\left(\frac{\alpha + \beta}{2}\right),$$

$$q_1 = -p \sin\left(\frac{\alpha + \beta}{2}\right) + q \cos\left(\frac{\alpha + \beta}{2}\right). \tag{5.2}$$

Kanade [29, p. 426] further proposes that the vertices of the hyperbola, which correspond to the least slanted orientation, are chosen within this one-parameter family. This proposal is in accordance with a heuristic observation of Stevens [35]. In the special case that skew symmetry is a real symmetry, that is, in the case that $\alpha - \beta = \pm \pi/2$, the hyperbola reduces to a pair of orthogonal lines [29, p. 426] passing through the origin. In such cases the slant is zero. In other words, Kanade's proposal predicts that real symmetries are inevitably interpreted as lying in the image plane, and hence having zero slant. Inspection of figure 1 shows that this is not the case. A (symmetric) ellipse is typically perceived as a slanted circle, particularly if the major and minor axes do not line up with the horizontal and the vertical.

Although Kanade's minimum-slant proposal does not seem to be correct, there is evidence [35] for Kanade's assumption that skew symmetries are interpreted as real symmetries. We now show that the assumption can in fact be deduced from our extremum principle. As a corollary, in appendix D we determine the slant and tilt of any given skew-symmetric figure; only in special cases does it correspond to the minimum-slant member of Kanade's one-parameter family.

Instead of using equations 4.25 and 4.26, we prove the result from first principles, since this enables us to use symmetry directly. First, we partition

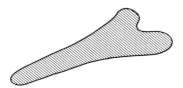

Figure 5
Partition of a skew-symmetric object into regions for the piecewise analysis presented in
section 5.

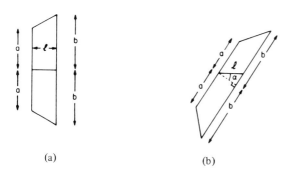

(a)   (b)

Figure 6
(a) A basic region before skewing. (b) The result of skewing the region shown in diagram
a through angle α.

the image into regions, as shown in figure 5. A typical region is shown in
figure 6(a), and we skew it by an angle α to get figure 6(b). We show that
the ratio of the area to the perimeter squared is greatest for figure 6(a) with
$\alpha = 0$. We show this is also true for the sum of the regions, and we take
the limit as the width of the regions goes to zero to complete the proof.

From figure 6(a) we calculate the area $A_i = \|\mathbf{A}\|$ and the portion P_i of the
perimeter of the shape to be

$$A_i = 2al + (b - a)l \tag{5.3}$$

and

$$P_i = 2[l^2 + (b - a)^2]^{1/2}. \tag{5.4}$$

From figure 6(b) we find

$$A_i' = 2al \cos\alpha + (b - a)l \cos\alpha$$

$$= A_i \cos\alpha \tag{5.5}$$

and

$$P_i' = [l^2 \cos^2\alpha + (b - a + l\sin\alpha)^2]^{1/2}$$
$$+ [l^2 \cos\alpha^2 + (b - a + l\sin\alpha)^2]^{1/2}. \tag{5.6}$$

We need to show that

$$\frac{\cos\alpha}{P_i'^2} < \frac{1}{P_i^2}. \tag{5.7}$$

This is equivalent to showing that

$$(2\cos\alpha - 1)[l^2 + (b - a)^2]$$
$$< [l^2 + (b - a)^2 + 2(b - a)l\sin\alpha]^{1/2}$$
$$\times [l^2 + (b - a)^2 - 2(b - a)l\sin\alpha]^{1/2}. \tag{5.8}$$

The condition clearly holds for $\pi/2 \geq \alpha \geq \pi/3$. Assume therefore that $0 \leq \alpha < \pi/3$. Squaring both sides of equation 5.8, we see that the condition is equivalent to

$$l^4 + (b - a)^4 + l^2(b - a)^2 \left(2 + \frac{\sin^2\alpha}{\cos^2\alpha - \cos\alpha}\right) > 0. \tag{5.9}$$

On completing the square, we see that this always holds provided

$$4\cos\alpha - 1 - 3\cos^2\alpha > 0. \tag{5.10}$$

This is so provided $\frac{1}{3} < \cos\alpha < 1$; that is, $0 < \alpha < \pi/3$. It follows that the ratio of the area to the perimeter squared is maximized for each region when $\alpha = 0$.

We now partition the shape into n regions as shown in figure 5. Let the ith block have area A_i' and permeter P_i' when the skew angle is α, and denote the area by A_i and the perimeter by P_i when $\alpha = 0$. It follows from the above results that

$$A_i' = A_i \cos\alpha \tag{5.11}$$

and

$$\frac{A_i'}{P_i'^2} < \frac{A_i}{P_i^2}. \tag{5.12}$$

We conclude from equations 5.11 and 5.12 that

$$P_i'^2 > P_i^2 \cos\alpha. \tag{5.13}$$

Hence, we obtain

$$\left(\sum_{i=1}^{n} P_i'\right)^2 > \cos\alpha \left(\sum_{i=1}^{n} P_i\right)^2 \tag{5.14}$$

and

$$\sum_{i=1}^{n} A_i' = \cos\alpha \sum_{i=1}^{n} A_i. \tag{5.15}$$

It follows that

$$\sum_{i=1}^{n} A_i' \bigg/ \left(\sum_{i=1}^{n} P_i'\right)^2 < \sum_{i=1}^{n} A_i \bigg/ \left(\sum_{i=1}^{n} P_i\right)^2, \tag{5.16}$$

and taking the limit as n tends to infinity shows that our extremum principle interprets a skew symmetry as an oriented real symmetry.

6 Strategy and Sensitivity

In section 3 we suggested that radially asymmetric, elongated, or non-compact contours most readily elicit three-dimensional interpretations. We then proposed a compactness measure A/P^2 and suggested that perceived surface orientation corresponds to the slant and tilt that maximize the measure. We briefly discussed the role of extremum principles in computer vision (Brady and Horn [12] present a fuller discussion) and criticized Barrow and Tenenbaum's measure on the grounds that it is highly sensitive to noise. In sections 4 and 5 we analyzed the extremum principle and showed that it interprets skew symmetries as oriented real symmetries.

In this section we return to the discussion in section 3, concentrating on two additional questions concerning our measure. First, we ask whether there are specific reasons why a visual system should adopt the strategy of extremizing our measure. We suggest that the extremum principle not only determines the orientation of the viewed curve but also provides an estimate of the stability of the interpretation. We relate this to the idea of general viewpoint. Second, we show that the compactness measure is relatively insensitive to noise and to the scale at which the image is sampled. To this end we consider two cases: adding a sinusoid to the contour and assuming that the image can be modeled in terms of fractals.

Viewing Position and Stability

Consider viewing a given planar curve from the hemisphere of all possible directions. Consider further the way the image changes when the viewpoint is shifted slightly. A smooth curve will hardly change with a slight change of viewpoint from most viewing directions. We call these viewing directions *stable viewpoints*. Stable viewpoints can be grouped into regions whose boundaries correspond to viewpoints where the contour changes rapidly for a slight change of viewing position. These stable regions will be quite large for images of smooth planar curves and smoothed curved surfaces. We suggest that image contours are interpreted as curves that are viewed from stable viewpoints. This is the essence of the *general viewpoint* constraint in computer vision. We are able to estimate how stable a given viewpoint is.

One way to find stable viewpoint positions is to define a *similarity measure* for viewpoints and then find the extrema of this measure. Sutherland (personal communication) has proposed A/P^2 as a similarity measure, based on empirical studies of animal perception. If this is correct, extremizing A/P^2 corresponds to finding the stable-viewpoint positions of a contour, and, as a result, the stable interpretations of a contour (defined to be those which observers at general positions are most likely to see). This suggests that assuming general viewing position corresponds to assuming interpretations around which our compactness measure is extremized and where it varies slowly.

For an ellipse, the stable viewing position corresponds to interpreting the ellipse as an oriented circle. Even if the circle is slanted by as much as $30°$, the value of A/P^2 hardly changes, as our algorithm demonstrates, and so the circle is a stable interpretation. If the algorithm is applied to an ellipse with large eccentricity, corresponding to large slant, A/P^2 changes rapidly for slight changes to the viewing position. If we look at an ellipse from all possible viewing angles it is most likely to appear as a circle, and so interpreting an ellipse as a slanted circle is a good strategy.

These results are preliminary.

Sensitivity of the Compactness Measure to Noise

The second question concerns the sensitivity of the measure to noise and to the scale at which an image is sampled. Since our measure involves fewer derivatives of the contour than measures such as the proposed by Barrow and Tenenbaum, it should be relatively insensitive to noise. Although our present algorithm and the sampling method are essentially equally sensitive, it is possible to develop a less sensitive algorithm to implement our measure. The sampling method inevitably involves calculating tangents, however, and hence it is inherently sensitive to noise and scale. For example, if the image contour is continuous but not differentiable, the sampling method cannot (strictly) be applied. Similarly, if the orientation of the tangent to the contour has a large high-frequency component, the sampling approach will be very sensitive to noise.

Consider the sensitivity to noise of the extremum principle. Clearly, the perimeter P depends on the scale at which the image is viewed, while the area A is much less dependent. It follows that the ratio A/P^2 varies with scale. If a sinusoid is added to a smooth contour, for example, the area will remain approximately the same but the perimeter will change significantly. This does not imply, however, that the extrema of A/P^2 vary with scale. For example, it is easy to show that if a sinusoid is added to the contour, the extremum of the area over the perimeter squared is effectively unchanged.

Similarly, suppose that the image can be approximated by a fractal. If we measure the image at a small fractal scale constant l, the perimeter will be given by

$$P(l) = Fl^{(1-d)},\tag{6.1}$$

where F is independent of l and where $d \geq 1$ is the fractal dimension. Provided l is small, the value of A is essentially independent of l, since the fractal tends to a limit contour, with finite area, as l goes to zero. Now we extremize A/P^2 for all contours that can be projected into the image contour. This is equivalent to extremizing $\log(A/P^2)$, which, using equation 6.1, we write as

$$\log\left(\frac{A}{P^2}\right) = \log A - 2\log F - 2(1-d)\log l.\tag{6.2}$$

We now extremize this over σ and τ (equations 4.24 and 4.25), and note that the term involving l is independent of σ and τ and disappears. It follows that the extrema of A/P^2 are independent of the scale of viewing for an image that can be approximated by a fractal.

7 Interpreting Image Contours as Curved Surfaces

Figure 3 shows a number of contours that are interpreted as curved surfaces. In this section we discuss one method for extending our extremum principle to this general case. The key observation, as it was for Witkin [39], is that our method can be applied locally. To do this, we assume that the surface is locally planar. At the surface boundary, corresponding to the deprojection of the image contour, the binormal coincides with the surface normal. The idea is to compute a local estimate of the surface normal by the extremum principle described in the previous sections and then to use an algorithm, such as that developed by Terzopoulos [36], to interpolate the surface orientation in the interior of the surface. The method is closely related to that proposed by Brady and Grimson [11] for perceiving subjective surfaces.

The main question concerns how to apply the extremum principle locally. We are currently investigating the following approach. Consider the circle of curvature to the space curve that is the deprojection of the contour. One way to define the circle of curvature is as the best-fitting local circle through three points (or more if one assumes noisy data and makes a least-squares estimate) on the space curve near the point in question. The circle of curvature projects into an ellipse. We compute the best-fitting ellipse at each point on the image contour, and compute from it a local estimate of the surface orientation by finding the slant and tilt of the corresponding circle, interpreted as the circle of curvature. It is easy to show that, so long as the surface foreshortening is differentiable, this is a good estimator of the circle of curvature and hence of the local surface normal.

It requires five parameters to define an arbitrary ellipse. Computing the best-fitting ellipse in the general case is a complex nonlinear problem best approach using a numerical descent method, although several algorithms have been published for computing best-fitting ellipse [2, 8, 31, 34]. If we assume that the normal to the space curve is not significantly foreshortened, we can compute the ellipse center and major axis from the curvature of the contour at the point in question. The slope of the contour at that point also defines the orientation of the ellipse, leaving a much simpler one-parameter problem.

Perceptually, the strongest local cues to surface orientation correspond to points of high curvature. This is consistent with our method of locally estimating surface orientation by fitting local ellipses. Our compactness measure was inspired by the observation (for example on ellipses) that large slant is an effective cue to surface orientation, and in the case of an ellipse this produces points of high curvature. In fact, we can show that numerical conditioning of the estimator of slant increases monotonically with the slant. Conversely, for straight-line portions of a contour, the curvature is zero and the surface is locally planar. Hence, surface orientation does not change along the length of the straight portion.

One issue that remains to be studied is the interface to the surface-reconstruction algorithm. Consider the image of a triangle shown in figure 1. There are, in general, three different perceived orientations of the triangle corresponding to propagating the interpretation of each of the (high-curvature) corners. Adjacent corners give inconsistent information, and so it seems necessary to use a labeling approach such as that proposed by Zucker et al. [41].

8 Related Work

Gibson [20] has argued that surface orientation is directly determined by certain "higher-order variables" in the proximal stimulus array. What exactly constitutes a "higher-order variable" has been the subject of extensive debate. Nevertheless, Gibson and his followers have proposed several such, especially for optical flow and texture gradients. Flock and co-workers [16, 17] have adopted a Gibsonian perspective on the judgement of slant in texture gradients. Flock has introduced a "higher-order variable" *optical slant* (actually "optical theta" in the original) as a possible basis for monocular slant perception [16, eq. 5] or, at least, as a discriminant for planarity. Flock's work implicitly assumes planarity [16, p. 381], and it assumes that the tilt direction has been computed previously. In fact, there are many assumptions in Flock's paper; Freeman [18, p. 502] counts 13. Moreover, several studies [13, 14, 18, 25] have shown that the determination of surface orientation from texture gradients—for example, using optical slant or as in [28]—is less effective than its determination from bounding contour.

Attneave [3; see also 4] describes an approach to determining surface orientation that has similarities to that developed here. First, he argues for a Praegnanz theory of perception, which stresses economy principles in perception. This has meant different things to different researchers. The Gestalt psychologists explicitly noted the link between Praegnanz and minimization principles (for example, the soap bubble) in mathematical physics. Attneave [3, p. 285] suggests that such minima may be computed by "hill-climbing techniques." The extremum principles discussed in section 3 of this paper and surveyed in [12], [22]–[24], and [36] can be considered more sophisticated formalizations of similar intuitions. In fact, Attneave adopts Hochberg's formulation of the Praegnanz theory as the tendency to keep differences to a minimum. In particular, he considers three-dimensional interpretations that equalize one or more angles, lengths of edges, and surface slopes in figures such as 7(a). The more of these that are in fact equalized in a particular three-dimensional interpretation of an image, the more likely that interpretation is to be chosen. In fact, the extremum principle developed in this paper will interpret figure 7(a) correctly. It will

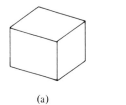   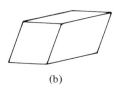

        (a)   (b)

Figure 7
(a) A boxlike figure typical of those studied by Attneave and Frost (ref. 4). (b) A sheared box.

also determine the shear in figure 7(b). Second, Attneave [3, figure 4] considers the judged orientation of rhombus figures. (See appendix D below for analysis of this case by our extremum principle). Surface orientation can be judged reliably for such shapes, more reliably in fact than for the box figures shown in figure 7, so long as the symmetries of the rhombus do not align with the horizontal and the vertical. It is well known that the horizontal and the vertical are important for shape description [10]. Note that surface slant is consistently underestimated.

In order to express depth constraints, Barnard [6] and Ikeuchi [28] have proposed alternative projections to the orthographic projection used in the development in section 3 and 4 above. The methods we have developed extend straightforwardly to these alternative projections. Barnard [6] finds surface orientation from vanishing points of families of parallel edges using central or perspective projection. He considers the projection of an angle, and, after the fashion of Hochberg and Attneave, heuristically assumes equiangularity to arrive at a three-dimensional interpretation of a triangle. As noted in appendix C, our method dispenses with the need for such a heuristic assumption. Similar remarks apply to Barnard's study of curvature. Ikeuchi [28] proposes a method for determining surface orientation for a surface that is covered with uniformly repeating texture elements. He assumes that the surface element corresponding to the texture element is planar. Most critically, it is assumed that the shape of the texture element is known *a priori*. For a particular slant and tilt, the orientation of the projection of the known figure changes. Ikeuchi proposes a measure that is superficially similar to the symmetry measure in section 4 to determine the slant and tilt of a texture element.

Olson [32] has studied a version of Ames's trapezoidal-window illusion. Surface slant is judged more accurately when the stimulus is moving consistent with the static three-dimensional interpretation than in the purely static case. Similarly, Wallach et al. [37] have shown that when an ellipse is roated in the image plane about an axis passing through its center and normal to the image it is perceived as a spinning oriented circle, like a settling spinning penny. The instantaneous surface orientation of the oriented circle can be computed by our method. Hildreth's dissertation on the perception of motion discusses the rotating ellipse and proposes a theoretical explanation of human perception of it.

Appendix A: The Maximum-Likelihood Method Applied to an Ellipse

Equation 4.30 gives the value F of the logarithm of the maximum-likelihood estimator for surface orientation:

$$F = \log \cos \sigma \oint dr - \oint \log(\cos^2 \sigma + \sin^2 \sigma \cos^2(\alpha - \tau)) \, dr. \qquad (A.1)$$

In this appendix we investigate the slant computed by the maximum-likelihood method for the ellipse

$$\frac{x^2}{a^2} + \frac{y^2}{b^2} = 1. \qquad (A.2)$$

It is convenient to use the standard parametrization,

$$x = a \cos\theta,$$

$$y = b \sin\theta, \quad 0 \le \theta < 2\pi \qquad (A.3)$$

$$dr = (a^2 \sin^2\theta + b^2 \cos^2\theta)^{1/2} \, d\theta.$$

Pending a more thorough analysis, we assume that the tilt $\tau = \pi/2$ is computed correctly by the maximum-likelihood method, and restrict attention to slant. Witkin [39, figure 5] and our own computational experiments suggest that this is reasonable; in any case, if it were not, the inequivalence of the maximum-likelihood and extremum-principle methods would be ensured. Without loss of generality, we assume that $a > b$, and denote a/b by $\lambda > 1$.

Since $\tau = \pi/2$,

$$\cos^2 \alpha = \frac{1}{1 + \tan^2 \alpha}$$

$$= \frac{a^2 \sin^2\theta}{a^2 \sin^2\theta + b^2 \cos^2\theta} \qquad (A.4)$$

since $\tan \alpha = dy/dx$. Also,

$$\sin(\alpha - \tau) = \sin\left(\alpha - \frac{\pi}{2}\right) = -\cos\alpha, \tag{A.5}$$

and so equation A.1 reduces to

$$F = \log\cos\sigma \oint dr - \oint \log(1 - \cos^2\alpha \sin^2\sigma)\, dr. \tag{A.6}$$

We are interested in extrema of F, and so we consider $dF/d\sigma$, which we write as

$$\cot\sigma \frac{dF}{d\sigma} = \oint \frac{a^2 \sin^2\theta \cos^2\sigma - b^2 \cos^2\theta}{a^2 \sin^2\theta \cos^2\sigma + b^2 \cos^2\theta}\, dr, \quad 1 \le \lambda. \tag{A.7}$$

Suppose that the maximum-likelihood method is extremized at $\sigma = \sigma'$. The slant that is necessary to interpret the ellipse as a circle is given by $\cos\sigma = 1/\lambda$. The maximum-likelihood method overestimates slant if and only if $\sigma' > \cos^{-1}(1/\lambda)$; that is, if and only if $\cos\sigma' < 1/\lambda$. This is true if $dF/d\sigma \ne 0$ for all σ such that $1 \le \lambda\cos\sigma < \lambda$. Denote $\lambda\cos\sigma$ by μ, so that $1 \le \mu < \lambda$. Substituting in A.7 and changing the limits of integration, we find

$$\frac{dF}{d\sigma} = 2b \int_0^\pi \frac{\mu^2 \sin^2\theta - \cos^2\theta}{\mu^2 \sin^2\theta + \cos^2\theta}(\lambda^2 \sin^2\theta + \cos^2\theta)^{1/2}\, d\theta. \tag{A.8}$$

We now split the range of integration into four equal intervals of size $\pi/4$. With suitable changes of variables to bring the intervals of integration to $[0, \pi/4]$, we find

$$\frac{dF}{d\sigma} = 4 \int_0^{\pi/4} \frac{\mu^2 \cos^2\theta - \sin^2\theta}{\mu^2 \cos^2\theta + \sin^2\theta}(\lambda^2 \cos^2\theta + \sin^2\theta)^{1/2}$$

$$- \frac{\mu^2 \sin^2\theta - \cos^2\theta}{\mu^2 \sin^2\theta + \cos^2\theta}(\lambda^2 \sin^2\theta + \cos^2\theta)^{1/2}\, d\theta. \tag{A.9}$$

Over the range of integration, $\cos\theta > \sin\theta$. Algebraic manipulation of A.9 shows it to be greater than zero, so that it is certainly not zero. Hence, the maximum-likelihood method overestimates the slant.

Appendix B: Why Square Curvature Is Inappropriate

In section 3 we rejected the measure

$$F = \int \kappa^2\, ds \tag{B.1}$$

because, despite popular belief to the contrary, it does not interpret an ellipse as a circle. In this appendix we substantiate that claim.

Consider the ellipse defined by equations A.2 and A.3. The curvature κ of the ellipse is given by

$$\kappa^2 = \left| \frac{d^2 r}{ds^2} \right|^2 \tag{B.2}$$

$$= \frac{a^2 b^2}{(a^2 \sin^2 \theta + b^2 \cos^2 \theta)^3}, \tag{B.3}$$

where s is the arc length. Substituting B.3 into B.1, we have

$$F(a, b) = \int_0^{2\pi} \frac{a^2 b^2}{(a^2 \sin^2 \theta + b^2 \cos^2 \theta)^{5/2}} \, d\theta. \tag{B.4}$$

Suppose, without loss of generality, that the ellipse is in the image plane and that $a > b$. Suppose further that the square curvature performance index (B.1) is correct and interprets the ellipse as a circle lying in a plane that is slanted with angle σ to the y axis, where

$$b = a \cos \sigma. \tag{B.5}$$

Equivalently, if we set $b' = b/\cos\sigma$, the measure will choose σ such that $b' = a$. Hence, if we write $b = \lambda a$ and consider $F(a, b)$ to be a function of λ, the measure should be extremized by $\lambda = 1$. We will now show that this is not the case.

Differentiating

$$F(\lambda) = \frac{1}{a} \int_0^{2\pi} \frac{\lambda^2}{(\sin^2 \theta + \lambda^2 \cos^2 \theta)^{5/2}} \, d\theta. \tag{B.6}$$

with respect to λ gives

$$\frac{\partial F}{\partial \lambda} = \frac{1}{a} \int_0^{2\pi} \frac{2\lambda \sin^2 \theta - 3\lambda^3 \cos^2 \theta}{(\sin^2 \theta + \lambda^2 \cos^2 \theta)^{7/2}} \, d\theta. \tag{B.7}$$

Evaluating this expression at $\lambda = 1$ gives

$$\left. \frac{\partial F}{\partial \lambda} \right|_{\lambda=1} = \frac{1}{a} \int_0^{2\pi} (2 \sin^2 \theta - 3 \cos^2 \theta) \, d\theta$$

$$= -\frac{\pi}{a} \tag{B.8}$$

Since the partial of F with respect to λ does not vanish when $\lambda = 1$, the circle does not extremize the ellipse for the square curvature measure.

Appendix C: The Interpretation of Some Simple Shapes

In this appendix we show that our method correctly interprets a number of simple shapes, namely an ellipse, a parallelogram, and a triangle.

Ellipse

Suppose the ellipse is given by equations A.2 and A.3. It is easy to show that the area A and the perimeter P are given by

$$A = \pi ab$$

and (C.1)

$$P = \int_0^{2\pi} (a^2 \sin^2\theta + b^2 \cos^2\theta)^{1/2}\, d\theta.$$

Maximizing A/P^2 is equivalent to minimizing $P/\sqrt{A}$. We set $b = \lambda a$ (λ is the eccentricity of the ellipse) and define $P/\sqrt{A} = f(\lambda)$. We find

$$f(\lambda) = \frac{1}{\sqrt{\pi}} \int_0^{2\pi} \left(\frac{\sin^2\theta}{\lambda} + \lambda \cos^2\theta \right)^{1/2} d\theta. \tag{C.2}$$

By the same argument presented in appendix B, the ellipse will be interpreted as a circle provided $\lambda = 1$ is a minimum of $f(\lambda)$. Changing the variable of the integral to $\phi = \theta + \pi/2$, we find that

$$f(\lambda) = f\left(\frac{1}{\lambda}\right), \tag{C.3}$$

which implies that $\lambda = 1$ extremizes $f(\lambda)$. It is also clear that extrema occur in pairs of the form λ, $1/\lambda$. Furthermore, both are stationary points or one is a maximum and the other a minimum. Observe that $f(\lambda)$ tends to infinity as λ tends either to zero or infinity. It follows that a sufficient condition for $\lambda = 1$ to be a global minimum is that all pairs of extrema be stationary points. Suppose that this is not the case, and let λ_0 be the smallest extremum that is not a stationary point. Since $f(\lambda)$ tends to infinity as λ tends to zero, λ_0 must be a minimum and $1/\lambda_0$ a maximum. But $1/\lambda_0$ is the largest nonstationary extremum, and so, by the same argument as above, it must be a minimum. This contradiction establishes the result.

Parallelogram and Triangle

In section 5 we showed that a skew symmetry is always interpreted as an oriented symmetry by our method. In particular, a parallelogram is interpreted as a rectangle. By the same argument, a rectangle is a skewed symmetry of a square. Hence, our method interprets a parallelogram as a square.

Similar reasoning shows that a triangle is interpreted as a skewed isosceles triangle, which is interpreted as a skewed equilateral triangle. The axes of the skewed symmetry join a vertex to the midpoint of the opposite side. Hence, our method interprets a triangle as an oriented equilateral triangle.

Appendix D: The Slant and Tilt of a Skewed Symmetry

In this appendix we calculate the slant σ and the tilt τ that correspond to the oriented real symmetry that is the interpretation of a skewed symmetry whose skew angle is δ.

As a simple but instructive example, consider a rhombus of side a and included angle γ (figure 8). To find the extremizing tilt, we substitute data from figure 8 into equation 4.24 and find

$$\frac{\sin\tau\cos\tau}{(1 - \sin^2\sigma\sin^2\tau)^{1/2}} + \frac{\sin(\tau - \gamma)\cos(\tau - \gamma)}{[1 - \sin^2\sigma\sin^2(\tau - \gamma)]^{1/2}} = 0. \tag{D.1}$$

We can rewrite this in the form

$$[\cos^2(\tau - \gamma) - \cos^2\tau]$$
$$\times \{\cos^2(\tau - \gamma) + \cos^2\tau$$
$$+ (1 - \cos^2\sigma)[1 - \cos^2(\tau - \gamma)](1 - \cos^2\tau) - 1\}$$
$$= 0. \tag{D.2}$$

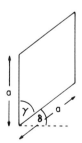

Figure 8
A typical skew-symmetric figure: a rhombus with side a, included angle γ, and skew angle $\delta = \pi/2 - \gamma$. The tilt direction is aligned with one of the axes of symmetry of the rhombus, determined by the angle δ.

We assume first that the first factor is zero. It follows that

$$\cos(\tau - \gamma) = \pm \cos\tau \qquad\qquad\qquad (D.3)$$

and so

$$\gamma - 2\tau = n\pi. \qquad\qquad\qquad (D.4)$$

Since $0 \leq \tau \leq \pi$ and $0 < \gamma < \pi$, there are two possible solutions:

$$\tau = \frac{\gamma}{2} \qquad\qquad\qquad (D.5)$$

and

$$\tau = \frac{\gamma + \pi}{2}. \qquad\qquad\qquad (D.6)$$

The tilt direction is one of the axes of symmetry of the rhombus shown in figure 8.

Having solved for the tilt, we now solve for the extremizing slant σ using equation 4.23. Recalling from D.4 that $\sin^2(\tau - \gamma) = \sin^2\tau$, we find upon substitution into 4.23

$$\tfrac{1}{2}(1 - \sin^2\sigma \sin^2\tau)^{1/2} = \cos^2\tau(1 - \sin^2\sigma \sin^2\tau)^{-1/2}, \qquad (D.7)$$

which we solve to get

$$\cos^2\sigma = \frac{\cos^2\tau}{\sin^2\tau}. \qquad\qquad\qquad (D.8)$$

The requirement that $|\cos\sigma| < 1$ picks out either D.5 or D.6, so we get a unique solution. In this case the skew angle is given by

$$\delta = \frac{\pi}{2} - \gamma. \qquad\qquad\qquad (D.9)$$

To summarize: If $\delta < 0$ we get

$$\tau = \frac{\pi}{4} - \frac{\delta}{2},$$
$$\cos\sigma = \frac{1 + \sin\delta}{\cos\delta}, \qquad\qquad\qquad (D.10)$$

and if $\delta > 0$ we get

$$\tau = \frac{3\pi}{4} - \frac{\delta}{2}, \tag{D.11}$$

$$\cos\sigma = \frac{\cos\delta}{1 + \sin\delta}.$$

These formulas were derived for an equal-sided parallelogram, but they will clearly apply to the more general case, and a rotation through the angles given by D.10 and D.11 will unskew any symmetry. It should be noted that τ is taken to be zero on the axis of symmetry, as in figure 8.

To conclude this appendix, we consider the case that the second factor in D.2 is zero and the first factor is nonzero. We introduce the angle ψ by analogy with 2.1, defining orthographic projection:

$$\tan^2\psi = \cos^2\sigma \tan^2(\gamma - \tau). \tag{D.12}$$

Then

$$\sin^2(\gamma - \tau) = \frac{\tan^2\psi}{\cos^2\sigma + \tan^2\psi}$$

and $\tag{D.13}$

$$\cos^2(\gamma - \tau) = \frac{\cos^2\sigma}{\cos^2\sigma + \tan^2\psi},$$

where, without loss of generality, we suppose $0 < \psi < \pi/2$. Now, by assumption, the second factor in D.2 is zero:

$$\cos^2\tau + \cos^2(\gamma - \tau) + \sin^2\sigma \sin^2\tau \sin^2(\gamma - \tau) - 1 = 0. \tag{D.14}$$

Using D.13, we find

$$\tan^2\tau \tan^2\psi = 1,$$

from which we deduce

$$\sin\tau = \cos\psi$$

and $\tag{D.15}$

$$\cos\tau = \mu \sin\psi, \quad \mu = \pm 1$$

since the ranges of the variables can be assumed to be $0 < \sigma < \pi/2$, $0 < \tau < \pi$, $0 < \psi < \pi/2$, and $0 < \gamma < \pi$. From D.13 we find

$$\sin(\gamma - \tau)\cos(\gamma - \tau) = \frac{v \tan\psi \cos\sigma}{\cos^2\sigma + \tan^2\psi}, \quad v = \pm 1 \tag{D.16}$$

and, since $\sin\tau\cos\tau$ has the same sign as $\sin(\gamma - \tau)\cos(\gamma - \tau)$, we have $\mu = \nu$. From D.1 we deduce

$$\frac{\sin\tau\cos\tau}{1 - \sin^2\sigma\sin^2\tau^{1/2}} = \frac{-\sin(\gamma - \tau)\cos(\gamma - \tau)}{1 - \sin^2\sigma\sin^2(\gamma - \tau)^{1/2}}$$

$$= \frac{\nu\sin\psi\cos\psi}{1 - \sin^2\sigma\cos^2\psi^{1/2}}. \tag{D.17}$$

So far in this appendix we have used only one of the constraints derived in section 4—namely 4.24, from which we derived D.1. We now use the second constraint, 4.23, which we can write in the form

$$\frac{2\cos^2\tau}{(1 - \sin^2\sigma\sin^2\tau)^{1/2}} - (1 - \sin^2\sigma2\tau)^{1/2}$$

$$+ \frac{2\cos^2(\gamma - \tau)}{(1 - \sin^2\sigma\sin^2(\gamma - \tau))^{1/2}} - [1 - \sin^2\sigma\sin^2(\gamma - \tau)]^{1/2} = 0. \tag{D.18}$$

After some algebraic manipulation, we deduce

$$\cos\sigma = -\tan^2\psi,$$

from which it follows that $\cos\sigma$ is negative, which is impossible in the range under consideration.

Acknowledgments

The authors thank R. Bajcsy, C. Brown, J. Canny, E. Grimson, E. Hildreth, T. Poggio, D. Terzopoulos, and A. Witkin for their comments. The work was supported in part by the Advanced Research Projects Agency of the Department of Defense under Office of Naval Research contract N00014-80-C-0505 and in part by the Systems Development Foundation.

References

1. G. J. Agin. Computer vision systems for industrial inspection and assembly. *IEEE Computer* 13 (1980): 11–20.

2. G. J. Agin. Fitting Ellipses and General Second-Order Curves. Report CMU-RI-TR-81-5, Robotics Institute, Carnegie-Mellon University, 1981.

3. F. Attneave. Representation of physical space. In *Coding Processes in Human Memory*, ed. A. W. Melton and F. Martin (Wiley, 1972).

4. F. Attneave and R. Frost. The determination of perceived tridimensional orientation by minimum criteria. *Perception and Psych.* 6 (1969): 391–396.

5. D. H. Ballard and C. M. Brown. *Computer Vision*. Prentice-Hall, 1982.

6. S. Barnard. Interpreting Perspective Images. SRI Report TR 271, 1983.

7. H. G. Barrow and J. M. Tenenbaum. Interpreting line drawings as three dimensional surfaces. *Artificial Intelligence* 17 (1981): 75–117.

8. F. L. Bookstein. Fitting conic sections to scattered data. *Computer Graphics and Image Processing* 9 (1979): 56–71.

9. M. Brady. Computational approaches to image understanding. *Comput. Surveys* 14 (1982): 3–71.

10. M. Brady. Criteria for representations of shape. In *Human and Machine Vision*, ed. J. Beck and A. Rosenfeld (Academic, 1983).

11. M. Brady and W. E. L. Grimson. The Perception of Subjective Surfaces. AI Memo 666, Massachusetts Institute of Technology, 1981.

12. M. Brady and B. K. P. Horn. Rotationally symmetric operators for surface interpolation. *Computer Graphics and Image Processing* 22 (1983): 70–95.

13. M. L. Braunstein and J. W. Payne. Perspective and form ratio as determinants of relative slant judgments. *J. Exp. Psychol.* 3 (1969): 584–590.

14. W. C. Clark, A. H. Smith, and A. Rabe. The interaction of surface texture, outline gradient, and ground in the perception of slant. *Canadian J. Psychol.* 10 (1956): 1–8.

15. L. S. Davis, L. Janos, and S. Dunn. Efficient Recovery of Shape from Texture. Report TR-1133, Computer Vision Laboratory, University of Maryland, 1982.

16. H. R. Flock. A possible optical basis for monocular slant perception. *Psych. Rev.* 71 (1964): 380–391.

17. H. R. Flock, D. Graves, J. Tenney, and B. Stephenson. Slant judgments of single rectangles at a slant. *Psychol. Sci.* 7 (1965): 57–58.

18. R. B. Freeman, Jr. Ecological optics and visual slant. *Psych. Rev.* 72 (1965): 501–504.

19. R. B. Freeman, Jr. Effect of size on visual slant. *J. Exp. Psychol.* 71 (1966): 96–103.

20. J. J. Gibson. *Perception of the Visible World*. Houghton Mifflin, 1950.

21. R. L. Gregory. *Eye and Brain*, second edition. McGraw-Hill, 1973.

22. W. E. L. Grimson. *From Images to Surfaces: A Computational Study of the Human Early Visual System*. MIT Press, 1981.

23. W. E. L. Grimson. A computational theory of visual surface interpolation. *Phil. Trans. Roy. Soc. Lond.* B 298 (1982): 395–427.

24. W. E. L. Grimson. An implementation of a computational theory of visual surface interpolation. *Computer Graphics and Image Processing* 22 (1983): 39—70.

25. H. E. Gruber and W. C. Clark. Perception of slanted surfaces. *Perception and Motor Skills* 6 (1956): 97—106.

26. B. K. P. Horn. Understanding image intensities. *Artificial Intelligence* 8 (1977): 201—231.

27. B. K. P. Horn. The Curve of Least Energy. Report AIM-610, Massachusetts Institute of Technology, 1981.

28. K. Ikeuchi. Shape from regular patterns. *Artificial Intelligence* 22 (1984): 49—75.

29. T. Kanade. Recovery of three-dimensional shape of an object from a single view. *Artificial Intelligence* 17 (1981): 409—460.

30. D. Marr. *Vision.* Freeman, 1982.

31. Y. Nakagawa and A. Rosenfeld. A note on polygonal and elliptical approximation of mechanical parts. *Pattern Recognition* 11 (1979): 133—142.

32. R. K. Olson. Slant judgments from static and rotating trapezoids correspond to rules of perspective geometry. *Perception and Psych.* 15 (1974): 509—516.

33. T. Pavlidis. *Structural Pattern Recognition.* Springer, 1977.

34. P. D. Sampson. Fitting conic sections to very scattered data: An iterative refinement of the Bookstein algorithm. *Computer Graphics and Image Processing* 18 (1982): 97—108.

35. K. A. Stevens. Surface Perception from Local Analysis of Texture. Report AI-TR-512, Massachusetts Institute of Technology, 1980.

36. D. Terzopoulos. Multi-level reconstruction of visual surfaces. *Computer Graphics and Image Processing* 24 (1983): 52—96.

37. H. Wallach, A. Weisz, and P. A. Adams. Circles and derived figures in rotation. *Am. J. Psychol.* 69 (1956): 48—59.

38. A. P. Witkin. Shape from Contour. Report AIM-TR-589, Artificial Intelligence Laboratory, Massachusetts Institute of Technology, 1980.

39. A. P. Witkin. Recovering surface shape and orientation from texture. *Artificial Intelligence* 17 (1981): 17—47.

40. A. Yuille. Zero Crossing on Lines of Curvature. Report AIM 718, Artificial Intelligence Laboratory, Massachusetts Institute of Technology, 1983.

41. S. W. Zucker, R. A. Hummel, and A. Rosenfeld. An application of relaxation labeling to line and curve enhancement. *IEEE Trans. Computers* 26 (1977): 394—403, 922—929.

11

Representational Axes and Temporal Cooperative Processes

John K. Tsotsos

This paper proposes a framework for the integration of time into "high-level" vision. Many characteristics of this framework have much in common with the handling of temporal concepts in low-level vision as well, but these will not be discussed. This framework addresses the integration of representations for temporal concepts with temporal reasoning schemes, temporal grouping, the discrimination and labeling of temporal concepts, and temporal sampling rates. Such issues are not addressed in most other "high-level-vision" methodologies.

Visual perception takes place within a spatio-temporal context, and thus the integration of time into every aspect of processing is crucial. One may draw an analogy here to the use of the term *pragmatics* in research on natural-language understanding. *Syntax* describes the rules for how individual tokens are grouped into larger tokens; *semantics* ascribes meaning to tokens; *pragmatics* relates that meaning to the remainder of the discourse or to the context in which the utterance was found. Most past computer-vision research has dealt with static images—a most unnatural kind of input, since biological visual systems are almost never presented with a single time slice of the visual world out of its spatial and temporal context. The temporal cooperative process that will be described is integrated with a hypothesize-and-test reasoning framework. The structure over which the cooperative process operates changes with time because of the status of interpretation, and iterations are defined by the passing of time for either static images (image contents do not change with time) or time-varying images, where in both cases the images are presented over a period of time. Since for computer vision we must deal with a discretized world, and since time is to be considered, temporal sampling must be an issue.

Is there anything special about time and the processing of time-varying information that does not allow us to treat it simply as a fourth dimension? Although significant effort has been expended on the analysis of time-varying images, this question has never been addressed completely. It is simply for the sake of covenience in processing that most computer-vision research has concentrated on single images, and that most motion research has concentrated on small numbers of images in a time sequence. In most past work on motion analysis and understanding it has been tacitly assumed that the techniques that have been used for analysis of static images apply directly for the time-varying case, and that time is strictly subsequent to spatial analysis. This is not necessarily the case; generally, time must be incorporated into each aspect of processing. The additional constraints provided by the temporal context of a scene are crucial for disambiguation and recognition.

There are three main constraints that time brings to bear on work in motion understanding. First, we cannot stop time. System response is required without unreasonable delay, since the environment continues to change. Yet computation requires a finite period of time. Thus, the processing rate must be sufficiently high to maintain an interpretation of the scene. Second, there is limited storage available. Whereas spatial data are presented in parallel, temporal data are presented serially. This implies that a finite temporal window must be used, and that events over a longer period of time must be sufficiently abstracted that they can be efficiently represented internally. Third, the system must be stable in a noisy environment and must degrade gracefully with increasing noise. Noise can take many forms: quantization noise, data irrelevant to the problem being tackled, and misleading data (including data at the wrong spatial and/or temporal scale). Therefore, some amount of smoothing must be present so that these confounding effects are minimized. This implies that rise and fall times must be chosen accordingly. Similarly, decision-making processes must exhibit procrastination and inertia. They cannot make decisions hastily, and they must temporally integrate results in order to take temporal context into account. A single noise point cannot undo the effect of many samples that exhibit some trend, yet enough samples must have been viewed in order to discover the trend. All this impacts the processing rate for the image sequence.

The problem of time and the interpretation of events in time is not new to psychologists. David Hartley (1749) set forth several propositions pertaining to groups of successive concepts and groups of compound synchronous concepts. He noted that an instance of such a group will raise in the mind expectations for the remaining concepts of the group, whether the concepts occur in a sequence or simultaneously. This is an example of top-down activation of grouping hypotheses. James Mill (1829) elaborated these thoughts and concluded that sensations have a naturally synchronous or successive order. To him, successive order implied order in time whereas synchronous order implied order in space. In addition, successive order implied notions of antecedent and consequent sensations. Grouping received large amounts of attention from the Gestalt psychologists, according to whom grouping principles can be summarized by the terms *proximity*, *similarity, continuity, symmetry*, and *familiarity* (Wertheimer 1923). Although most studies of such grouping principles were performed mainly by considering the partitioning of a stimulus array in space, each of these has a temporal analogue. For example, the smaller the temporal separation, the greater the tendency to be grouped into a sequence; similarity of temporal primitive; temporal symmetry could refer to oscillatory motions, etc. Unfortunately, for both temporal and spatial versions, these require much elaboration and quantification before they can be immediately applied.

Synchronous order in time was discussed by Gibson (1957) and Hay (1966), who considered the distinctions between physical and optical motions. They, particularly Hay, defined a variety of optical motions as combinations of simultaneous physical motions, thus decomposing complex motions into aggregates of simpler ones. Such decompositions are important notions in my work.

The following experiments point to a strong relationship between expectation and the specialization/generalization of concepts. The experiments of Cooper and Shepard (1973) show the strong positive effect of *a priori* expectations on time for interpretation; those of Bugelski and Alampay (1962) and Palmer (1975) show the effects of generalization of expectation classes. Cooper and Shepard reported that in the identification of letters presented at varying orientations the time taken to identify the letter varied with the amount of rotation (to a maximum value at 180°); this implied that mental rotation and matching were being performed by the visual system, and that if identity and orientation were given before the stimulus the response time was flat across all orientations as long as sufficient time was allowed before the stimulus was presented for expectation formation.

Bugelski and Alampay showed that if a subject is conditioned to expect a given category (or generalization) of stimulus, then the identification time of the stimulus is reduced. They presented stimuli all belonging to the same class of concept (animals); when nonanimal stimuli were presented, the response time increased. This was further examined by Palmer, who also noted the impairment of identification if the context is misleading. (The mechanisms that produce such behavior are not understood.)

Dretske (1981) emphasized temporal integration:

To understand how certain sets of information are registered, it is important to understand the way a sensory representation may be the result of a temporal summation of signals. To think of the processing of sensory information in static terms, in terms of the kind of information embodied in the stimulus at a particular time, is to completely miss the extent to which our sensory representations depend on an integrative process over time.

The importance of time in sensory perception is given additional credence by the fact that sensory neurons have the ability to sum their input signals not only spatially but also temporally (Kandel and Schwartz 1981). Within the domain of computer vision, the study of motion interpretation has not adequately addressed the issue of temporal integration of results; indeed, much of the work concentrates on the processing of motion information by considering a set of static images. The methodologies developed do not, for the most part, have the ability to combine events into higher-order concepts such as sequential or synchronous events.

The remainder of this paper deals with the representation and organization of temporal concepts, and describes how this organization drives a hypothesize-and-test reasoning process as well as the cooperative process that forms the structure within which the hypothesis response is computed. This research is distinguished from other research on cooperative processes in a number of ways. Schemes such as those of Glazer (1982) and Terzopoulos (1982) use cooperative methods in arriving at a solution to a numerical approximation problem. They use hierarchies of data, but the type of information is uniform; only resolution differs by level of hierarchy. Their problems are posed as numerical ones, and in those cases relaxation methods assist in obtaining a solution. Our case differs in four respects:

• Our information is not uniform but rather different concepts are represented at different levels of the hierarchies.

• There are multiple interacting networks, each organized according to different semantics.

• The data are time-varying (and, more important, the structive over which relaxation is performed is time-varying).

• We are interested in an interpretation task, not an approximation one.

Research such as that of Hummel and Zucker (1980) deals with theoretical foundations underlying relaxation methods. My work should not be considered in such a light. The cooperative process to be described has the qualitative properties I believe are desirable for temporal interpretation, and its performance will be described empirically and in a qualitative fashion through the use of several examples. It should be regarded as an extension of relaxation methods into a domain where they have previously not been used.

There are similarities between the present work and that of Hinton and Sejnowski (1983). They too employ a hypothesize-and-test framework where hypotheses are in one of two states (true and false) and apply a cooperative process to find optimal combinations of hypotheses. Differences exist in that a representation for hypotheses was not presented, nor were specific search mechanisms, and their mathematical analysis (which they based on system energy) is not directly applicable. The work presented in this paper can also be seen as an elaboration and an extension of the vertical and horizontal relaxation processes of Zucker (1978a).

One further major difference exists with past cooperative-computation research. We are dealing with a time-varying data-interpretation task. Past work has shown that, in general, relaxation schemes require large, and potentially very large, numbers of iterations in order to converge to stable solutions. We cannot afford this luxury. In a time-varying context, decisions must be made relatively independent of the number of iterations, so that new data can be considered. Therefore, what is required is a cooperative process that can be characterized in the following way: The only decisions that will be made are those that can be made within a small, fixed number of iterations. We must discover the conditions under which this is possible, for all events of interest, given small amounts of noise in the data. These conditions will be developed in the course of the paper, and will lead to a relationship between image sampling rate and iterations.

In order to describe our scheme—that is, a temporal, high-level vision framework—we must first decide on what we mean by "high level." The approaches of Marr (1982) and Julesz (1980) certainly do not fall within the meaning of high level. On the other hand, work described by Hanson and Riseman (1978), Levine (1978), Ballard et al. (1978), Brooks (1981), O'Rourke and Badler (1980), and Tenenbaum and Barrow (1977) certainly does. What distinguishes these approaches? It is not (as is commonly thought) the use of domain-specific knowledge. The work conducted and motivated by Marr utilized physical constraints of the world, while the VISIONS system of Hanson and Riseman employs knowledge of the appearance of houses; both are forms of knowledge. I believe that the distinction is a deeper one. We can gain insight by looking at some recent distinctions drawn by psychologists between "pre-attentive" and "attentive" vision.

Briefly, the pre-attentive system is a parallel one that can cope with single disjunctive features only, such as the distinction between differently oriented black bars on a white background. (See Treisman and Gelade 1980; Treisman 1982; Treisman and Schmidt 1982.) The attentive system, on the other hand, can handle much greater complexity of visual input. Treisman and co-workers claim that it is a serial system incorporating a focus of attention, and that it thus can deal with the conjunction of features such as color and shape. Moreover, it must play a role in the discrimination of feature conjuncts within a field of conjunctions of similar features. For example, the attentive system must be used to find a green vertical bar in a field of many randomly oriented bars, each a different color. Several discussions on the differences between attentive and pre-attentive vision may be found in the literature; see Julesz and Schumer 1981. Curiously, only static images had been considered in those works. On the other hand, the so-called short-range and long-range motion processes of Braddick (1974) and Anstis (1978) describe perceptual processes that can cope with motions involving small displacements and not requiring form recognition or correspondence (Braddick) and with motions requiring form recognition and larger displacements, necessitating correspondence (Anstis). It would be startling indeed if the static and temporal distinctions drawn in the above works were simply instances of the same process.

The most obvious manifestation (but not the only one) of serial visual processing is visual search. Given a complex image, our gaze typically moves around the image, tracing contours and interesting features until the image has been interpreted to our satisfaction. What could trigger such a search? If one believes that the purpose of vision is to construct some internal representation of the physical world, then one may also hypothesize that, on the basis of pre-attentive vision, a "skeleton" structure is created, which may then, if required, be filled in by the attentive process. This filling in or completion could be driven by the need for completeness of description and disambiguation. For single disjunctive visual features, this skeleton may be complete—it may be compared to Marr's (1982) primal sketch or to Julesz's (1980) textons. Labeling of features of such a ·skeleton of isolated, disjunctive features proceeds in a "pre-attentive-like" manner, that is, bottom-up and in parallel. Whereas visual search in the static case involves changes of fixation in some manner, search in the dynamic case may involve both search for features that complete the skeleton of objects and temporal search or the generation of expectations in time for completion of the motion skeleton. The motion skeleton may be the result of short-range processes, or what Braddick and Anstis call

Real Motion, whereas Apparent Motion requires the filling in of form-related and correspondence-related information.

Search schemes are common components of systems that claim reasoning capabilities. In addition, all such systems exhibit foci of attention that are derived from the "best guesses" for the solution of the problem at hand. However, search in vision can take many forms. In order to conjoin features (such as "red" and "the letter B") into a single percept, search for corresponding features in different portions of processing hierarchies may be required. This, of course, assumes static images. It may be that the feature being searched for has no corresponding instance and thus a visual search—eye motion—must be initiated. (There clearly are other reasons for eye movement as well.) This would be accompanied by establishing expectations as to what the attentive system was looking for, thus biasing the computation. Finally, in the time-varying case, it may be that the corresponding feature is an event that has not yet occurred. In this case, expectations are set up in time, again biasing the computation. These biases may be regarded in one of two ways: as "priming" signals (that is, signals that may facilitate the computation of particular units or concepts) or as manifestations of internal focus of processing attention.

Search for missing discriminatory features will be considered as the main distinction between "high-level" and "low-level" vision. Search for globally consistent results, such as manifested by relaxation schemes, is not included within this distinction, since global consistency must play a role in both levels of vision.

In summary, the major capabilities that an attentive vision system—particularly one addressing time-varying phenomena—must possess are the following:

prototype concept representation, manifested as stereotyped computing units

temporal grouping

temporal expectations

generalization of concepts in relation to expectations

rich search dimensions that enable and distinguish search in image space from search in hypothesis space

spatial and temporal integration of results

generation and maintenance of a focus of attention

an interface to the tokens that may be abstracted from images by early processes.

This paper discusses a framework for the realization of such capabilities. Although it is claimed that attentive vision systems must possess at least the capabilities just summarized, the realization presented here is only one of many possible realizations with the same capabilities. There are no claims on necessity. On the other hand, this framework is indeed sufficient and does satisfy the requirements laid out. All the machinery described in this paper has been implemented as part of the ALVEN expert vision system (Tsotsos 1981a, 1983; Tsotsos et al. 1984), which assesses the performance of the human left ventricle from x-ray image sequences. The experimental work described in this paper was done with that implementation.

Overview

The basic properties of an attentive vision framework involving temporal phenomena were described in the preceding section, and they are manifested in a clear manner in our attentive vision framework. Knowledge organization plays a significant role. The key elements of the framework are the following:

• Four dimensions of knowledge organization, namely IS-A (generalization/specialization), PART-OF (aggregation/decomposition), SIMILARITY, and Temporal Precedence.

• Frames as the prototype knowledge or computing unit, organized along the four dimensions just mentioned. These may be considered as declarative structures, specialized procedures, or some combination of these two. It is not important how they are implemented for the purposes of this framework. The important point is that specialized units are present that interpret specific visual entities, which may be as simple as "change detection" or as sophisticated as "left ventricular systole" and which may involve spatial relations, such as "above" or "inside," and temporal quantities such as velocities or rates of area change. These computing units must have several important properties: they realize when they cannot successfully interpret some visual feature, they can create a data structure (an exception record) describing why they cannot, they can create instance representations of themselves when appropriate, and they can communicate with other units.

• The "leaves" of the PART-OF hierarchy of frames represent the primitive types of features that may be abstracted in a pre-attentive fashion from the images, thus forming the interface between early and attentive processing.

• Hypothesize and test as the basic interpretation paradigm, with hypotheses being activated from the knowledge frames as a result of four interacting search dimensions, namely hypothesis-driven, data-driven, failure-driven, and temporal search. Since hypotheses are derived from prototype knowledge frames, and those frames are organized, hypotheses are also organized in the same fashion.

• A projection mechanism to transduce hypothesis-specific expectations to image-specific ones, and a scheme to recover from inadequate expectations through upward traversal of the IS-A hierarchy, thereby relaxing constraints.

• A cooperative process that integrates results over time and space in order to enforce global hypothesis consistency and determine the best hypotheses, and thus the system focus of attention. The focus exhibits levels of abstraction because of the hypothesis organization. This process should also be able to deal with noisy and incomplete data.

It will be shown that knowledge organization is the driving force behind the interpretation strategy, and that, in addition to the knowledge-structuring properties used in many other knowledge-based systems, the dimensions of knowledge organization have many other important uses, ranging from restricting the temporal sampling rate to supplying the feedback necessary for stability for the cooperative process. These aspects and others will be discussed in detail.

Representation and Organization

A popular form of knowledge representation for "packets" of knowledge is the *frame* (Minsky 1975). Frames may be thought of as primitive computing units, declarative definitional structures, or some combination of the two. Their exact form is not important; it suffices that each is specialized for the computation of some specific visual entity. A version of frames called *classes* is presented in the PSN (Procedural Semantic Networks) formalism of Levesque and Mylopoulos (1979). The remainder of the discussion focuses on knowledge class organization, since organization is of greater importance than the form of the actual knowledge packages.

Class Organization: Generalization, Aggregation, Instantiation

When one is confronted with a large, complex task, "divide and conquer" is an obvious tactic. Task partitioning is crucial; however, arbitrary task subdivision will yield structures that are unwieldy, unnecessarily complex, or inappropriately simple. Furthermore, such structures have poorly defined semantics, lead to inefficient processing, and lack clarity and perspicuity. Within the existing representational repertoire, there exist two common tools for domain subdivision and organization: the IS-A relationship (or generalization/specialization axis) and the PART-OF relationship (or part/whole axis). Brachman (1979, 1982) and Levesque and Mylopoulos (1979) discuss the properties, semantics, and use of these relationships. The IS-A (generalization/specialization) relationship was included in order to control the level of specificity of concepts represented. IS-A provides for economy of representation by representing constraints only once and enforcing strict inheritance of constraints and structural components. It is a natural concept-organization scheme, and it provides a partial ordering of knowledge concepts that is convenient for top-down search strategies. In conjunction with SIMILARITY (another representational construct), IS-A siblings may be implicitly partitioned into discriminatory sets. The PART-OF (aggregation) relationship allows control of the level of resolution represented in knowledge packages and thus control of the knowledge granularity of the knowledge base. It provides for the implementation of a divide-and-conquer representational strategy, and it forms a partial ordering of knowledge concepts that is useful for both top-down and bottom-up search strategies. Concept structure can be represented using slots in a class definition. The slots form an implicit PART-OF relationship with the concept. Representational prototypes (classes) are distinguished from and related to tokens by the INSTANCE-OF relationship. Instances must reflect the structure of the class they are related to; however, partial instances are permitted in association with a set of exception instances, or the exception record, for that class. In addition, a third type of incomplete instance is permitted: the potential instance or hypothesis. It is basically a structure that conforms to the "skeleton" of the generic class, but that may have only a subset of slots filled, and has not achieved a certainty high enough to cause it to be an instance or a partial instance. Details on the precise semantics of IS-A, PART-OF, and INSTANCE-OF may be found in Levesque and Mylopoulos 1979.

Such knowledge organization dimensions have been used in many other knowledge-based vision systems. (See, e.g., Hanson and Riseman 1978; Levine 1978; Sabbah 1981; Brooks 1981; Mackworth and Havens 1983.) Yet, their integration into the interpretation scheme was not completely developed within those works. The knowledge organization was used to structure knowledge and to provide access mechanisms for it. This work will show that knowledge organization can really do much more.

Time

A representation of general temporal concepts is beyond the scope of this work. In fact, many of the details of such representations, such as the calculus presented by Allen (1981), are not relevant. We are concerned with the impact of time-varying concepts on knowledge organization. From this point of view, time-varying aspects impose a partial ordering on elements of a concept; that is, a concept's parts are ordered in time. This ordering involves relationships such as *next*, *previous*, *simultaneous*, and *overlap*. Temporal precedence relationships interact with the PART-OF relationship.

Arbitrary groups or sets of events can be represented. If temporal concepts are grouped within some class, then whenever they represent a sequence of events, the particular concept representing the group exhibits a "coarser" temporal resolution than its components. To carry this further: A PART-OF hierarchy of temporal concepts displays levels of temporal resolution.

Description via Comparison: Similarity

Similarity measures that can be used to assist in the selection of other relevant hypotheses on the failure of hypothesis matching are useful to control the growth of hypothesis space. These measures usually relate classes that together make up a discriminatory set (i.e., only one of them can be instantiated at any one time). As such, they relate classes that are at the same level of specificity on the IS-A hierarchy and have the same IS-A parent class. Multiple IS-A parents are permitted as long as each class of the discriminatory set has the same set of IS-A parents. Similarity links are components of the frame scheme of Minsky (1975), and a realization of SIMILARITY links as an exception-handling mechanism based on a representation of the common and differing portions between two classes is presented in Tsotsos et al. 1980. Thus, they are an element of embedded declarative control, and they add a different view of frame representation, thereby enhancing the redundancy of the representation. The three major components of a SIMILARITY link are the list of target classes, the "similarities" expression (the important common portions between the source and target classes—remember that during interpretation the target classes are not active when the SIMILARITY link is being evaluated; thus, in time-dependent reasoning situations the components of the target class that are the same as those in the source class before activation of the

SIMILARITY link can be verified using the similarities expression), and the "differences" expression (the time course of exceptions that would be raised through inter-slot constraints of the source class or in parts of the source class).

Transduction between Domains: Projection

Projection is a transformational link relating representations of the same concept but in differing representational domains. In other words, projection is used to represent hypothesis-to-signal transductions. It is important because this enables the implementation of "priming" signals from "high-level" hypothesis expectations down to image-specific computing units. It is, for example, the relationship between a prototypical object and its actual appearance in an image. The ALVEN system employs such projections in creating predictions for low-level image operators.

The need for expectations and their use in high-level vision is not a new idea. Its importance was emphasized by Mackworth (1978) and Kanade (1980). However, no clear models exist. We believe that rich and well-defined knowledge organizations are a prerequisite for such expectation capabilities.

The generation of expectations is driven by current best hypotheses. Clearly, if the set of best hypotheses does not include the correct one at some point then the expectations produced will not be verified by the data. A mechanism that utilizes the hypothesis level of specificity in recovering gracefully from such incorrect expectations is required, and it is here that the above-mentioned link between specialization of concepts and expectations is used. Recovery from incorrect predictions involves upward movement along the IS-A hierarchy of hypotheses. This has the effect of relaxing the constraints that generated the original incorrect prediction and allowing for the creation of a more general prediction as the next plan.

Down (1983) presented examples of prediction specifications for simple shapes (such as points, lines, arcs, and circles) and aggregations of these shapes into more complex forms, as well as the methodology for their use. Predictions are classes in their own right and are thus treated as are all other classes. They are a version of limited planning capability.

Attentive Vision and Search

As described earlier, attentive vision can be characterized by several basic characteristics. One of these characteristics, perhaps the most important, is the presence of rich dimensions of search that allow for an interface between data tokens and the interpretation process, distinguish between search in the image and search in hypothesis space, and enable model-driven, goal-driven, and data-driven interpretation. This section addresses the search schemes in our framework and the basic processing cycle within which they operate.

Hypothesize-and-test is the basic recognition paradigm. However, activation of hypotheses proceeds along each of four dimensions concurrently, and hypotheses are considered in parallel rather than sequentially. These dimensions are the same class-organization axes that have been described above. Hypothesis activation is a cyclic process, beginning with data-driven activation and then alternating with goal-driven, model-driven, temporally directed, and failure-directed activations. For a given set of input data, in a single time slice, activation is terminated when none of the four activation mechanisms can identify an unactivated viable hypothesis. Termination is guaranteed by the finite size of the knowledge and the explicit prevention of reactivation of already active hypotheses. Furthermore, the activation of one hypothesis has implications for other hypotheses. Because of the multidimensional nature of hypothesis activation, the "focus" of the system also exhibits levels of attention. In its examination, the focus can be stated according to the desired level of specificity or resolution (the two are related), discrimination set, or temporal slice.

Each newly activated hypothesis is recorded in a structure that is similar to the class whose instance it has hypothesized. This structure includes the class slots awaiting fillers, the relationships that the hypothesis has with other hypotheses (its "conceptual adjacency"), and an initial certainty value determined by the activating hypothesis.

The "test" part of hypothesize-and-test is accomplished by the evaluation of constraints specified in the knowledge classes. The matching result of a hypothesis for the purpose of hypothesis ranking is summarized as either success or failure. Matching is defined as successful if each hypothesis component that is expected to be present at the time of matching has a corresponding active hypothesis that matches successfully and each slot and inter-slot constraint within the hypothesis evaluates to true. Matching is defined as unsuccessful if any slot or inter-slot constraint evaluates to false, or if any expected hypothesis component fails matching or does not exist and cannot be found through any mechanism.

Goal-Directed and Model-Directed Search

Top-down traversal of an IS-A hierarchy (that is, moving downward when concepts are verified) implies a constrained form of hypothesize-and-test

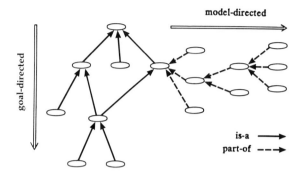

Figure 1
The directions of search for goal-directed and model-directed search processes.

for more specialized concepts. Similarly, top-down traversal of the PART-OF hierarchy implies a constrained form of hypothesize-and-test for components of classes that reflect greater resolution of detail. This search dimension along either representational axis is success-driven (figure 1).

A successful match (distinguished from "instantiation") of an IS-A parent concept implies that perhaps one of its IS-A children applies; a successful match of an IS-A child implies that its parents should also be true. Multiple IS-A children can be activated by a parent, but a more efficient scheme would be to activate one of the children if all children form a mutually exclusive set, or one child from each of several such sets, and then allow lateral search to take over. This selection may be guided by meta-knowledge associated with the IS-A parent hypothesis class. The lateral search mechanism will then determine how many IS-A children in a discriminatory set are viable possibilities. Note that hypotheses are activated for each class in a particular IS-A branch as the hierarchy is being traversed, and thus tokens will be created for each on instantiation. The activation of a hypothesis implies activation of all its PART-OF components as hypotheses as well. Cycles are avoided since at most one hypothesis for a particular class can exist for each time interval and set of structural components.

In the case of top-down PART-OF hierarchy traversal, activation of a hypothesis forces activation of hypotheses corresponding to each of its components, i.e., slots. The implication is that all slots must be filled in order for the parent hypothesis to be instantiated. Slots may have a temporal ordering, a feature handled by the temporal search mechanism interacting with this one. The search is therefore for all components of a class, increasing the resolution of the class definition.

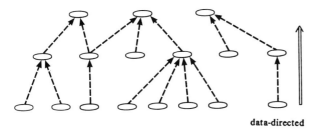

data-directed

Figure 2
The direction of search for the data-directed search process.

Data-Directed Search

The PART-OF hierarchy can also be traversed bottom-up in aggregation mode (figure 2). Bottom-up traversal implies a form of hypothesize-and-test where hypotheses activate other hypotheses that may have them as components, i.e., data-directed or event-driven search. This form of search has important implications for the definition of the knowledge base. The leaves of the PART-OF hierarchy are required to represent the types of tokens that can be abstracted from images, thus interfacing attentive with early vision processing components. This definition of the interface is independent of the number or form of "intrinsic" images computed during early vision.

This form of search also is success-driven. A successful match of a hypothesis implies that it may be a component of a larger grouping of hypotheses, and thus each possible PART-OF parent hypothesis is activated. Guidance for limiting the number of activations can be obtained from relevant meta-knowledge associated with the activating hypothesis class. Activation of hypotheses in this direction implies activation of all IS-A ancestors of new hypotheses. Arbitrary hypothesis groupings can be accomplished, but specific groupings can be recognized only if defined as a class.

Lateral Failure-Directed Search

Lateral search is a very different process than the previous two, since it is failure-driven. The search is along the SIMILARITY dimension (figure 3) and depends on the exception record of a particular hypothesis. Typically, several SIMILARITY links will be activated for a given hypothesis, and the resultant set of hypotheses is considered as a discriminatory set (i.e., at most one of them may be correct). Discriminatory sets are not allowed to

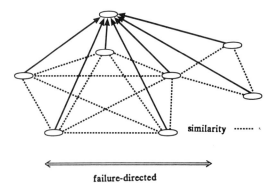

Figure 3
The directions of search for the failure-directed search process.

intersect. SIMILARITY interacts with the PART-OF relationship in that exceptions raised that specify missing slot tokens are handled by the hypothesis's PART-OF parent. Of course, the source and target classes of those links are at a different level of resolution.

Two situations may arise that require special consideration. The first occurs when the failing hypothesis has no PART-OF parent, as may occur during the first stage of data-driven search. The second may occur when no similarity link can be found that handles some of the exceptions raised. The goal of the exception-handling mechanism is to use all raised exceptions in some way through the similarity links. In the former case, when the failing hypothesis has no PART-OF parent, the similarity links found within its own structure are tried. In the latter case, when no similarity link can be found that can handle certain exceptions, the IS-A inheritance mechanism plays a role. If no similarity link can be found within the hypothesis itself or within a PART-OF parent, this means that the exhibited phenomena disagree with the hypothesized ones in a major way. For example, suppose that a hypothesis defining a particular type of "contract" motion was under consideration. The immediately avilable similarity links may be set up handle differences in rate of contraction. They would not point to appropriate hypotheses if the motion simply ceased. Therefore, similarity links are inherited from IS-A ancestors by either the PART-OF parent or the hypothesis itself as necessary. The IS-A ancestors of each hypothesis are also active hypotheses. The end result would be that the exception causes new hypotheses to be activated at some higher level of general-ization, rather than at the same level. In this way traversal back up the IS-A hierarchy can be accomplished. This is not necessarily a form of

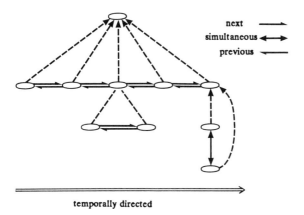

Figure 4
The direction of search for the temporally directed search process.

backtracking. It will indeed be backtracking in situations where wrong hypotheses are activated. However, since the context is time-varying, this mechanism also allows fast reaction to changes in data from hypotheses that are no longer viable because their expectations in time are no longer exhibited in the data.

Temporally Directed Search

Temporal search, a special case of hypothesis-driven search along the PART-OF dimension, is relevant whenever a class has an IS-A relationship with the SEQUENCE class. This is shown in Figure 4. Elements of a sequence may be compound events, such as other sequences, simultaneous events, or overlapping events. In a sequence, each element has a PART-OF relationship with the event class. Thus, on activation of the class, it is meaningless to activate all parts, as stated above, at the same time. Activation of the parts occurs only when their particular temporal specifications are satisfied. This form of search can take place only when temporal ranges are known. Arbitrary forms of temporal grouping can otherwise occur in a data-driven fashion, and specific groupings, if labeled by the creation of a class, can be recognized from them. (Causal or existential dependencies, a special case of temporal search, are not discussed here.)

The Search Cycle

The four search dimensions described must be coordinated in order to achieve the desired results, namely that each is used when appropriate.

Decisions on which dimension to use are governed by the following:

• There is a drive to instantiate the most specific classes for each data item at each time interval. Therefore, as soon as a successful match is obtained for a hypothesis, activate the next most specialized hypothesis for that data grouping.

• Instantiation implies a drive for completeness of description involving all components of a class description.

• There is a need to achieve instantiation in as few time samples as possible. Thus, as soon as an unsuccessful match is obtained, activate the relevant alternate hypotheses for that data grouping.

• Acquisition of new data items, regardless of whether they be acquired as the basic sampled data or as data found by specialized procedures initiated by hypotheses, necessitates data-driven search.

• Specific data items or groupings of data items must be considered individually with respect to the appropriate search scheme at specific points in time.

• Activation of a hypothesis by any method implies activation of all IS-A ancestors (perhaps several levels) and each direct PART-OF component (unless already active).

These basic rules ensure that the search schemes are indeed mutually complementary and are used only when appropriate.

Figure 5 presents the coordination of the different search modes within the processing cycle.

Hypothesis Structure and Its Properties

Hypotheses, like generic knowledge classes, are organized in specific ways. Connections among hypotheses are referred to as *conceptual adjacencies*. If a knowledge organization relation (IS-A, PART-OF, SIMILARITY, Temporal Precedence) exists between two classes and hypotheses are active for those two classes such that one hypothesis was activated by the other, then the hypotheses also have that same relation. The conceptual adjacency is one of the major components of hypothesis ranking, since it specifies what kinds of global and local consistencies play a role for a given hypothesis. In fact, the certainty updating scheme only uses information about conceptual adjacency and hypothesis matching. The set of conceptual adjacencies for a given hypothesis varies with time, as do its matching characteristics.

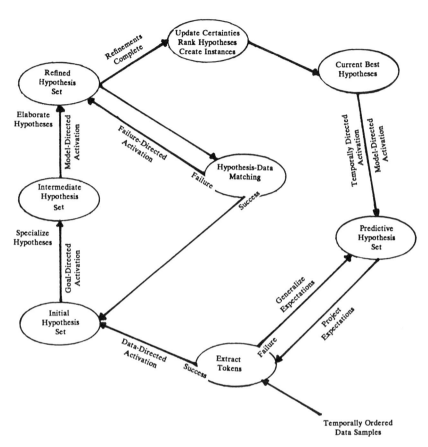

Figure 5
An attentive control strategy.

Temporal order satisfaction plays a role in the determination of component grouping strength, but is not the only actor. Each hypothesis has a self-contribution as well, which is based on the matching result of internal constraints.

Basically, hypotheses that are connected by conceptual adjacencies that imply consistency support one another, and those linked by adjacencies that imply inconsistency compete with one another by inducing inhibition. The IS-A relationship is in the former group; the SIMILARITY relationship is in the latter group. The *focus* of the system is defined as the set of hypotheses whose elements are the highest-ranked hypothesis at each level of specificity for each set of structural components being considered in the given time slice. Because of the slow change of certainties inherent in relaxation schemes, this focus exhibits inertia, or procrastination; i.e., it does not alter dramatically between certainty updates. It is a nonlinear scheme. Both global and local consistency are enforced through the contributions of hypotheses to one another via their conceptual adjacencies.

For the cooperative process, there are four major components that contribute to the certainty for each hypothesis: contributions from more general hypotheses along IS-A; contributions from competing hypotheses along SIMILARITY; contributions from component hypotheses along PART-OF; and the grouping strength of those components due to the satisfaction of temporal ordering considerations, spatial constraints or other component interrelationships, and matching results. Each of these is relevant only among active hypotheses.

Hypothesis Structure Consistency

It is important to define the notion of "consistency" in such a network of hypotheses. Within our framework, there are really three views of consistency that are considered:

global consistency (Are all the instances resulting from interpretation related to one another in reasonable ways?)

internal consistency (Does each instance have sufficient support from the data elements that directly constitute it?)

competition consistency (Do the competing hypotheses for each instance "believe" that the correct hypothesis was instantiated?)

These three considerations will be assumed to have equal importance.

Global consistency is required among all instances along their IS-A relationships. The semantics of IS-A imply strict inheritance, so that if a hypothesis is instantiated, then all its IS-A ancestors must also be instantiated. Thus, along the IS-A dimension, hypothesis responses are related by

$$R(h, t) \leq \min_{j \in N_{\text{IS-A}}(h, t)} R(j, t),$$

where $N_{\text{IS-A}}(h, t)$ is the set of IS-A ancestors for hypothesis h at time t, the hypotheses j are elements of that set, and $R(h, t)$ is the response of hypothesis h at time t.

Internal consistency, or sufficient internal support, is reflected by specific mechanisms within the updating rule. Unfortunately, no characterization is possible, and instances are created when their total support from all sources causes their certainty to achieve a threshold.

Competition consistency is defined along the SIMILARITY dimension. Each competing group has the same set of direct IS-A ancestors by definition (because otherwise the competition would not be meaningful). Moreover, the hypotheses in a competing group are mutually exclusive, so only one can be instantiated. Therefore, responses of a discriminatory group are related by

$$\sum_{h \in N_{SIM}(*, t)} R(h, t) = \min_{j \in N_{IS\text{-}A}(*, t)} R(j, t),$$

where $N_{SIM}(*, t)$ is the set of competing hypotheses at time t and where $N_{IS\text{-}A}(*, t)$ is the set of IS-A ancestors for that group. If the IS-A ancestors have been instantiated, then the right-hand side reduces to 1.0, which is the same as in standard relaxation. Consistency is enforced through the response-normalization process, and these relationships will appear in the updating rule to be presented below.

Compatibilities for the Cooperative Process

The conceptual adjacency relations manifest themselves as compatibilities in the updating of hypothesis certainty. In standard relaxation (Zucker et al. 1977), compatibility factors form the "model" (the view of consistency that the RLP has). In our scheme, each organizational relation has an associated compatibility. Each has a very intuitive meaning, and they are all listed below.

• self-compatibility: If a hypothesis succeeds—that is, if its internal constraints match the data successfully (the "glue" or "grouping strength" that binds its parts together)—it supports itself. If it fails, it inhibits itself. A failing hypothesis is not deleted from consideration on match failure alone.

• PART-OF compatibility: If a hypothesis has parts (features that can be observed), it receives a positive contribution from each part. A hypothesis cannot inhibit a part, because that part must be allowed to participate in other groupings in an unfettered manner.

• IS-A compatibility: Let hypothesis h_1 be IS-A related to h_2, i.e., h_1 IS-A h_2. When updating h_1, if both h_1 and h_2 match successfully, h_2 supports h_1. If h_1 succeeds and h_2 fails, h_2 inhibits h_1. Failure of h_1 has no effect on h_2.

• SIMILARITY compatibility: Hypotheses related by SIMILARITY are competitors—only one out of such a discriminatory set can be instantiated.

Let h_1 be related via a SIMILARITY link to h_2. When updating h_1, if h_2 fails, h_2 supports h_1, and if h_2 succeeds, h_2 inhibits h_1.

• temporal compatibility: Let the temporal relation between hypotheses h_1, h_2, and h_3 be

$$h_1 \leftarrow \text{previous} - h_2 \leftarrow \text{previous} - h_3.$$

Also let h_{sequence} be the hypothesis that represents this sequence, so that each of h_1, h_2, and h_3 is PART-OF h_{sequence}. When updating h_{sequence}, each of h_1, h_2, and h_3 would contribute to h_{sequence} when they appear through PART-OF. If no special mechanism were present for temporal order, the PART-OF contribution alone would not provide a discriminatory effect if the order were wrong. Therefore, there is a bonus contribution to h_{sequence} during the event h_2 due to the last nonzero response of h_1 if it appeared in the correct order, and likewise if h_3 follows h_2. This contribution decays exponentially; thus, the further in the past it happened, the smaller the force of the "glue" that groups these elements together. This will be termed *"previous" support*. Similarly, h_{sequence} receives a bonus inhibition due to h_3 that does not decay with time if h_3 appears before h_2 and this is the "next" inhibition. The same occurs if h_2 occurs before h_1. Clearly, "next" and "previous" are reciprocal relations except at the ends of the sequence.

Compatibilities are set to values between 1.0 and -1.0, where 1.0 means that the hypotheses are strongly compatible, 0.0 means that they are independent, and -1.0 means that they are strongly incompatible. They will appear in the form $1/k_{i,j}$ in the remainder of the discussion, where the absolute value $|k_{i,j}| \geq 1.0$, so that $-1.0 \leq 1/k_{i,j} \leq 1.0$. Here "$i$, j" corresponds to the type of compatibility between hypotheses i and j and can be of the following types:

self-compatibility: k_{self}

SIMILARITY compatibility: k_{SIM}

IS-A compatibility: $k_{\text{IS-A}}$

PART-OF compatibility: $k_{\text{PART-OF}}$

temporal compatibility: "previous" support is embodied in k_{prev}

temporal compatibility: "next" inhibition is given by k_{next}.

Each compatibility value is positive unless explicitly prefixed with a minus sign. A set of empirically derived inequalities that constrain the values of each of these compatibilities will be presented.

Initial Certainties of Hypotheses

The activation of hypotheses is the first step of processing. Once an initial set has been activated, matching is performed for each of those active hypotheses. Then, depending on those results, other hypotheses may be activated. On activation, each hypothesis receives an initial certainty, and this certainty is updated after all hypothesis activation and matching has been completed for that time interval.

Hypotheses are activated via the search mechanisms outlined above. Each hypothesis has an associated structure that conforms to the generic class to which it is related. In addition, each is assigned an initial certainty depending on how it was activated and ensuring that consistency relationships are maintained. Let the activated hypothesis be h, a single activating hypothesis be h_a, a set of simultaneously activating hypotheses be H_a, the activation time be t_0, and the hypothesis response be R. Initial certainties are assigned depending on the following activation types.

• Data-driven activation along PART-OF. The parts of a class, from which a hypothesis is derived, are represented by the set $N_{PART-OF}(h, *)$ and each of those parts can activate the hypothesis. (Of course, there can be only a single activator as well.) Thus, $H_a \subset N_{PART-OF}(h, *)$, and the initial certainty is given by

$$R(h, t_0) = \frac{\sum_{j \in H_a} R(j, t_0)}{|H_a|}.$$

• Hypothesis-driven activation along PART-OF: $R(h, t_0) = R(h_a, t_0)$.

• Hypothesis-driven activation along IS-A where several hypotheses in the set $H_a \subset N_{IS-A}(h, *)$ may participate in the activation: $R(h, t_0) = \min_{j \in H_a} R(j, t_0)$.

• Temporally driven activation. This is a special case of hypothesis-driven activation along PART-OF, and thus the initial certainty is computed in the same manner.

• Failure-driven activation along SIMILARITY: When a competitive set N_{SIM} first comes into being at time t_0, it does so by hypothesis-driven activation along IS-A, so that each hypothesis receives an equal share of the minimum certainty of their activating IS-A ancestors $H_a \subset N_{IS-A}(h, *)$:

$$\frac{\min_{j \in H_a} R(j, t_0)}{|N_{SIM}|}.$$

Suppose there is currently a set of competitors $N_{SIM}(*, t_0 - 1)$ and K new hypotheses are added to that set at time t_0. The already existing hypotheses donate half of their response to a pool, and then that pool is shared equally over the new and old hypotheses. Thus, the initial certainty of each of those K new hypotheses is given by

$$\frac{\sum\limits_{j \in N_{SIM}(*, t_0 - 1)} R(j, t_0 - 1)/2}{|N_{SIM}(*, t_0 - 1)| + K}$$

and each of the hypotheses h in $N_{SIM}(*, t_0 - 1)$ has its certainty adjusted to

$$\frac{R(h, t_0 - 1)}{2} + \frac{\sum\limits_{j \in N_{SIM}(*, t_0 - 1)} R(j, t_0 - 1)/2}{|N_{SIM}(*, t_0 - 1)| + K}.$$

These certainties are the adjusted ones before updating is done for time t_0. This sharing scheme maintains that the sum of the certainties in the competing set satisfies the definition of IS-A consistency. The design of the certainty sharing was motivated by the fact that the addition of a competing hypothesis must not undo the accumulated results of the activating hypothesis's matching history, i.e., hypothesis's matching inertia. It is an assignment that preserves hypothesis relative ranking.

Certainty Updating in Time

A variant of the temporal relaxation rule introduced in Tsotsos et al. 1980 will be used for hypothesis certainty updating. Basically, a neighborhood whose members change with time is responsible for the contribution part of the update. The hypothesis must reflect the same IS-A and PART-OF relationships with other hypotheses as does the generic class of which it may be an instance, with classes the generic class is related to. However, the temporal and SIMILARITY relationships of the hypothesis may only be a subset of those in the class. It will not, for example, always be the case that the discrimination will take place among all possible choices, nor will it always be the case that the correct temporal sequence of events will occur. Figure 6 shows a typical set of relationships among generic classes and hypotheses during the recognition process. This neighborhood, derived from the conceptual adjacencies described above, may be thought of as a "conceptual receptive field" for the hypothesis, because changes in response in any of the neighborhood members will result in changes in the hypothesis itself. Although the numbers of contributors may vary widely for given hypotheses, this variation has no adverse effect on the certainty

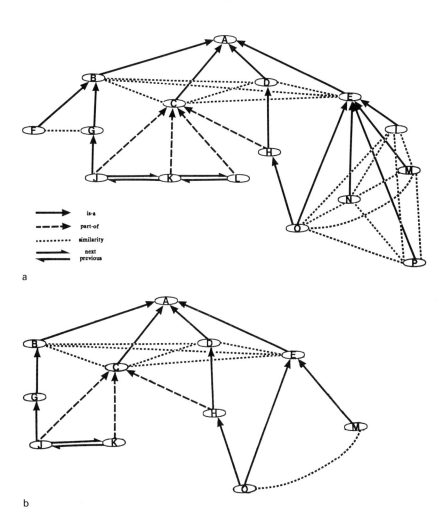

a

b

Figure 6
The relationship between generic knowledge (a) and a representative hypothesis structure
(b) that may be created from it.

updating, since the magnitude of each contribution is weighted by the number of contributors where necessary.

The rule is now presented. The response of hypothesis h at time $t + 1$ is defined by

$$R(h, t + 1) = \frac{R(h, t) \left(\sum_{j \in N(h, t)} w(h, j, t) \frac{R(j, t)}{k_{h, j}(t)} \right) \min_{a \in N_{\text{IS-A}}(h, t)} R(a, t + 1)}{\sum_{m \in N_{\text{SIM}}(h, t)} \left(R(m, t) \sum_{n \in N(m, t)} w(m, n, t) \frac{R(n, t)}{k_{m, n}(t)} \right)},$$

where $R(h, t)$ is the hypothesis response (or certainty) at time t and is restricted to the range from 0.0 to 1.0, and where $N(h, t)$ is the set of all hypotheses that are neighbors to h at time t and is the union of the following five sets:

$N_{\text{SIM}}(h, t)$, the set of all hypotheses that are neighbors to h through a SIMILARITY connection at time t (including h),

$N_{\text{IS-A}}(h, t)$, the set of all hypotheses that are neighbors to h through an IS-A connection at time t,

$N_{\text{PART-OF}}(h, t)$, the set of all hypotheses that are neighbors to h through a PART-OF connection at time t,

$N_{\text{previous}}(h, t)$, the set of all hypotheses that are neighbors to h through the temporal sequence connection "previous," and

$N_{\text{next}}(h, t)$, the set of all hypotheses that are neighbors to h through the temporal sequence connection "next."

Also in the above equation, $w(h, j, t)$ is the weight of the contribution by hypothesis j to hypothesis h at time t in relation to the other contributions. The sum of the weights over the set $N_{\text{SIM}}(h, t) \cup N_{\text{IS-A}}(h, t) \cup N_{\text{previous}}(t) \cup N_{\text{next}}(t)$ must be 1.0, and the sum of the weights over the set $N_{\text{PART-OF}}(h, t)$ must be 1.0 for convergence purposes. Since the hypothesis structure varies with time, so clearly do the assignments of weights. Furthermore, $k_{h, j}(t)$ is the compatibility between hypotheses h and j at time t and is determined by the type of relationship between the two hypotheses. There are six types, as described above, and the hypothesis matching result at time t determines whether the value is positive or negative for certain ones.

The contribution portion of this rule, through judicious choices of weighting factors, is restricted to the range $0.0 \leq$ contribution ≤ 2.0, as it is in Zucker et al. 1977. However, normalization takes place only among hypotheses that are comparable, that is, elements of the same discriminatory set. It would be meaningless to try to normalize between levels of abstraction. Moreover, because of the definition of IS-A consistency, the sum of the responses over a discriminatory set is not normalized to 1.0 necessarily, but rather to the minimum updated response of the IS-A ancestors of the hypothesis, thus the last term of the numerator. This implies that the normalization process must be done in a strict order, from general hypotheses to specific ones along the IS-A relationship. If there is no discriminatory set the denominator is set to 1.0, and if there are no IS-A ancestors that term is also 1.0.

If we expand the contribution portion of the rule, the values of the weights will become apparent.

$$\sum_{j \in N(h,t)} w(h, j, t) \frac{R(j, t)}{k_{h,j}(t)}$$

expands out to the sum of the following terms:

- self-contribution: $w(h, h, t) \dfrac{R(h, t)}{k_{\text{self}}(t)}$.

- SIMILARITY contribution: $\displaystyle\sum_{j \in N_{\text{SIM}}(h, t), j \neq h} w(h, j, t) \frac{R(j, t)}{k_{\text{SIM}}(t)}$.

- IS-A contribution: $\displaystyle\sum_{j \in N_{\text{IS-A}}(h, t)} w(h, j, t) \frac{R(j, t)}{k_{\text{IS-A}}(t)}$.

- PART-OF contribution: $\displaystyle\sum_{j \in N_{\text{PART-OF}}(h, t)} w(h, j, t) \frac{WR(j, t)}{k_{\text{PART-OF}}(t)}$,

where $WR(j, t)$ is the weighted response of the PART-OF subtree rooted at hypothesis j.

- previous contribution: $\displaystyle\sum_{j \in N_{\text{previous}}(h, t)} w(h, j, t) R(j, t_{\text{last}}) e^{(-t + t_{\text{last}})/k_{\text{prev}}}$.

- next contribution: $\displaystyle\sum_{j \in N_{\text{next}}(h, t)} w(h, j, t) \frac{R(j, t_{\text{last}})}{k_{\text{next}}}$.

The following are the weight assignments.

- for PART-OF contributors: $w(h, j, t) = \dfrac{1}{|N_{\text{PART-OF}}(h, t)|}$,

so that $\sum_{j \in N_{\text{PART-OF}}(h, t)} w(h, j, t) = 1.0$. Of course, the number of PART-OF contributors varies with time.

- The sum of the weights of all the remaining contributors, including the self contribution, must be 1.0. The weights, therefore, are not fixed but vary with time depending on which contributors are present. The remaining major contributions reflect the hypothesis's internal consistency, its global consistency, and its consistency as viewed by its competitors. Each of these three contributions is weighted equally. In the case that all are present, the following weights are assigned: For IS-A contributors, $w(h, j, t) = 1/3 |N_{\text{IS-A}}(h, t)|$. (The number of IS-A contributors changes with time.) For SIMILARITY contributors, $w(h, j, t) = \frac{1}{3}$. (The weighted sum is not required here, since the sum of responses may be at most 1.0, and this is enforced through normalization.) For grouping strength, self-contribution, previous support, and next inhibition are equally weighted, and when all are present $w(h, j, t) = \frac{1}{9}$ so that the sum of the weights is $\frac{1}{3}$. If only the self-contribution is present, then it is weighted by the entire $\frac{1}{3}$ amount. If the self-contribution and (say) the next inhibition are present, each is weighted by $\frac{1}{6}$.

The PART-OF contribution is always present and is positive. The weights on any other contributions may vary, but the sum of those weights must always be 1.0.

Result Propagation through the Network

Since iterations are related to time samples, it is important to address the problem of result propagation through the network of hypotheses. In standard RLPs, results propagate to neighboring processes, as a result of several iterations, and the field of influence of a given process is determined directly by the number of iterations; the greater the number of iterations, the larger the field. In our case, all results must propagate to any other processes that may need them during a small fixed number of iterations, because for the next iteration new data will be presented to the system. This does not mean that a consistent solution is also found within that same small number of iterations; iterations are required for the temporal integration of results.

The results that must be communicated are of two types: changes in certainty and changes in hypothesis matching state. The hypotheses are organized in the same fashion as the generic knowledge classes from which they are derived, namely along the IS-A, PART-OF, SIMILARITY, and Temporal Precedence dimensions. The first three of these (Temporal Precedence is a special case of PART-OF) enable results to propagate as desired. SIMILARITY networks pose no problem, since each active hypothesis is directly connected to each other active hypothesis.

PART-OF also poses no problem, because the PART-OF contribution is computed as a weighted sum of the entire subtree rooted at the contributing hypothesis. This, in addition, imposes an ordering on the computation of updated certainty values.

The role of the IS-A dimension requires more elaboration. Because of inheritance, match results are conveyed down the IS-A hierarchy implicitly. There is no upward communication along this dimension. Because of the strict order of normalization (downward along IS-A), changes in an IS-A ancestor's certainty will result in changes in the normalization factor for the IS-A child. Increases in ancestor certainty will allow the child's certainty to increases, and vice versa. Communication along all relevant branches of the hypothesis network, both of match results and of certainty changes, is thus guaranteed by the nature of the knowledge organization and definitions of network consistency.

Nonlinearity and Feedback

A linear system has response that is computed according to current input and current state, independent of the rate at which response is changing. The updating rule presented above is nonlinear. Because of the multiplicative nature of the rule's numerator, the change in response is greater with increasing previous response, and with increasing IS-A parent response. The question that must be asked here is: "Are the nonlinearities inherent in the theory, or do they appear as a result of the particular realization of the theory?" This will be only partially addressed here. However, owing to other aspects of the theory, the effect of the nonlinearities is minimal.

One important aspect of the updating rule is the normalization of response. This is necessary because of the definitions of network consistency, and is thus an inherent nonlinearity of the theoretical foundations of this framework. Moreover, from a practical point of view, normalization is necessary in order to ensure that responses do not grow unchecked, something that would occur even with a linear rule. A second source of nonlinearity is due to the first term of the numerator, the multiplication by the response of the hypothesis under consideration. This is present in the original RLP model of Zucker et al. 1977, and is a carryover from there. It is an implementation-dependent nonlinearity, and no attempts were made to reformulate this in a linear manner.

Nonlinear, time-varying systems in open loop configuration are rather difficult to characterize and control. The incorporation of feedback, on the other hand, has definite advantages. Feedback reduces sensitivity of response to parameter variations (in this case, compatibility values), reduces the effect of noise disturbances, and makes the response of nonlinear elements more linear.

The essential property of feedback is its iterative comparison of the current state with the desired state in such a way that results of comparison can be used to correct the system toward the desired state (Zucker 1978b). The desired state in a recognition task is unknown, yet global consistency is sufficient to ensure that a correct interpretation can be obtained. Feedback is inherent in this framework in two ways: exception recording and handling via the similarity mechanism, and levels of IS-A abstraction and downward communication between them. It is evident from the experimental results that the resulting scheme is well behaved, yet analytic proof is elusive.

Performance of the Temporal Cooperative Process

Let us take a simple situation and see how this updating rule performs. Figure 7 presents a single hypothesis, totally disconnected from any other hypotheses, whose contributions come from its own matching success or failure and from its PART-OF elements.

The PART-OF contribution, for purposes of the first few examples, is 1.0. There is no need for normalization, since there is no discriminatory set.

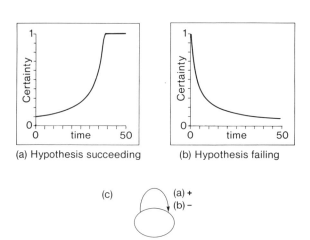

(a) Hypothesis succeeding   (b) Hypothesis failing

(c)   (a) +
       (b) −

Figure 7
Certainty changes with time for a single hypothesis with self-contribution and PART-OF contributions.

On the other hand, this forces the need for a careful analysis. Normalization forces all responses to behave, that is, to stay between 0.0 and 1.0. Without it, response may be unbounded. Figure 7c shows the hypothesis configuration, while figures 7a and 7b show the certainty over time if the hypothesis always succeeds or always fails in matching, respectively. The updating rule in this case reduces to

$$R(1, t) = R(1, t - 1) + \frac{R(1, t - 1)^2}{k_{self}}$$

for figure 7a and to

$$R(1, t) = R(1, t - 1) - \frac{R(1, t - 1)^2}{k_{self}}$$

for figure 7b. Approximating each of these with an ordinary differential equation and solving, the response functions become, respectively,

$$R(1, t) = \frac{R(1, 0)}{1 - R(1, 0) * t / k_{self}}$$

and

$$R(1, t) = \frac{R(1, 0)}{1 + R(1, 0) * t / k_{self}}.$$

In the constant failure case, the response smoothly tends toward 0 with increasing time and the speed of decrease can be controlled by adjusting k_{self}. For the constant success case, as is intuitively clear, there is no such nice property. Indeed, the response will achieve 1.0 at time

$$\frac{k_{self} * (1 - R(1, 0))}{R(1, 0)}$$

and keep on increasing. Clearly, the smaller k_{self} is, the faster this occurs. We will want decisions on interpretation to occur as close to the end time of an event as possible, but most definitely not after the event has ended. Therefore,

$$k_{self} \leq \text{minimum event duration} * \frac{R(1, 0)}{1 - R(1, 0)},$$

where the minimum event duration has units of "temporal measurements." A temporal measurement is taken "between" two data samples. For simplicity we will ignore the final term due to initial hypothesis response.

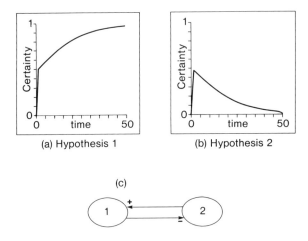

(a) Hypothesis 1   (b) Hypothesis 2

(c)

Figure 8
Certainty changes with time for a pair of competing hypotheses with SIMILARITY and PART-OF contributions.

It will be apparent that this does not ill affect the remainder of the analysis, since a structure with an isolated hypothesis can never occur. We will require that the number of iterations (or the number of temporal measurements) required in order to "recognize" a particular concept always be less than or equal to k_{self}. In other words, we equate iterations with temporal measurements.

Hypotheses are never alone; they have neighbors. The first neighbor that will be investigated is the one connected via SIMILARITY. Figure 8 presents hypotheses where both PART-OF and SIMILARITY contributions are present, but not self-contributions. Hypothesis 1 always succeeds; hypothesis 2 always fails. The updating rule for this situation reduces to the pair

$$R(1, t) = R(1, t - 1) + \frac{R(1, t - 1) * R(2, t - 1)}{k_{\text{sim}}},$$

$$R(2, t) = R(2, t - 1) - \frac{R(2, t - 1) * R(1, t - 1)}{k_{\text{sim}}}.$$

In this case the normalization factor has a value of 1.0. The initial values $R(1, 0)$ and $R(2, 0)$ sum to 1.0, and it is clear from the updating rule that the denominator of the updating rule will always be $R(1, t - 1) + R(2, t - 1)$, or 1.0. By the same approach as in the preceding example, the response curves can be approximated by

$$R(1, t) = \cfrac{1}{\cfrac{1 - R(1, 0)}{R(1, 0)} * e^{-t/k_{\text{SIM}}} + 1},$$

$$R(2, t) = \cfrac{1}{\cfrac{1 - R(2, 0)}{R(2, 0)} * e^{t/k_{\text{SIM}}} + 1}.$$

In both cases, desirable properties are exhibited. The response for hypothesis 1 tends to 1 with increasing time, and the rate can be controlled by adjusting k_{SIM}. The response for hypothesis 2 tends to 0 with increasing time, and again the rate is set by k_{SIM}.

Let us now join these two examples and investigate the situation where there is both self-contribution and SIMILARITY contribution. This is portrayed in figure 9.

Two hypotheses are present: that hypothesis 1 always succeeds and that hypothesis 2 always fails. The updating rule for this situation is

$$R(1, t) = \cfrac{R(1, t - 1) + \cfrac{R(1, t - 1)^2}{2k_{\text{self}}} + \cfrac{R(1, t - 1)*R(2, t - 1)}{2k_{\text{SIM}}}}{\text{NORM}},$$

$$R(2, t) = \cfrac{R(2, t - 1) - \cfrac{R(2, t - 1)^2}{2k_{\text{self}}} - \cfrac{R(2, t - 1)*R(1, t - 1)}{2k_{\text{SIM}}}}{\text{NORM}},$$

where

$$\text{NORM} = 1 + \frac{R(1, t - 1)^2}{2k_{\text{self}}} - \frac{R(2, t - 1)^2}{2k_{\text{self}}}.$$

This is not easy to deal with analytically, and thus an approximation will not be presented. However, figures 9a and 9b show the typical response profiles that such a configuration produces. It appears as if these results are well behaved, and indeed through experimentation it was found that this is the case.

All response computations are subject to lower and upper thresholds for hypothesis deletion and instantiation, respectively. The curves shown in the preceding figures have a passing resemblance to exponential functions. A common notion for exponentials is the time constant, or the amount of time required for the function to reach $1/e$ of its initial value if decreasing

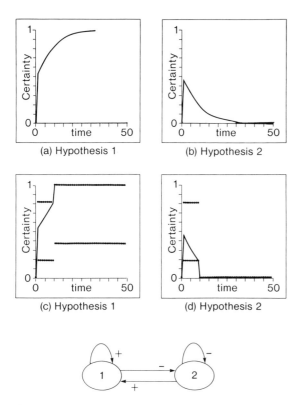

Figure 9

Two competing hypotheses with SIMILARITY, PART-OF, and self-contributions.
Diagrams c and d show the effect of applying the dynamic threshold mechanism for
hypothesis instantiation and deletion. Upper (instantiation) and lower (deletion) thresholds
are shown as dotted lines. The change in threshold values with time is apparent.

or $(1 - 1/e)$ of its final value from an initial value of 0.0 if increasing. Using the initial values of hypotheses in competing sets defined earlier to compute the height of the exponential, we set the instantiation threshold at

$$\left(1 - \frac{1}{|N_{SIM}|}\right) * (1 - e^{-1}) + \frac{1}{|N_{SIM}|}.$$

$|N_{SIM}|$ is the number of competing hypotheses in the discriminatory set, and this relationship is derived under the assumption that all hypotheses start at equal certainties (which is the case when they are all activated at the same time.) The corresponding deletion threshold is set at

$$\frac{e^{-1}}{|N_{SIM}|}.$$

The effects of applying these thresholds to the previous case are shown in figures 9c and 9d. The amount of time required to reach the instantiation threshold is the response time of the system. With contributions other than the self-contributions, this response time is significantly shorter than with self-contribution alone. For the remainder of this discussion, a given hypothesis will have achieved *convergence* (or the reaching of a decision) when the hypothesis's response achieves the instantiation threshold. It will have achieved *useful convergence* if the number of iterations (or time samples) is less than or equal to the minimum duration of the event represented by that hypothesis.

Using the above definition of convergence, I now elaborate on the experimentation performed for the current configuration. Figure 10 (a solid family of curves) shows the empirical relationships found between k_{self} and k_{SIM} for varying values of $|N_{SIM}|$. It was found that in order to ensure the required behavior, namely convergence in no more than k_{self} iterations, k_{self} must be greater than or equal to k_{SIM}. More precisely, the following was found to be the relation among k_{self}, k_{SIM}, and the number of competitors in the set N_{SIM}:

$$k_{SIM} = 1.0 \quad \text{for } 2|N_{SIM}| \leq k_{self} < \frac{7|N_{SIM}|}{3},$$

$$k_{SIM} \leq \frac{3(k_{self} - |N_{SIM}|)}{4|N_{SIM}|} \quad \text{for } k_{self} \geq \frac{7|N_{SIM}|}{3}.$$

These relationships are conservative approximations to the family of curves presented in figure 10. Spot checks for values of $|N_{SIM}|$ not on this graph were tested with satisfactory results. There is no convergence within k_{self}

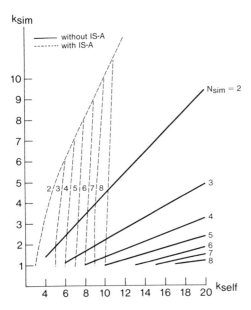

Figure 10
The empirical relationship between the self-contribution compatibility k_{self} and the
SIMILARITY compatibility k_{SIM} for varying numbers of competing hypotheses. The solid
curves show the relationship without the IS-A compatibility; the dotted curves show the
effect with IS-A.

time units (iterations) for values of $k_{self} < 2|N_{SIM}|$. The fastest convergence
occurs when $k_{SIM} = 1.0$ (approximately $2|N_{SIM}|$ time units).

The next compatibility type we will discuss in IS-A compatibility. A
hypothesis configuration with IS-A comtribution is shown in figure 11.
IS-A contributions may be considered as a "high-level bias" mechanism. If
the biased hypothesis is succeeding, it should speed up its increase in
response. Indeed, for an IS-A hypothesis with response 1.0 the updating
rule reduces to

$$R(1, t) = R(1, t-1) + \frac{R(1, t-1)^2}{2k_{self}} + \frac{R(1, t-1)*R(2, t-1)}{2k_{IS\text{-}A}},$$

where hypothesis 1 IS-A hypothesis 2. The normalization factor is 1 since
there are no competitors, and it is assumed that the IS-A parent hypothesis
has response 1.0. This will cause the response of hypothesis 1 to increase
faster than the hypothesis with self-contribution alone, and the degree of
speedup can be controlled by $k_{IS\text{-}A}$. If the hypothesis fails, there is no IS-A
contribution. Thus, failing hypotheses are allowed to decay on the basis

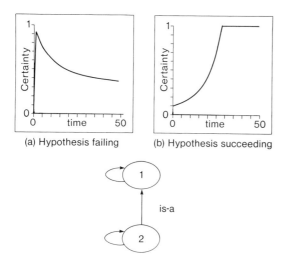

(a) Hypothesis failing   (b) Hypothesis succeeding

Figure 11
Certainty changes with time for two hypotheses related by IS-A with IS-A, PART-OF, and self-contributions present.

of their self-contribution, while succeeding hypotheses are given an extra boost.

An important question, however, is: How much faster is the increase in response? In the case where self, SIMILARITY, and IS-A contributions are present, experiments reveal the results shown in figure 10 (the dashed family of curves) for the empirical relationship between k_{self} and k_{SIM} for varying values of $|N_{\text{SIM}}|$ and where the largest value of $k_{\text{IS-A}}$ that allowed useful convergence was used. This largest value and its relationship with k_{self} are shown in figure 12. Without IS-A useful convergence could not be achieved for $k_{\text{self}} < 2|N_{\text{SIM}}|$, but with IS-A it is possible for $k_{\text{self}} \geq |N_{\text{SIM}}| + 2$ with $k_{\text{SIM}} = 1.0$ and $k_{\text{IS-A}} = 1.0$ in time approximately $|N_{\text{SIM}}| + 1$. For $k_{\text{self}} \geq |N_{\text{SIM}}| + 3$, we have $k_{\text{SIM}} \leq k_{\text{self}}$ and $k_{\text{IS-A}} \leq k_{\text{self}}/(|N_{\text{SIM}}| + 1)$. (This is a very conservative estimate when $|N_{\text{SIM}}| = 2$.) Of course, $k_{\text{IS-A}} = 1.0$ will ensure the fastest decision.

Two final considerations will complete the characterization of the above three types of compatibilities. For the case where h_1 IS-A h_2, the values of the compatibilities should ensure that if h_1 succeeds and h_2 fails then the response of h_1 decays. This will be true if

$$\frac{R(h_1, t)^2}{k_{\text{self}}} - \frac{R(h_1, t)R(h_2, t)}{k_{\text{IS-A}}} < 0.$$

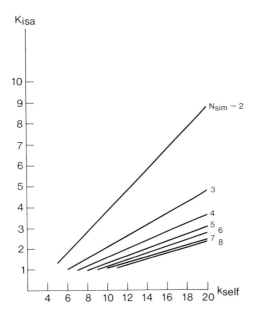

Figure 12
The empirical relationship between the largest value of the IS-A compatibility that enables useful convergence and the corresponding values of the self-contribution compatibility for varying numbers of competing hypotheses.

Since by IS-A consistency $R(h_2, t) \geq R(h_1, t)$, necessarily $k_{\text{self}} > k_{\text{IS-A}}$. If a third hypothesis h_3 is added such that h_3 IS-A h_2 and h_1 SIMILARITY h_3, and if h_1 and h_2 succeed and h_3 fails, we want to ensure that h_3 decays more rapidly than without the IS-A relation. This will be the case if

$$\frac{-R(h_3, t)}{k_{\text{SIM}}} + \frac{2R(h_2, t)}{k_{\text{IS-A}}} > \frac{R(h_1, t)}{k_{\text{self}}}.$$

This comes from the differences in the denominators of the rule between the two cases. Since $R(h_2, t) \geq R(h_3, t)$, and $k_{\text{self}} > k_{\text{SIM}}$ as described previously, then necessarily $k_{\text{SIM}} > k_{\text{IS-A}}$. The result is that $k_{\text{self}} > k_{\text{SIM}} > k_{\text{IS-A}}$, with specific values being set using the relationships derived experimentally.

For the previous discussion, it was assumed that the PART-OF contribution was always 1.0. In general, this is clearly not the case. Experiments were conducted on the full range of acceptable values for the compatibilities discussed above, for sets of competitors that had all manner of varying PART-OF contributions, and with $k_{\text{PART-OF}} = 1.0$. The longer the event duration (that is, the larger the value of k_{self}), the smaller the difference of

PART-OF contribution that could be present if a proper decision was to be made. (Roughly speaking, for short events the difference required was about 50 percent; for longer events it could be as little as 20 percent.) Large values of k_{self} coupled with relatively small values of k_{SIM} and k_{IS-A} were preferred so that the the number of iterations (time samples) would be large enough to accumulate information over the entire duration of the event. No additional restrictions on the values of the other compatibilities were necessary, and the ranges for convergence defined above still held. Therefore, the final ordering of compatibility values was

$$k_{self} > k_{SIM} > k_{IS-A} \geq k_{PART-OF} = 1.0,$$

with further restrictions on k_{self} and k_{IS-A} as defined above.

The next example is a simple sequence group that embodies the PART-OF contribution as well as the support and inhibition available for temporal grouping (figure 13). The hypothesis representing the sequence is labeled 1. The stimuli, numbered 2 through 6, have a high response of a given duration beginning at a specific time and a zero response elsewhere. The response of group 1 decays rather quickly but recovers when a new stimulus of the sequence appears. In figure 13a the stimuli are on for one time unit and off for nine. During those nine time units, the sequence hypothesis self-inhibits because there are no component parts to support it and cause it to match successfully. The sequence in figure 13a is never very sure of itself. In figure 13b, each stimulus is on for three time units and off for seven. In this case, there is some consistency to the response, and as the stimulus-on period increases to five in figure 13c and nine in figure 13d the sequence becomes more consistent with time.

There are three mechanisms at work in this example: self-contribution, PART-OF contribution, and PREVIOUS contribution. In this example, the stimuli were moving in the correct direction. A PREVIOUS contribution (always positive) appears only if the hypothesis IS-A SEQUENCE. NEXT contributions are always negative.

The value of the PREVIOUS compatibility is set depending on the temporal separation of events for which it is desired to cause a strong "gluing" effect. This can be accomplished if k_{prev} = maximum temporal separation in time units (or iterations). Therefore, for temporal separations between events in a sequence less than this value the compatibility will be greater than $1/e$; if the separation is greater, the compatibility will be less than $1/e$.

The situation when the correct direction is observed causes faster response time for the sequence hypothesis due to the PREVIOUS contribution than

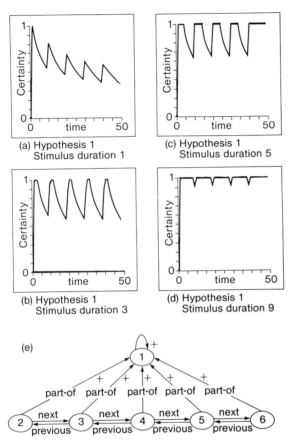

Figure 13

Certainty changes with time for a simple sequence grouping of hypotheses, with varying durations for the hypotheses 2, 3, 4, 5, and 6. PART-OF, PREVIOUS, and self-contributions play a role.

without it. However, in cases where the data are not in the correct order the setting of compatibilities requires more care. The contributions from previous or next events are taken into account each time the contribution from any single event is computed. Only the previous or next events of that single event are considered. The certainty of the previous or next contribution is determined using its most recent certainty value, denoted by t_{last} below. In the case where both the previous elements and next elements are present, there are two competing contributions, weighted equally, to the updating of the sequence hypothesis (that are different from previous situations):

$$R(h_2, t_{last}) * e^{(-t + t_{last})/k_{prev}} - \frac{R(h_4, t_{last})}{k_{next}}.$$

The sequence constraints of the hypothesis are violated, so the hypothesis itself is self-inhibiting. It is important that the positive term due to the previous event not outweigh the negative term due to the next event. Indeed, the desired result is that the decay is accelerated because of the next effect, and this would be ensured if the negative term were larger in magnitude than the positive term of the above contributions. Therefore, if both next and previous events were of the same strength, and in the worst case where t_{last} is just the previous time interval rather than farther back in time, the following relation should hold in order to ensure this:

$$k_{next} < e^{1/k_{prev}}.$$

The situations presented above make it possible to derive empirical constraints on the values of the compatibilities and to relate those values to characteristics of the temporal domain being considered.

A Brief Look at Some More Complex Examples

The remaining several examples are too complex to permit any specific quantitative analysis. They do, however, represent common situations in low-level and high-level vision. They are presented to demonstrate that the machinery presented does indeed function in complex situations as long as the guidelines for the setting of compatibility constants are obeyed. Figure 14 illustrates a rather common situation, that of orientation selection, with static data. Assume that all eight orientations are considered here, even though pictorially is it difficult to portray both orientations along a single line.

The stimulus array is 5 × 5; the darker the element, the higher the

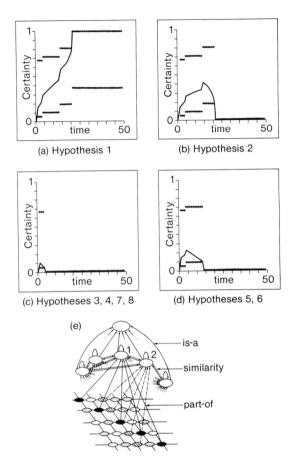

Figure 14
An orientation-selection hypothesis structure, with stimuli on a grid, of varying strengths (coded by shading), and the resulting certainty-vs.-time profiles for each of the eight orientation hypotheses. As the hypothesis number increases, the orientation it represents rotates 45° clockwise, with the orientations for hypotheses 1 and 2 shown.

response value. (The black ones have response 1.0, the striped ones 0.5, the white ones 0.0, and the remainder 0.2.) Eight hypotheses are in competition here, with hypothesis 1 representing the dark elements (which form a consistent orientation grouping going from the top left of the array to the bottom right) and with hypothesis 2 representing the striped elements (which form a consistent orientation grouping from the top to the bottom of the array). The 180° opposite orientation to these, we assume, is inconsistent. Both hypotheses 1 and 2 succeed in their matching, since they are looking at elements that semantically form an orientation group. The other hypotheses fail. The result for hypothesis 1 is shown in figure 14a, and that for hypothesis 2 in figure 14b. The results for hypotheses 3, 4, 7, and 8 are the same and are shown in figure 14c. The results for hypotheses 5 and 6, which also are the same, are shown in figure 14d. The clear winner is hypothesis 1 after about 25 time units (iterations). The other hypotheses are never even close to the instantiation threshold. The threshold dependency on the number of competitors is very clear. It jumps when hypotheses 3, 4, 7 and 8 are deleted, when hypotheses 5 and 6 are deleted, and again when hypothesis 2 is deleted.

Figure 15 shows exactly the same setup, except that there is an IS-A constraint that affects each of the eight competing orientation hypotheses.

Basically, it is a hypothesis that biases the situation—it communicates to each hypothesis that there is indeed an orientation element in the stimulus array. It does not identify which one, however. The successful hypotheses accept this bias, while the failing ones reject it. The effect is that the only change from the previous case is that the instantiation of the correct hypothesis occurs sooner, by about five time units. Response time is decreased by the addition of top-down biases.

Using the same stimulus array but adding the time dimension, figure 16 portrays a direction-selection experiment.

Each stimulus is on for eight time units and off for two. The correct ordering for hypothesis 1 is from the top left corner to the bottom right corner. For hypothesis 2, each of the stimuli has the same characteristics as for hypothesis 1 except for strength, and the correct order is from top to bottom. In fact, all hypotheses share an event: the middle one. Hypotheses 1 and 2 succeed in matching; the remainder do not. Each stimulus, when it becomes active, activates of reactivates each higher-order hypothesis that it is PART-OF. The life span of hypothesis 5, whose elements are as strong as its correctly matching counterpart 1 but whose ordering is wrong, is rather short. In fact, as soon as the inhibition due to the reversal in order comes into play at the start of the second stimulus, it is quickly removed.

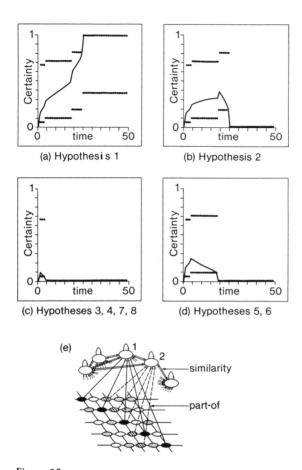

Figure 15

An orientation-selection hypothesis structure, with stimuli on a grid, of varying strengths (coded by shading), and the resulting certainty-vs.-time profiles for each of the eight orientation hypotheses. As the hypothesis number increases, the orientation it represents rotates 45° clockwise, with the orientations for hypotheses 1 and 2 shown. This structure has an IS-A relationship for each of the orientation hypotheses that acts as a top-down bias. The resulting speedup in time to convergence can be seen.

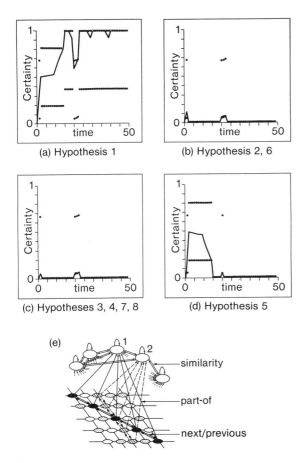

(a) Hypothesis 1

(b) Hypothesis 2, 6

(c) Hypotheses 3, 4, 7, 8

(d) Hypothesis 5

(e)

—similarity

—part-of

—next/previous

Figure 16
A direction-selection hypothesis structure, with stimuli on a grid, of varying strengths (coded by shading), and the resulting certainty-vs.-time profiles for each of the eight direction hypotheses. As the hypothesis number increases, the direction it represents rotates 45° clockwise, with the directions for hypotheses 1 and 2 shown. For example, hypothesis 5 represents the exact opposite direction to hypothesis 1. The temporal precedence relations among the grid stimuli are shown. Each stimulus is allowed to (re-)activate its PART-OF parent hypothesis.

Hypothesis 1 is again the clear winner. During the stimulus-off period, however, there is self-inhibition. The total decrease in response is, of course, a function of the duration of the off time as well as the decay constant.

Figure 17 shows the results of the same direction-selection task, with an added IS-A constraint. The effect of the IS-A constraint should be the same as was shown for the orientation-selection case. Indeed, the slope of initial increase of response for hypothesis 1 is slightly higher, but the time for instantiation could not be shorter since the second stimulus must appear before discrimination can occur. The decays are compensated slightly. Figure 18 shows the results from the same structure, but with a different definition of SEQUENCE; only the first stimulus of a sequence can activate the higher-order SEQUENCE unit. This is included for purposes of comparison with the previous example. The definition of SEQUENCE used here leads to a more stable response curve for hypothesis 1. It is clear that one may experiment with a variety of schemes. With these more complex examples, in each case the structure over which the cooperative process operates changes with time; however, even more complex situations arise in a real application.

To summarize: The temporal cooperative process displays qualitative results in both static and dynamic situations that are both desirable and consistent. Guidelines were presented for the setting of compatibility values that would achieve such results. The process is remarkably insensitive to actual compatibility values so long as the guidelines are obeyed. Since iterations are considered in time and have the same meaning in either static or dynamic situations, we can begin to relate system response time in static cases using the same terms as for dynamic cases.

Noise Effects

Up to this point, the effect of noisy data has not been addressed. Experiments conducted with randomly generated, normally distributed, noisy matching data are described in detail in Tsotsos 1981b. Basically, a set of competing hypotheses are created, with no semantics, and a match result over time is generated for each. For example, for two competing hypotheses where one is correct, the other is false, and the data are perfect, true matching data would be generated for the former and false data for the latter. With the addition of 10 percent noise, the matching data for the correct hypothesis would be true only for 90 percent of the samples generated; they would be false for only 90 percent of the samples

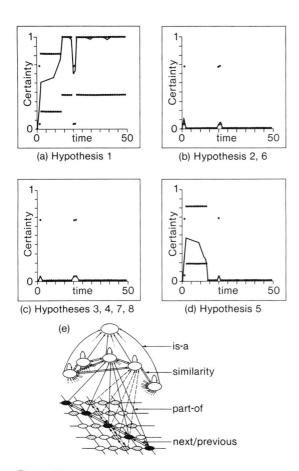

Figure 17

A direction-selection hypothesis structure, with stimuli on a grid, of varying strengths (coded by shading), and the resulting certainty-vs.-time profiles for each of the eight direction hypotheses. As the hypothesis number increases, the direction it represents rotates 45° clockwise, with the directions for hypotheses 1 and 2 shown. For example, hypothesis 5 represents the exact opposite direction to hypothesis 1. The temporal precedence relations among the grid stimuli are shown. Each stimulus is permitted to (re-)activate its PART-OF parent hypothesis. An IS-A relationship as top-down bias is added to this structure.

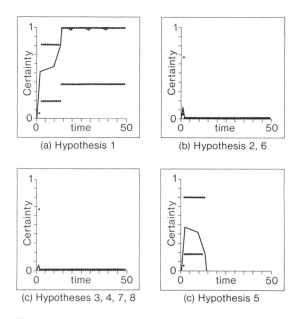

Figure 18
A direction-selection hypothesis structure, with stimuli on a grid, of varying strengths (coded by shading), and the resulting certainty-vs.-time profiles for each of the eight direction hypotheses. As the hypothesis number increases, the direction it represents rotates 45° clockwise, with the directions for hypotheses 1 and 2 shown. For example, hypothesis 5 represents the exact opposite direction to hypothesis 1. The temporal precedence relations among the grid stimuli are shown. The IS-A relationship is also present. Only the expected first stimulus of a hypothesized sequence is permitted to activate a hypothesis.

generated for the false hypothesis. The figures from Tsotsos 1981b that summarize the experimental findings are reproduced here as figure 19 and 20. The main results can be summarized as follows:

• When the number of competitors increases, the time to reach a decision also increases, roughly linearly.

• When varying amounts of noise are added, the slope of the curve increases in a smooth manner. The more noise, the longer it takes to reach a decision.

• When there is 50 percent noise (no information), no decisions can be reached.

These results are all very intuitive, yet it is satisfying to know that the temporal cooperative process possesses these characteristics.

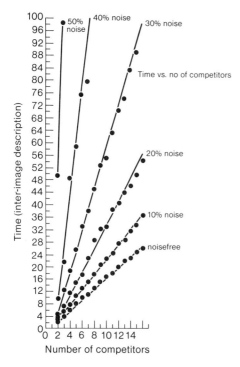

Figure 19
The results of experiments on time to decision with respect to size of discriminatory set for a particular setting of parameter values. In addition, varying amounts of random noise were included and the experiments repeated. The plots show a roughly linear relationship between time and number of competitors (as would be expected). Also, the addition of noise causes a graceful degradation of performance.

The effect on the exact same set of experiments of an added IS-A constraint are also described in Tsotsos 1981b. The slope of each curve, except the 50 percent noise curve, drops significantly. The added constraint can actually compensate for noise, to some degree, through feedback.

Temporal Sampling

Temporal sampling is an important issue. The guidelines presented earlier for the setting of compatibility values have presented some interesting possibilities for the determination of sampling rate. Intuitively, one might believe that the following play a role in the calculation of the sampling rate: the size of the discriminatory set, the expected noise level of the data, the

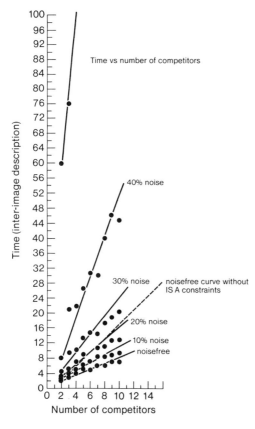

Figure 20

The same experimental setup as for figure 19 was used, with the addition of an IS-A constraint on the discriminatory set. It is clear that the time to decision is significantly decreased, even in the presence of moderate amounts of noise.

shortest duration for events in each discriminatory set, and, of course, the system response characteristics. With the size of the discriminatory set known, the time in iterations to make a useful decision was designed into the compatibilities; it is given by k_{self} for discriminatory set N_{SIM}. Proper performance is guaranteed for $k_{self} \geq |N_{SIM}| + 3$, and thus this compatibility can be set independently. Since k_{self} has units of "temporal measurements" where measurements are made "between" time samples, $k_{self} + 1$ gives the number of time samples required for k_{self} temporal measurements. The minimum event duration in seconds for a given discriminatory set is dur_{min}. If we assume the possibility of individualized compatibility values, where the subscript j ranges over all the individual groups, the minimum sampling rate can be given by

$$SR_{min} = \max_{j} \frac{(|N_{SIM}| + 4)_j}{(dur_{min})_j}.$$

Appropriate settings of k_{SIM} and $k_{IS\text{-}A}$ (that is, increasingly larger values) will compensate for reasonable amounts of noise. The resulting sampling rate must clearly be within the physical capabilities of the sampling system. If this is not true, it may be that changing k_{self} (that is, increasing this parameter) may shift it appropriately. If this is not possible, then the framework presented here is not applicable to the domain under consideration.

Note that $1/dur_{min}$ may be considered as the temporal frequency of the shortest event. If all discriminatory sets are considered, the value used in the sampling-rate determination is the maximum temporal frequency that is represented in the knowledge of the system, and thus the maximum temporal frequency that must be recognized. The standard Nyquist sampling rate for signal reproduction is $2F_{max}$, where F_{max} is the maximum frequency present in the signal. Therefore, we know that sampling at a higher rate will not yield new information. We can conclude that $[(|N_{SIM}| + 4)/2]_t$ must be performed per time sample. This satisfies our original goal, namely, that we are interested in a cooperative process such that the only decisions that are made are those that can be made within a small fixed number of iterations, and that this small number be sufficient for all events of interest. From an efficiency point of view, the smaller $|N_{SIM}|$ is, the fewer the iterations. This value can be kept small by appropriate use of concept organization along the IS-A dimension.

Finally, the PART-OF hierarchy of temporal concepts implicitly represents increasingly coarser levels of temporal as well as spatial resolution for concepts such as sequences. Using the relationship for sampling rate presented earlier, it is clear that, as temporal resolution becomes coarser, the sampling rate and thus the number of applications of the cooperative process iterations becomes smaller. This poses interesting possibilities for increasing the efficiency of the scheme, and it requires further exploration.

Discussion

Representational dimensions such as those described in the third major section of this paper have been prominent for some time in the literature on the representation of knowledge. The arguments for their use have been mostly qualitative, that is, they seem to have nice formal properties and lend themselves naturally to the construction of knowledge bases. In this work, it has been shown not only that these aspects are present but also that each representational dimension has a distinct role to play in an interpretation scheme. In fact, each has two important roles. One role is that of enabling multiple, interacting search mechanisms. This function should not be underestimated. Rule-based recognition paradigms, for example, only offer a single dimension of search. As was pointed out by Aiello (1983), such systems suffer from serious problems due to the one-dimensionality of the inference procedure. The conclusion is that goal-directed, event-directed, and model-directed inference mechanisms can most effectively compensate for one another's deficiencies if used in concert. For example, a data-directed scheme considers all the data and tries to follow through on every event generated. It can be nonconvergent, can produce only conclusions that are derivable directly or indirectly from the input data, and cannot focus or direct the search toward a desired solution. The goal-directed strategy is easy to understand and implement, and at each step of the execution the next step is predetermined. Rules are evaluated in the same order regardless of the input data. Thus, this strategy is inefficient and cannot exhibit a focus with respect to the problem being solved, since there is no mechanism that determines what is important and what is not. Finally, the model-directed approach, although the most efficient and the one that exhibits correct foci of problem-solving activity, has the disadvantage that its conclusions depend heavily on the availability of the correct model and initial focus. An incorrect initial focus will lead it to the examination of useless and incorrect analyses and will cause some perhaps relevant data to be ignored.

In our scheme, each dimension of search compensates for the failings of another, and thus as a whole the scheme offers a rich and robust framework. The several dimensions of search are tied to the knowledge-organization principles. Also, each organization dimension offers distinct and necessary contributions to the updating of hypothesis certainty, to the definition of neighborhoods and compatibilities, and to the maintenance of consistency within an interpretation:

• IS-A, besides offering a definition of global consistency of hypothesis certainty, plays the role of speeding up the convergence of results. This allows smaller temporal sampling rates. Owing to inheritance, the problem posed by the propagation of results disappears. IS-A also has an important part in the graceful recovery from poor predictions. Finally, feedback imposed by the IS-A hierarchy increases the stability of the cooperative process and partially compensates for the effects of noise disturbances.

• SIMILARITY plays the discrimination role, and is the only mechanism that allows for competition between hypotheses, enabling "best choice" selection. In conjunction with the exceptions that drive SIMILARITY activations, this is a strong feedback mechanism, enhancing the stability of the cooperative process. Moreover, it is central to the definition of temporal sampling rate and of compatibility values.

• PART-OF is the mechanism that permits the selection of the stronger of two equally consistent hypotheses on the basis of the strength of their components.

• Temporal Precedence assists in the discrimination of proper temporal order, which is important for temporal grouping and for temporal "gluing" of events into higher-order ones.

Moreover, each of these representational dimensions is integrated into the certainty updating scheme in an intuitive manner through the use of separate compatibility values and the use of neighborhoods or "conceptual receptive fields" for hypotheses.

It should be clear from the discussions in this section that there is no optimal setting of compatibility values for an entire knowledge base. Setting the values to accommodate the worst case may cause too quick a decision for other cases. Thus, it is natural to consider individualized settings of compatibilities, with a particular set of values holding over each hypothesis in a discriminatory set. This would allow for the best performance characteristics. Each conceptual receptive field thus has an individualized compatibility profile that is computed automatically and dynamically depending on the hypothesis structure that it is involved with and on the only three domain-specific constants required for each hypothesis (namely, minimum duration, number of active competitors, and—if it is a sequence—maximum temporal separation of its parts).

We have achieved one of our original goals: that of discovering the conditions under which this cooperative process can reach decisions about time-varying events within a small, fixed number of iterations. This result has led to the first stages of a sampling theory. Sampling considerations, woefully missing from much of computer-vision research, are clearly necessary within the spatio-temporal context that is required for visual perception.

Conclusion

A framework for the integration of time into high level or attentive vision was described. The key elements are an organization of knowledge along several axes, including time; several search modes facilitated by the knowledge organization; a hypothesize-and-test reasoning framework; and a temporal cooperative process driven by the knowledge organization. The goal of the research was to tie together work in knowledge-representation theory with cooperative processes, which are important for vision. Knowledge or concept organization is seen as the key and not the internal form of knowledge packages. The analysis and the examples presented demonstrate that each of the common representational axes—IS-A, PART-OF, SIMILARITY, and Temporal Precedence—has a natural place within the temporal cooperative process, and, moreover, make important contributions to it. Temporal considerations have played a key role, and have led to a useful version of a relaxation rule for time-varying interpretation under the severe constraints that a changing environment places on the number of iterations that can be performed. Although this scheme has been successfully implemented within the ALVEN expert system, much work remains, particularly with its mathematical foundations.

Acknowledgments

I am indebted to Allan Jepson for his useful suggestions. David Fleet and Niels da Vitoria Lobo read drafts and provided many useful comments. Niels also assisted with the implementation and experimentation. This paper also benefited from discussions with Allen Hanson, Ed Riseman, and Roger Browse. Financial support was received from the Canadian Heart Foundation and from the Natural Sciences and Engineering Research Council of Canada. The author is a Fellow of the Canadian Institute for Advanced Research.

References

Aiello, N. 1983. A comparative study of control strategies for expert systems: AGE implementation of three variations of PUFF. In Proceedings of AAAI, Washington.

Allen, J. 1981. Maintaining Knowledge about Temporal Intervals. Report TR-86, Department of Computer Science, University of Rochester.

Anstis, S. 1978. Apparent motion. In *Handbook of Sensory Physiology*, ed. Held, Leibowitz, and Teuber (Springer).

Ballard, D., C. Brown, and J. Feldman. 1978. An approach to knowledge-directed image analysis. In *Computer Vision Systems*, ed. Hanson and Riseman (Academic).

Brachman, R. 1979. On the epistemological status of semantic networks. In *Associative Networks*, ed. Findler (Academic).

Brachman, R. 1982. What IS-A and isn't. In Proceedings of CSCSI-82, Saskatoon.

Braddick, O. 1974. A short range process in apparent motion. *Vision Research* 14: 519–528.

Brooks, R. 1981. Symbolic reasoning among 3D models and 2D images. *Artificial Intelligence* 17: 285–348.

Bugelski, B., and D. Alampay. 1962. The role of frequency in developing perceptual sets. *Canadian Journal of Psychology* 15: 205–211.

Cooper, L., and R. Shepard. 1973. Chronometric studies of the rotation of mental images. In *Visual Information Processing*, ed. Chase (Academic).

Down, B. 1983. Using Feedback in Understanding Motion. M. Sc. thesis, University of Toronto.

Dretske, F. 1981. *Knowledge and the Flow of Information.* MIT Press.

Gibson, J. J. 1957. Optical motions and transformations as stimuli for visual perception. *Psychological Review* 64, no. 5: 288–295.

Glazer, F. 1982. Multilevel Relaxation in Low Level Computer Vision. Report TR 82-30, Department of Computer and Information Science, University of Massachusetts, Amherst.

Hanson, A., and E. Riseman. 1978. VISIONS: A computer system for interpreting scenes. In *Computer Vision Systems*, ed. Hanson and Riseman (Academic).

Hartley, D. 1749. Observations on man, his frame, his duty, and his expectations. Reprinted in *A Source Book in the History of Psychology*, ed. Herrnstein and Boring (Harvard University Press, 1968).

Hay, J. 1966. Optical motions and space perception: An extension of Gibson's analysis. *Psychological Review* 73, no. 6: 550–565.

Hinton, G., and T. Sejnowski. 1983. Optimal perceptual inference. In Proceedings of the IEEE Conference on Computer Vision and Pattern Recognition, Washington, D.C.

Hummel, R., and S. Zucker. 1980. On the Foundations of Relaxation Labelling Processes. Report TR-80-7, Department of Electrical Engineering, McGill University.

Julesz, B. 1980. Spatial nonlinearities in the instantaneous perception of textures with identical power spectra. *Philosophical Transactions of the Royal Society of London* 290: 83−94.

Julesz, B., and R. Schumer. 1981. Early visual perception. *Annual Review of Psychology* 32: 575−627.

Kanade, T. 1980. Survey: Region segmentation: Signal vs. semantics. *Computer Graphics and Image Processing* 13: 279−297.

Kandel, E., and J. Schwartz, eds. 1981. *Principles of Neural Science.* Elsevier/North-Holland.

Levesque, H., and J. Mylopoulos. 1979. A procedural semantics for semantic networks. In *Associative Networks*, ed. N. Findler (Academic).

Levine, M. 1978. A knowledge-based computer vision system. In *Computer Vision Systems*, ed. Hanson and Riseman (Academic).

Mackworth, A. K. 1978. Vision research strategy: Black magic, metaphors, mechanisms, miniworlds, and maps. In *Computer Vision Systems*, ed. Hanson and Riseman (Academic).

Mackworth, A., and W. Havens. 1982. Representing visual knowledge. *IEEE Computer* 16, no. 10: 90−98.

Marr, D. 1982. *Vision.* Freeman.

Mill, J. 1829. Analysis of the phenomena of the human mind. Reprinted in *A Source Book in the History of Psychology,* ed. Herrnstein and Boring (Harvard University Press, 1968).

Minsky, M. 1975. A framework for representing knowledge. In *Phychology of Computer Vision,* ed. Winston (McGraw-Hill).

O'Rourke, J., and N. Badler. 1980. Model-based image analysis of human motion using constraint propagation. *IEEE Transactions on Pattern Analysis and Machine Intelligence* 522−536.

Palmer, S. 1975. The effects of contextual scenes on the identification of objects. *Memory and Cognition* 3: 519−526.

Sabbah, D. 1981. Design of a highly parallel visual recognition system. In Proceedings of the International Joint Conference on Artificial Intelligence, Vancouver.

Tenenbaum, J., and H. Barrow. 1977. Experiments in interpretation guided segmentation. *Artificial Intelligence* 8: 241–274.

Terzopoulos, D. 1982. Multi-Level Reconstruction of Visual Surfaces. AI Lab Memo 671, Massachusetts Institute of Technology.

Treisman, A. 1982. Perceptual grouping and attention in visual search for features and for objects. *Journal of Experimental Psychology* 8, no. 2: 194–214.

Treisman, A., and G. Gelade. 1980. A feature-integration theory of attention. *Cognitive Psychology* 12: 97–136.

Treisman, A., and H. Schmidt. 1982. Illusory conjunctions in the perception of objects. *Cognitive Psychology* 14: 107–141.

Tsotsos, J. 1981a. Temporal event recognition: An application to left ventricular performance assessment. In Proceedings of the International Joint Conference on Artificial Intelligence, Vancouver.

Tsotsos, J. 1981b. On classifying time-varying events. In Proceedings of the Conference on Pattern Recognition and Image Processing, Dallas.

Tsotsos, J. 1983. Medical knowledge and its representation: Problems and perspectives. In Proceedings of IEEE MEDCOMP' 83.

Tsotsos, J. K., J. Mylopoulos, H. D. Covvey, and S. W. Zucker. 1980. A framework for visual motion understanding. *IEEE Transactions on Pattern Analysis and Machine Intelligence* 563–573.

Tsotsos, J. K., D. Covvey, J. Mylopoulos, and P. McLaughlin. 1984. The role of symbolic reasoning in left ventricular performance assessment: The ALVEN system. In *Ventricular Wall Motion*, ed. Sigwart and Heintzen (Georg Thieme Verlag).

Wertheimer, M. 1923. Untersuchung zur Lehre von der Gestalt. II. *Psychologische Forschung* 4: 301–350.

Zucker, S. W. 1978a. Vertical and horizontal processes in low level vision. In *Computer Vision Systems*, ed. Hanson and Riseman (Academic).

Zucker, S. W. 1978b. Production systems with feedback. In *Pattern-Directed Inference Systems*, ed. Waterman and Hayes-Roth (Academic).

Zucker, S. W., R. A. Hummel, and A. Rosenfeld. 1977. An application of relaxation labelling to line and curve enhancement. *IEEE Transactions on Computers* 26: 394–403.

12

Computational Techniques in Motion Processing

Daryl T. Lawton,
Joachim Rieger, and
Martha Steenstrup

Introduction

A general outline of motion processing is shown in figure 1. This figure indicates a basic loop in which the changes in a sequence of images are determined and represented, a model is inferred from these transformations, and the model is used to predict and constrain the processing of ongoing image transformations.

Each of these elements—the image transformations, the inference of the model, the model itself, and the predictions—typically corresponds to several different processes and representations, which can vary significantly with application. There is almost always some type of initial model incorporating domain-specific information about expected image transformations. In many applications, these assumptions are very specific and task dependent, as in target tracking. In others, the assumptions are more abstract, involving general environmental properties such as continuity of motion and environmental surfaces. One aspect of this is the *start-up* problem, which is concerned with how to determine image transformations without any initial description of the environment. Most research in motion processing has been concerned with the analysis of image sequences produced by rigid body motions. This problem lends itself to a theoretical development that does not become overly complex yet reflects a common situation in the world. The particular image transformation associated with this analysis is *optic flow*. This may be thought of as a classical problem in image processing: the inference of environmental information from the optic flow field generated by rigid body motions.

Optic Flow

Optic flow was introduced by the psychologist J. J. Gibson (1950, 1966, 1979), who was struck with how different patterns and extents of image

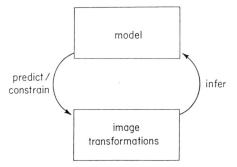

Figure 1
The general structure of motion processing.

displacements could specify critical environmental information for the control of behavior, such as heading, immediacy of collisions, and environmental layout. Gibson's analysis was extremely suggestive and stimulating, but it was incomplete because he did not analyze computationally how environmental information was extracted from flow fields or how flow fields were determined. Recently, a variety of techniques have been developed for computing flow fields and inferring motion parameters and environmental layout. For instance, it has been shown that the three-dimensional motion and the relative depth of an arbitrarily moving rigid object can be computed from transformations acting on an infinitesimally small image patch or from image displacements of a small number of points. However, none of these schemes has proven sufficiently robust to be applied to the typically noisy and sparse displacement fields obtained from successive images in the case of unrestricted motion between camera and scene.

Computing Optic Flow

Optic-flow computation involves the determination of the displacements of image points over a sequence of images. There are several problems in this, involving the effects of image resolution, the dramatic changes in image structure that can occur during motion (such as occlusion), and the well-known *stimulus matching* or *correspondence* problem. To begin with, the notion of an environmental point corresponding to a distinguishable image point is an abstraction that is difficult to realize computationally. An image point is actually a small image area that can correspond to an appreciable area in the environment. One aspect of this is that actual flow

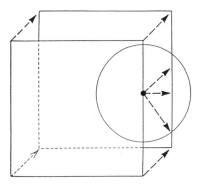

Figure 2
The stimulus-matching problem.

fields do not have an arbitrarily high level of precision. The flow vector at a point summarizes a composite area in the environment. Another implication is the emergence or disappearance of detail as environmental surfaces are approached or receded from. In such situations, features that are meaningful and trackable at one environmental distance may no longer be meaningful at another distance. This partially motivates hierarchical procedures for flow-field computation. It also reflects an important assumption applied throughout motion processing: During motion, image structures will change sufficiently slowly to allow changes to be determined, but not so dramatically that correspondence becomes unrecognizable at successive instants. Often this is not a valid assumption. In fact, significant information can be obtained from particular situations at which the optic-flow field becomes nonexistent or singular and thus difficult to compute because of such things as occlusion, the motion of specularities, and the changing projections of smooth extremal boundaries.

The stimulus matching or correspondence problem (Burt 1976; Huang 1981; Thompson and Barnard 1981) refers to the ambiguity in determining image displacements, and is particularly problematic with nondistinctive portions of image structures or homogeneous image areas. The difficulties are exemplified by the situation illustrated in figure 2, which shows a square undergoing a diagonal displacement. The information obtainable locally along an edge only constrains the potential edge motion to a wide range of displacements. The general solution to the stimulus-matching problem involves the manner in which local determination of displacements can result in a globally coherent interpretation of the changes in an image sequence.

The techniques developed to date for computing optic flow can be grouped into matching techniques and differential techniques. Both of these have to deal with the problems just described and are distinguished by the different assumptions under which they operate.

Matching Techniques
Matching techniques are roughly categorized by the types of image structures they use and the criteria by which matches of image structures in successive images are determined. Image structures can be ordered by the extent and the locality of processing required in their extraction and the complexity of the structural relations in their description. In general, the more abstract the image structure, the more stable it becomes over a sequence of images because the ambiguity in determining matches is reduced. For example, if a complete semantic analysis of each image has been performed in a sequence taken from a sensor moving relative to a house, it is easier to match at the level of extracted houses in the successive images than at a less abstract and more local feature level, such as a vertical edge. There are fewer things to match and they cover an area of the image significantly larger than their potential displacements.

Examples of image structures that have been used in motion analysis, organized in terms of increasing abstraction, are distinctive raw image subareas (Aggarwal et al. 1981; Barnard and Thompson 1980; Dreschler and Nagel 1981; Hannah 1974; Quam 1971), parametrized tokens describing local image subareas (Haralick 1982, 1983), edges (Aggarwal and Martin 1981; Burr 1977), regions (Radig 1981; Roach and Aggarwal 1979), structural descriptions of edges and regions (Brady 1983; Jacobus et al. 1980), instantiated environmental surfaces (Williams 1980), and various high-level semantic interpretations (Badler 1975; Tsotsos et al. 1980).

Procedures for determining optic flow have generally been restricted to matching features whose extraction involves very little processing. This is a consequence of the view of optic flow as a primitive description of image motion from which much information will be derived that is useful for higher-level processes. From this perspective, flow processing should not depend on the processes to which its results will contribute. Also, when more abstract descriptions are used, although the determinations of matches become more viable, the determination of specific image displacement becomes less exact. This reflects a general problem that has been largely ignored by researchers in motion, with some important exceptions, notably Tsotos et al. (1980): The mechanisms by which matches at different semantic levels of image descriptors can be combined so that the matches between lower-level image structures are constrained by the matches at higher-level surface or semantic descriptions.

In general, most matching procedures do not deal explicitly with the dramatic-change and resolution problem. Because of the assumption that most image structures will change slowly over time, if dramatic changes do occur they are reflected by a breakdown in the matching processes. The basic approach to the stimulus-matching problem has been to characterize global properties of the displacement field in a manner that directs the evaluation of image displacements. This is done in different ways. Matching structures at a more abstract or symbolic level typically involves matching strings or graphlike structures. Solutions to this type of problem use dynamic programming or heuristic search techniques to minimize some global distortion measure reflecting the extent of graph similarity (Barrow et al. 1972; Cheng and Huang 1982; Haralick 1978; Shapiro and Haralick 1982). In another form of match processing applied to less abstract features, a global property such as smoothness or continuity of the displacement field is used to form a local constraint on the flow-field computation. This constraint leads to a local, iterative, relaxation-type procedure in which a given feature displacement must be consistent, under the criteria of smoothness, with the displacements of its spatially neighboring features (Barnard and Thompson 1980). Updating rules take the form of setting a feature's estimate of its correct displacement to the average of its neighbors.

Generalized Hough transform approaches to matching (Aggarwal et al. 1981; Ballard 1981; Davis et al. 1983) somewhat reverse the relation between local computations and global field properties when compared with such relaxation-based matching approaches. In the generalized Hough approaches, the properties of a displacement field are parametrized and represented in an N-dimensional histogram to which the local image measurements contribute. For example, the global structure of the flow field can be restricted to being a particular type of transformation, such as an affine transformation in the plane (Adiv 1983). Each local process for determining an image displacement evaluates the consistency of its potential displacements with the values of the parameters describing each affine transformation (up to some level of parametric resolution). Globally, the parameter value most consistent with all the potential image displacements will have the most favorable evaluation (or response in the histogram). Once a global interpretation has been determined, it can then be refined with increased resolution in the parameter space about the coarse solution.

Differential Techniques

Differential techniques are based on direct measurements of intensity changes perpendicular to an image gradient in order to determine one component of the optic flow at a point. These measurements are expressed as a function of the temporal changes in image intensity and the image gradient at a point. The other component is then determined by using an additional constraint derived from assumptions concerning the global structure of the flow field. These generally involve the smoothness of the flow field or the type of transformations that can describe the displacement field. In a manner similar to the matching techniques, these constraints are developed computationally as local, iterative processes in which global consistency is achieved via propagation similar to solutions of diffusion equations (Horn and Schunck 1980; Glazer 1981, 1983; Terzopoulos 1983). In a few applications (Fennema and Thompson 1979; Thompson and Barnard 1981), the local measurements can also be integrated by their independent contributions to a global histogram which expresses the parameter values of particular types of image transformations. Differential techniques can also be used to roughly constrain the motion of boundaries without trying to derive the optic flow. These constraints can be used to get rough qualitative motion information along closed contours, such as expansion, image motion in a rough direction, or the occurrence of rotation.

The key attribute of differential techniques is that they are based on very local, simple computations at a low level of processing. They are also based on some unrealistic assumptions that affect computations when these techniques are uniformly applied to actual image sequences. These assumptions concern smoothness and often linearity in the image intensity gradients, limited extents of motion, and the constancy of image brightness over time. The smoothness assumption breaks down at surface occlusion boundaries, or wherever dramatic image changes occur, such as at reflectance boundaries. Differential techniques also tend to produce dense fields, whose value is not clear, especially since the interpolation is performed in a manner that may adversely affect the inference of motion parameters. Researchers have focused on some of these problems. Schunk (1983) has tried to characterize the effects of occlusion so that the computation of image displacements is selectively shut off in such areas. Hildreth (1982) and Kearney et al. (1982) are working with more complex image gradients and integrating the components of information to the degree that they provide unambiguous displacement information at boundaries.

Hierarchical Processing

A fundamental paradigm in computer vision is the use of hierarchical representations and processes (Burt 1982; Hanson and Riseman 1980; Rosenfeld 1983; Tanimoto and Klinger 1980; Uhr 1978)). This allows different resolutions and scales of image events to be handled uniformly. Additionally, the consistent agreement among hierarchically organized processes is a basic control strategy for a wide range of high-level and low-level interpretation tasks. Hierarchical processing can produce significant computational reductions, wherein results from processing performed rapidly at lower resolutions of image information are used to direct and constrain more detailed and extensive processing of higher-resolution image information. Given the increase in computational requirements over static image processing, hierarchical mechanisms are extremely important in motion processing.

The use of hierarchical processing in motion typically involves representing an image at different filtered spatial frequencies and using the processing at lower spatial frequencies to constrain the processing at higher spatial frequencies (Burt 1982; Glazer et al. 1983; Grimson 1981; Wong and Hall 1978). The matches determined for the larger spatial structures in an image are used to initialize the computation for the displacements of the smaller structures. In hierarchically organized processing, the resolution problem is handled implicitly by representing an image sequence at multiple resolutions simultaneously. The stimulus-matching problem is dealt with by taking advantage of the fact that matches have a tendency to be less ambiguous at lower spatial frequencies because there are fewer gross image structures and they are large relative to their potential displacements. However, the problem of dramatic change associated with flow-field computation affects hierarchical processing because image structures may appear and disappear at different levels of resolution and errors produced at a lower image resolutions can propagate to the higher-resolution images. Some filtering schemes (Burt et al. 1983; Glazer et al. 1983) have been proposed to deal with this inherent problem by detecting the occurrence of a failure in the matching procedure and shutting off the initialization of image displacements in the higher-resolution images. Others have developed error measures that direct the propagation of displacement estimates from lower to higher spatial frequencies (Anandan 1984).

Inference from Optic Flow

Work in the inference of environmental information from flow fields has generally been restricted to the case of rigid body motion or linked systems of rigid bodies (Webb and Aggarwal 1981). There is very little general understanding in the interpretation of nonrigid environmental motions. Often such work is task dependent, as in the interpretation of image sequences of moving cloud formations and beating hearts (Tsotsos et al. 1980).

The problem of inferring environmental information from a flow field produced by rigid body motion is often termed the shape-from-motion problem (i.e., how to determine the shape of objects or environmental depth from a flow field or a sequence of flow fields) or, somewhat confusingly, the motion-from-motion problem (i.e., how to determine the parameters of object or sensor motion from a flow field or a sequence of flow fields). Theoretically, these problems are equivalent, though there are some practical difficulties in inferring one from the other.

There have been significant milestones in formulating solutions to these problems. One set of results has dealt with the minimal conditions that are necessary for determining object shape and sensor motion in terms of the number of flow vectors across an image sequence (Fang and Huang 1983; Lawton 1980; Roach and Aggarwal 1980; Ullman 1979b; Webb and Aggarwal 1981; Yen and Huang 1983). In this work, researchers derive various sets of simultaneous nonlinear equations whose solution would constitute the appropriate inference. Since these equations cannot be solved directly, various optimization procedures are required. In another set of formulations, developed primarily by Nagel and by Prazdny (1981), the inference of sensor motion parameters is expressed as a search through the rotational subspace of the total set of rigid-body motion parameters. Prazdny's development is rather geometrical and Nagel's is more algebraic, but they are basically similar. In 1981, Tsai and Huang (1982) and Longuet-Higgins (1981) simultaneously developed closed-form solutions that could be solved by direct means.

In view of these developments it is somewhat alarming that none of these techniques have been successfully applied to flow fields computed from anything like realistic image sequences. In fact, only in the recent work of Fang and Huang (1983a, b) and Jerian and Jain (1983) has there even been an explicit evaluation of a procedure on such images. This work has shown the particular difficulties familiar to motion researchers: extreme sensitivity to noise and resolution, dependence on the type and extent of motion, and general instability.

There are many reasons, not all of which are fully understood, why the inference of motion parameters and environmental depth has been difficult. Some of the formulations involve image measurements, such as higher-order derivatives of an instantaneous vector velocity field, which are difficult to obtain and are also quite noise sensitive when applied to discrete image sequences (Prazdney 1980; Longuet-Higgins and Prazdny 1980). There are also many inherently ambiguous cases of motion where the structures of the translational and rotational fields are indistinguishable. In recent work concerning the interpretation of images containing multiple independently moving objects, Adiv (1984) has found cases in which independently moving objects with different parameters of motion can, when considered together, result in a globally consistent but incorrect interpretation. Another problem affecting shape-from-motion formulations is the baseline effect common to stereo, which expresses the resolution and accuracy of depth inferences as a decreasing function of the distance between the sensor locations at which images are formed. For motion, where the sensor displacements are generally small between successive instants, the environmental inference would tend to be poor, but could be compensated by the availability of more and more images over time. Finally, there has been almost no stability analysis of the systems of equations for inference from optic flow.

There have been several responses to these difficulties. One approach has been to utilize optimization procedures based on global evaluation of the expressions for the inference of motion parameters from flow fields instead of local iterative optimization procedures. Examples of these approaches are the work with generalized Hough transforms (Adiv 1984; Ballard 1981) and the procedure involving highly parallel architectures (Steenstrup et al. 1983). Some researchers are beginning to perform explicit analyses of the stability of the different solutions (Shaw 1983), others are trying to develop more robust qualitative inference techniques (Thompson et al. 1983), and still others are beginning to investigate the inference of motion and shape from image transformations other than optic flow, such as the analysis of contour shape changes (Davis et al. 1982).

Another response to these inadequacies has been to deal with restricted cases of motion. Here too, the work has been limited in application to realistic image sequences; the principle results have been those achieved by Williams (1980) and Dreschler and Nagel (1981) and those described below. These restricted cases of motion can be of significant practical use, since in many cases some of the parameters of motion can be determined by other sensing devices. In some cases, general motion can be locally interpreted, temporally and spatially, as consisting of certain restricted types of motion.

Coordinate Systems

To describe environmental inferences, we need to review some of the basic structural properties of flow fields. We describe both continuous and discrete optic flow fields in terms of inferences based on flow-field decomposition and environmental rigidity.

It is useful to have terms for describing the motion of features in an image sequence and the corresponding motion of environmental points. An *image-displacement vector* is the two-dimensional vector describing the displacement of an image feature from one image to the next. An *image-displacement field* is the set of image-feature-displacement vectors for successive images. An *image-displacement sequence* indicates the positions of an image feature over several successive images. Though we often deal with discrete image sequences, it is possible to describe the continuous curve along which an image feature point is moving. This is called the *image-displacement path*. Corresponding to image motions, we use a set of terms for describing environmental motions. An *environmental displacement field* is the set of three-dimensional vectors indicating the positions of environmental points at successive instants. An *environmental displacement sequence* indicates the position of an environmental point over several successive instants. An *environmental displacement path* describes the three-dimensional curve that an environmental point is moving along for a particular motion.

The coordinate system we use is shown in figure 3. It corresponds to a camera O moving relative to a static scene. Let $\tilde{P}$ at the image position $\tilde{\mathbf{r}} = (\tilde{x}, \tilde{y}) = (x, y)/z$ be the projection of the visible point P at the location $\mathbf{r} = (x, y, z)$. We obtain the image velocity $\mathbf{u}$ of $\tilde{P}$ by differentiating $\tilde{\mathbf{r}}$ with respect to time:

$$\mathbf{u} = (\dot{x} - \tilde{x}\dot{z}, \dot{y} - \tilde{y}\dot{z})/z. \tag{1}$$

If we let $\mathbf{v} = (v_x, v_y, v_z)$ and $\mathbf{w} = (w_x, w_y, w_z)$ denote the translational and rotational velocities of O, the relative motion $\dot{\mathbf{r}} = (\dot{x}, \dot{y}, \dot{z})$ of P becomes

$$\dot{\mathbf{r}} = -\mathbf{v} - \mathbf{w} \times \mathbf{r}. \tag{2}$$

Eliminating $\dot{x}$, $\dot{y}$, and $\dot{z}$ between the above equations, the translational and rotational components of image velocity $\mathbf{u}$ may be written as

$$\mathbf{u}_T = (\tilde{x}v_z - v_x, \tilde{y}v_z - v_y)/z \tag{3}$$

and

$$\mathbf{u}_R = [\tilde{x}\tilde{y}w_x - (\tilde{x}^2 + 1)w_y + \tilde{y}w_z, (\tilde{y}^2 + 1)w_x - \tilde{x}\tilde{y}w_y - \tilde{x}w_z]. \tag{4}$$

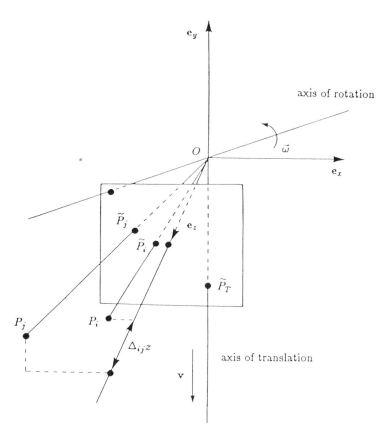

Figure 3
Camera model employed. The image plane is at a unit distance along the z axis, which sets
the focal length to unity. O is the nodal point of the camera's lens. P_i and P_j are visible
details in the scene.

The reason for this decomposition into rotational and translational components will become clear shortly.

For image sequences indexed by discrete times, we add a time index to the environmental points and image locations. Thus, the vector P_{mi} refers to the ith point at time m and $\tilde{r}_{mi}$ is the image of this point. We refer interchangeably to an image point as $\tilde{r}_{mi}$ or I_{mi} or $\tilde{P}_{mi}$. With the focal length set to unity, the relations between P_{mi}, z_{mi}, and positions in the image plane determined by perspective projection are

$$P_{mi} = (x_{mi}, y_{mi}, z_{mi}),$$

$$I_{mi} = \left(\frac{x_{mi}}{z_{mi}}, \frac{y_{mi}}{z_{mi}}, 1 \right),$$

$$I_{mi} = (\tilde{x}_{mi}, \tilde{y}_{mi}, 1),$$

$$P_{mi} = z_{mi} I_{mi}.$$

(5)

Flow-Field Decomposition

Basic results from kinematics allow rigid body motions to be expressed as a rotation about an axis positioned at an arbitrary point followed by a translation (Whittaker 1944). This implies that the axis of rotation can be positioned anywhere so long as it is followed by the appropriate translation. Thus, it is typical to canonically describe sensor motion as an initial rotation about an axis positioned at the origin of the sensor coordinate system (bringing the sensor into the same orientation at successive instants when considered discretely) followed by a translation (bringing the sensor in coincidence at successive instants). This decomposes an image-displacement field into a field produced solely by the rotation of the sensor and a field produced solely by the translation of the sensor. Each of these fields contains different information.

For pure rotational fields, image displacements are totally a function of image position and yield no information concerning environmental depth. That is, given the position of an image point at time t and the sensor rotation R, its position at time $t + 1$ is completely determined. To describe the general structure of rotational flow fields, consider the image-displacement path generated by a particular image point under sensor rotation. In figure 4, we see an axis of rotation positioned at the origin of the coordinate system and a ray of projection determined by some image point I_{mi}. The effect of the rotation will be that the ray of projection will generate the surface of a cone. The image-displacement path for the rotation of this image point will then be determined by the intersection of this cone with

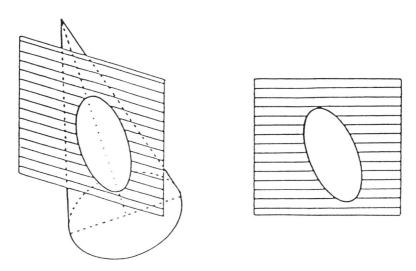

Figure 4

Rotational-displacement paths. Left: The intersection of an image plane with the cone determined by the axis of rotation positioned at the focal point and a given image-position vector. Right: The resulting conic image-displacement path.

the image surface, i.e., a conic section. For points along the same ray of projection, the image displacements under a given rotation will all be the same. Thus, there is no basis upon which to infer environmental depth under rotational motion, because the angles between rays of projection remain fixed.

For pure translational motion, image-displacement paths are determined by the intersection of the translational axis with the image plane. If the translational axis intersects the image plane on the positive half of the axis, the point of intersection is called a *focus of expansion* (FOE) and the image motion is along straight lines radiating from it. This corresponds to sensor motion toward visible environmental points. If the translational axis intersects the image plane on the negative half of the axis, the point is called a *focus of contraction* (FOC) and the image-displacement paths are along straight lines converging toward the FOC. This corresponds to camera motion away from visible environmental points. The intersections of axes parallel to the image plane are points at infinity and thus may be considered to be either an FOE or an FOC in opposite directions. This ambiguity is one reason we refer to the directions of motion determined by the translational axes themselves instead of the intersections with the image plane.

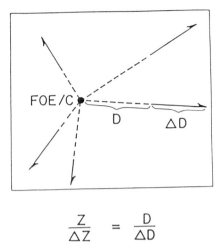

$$\frac{Z}{\Delta Z} = \frac{D}{\Delta D}$$

Figure 5
Relation between relative environmental depth and extent of image displacement with respect to FOE/C.

Given the direction of translation and the image displacements of a set of environmental points, the relative depths of these points can be computed by solving the inverse perspective transform (Rogers and Adams 1976). Relative depth can also be simply inferred from the position of a feature and the extent of its displacement relative to an FOE or an FOC. This relation is expressed as

$$\frac{D}{\Delta D} = \frac{Z}{\Delta Z}, \tag{6}$$

where Z is the value of the Z component of an environmental point at time $t + 1$, ΔZ is the extent of environmental displacement along the Z axis from time t to time $t + 1$, D is the distance from the corresponding image point from the FOE or FOC at time t, and ΔD is the displacement of the image point from time t to time $t + 1$. Thus, the Z value of an environmental point can be recovered from image measurements in units of ΔZ, or what has been termed *time-until-contact* by Lee (1980). See figures 5 and 6.

The effects of composite image motions produced by sensor rotation and translation can be analyzed as follows for an image feature I_{mi} that undergoes a displacement D to position I_{ni} at time n (figure 7). The motion can be described as an initial displacement R to a position J_{mi} due solely to the rotation of the sensor, which is followed by a displacement T from J_{mi} to I_{ni} along the translational displacement path determined by the straight

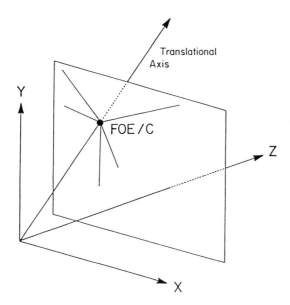

Figure 6
FOE/C is determined by intersection of image plane with translational axis.

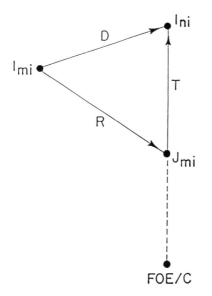

Figure 7
Composite field structure.

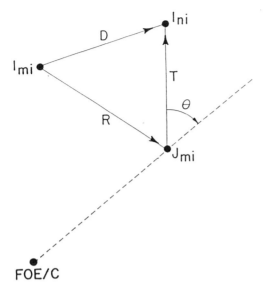

Figure 8
Error measure from composite field structure..

line containing image points J_{mi} and the FOE determined by the translational parameters.

These structural properties provide measures for the consistency of a given image displacement with hypothesized sensor rotation and translation parameters (figure 8). As above, for an image point I_{mi}, the rotational parameters induce an image displacement to some position J_{mi}. This point and the FOE corresponding to a particular translational axis determine an expected translational displacement path. The angle between this displacement path and the vector $I_{ni} - J_{mi}$ corresponds to the discrepancy between the image displacement and the hypothesized values of the sensor motion parameters.

Rigidity Constraints

An alternative development to environmental inference from optic flow is to use the constraints provided by environmental rigidity between points (Lawton 1980). This is a basic paradigm in computer vision: to express an environmental property in terms of the constraints it imposes on image structures and events (Barrow and Tenenbaum 1981). In particular, equation 5 transforms relations between environmental points into equations in terms of image-position vectors and unknown Z values which correspond to environmental depth values. Solutions to the resulting equations yield a set of Z values providing a consistent interpretation over time for the positions of the corresponding set of environmental points.

For two points i and j on a rigid body at times m and n, rigidity is expressed as

$$\|P_{mi} - P_{mj}\| = \|P_{ni} - P_{nj}\|, \tag{7}$$

which can be expanded, by using the substitution specified by equation 5 and squaring both sides, into the image-based equation

$$z_{mi}^2(I_{mi} \cdot I_{mi}) + z_{mj}^2(I_{mj} \cdot I_{mj})$$

$$- 2z_{mi}z_{mj}(I_{mi} \cdot I_{mj}) - z_{ni}^2(I_{ni} \cdot I_{ni})$$

$$- z_{nj}^2(I_{nj} \cdot I_{nj}) + 2z_{ni}z_{nj}(I_{ni} \cdot I_{nj}) = 0, \tag{8}$$

where the inner-product terms in parentheses are constants determined from the positions of image points. To determine a solution, we will find the minimum number of points and frames for which the number of independent constraints (in the form of equation 8) equals or exceeds the number of unknown Z values.

We begin with the number of unknown Z values. For N points in K frames (where $N > 2$ and $K > 1$), there are $(NK - 1)$ unknown Z values. The decrease by 1 in the number of unknowns reflects the loss of absolute scale information. Thus, one of the Z values can be set to an arbitrary value, which can be recovered from the actual sensor displacement if such absolute measurements are available.

The number of rigidity constraints generated by a set of N points in K frames is the product of $3 \times (N - 2)$ and $(K - 1)$. The first term is the minimum number of unique distances that must be specified between pairs of points, in a body of N points with no three points being collinear, to ensure its rigidity. Thus, four points require six pairwise distances (all that are possible). For configurations of more than four points, it is necessary to specify the distance of each additional point to only three other points to ensure rigidity. The second term is the number of interframe intervals, with each interval providing a set of additional constraining points. Each distance specified must be maintained over each interframe interval.

A solution is possible when the number of constraints is greater or equal to the number of unknowns. This occurs when

$$2NK - 6K - 3N + 7 \geq 0. \tag{9}$$

Thus, minimal solutions can be found when $N = 5$ and $K = 2$, producing nine constraint equations, or when $N = 4$ and $K = 3$, producing twelve constraint equations.

Processing Restricted Environmental Motion

Certain cases of restricted motion allow for processing that combines the determination of motion parameters, image displacements, and environmental depth in a single, mutually constraining computation. In this section we consider such processing for image sequences produced by environmental translations (Lawton 1983). This is an especially useful case since it can be used as a basic component for visually guided navigation when other parameters of sensor motion are obtained using associated devices or removed by sensor stabilization.

The procedure consists of a feature-extraction process applied to the initial image of a sequence followed by a search for the translational axis most consistent with the potential displacements of the extracted features. The search process is defined with respect to a unit sphere with each point corresponding to a different direction of sensor translation. We use a simple measurement that associates with a point on the unit sphere, corresponding to a particular translational axis, a number describing the total extent of feature match along the displacement paths corresponding to the translational axis. Experiments in several image sequences have shown this measure to be smooth and to have a distinct maximum in a large neighborhood about the correct translational axis.

Feature Extraction

The feature-extraction process finds small areas (referred to as *image points* or *features*) in an image that are distinct from surrounding portions of the image. This distinctiveness limits the potential matches of features in succeeding images and may also reflect a correspondence to actual and significant features in the environment, such as points of high curvature on object boundaries, texture elements, and surface markings. There are also false features, which result from noise, occlusion, and light-source effects whose dynamic behavior can be difficult to interpret. Features can be represented either as arrays of numbers extracted directly from an image or as parametrized tokens describing local image properties. We refer to features exclusively as small arrays of data values centered at some point in an image at some time t.

The method of feature extraction we have used (following Moravec) is based on the use of correlation measures bounded between 1 (for perfect correlation) and 0. The *distinctiveness* of a feature is 1 minus the best correlation value obtained when the feature is correlated with its immediately neighboring areas (excluding correlation with itself). Good features are selected by finding the local maxima in the values of the distinctiveness measure over an image. There are several metrics available for similarity of two $n \times n$ arrays $A_{i,j}$ and $B_{i,j}$, such as the following.

Normalized correlation:

$$\frac{\sum_i \sum_j A_{i,j} B_{i,j}}{\sqrt{\sum_i \sum_j A_{i,j} A_{i,j}} \times \sqrt{\sum_i \sum_j B_{i,j} B_{i,j}}}.$$

Moravec correlation:

$$\frac{\sum_i \sum_j A_{i,j} B_{i,j}}{(\sum_i \sum_j A_{i,j} A_{i,j} + \sum_i \sum_j B_{i,j} B_{i,j})/2.0}.$$

Normalized absolute value difference:

$$1.0 - \frac{\sum_i \sum_j |A_{i,j} - B_{i,j}|}{\sum_i \sum_j A_{i,j} + \sum_i \sum_j B_{i,j}}.$$

Each of these measures has a value of 1 for a perfect match. Of these, the first choice is the most conventional, the second is a good approximation to the first and more efficient, and the third is the quickest to evaluate.

We further constrain the neighborhoods over which the features are selected to contours determined by other processes, such as zero-crossing extraction, that are sensitive to edges. This yields interesting points that are locally distinctive and exhibit high curvature along extracted contours containing the point. Further filtering is based on local approximations to contour curvature.

The images in figures 9 and 10 were taken from a gyroscopically stabilized movie camera held by a passenger in a car traveling down a country road in Massachusetts (Williams 1980). They are 128×128-pixel images with six bits of resolution in intensity and will be referred to as the *road-sign images*. Figure 11 shows the zero crossings extracted from the initial road-sign image using a $\nabla^2 G$ mask with a positive width of 5 pixels. The distinctiveness values were computed using features that were 5×5-pixel arrays extracted from the convolved image and centered on pixels that were adjacent to the zero-crossing contour and of positive value.

Figure 9
Road-sign image 1.

Figure 10
Road-sign image 2.

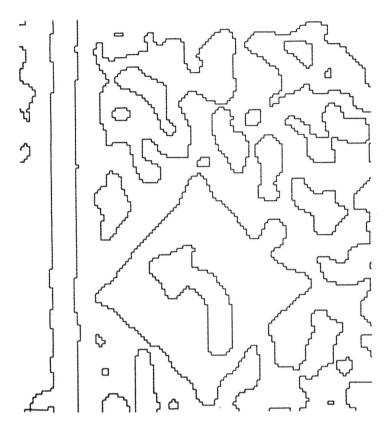

Figure 11
Zero-crossing contours of road-sign image I.

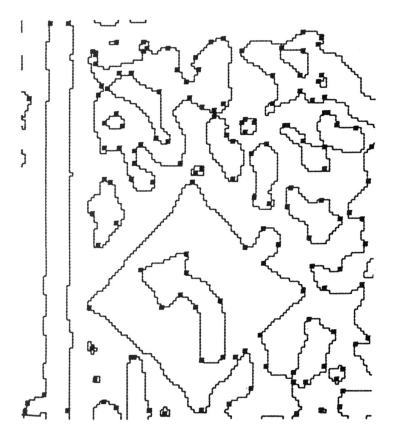

Figure 12
High-curvature points along zero-crossing contour.

These features were correlated, using Moravec's norm, with their eight immediately neighboring features. Figure 12 shows the results of suppressing low-curvature feature points along this contour.

Determining the Axis of Translation

The translational axis is determined by optimizing a measure that describes the extent of feature match along the image-displacement paths determined by a hypothesized translational axis. During this optimization, the image displacements are determined simultaneously with the direction of motion. Figure 13 shows an FOE corresponding to a potential translational axis and the corresponding image-displacement paths for some extracted features.

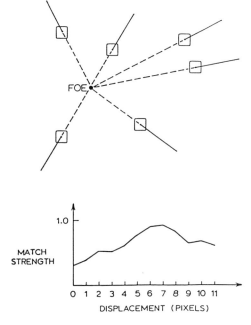

Figure 13
Translational-displacement paths for a hypothesized FOE and a match function on one feature.

Also shown is the match profile of a particular feature along a segment of its displacement path in the succeeding image. The adequacy of a potential translational axis for describing the motion between successive images is measured simply by summing the best matches for each of the features along their respective image-displacement paths.

The set of all possible translational axes describes a unit sphere called the *translational direction sphere*. The search procedure is defined with respect to this sphere instead of the potential positions of FOEs and FOCs in the image plane. The sphere is a bounded surface which makes uniform global sampling of the error measure feasible. When the image plane is used directly, the resolution in the position of the translational axis varies. Special criteria must be used to distinguish between FOEs and FOCs if the error measure is defined relative to the image plane. Roughly parallel image displacements could correspond to an FOE off to one side or an FOC off to the opposite of the image plane. On the translational-direction sphere the corresponding translational axes would be close, whereas on the plane they are widely separated at plus and minus infinity.

The search measure is computed by finding the best matches for all the features along a segment of their image-displacement paths using one of the normalized match metrics above and summing them. Thus, for a set of N features in an initial image, a hypothesized translational axis, and one of the match metrics given above, the measure M is

$$\sum_{i=1}^{N} \text{bestmatch}(i), \tag{10}$$

where bestmatch(i) is the best-match value associated with feature i along the appropriate image-displacement path.

The measure can utilize the different correlation norms described above and different interpolation processes for determining positions along an image-displacement path. The choices among these involve a tradeoff between the speed of evaluating the error measure and the precision with which the translational axis can be determined. Depending on the accuracy required, positions along the image-displacement path can be approximated roughly by setting the coordinates of the feature's position to the nearest integer value or, more accurate, by performing a subpixel interpolation of the feature at each of a set of selected positions along the image-displacement path. The basic tradeoff is between speed and accuracy; subpixel interpolation is more expensive. To reflect this, the measure was computed in two forms in the experiments below: a *fast-evaluation* form and a *precise-evaluation* form. The fast form uses the absolute-value norm and the nearest-integer approximation to determine feature position along the image-displacement paths. The fast form is useful for evaluating image sequences with several extracted features to determine the rough position of the global minimum.

Search Organization

The search process used here consists of two phases: An initial global sampling of the measure to determine its rough shape and then a local search to determine a maximum. The local search begins at the position where the maximum value was determined by the global sampling. The local search begins with an initial fixed step size and determines a local minimum using it. The step size is then reduced and the procedure repeated until the step size is at the desired resolution for the determination of the translational axis. In the experiments below the initial step size was set to 0.1 and then reduced successively to 0.025 and 0.005 radians. In general, the global sampling can be quite sparse or the initial step size of the local search quite large.

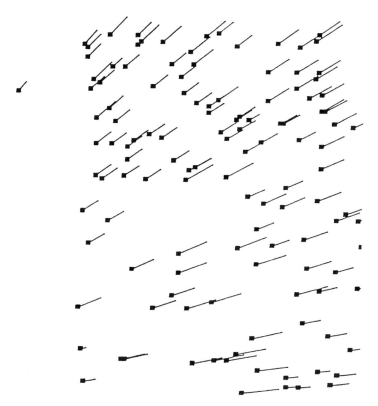

Figure 14
Scaled displacements for road-sign images.

Road-Sign Image Experiments

The procedure was applied to the road-sign image sequence using the features extracted at the positions indicated in figure 13. The translational axis was determined to be $(-0.837, -0.420, 0.349)$. The image displacements for the feature points shown in figure 12 that are associated with this translational axis are shown in figure 14. From the translational axis and image displacements, the relative environmental depths of image points can be recovered by the simple relation in equation 6. When image displacements are small, the inferred depth values can be quite erratic because of the sensitivity to small numbers in the denominator in the left-hand side of equation 6. It is best to use image pairs for which large displacements can be determined. One way to do this for image sequences that are related by successive sensor translations is to track the FOE from a given image

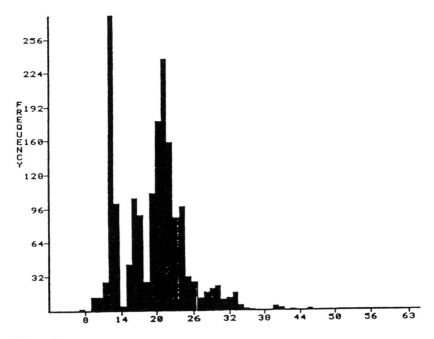

Figure 15
Depth histogram.

with respect to successive later images. This was done with four successive images from the roadsign sequence beginning with road-sign images 1 and 2. The position of the translational axis determined from images $I(t)$ and $I(t + 1)$ is used as the initial value in the local search for determining the translational axis for images $I(t)$ and $I(t + 2)$. The displacements of all features along the contour in figure 11 were determined along the image-displacement paths determined by the FOE found for images $I(1)$ and $I(4)$. To compute depth along the contours, 5×5 windows, centered at each contour point, were matched along the image-displacement paths, and the displacements corresponding to the best match were determined. Alternatively, the entire extracted segment between distinctive points could be matched. The road-sign sequence is particularly nice for presenting depth-processing results, because the three environmental objects in the images are at three distinct depth intervals. This is shown in figure 15 by the three distinct clusters in the histogram of the depth values calculated for the points along the contour. The units in the histogram are cumulative time-until-contact values. That is, the depth is given in units of the displacement

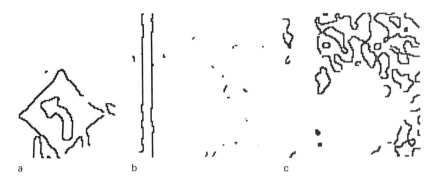

a   b   c

Figure 16
(a) Sign depth cluster. (b) Pole depth cluster. (c) Trees depth cluster.

of the camera from $I(1)$ to $I(4)$ along the Z axis. From left to right, the first peak corresponds to the sign, the second to the pole, and the third to the trees. As can be seen, there is a wide range of depths associated with the trees. Mapping these clusters back onto contour points from figure 11 yields the following distinct objects: the boundary shown in figure 16 (the sign), the boundary shown in figure 16 (the pole), and the boundary segment shown in figure 16 (the trees). Points near the image boundary of $I(1)$ were ignored because the processing did not take into account occlusion effects along the image boundaries.

Further experiments were conducted to test the accuracy of the algorithm when applied to small areas of the visual field. For example, the procedure was applied to the roadsign image sequence with features restricted to the rectangular area shown in figure 17 corresponding to texture in the distant trees. The translational axis was determined to be $(-0.843, -0.429, 0.325)$, within a few degrees of the translational axes determined previously.

The search measure generally has a distinct global minimum at the point on the unit sphere corresponding to the correct translational axis. This is reasonable, since it is unlikely that translational axes that are from the correct position will define image-displacement paths that simultaneously allow good matches for many features. Thus, competing candidates for the global minimum are not expected to be widely separated. This reasoning implies strong unimodality and smoothness of the error measure over a large neighborhood, and this has been confirmed empirically. Therefore, the optimization procedure used here could be replaced by other techniques having faster convergence.

The error measure is affected by both nondistinctive and false features.

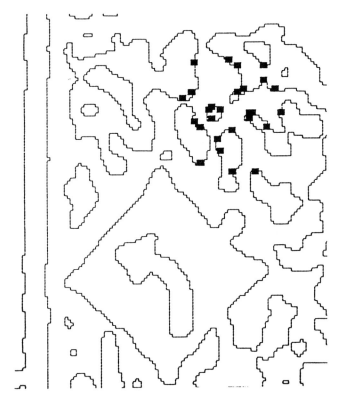

Figure 17
Road-sign subimage features.

Nondistinctive features will match well for many different translational axes. Large numbers of these weak features will flatten the response of the error measure. False features will also distort the error measure, since they will often have their best matches with incorrect translational axes. The effects of these poor features should be compensated by the agreement of good features. Every one of the good features will tend to have a bad match for the incorrect translational axis, and their unanimity is expected to override the lack of discrimination of weak features and the random quality of the matches of false features. However, there is a limit in the percentage of weak and false features before the algorithm will degrade. This limit has not been explored, but our experience suggests that it may be quite high, with perhaps as many as 50 percent of the features ineffective.

Restricted Motion and Rigidity Constraints

As one would expect, the rigidity constraints are also simplified by the addition of restrictions on allowable motions of environmental points. Consider motion constrained to a plane. For simplicity we assume that it is parallel to the XZ plane of the camera coordinate system; however, an appropriate transformation can be applied so that the results are valid for motion constrained to an arbitrarily oriented but known plane. Here, the Y component of an environmental point is assumed to remain constant over time. For a point i at times m and n, this is expressed as

$$y_{mi} = z_{mi}\tilde{y}_{mi} = z_{ni}\tilde{y}_{ni} = y_{ni} \tag{11}$$

and solving for z_{ni} yields

$$z_{ni} = z_{mi}(\tilde{y}_{mi}/\tilde{y}_{ni}). \tag{12}$$

This allows a substitution for points i and j in equation 8, which simplifies (at least in terms of the number of unknowns) the rigidity constraint to

$$z_{mi}{}^2\left[(I_{mi}\cdot I_{mj}) - \left(\frac{\tilde{y}_{mi}}{\tilde{y}_{ni}}\right)^2(I_{ni}\cdot I_{ni})\right] + z_{mj}{}^2\left[(I_{mj}\cdot I_{mj}) - \left(\frac{\tilde{y}_{mj}}{\tilde{y}_{nj}}\right)^2(I_{nj}\cdot I_{nj})\right]$$

$$+ z_{mi}z_{mj}\left\{2\left[\left(\frac{\tilde{y}_{mi}}{\tilde{y}_{ni}}\right)\left(\frac{\tilde{y}_{mj}}{\tilde{y}_{nj}}\right)(I_{ni}\cdot I_{nj}) - (I_{mi}\cdot I_{mj})\right]\right\}$$

$$= 0. \tag{13}$$

The planarity constraint has removed two unknowns. Note that the bracketed expressions are again constants that can be determined from the locations of the image points. This equation can be solved given two points in two frames. Thus, for points i and j at times m and n with the corresponding unknown depth values z_{mi}, z_{mj}, z_{ni}, and z_{nj}, equation 13 reduces these to a system of two unknowns, z_{mi} and z_{mj}. One of these variables, say z_{mi}, can be set to an arbitrary value, reflecting scale independence, allowing z_{mj} to then be determined by solving the quadratic in terms of z_{mi}.

Rigidity Constraints Applied to Translational Motion

The constraint imposed by translational motion of points i and j on a rigid body at times m and n is expressed by

$$P_{mi} - P_{mj} = P_{ni} - P_{nj}, \tag{14}$$

which is similar to equation 7 except that the operation is vector subtraction, reflecting the preservation of length and orientation under translation. Setting z_{mi} to a constant value 1, to reflect scale independence in equation 14, yields three simultaneous linear equations in three unknowns:

$$(\tilde{x}_{mi}, \tilde{y}_{mi}, 1) = z_{mj}(\tilde{x}_{mj}, \tilde{y}_{mj}, 1) + z_{ni}(\tilde{x}_{ni}, \tilde{y}_{ni}, 1) - z_{nj}(\tilde{x}_{nj}, \tilde{y}_{nj}, 1). \tag{15}$$

Thus, not surprisingly, environmental inference from translation requires two points in two frames.

Translational Motion Processing Extensions

There are several extensions to the translational-motion procedure for such things as expressing the computation hierarchically, processing image sequences containing multiple independently translating objects, and using it for autonomous vehicle navigation by using devices to stabilize the sensor or to obtain the rotational parameters directly. The procedure can also be applied to general and nonrigid motion by treating them as local environmental translations.

Hierarchical Computation

Hierarchical organized representations and processes (Burt 1982; Glazer 1983; Glazer et al. 1983; Hanson and Riseman 1980; Tanimoto and Klinger 1980; Uhr 1978) allow different scales of image events to be handled uniformly. The consistent agreement among hierarchically organized processes is a basic control strategy for a wide range of high- and low-level interpretation tasks. Hierarchical processing produces significant computational reductions, wherein results from processing performed rapidly at lower resolutions of image information are used to direct and constrain more detailed and extensive processing of higher-resolution image information. Translational motion processing can be done hierarchically with the benefits of increased speed and dealing with larger image displacements.

In our initial work, images have been represented in the VISIONS image operating cone structure of Hanson and Riseman (1980). This consists of a sequence of images $I_0, I_1, I_2, \cdots, I_n$, where the successive sizes of the images are $1 \times 1, 2 \times 2, 4 \times 4, \ldots, 2^n \times 2^n$. The value n is the *level* of the image in the cone. Each pixel in the mth image, except for the first and last images, has a connected neighborhood of *immediate descendants* in the $m + 1$ image and a parent in the $m - 1$ image. The size and shape of the immediate-descendant neighborhood can be arbitrary, and the immediate-descendant neighborhoods of adjacent pixels may or may not overlap. There are several ways to reduce image resolution in pyramid architecture (Burt 1982; Hanson and Riseman 1980; Tanimoto and Klinger 1980; Uhr 1978). These usually involve smoothing the image with some operator and then sampling at a reduced interval. We have used Burt's (1982) 5 × 5 mask, which approximates Gaussians. A reasonable change to this would be to use band-passed filtered images instead of smoothed ones. Work by Burt (1982) and Glazer et al. (1983) indicates that the matches of features from successive band-passed images are much more distinctive than using features from low-pass images.

The positions of the extracted features for translational processing are also represented at different levels of resolution. There are multiple ways of doing this. It may possible to simply apply the procedure uniformly at each image position, without extracting features at all. Alternatively, the feature-extraction process can be applied to each image at each level of image resolution. Or features can be extracted in the highest-resolution image and their ancestors in the lower-resolution images then also treated as features. In this case, the immediate-descendant neighborhoods should not overlap (so each features has unique ancestors) and a feature is positioned at a parent pixel if any of its descendants are at positions where a feature has been extracted. These approaches may interact in interesting ways if the strength of a feature is expressed as a function of its own distinctiveness and that of its descendants. We have thus far utilized the approach based on extracting features at the highest image resolutions.

Translational Processing at Different Resolutions

The translational processing can be applied to successive images at any level of resolution for which features have been extracted from an initial image. The basic questions concern how processing at one level affects processing at another level. In particular, how do processing results at a coarser level of resolution constrain the processing at finer levels of resolution? At what level in the cone can processing be meaningfully initialized? How do the various parameters involving feature window size, displacement resolution along a flow path, and resolution of the optimization procedure change at different levels of the cone?

We currently use the position of the optimally determined translational axis at level m to initialize the optimization for the images and feature positions at the $m + 1$ level in the cone. In addition to constraints on the position of the error-function minimum, processing at lower resolutions

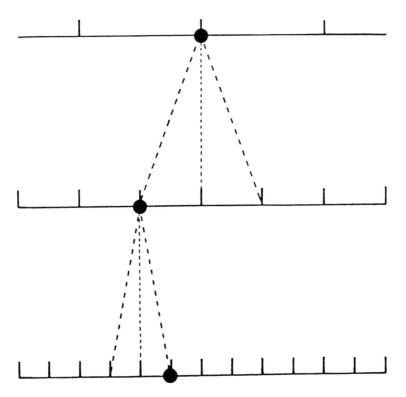

Figure 18
Relations between displacements at different resolutions.

constrains the evaluation of the potential displacements of extracted features along their displacement paths. Figure 18 shows flow paths at different levels of resolution. For each displacement determined at level m,
only three positions have to be evaluated at level $m + 1$. Thus, not only
is the minimum of the error function passed on, but also the displacements
of parent features, which are then used to constrain the evaluation of the
displacements of descendant features (Glazer et al. 1983).

   There are several possibilities for relating the error-function minimization across the different image resolutions. One strategy that has been
employed involves the use of different step sizes in the error-function
evaluation correlated with particular image levels. That is, as processing
moves to increased image resolutions, the step size of the search process
decreases. Alternatively, a complete search could be done at a given level
before proceeding to the higher resolutions. In the experiments illustrated
in figure 19, processing was initialized at level 4 by performing the global

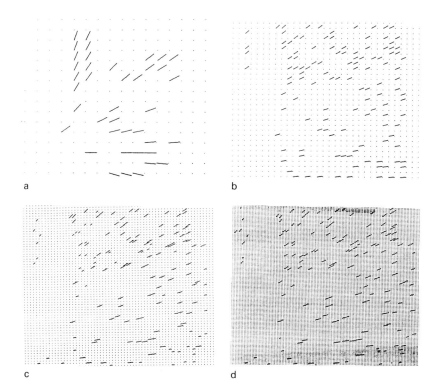

Figure 19
Image displacements at resolutions of (a) 16 × 16, (b) 32 × 32, (c) 64 × 64, and (d) 128 × 128.

sampling of the error measure at a separation of $\pi/10$ radians. The resulting flow field is shown in figure 19a. The first step of the local processing, which was initialized at the minimum determined by global sampling, used a step size equal to 0.1 radians for the images and features at level 5. The resulting flow field is shown in figure 19b. At level 6, the step size was reduced to 0.025 and the local search initialized at the minimum determined by the processing done at level 5. At level 7, the step size was reduced to 0.005 and the search was initialized at the minimum determined at level 6. 5 × 5 windows were used at each level, with convergence to the results obtained previously at the highest level of resolution.

Multiple Independently Moving Objects

The procedure described here assumes a sensor moving relative to a stationary environment or a single object moving relative to a translating sensor. A useful extension would allow the presence of multiple independently moving objects while maintaining the ability to determine image displacements concurrently with the direction of translation. One technique for this is to utilize generalized Hough transforms (Ballard 1981) for decomposing the responses in the search measure into corresponding independently moving image segments.

The global component of the optimization process is an instance of a generalized Hough transform in which each feature scales its vote for a particular translational axis as a function of the best match it can find that is consistent with the translational axis. Associated problems are typical for Hough transforms: how to associate labels corresponding to the resulting peaks in the histogram with image points or features. The general form of this processing is to find the translational axis with the greatest response in the histogram, associate a label with it, and then associate this label with image features that match above some threshold along the image-displacement paths determined by the corresponding translational axis. The resulting set of features are then removed, and a new histogram is produced. The peak in this new histogram is extracted, and the process is repeated until there are no more distinct peaks in the resulting histograms, or until all image features are labeled (Adiv 1983).

This procedure will have difficulties with weak or homogeneous feature points that have strong matches consistent with several distinct translational axes. Thus, when rehistogramming occurs it is necessary to establish which image features already labeled are consistent with the newly extracted peak. An alternative is to proceed in the conventional manner and determine a set of labels corresponding to translational axes for which there is evidence. Each feature is then labeled with each translation axis from this set with which is it consistent. A given feature could have several labels. A unique consistent labeling is then obtained by using other information: segmentation grouping using other image attributes, depth consistency with neighbors, and common magnitude of image displacements. Additionally, this disambiguation can occur over several successive images. In fact, a potentially significant aspect of generalized Hough technique may be the correlation of histograms from successive instants to bring out structures that are moving consistently.

Hybrid Sensor Systems

Translational processing is useful for vision-based navigation in a stationary environment if the orientation of the optic sensor can be fixed relative to the environment over time. In this case, sensor motion amounts to a sequence of translations. In some work on sensor stabilization, electro-optical systems have been suspended in magnetic fields; in other work, more conventional gimbel-based stabilization has been used.

One difficulty with a stabilized retina is that it is not able to rotate in order to focus on particular parts of the environment. This could be corrected by using a set of stabilized retinas arranged to yield a complete view of space. There would then be no need to rotate the sensor to view a particular environmental point. A possible arrangement of retinal surfaces is a cubical one. One of the retinal planes will always contain an FOE, and another will always contain an FOC (unless the direction of motion is right on an edge of the cube and the focal length has not been properly adjusted). There will also be several independent estimates of the direction of translation, which can be integrated.

Alternatively, if the sensor cannot be stabilized, there are other devices that can determine the rotational parameters of sensor motion. A particular technology that is very attractive for this use is that of *fiber-optic rotation sensors* (Ezekiel and Arditty 1982). These sensors are expected to be the low-cost gyroscope of the near future, since they are small, cheap, and precise. Because they have no moving elements, they are not as affected by rapid accelerations as conventional gyroscopes. There are currently slow drift problems when sensor orientation is considered over long periods of time. In our processing, though, we would be concerned with measurements of rotation over much shorter periods. Additionally, when such sensors are coupled with an image-processing system for guidance and navigation, the effects of such long-term drifts could be recognized and accounted for by noting the position of specified landmarks.

The Local Translational Decomposition

The procedure for translational motion processing can be extended to more general and arbitrary sensor motions by applying the procedure to small areas over an image. This approximates more general motion as an array of local environmental translations by interpreting local image motions as if they resulted from translational motion of the corresponding portions of the environment. The resulting description of motion is an approximation to the *environmental direction-of-motion field* (EDMF), which associates with a set of image points (or small image areas) the relative direction of motion of the corresponding environmental points (or small environmental surface areas). This low-level representation of environmental motion simplifies the recovery of the sensor motion parameters considerably.

Computing the Environmental Direction-of-Motion Field

The environmental direction-of-motion field (EDMF) that associates with each feature or small image area a three-dimensional unit vector describing the direction of motion of the corresponding feature or small surface area in the environment relative to the observer. It can be computed from image sequences directly or from computed flow fields.

Analysis of Raw Image Sequences

The procedure for translational motion yields a set of image displacements consistent with a determined translational axis. Application of this procedure to a small area of an image containing extracted features yields a set of image displacements consistent with an interpretation of the local image motion as a relative translation of the corresponding part of the environment. Where the translational approximation is poor, there will be a small value of the measure, reflecting the weaker confidence in the validity of the approximation.

This use of the translational procedure can be seen as a local constraint on the determination of image displacements. Typically, most such constraints are based on the smoothness of the resulting displacement field (Barnard and Thompson 1980; Glazer 1981; Horn and Schunck 1980) where image displacements are computed under the constraint of being a local average of the displacements in their surrounding neighborhood. In our case, image displacements are determined such that the corresponding environmental motion can be interpreted locally as being translational. This constraint does not necessarily imply local smoothness in the displacement field.

Computing the EDMF from raw image sequences depends on how the images are divided into subareas. The image could be divided into small, regular, square subareas across the image; the procedure for determining the axis of translation is then applied to each subarea independently. Alternatively, the procedure could be applied to individual regions determined by some segmentation procedure. In our work to date, we have used another approach in which the image subareas are neighborhoods centered on single features and the computation is applied independently over the neighborhood of each feature.

Computing the EDMF can be expensive for such feature-based neighborhoods, since the feature displacements of many points are being determined simultaneously for different, overlapping image subareas. An approximation is used to simplify this computation. For each feature, its

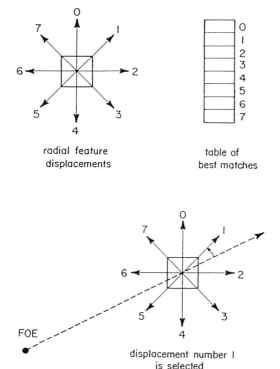

radial feature
displacements

table of
best matches

FOE

displacement number I
is selected

Figure 20
Approximating match values along translational flow paths.

best match and corresponding displacement along each of a set of radial directions are determined from one image into the next. These values are then stored in a one-dimensional array where each index corresponds to a particular radial direction centered at the feature and the associated best match value for the corresponding direction (figure 20).

In the determination of the value of a particular translational axis with respect to a the neighborhood of a feature, each feature in the neighborhood finds its best match along the direction closest to that determined by the translational axis. The resulting values are then summed up. In this way, redundant evaluations of feature matches are avoided.

Figure 21 and 22 are referred to as the grass sequence. Figure 21 is a 128 × 128-pixel image of some grass texture with seven bits of intensity. Figure 22 was derived from figure 21 by applying a rotation of 0.1 radians about the Y axis of the camera coordinate system. Features were selected from the image in figure 21 by determining image points where the

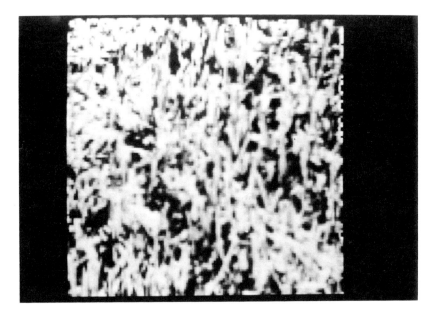

Figure 21
Grass sequence image 1.

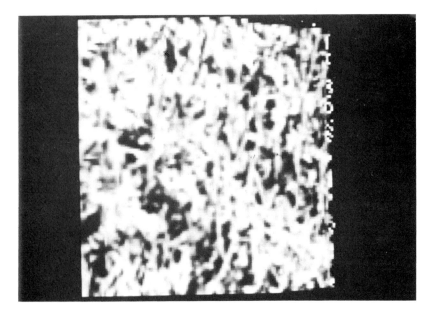

Figure 22
Grass sequence image 2.

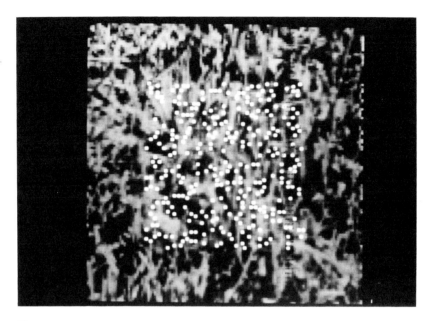

Figure 23
Selected features.

contrast was greater than 20 intensity levels and which were also local maxima in the distinctiveness values associated with 5×5-pixel square features centered at those points. The resulting feature positions are shown in figure 23.

The direction of translation was determined for 11×11-pixel neighborhoods centered at each feature in figure 23. Each feature determined its best displacements in 256 evenly spaced directions for distances of up to 10 pixels. The image displacement associated with a feature was the displacement that was consistent with the FOE/C determined by the translational approximation for the feature's neighborhood. The resulting image-displacement field, shown in figure 24, has the correct form for rotational motion about the Y axis.

Figure 25 shows the X, Y, Z components of the EDMF for the corresponding image points. The values in the EDMF are between 1.0 and -1.0, since it consists of unit vectors. All the features have displacements in the same X direction (figure 25a), because the camera rotation about Y induces all points to move left or right. The Y displacements are all very close to zero (consistent with motion constrained to planes parallel to the Y axis). The mean Y displacement is -0.003 (figure 25b). The Z com-

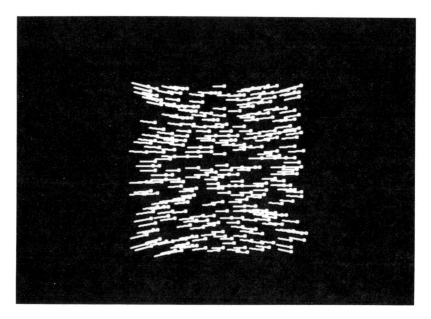

Figure 24
Determined image displacements.

ponents are positive for the right half and negative for the left half of
the image (figure 25c). (The scale of the display has also been increased.)
This motion occurs in pure rotation about Y, because the environmental
motions lie on circular paths with one side going away from the observer
and the other side going toward the observer.

Analysis of an Existing Displacement Field
To compute the EDMF from image sequences for which image displacements have already been determined, it is necessary to use a measure
describing the fit of the displacement paths corresponding to a particular
translational axis and a computed displacement field. One of these is a
simple function of the angles between the image-displacement paths deter-
mined by the FOE and the image-displacement vectors, such as $\sum_i^N |\cos\theta_i|$,
expressed as a least-squares fitting procedure.

Processing of Motion Constrained to an Unknown Plane

The EDMF produced by motion constrained to an unknown plane is
particularly simple. For this case, all the EDMF vectors are constrained to
lie in a plane that is parallel to the plane of environmental motion. By

a

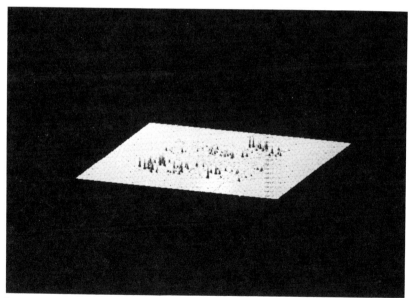

b

Figure 25

Computed components of EDMF. (a) X component, (b) Y component, (c) Z component.

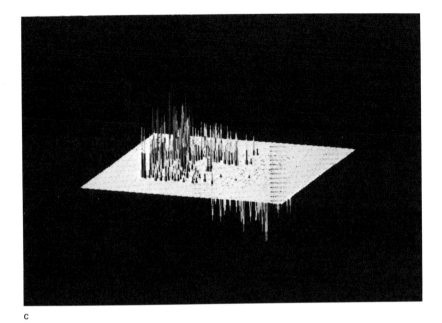

c

Figure 25 (continued)

calculating the EDMF vectors and fitting a plane to them, the plane of motion and thus the axis of rotation can recovered. If the motion occurs over several successive instants and remains constrained to the same plane, then the vectors in the successive EDMFs are also constrained to lie in a plane parallel to it and containing the origin on the direction-of-translation sphere. Thus, more and more values for the fit can be collected over time, thereby increasing the accuracy of the processing. The grass sequence involving pure rotation is a case of motion constrained to a plane, since the environmental displacement paths all lie in planes perpendicular to the axis of rotation. Using the EDMF determined for the grass texture sequence described above, the normal to the best plane determined by an eigenvector fit procedure (Duda and Hart 1973) was $(0.003, 0.999, -0.014)$. This is off by $0.836°$ from the correct rotational axis.

Solving the Rigidity Constraints Using the EDMF

The rigidity constrains are significantly simpler when they are integrated with information concerning the environmental direction of motion from the local translational decomposition. To do this, the EDMF is used first to

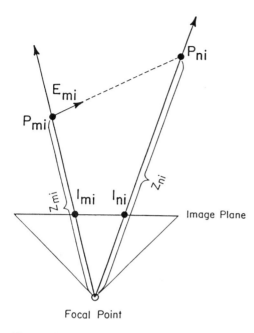

Figure 26
Relative depths for a point over time from the EDMF.

find consistent relative depths for individual points over successive images. Consistent relative depths for several points are then determined by scaling the particular depth values for the individual points using the rigidity constraint.

We first examine the use of the EDMF in the determination of consistent relative depths for a single point over time. Consider the image-position vectors I_{mi} and I_{ni} (for the successive image positions of point i at times m and n) and the environmental direction of motion associated with point i at time m: E_{mi} (figure 26). Assuming the ideal case, in which there is no error in any of these quantities, the EDMF vector E_{mi} will lie in the plane determined by I_{mi} and I_{ni}. Thus, given a depth z_{mi} along the ray of projection corresponding to I_{mi}, one can find a depth value z_{ni} along the ray of projection associated with I_{ni} from the intersection of the lines $P_{mi} + tE_{mi}$ and $z_{ni}I_{ni}$. In the usual case of error in these measurements, these lines will not intersect because they are skewed in three dimensions. In these instances we can solve for the line segment perpendicular to both these lines. Let us express the point along the ray of projection determined by I_{ni} that is closest to the line determined by the point $P_{mi} = z_{mi}I_{mi}$ and the direction of motion E_{mi} from the EDMF:

$$t(E_{mi} \cdot E_{mi}) - z_{ni}(E_{mi} \cdot I_{ni}) = -z_{mi}(I_{mi} \cdot E_{mi}),$$

$$t(E_{mi} \cdot I_{ni}) - z_{ni}(I_{ni} \cdot I_{ni}) = -z_{mi}(I_{mi} \cdot I_{ni}). \tag{16}$$

These equations can be expressed in terms of the ratio of the relative distances along the successive rays of projection consistent with the environmental direction of motion E_{mi} (with t treated as a dummy variable):

$$t(E_{mi} \cdot E_{mi}) - r_{mni}(E_{mi} \cdot I_{ni}) = (I_{mi} \cdot E_{mi}),$$

$$t(E_{mi} \cdot I_{ni}) - r_{mni}(I_{ni} \cdot I_{ni}) = (I_{mi} \cdot I_{ni}), \tag{17}$$

where

$$r_{mni} = \frac{z_{mi}}{z_{ni}}.$$

This yields the relative depths of a single point over time. We now use the rigidity constraint to determine the appropriate scaling of each of these ratios for all the points.

Assume that we have two points, i and j, at times m and n. Let z_{mj} be set to an arbitrary value. Then z_{nj} may be obtained by the product

$$z_{mj} \times r_{mnj} = z_{mj} \times \frac{z_{nj}}{z_{mj}},$$

where the ratio r_{mnj} is obtained through the relation expressed in equation 17. This yields the environmental points P_{mj} and P_{nj}. We can now use the rigidity constraint to determine a scale factor expressing $P_{mi} = z_{mi}I_{mi}$ and $P_{ni} = z_{ni}I_{ni} = z_{mi}r_{mni}I_{ni}$ in terms of P_{mj} and P_{nj}. Substitution into the rigidity constraint yields

$$\|z_{mi}I_{mi} - P_{mj}\| = \|z_{mi}r_{mni}I_{ni} - P_{nj}\|, \tag{18}$$

where z_{mi} is the scale factor. Equation 18 can be expanded as

$$z_{mi}^2[(I_{mi} \cdot I_{mi}) - (r_{mni}I_{ni} \cdot r_{mni}I_{ni})] + [(P_{mj} \cdot P_{mj}) - (P_{nj} \cdot P_{nj})]$$

$$- 2z_{mi}[(I_{mi} \cdot P_{mj}) - (r_{mni}I_{ni} \cdot P_{nj})] = 0 \tag{19}$$

The resulting equation is quadratic in one unknown. Thus, given successive depth values determined for a particular point from its EDMF vector, one can determine consistent depths for every other pair of successive depth values by solving this equation for each resulting pair of points.

In summary: Given a flow field and an EDMF, one can find a pair of depth values for each image point at successive instants that are consistent with the determined EDMF vectors. Once the relative, successive depth values are determined for each point, they may then be scaled relative to any selected point. Several depth maps can thus be computed (one for each selected image point), and the certainty of a particular depth inference could be based on agreement in the relative depth values in all the resulting depth maps. If there were further spatial constraints, such as motion relative to a planar surface, all the determined depth maps would have to be in agreement with respect to the shape; for example, all the determined depth maps for a plane would have to correspond to a single plane at the same orientation.

If the EDMF could be computed reliably, it would be a very useful low-level representation for the analysis of rigid body motion. This appears possible for densely textured image sequences for which the camera motion parameters to be recovered correspond to motion constrained to an unknown plane. The local translational decomposition may also be applicable to inferring qualitative descriptions of nonrigid motions by noting certain patterns in the relative directions of motion as would typify such motions as expanding or twisting.

Using a Content-Addressable-Array Parallel Processor

Motion perception in artificial systems will require highly parallel architectures. Here we demonstrate the use of a content-addressable-array parallel processor (CAAPP) as an effective means of decomposing a computed flow field into its rotational and translational components to recover the parameters of sensor motion (Weems 1984). The algorithm is a straightforward implementation of exhaustively checking 200,000 potential rigid-body motions using the decomposition technique described above. Since this work was done, in 1983, CAAPP has undergone extensive redesign; it is now considerably larger and faster.

Organization of the CAAPP

The CAAPP is a VLSI-based single instruction, multiple data (SIMD) machine designed at the University of Massachusetts. It consists of a parallel processor containing 512 × 512 cells and a central controller. The central controller issues instructions to the parallel processor, controls the loading and unloading of data in the parallel processor, and serves as an interface to the host computer and to secondary storage devices. It broadcasts data to the parallel processor bit serially, and the entire memory may be bulk-loaded in one video-frame time ($\frac{1}{30}$ second). The central controller contains a set of microcoded subroutines in ROM for performing high-level CAAPP routines and a writable control store for adding microcode.

The parallel processor consists of an 8 × 8 array of processing circuit boards and a set of boards which control CAAPP edge treatment. Each processor board, in turn, consists of an 8 × 8 array of special-purpose CAAPP IC chips plus random buffer logic. Each chip contains 64 cells, an instruction decoder, and some miscellaneous logic. There are eight basic instruction types recognized by the chip, each performed in parallel by the constituent cells. Most instructions take one minor cycle time (100 nanoseconds) to execute. Intercell communication is bit serial and is accomplished by a four-way (N, S, E, W) cell interconnect network, allowing for three types of edge treatments: dead-edging, circular wrap, and zig-zag wrap.

Each unit cell consists of 64 bits of fully static memory, four one-bit static "tag" registers (A, B, X, and Y), a static carry bit register Z, and an ALU which continuously generates X NAND Y, X NOR Y, and X + Y + Z. Also, each cell contains logic for selecting a data source [a register (excluding Z), memory, an ALU function, broadcast data, or a neighboring cell (N, S, E, or W)], possibly inverting the selected signal, and storing it in a destination (a register or memory). The X register is the main tag register. Its output is connected to Some/None logic, indicating cell response, and to the neighbor communication network. The A register controls whether or not a cell is active. An inactive cell ignores all but a small set of instructions broadcast by the central controller. The Y register provides a secondary store for tag bits; the B register provides a secondary store for activity bits.

Flow-Field Decomposition Procedure

Our algorithm is an exhaustive procedure that uses a set of rotational and translational flow-field templates to find a component pair that can account for the motion depicted in a given flow field. Currently, 1,000 rotational templates and 200 translational templates are used. These are generated from 100 axes, which are uniformly distributed with respect to a unit

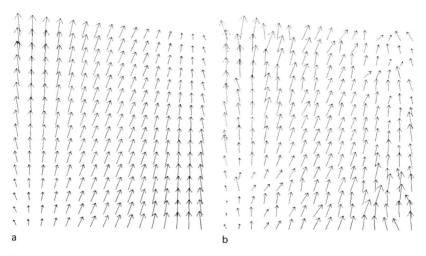

Figure 27

hemisphere and which all pass through the origin of the sensor coordinate system. Each flow field consists of 16 × 16 vectors and is stored on a 2 × 2 square of chips consisting of 256 cells. The 2 × 2 chip arrangement facilitates flow-field addressing. Each cell contains the horizontal and vertical components of a flow vector, each specified with ten bits of precision.

The algorithm consists of four basic steps:

(0) The rotational templates are loaded into the CAAPP, one template for each flow-field location. Each flow-field location corresponds to one of the squares in the CAAPP response diagrams shown in figures 28–30. The rotational templates need be loaded only once, since they are used in determining any flow-field decomposition.

(1) A copy of the input flow field is loaded into each flow-field location in the CAAPP. Figures 27a and 27b show two sample input fields, both produced by the same motion and environment except that figure 27b was produced by adding random spike noise to figure 27a.

(2) A set of difference fields is formed by subtracting each rotational template from the copy of the input flow field stored with it. For each resulting difference field, the slope of each difference vector is computed by dividing the vertical component by the horizontal component. These subtraction and division procedures are performed in parallel across all flow fields represented in the CAAPP.

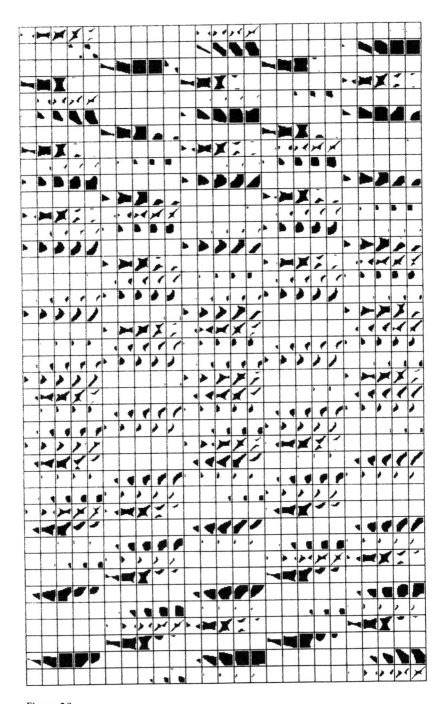

Figure 28

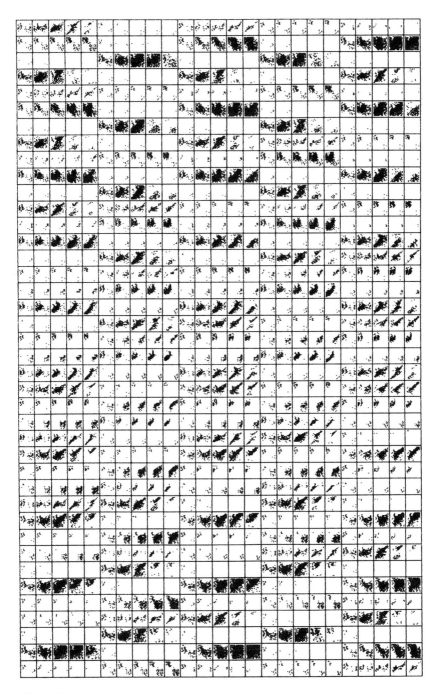

Figure 29

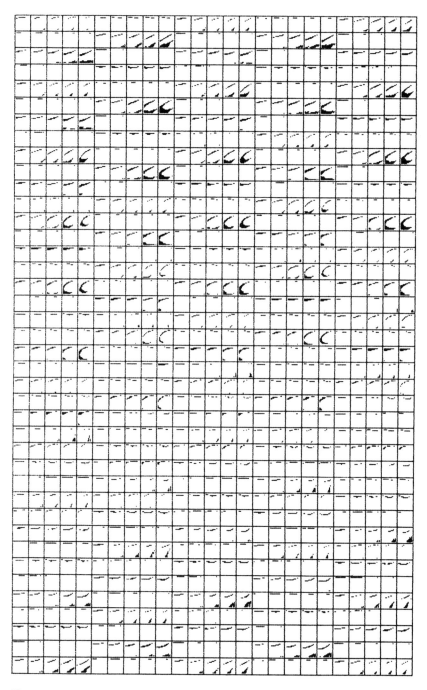

Figure 30

(3) The similarity between the difference fields and each of the translational templates is evaluated, proceeding sequentially through all the translational templates. For a given translational template, this comparison is done in parallel with all difference fields stored in the CAAPP and consists of the following steps:

(3a) The slope of each component vector of the translational template is loaded into the corresponding vector location of each difference field. The sign of the slope of each difference vector is compared with the sign of the slope of the corresponding translational-template vector. If the signs agree, the absolute value of the difference between the slope of the difference vector and the slope of the translational-template vector is computed and then scaled according to the absolute value of both slopes. If the scaled slope difference does not exceed a predetermined maximum error value, then a vector match is designated at that position. The quantity of error permitted here allows the algorithm to be resistant to uniformly distributed Gaussian noise of low variance present in the original flow field.

(3b) For each difference field the number of vector slope matches is counted. If this sum exceeds a predetermined minimum number of matches (in our implementation, 75 percent of the field size), then the associated rotational and translational templates become a candidate pair for the flow-field decomposition. Utilization of a minimum number of required matches ensures that only templates that are reasonably close to the actual motion will be chosen and permits some resistance to random spike noise. Figure 28 shows, for difference fields resulting from the input field in figure 27a, the CAAPP response to the translational motion. Each black dot within a square represents a position in a difference field at which the slope of the difference vector matches the slope of the translational template. Figure 29 shows, for difference fields resulting from the input field in figure 27b, the CAAPP response to the translational template that is closest to the actual translational motion. Figure 30 shows the CAAPP response to a translational template that is not close to the actual translational motion. This translational template is shown in figure 31.

(3c) For all difference fields yielding at least the required minimum number of matches, the variance of the scaled slope difference is computed and the difference field with the minimum variance is determined. This value is compared with the minimum variance found from processing the preceding minimum. It becomes the new global minimum. The rotational template associated with the difference field and the current translational template become the current best candidate pair for the flow-field decomposition.

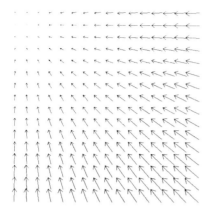

Figure 31

Steps 3a, 3b, and 3c are performed for each translational template.

(4) The flow-field decomposition considered to be the best is the rotational and translational template pair resulting in the difference field yielding at least the required minimum number of matches and the least slope difference variance. Utilizing minimum variance instead of the maximum number of matches, the algorithm has achieved better results, particularly for motions whose component parts lie between sets of templates. Figures 32a and 32b show the rotational and translational templates selected by the algorithm in the presence of and in the absence of noise for the input fields in figures 27a and 27b. These templates are the closest ones to the actual motions. Figures 33a and 33b show the difference fields resulting from subtracting the rotational motion in figure 32a from the original fields in figures 27a and 27b, respectively.

Experiments

Experiments have been performed with a CAAPP simulator on a VAX 11/780 using a wide variety of motions and simulated environments. In all cases examined, the translational template closest to the actual translational motion was selected. The rotational template was always close to the actual rotational motion, but was sometimes not the closest template. The procedure proved to be resistant to limit Gaussian noise as well as to limited random spike noise in the original flow field. Applying motion to points at random depths produced results similar to those obtained in the noise experiments. The algorithm's performance was degraded slightly if

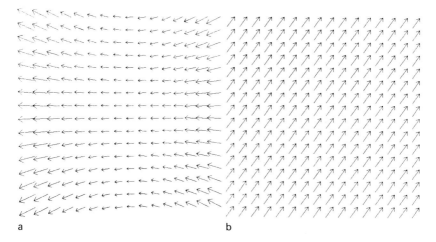

a   b

Figure 32

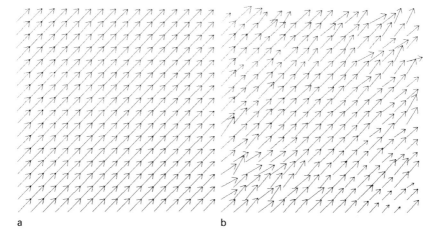

a   b

Figure 33

each flow vector component was specified by eight bits of precision instead of by ten.

The CAAPP timing calculations revealed that the algorithm could perform the rotational-translational decomposition in slightly more than $\frac{1}{4}$ second. If two CAAPPs are used in parallel, the time can be reduced to less than $\frac{1}{5}$ second, since only half of the translational templates need be tested on each CAAPP. Given fabrication techniques available in the immediate future, we expect execution times to be significantly improved. We also suspect that performance will improve because of increases in the number and the size of the rotational and translational templates.

Processing Differential Image Motion

The inference of sensor motion and environmental depth can be significantly simplified when there are environmental depth variations, such as at occlusion boundaries. Under this condition, differential image motion—the directed variance of optic flow over some area—yields a simple estimate of the translational field lines at image locations corresponding to environmental depth discontinuities. We have used this condition to develop a simple and robust procedure for processing unrestricted motion relative to a static scene in which the axis of translation is recovered from the differential image motion (Rieger and Lawton 1985). The translational field lines are then used as a constraint for solving for the 3D rotation. The procedure is inexpensive, since it requires only computation of local differences, thresholding, and solving systems of linear equations. It also appears to be insensitive to noise.

Computing the Axis of Translation

The geometrical structure of optic flow within image regions corresponding to environmental depth changes has a particularly simple form, allowing for the recovery of the translational axis. In such regions, the difference vectors between flow vectors computed over some neighborhood are oriented along translational field lines. This can be easily seen in the case of details (such as points along occluding boundaries) that are located in exactly the same direction from the camera but lie at difference depths; as observed by Longuet-Higgins and Prazdny (1980), such points will differ in their image velocity vectors by the difference of their translational components only. Since image flows obtained from actual image sequences are sparse in regions corresponding to depth variation in the scene, to develop this computationally we have to consider the effects of subtracting spatially separated flow vectors. To this end we decompose a difference vector into a signal component (oriented along the correct translational field line) and a noise component. We find that the signal components of difference vectors increase in regions corresponding to environmental depth variation and increased angular deviation from the translational axis.

Using the coordinate system from figure 3 and the flow paths described by equations 3 and 4, two image points $\tilde{P}_i$ and $\tilde{P}_j$ at relative image positions $\tilde{\mathbf{r}}_j - \tilde{\mathbf{r}}_i = (d_x, d_y)$ differ in their rotational flow vectors by

$$\Delta_{ij}\mathbf{u}_R = \mathbf{u}_{jR} - \mathbf{u}_{iR}$$

$$= w_z(d_y, -d_x) + (\tilde{y}_j w_x - \tilde{x}_j w_y)(d_x, d_y) + (d_y w_x - d_x w_y)\tilde{\mathbf{r}}_i. \tag{21}$$

Letting $\tilde{\mathbf{r}}_T = (v_x, v_y)/v_z$ denote the intersection of the translational axis with the image plane, we can rewrite the translational component of the flow as $\mathbf{u}_T = v_z(\tilde{\mathbf{r}} - \tilde{\mathbf{r}}_T)/z$. (Here and in the following we assume, for brevity, that v_z does not vanish. Allowing for translations parallel to the image plane requires simple modifications.) Then the difference vector of the translational flow of separated image points $\tilde{P}_i$ and $\tilde{P}_j$ becomes

$$\Delta_{ij}\mathbf{u}_T = \mathbf{u}_{jT} - \mathbf{u}_{iT}$$

$$= \frac{v_z}{z_j}\left[\tilde{\mathbf{r}}_j - \tilde{\mathbf{r}}_i + \frac{\Delta_{ij}z}{z_j}(\tilde{\mathbf{r}}_T - \tilde{\mathbf{r}}_i)\right], \tag{22}$$

where $\Delta_{ij}z = z_j - z_i$ is the depth separation of the corresponding points P_i and P_j in the scene. In general, then, a difference vector $\Delta_{ij}\mathbf{u} = \Delta_{ij}\mathbf{u}_T + \Delta_{ij}\mathbf{u}_R$ of spatially separated flow vectors consists of a signal component along a translational field line and a noise component:

$$\Delta_{ij}\mathbf{u} = \underbrace{\left[\frac{v_z\Delta_{ij}z}{z_i z_j}(\tilde{\mathbf{r}}_T - \tilde{\mathbf{r}}_i)\right]}_{\text{Signal}} + \underbrace{\left[\frac{v_z}{z_j}(\tilde{\mathbf{r}}_j - \tilde{\mathbf{r}}_i) + \Delta_{ij}\mathbf{u}_R\right]}_{\text{Noise}}. \tag{23}$$

If $\|\tilde{\mathbf{r}}_i - \tilde{\mathbf{r}}_j\|$ is kept small and $\|\Delta_{ij}\mathbf{u}\|$ is large compared with the local average magnitude of difference vectors, then $\Delta_{ij}\mathbf{u}_{\text{Signal}}$ must be the dominating term in equation 23. ($\Delta_{ij}\mathbf{u}_{\text{Noise}}$ tends to zero as $\|\tilde{\mathbf{r}}_i - \tilde{\mathbf{r}}_j\|$ approaches zero.)

The structure of such difference vectors suggests the following scheme for recovering the field lines of the translational component field (and thus the axis of translation). First, for each flow vector $\mathbf{u}_i$ compute the difference vectors with adjacent flow vectors $\mathbf{u}_j$ that are located within some image distance ε, i.e., $\|\tilde{\mathbf{r}}_i - \tilde{\mathbf{r}}_j\| \leq \varepsilon$. Determine an average orientation of the resulting difference vectors $\Delta_{ij}\mathbf{u}$ by fitting a line l_i passing through $\tilde{\mathbf{r}}_i$ that minimizes the sum of the squared perpendicular distances to the set of points defined by $\{\tilde{\mathbf{r}}_i + \Delta_{ij}\mathbf{u}\}$. As desired, the larger difference vectors $\Delta_{ij}\mathbf{u}$ within a neighborhood will essentially determine the orientation of l_i resulting from such an eigenvector lined fit. This line l_i will be a good estimate of the translational field line at $\tilde{\mathbf{r}}_i$ if the points follow the line closely. This is so because the noise components of the set of difference vectors $\{\Delta_{ij}\mathbf{u}\}$ will have varying orientations depending on the locations of the flow vectors $\mathbf{u}_j$ relative to $\tilde{\mathbf{r}}_i$ (equation 23), whereas the signal components, by definition, will be oriented along the translational field line at $\tilde{\mathbf{r}}_i$. Thus, the distribution of $\{\tilde{\mathbf{r}}_i + \Delta_{ij}\mathbf{u}\}$ yields an estimate of the signal-to-noise ratio of the difference vectors. The second step, then, is to threshold the lines l_i that have been obtained for each flow vector $\mathbf{u}_i$ on the basis of the anisotropy of the points $\{\tilde{\mathbf{r}}_i + \Delta_{ij}\mathbf{u}\}$. Thus, we require that the ratio between the small and the large eigenvalue of each fitted line l_i not exceed some constant δ, i.e., $\|\lambda_{i\,\text{Small}} / \lambda_{i\,\text{Large}}\| \leq \delta$. Finally, the position of the translational axis may be determined by solving for the intersection of the remaining set of lines l_i (involving a linear least-squares fit).

The distribution of difference vectors obtained over an isotropic set of relative positions (d_x, d_y) may be determined from equations 21 and 23. Unfortunately, owing to unknowns such as camera rotation, there does not exist a direct relation between the error of l_i and the distribution of $\Delta_{ij}\mathbf{u}$ within a window. However, a worst-case analysis (assuming some maximal field of view and related maximal interframe camera rotation beyond which the computation of image motion becomes impossible) in computer simulations indicates that the distribution of $\Delta_{ij}\mathbf{u}$ can turn anisotropic ($\|\lambda_{i\,\text{Small}} / \lambda_{i\,\text{Large}}\| < 0.1$) only within windows of dominating signal component. For sparse image flows, as obtained by interframe matching of gray-value corners, this procedure can be modified in that only difference vectors that exceed some minimal length threshold are used to estimate l_i.

Computing the Camera Rotation

Computing the 3D rotation (up to focal length) from an image flow field is straightforward once the translational axis is known. The components of the flow prependicular to the radial (translational) field lines must be induced by rotation. Thus, introducing polar image coordinates ρ, θ centered at $\tilde{P}_{\mathrm{T}}$, we obtain for each flow vector $\mathbf{u}$ the constraint $\mathbf{u}_{\mathbf{R}} \cdot \mathbf{e}_\theta = \mathbf{u} \cdot \mathbf{e}_\theta$ (where $\mathbf{e}_\theta$ denotes a unit vector in the direction of increasing θ). The rotational components $\mathbf{u}_{\mathbf{R}}$ of the flow are linear in w_x, w_y, and w_z (see equation 3); thus, the parameters of the 3D rotation may be calculated by a linear least-squares method.

Calculating a Relative Depth Map of the Scene

Knowing the 3D rotation yields the rotational components of the flow and thus the desired decomposition of an image flow into its component fields. Now the relative depth of a point in the scene is simply

$$\frac{z}{v_z} = \frac{\|\tilde{\mathbf{r}} - \tilde{\mathbf{r}}_T\|}{\|\mathbf{u}_T\|},$$

which is the time-unit-contact measure referred to above.

Summarizing the steps of the procedure: (1) Locally compute difference vectors within some neighborhood of each flow vector and determine the line l_i representing their general orientation. (2) Select the lines l_i representing anisotropic sets of difference vectors. (3) Determine the translational axis from the remaining set of lines. (4) Calculate 3D rotation satisfying $\mathbf{u}_R \cdot \mathbf{e}_\theta = \mathbf{u} \cdot \mathbf{e}_\theta$, where $\mathbf{u}_R$ is linear in w_x, w_y, and w_z. (5) Compute component fields of the image flow and a relative depth map.

Experimental Results

The procedure has been applied to several displacement fields obtained from both simulations and flow fields computed from image sequences. Although the procedure has been derived using a continuous formulation in terms of image velocities, it is directly applicable to discrete image sequences. The expected effects of the parameters controlling the signal-to-noise ratio of the difference vectors on the precision of the procedure in locating the axis of translation have been observed in all experiments.

The first example illustrates the performance of the procedure as a function of the depth variation of a scene. Image-displacement fields simulating camera motion relative to points located on two transparent (x, y) planes, at depths z_1 and z_2, were used as input. The depth z_2 was gradually increased while all other parameters were kept constant. The curves shown in figure 34 represent the angular error of the computed translational axis as a function of the depth separation of the planes over the viewing distance $\Delta z/z_1$. The translational axis approaches, as expected, the correct location for increasing $\Delta z/z_1$, where the rate of convergence is higher when difference vectors are computed over smaller neighborhoods ε. To understand the effects of errors in the displacement fields on the procedure, we added to each displacement vector some random component. The parameters in this experiment were the same as those used in the first example, except that $\Delta z/z_1$ was kept constant. Figure 35 shows an approximately linear

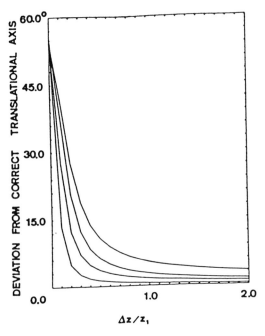

Figure 34
Effects of depth variation. The family of curves corresponds to window sizes of $\varepsilon \approx 1.5°$, $3.0°$, $4.5°$, and $6.0°$. The flow field was induced by an observer motion composed of a translation of one unit along $(-1, 1, 1)$ and a rotation of $6°$ about $(0, 1, 0)$. The nearer surface was at a depth of $z_1 = 10$ units.

increase in the angular error of the computed translational axis with increasing amount of error in the displacement field.

The relations among depth variation, the distribution of $\Delta_{ij}\mathbf{u}$ within a neighborhood, and the error in the estimate l_i are indicated by the results shown in tables 1 and 2. Here 100×100-pixed images were simulated (with a field of view of $45° \times 45°$ and image motion determined at each pixel). The difference vectors were determined over square windows with the same extent of environmental depth variation in each window. The average magnitude of $\|\lambda_{i\,Small} / \lambda_{i\,Large}\|$ (table 1) and the deviation of l_i from the correct translational field lines at $\tilde{\mathbf{r}}_i$ (table 2) were evaluated for different depth variations and window sizes. The measure in table 2 is the average value of the inner product of the small eigenvector with the unit vector along the corresponding translational field line. The increase in depth variation is mirrored in the rapid decrease of both the error in the estimate of l_i and the isotropy of the distribution of $\Delta_{ij}\mathbf{u}$ within a window.

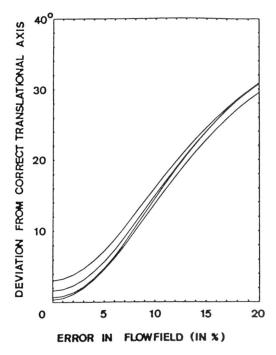

Figure 35

Effects of errors in the flow field. The parameters were the same as those in the previous experiment (figure 34) except for a constant depth variation of $\Delta z-z_1 = 2.0$. The summed magnitudes of the added random components are expressed as percentages of the summed magnitudes of the correct flow vectors.

The flow field computed from successive 128×128-pixel images taken from a camera mounted on a robot arm with a field of view of $29.5° \times 29.5°$ is shown in figure 36. The scene consists of two textured planar surfaces, the nearer one at a depth of 50 cm and the more distant one at a depth of 150 cm along the z axis. The camera motion was a translation of 10 cm toward the background followed by a rotation of about $3.5°$ to the left. The flow field was computed using a procedure developed by Anandan (1984) that is based on a coarse-to-fine correlation matching strategy (Glazer 1983) with certainty measures reflecting the reliability of the computed flow. On the basis of these measures and other local variance measures, the flow can be filtered to remove effects that correspond to occlusion or various kinds of error and distortion. The field of lines l_i representing the local orientation of difference vectors that have been computed over window sizes of $\varepsilon = 12$ pixels has been thresholded by removing the lines

Table 1
Effects of depth variation on the distribution of difference vectors.

$$\frac{\sum_{i=1}^{N} \|\lambda_{i\,\text{Small}} / \lambda_{i\,\text{Large}}\|}{N}$$

	Neighborhood size (pixels)			
$\Delta Z/Z$	5×5	13×13	21×21	25×25
0.0	0.448	0.480	0.512	0.531
0.1	0.035	0.162	0.313	0.374
0.2	0.010	0.056	0.130	0.165
0.3	0.005	0.029	0.073	0.094
0.4	0.003	0.019	0.048	0.062
0.5	0.002	0.014	0.035	0.045
0.6	0.002	0.010	0.027	0.035
0.7	0.001	0.009	0.022	0.029
0.8	0.001	0.007	0.019	0.025
0.9	0.001	0.006	0.016	0.021
1.0	0.001	0.005	0.014	0.020

Table 2
Effects of depth variation on the error of l_i.

$$\frac{\sum_{i=1}^{N} \|[(\tilde{\mathbf{r}}_i - \tilde{\mathbf{r}}_\text{T}) \cdot \mathbf{e}_{i\,\text{Small}} / \|\tilde{\mathbf{r}}_i - \tilde{\mathbf{r}}_\text{T}\|]\|}{N}$$

	Neighborhood size (pixels)			
$\Delta Z/Z$	5×5	13×13	21×21	25×25
0.0	0.721	0.720	0.707	0.708
0.1	0.007	0.037	0.093	0.122
0.2	0.002	0.011	0.029	0.037
0.3	0.001	0.006	0.016	0.020
0.4	0.001	0.004	0.011	0.014
0.5	0.001	0.003	0.008	0.011
0.6	0.000	0.003	0.007	0.009
0.7	0.000	0.002	0.006	0.008
0.8	0.000	0.002	0.005	0.007
0.9	0.000	0.002	0.005	0.006
1.0	0.000	0.002	0.004	0.006

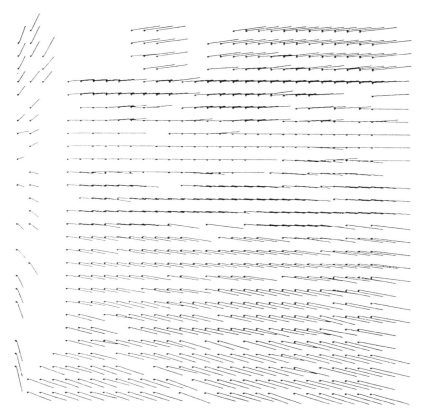

Figure 36

whose ratio of small to large eigenvalues exceeded $\delta = \frac{1}{10}$. The resulting field is shown in figure 37 together with the computed location of the translational axis, which deviated from the correct axis by 0.25°. The procedure determined that the camera rotation was 3.44° about an axis given by $(-0.035, 0.998, 0.047)$, which is within the rotational-error tolerance of the robot arm. Figure 38 and 39 show the resulting rotational and translational components of the flow field. The relative depth map extracted from the translational-component field is shown in figure 40.

Implications for Human Motion Perception

Currently, many researchers in human vision believe that optic flow may be utilized for a rough figure/ground segmentation of a scene but not for more detailed motion and depth perception. This opinion seems to be

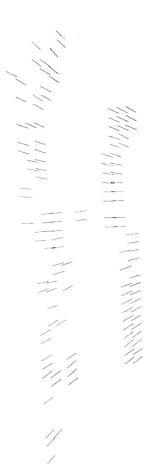

Figure 37

Figure 38

supported by the poor judgments of human observers about their direction of translation when a single approaching plane is displayed on a screen (Llewellyn 1971; Johnston et al. 1973; Regan and Beverley 1982) and by studies of the sensitivity of the human visual system to differential image motion (Van Doorn and Koenderink 1982a, b, 1983; Nakayama 1981; McKee 1981) that rule out measurements of spatial derivatives of image flows under the condition of common image motion. If, however, humans were to employ a scheme that required the presence of depth variation for parts of the field of view to determine their motion and the depth of the scene, the above results would be expected.

Most of the studies investigating the accuracy of human observers in locating their direction of translation simulated an approaching plane that was perpendicular to the translational axis (Llewellyn 1971; Johnston et al. 1973; Regan and Beverley 1982). In these studies, the judged translational axes deviated from the correct axes by $10°$ on the average (and for large

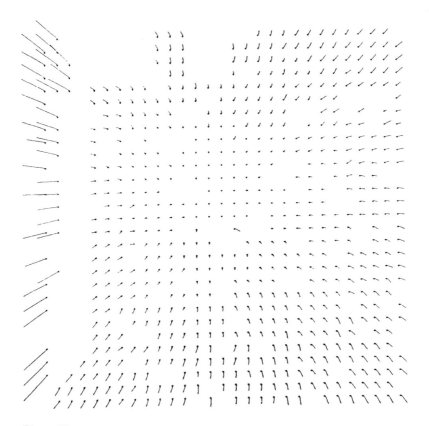

Figure 39

Figure 40

rotational component flows by as much as $20°$). However, the signal components of the image flows were identically equal to zero in these simulations, since a single plane perpendicular to the axis of translation contains no depth variation. In a similar study in which motion across a ground plane (where the local depth variations are still small but differ from zero) was simulated, Warren found smaller errors of about $5°$ in the judgments. Cutting (1983) also found a strong dependency on inferring the direction of observer motion and the presence of environment on depth variation.

Acknowledgments

The work described in this paper was mostly done while the authors were graduate students at the University of Massachusetts at Amherst. We would like to acknowledge the support, friendship, and guidance of Ed Riseman, Al Hanson, and the entire University of Massachusetts VISIONS group. This work was supported by DARPA grant N00014-82-K-0464. We would also like to acknowledge Angela Erickson, Nancy English, and Milissa Feeny.

References

Adiv, G. 1983. Recovering Motion Parameters in Scenes Containing Multiple Moving Objects. In Proceedings of IEEE Conference on Computer Vision and Pattern Recognition, Washington, D.C.

Adiv, G. 1984. The Interpretation of Optical Flow Fields. Ph.D. thesis, University of Massachusetts, Amherst.

Aggarwal, J. K., and W. N. Martin. 1981. Analyzing dynamic scenes containing multiple moving objects. In *Image Sequence Analysis*, ed. T. S. Huang (Springer-Verlag).

Aggarwal, J. K., L. S. Davis, and W. N. Martin. 1981. Correspondence processes in dynamic scene analysis. *Proceedings of the IEEE* 69, no. 5: 562–575.

Anandan, P. 1984. A Confidence Measure for Correlation Matching. COINS Technical Report, University of Massachusetts, Amherst.

Badler, N. I. 1975. Temporal Scene Analysis: Conceptual Descriptions of Object Movements. Report TR 80, University of Toronto. Also available as Technical Report 80 from University of Pennsylvania.

Ballard, D. H. 1981. Parameter networks: Towards a theory of low-level vision. In Proceedings of the International Joint Conference on Artificial Intelligence, Vancouver.

Barnard, S. T., and W. B. Thompson. 1980. Disparity analysis of images. *IEEE Transactions on Pattern Analysis and Machine Intelligence* 2, no. 4: 333–340.

Barrow, H. G., and J. M. Tenenbaum. 1981. Interpreting line drawings as three dimensional surfaces. *Artificial Intelligence* 17: 75–117.

Barrow, H. G., A. P. Ambler, and R. M. Burstall. 1972. Some techniques for recognizing structures in pictures. In *Frontiers of Pattern Recognition*, ed. S. Watanabe (Academic).

Brady, M. 1983. Criteria for shape representations. In *Human and Machine Vision*, ed. J. Beck and A. Rosenfeld (Academic).

Burr, D. 1977. A System for Stereo Computer Vision with Geometric Models. Ph.D. dissertation, University of Illinois.

Burt, P. J. 1976. Stimulus Organizing Processes in Stereopsis and Motion Perception. COINS Technical Report 76-15, University of Massachusetts, Amherst.

Burt, P. J. 1982. Pyramid-based extraction of local image features with application to motion and texture analysis. In Proceedings of SPIE Conference on Robotics and Industrial Inspection, San Diego.

Burt, P. J., C. Yen, and X. Xu. 1983. Multi-resolution flow-through motion analysis. In Proceedings of IEEE Conference on Computer Vision and Pattern Recognition, Washington, D.C.

Cheng, J. K., and T.S. Huang. 1982. Recognition of curvilinear objects by matching relational structures. In Proceedings of the Pattern Recognition and Image Processing Conference, Las Vegas.

Cutting, J. E. 1983. Perceiving and recovering structure from events. In Proceedings of the ACM SIGGRAPH/SIGART Conference on Motion: Representation and Perception, Toronto (Association for Computing Machinery).

Davis, L. S., Z. Wu, and H. Sun. 1982. Contour-Based Motion Estimation. Report TR-1179, Center for Automation Research, University of Maryland, College Park.

Davis, L. S., K. Kitchen, F. P. Hu, and V. Hwang. 1983. Image Matching Using Generalized Hough Transforms. Report CAR-TR-27 or CS-TR-1335, Center for Advanced Automation Research, University of Maryland, College Park.

Dreschler, L., and H.-H. Nagel. 1981. Volumetric model and 3-D trajectory of a moving car derived from monocular TV-frame sequences of a street scene. In Proceedings of the Seventh International Joint Conference on Artificial Intelligence, Vancouver. Also published in *Computer Graphics and Image Processing* 20 (1982): 199–228.

Duda, R. O., and P. E. Hart. 1973. *Pattern Classification and Scene Analysis*. Wiley.

Ezekiel, S., and H. J. Arditty. 1982. *Fiber Optic Rotation Sensors and Related Technologies*. Springer-Verlag.

Fang, J. Q., and T. S. Huang. 1983a. Estimating 3-D movement of a rigid object: Experimental results. In Proceedings of the International Joint Conference on Artificial Intelligence, Karlsruhe, Federal Republic of Germany.

Fang, J. Q., and T. S. Huang. 1983b. Solving three-dimensional small-rotation motion equations. In Proceedings of the IEEE Conference on Computer Vision and Pattern Recognition, Washington, D.C.

Fennema, C. L., and W. B. Thompson. 1979. Velocity determination in scenes containing several moving objects. Computer Graphics and Image Processing 9, no. 4: 301–315.

Gibson, J. J. 1950. The Perception of the Visual World. Houghton Mifflin.

Gibson, J. J. 1966. The Senses Considered as Perceptual Systems. Houghton Mifflin.

Gibson, J. J. 1979. The Ecological Approach to Visual Perception. Houghton Mifflin.

Glazer, F. 1981. Computing optic flow. In Proceedings of the Seventh International Joint Conference on Artificial Intelligence, Vancouver.

Glazer, F. 1983. Multilevel relaxation in low-level computer vision. In Multiresolution Image Processing and Analysis, ed. A. Rosenfeld (Springer-Verlag).

Glazer, F., G. Reynolds, and P. Anandan. 1983. Scene matching by hierarchical correlation. In Proceedings of the IEEE Conference on Computer Vision and Pattern Recognition, Washington, D.C.

Grimson, W. E. L. 1981. From Images to Surfaces: A Computational Study of the Human Early Visual System. MIT Press.

Hannah, M. J. 1974. Computer Matching of Areas in Stereo Images. AI Memo 239, Stanford University.

Hanson, A. R., and E. M. Riseman. 1980. Processing cones: A computational structure for image analysis. In Structured Computer Vision, ed. S. Tanimoto and A. Klinger (Academic).

Haralick, R. M. 1978. Scene analysis, arrangement and homomorphisms. In Computer Vision Systems, ed. A. H. Hanson and E. M. Riseman (Academic).

Haralick, R. M. 1982. Zero-crossings of second directional derivative edge operator. In Proceedings of the SPIE Symposium in Robot Vision, Washington, D.C.

Haralick, R. M. 1983. Ridges and valleys on digital images. Computer Graphics and Image Processing 22, no. 1: 28–39.

Hildreth, E. C. 1982. The integration of motion information along contours. In Proceedings of the IEE Workshop on Computer Vision: Representation and Control.

Horn, B. K. P., and B. G. Schunck. 1980. Determining Optical Flow. AI Memo 572, Massachusetts Institute of Technology.

Huang, T. S., ed. 1981. *Image Sequence Analysis.* Springer-Verlag.

Jacobus, C. J., R. T. Chien, and J. M. Selander. 1980. Motion detection and analysis by matching graphs of intermediate-level primitives. *IEEE Transactions on Pattern Analysis and Machine Intelligence* 2, no. 6: 495–510.

Jerian, C., and R. Jain. 1983. Determining motion parameters for scenes with translation and rotation. In Proceedings of the SIGGRAPH/SIGART Interdisciplinary Workshop on Motion: Representation and Perception, Toronto.

Johnston, I. R., G. R. White, and R. W. Cumming. 1973. The role of optical expansion patterns in locomotor control. *American Journal of Psychology* 86: 311–324.

Kearney, J. K., W. B. Thompson, and D. L. Boley. Gradient-based estimation of disparity. In Proceedings of the Pattern Recognition and Image Processing Conference, Las Vegas.

Lawton, D. T. 1980. Constraint-based inference from image motion. In Proceedings of AAAI-80, Stanford, Calif.

Lawton, D. T. 1983. Processing translational motion sequences. *Computer Vision, Graphics, and Image Processing* 22: 116–144.

Lee, D. N. 1980. The optical flow field: The foundation of vision. *Philosophical Transactions of the Royal Society (London)* B 290: 169–179.

Llewellyn, K. R. 1971. Visual guidance of locomotion. *Journal of Experimental Psychology* 91: 1245–1261[?].

Longuet-Higgins, H. C. 1981. A computer algorithm for reconstructing a scene from two projections. *Nature* 293: 133–135.

Longuet-Higgins, H. C., and K. Prazdny. 1980. The interpretation of a moving retinal image. *Proceedings of the Royal Society (London)* B 208: 385–397.

McKee, S. P. 1981. A local mechanism for differential velocity detection. *Vision Research* 21: 491–500.

Nakayama, K. 1981. Differential motion hyperacuity under conditions of common image motion. *Vision Research* 21: 1475–1482.

Prazdny, K. 1980. Egomotion and relative depth map from optical flow. *Biology and Cybernetics* 36: 87–102.

Prazdny, K. 1981. Determining the instantaneous direction of motion from optical flow generated by a curvilinearly moving observer. *Computer Graphics and Image Processing* 17: 238–248.

Quam, L. H. 1971. Computer Comparison of Pictures. AI Memo AIM-144, Stanford University.

Radig, B. M. 1981. Image region extraction of moving objects. In *Image Sequence Analysis*, ed. T. S. Huang (Springer-Verlag).

Regan, D., and K. I. Beverley. 1982. How do we avoid confounding the direction we are looking and the direction we are moving? *Science* 215: 194–196.

Rieger, J. H., and D. T. Lawton. 1985. Processing differential motion. *Journal of the Optical Society of America* A 2, no. 2.

Roach, J. W., and J. K. Aggarwal. 1979. Computer tracking of objects moving in space. *IEEE Transactions of Pattern Analysis and Machine Intelligence* 1: 127–134.

Roach, J. W., and J. K. Aggarwal. Determining the movement of objects from a sequence of images. *IEEE Transactions on Pattern Analysis and Machine Intelligence* 2: 554–562.

Rogers, D. F., and J. A. Adams. 1976. *Mathematical Elements of Computer Graphics.* McGraw-Hill.

Rosenfeld, A. 1983. *Multiresolution Image Processing and Analysis.* Springer-Verlag.

Schunck, B. G. 1983. Motion Segmentation and Estimation. Ph.D. thesis, Massachusetts Institute of Technology.

Shapiro, L. G., and R. M. Haralick. 1982. Organization of relational models for scene analysis. *IEEE Transactions on Pattern Analysis and Machine Intelligence* 4: 595–602.

Shaw, G. B. Determining Motion Parameters Using a Perturbation Approach. Technical Report 83-30, Department of Computer and Information Science, University of Massachusetts, Amherst.

Steenstrup, M. E., D. T. Lawton, and C. Weems. 1983. Determination of the rotational and translational components of a flow field using a content addressable parallel processor. In Proceedings of the IEEE Conference on Computer Vision and Pattern Recognition, Washington, D.C.

Tanimoto, S., and A. Klinger, eds. 1980. *Structured Computer Vision: Machine Perception through Hierarchical Computation Structures.* Academic.

Terzopoulos, D. 1983. The role of constraints and discontinuities in visible-surface reconstruction. In Proceedings of the International Joint Conference on Artificial Intelligence, Karlsruhe, Federal Republic of Germany.

Thompson, W. B., and S. T. Barnard. 1981. Lower-level estimation and interpretation of visual motion. *IEEE Computer* (August).

Thompson, W. B., K. M. Mutch, and V. A. Berzins. 1983. Determining qualitative spatial properties from optical flow fields. In Proceedings of the Workshop on Vision, Brain, and Cooperative Computation, University of Massachusetts, Amherst. Also available as a technical report form the Department of Computer Science of the University of Minnesota.

Tsai, R. Y., and T. S. Huang. 1982. Uniqueness and estimation of three-dimensional motion parameters of rigid objects with curved surfaces. In Proceedings of the Pattern Recognition and Image Processing Conference, Las Vegas.

Tsotsos, J. K., J. Mylopoulos, H. D. Convey, and S. W. Zucker. 1980. A framework for visual motion understanding. *IEEE Transactions on Pattern Analysis and Machine Intelligence* 2: 563–573.

Uhr, L. 1978. Recognition cones and some test results. In *Computer Vision Systems*, ed. A. R. Hanson and E. M. Riseman (Academic).

Ullman, S. 1979a. *The Interpretation of Visual Motion.* MIT Press.

Ullman, S. 1979b. The interpretation of structure from motion. *Proceedings of the Royal Society (London)* B 203: 405–426.

Van Doorn, A. J., and J. J. Koenderink. 1982a. Temporal properties of the visual detectability of moving spatial white noise. *Experimental Brain Research* 45: 179–188.

Van Doorn, A. J., and J. J. Koenderink. 1982b. Visibility of movement gradients. *Biological Cybernetics* 44: 167–175.

Van Doorn, A. J., and J. J. Koenderink. 1983. Detectability of velocity gradients in moving random-dot patterns. *Vision Research* 23: 799–804.

Webb, J. A., and J. K. Aggarwal. 1981. Visual interpretation of the motion of objects in space. In Proceedings of the Pattern Recognition and Image Processing Conference, Dallas, 1983.

Weems, C. 1984. A Content Addressable Array Processor for Image Processing. Ph.D. dissertation, University of Massachusetts, Amherst.

Whittaker, E. T. 1944. *A Treatise on the Analytical Dynamics of Particles and Rigid Bodies.* Dover.

Williams, T. D. 1980. Depth from camera motion in a real world scene. *IEEE Transactions on Pattern Analysis and Machine Intelligence* 2: 511–516.

Wong, R. Y., and E. L. Hall. 1978. Sequential hierarchical scene matching. *IEEE Transactions on Computers* 27, no. 4: 359–366.

Yen, B. L., and T. S. Huang. 1983. Determining 3-D motion parameters of a rigid body: A vector-geometrical approach. In Proceedings of the ACM Workshop on Motion, Representation, and Perception, Toronto.

13

Schemas That Integrate Vision and Touch for Hand Control

Michael A. Arbib,
Thea Iberall, and
Damian Lyons

Conventional control theory is based on the interactions of a fixed network of dynamic systems (controller, plant, sensors, and so on); conventional serial programs are based on the execution of a single instruction at a time. Lines in a block diagram of a control system represent flow of data; lines in a program flow diagram represent transfer of activation. We argue (see Arbib 1981) for a style of cooperative computation that involves concurrent activity in a dynamic network of entities called *schemas*, which combine attributes of both control elements and instruction instantiations.

In the present paper, we focus the study of schemas by considering how a robot control program or a primate central nervous system could control complex interactions with the environment, such as the grasping and manipulation of visually recognized objects. The recognition of those objects and the knowledge of their use depend on an internal model of the world (MacKay 1966; Gregory 1969). In the context of the present volume, we view the current internal model as a *task-dependent* representation based on the activity of perceptual schemas which provide parameters for the coordinated activity of motor schemas which guide movement.

In reaching to grasp an object during a task, the arm moves the hand toward the object and the hand grasps it. In the present paper, we use a task-analysis approach to determine which schemas might be controlling the various movements performed during the task. The top half of figure 1 shows a collage of hand shapes as the hand moves from its initial position to pick up a ball. Not only has the hand moved, but the hand has *preshaped* so that when it has almost reached the ball it is of the right shape and orientation to enclose the ball before gripping it firmly. The lower half of the figure indicates with a sequence of dots the position of the tip of the thumbnail in consecutive frames of a movie. The spacing of these dots reveals that the movement can be broken into two parts: a fast initial movement and a slow approach movement. Moreover, Jeannerod has shown

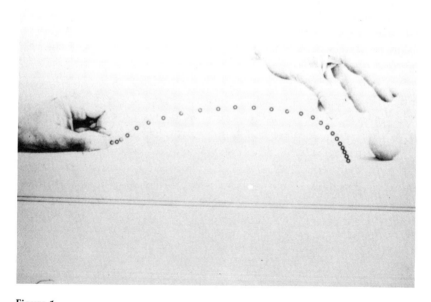

Figure 1
(a) Hand shapes anticipating the shape of an object during the reaching movement.
(b) Small circles indicate position of thumbnail tip at equally spaced moments, indicating
a fast phase followed by a slow movement. (Jeannerod 1984)

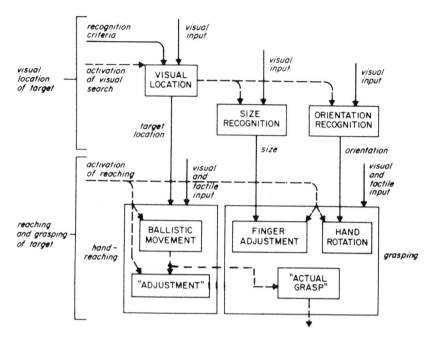

Figure 2

Hypothetical coordinated-control program for visually directed reaching to grasp an object by a human. Dashed lines carry activation signals; solid lines transfer data. (Adapted from Arbib 1981.)

that the transition from the fast to the slow phase of the hand transfer movement is coupled with a transition from the preshape of the hand itself to the closing in of the fingers so that touch may take over in controlling the final grasp.

Figure 2 provides a broad-brush view of how schemas might interact to perform such visually directed reaching to grasp an object. *Perceptual schemas*, seen in the upper half of the figure, are internal representations of objects, domains of interaction, or properties of the environment: the size of the object, its location, its orientation, its relative motion, etc. They pass parameter values to motor schemas. For example, analysis of the visual input locates the object within the subject's reaching space (it is not the job of this system to choose the target), and this information is passed to a motor schema to perform the reaching action. *Motor schemas*, as seen in the bottom half of the figure, are units of motor control. They continually monitor feedback from the system they control in order to determine the appropriate pattern of action to achieve their goals. On activation, the hand reaching system directs a ballistic movement toward the target. Thereafter, it activates a final phase of the movement in which visual and tactile feedback are used. Before the actual reaching, however, analysis of visual input also extracts the size and the orientation of the target object and feeds this information to the grasping schema. Next, finger adjustments are made by a schema that preshapes the hand into a shape suitable for the interaction, and, in parallel, another schema is activated which rotates the wrist in order to orient the hand correctly. This is followed by inactivity within the grasping schema, which lasts until its reactivation on the completion of the fast phase of the reach. The "actual" grasping movement shapes the hand on the basis of a spatial pattern of tactile feedback.

The internal model of the environment is an active process, composed of an *assemblage* (or interacting group) of schemas, that attunes the animal or robot for possible interactions with its environment. The level of activation of any schema depends on its credibility within the assemblage; schemas are activated on the basis of that credibility (or activation) level. The reaching-and-grasping example shown in figure 2 involves only schemas with high credibility, since they were the ones needed for that task. The activation level of a motor schema is an indication of how useful the schema is for dealing with the present environment as perceived by perceptual schemas. A motor schema may have its activation level affected by other motor schemas as well as by dynamic perception. Cooperating schemas will increase one another's activity; competing schemas will attempt to decrease one another's activity. The overall behavior of the system is the combined behavior of all its component schemas, and it is a *coordinated-control program* that interweaves the activation of motor schemas to control action. The example in figure 2 is thus a coordinated-control program for reaching and grasping visually perceived objects. Although the perceptual schemas are shown separately for clarity, they may be embedded within the motor schemas so as to provide the parameters relevant to the controlled system.

The key suggestion of the discussion so far is that vision is to be seen not as a unitary process that delivers a completely general representation of the seen environment, but rather as a task-directed process that delivers partial representations under the direction of the regnant coordinated-control program (though this will, in general, be responsive to unexpected visual input).

Two-Phase Analysis of a Motor Schema

In an informal study of the motor skills involved in drinking beer, Lyons (1982) observed that the placing of a beer mug could be separated into two phases: a fast movement to a target above the table and a slower movement in which the mug is gently lowered to make contact with the table top (figure 3a). The distance δ_1 of the first target above the table seemed to increase with decreasing sobriety, suggesting a deliberate undershoot to ensure that the rapid first movement would not end in too sharp a contact with the table top. This led us (Arbib et al. 1983) to posit that such a movement can be seen as involving two activations of a basic motor schema, but with different parameters. The basic schema MOVE(B, T, C) is shown in figure 3b: Move to target B with timing parameters T and expected contact C. In the beer-mug example, C is the subtle spatiotemporal tactile pattern to be experienced on the hand when the mug hits the table from above. (Note the need for a complex visual-tactile transformation to anticipate C.) Just what constitutes the timing parameters T is a matter for experiment; candidates include movement duration, peak velocity, average velocity, and peak force. All that matters for the present discussion is that we can speak of "fast T" and "slow T." MOVE(B, T, C) has three paths whereby activation can be transferred to other schemas: B (move completed, though probably near B rather than exactly at B; thus the need for feedback tuning), C (if contact is made with an expected tactile pattern), and $\bar{C}$ (if contact is made with the "wrong" tactile pattern).

Figure 3c shows the coordinated-control program for the two-phase movement of figure 3a. Activation of the overall program activates MOVE($A + \delta_1$, T fast, C), with an appropriate activation level, which should normally terminate by reaching the position (near to) $A + \delta_1$. If contact $\bar{C}$ is made there is a "failure exit" (some error-correction schema must be activated), whereas contact C may be treated either as failure (completion unexpected; check for spilled beer) or success (mug on table). On normal exit from the first schema, control is transferred to MOVE($A - \delta_2$, T slow, C), with a normal exit occurring on contact C (termination under tactile feedback "in the right ballpark"). Both $\bar{C}$ (unexpected contact) and $A - \delta_2$ (the table is not where it was thought to be) are failure exits from the overall schema. A smoothing of the transition from the first schema to the second is achieved by the lowering and raising of the activation of the schemas.

However, we would now like to address the question of whether there is a single schema MOVE(B, T, C) for which "fast" and "slow" are possible values of the parameter T, or whether there are really two distinct schemas (i.e., different neural circuits in the brain; different programs in a robot control system): MOVE$_{fast}$(B, C) and MOVE$_{slow}$(B, C). We may compare the first schema to a ballistic phase and the second schema to a feedback

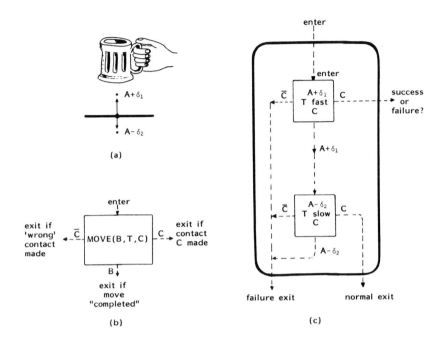

Figure 3
(a) The placing of a mug on a table may be seen as composed of two movements: a fast
movement to a target $A + \delta_1$ above the intended resting point A on the table (with the
"safety undershoot" increasing with an estimate of decreasing accuracy of the movement),
and a slow movement toward a point $A - \delta_2$ just below the table (designed to terminate
under feedback control on contact). (b) The basic move schema: Move to visually defined
target B with speed parameter T and expected tactile contact C. Three separate exit
conditions are stipulated: B if no contact is made, C if the expected contact is made,
and $\bar{C}$ if an unexpected contact is made. (c) The coordinated-control program for the
movement of diagram a, involving two calls of the schema of diagram b with different
parameters.

phase, refining the discrete-activation feedforward schema of Arbib 1981 (figure 11). (Compare with Navas and Stark 1968 for the idea that the low-velocity terminal part of the trajectory is a guided phase whereas the earlier, high-velocity phase is ballistic.) Jeannerod (1984) posits that the reaching and grasping components are temporally coordinated—that the fingers, having formed the pregrasp, begin to close in anticipation of contact at the transition from the high-velocity to the low-velocity phase of reaching. However, whereas Jeannerod would suggest that the timing of the two components is achieved by a centrally generated temporal pattern, we would hypothesize that the activation signal (figure 3c) from the first schema to the second schema of a reach movement also serves to activate a second schema in the grasp—precisely the hypothesis (though with a more primitive analysis of the schemas) embodied in figure 2.

We now develop evidence that, at least in the case of human movements, two different control systems are involved in the two stages of a movement. It may well be that the initial stage of the movement involves "bang-bang" control, analogous to that involved in making an elevator move from one floor to another in minimal time. Here, the time-optimal strategy is to accelerate the elevator maximally to the midpoint between the two floors and then decelerate maximally for the rest of the journey. Clearly, the calculation of such a trajectory requires that the system know both the initial point and the endpoint of the movement so that the midway transition point can be recognized and acted upon. Similarly, in fast limb movements we can see a burst of initial muscle contraction to move the arm upon its way and a second burst of antagonist muscle contraction to slow the arm down and bring it to rest at or near the desired point. However, the body consists of a skeleton whose movement is controlled by muscles, and these muscles can be thought of as somewhat like springs whose stiffness is under the control of the nervous system. Thus, we can also bring the body to a desired position by resetting the stiffness and then letting the muscles relax into a new equilibrium position. But the desired equilibrium may take quite a while to attain, and may be replaced by a "wrong" intermediate semi-equilibrium if the initial position is too far from the end position. Thus, this mode of control would seem appropriate for the small, slow second stage of the two-stage movement described above rather than for the fast initial stage.

Possible evidence for this separation of the two stages may be found in observations made by Jeannerod et al. (1984) on a patient who underwent neurosurgery in Lyon, France. At the end of the surgery, a small piece of surgical gauze was left in one of the arteries. It blocked blood flow to the somatosensory cortex on the left side of the brain. As a result, the patient not only lost the sense of touch for the right side of her body—most acutely in the extremities—but also lost position sense (the ability to sense how the body or parts of it are being held). Figure 4 gives a sequence of diagrams showing her moving to grasp a ball with her right hand. The dashed line separates the visual field (to the left) from the area that she could not see (to the right). Initially, her hand was placed in a bizarre posture by the clinician, and her brain had no way to tell what that shape was. She was able to see the ball and use this information to direct the arm to carry the hand, but, lacking precise information about the initial shape of the hand, she did nothing to start preshaping the hand until the hand came into view. Thereafter, since only visual shaping was available, and not tactile information or position sense, the preshaping was somewhat clumsy. Nonetheless, the crude preshape was formed, and then the hand shaped itself around the ball. This grasping was also clumsy, since only the mechanical force stopping the movement of the fingers now controlled this movement in addition to visual information—there was no tactile feedback that could be used by the brain. The inability of the patient to preshape her hand before it came into view suggests very strongly that the initial preshape is of the ballistic kind in which knowledge of initial position as well as final position is required to compute the necessary control forces. By contrast, we would suggest that the second stage involves the passage to mechanical equilibrium.

Detailed Schemas for Grasping a Mug

To pinpoint the subtle transformations required of a brain (or a robot controller) in using vision and touch to direct hand movements, we shall specify the schemas of figure 2 in more detail for the case in which the target is a cup or a mug (figure 5). The following data and analysis are taken from Arbib et al. 1983, although the figures here are new. For a related analysis of the uses of schemas in a robotic assembly task, see the paper by Overton in this volume.

The task domain has been structured as follows. The task is performed by a subject seated in front of a table on which a mug has been placed within arm distance. No obstruction lie between the mug and the subject's hand. As the hand moves toward the mug, the hand is simultaneously preshaping to grasp the handle. This preshaping depends on object parameters, such as a visually determined estimation of the handle's size and orientation. In this task, the five fingers of the hand have three major functions: to provide a

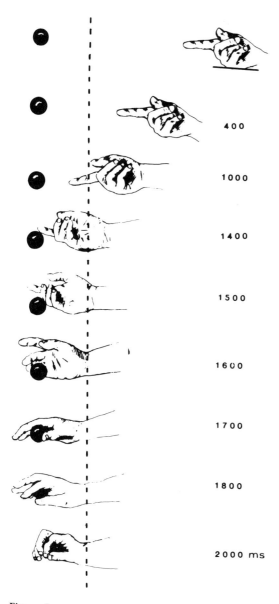

Figure 4
Reaching and grasping without tactile sensory information. (Jeannerod 1984)

TO MOVE ARM: Where is mug? Where is body referent to move?

TO PRESHAPE HAND: What is the size of the handle?

Figure 5
In reaching for a mug, estimated parameters are needed from a vision system. An estimated weight of object could also be a parameter.

downward force from above the handle, to provide an upward force from within the handle, and, if necessary, to stabilize the handle from below. We hypothesize that each of these functions can be represented as the task of a *virtual finger*, i.e., a group of fingers working together. The real fingers within a virtual finger move in conjunction. This limits the degrees of freedom to those needed for a given task and provides an organizing principle for task representation at higher levels in the brain. In this example, the task would direct VF1 to provide an opposing force on the top of the handle against VF2, direct VF2 to grasp the handle and provide stabilization, and direct VF3 to provide stabilization against the bottom of the handle (if needed).

As evidence for the concept of virtual finger, consider the behaviors pictured in figure 6. All four examples show a subject reaching for and grasping a mug. In each of them, the thumb is mapped into VF1, which provides a force from above the handle. For a teacup with a very small handle (figure 6a), only one finger will fit inside the handle. During the preshaping, only the forefinger is mapped into VF2 (the second virtual-finger function), acting to provide an upward force from within the

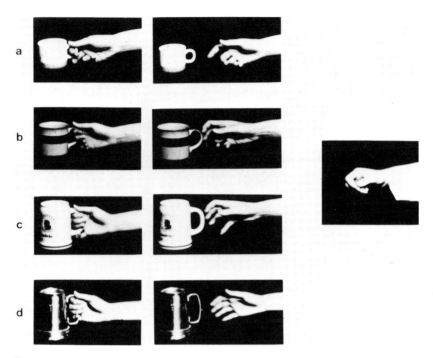

Figure 6
Various combinations of real fingers can be mapped into virtual fingers for objects of
different sizes.

handle. The rest of the fingers become VF3, to provide support for cup
stabilization. For a coffee mug of the kind pictured in figure 6b, two fingers
will fit within the handle to form VF2; the other two fingers become VF3.
For the mug of figure 6c, VF2 will comprise three fingers. Figure 6d
demonstrates the case in which all four fingers are mapped into VF2, with
VF3 the empty virtual finger. The actual mapping to real fingers is then a
subtask to be performed by another schema, making task implementation
somewhat "tool independent"; there would be a single rask representation
in terms of the actions of virtual fingers, rather than four different task
representations (one for each choice of the number of fingers to be inserted
into the handle). For each such choice, the hand is configured as a different
"tool" for grasping; thus, the sense in which the program we are developing
is "tool independent."

With this background, we now describe our third coordinated-control
program. This program for grasping a mug stresses the interaction of
vision, touch, and internally generated parameters.

Schemas can be generated from the task description in a top-down fashion. The arm move and the hand preshape are concurrent. Both work from a feedforward model supplied by the Grasp Schema, the highest-level schema under consideration in this task, which calls on the schemas in figure 2 to perform the actions on the basis of the perceptions passed by the perceptual schemas. The move terminates when the hand is at the required working offset from the mug. The preshape terminates when a satisfactory shape (a model-determined set of finger positions) has been assumed, or when the move terminates.

The motor schema controlling arm movement has a visually determined target parameter, A, which in this task we assume to be inside the hole defined by the handle (figure 7a), and a handle orientation. However, the body referent for this movement (which we posit could be located at the center of the wrist, W) must be aimed not at A but at a point displaced from A by the vector X linking the wrist to the intended contact point on the hand. This contact point, say the tip of VF2, is also passed from the Grasp Schema. The hand, no matter what its shape (which is changing during the movement) or what it is carrying, will thus have this vector parameter X (provided by the Preshape Schema), to which the Reach Schema must adjust. The Reach Schema will then call the Move Wrist Schema (figure 7b) to move the wrist reference point to the target, and the Orient Hand Schema to point the hand in the right direction. It will terminate successfully either when contact is made on the tip of VF2 or when it is near the target (which was visually determined). The current location of the body referent redefines the target location. If the termination was by contact being made, the location is determined tactilely instead of visually. If contact is made anywhere else, this schema will terminate with a failure.

The Virtual Finger Mapping Schema maps virtual fingers onto real fingers, depending on the visually determined size of the handle, as described in our discussion of figure 6. A full geometrical model of the mug is not required for it to function. All other schemas will deal with virtual fingers. If this schema remains active as long as the hand is preshaping, the fingers can be remapped dynamically (i.e., on finding that the initial estimate of the handle size was wrong). The mapping of virtual fingers onto real fingers is dependent on object parameters (such as shape, size, and weight) and on how the object is used within the task. A complete analysis of this issue is given in Iberall et al. 1984.

We now briefly expand the description of the two schemas embedded

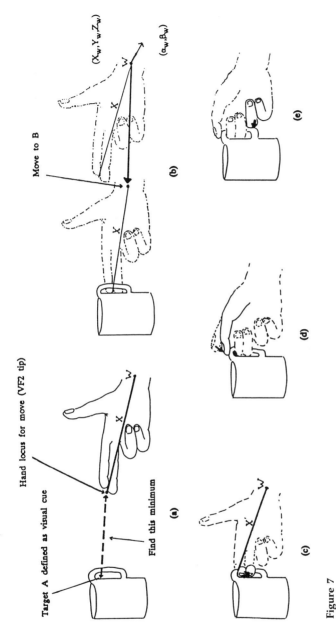

Figure 7

(a) The task of the Move Hand to Mug Schema is to aim VF2 tip to target *A* by calling the Move Wrist Schema with the distance between tip of VF2 and *W*. (b) The Move Wrist Schema. (c) The Hook VF2 Around Handle Schema. (d) The Oppose Thumb Schema. (e) The VF3 to Support Position Schema.

within the Reach Schema. The Move Wrist Schema (figure 7b) will inspect the position of the desired object in body-centered coordinates. The coordinates are mapped onto arm extension coordinates, and the wrist referent point W with coordinates (X_W, Y_W, Z_W) is moved to a location B near the target but offset by the hand size X. If any tactile contact is made in the duration of this schema activation, it will return, indicating failure. It is up to the higher-level Reach Schema to decide if this return is acceptable. This schema must call motor-servo routines to actually move the arm joints. The Orient Hand Schema is responsible for aligning the hand with the axis of the handle of the mug. It rotates the wrist, using vector (α_W, β_W), until VF2 is in a position to slide through the mug handle. It must call elementary motor-servo routines to control the actual joints in the hand.

Concurrent with the arm movement is hand preshaping, directed by the Preshape Schema, which defines the hand in terms of three virtual fingers (one for each of the forces needed in the grasping of the handle). The Preshape Schema positions the three virtual fingers in anticipation of their roles, depending on whether they are applying the force on top of the handle (VF1), inside the handle (VF2), or against the bottom of the handle (VF3). This schema is provided with the visually defined target, handle orientation, and handle size as parameters, and it will call upon low-level schemas to move the virtual fingers into some standard preshaped pattern relative to the handle. It will also provide other schemas with the pre-shaped size of the hand; in this task, it will provide the Reach Schema with the vector X from the tip of VF2 to the wrist reference point W. It will terminate with success when the shape is achieved, or when the tip of VF2 comes into contact with the handle. Actual contact is not really necessary, and so it also terminates when the tip gets to a near enough location. The Preshape Schema fails if there is contact anywhere else, letting higher-level schemas know. Once the Preshape Schema terminates, other schemas will call upon the same low-level move schemas to move the virtual fingers. This provides a smooth transition from contact-free preshaping to contact-oriented grasping movements.

Once the hand is preshaped and in a position to grasp, the grasping process begins. This consists of the parallel actions of hooking VF2 around the handle, bringing VF1 down onto the top of the handle, and bringing VF3 up to a position of support. The visually defined target provided by the embedded perceptual schema becomes tactilely defined after the successful completion of the Reach Schema. Schemas activated in the grasping process can use the redefined target.

The Hook Virtual Finger Schema (figure 7c) will incrementally close all joints of (in this case) VF2 until all fingers within the VF have achieved tactile contact against the handle. Once the correct tactile contact is achieved for a finger, it stops moving. When all are stopped, the schema terminates. The schema curls the finger toward the handle even before tactile stimuli. This schema may activate the Reach Schema if it has determined that the wrist reference point W must be moved backward in order to achieve contact. It will do so using the inside of VF2 as the expected contact point. However, in order for this movement (which feels as if it is a movement of the fingers along the handle) to be accomplished, the wrist must be moved in such a way as to allow the fingers to curl around the handle in the appropriate fashion. Thus, the brain must compute an elaborate inverse transformation from tactile information from the fingers to obtain appropriate patterns of muscle contraction for finger, wrist, and arm control.

In the Oppose Thumb Schema (figure 7d), the thumb (VF1) is brought to a tactilely defined target. In this case, VF1's target is where VF2 is touching below the top of the handle. The movement is made as a "curl" of the virtual finger until it makes contact on its tip; contact anywhere else is a failure. It terminates successfully on contact with the handle, before it actually reaches its target.

If there is a VF3, it is extended toward the underside of the handle by the Extend Virtual Finger Schema (figure 7e). When contact is made with the handle, or when the virtual finger cannot move anymore, successful termination is made.

Figure 8 shows the result of implementing such a program of hierarchical control so that it can drive the graphics display of a hand moving toward a mug. This program has no explicit control of the individual fingers as such by the overall coordinated program, but instead uses schemas in terms of the three fingers. The development of such programs is now taking the form of the development of an explicit schema-programming language PRL, the Perceptual Robotics Language. The goal of our research is now threefold: to use an implementation of this language to control computer graphics to allow us to simulate the effects of different types of program; to use this simulation testbed to come up with better models of human movements, which can eventually be tied to an understanding of the effects of brain damage, and models of the underlying neural circuitry; and to study how schema programs may be played out over a network of microprocessors for distributed dynamic sensing control of robot behavior.

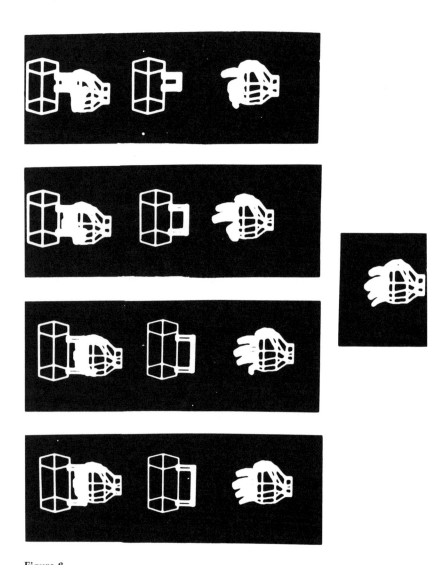

Figure 8
Computer simulation of the handle-dependent virtual-finger formation, preshaping, and grasping behaviors of figure 6.

Neural Correlates of Schemas

The description of coordinated-control programs given above is essentially phenomenological and is based on informed observations of human performance. However, it has been guided by the constraint that the schema language be precise enough to be used for robot programming (figure 8) and to help refine the language used in specifying the search for neural mechanisms of hand control. To the latter end, we now discuss probable neural and behavioral correlates of the schema concepts presented in this paper. For a discussion of possible neural correlates for the processes whereby coordinated-control programs are planned, see Arbib 1981, Brooks 1979, and Evarts 1981. The paper by Arbib and House in this volume looks at the neural instantiation of schemas in another setting, the control of detour behavior in the frog and the toad, and places especial stress on the role of cooperative computation in depth perception.

Concurrency and Localization of Schema Activation

Our coordinated-control program of figure 2 was designed to formalize the observations of Jeannerod and Biguer (1982) on the concurrent initiation of reaching and hand preshaping. As Jeannerod (1981) noted, our program shows that the existence of separate perceptual schemas activated in parallel to extract different, task-related parameters (such as shape and location in space) of an object does not deny the existence of an overall program that can orchestrate the use of these channels. Moreover, there is neurophysiological evidence for dividing the act into a reaching component (proximal muscles) and a preshaping-and-manipulation component (distal muscles). Figure 9 is based on the work of Brinkman and Kuypers (1972) and Haaxma and Kuypers (1974), who were able to show that finely coordinated visually guided behavior involved the cooperative computation of two different systems. A pathway involving the brain stem controls the undifferentiated hand movements in a manner akin to the simple grasping schema of figure 2. A pathway from visual cortex to precentral gyrus and thence directly via the pyramidal tract to motor neurons controls the distal musculature and is responsible for the control of relatively independent finger movements. With interruption of either the cortico-cortical connections or the pyramidal tract, the animal was unable to shape its hand in such a way as to dislodge a pellet from a groove whose orientation could be determined visually. Instead, the animal could reach for the pellet, but without preshaping its

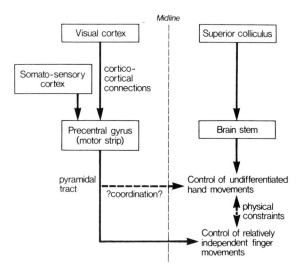

Figure 9
The pyramidal pathway supports schemas for differentiated finger movements; the
extrapyramidal system provides the substrate for a rough grasp schema.

hand, and would then move its hand back and forth under tactile control
until by chance the pellet was dislodged. At that time, the tactile freedback
sufficed to allow the animal to grasp the pellet efficiently and bring it to its
mouth.

Muir amd Lemon (1983) added further support to the hypothesis that
direct corticomotoneuronal connections confer the ability to perform discrete finger movements, but their work suggests that cells of motor cortex
may be seen as related not so much to specific muscle contractions as to
the activation of muscles within the execution of a specific motor schema.
They identified a subpopulation of pyramidal-tract neurons (PTNs) with
direct influences on motor neurons of small hand muscles, finding that
these PTNs are active in the "precision grasp schema" (when the muscles
are used to position the fingers independently) but not in the "power grasp
schema" (when a generalized co-contraction flexes all the muscles together).
The "power grasp schema" must thus be represented by neurons elsewhere. (For more on the power and precision grips, their anatomical basis,
and how the decision about which grasp to use depends on the task rather
then the shape of the tool, see Napier 1956 and 1962.)

Distributed Motor Control

Pitts and McCulloch (1947) offered a model of the superior colliculus in which each collicular neuron was connected to motoneurons, whose firing would cause a contraction of oculomotor muscles that would turn the eye in such a way as to center the gaze in the direction corresponding retinotopically to the given point in the superior colliculus. Crucially, their model predicts that the response to a complex visual stimulus will drive the gaze to the center of gravity of the visual pattern. This led Arbib (1972, p. 160) to postulate a topographically structured "distributed motor controller" as a basic component of motor systems. The controller has an input surface, stimulation at a point of which will be transformed into the appropriate sequence of motoneuron commands for movement to a spatially corresponding target position. An array of inputs would then yield movement to the average of the encoded motor targets. (See the corresponding discussion of "maps as control surfaces" in Arbib 1981.) The hypothesis, then, is that when we look for motor schemas as instantiated in the brain, we should look for a brain region in which inputs are coded retinotopically or somatotopically and in which activity of an input population yields movement to an average target. Such structures have been found by McIlwain (1982) and by Georgopoulos et al. (1983a, b), who worked independent of each other.

McIlwain (1982) found that microstimulation in the intermediate gray layer of the cat's superior colliculus yielded widespread synaptic activation of the layer. Yet such stimuli evoked saccades whose metrics seemed to depend primarily on the location of the stimulating electrode. This led McIlwain to postulate, in what may be seen as an updating of the Pitts-McCulloch model in the light of the findings of Robinson (1972, 1981) in monkeys, that the spatial densities of the cells projecting to vertical and horizontal generators of the saccadic system vary systematically beneath the retinotopic collicular map.

In studies more closely related to hand control, Georgopoulos et al. (1983a,b) recorded neurons in motor cortex of rhesus monkeys contralateral to the arm engaged in moving a manipulandum to capture a visual target. They found that 75 percent of the task-related cells discharged at higher frequencies with movements in a particular direction and at progressively lower frequencies with movements made in directions farther and farther from the preferred one. Thus, a large population of cells was involved in each movement. In their variant of the Pitts-McCulloch hypothesis, the vector model, Georgopoulos et al. advanced the hypothesis that each cell should be viewed as casting a "vote" for movement in its preferred direction, with the weight of that vote given by the amount (positive or negative) by which its firing rate exceeded the average rate; they were then able to show that the corresponding vector sum of neurally coded directions did indeed closely match the direction of arm movement.

However, the results of Georgopoulos et al. suggest that for this motor schema it is the direction of movement and not its endpoint that is the principal determinant of cell discharge. Since Polit and Bizzi (1979) have posited that the endpoint of the movement is the controlled spatial variable, this suggests that we must search for a re-coding process other than in motor cortex. Of course, the problem is ever more subtle, as can be seen by examining figure 3 of Georgopoulos et al. 1983b, which shows the time course of EMG activity of thirteen muscles during movements in one direction. Not only is there a (frequently bimodal) time course for each EMG trace, but most muscles have different resting levels of EMG before and after the movement. Thus, these traces exhibit the activity of the two classes of motor schemas discussed above: the "fast move" (which involves both acceleration and deceleration) and the "hold" (which also serves as the second "slow move" schema of our two-phase analysis).

Conclusion

In exploring the theme of vision, brain, and cooperative computation, we have stressed the cooperative use of vision and touch in the control of movement, be it in humans or in robots. We have suggested that a complex behavior is controlled by a coordinated-control program in which perceptual schemas provide appropriate parameters to motor schemas. Thus, we stress vision neither as a labeling process nor as a process of generating a geometric model (though both classification and approximate geometric modeling do play roles) but rather as a process for delivering task-dependent information.

On the motor side, we have stressed the notion of virtual fingers as a concept for hierarchical structuring of movement, and have analyzed the way in which many movements are divided into an initial fast phase and a subsequent slow phase. Our suggestion is that this is appropriate for a system that is to move quickly but which is not completely accurate. The initial target is calculated so as to make it highly unlikely that, with any expectable error of movement, contact will be made during the fast phase of the movement. However, if this offset is judged carefully so that only a small distance remains, the second phase, although executed slowly, will not take much time. The combination achieves overall speed while minimizing the risk of collision.

Acknowledgment

The preparation of this paper was supported in part by grant ECS-8108818 from the National Science Foundation.

References

Arbib, M. A. 1972. *The Metaphorical Brain: An Introduction to Cybernetics as Artificial Intelligence and Brain Theory.* Wiley-Interscience.

Arbib, M. A. 1981. Perceptual structures and distributed motor control. In *Handbook of Physiology—The Nervous System, II. Motor Control,* ed. V. B. Brooks (American Physiological Society).

Arbib, M. A., T. Iberall, and D. Lyons. 1983. Coordinated Control Programs for Movements of the Hand. Technical Report 83-25, Department of Computer and Information Science, University of Massachusetts, Amherst; *Experimental Brain Research Suppl.* (1985): 111–129.

Brinkman, J., and H. G. J. M. Kuypers. 1972. Splitbrain monkeys: Cerebral control of ipsilateral and contralateral arm, hand, and finger movements. *Science* 176: 536–539.

Brooks, V. B. 1979. Motor programs revisited. In *Posture and Movement,* ed. R. E. Talbot and D. R. Humphrey (Raven).

Evarts, E. V. 1981. Role of motor cortex in voluntary movement in primates. In *Handbook of Physiology—The Nervous System, II. Motor Control,* ed. V. B. Brooks (American Physiological Society).

Georgopoulos, A. P., R. Caminiti, J. F. Kalaska, and J. T. Massey. 1983a. Spatial coding of movement: A hypothesis concerning the coding of movement direction by motor cortical populations. In *Neural Coding of Motor Performance,* ed. J. Massion, J. Paillard, W. Schultz, and M. Wiesendanger (Springer-Verlag).

Georgopoulos, A. P., J. F. Kalaska, M. D. Crutcher, R. Caminiti, and J. T. Massey. 1983b. The representation of movement direction in the motor cortex: Single cell and population studies. In *Dynamic Aspects of Neocortical Function,* ed. G. M. Edelman, W. M. Cowan, and W. E. Gall (Wiley).

Gregory, R. L. 1969. On how so little information controls so much behavior. In *Towards a Theoretical Biology, 2: Sketches,* ed. C. H. Waddington (Edinburgh University Press).

Haaxma, R., and H. G. J. M. Kuypers. 1974. Role of occipitofrontal cortico-cortical connections in visual guidance of relatively independent hand and finger movements in rhesis monkeys. *Brain Research* 71, no. 2–3: 361–366.

Iberall, T., G. Bingham, and M. A. Arbib. 1984. Opposition Space as a Structuring Concept for the Analysis of Skilled Hand Movements. Presented at Generation and Modulation of Actions Patterns Symposium, Bielefeld, Federal Republic of Germany. *Experimental Brain Research Suppl.* (in press).

Jeannerod, M. 1981. Intersegmental coordination during reaching at natural visual objects. In *Attention and Performance IX*, ed. J. Long and A. Baddely (Erlbaum).

Jeannerod, M. 1984. The timing of natural prehension movements. *Journal of Motor Behavior* 16, no. 3: 235–254.

Jeannerod, M., and B. Biguer. 1982. Visuomotor mechanisms in reaching within extrapersonal space. In *Analysis of Visual Behavior*, ed. D. J. Ingle, M. A. Goodale, and R. J. W. Mansfield (MIT Press).

Jeannerod, M., F. Michel, and C. Prablanc. 1984. The control of hand movements in a case of hemianaesthesis following a parietal lesion. *Brain* 107: 899–920.

Lyons, D. 1982. The Use of Hands in Providing a Mechanism for Achieving the State of Non-Sobriety in a Human. Department of Computer and Information Science, University of Massachusetts, Amherst.

MacKay, D. M. 1966. Cerebral organization and the conscious control of action. In *Brain and Conscious Experience*, ed. J. Eccles (Springer-Verlag).

McIlwain, J. T. 1982. Lateral spread of neural excitation during microstimulation in intermediate gray layer of cat's cuperior colliculus. *Journal of Neurophysiology* 47, no. 2: 167–178.

Muir, R. B., and R. N. Lemon. 1983. Corticospinal neurons with a special role in precision grip. *Brain Research* 261: 312–316.

Napier, J. 1956. The prehensile movements of the human hand. *Journal of Bone and Joint Surgery* 38B, no. 4: 902–913.

Napier, J. 1962. The evolution of the hand. *Scientific American* 207, no. 6: 56–62.

Navas, F., and L. Stark. 1968. Sampling or intermittency in hand control system dynamics. *Biophys. Journal* 8: 252–302.

Pitts, W. H., and W. S. McCulloch. 1947. How we know universals, the perception of auditory and visual forms. *Bull. Math. Biophys.* 9: 127–147.

Polit, A., and E. Bizzi. 1979. Characteristics of motor programs underlying arm movements in monkeys. *Journal of Neurophysiology* 42, no. 1: 183–194.

Robinson, D. A. 1972. Eye movements evoked by collicular stimulation in alert monkey. *Vision Research* 12, no. 11: 1795–1808.

Robinson, D. A. 1981. Control of eye movements. In *Handbook of Physiology— The Nervous System, II. Motor Control*, ed. V. B. Brooks (American Physiological Society).

14   Robot Tactile Sensing and Schema Control

Kenneth J. Overton

Rapid developments in the field of robotics are making the machines more numerous, adaptable, reliable, precise, and inexpensive. Current robots, ranging from those available commercially to experimental prototypes, are beginning to be equipped with optical, tactile, and force sensors and a variety of special-purpose sensors. While they are making increasing use of sensory feedback regarding their relation to the work environment, most industrial robots remain "blind," "deaf," "dumb" and lack the "sense of touch." The development of more sophisticated robots requires research on the increasingly subtle use of sensory input in the control of robots. The intent is to develop robots that will react to the particulars of a dynamic environment in a flexible way.

To a great extent, work to date has exhibited a distinct task-by-task approach, with little regard for a general theory concerning the integration of sensory information into the control of robots. In most cases, the task is completely specified and is performed in a heavily constrained, known environment (Rosen et al. 1978). Recently, vision systems and certain forms of force compensation have found increasing use in helping to remove the requirement of complete specificity (VanderBrug et al. 1979). The state of the art in robotics, however, has yet to include tactile sensation and dynamic visual input, flexible control structures, and data-driven models of the environment.

This paper discusses two areas relevant to these issues. In the first section, tactile array sensors are reviewed and the device used for the experimentation discussed in this paper is presented. The characteristics of the tactile domain are outlined, and some experiments in tactile image processing are presented. In the second section I suggest a method of control using multimodal sensory information through the development of schemas.

Tactile Perception

Tactile array sensors are devices that provide information regarding the distribution of force, or deflection present at the interface between the sensory surface and the object. These devices produce an array of numbers corresponding to the magnitudes of the stimulus at each sensing point. The arrays of numbers, called *force images,* are composed of individual force elements, or *forcels.* The "ideal" tactile sensor would exhibit several desirable characteristics (Harmon 1981): physical ruggedness, reasonable fabrication cost, high spatial resolution, low hysteresis, high sensitivity, large dynamic range, and monotonic response. A number of researchers have been developing and using tactile array sensors. A hand constructed by Hill and Sword (1979) employed analog force-sensing arrays. Larcombe (1976) developed a sensor utilizing woven graphite fibers as the physical transducer. The "artificial skin" tactile array sensor developed by Clot and Briot at the LAAS in Toulouse utilizes pressure-variable transverse resistance to transduce the forces present on the pad (Clot and Faliou 1977, 1978; Briot 1979). This sensor, originally developed to assist in the analysis of the pressure distribution on the sole of the foot during walking, has sparked great interest in the field of robotics. The device used by Briot in the robot experiments consisted of 100 points arranged in a 10 × 10 array with 1-cm spacing between the centers of adjacent transducers. Each transducer consisted of a center measurement electrode surrounded by an annular electrode. A homogeneous pad composed of a conductive elastomer 5 mm thick was placed on top of the contact array. A reference voltage was applied to the annular electrode, and the current entering the center electrode was measured. Since this current is proportional to the resistance through the pad, it is an indication of the force present in that area. Hillis, at MIT, has demonstrated an array sensor with 256 forcels per square centimeter utilizing a carbon-filled elastomer mounted on a mechanical finger (Hillis 1981). Purbrick, also at MIT, is investigating a slightly different sensor design (Hapgood 1983).

A number of companies have developed and are marketing tactile array sensors. The Barry Wright Corporation (1983) has demonstrated prototypes of a 16 × 16-forcel sensor, with 100 forcels per square inch, that uses the technology developed at MIT. The Lord Corporation (1983) is marketing a 12 × 8-element array sensor using an optical technology, also with a spatial density of 100 elements per square inch. Transensory Devices (1984) markets one-element tactile sensors based on a micromechanical technique. Nine of these elements are configured in a 3 × 3 matrix to produce an array sensor with sensitive sites on 0.08-inch centers. Tactile Robotic Systems (1984) is bringing to market a 16 × 16-element array that utilizes an optical transduction technique; a number of other sizes in two resolutions are also available.

The tactile array sensor used in this work is similar to the devices of Briot and Hillis in that the basic phenomenon being measured is a resistance that is proportional to the pressure being applied to the forcel. The differences, however, are significant (Overton and Williams 1981). The device is a scanned sensor, in that the pad used to transduce the force distribution is probed by scanning an array of sites in a grid of electrodes. The most difficult characteristic to be dealt with in a scanned sensor involves the electrical decoupling of the transducers. Each of the transducers is electrically isolated from the others in the pad by virtue of the fact that they are constructed as discrete entities. In addition, each forcel is connected in series with a diode, thus eliminating multiple conduction paths during scanning. The version presented here (figure 1), contains 128 forcels in a

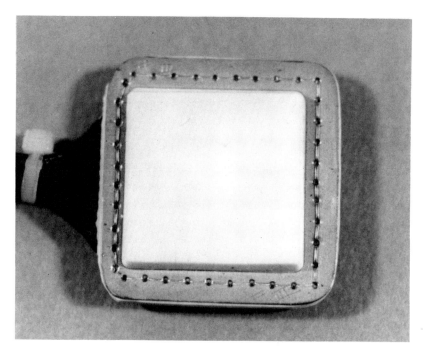

Figure 1
Tactile array sensor containing a 16 × 8 matrix of forcels in an area of 1 square inch.

1-inch-by-1-inch surface. The device is easily scanned and produces an image with no ghost images.

The generic sensor pad utilized in this design consists of a spatial array of carbon-filled elastomeric columns embedded in a nonconductive body. Each column acts as a variable resistor whose response is correlated to compression, or force. This material's resistance decreases as it is compressed. (Since the terms *compression* and *force* are related by essentially a scaling factor, they will be used interchangeably.) In addition, there are two pressure-variable contact resistances resulting from the junctions between the sensing electrodes and the elastomeric columns. These three resistances are lumped together and measured as a single variable resistance, which is indicative of the force present between the sensor element and the object being sensed.

The fact that the pad is a homogeneous block implies that there will be some mechanical interaction among neighboring elements. A great deal of my work has centered on developing an understanding of the response characteristics of the sensor. The features studied include hysteresis, the spread function, and settling of the sensor/data acquisition system. Although this information is important, it is not central to this paper, and it is discussed elsewhere (Overton 1984).

Work in tactile image processing has been done by Wolfeld (1981), Briot (1979), and Hillis (1981). Rather than detail their approaches, I will briefly discuss the constraints and assumptions that are applicable in the tactile domain. Once these have been outlined, it will be possible to develop techniques for extracting the needed information in an organized fashion. Since most of the image-processing work to date has occurred in the visual domain, it is useful to contrast the properties of that domain with those of the tactile domain. The following list summarizes the characteristics of the tactile domain, which can be used to make explicit assumptions about the domain and thereby reduce the complexity of the processing algorithms:

- Tactile data provide explicit three-dimensional information.

- There is no specularity (compared with vision).

- There are no shadows (compared with vision).

- There is no scaling distortion (compared with vision).

- There is no perspective distortion (compared with vision).

- Separation of objects from the background is straightforward.

- The information provides a local "view" of the environment.

• The act of sensing may produce a physical distortion of the stimulus.

• Occlusion assumes a form different from that in vision.

My approach to tactile image processing has developed from work in machine vision. In particular, I have been investigating the use of well-known visual image processing techniques, modified and refined in response to the characteristics of the tactile domain.

The array of numbers obtained by scanning the sensor contains a great deal of information about the shape of the object sensed, such as deflections, as well as the distribution of forces present at the interface with the object. Because of the nature of the sensor and the construction process, the individual transducers vary in response. This means that the number produced by one transducer for a given force or deflection may not be the same number produced by another transducer under the same conditions. In order for the spatial information inherent in the nature of the array sensor to be utilized, the relationship between the applied force or deflection and the output must be known for each forcel. The computational overhead of the correction algorithm and its effectiveness are of interest, since we need not only to correct images but to do so in an amount of time small enough to allow the transformed image to be processed and the resulting information to be used in robot control. Figure 2 contains a tactile image from the sensor shown in figure 1 after a simple correction algorithm has been applied. (The image was produced by pushing a cylinder onto the pad. The cylinder measured $\frac{3}{4}$ inch in length and $\frac{1}{8}$ inch in diameter and was oriented such that its major axis was inclined 30° from the vertical axis of the image.) The correction method consisted of normalizing the response of each transducer within a range determined by individually stimulating the transducers over a known force range.

A common task performed by a robot involves handling long, thin components, such as motor shafts. A very important piece of information is the angle of the shaft relative to the robot's fingertip. A tactile array sensor was affixed to the fingertip of a simple gripper, and an algorithm that determined the angle of long, thin objects held by the machine was implemented. A line was fitted to the above-threshold forcels in the image by a least-squares technique. A coefficient relating how well the scatter of the above-threshold forcels fits a line was used to determine whether a given image contained a long, thin object. If the correlation coefficient was above a threshold, it was assumed that a long, thin object was being touched, and the angle of the axis (defined by the regression line) was returned as the angle of the object relative to the robot's gripper.

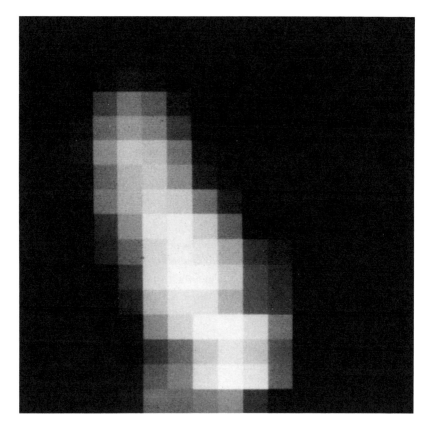

Figure 2
Image of $\frac{3}{4} \times \frac{1}{8}$-inch cylinder after application of simple correction technique.

A second algorithm demonstrates the usefulness of the tactile array sensor in determining the salient information about a feature of the object(s) being felt. The sensor provides an "image" of the forces felt by (or the deflections of the surface of) the sensor, produced by contact between the sensor and an object in the environment. This algorithm was designed to find the center of a circular depression or peak. Such information is useful in the case where a robot must insert something in a hole. Since the tactile sensor provides explicit three-dimensional information, the result of the algorithms can be interpreted directly in terms of the robot's coordinate system. This algorithm uses two basic assumptions: that a circular feature is located somewhere in the image and that the circle has a fixed, pre-specified radius. A coordinate pair is returned every time an image is processed, regardless of whether or not there is actually a circular region in the image. In addition, it searches for regions of a specific size. It may or may not find holes of different sizes. Extensions to the algorithm have been made that alleviate the need for these assumptions.

The final algorithm to be discussed was an attempt to perform object recognition from tactile sensation. The experimental setup was again a simple two-fingered gripper with a tactile array sensor on one fingertip. The information used by this algorithm is very similar to that used by Briot in that both a tactile image and the separation of the fingertips are needed. An unknown object is grasped, and, as the manipulator begins to move, a parallel process analyzes the tactile image to identify it from a limited set of objects. The system has two phases: a presentation phase, in which each of the objects to be recognized in the future is presented to the gripper/tactile sensor system and certain data are stored, and a run-time phase, in which an object from the learned set is presented to the gripper and identified. The information stored includes a raw tactile image and the separation of the fingertips as derived from the position-sensing system in the gripper.

In the run-time phase, the gripper closes on the unidentified object, and the tactile image and the fingertip separation are stored. The new sensory information is compared with the information stored during the presentation phase, and the best match is picked as the identity of the new object. The comparison consists of normalized cross-correlation between the new and the stored tactile images and differencing of the new and the stored fingertip separation. In the correlation phase, the new image is shifted around in a small window to find the point of maximum correlation. The maximum correlation value and the (normalized) separation difference are combined in a weighted measure. The identity of the stored data producing the best match is used as the identity of the new object.

This algorithm was tested on a set of seven objects, three of which were transformers of approximately the same size but different coil/lamination orientations. The system proved to be reasonably accurate in its identification of the objects. For some objects discrimination based on the fingertip separation alone was possible, but for others the tactile image data were required.

This discussion has focused on work in the area of tactile perception, including transducer design and tactile image processing. Historically, the most active area of robot sensory research has been vision. In addition, knowledge surrounding the use of other sensory modalities, such as laser range finding and acoustic and radar imaging, is ever increasing. We are able to impart sensing capabilities of increasing sophistication to our robots.

The question that immediately arises concerns how this increased sensory input is to be used. The next section presents some ideas relating to this topic and is intended more as a basis for discussion than as a total solution.

An Informal Theory of Schemas

A robot system consists of an articulated mechanical device capable of interacting with the environment, sensors of various sorts (including vision and tactile), and a network of logical units given the responsibility of controlling the system. At present, sensory information is typically integrated into robot control at two very different levels, depending on the type of information involved. At the servo control level, velocity and position information for a given actuator are used by the control algorithms in order to achieve satisfactory performance. Force feedback information is used at a level involving the interactions of several joint/link pairs. The other extreme is exemplified by what might be called the "snapshot" paradigm for the use of visual information, in which the actions of the robot are halted, processing of visual input is requested of another unit, and this other unit collects and processes the data and returns a coded form of the information. The robot system then proceeds "blindly" on the basis of this new glimpse of the world. This approach requires the environment to be relatively static and well specified. Moreover, in this approach the functioning of the robot tends to be viewed as a serial progression of events, with only a single task or subtask implemented at any given instant. This implies discrete switching to new subtasks and an inability to change attention smoothly from one set of activities to another.

By contrast, we humans are constantly sensing the environment. Our actions provide new sensory input, which is used to modify our actions, which in turn produce more sensory input. This cycle has been termed the action perception cycle (Arbib 1981). In addition to new sensory information, an action yields an expectation of certain types of sensory stimuli. This expectation combines with the actual sensory input to provide a complex error signal, which we use in verifying and fine-tuning our movement. This section discusses a schema-theoretic approach to making such use of available sensory information in a paradigm for distributed planning and control for a robot. Such a framework must be capable of dealing with smooth transitions from one task to another in a context in which any number can be partially active. These units represent a modification of Arbib's (1981) concept of a schema.

I shall relate my schemas not so much to objects, such as coffee mugs and chairs, as to the actions afforded by them and the way humans or robots can interact with them. I shall analyze actions, or motor behavior, in terms of units of behavior called *motor schemas*. One such unit would direct a hand to grasp an object, such as a pole, given its location, size, and orientation as input. A useful motor schema for the control of locomotion would generate, given a path plan as input, the first step along that path as output. The raw patterns of sensory stimulation cannot guide movement directly. Rather, they must be interpreted in terms of objects or other "domains of interaction" in the environment (Gibson 1966, 1977). I use the term *perceptual schema* for the process whereby the system determines whether a given domain of interaction characterizes the environment. In obtaining information to guide action, a schema may fall far short of a detailed representation of an object per se. When moving beyond simple tasks, the system will be in an environment whose representation will involve the activation of a whole assemblage of schemas. The activation level of a perceptual schema represents the credibility of the hypothesis that the task represented by the schema is indeed relevant to the environment; other schema parameters will represent further properties (such as size, orientation, location, and relative motion) that should be passed to the motor schemas. The process of sensory-input matching will be carried on in parallel by any number of schemas. The activity of any particular schema is determined by how well it fits the sensory input and by the influence felt from other schemas. One type of action could be to bolster or quell the activity in another schema via cooperation and competition routines designed to facilitate these interactions.

A motor schema is a control system that continually monitors feedback from the system it controls to determine the appropriate pattern of action to achieve the motor schema's goals (which will, in general, be subgoals within some higher-level coordinated-control program). Since the controlled system may itself be variable, the motor schema must be supplied with the relevant parameters of the controlled system (for example, a grasp schema needs to know the position, size, and orientation of what is to be grasped) or must itself estimate them using a learning procedure or "identification algorithm." The identification procedure may be viewed as a perceptual schema embedded within a motor schema. (A further consideration of learning involves how schemas are constructed initially and how a particular set of instances are generalized into a new schema.)

To gain some idea of what is involved in one of these schemas, consider the process used to lift a coffee mug from a table and raise it to drink. Unless the hand is resting on the mug, the first phase of this task will involve visually locating the mug. This information provides the initial target location for a reaching movement. In some cases, knowledge from the last interaction with the mug will include positional information that eliminates the need for a visual search. The reach is intended to bring the hand into contact with the mug. Even this simple task requires planning to choose one of at least three courses of action: grasp handle to lift, grasp mug to lift, or grasp mug to turn it to bring handle into position. During the reaching, the fingers and the hand are preshaped in a way that will allow grasping of the mug. The grasp configuration is derived from percep- tions about the shape of a mug, orientation information provided from vision or from previous knowledge, and, in general, the action to be performed with the mug. This preshaping puts the fingers in the "right ballpark" for grasping.

Once the fingers are in contact with the object, they are used to haptically search the surface. As tactile information is gained, a detailed model of the object can be constructed or verified. Orientation and position information is also acquired and is used to refine the finger positions for grasping. In the "mug task," the exact position and orientation of the mug relative to the hand can be determined through tactile sensation from the shape of the cylinder of the mug or the handle. The finger and hand configurations are refined, and the mug is firmly grasped. In this stage, tactile sensation is used to provide the location and the orientation of features relevant to the task at hand (in this case, the handle and lip of the mug). For an industrial task, the features of interest could include the orientation of long, thin regions or the locations of holes in the manipulanda.

The transportation phase moves the mug from the table to the lips. This requires that the mug be accelerated and decelerated in such a manner that the contents are not spilled. In addition, the mug must remain upright. The trajectory along which the mug is moved is derived from the known (via experience) kinematics of the body. The velocity and acceleration parame- ters used in drinking from a mug, as well as the trajectory, are very dif- ferent from those employed when the mug is moved to the coffee pot to be filled. Further, when the mug is empty, a different grasp may be used, since the orientation of the mug is critical only while coffee is poured.

Motor and sensory processes contain both serial and parallel processing. Motor activity contains parallel components which are exemplified by the coactivation of reaching and preshaping the hand for grasping. In addition, serial components are required in order to allow the temporal nature of coordinated activity. Actions require direct sensory feedback and produce expectations regarding sensory input. Sensory input, in turn, provides access to further actions. This, again, is the action-perception cycle.

A schema that is to be implemented for robot control using dynamic sensing should, in some way, code both the motor activity and the sensory processing associated with some behavior. The next question that arises involves how one or more of these units become active and how they terminate their activity (either because their piece of behavior has been completed or because of some overriding external event). In short, how does a particular schema determine that the robot is in the correct domain of interaction for that schema to become active?

Consider two possible activation paradigms: forced activation by a master scheduler and activation through a competition-and-cooperation scenario. In the first case, a unit is needed that plans the activity of the robot and decomposes the plan into the appropriate temporal sequence of activations. This requires that the scheduling unit contain models of the task, of the system it controls, and of the environment, as well as specific knowledge regarding the details of the activation sequence. The use of a master scheduler sidesteps the question of activation by placing the control in the scheduler. The problem with this paradigm is not the direct activation of units but rather the amount of knowledge that must be contained in a master scheduler. I do not deny that, in some applications, a master scheduler may be appropriate. However, my interest concentrates on distributed control strategies.

Distributed control can be accomplished by having all the units continually monitor appropriate signal sets (which may include, but need not be restricted to, the sensory input and the goal state of the system). A particular unit becomes active only when the input matches the prerequisites for that unit or when directly activated by another unit. Once an action has been initiated, temporal activation of additional units is not only reasonable but required. Distributed control eliminates the need for a single unit to possess knowledge of the entire world, goal state, and specific details of the way in which the robot should act.

These units then need the following major components: an activation mechanism, an event section, and a tuning component. The activation mechanism monitors both the current goal state(s) of the system and part or all of the sensory input and activates or deactivates the unit upon preset conditions in both areas. The event section consists of a number of components which yield both parallel and serial activity, and comprises the "behavioral" section of the unit. There may also be a "tracing component" (not necessarily disjoint from the others) to allow adaptation, or tuning, of the schema over time.

This idea of input matching activating an "event" section of the schema may, at first pass, appear very similar to a production system. When examined in more detail, several differences become apparent. Recall that in a production system an exact match of the preconditions of a rule elicits immediate execution of the corresponding action. In schema activation, not only are the preconditions usually extremely complicated and parametrized but the efficacy of the event, or the action on a given actuator, is determined by both the activation level of the schema and the set of other active schemas also providing input to that actuator. In addition, the tracing component of a schema provides some history of the schema activation. Such a mechanism is not inherent in production systems.

Communication between the units is accomplished via the activation sections. Cooperation is accomplished when one unit's activity bolsters the activity level of another unit by changing the other's goal state or increasing the desired input through its own activities, or both. Competition occurs when one unit's activities change the goal state away from that needed for another to activate or reduce the positive sensory input, or both.

This "information" can be used in discussing the last experiment outlined in the preceding section. Recall that the purpose of this experiment was to recognize a part being "felt" by a tactile-sensor-equipped gripper from a set of known parts. The tactile-sensor image and the fingertip separation were used in the identification process. This process could be viewed in a number of ways according to the preceding discussion of schemas. One approach would require that each object (and the set of actions it affords) be represented by a separate schema. At any given instant, all these schemas would be monitoring the tactile-sensor image and the gripper-position feedback system. The activation of a schema would reflect the degree of match between the sensed tactile image and the image stored during the presentation phase and the sensed and stored fingertip separation. In the experiment, the only action taken once an object was identified, i.e., its schema's activation level became elevated relative to those of the other objects, was to display a message. In practice, the increased activation of the perceptual schema corresponding to a given object would initiate the associated event section. This latter section would contain actions as well as further sensing and would encode how the robot is to interact with the object under the current sensory conditions.

Acknowledgment

This work was supported by the Laboratory for Perceptual Robotics in the Department of Computer and Information Science at the University of Massachusetts under NSF grant ECS-8108818.

References

Arbib, M. A. 1981. Perceptual structures and distributed motor control. In *Handbook of Physiology*, Neurophysiology section, volume III: Motor Control, ed. V. B. Brooks (American Physiological Society).

Barry Wright Corporation, Watertown, Mass. 1983. Product literature on Model TS 402 Tactile Sensor System.

Briot, M. 1979. The utilization of an "artificial skin" sensor for the identification of solid objects. In Proceedings of the Ninth International Symposium and Exposition on Industrial Robots, Washington, D.C.

Clot, J., and J. Faliou. 1977. Project Pilote SPARTACUS: Etude d'un capteur tactile (eau artificielle) utilize comme detecteur d'efforts de pression et de glissement. Publication LAAS 1629, Centre National de la Recherche Scientifique, Laboratoire d'Automatique et d'Analyse des Systems, Toulouse.

Clot, J., and J. Faliou. 1978. Realization d'otheses pneumatiques madulaires, Etude d'un detecteur de pressions. Publication LAAS 1852, Centre National de la Recherche Scientifique, Laboratoire d'Automatique et d'Analyse des Systems, Toulouse.

Gibson, J. J. 1966. *The Senses Considered as Perceptual Systems.* Allen and Unwin.

Gibson, J. J. 1977. The theory of affordances. In *Perceiving, Acting and Knowing*, ed. R. E. Shaw and J. Bransford (Erlbaum).

Hapgood, F. 1983. Inside a robotics lab: The quest for automatic touch. *Technology Illustrated*, April, pp. 18–22.

Harmon, L. D. 1981. Automated Tactile Sensing. Department of Biomedical Engineering, Case Western Reserve University.

Hill, J. W., and A. J. Sword. 1979. Manipulation based on sensor-directed control: An integrated end effector and touch sensing system. In Proceedings of the Annual Human Factor Society Convention, Washington, D.C.

Hillis, W. D. 1981. Active Touch Sensing. AI Memo 629, Artificial Intelligence Laboratory, Massachusetts Institute of Technology.

Larcombe, M. H. E. 1976. Tactile sensors, sonar sensors, and parallax sensors for robot applications. In Proceedings of the Third Conference on Robot Technology and Sixth International Symposium on Industrial Robots, University of Nottingham.

Lord Corporation. 1983. Technical description of Lord Corporation Touch Sensor, Model LTS200. Industrial Automation Program, Lord Corporation, 407 Gregson Drive, Cary, N.C. 27511.

Overton, K. J. 1984. The Acquisition, Processing and Use of Tactile Sensor Data in Robot Control. Ph.D. dissertation, University of Massachusetts, Amherst.

Overton, K. J., and T. W. Williams. 1981. Tactile sensing for robots. In Proceedings of the Seventh International Joint Conference on Artificial Intelligence.

Rosen, C., et al. 1978. Machine Intelligence Research Applied to Industrial Automation. Eighth report, SRI International.

Tactile Robotics Systems, Sunnyvale, Calif. 1984. Product literature on TRS1616 tactile array sensor and interface.

Transensory Devices, Fremont, Calif. 1984. Tactile Perceptions product literature, TP40xx series.

VanderBrug, G. J., J. S. Albus, and E. Barkmeyer. 1979. A vision system for real time control of robots. In Proceedings of the Ninth International Symposium and Exposition on Industrial Robots, Washington, D.C.

Wolfeld, J. A. 1981. Time Control of a Robot Tactile Sensor. M.S. thesis, Moore School of Engineering, University of Pennsylvania.

IV

Connectionism and Cooperative Computation

The term *connectionism* has recently come to refer to a parallel style of computing carried out by networks composed of locally interconnected computing elements. The elements of such networks are often simple; their inputs are restricted to local areas of data and information obtained from their neighboring elements in the network. Each processing element generally maintains one or more competing plausible interpretations of the local data. Information from neighboring elements is used to inhibit or excite subsets of the interpretations, which causes the local element to update its interpretations. The networks are typically iterative (that is, several update cycles are necessary), and the goal is the formation of a globally coherent interpretation of the data. These networks bear a strong resemblance to early models of neural networks, to the relaxation algorithms used in computer vision (see the papers by Zucker and Tsotsos in this volume), and a variety of natural phenomena (e.g., heat flow in planar sheets). The following papers explore various formulations of the connectionist style of computing, examine its relevance to computer vision and neuroscience, and attempt to relate it to the mechanisms underlying biological computing.

Sejnowski and Hinton explore the role of parallel search in early vision. Noting that many early-vision problems can be formulated as search problems (such as stereopsis, grouping, and figure-ground separation), they propose a relaxation-type stochastic search process for a simplified figure-ground separation task. Their search process is similar to classical relaxation, but is cast in the connectionist paradigm. Figure units and edge units, organized retinotopically, are interconnected so that figure units support other figure units and collinear bounding edge units. Each state of each unit is assigned an energy level as a function of active neighbors and any other more global information. The search problem is then one of finding a combination of states that has a local energy minimum; the solution is based on statistical mechanics and, in particular, on a procedure known as simulated annealing. The resulting system and its components have a number of properties in common with networks of neurons. An interesting observation is that noise in the system ensures convergence (by randomly forcing the system to consider locally nonoptimal states); Sejnowski and Hinton conjecture that noise in neural networks may function in the same fashion.

How the weights between interconnecting units are set is an open question. Sejnowski and Hinton chose them carefully by hand, but it should be possible to "learn" them. Barto considers the problem of learning control surfaces (functions that map input situations into actions) by means of the connectionist paradigm, and discusses the credit-assignment problem as it applies to learning networks of this type. Barto's approach is to endow each of the local elements in a network with learning capabilities that are sophisticated enough to enable it to improve its own performance (uncertainty notwithstanding) by using locally available information. His goal is to demonstrate that components that are already capable of solving problems can interact cooperatively to solve more complex problems. Barto presents a series of learning examples illustrating parameter acquisition and modification in a variety of tasks.

Ballard examines the utility of the connectionist paradigm as a model for cortical computing by looking at two related issues: how information about the world is captured in cortical anatomy (representation) and how information is dynamically accessed and modified in order to produce interesting behaviors. His approach is to combine current computational views based on connectionism and parallel computing with emerging neurophysiological and anatomical knowledge of the cortex. His model posits two types of computing elements: value units and variable units. Value units represent the values of important parameters, although the meaning of a unit's output can change depending on the states of other units. Using this notion, abstract computations (such as finding a line in terms of oriented edges) can be defined in a distributed manner over a network that bears a strong resemblance to cortical structure.

Trehub presents a connectionist model for human visual-cognitive competence. He is concerned not only with low to intermediate-level vision, where the processed data are organized retinotopically, but also with high-level representations of objects and scenes. The basic system is composed of two modules: a synaptic matrix, which constructs associative spatial filters, and a retinoid matrix, which organizes successive retinocentric patterns into egocentric representations of object space and models spatial relationships between the system and the observed world. The second part of the paper is concerned with extending the two-dimensional system into one capable of stereopsis and with episodic learning and associative recall.

Feldman presents a connectionist model of how primates perceive objects and deal with visual space, particularly with how objects might be located and their location in space determined. The model, which is based on an action-oriented view of perception, is organized around four frames, which maintain the representation of the external world as well as the observer's relation to it. The first frame represents the features processed at each eye fixation; this information is integrated into a stable view of the world in the second frame. The third frame represents the observer's knowledge about the world (not necessarily restricted to vision), and the fourth frame captures the observer's representation of the surrounding space. An assumption of the model is that all visual features of interest can be represented as explicit parameter values in a suitably defined representation (cf. Ballard). Feldman's model may be viewed as operating primarily at the symbolic level, and hence is quantitatively and qualitatively different from those considered in the other papers in this part.

15   A Functional Model of Vision and Space

Jerome A. Feldman

There is a standard way of designing large, complex information-processing systems. One starts with the functional requirements (what the system must do) and the constraints on the available resources. The first step is to divide the system into functional components that partition the overall task into relatively autonomous parts. Second, one chooses the representation of information within the subsystems and the languages of communication among them. Hanson and Riseman (1985) analyzed several computer-vision systems at this level. Third, the details of the subsystems are specified and coded. Finally, the subsystems are tested individually, pairwise, and in toto. Essentially the same methods are employed for analyzing unknown large information-processing systems when circumstances require it. It is at least possible that a similar paradigm would be of some use in studying complex biological systems, such as the primate visual system. Such system analysis complements the detailed study of particular mechanisms that characterizes most of visual science.

I have been engaged for some time in attempting to use this approach to develop a provisional model of how primates perceive objects and deal with their visual environments. The model tries to cover the entire range from behavior and phenomenological experience to detailed neural encodings in crude but computationally plausible reductive steps. The problems addressed include perceptual constancies, eye movements and the stable visual world, object descriptions, and the representation of extrapersonal space. All these problems have received extensive attention, and many of the theoretical constructs have long histories. But the attempt to treat all these issues in a coherent computational framework appears to be new and potentially promising. The entire development is based on an action-oriented notion of perception. The observer is assumed to be continuously sampling the ambient light for information of current value. The central problem of vision is taken to be the categorizing and locating of objects in

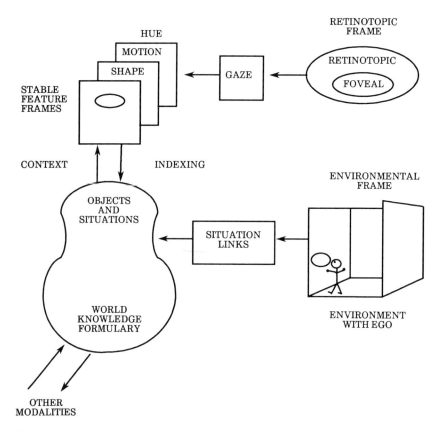

Figure 1
Four frames.

the environment. The critical step in this process is the linking of visual information to object descriptions; this is called *indexing,* from the analogy with identifying a book from terms in its index. The system must also identify situations and use this knowledge to guide movement and other actions in the environment. My treatment focuses on the different representations of information used in the visual system. I suggest that the following kind of loose discussion provides an adequate reason to suppose that at least four frames of reference will be needed to describe vision and space.

The representation of information in the first frame of figure 1 is intended to model the view of the world that changes with each eye movement. The second frame must deal with the phenomena surrounding what used to be called "the illusion of a stable visual world." A static observer has the experience of (and can perform as if he held) a visual scene much more uniform than the one the foveal-periphery first frame is processing at each fixation. One can think of the second frame as associated with the position of the observer's head; this is an oversimplification, but it conveys the right kind of relation between the two frames. Of course, neither of these frames is like a photographic image of the world, as even a casual examination of the structure of the visual system shows. Light striking the retina is already transformed, and the layers of the retina, the thalamus, and the visual cortex all compute complex functions. The crucial difference between the first two frames is that the first one is totally updated with each saccade and the second is not. The current model also assumes that the first frame—the *retinotopic frame* (RF)—computes proximal stimulus features and the second captures distal (constancy, intrinsic) features as well as being stable (it is therefore called the *stable feature frame*, or SFF). As a crude approximation, one can identify the RF with striate and the SFF with extrastriate visual cortex (Ballard, this volume).

The third and fourth representational frames are both multimodal and thus are unlikely to be the same as the first two. The third representation is not primarily geometrical and will be described in the next paragraph. The fourth frame—the *environmental frame* (EF)—is intended to model an animal's representation of the space around it at a given moment. It captures the information that enables one to locate quickly the source of a stimulus from sound, wind, smell, or a verbal cue, as well as maintaining the relative location of visual phenomena not currently in view. For a variety of reasons, the model proposes a single allocentric environmental frame, which gets mapped, by *situation links*, to the current situation and the observer's place in it. The EF corresponds loosely to posterior parietal cortex (Sakata et al. 1980).

The final representational frame to be considered is the observer's general knowledge of the world, including items not dealing with either vision or space. I follow the conventional wisdom in assuming that this knowledge is captured in relational form, modeled in this case by a special kind of semantic network. One kind of knowledge encoded will be the visual appearance of objects. These descriptions have much of the character of Minsky's (1975) frames and of the object-centered frames of Hrechanyk and Ballard (1983) and Hinton (1981). Since the other three representations are organized geometrically, I will refer to the collection of semantic knowledge as the *world knowledge formulary* (WKF), to emphasize its nature as a collection of information in abstract form. The substrate of phenomenological perception is assumed to be the stable feature frame, but to respond to a percept requires its categorization in the WKF. The WKF representation is independent of viewing conditions and is more like a verbal description of something not currently in view. The WKF will carry much of the burden of integrating information from the other three frames. It is far from adequately worked out in this paper, but all we need for now is the notion that the semantic-network representation is likely to be quite different from that of the RF, the SFF, or the EF. All this suggests that even a provisionary model of vision and space will require at least four representational frames.

The initial exposition of four frames was based on a static observer and a basically static environment. Most of the detailed discussion in subsequent sections retains this restriction, but the model does attempt to cover motion as well. One major additional construct needed is to postulate explicitly that the entire system has a second mode of operation: the *pursuit mode.* To get a feeling for the difference between the two modes, track your finger as you move it along the second line of text on this page. Now go back and read the line of text, using your finger as a pointer. There is considerable evidence that the pursuit mode is computationally distinct and is used for navigation while moving as well as for tracking.

One of the principal devices employed in the current model is the assumption that all the visual features of interest can be reduced to explicit parameter values in some representational space. Typical parameter spaces include color spaces, spatial-frequency channels, and slant-tilt maps for surface orientation. The mapping of primitive shapes, textures, and motions to parameter spaces remains problematic, but the model assumes that it must be done (Ballard, this volume). A computational advantage of this total parametrization of visual features is that all of the subsequent discussion can be framed as discrete computational problems. More important, the assumption that early vision computes discrete values of fixed parameters supports a clear view of such phenomena as apparent motion. From the stream of visual input, the visual system continuously calculates the best fit to the critical parameters. The best fit is, of course, sometimes nonveridical, giving rise to apparent motion, shape, and so on. If the computational model is sound, then careful study of illusions, metacontrast, and the like should lead to an understanding of the critical parameters and their possible values. This is the traditional goal of perceptual psychology; an explicit computational model permits the expression of more comprehensive and quantitative theories.

One essential requirement of a computational model of vision and space is that it be massively parallel. In addition to the obvious parallelism of the

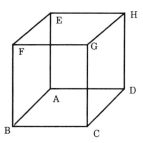

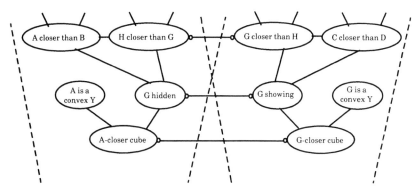

Figure 2
The Necker cube.

retina and early vision, simultaneous massive interaction between computational units within and across levels of organization of the visual system
is required. A great deal of recent work has been dedicated to defining and
studying massively parallel systems of neuron-like units (Feldman and
Ballard 1982; Feldman 1982; Sejnowski and Hinton, this volume). In this
paper I will treat computational units informally and just assume that each
unit's activity reflects the confidence that some feature has a particular
value. Exploiting the reduction of all visual features to explicit parameters
makes it possible to devote an individual computational unit to each
separate value of each parameter and allow all these units to interact.
Competing *coalitions* of such units will be the organizing principle behind
most of the models. Consider the two alternative readings of the Necker
cube (figure 2). At each level of visual processing, there are mutually
contradictory units representing alternative possibilities. The dashed lines
denote the boundaries of coalitions which embody the alternative interpre-

tations of the image. The units connected by circular-tipped arcs are assumed to inhibit one another, and the others to excite one another. The units in figure 2 each represent a distinct entity and are thus like the infamous "grandmother cells." Most of my constructions will employ such dedicated units for simplicity; my suggestions on how this relates to neural encodings are outlined below and discussed in detail in Ballard's paper.

The four-frames model is mainly an attempt to provide a coherent structure for relating the myriad findings on vision and space. To keep the paper of manageable size, emphasis is placed on filling in the gaps between existing theories and models of different aspects of vision and space. Somewhat surprisingly, I have encountered no other contemporary effort to do this, even at a discursive level. There are, of course, a large number of researchers whose ideas have had a marked effect on the enterprise, Barlow (1981) has stressed the use of computational as well as physiological constraints in studying the visual system and suggested an important role for parameter spaces. Among perceptual psychologists, Gregory (1970) and Hochberg (1978) are closest in spirit to the current enterprise. Haber (1983) has suggested a synthesis of this line of thought with Gibsonian ideas on early vision, and his treatment of low-level vision and space appears to agree with mine.

My approach to the problem is like that of Marr (1982) in that I place primary emphasis on computational adequacy while requiring consistency with biological and behavioral findings. Much of Marr's effort was directed toward problems at a lower level than those addressed here. His primal sketch (augmented with motion, color, and disparity data) could serve as the RF. In the areas of overlap, the two models agree on the use of hierarchical, object-oriented descriptions and disagree on the SFF and the importance of context and visual cues other than shape. More generally, my treatments of the SFF and the WKF, indexing, and context appear to be natural extensions of current computer-vision practice (Ballard and Brown 1982) to massively parallel hardware. There has been relatively little computational work on space models, but the work that has been done (Kuipers 1973; McDermott 1980) fits well into "situation" treatment. Before discussing how the four-frames model articulates with behavioral and biological studies, I will give a computational analysis of the model.

The Four-Frames Model in a Small World

One problem in trying to think coherently about vision and space is the enormous number of entities involved at every level. In this section I will

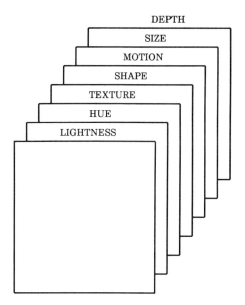

Figure 3
The six feature (and depth) planes for the small world SFF.

present a fairly detailed examination of the interactions among the four frames, but at a very coarse grain. The small-world development has been crucial to the elaboration of the current model and will hopefully also be easier for others to work with. The idea is simply to reduce the problem to a manageable size while retaining the essential structure of the real visual system. The maps representing visual information have 10 × 10 units rather than the realistic value of 1,000 × 1,000. Other parameters, such as the number of stimulus dimensions (features) and their possible values, are similarly reduced in scale. The computational issues arising in moving to realistic scale are discussed in Feldman 1985 and in Ballard's paper.

The present discussion begins with the problem of linking visual-feature information with the knowledge of how objects in the world can appear. The problem of going from a set of visual features to the description of a situation—the *indexing problem*—is taken to be the central problem of vision. The small world we will consider in detail has six distinct visual features, each with ten possible values (figure 3). Assume for now that any object in the small world can be characterized by some particular set of values for the six features. This would mean that each object has a distinct six-digit visual code. If the system could always reliably extract the values for the visual features, it would not be hard to identify which objects were in which places in the current environment. No additional problems would arise if some objects had multiple codes among the 1 million available. But the system, as specified, would break down if two objects needed to share the same code (i.e., looked identical relative to our set of features and values).

The six particular visual features that have been chosen are intended to elucidate the major scientific problems in intermediate-level vision, and would not be the best choice for a practical computer-vision system. It is assumed for now that the best value at each position of the current view is continuously maintained by parameter network computations (Ballard 1984). Some of the parametrizations are turning out to be rather subtle. For example, it appears that natural textures can be well characterized by fractal parameters (Pentland 1984). Features such as size and shape, which cover several units, are assumed to be represented by a single unit at the center of the region covered. This formulation assumes the solution of the segmentation problem, the partitioning of the image into meaningful regions. This is a major concern of computer vision (Ballard and Brown 1982; Riseman and Hanson, this volume). Its relation to the four-frames model is discussed in Feldman 1985.

The feature values are used mainly for indexing and are chosen to be maximally useful for that purpose. Typical cases are shape = cylindrical, hue = violet, and motion = flying. The treatment of motion as just another feature entails a significant scientific commitment. There is currently no satisfactory treatment, at any level, of how time and space changes are integrated into perceptual units. My model assumes that the time-space signal is separated into object features and motion parameters in early vision. This appears to be consistent with the findings of Burt and of Burr and Ross (this volume) and with the computational work of Ballard (1984). In addition to its computational advantages, the idea of best fit to motion parameters helps explain various apparent motion phenomena.

The model specified so far has almost no content, but several important points can already be seen. The most important point is that discrete values for a fixed set of visual features provide a natural base for indexing, and all my models will assume this structure. The second point is that the visual features chosen will determine which distinctions the system is capable of, as is already well known in classical pattern recognition. An obvious consequence is that the features used for indexing should be as invariant as possible under different viewing conditions. This suggests that, for indexing, the "constancy" properties (e.g., reflectance, physical size, and solid shape) should be used rather than proximal or image features.

The six visual features used in indexing are lightness, hue, texture, shape, motion, and size. Obviously enough, ten values of these features (even in logarithmic scales) are not enough to characterize visual appearance in the real world; but the small world is rich enough to exhibit most of the required problems. The model assumes that the six features are continuously updated in six parallel 10×10 arrays intended to map the currently visible external world. There is also assumed to be a (ten-valued logarithmic) depth map maintained as part of the same structure (figure 3). The depth map is needed for calculating constancy features such as object size and is also used directly in mapping the environment. The depth map is calculated cooperatively with the six feature planes, using binocular and other cues. These seven parallel arrays, along with some auxiliary structure, constitute the stable feature frame.

The stable feature frame takes its name from its two main properties: it encodes visual feature values and it is stable over fixations. The SFF is the basic interface between the visual system and the more general world knowledge represented in the WKF. The idea is that the SFF at all times maintains a map of the visual properties of the part of the world that is currently in view. I will describe later in this section how the SFF interacts with the RF in maintaining a stable visual world. Assuming that the SFF is successfully maintained, I now address the problem of how its feature values can be employed to capture knowledge of the objects in the current environment (and their activities). Thus, I return to the indexing problem.

The first notion of appearance models was that each object could be characterized by one or more sets of feature values. For objects that are sufficiently simple, this is not a bad approximation. You can probably name an object that is an approximately 1.5-inch white sphere and is uniformly pockmarked even before seeing it hook into the rough. But for complex objects like a horse or Harvard Square, the single feature set is not even the right kind of visual information. My way of handling the appearance models for complex objects and situations is, again, taken directly from current artificial-intelligence practice. I assume that the appearance of a complex object is represented (as part of one's world knowledge) as a network of nodes representing the "appearance possibilities" of components and relationships among them. This is a simplification of current AI practice (Tsotsos, this volume), but it is adequate for the present purposes.

Recall that the naive version of indexing was to use the six-digit visual feature code to look up the name of the object with that description. Complex objects are taken to be composed of parts, each part being either another complex object or a visual element that can be indexed by the six-

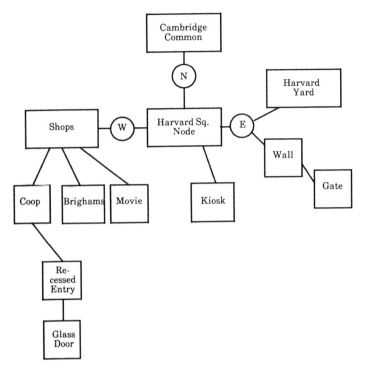

Figure 4
Harvard Square situation network. Rectangles are situations; squares are (complex) objects.

digit code. Now recall that all of our structures are assumed to be parallel and continuously active. This means that "indexing" can be continuously in progress between different areas of the SFF and networks of visual-appearance knowledge in the WKF. The crude version of this idea is to assume that each set of visual features (for a point in the 10 × 10 SFF map) picks out (indexes) the appropriate visual element. If this were to happen, a visible complex object would have many of its visual element parts activated simultaneously and should therefore be recognizable. Recognition of an object or a situation is modeled as a mutually reinforcing coalition of active nodes in the WKF. The relaxation of feature and model networks also involves top-down, context links from visual elements to the appropriate feature units (Weisstein and Wong, this volume). The network representation of a situation, such as Harvard Square (figure 4), includes objects not currently in view.

To make these notions more precise and eliminate the ghosts from our machine, one must describe all this in considerably more detail, using units

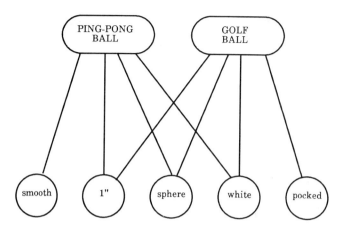

Figure 5
Ping-pong-ball and golf-ball descriptions.

like those of figure 2. (Technical definitions are given in Feldman and Ballard 1982 and in Ballard's paper in the present volume.) The various components of the SFF and the WKF will be elaborated in terms of the units. Separate units will be needed for each of the 100 spatial positions in each of the seven separate maps. It is also important to follow the unit/value principle and require a separate unit for each value of each cell in the maps above, giving a total of 7,000 units. In line with the connectionist dogma, it is assumed that visual elements are units which are connected to the appropriate set of visual-feature-value units. For example, figure 5 shows how golf-ball and ping-pong-ball descriptions in the WKF might be connected (indexed) by visual features. It is easy to see how to make connections do the same job as the index codes. Each code for a visual element is encoded as a conjunction of links from units representing the appropriate value of each feature. Using one extra collecting network, the model avoids repeating the visual element for every position in space (Feldman 1985). A visual element with multiple codes has several disjunctive "dendrites," one for each code. Visual elements that are part of a complex object are also linked into a network for representing the appearance of the object (figure 4). The general notion of representing a complex object as a network or graph of nodes is common in machine perception and will be followed here. In the small world, it will be assumed, a node corresponds to one visual element (set of feature values) and is represented by a single unit. The links between nodes are assumed to be conceptually labeled.

An important aspect of the small-world model is that situations have the same representation as complex objects in the WKF but may include several complex objects and relations among them. A *situation* is any oriented WKF network that can be mapped to the environmental frame to guide behavior. The question of whether a given network should be viewed as a situation description is not fixed in advance but is determined by the way the description is being used. Intuitively, it seems reasonable enough that a room or Harvard Square can be treated either as a situation or as an object viewed from some distance, and that the same relational knowledge could be employed in each use. Both object and situation descriptions allow for nested subdescriptions, and both can accommmodate some stylized movement.

The question of when a network description is playing the role of a situation is quite sharply defined in the model. It is assumed that at any given time there is exactly one active situation description, and that it represents the environmental situation at that time. Loosely speaking, the model has situation descriptions for places, routes, and so on, and these are linked in the WKF as a "patchwork cognitive map" (Kuipers 1973). The technical questions to be addressed here are how these situation descriptions interact with early vision (SFF) and with the (modality-independent) frame that encodes knowledge of the space around us at any time. The EF is the fourth pillar of the framework; the others are general world knowledge (WKF), features of the stable visual scene (SFF), and the instantaneous retinotopic information (RF). Again, it is crucial to think of all these frames as continuously active and interacting with one another.

The environmental frame in the small world is again unrealistically rectilinear. It postulates that the world around us is always represented as a box-like three-dimensional spatial map, as shown in figure 6. The nodes of the EF each represent a position in the space surrounding the observer, and the activation of these nodes varies with the direction of gaze. There is a mapping to nodes in the currently active situation (in the WKF) from appropriate units in the environmental frame. Every node in the currently active situation will get some potentiation just from being part of the active situation. Additionally, if one of these nodes is mapped to a position in space that is currently being gazed upon, it will receive much more potentiating input and can be said to be "anticipated." In the case of ambiguous visual input, as with the Necker cube, mechanisms like this could lead to one interpretation being preferred over another, depending on the situation.

The model includes three levels of top-down input to nodes represent-

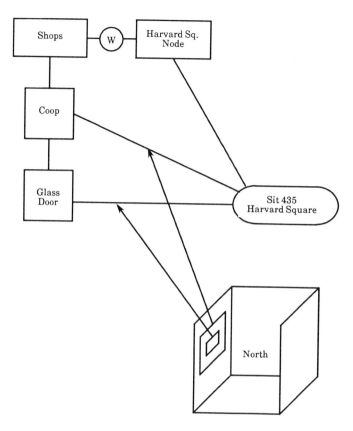

Figure 6
Two EF units of different scales activate different objects in ⟨⟨Sit. 435 = Harvard Square⟩⟩.

ing visual objects in the WKF: current situation, visible, and foveated. The proposed representation for situations and the EF are described in more detail in Feldman 1985 and in Feldman and Shastri 1984.

The model of the EF includes a subnetwork that continuously updates the position and orientation of the observer within his environment. This is clearly necessary for computing which parts of the environment are visible and foveated. The same information is assumed to be used in the gaze mapping (figure 1) linking the RF and the SFF. Although it is not so obvious, the ego position within the frame also can provide scale information, making it possible to anticipate more precisely what should be visible from a given viewpoint in the environment. This scale information combines nicely with the hierarchical nature of the visual descriptions suggested for the WKF. As the observer approaches some object, different levels of substructure become visible; the operation of the current model incorporates this in a natural way. The relative position of objects to the current egocentric position is also the basis for physical actions on objects. The model suggests that the SFF-WKF system is crude and needs visual or other sensory guidance for accurate location of objects.

For concreteness, it is assumed that the (fixed) environment frame has four directions (N, E, S, W); objects above or below the observer are omitted. Starting from the center of the map, there are four (logarithmic) distances in each direction. For things at distance 1, the observer can resolve 10×10 spatial positions. At distance 2, the resolution is 5×5. At distance 3 it is 2×2, and at distance 4 only one unit is active or not. Situations (in the WKF) are encoded in a compatible way. Each object description in a situation network has a scale at which it could be visible if gazed upon.

As the observer moves, the visible scale and position values are continuously updated. There is no apparent difficulty in also computing occlusion information, either generally through the EF or specifically in the situation description. It is assumed that situations are mapped as the active current environment, on the basis of how the observer has organized his situation memory. Some general cues as to when situations would change are going through a door, changing to a different scale of consideration, and switching from planning to acting. The technical question is exactly how the EF interacts with the current situation network. The major difficulty is providing for the mapping of a great number of possible situations onto the single fixed EF. Any connectionist model will face the problem of coupling distributed knowledge to fixed input and output systems; the scientific questions are where and how to carry out this coupling. The keys to solving the situation-EF mapping problems are situation nodes, conjunctive connections, and directly encoding only the inverse mapping. It is assumed that the EF consists of (inter alia) units that each represent a region of the currently surrounding space. Each of these units will conjunctively connect to all the objects that might be visible in its region of space in some situation. Not surprisingly, the other half of the conjunctive connection comes from a unit that is active for one particular situation. Figure 6 depicts a typical example. If the current situation is "Harvard Square" = S435, then all the objects in that situation will be receiving some activation. This means that there will be some greater than usual expectation that these objects will be chosen over their rivals in nonvisual as well as visual computations. When gaze is of a direction and a scale appropriate for some object, its node (in the WKF network) will be more strongly activated beacuse the corresponding position in the EF will be active, and this plus the currency of S435 will cause high activation of, for example, "The Coop" and "Brighams." This provides top-down bias to the relaxation between the WKF and the visual features of the SFF, the details of which are given in Feldman 1985. Finally, if a particular known object (say, the door of the Coop) is foveated, there will be even stronger top-down bias through the WKF to both the SFF and retinotopic computations.

The advantages accruing to a visual system with foveation are the focus of the description of the first basic component of the model: the retinotopic frame. Even before the details are filled in, one can see that there are several reasons why foveating an object of interest leads to better recognition:

• Certain complex calculations (e.g., color, texture) can only be done foveally.

• Bottom-up indexing of features to visual elements can be restricted to the area of the SFF being foveated (by spatial focus units), greatly reducing the possible confusions. There are also nonfoveal attentional factors (Posner and Cohen 1984; Weisstein and Wong, this volume).

• In a known environment, top-down activation from the conjunction of situation and gaze information can significantly raise the activation of an expected object or element.

These advantages reinforce one another, leading to an overwhelming advantage for foveal vision in the model. The role of peripheral vision in the model is to set and maintain contexts and to continuously monitor for change.

The retinotopic frame is primarily concerned with bringing the enormous spatial resolution and processing power of the fovea and its maps to bear on points of interest. The RF calculates the values of disparity, retinotopic motion, intensity change, etc., which are the primary inputs to the SFF. The current model assumes that there are local grouping and smoothing processes active within each feature network, but that interactions among features are carried out in the SFF. The SFF also is the means for combining the detailed descriptions of tiny patches computed by the RF.

In keeping with the rest of the development, I will describe a specific incarnation of the RF that is much too small and rectilinear but should be easier to understand. This RF has 100 spatially organized units, like the SFF, but they are laid out very differently. In the RF, 64 of the 100 spatial units are uniformly packed into an area equivalent to a 2 × 2 array of the SFF.

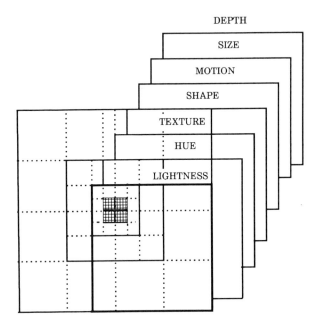

Figure 7
Retinotopic frame mapped to stable feature frame.

The remaining 36 units are formed into three surrounding rings of logarithmically decreasing resolution. In terms of SFF units, the units in the outer rings of the retinal frame cover 1, 4, and 16 squares, respectively. All this is depicted in figure 7.

Assume that the RF can (logically) move with respect to the SFF. The center of the RF can "move" to any position in the SFF except the two outermost rings. Under these conditions, the entire SFF is covered by the RF at all times. Naturally, the parts of the SFF mapped by the coarse units of the RF get only coarse information while the fovea is mapped elsewhere. Figure 7 depicts the situation where the fovea is mapped to the upper left extreme of its range, leaving most of the SFF covered by 2 × 2 and 4 × 4 retinotopic units.

The relative motion of the RF must be implemented in this scheme by a switchable conjunctive mapping. Assume that each RF unit is linked appropriately with every combination of SFF units to which it could map. Every such RF-SFF link is conjoined with a connection that specifies the currently active GAZE mapping. For example, in figure 7 the top left corner unit of the RF arrays will be mapped to the unit just beyond the fovea which is at the top left of its ring. The mappings for units other than those in this ring are not one-to-one; this will be important as we consider the interactions of the retinotopic and feature frames.

The results of Weisstein and Wong (this volume) suggest that there may be top-down priming from the SFF to the RF. This would require an inverse gaze link not shown in figure 1 but compatible with it. The flow of information in the other direction is, of course, the basic problem of low-level visual processing. The model postulates a distinct fovea and periphery in the RF and assigns quite different functions to them. The fovea (8 × 8 in this case) is assumed to have enough resolution to determine which of the discrete (ten in our case) values of the stimulus features are present in the area foveated. The SFF is assumed to be able to integrate and retain information about hue, texture, and shape, but not the direct computation of the feature values. The main purpose of the SFF is incorporating and maintaining information about the entire visible scene that is only computable foveally. The SFF does not simply transcribe retinotopic input; the seven planes interact continuously to produce a feature frame that encodes "constancy" values of size, hue, etc. The depth map is needed in the SFF to aid in constancy calculations; a number of other auxiliary calculations appear to be needed as well (Ballard, this volume). The four spatial units of the SFF planes currently mapped to the fovea of the RF dominate the calculation of feature values, but an overall consistancy must be maintained.

The peripheral 36 units of the RF play a different role. If the SFF is blank, as when a new scene is first encountered, each unit in the RF provides the same value to all the (one, four, or sixteen) units in the SFF to which it is currently mapped. These crude values become the basis for the initial relaxation toward constancy features in the SFF and (because they are there) begin indexing the visual elements in the WKF. This crude indexing provides some guidance in the choice of fixation points for further analysis of the scene (Navon 1981).

When analysis is well underway and the SFF is not blank, the periphery is assumed to function in a "change-detection" mode. The coarse values computed by peripheral units are compared with average values from the (one, four, or sixteen) SFF units covered. If there is too large a difference, an alerting signal is activated, leading (in the simple case) to a saccade to the place of change. The SFF is also assumed to contain networks for "smooth continuation" of visual properties across fixations. The networks for continuity and "filling in" phenomena are assumed to interact with the coarse values computed by the peripheral RF. The wealth of data on visual illusions and other perceptual phenomena constrains the choices of how these networks function and interact. Some of these are considered in the next section.

The Small World and the Real World

The major claim made for the four-frames model is that it is consistent with all the established facts about vision and space. It will now be clear to the reader that the claim is, at best, a qualitative one; no particular systems or range of phenomena have been modeled at a scientifically adequate level of precision. The purpose of this section is to explore the qualitative adequacy of the four-frames model and to describe some of the experimental results that led to its current form. The behavioral and neurobiological constraints on the model were chosen as broadly as possible. I deliberately attempted to incorporate only the least controversial and best established findings. This decision fits well with the relatively abstract level of the current model. It should not require delicate experiments or arguments to point out structural flaws in the four-frames model. Some potentially revealing experiments will be suggested later in this section. It is, of course, much easier to suggest experiments than to carry them out. A major purpose of this or any other model is to help suggest questions that are worth the experimental effort.

Many of the elements of the four-frames model will be easily recognizable to workers in artificial intelligence. The SFF has much in common with Ballard's (1984) parameter network, which is itself an extension of the intrinsic-image notion that is currently a major topic in computer vision. The active semantic net of the WKF fits into almost any current knowledge-representation scheme in AI or cognitive psychology. The EF and situation links are also quite like the AI models of space (Kuipers 1973; McDermott 1980) to the extent that they have been worked out. This suggests that the basic computational paradigms selected for the four frames are consistent with current mainstream AI notions of how these functions can be accomplished. The translation to connectionist modeling terms (Feldman 1985) is only partially specified in this paper, but there should be enough material to indicate that the standard AI structures and algorithms can be expressed in terms of neuron-like computing units in a way that is compact and fast enough to be biologically plausible.

A large number of technical and scientific questions will have to be answered before a functioning four-frames model can be constructed (Feldman 1985). For example, in order even to define SFF features, such as shape and size, the image must already be segmented into regions, and it has not been specified how this segmentation is to happen. How region analysis and feature extraction are cooperatively computed is described in detail in Ballard 1984. The basic idea is that the SFF also contains parameter-space networks representing the relative importance of different feature values in a given scene. Color is a particularly easy example to examine. Our ten values of hue and lightness yield 100 color values that could be present in a scene. Imagine one unit for each of these 100 values whose activity is a measure of how much of this color is in the scene. Now consider the most active color and the points in the SFF whose hue and lightness yield that color. This collection of identically colored points is a good candidate for a meaningful region, especially if the points are adjacent. If there is no significant variance in depth, texture, or motion over such a region, it will almost certainly be segmented out, and its size and shape will be computable. When the various features do not agree, humans have trouble with segmentation (as in the case of camouflage). Algorithms for forming distinct regions within a cellular computer (Minsky and Papert 1972) are not trivial. The size and the crude shape of an identified region could be calculated by a parameter network (Ballard 1984). It is assumed here that for indexing, the properties of a region are represented by the unit at its center of mass, with the other units reporting null values.

Most current research in computer vision is directed at a less abstract set of constancy features emphasizing (e.g.) local surface slant and tilt instead of shape features. Such detailed intrinsic image information could be used to compute more qualitative features, but there are alternative ways to do so (Witkin and Tenenbaum 1983). The model should be elaborated to include more details on these computations as well as those of global parameters such as the direction and color of illumination. The model should also be refined to account for the fact that there are order relationships among the features. For example, depth appears to precede lightness (Gilchrist 1977), and region properties such as size and shape presume some segmentation by depth, color, motion, and texture. All these calculations interact with one another as well as with the bidirectional (indexing and context) links to knowledge of the appearance of objects (WKF).

Another important issue is the role played by points of discontinuity (edges) in the feature frame. Both the behavioral and the physiological data indicate strongly that the visual system responds primarily to differences (e.g. in color), but the feature frame encodes point values of features. The model uses the feature frame primarily as a buffer memory and for indexing—functions that are better served by attempting to capture the (constancy) values of visual features. It might be useful to add planes representing depth discontinuities to the feature frame, and there is no problem in doing so. Depth-discontinuity points would be particularly useful in grouping regions into separate objects, and this, in turn, would greatly simplify indexing. More generally, the conversion from retinotopic (difference) information to SFF (constancy-value) information is a major prediction of the model. The model postulates that the feature frame continuously computes, among other things, smooth continuation values for feature-plane units not foveated recently.

The most difficult computational issue in the model concerns the mapping from spatially organized features in the SFF to spatially independent visual elements needed in the WKF. This classic problem in the study of vision is treated in detail in Feldman 1985. The basic idea is to have spatially independent units for certain pairs of features. These units are activated only when the two features coincide in space. Related problems addressed in Feldman 1985 include occlusion, articulated objects, and multiple instances of objects in a scene.

Another general issue is the choice of one unit per feature value as a basis for representing information. Although this unit/value principle is a convenient way to build models and appears to be a reasonable abstraction of the experimental data, the real situation is more complex. Even on pure computational grounds, it is much more efficient to use some encoding tricks, such as the coarse coding described by Ballard in this volume. These tricks also exploit conjunctive connections to reduce by a large fraction the number of units that would be required to capture a given level of precision for a feature value. The assertion here is that these technical tricks are sufficient to solve the problem of combinatorial explosion in the number of units as one moves to realistic numbers (Feldman and Ballard 1982). In this exposition I will continue to use pure value units (e.g. in the planes of the feature frame), with the understanding that any physiological predictions would have to be translated to realistic encodings.

There are two lines of computational experiments that might be added to the work already underway. The small-world system could be simulated as specified. The performance range would be limited, but one could learn quite a lot, especially from the SFF-WKF interactions. One of the nice features of the model is that it solves the classic AI problem of converting from numerical to symbolic representations of a scene. A second line of experimental AI work could focus on situation maps and the EF. It would be very informative to see if hierarchical and sequential situations could be implemented and whether multiple situations could be worked out computationally.

But it is not computational experimentation that is most needed at this stage. The four-frames model makes a number of predictions that should be behaviorally and physiologically testable. Computational requirements have played an important role in the development of the model, but major constraints have come from the structure and the behavior of the visual system. Most of the assumptions in the four-frames model are part of a widely shared current world view and will not be explicitly addressed. What does need more discussion is the rationale for the choices made in the novel integrative aspects of the work. The experimental basis for these choices is in no instance compelling; more research needs to be done in all these areas. Various experimental findings indicating the central features of the four-frames model are presented as suggestive.

For the RF, the data are far ahead of the model and the theory has relatively little to offer experimentalists. There are some new questions to be asked, but they are mainly concerned with the relation between the RF and the SFF. The four-frames model assumes that the detailed calculations of color, texture, and so on are carried out by the RF and integrated by the SFF. It is assumed that striate cortex and the various psychophysical "channels" are at the RF level. Obviously any foveal functions are part of the RF. The RF is clearly involved in indexing, and there should be an extra link in figure 1 for this. Some insights into RF structure and function might arise from the computational constraints brought out by the connectionist model; Ballard explores these issues in detail in this volume. The most interesting predictions of the model concern the interactions between the RF and the (hypothesized) SFF. One would expect mappings to extrastriate cortex that depended on gaze and mapped RF units with similar response characteristics. Graybiel and Berson (1981) suggest that at least the gaze information of figure 1 is available for this mapping through the LP-pulvinar complex.

The SFF is a major prediction of the four-frames model. It presents a computationally plausible and relatively well-specified theory of the functioning of extrastriate visual cortex. It is well established that there are reciprocal connections among most extrastriate visual areas and that the features to which each area is most responsive vary (Allman et al. 1981; Cowey 1981). There is some evidence that extrastriate visual maps are concerned with constancy features (Zeki 1980). Experiments like those of Sparks and Jay (this volume) demonstrate that saccades are directed toward points in space, not coded as relative displacements from the current fixation. With one major proviso, the SFF makes predictions that are subject to immediate experimental exploration. The proviso is (as mentioned above) that SFF units are assumed for simplicity to respond only to a single feature. This is neither biologically plausible nor computationally efficient.

In view of the multifeature nature of the units, the SFF's predictions are strong and perhaps surprising. One should find visual maps that are spatially organized by head position (in an upright stationary animal) and that respond to constancy values of visual stimuli. These should interact bidirectionally with parameter maps that are organized along nonspatial axes; this latter hypothesis is currently being tested (Ballard, this volume).

The obvious alternative to the SFF hypothesis is one that suggests that constancy and indexing computations are done separately at each fixation, with integration of the scene occurring only at the WKF level. The crucial question concerns the existence of spatial maps that are independent of eye position. There are isolated reports of units whose properties are independent of eye movement (Schlag et al. 1980; Tomko et al. 1981), but the usual description of extrastriate maps is in retinal terms. However, the vast majority of neurophysiological experiments have been done on anaesthetized or fixated animals and would not distinguish retinal from spatial organization. It has also been noted that the receptive field is much larger (up to the entire field) as one moves toward more anterior visual areas (Gross et al. 1981). Since most fixations are within 15°, the effective size of the SFF could be of the order of the receptive field sizes found in the extrastriate areas described by Allman et al. (1981). This is just what one would predict from the results of Rayner et al. (1981) on parafoveal priming. Visually responsive areas anterior from these will be discussed in connection with indexing and the WKF.

The psychological literature already contains extensive data on nonretinal (spatial) encoding of visual data and on constancy calculations (Fisher et al. 1981; Epstein 1977; Howard 1982). The notion that these are carried out (along with perceptual filling) by a single structure seems to be consistent with the literature, and is certainly testable. Behavioral experiments, such as the masking work of Davidson et al. (1973), give some idea of the interactions of the retinotopic and spatial frames. In these letter-naming experiments, masks were perceived to overlie the target letter that was in the appropriate SFF position, but it was the RF position that could not be identified. A wide range of psychological data are best explained by the assumption of an environmentally (not retinally) based spatial buffer. In an orthocopic projection (Rock 1983), humans are able to recognize simple objects seen passing behind a narrow slit. The results of Coren et al. (1975) provide convincing evidence that humans take eye movements into account when working out the shape of an object. Coren et al. found that subjects tracking a spot in the dark systematically underestimated the diameter of a circular trajectory while in pursuit mode. The underestimate was proportional to velocity up to a speed where saccades became predominant and the perceived size became much more accurate. A simple demonstration can be obtained by gently pushing one's eyeball to the side while fixating a distant object. No such phenomenological jump accompanies a volitional eye movement of the same kind. There are several models of this behavior in the literature; see MacKay 1973. There is also evidence of important interactions among SFF computations. For example, apparent motion will not occur for objects that appear to be at great depth no matter what choices of retinal spacing and interstimulus interval (Haber 1983) are used. A wide range of experiments on the interactions of perceived depth, shape, and motion are directly relevant; see Johansson 1977. Another example is the work of Gilchrist (1977) showing that lightness constancy is applied only to adjacent areas of the same apparent depth. If the different intrinsic-image calculations interact in the way I suggest, one should be able to predict the perceptual effects of anomalous combinations. An effort to deal comprehensively with existing illusion data would be a strong test for the model.

The main use of the SFF in the model was in indexing from its visual features to visual primitives in the WKF. The particular networks used (figure 8) call for spatially independent units that respond to pairs of visual features. The most likely anatomical site for such units would be the inferotemporal (IT) cortex. Gross et al. (1981) report that units in this area are spatially independent and respond to complex stimuli and multiple features. Desimone et al. (1984) found cells in monkey IT cortex that responded well to frontal views of monkey faces and much less well to partial faces, scrambled pieces, or other stimuli. Faces and hands are special stimuli, but many other cells responded well to feature pairs, as the model would suggest. The large receptive fields found and the consistency of response over position and size change fits nicely with the model. The connections known for IT cortex are also consistent with the model (Allman et al. 1981). The outputs from IT cortex include ones that could embody the spatial focus units and indexing links to the WKF, which I presume to be subsumed by anterior temporal and parietal structures. Alternative treatments of the relatively small amount of information known about this large area of cortex exist, of course.

Indexing by spatially independent feature-pair units is only one of a number of possibilities. Treisman (1983) reported a collection of experiments that limit the possible performance of such a mechanism in humans. She has shown that, under overload conditions, subjects cannot detect parallel targets requiring feature pairs but can do quite well at single-feature detections. Treisman hypothesizes that all feature-pair detections require an

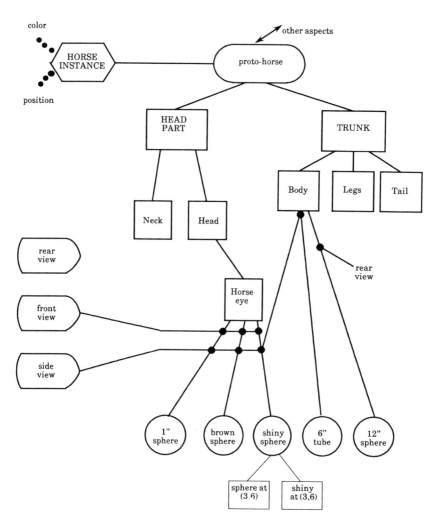

Figure 8
General views of horse.

internal focus of attention (like our spatial focus), but this seems to me to be much too slow for coping with natural scenes. Perhaps the best current reconciliation of the various results is the postulate that attention is needed to inhibit unwanted indexing. In conventional scenes, the constraints imposed by structured world knowledge (e.g., figure 8) can permit recognition with sequential attention, but tasks like Treisman's can be done only if they are very simple. This is another area in which the model is close enough to existing experiments for useful interactions.

One of the strongest links between the four-frames model and current research is the perceptual-constancy literature, which I will consider in moderate detail, following the terminology of Epstein (1977). Inherent in an overall system model, such as the four-frames model, are teleological statements about what role the constancies play in the system. In my model, constancies of space and form are critical features that allow a stable computational base for the apprehension of objects and situation. Visual position constancy (over eye movements) is the major reason for introducing the SFF, mapped by perceived gaze from the RF. Visual direction constancy (over head and body movements) is addressed by the allocentric environmental frame.

The various constancies of form are primarily functions of the feature frame. The related constancies of size and depth are assumed to be mediated by networks which directly embody the mutual constraints; these play an important role in SFF calculations (Feldman 1985). Color and lightness constancies are similarly assumed to arise from constraint networks described above. The fact that particular constancies are not always fully realized is a consequence of the need to mutually satisfy all the constraints in the SFF network. The effects of subject instructions and other context factors are captured in the "context" links of figure 1. Motion constancy is part of the missing treatment of temporal change and will be a significant constraint in working this out.

Shape constancy is quite different from other form constancies in the four-frames model. One form of shape constancy, the determination of three-dimensional surface orientations, is part of the relaxation network of the feature frame; however, most work on shape constancy has been concerned with the fact that shapes (usually two-dimensional) are treated as the same under various perspective transformations. In the four-frames model, such phenomena belong to the indexing network linking features to descriptions in the WKF. The principal-views representation (figure 8) captures the qualitative nature of shape constancy. The detailed calculation of the perspective transforms by networks, not done in detail here, is described in Hrechanyk and Ballard 1983 and in Plaut 1984. Shape constancy will be more labile and more context dependent than the others because it is based on the knowledge structure.

The WKF is the least susceptible to direct biological experiments of the four frames. In the model, the WKF is recruited from all modalities and output areas. Its functions would be subsumed by a number of areas, presumably in the anterior portions of temporal and parietal cortex. Bulk metabolic experiments give some corroboration of this view, but all this is not much more than a restating of the classical notion of association areas. There is some evidence that multimodal-feature cells of the sort required for the WKF are found in the superior temporal polysensory area (Bruce et al. 1981). Direct neurophysiological investigation of the WKF does not appear promising.

Behavioral testing of the WKF does seem to be feasible at present. There is considerable work in experimental psychology on spreading activation in semantic networks (Anderson 1983; Collins and Loftus 1975; Smith et al. 1974) and a fair amount on the perception of scenes (Hintzman et al. 1981; Palmer 1981). The results of Palmer et al. (1981) on the perception of objects (e.g. horses) from different perspectives support the principal-views representation chosen for complex objects. The four-frames model suggests a number of experiments on priming, confounding, and other issues based on the proposed network structure of appearance models. The results of Sperber et al. (1979) that showed significant cross-modal priming between pictures and words are best explained by a shared structure like the WKF. In fact, a major paradigm in psycholinguistics relies on the fact that a flashed word activates both related words and other senses of those words (Swinney 1982; Tanenhaus et al 1979). The results of Lucas (1984) suggest a time lag of about 100 milliseconds, which is not much more than the transmission time. Again, a shared conceptual representation is the simplest explanation of these effects.

The cortical structure most likely to subsume the functions of the EF appears to be the posterior parietal region (Lynch 1980; Robinson et al. 1978; Sakata et al. 1980). The four-frames model suggests that it is multimodal and allocentrically organized and contains substructures that encode the current ego position. The environmental frame should play a crucial role in hand-eye tasks and in other visually guided tasks. Most of these characteristics have been attributed to the posterior parietal area, but there is still quite a lot of disagreement on specifics (Lynch 1980). The EF is assumed to act through situation links connecting to WKF networks. There is considerable behavioral evidence that humans use relational, network-like descriptions of spatial situations (Brewer and Treyens 1981; Hintzman et al. 1981). The four-frames models entails a number of specific predictions about these networks and about cortical connections between EF, WKF, and gaze structures. The constraint of one-way EF-WKF links is a computational one—it seems unreasonable to have every object link to its places in the EF. The model assumes that objects in a situation are located relationally (in the WKF) rather than in absolute space (Hintzman et al. 1981). The particular representation choices for extrapersonal space in the current model are supported by some findings of Bisiach and Luzzatti (1978), who reported that two patients with parietal lesions were unable to describe whatever details of a remembered scene happened to be on their left from a (changing) imagined viewpoint. Results from child-development studies could also be helpful here; it is already known that the ability to use allocentric frames of reference develops rather late (Piaget and Inhelder 1967).

One way in which the four-frames model greatly oversimplifies the visual system is by ignoring hemispheric laterality. Each hemisphere performs visual computations for the contralateral hemifield with very little communication before the inferotemporal areas. The only systematic mapping across the hemispheres for earlier areas is of the vertical meridian, which is the border between the two hemifields. In terms of the model, this means that the retinotopic frame and the feature frame are duplicated and that the spatially-independent-feature units (figure 8) are probably also separate but communicate across hemispheres. The WKF obviously would cover multiple modalities and hemifields and would represent the first fully centralized level. A number of aspects of external space are known to be coded separately in the two parietal lobes, but I postulate that the EF is subsumed by the right posterior parietal region. The major problem for the model is explaining how early vision (the feature frame) copes with the switching of inputs between hemispheres with gaze shifts. This appears to be a difficult and important issue in any account of vision and space.

The most serious omission from the current treatment is temporal effects. Time-varying changes pervade the visual system, and taking them seriously will certainly lead to significant modifications in the model. From the lowest level of edge detection to the highest level in tasks such as route planning, time is of the essence. One view of the four-frames model is that it addresses seriously only the ventral ("what") portion of the two visual systems (Macko et al. 1982; Leibowitz et al. 1982). The required despacing of feature information in indexing (figure 8) suppresses detailed localization information, as the two-systems view would suggest. The dorsal ("where" or navigational) system might be viewed as splitting from the model at the feature-frame level and as making only minor contact with the WKF. The fact that one can read while walking suggests this possibility. The model predicts that one would not be able to read material requiring spatial reasoning while walking. But this is just one aspect of temporal vision; taking time seriously appears to be an effort of the magnitude of the four-frames model.

Even without new experiments, a great deal might be learned from trying to fit the four-frames model to existing bodies of data. Doing this at a crude level has forged the current form of the model. Subsequent efforts are of two different kinds: detailed fitting of small segments of data and further refinement of the global model. Detailed studies are underway at the University of Rochester on parameter networks in extrastriate cortex and on computational models of specific feature-frame and WKF computations. At the least, more attention will be directed to the global properties of the visual system, which is often treated as a large number of totally separate problems. The rationale of the whole enterprise is that it is not too early to benefit from more general considerations of the problems of vision and space.

Acknowledgments

The preparation of this paper was supported in part by Defense Advanced Research Projects Agency grant N00014-82-K-0193 and in part by Defense Advanced Research Projects Agency grant N00014-78-C-0164.

References

Allman, J. M., J. F. Baker, W. T. Newsome, and S. E. Petersen. 1981. Visual topography and function: Cortical visual areas in the owl monkey. In *Cortical Sensory Organization*, ed. C. N. Woolsey (Humana).

Anderson, J. R. 1983. *The Architecture of Cognition*. Harvard University Press.

Ballard, D. H. 1984. Parameter networks. *Artificial Intelligence* 22: 235–267.

Ballard, D. H., and C. M. Brown. 1982. *Computer Vision*. Prentice-Hall.

Barlow, H. B. 1981. Critical limiting factors in the design of the eye and visual cortex. *Proc. Roy. Soc. Lond.* B 212: 1–34.

Bisiach, E., and C. Luzzatti. 1978. Unilateral neglect of representational space. *Cortex* 14: 129–133.

Brewer, W. F., and J. C. Treyens. 1981. Role of schemata in memory for places. *Cognitive Psychology* 13: 207–230.

Bruce, C., R. Desimone, and C. G. Gross. 1981. Visual properties of neurons in a polysensory area in superior temporal sulcus of the macaque. *J. Neurophysiology* 46, no. 2: 369–384.

Collins, A. M., and E. F. Loftus. 1975. A spreading-activation theory of semantic processing. *Psych. Rev.* 82: 407–429.

Coren, S., D. R. Bradley, P. Hoenig, and J. S. Girgus. 1975. The effect of smooth tracking and saccadic eye movements on the perception of size: The shrinking circle illustration. *Vision Research* 15: 49–55.

Cowey, A. 1981. Why are there so many visual areas? In *The Organization of the Cerebral Cortex*, ed. F. O. Schmitt, F. G. Worden, G. Adelman, and S. G. Dennis (MIT Press).

Davidson, J. L., M. J. Fox, and A. O. Dick. 1973. Effect of eye movements on backward masking and perceived location. *Perception and Psychophysics* 14, no. 1: 110–116.

Desimone, R., T. D. Albright, C. G. Gross, and C. Bruce. 1984. Stimulus-selective properties of inferior temporal neurons in the macaque. *J. Neuroscience* 4, no. 8: 2051–2062.

Epstein, W., ed. 1977. *Stability and Constancy in Visual Perception: Mechanisms and Processes.* Wiley.

Feldman, J. A. 1982. Dynamic connections in neural networks. *Biological Cybernetics* 46: 27–39.

Feldman, J. A. 1985. Four frames suffice: A provisional model of vision and space. *Behavioral and Brain Sciences* 8: 265–289.

Feldman, J. A., and D. H. Ballard. 1982. Connectionist models and their properties. *Cognitive Science* 6: 205–254.

Feldman, J. A., and L. Shastri. 1984. Evidential inference in activation networks. In Proceedings of the Cognitive Science Conference, Boulder.

Fisher, D. F., R. A. Monty, and J. W. Senders, eds. 1981. *Eye movements: Cognition and Visual Perception.* Erlbaum.

Gilchrist, A. L. 1977. Perceived lightness depends on perceived spatial arrangement. *Science* 195: 185–187.

Graybiel, A. M., and D. M. Berson. 1981. Families of related cortical areas in the extrastriate visual system: Summary of an hypothesis. In *Cortical Sensory Organization*, ed. C. N. Woolsey (Humana).

Gregory, R. L. 1970. *The Intelligent Eye.* McGraw-Hill.

Gross, C. G., C. J. Bruce, R. Desimone, J. Fleming, and R. Gattass. 1981. Cortical visual areas of the temporal lobe: Three areas in the macaque. In *Cortical Sensory Organization*, ed. C. N. Woolsey (Humana).

Haber, R. N. 1983. Stimulus information and processing mechanisms in visual space perception. In *Human and Machine Vision*, ed. J. Beck, B. Hope, and A. Rosenfeld (Academic).

Hinton, G. E., 1981. Shape representation in parallel systems. In Proceedings of the Seventh International Joint Conference on Artificial Intelligence, Vancouver.

Hintzman, D. L., C. S. O'Dell, and D. R. Arndt. 1981. Orientation in cognitive maps. *Cognitive Psychology* 13: 149–206.

Hochberg, J. 1978. *Perception*. Prentice-Hall.

Howard, I. P. 1982. *Human Visual Orientation*. Wiley.

Hrechanyk, L. M., and D. H. Ballard. 1983. Viewframes: A connectionist model of form perception. In Proceedings of CVPR, Washington, D.C.

Johansson, G. 1977. Spatial constancy and motion in visual perception. In *Stability and Constancy in Visual Perception: Mechanisms and Processes*, ed. W. Epstein (Wiley).

Kuipers, B. J. 1973. Modeling spatial knowledge. *Cognitive Science* 2: 129–153.

Lucas, M. 1984. Frequency and Context Effects in Lexical Ambiguity Resolution, Technical Report 14, Cognitive Science Department, University of Rochester.

Lynch, J. C. 1980. The functional organization of posterior parietal association cortex. *Behavioral and Brain Sciences* 3: 485–534.

MacKay, D. M. 1973. Visual stability and voluntary eye movements. In *Central Processing of Visual Information. A: Integrative Functions and Comparative Data*, ed. R. L. Jung (Springer-Verlag).

Macko, K. A., et al. 1982. Mapping the primate visual system with [2-^{14}C]de-oxyglucose. *Science* 218, no. 4570: 394–396.

Marr. D. 1982. *Vision*. Freeman.

McDermott, D. 1980. Spatial Inferences with Grounds, Metric Formulas on Simple Objects. Research Report 173, Department of Computer Science, Yale University.

Minsky, M. 1975. A framework for representing knowledge. In *The Psychology of Computer Vision*, ed. P. H. Winston (McGraw-Hill).

Minsky, M., and S. Papert. 1972. *Perceptrons*. MIT Press.

Navon, D. 1981. The forest revisited: More on global precedence. *Psychological Research* 43: 1–32.

Palmer, S. E. 1981. Transformation structure and perceptual organization. In Proceedings of the Third Annual Meeting of the Cognitive Science Society, Berkeley, Calif.

Palmer, S. E., E. Rosch, and P. Chase. 1981 Canonical perspective and the perception of objects. In *Attention and Performance IX*, ed. J. Long and A. Baddeley (Erlbaum).

Pentland, A. P. 1984. Shading into texture. In Proceedings of AAAI.

Piaget, J., and B. Inhelder. 1967. *The Child's Conception of Space.* Norton.

Plaut, D. C. 1984. Visual Recognition of Simple Objects by a Connection Network. Report TR143, Computer Science Department, University of Rochester.

Posner, M. I., and Y. Cohen. Components of visual orienting. In *Attention and Performance X*, ed. H. Bouma and D. Bouwhuis (Erlbaum).

Rayner, K., A. W. Inhoff, R. E. Morrison, M. L. Slowiaczek, and J. J. Bertera. 1981. Masking of foveal and parafoveal vision during eye fixations in reading. *J. Experimental Psychology: Human Perception and Performance* 7, no. 1: 167–179.

Robinson, J. G. 1983. Frequency domain visual processing. In *Physical and Biological Processing of Images*, ed. O. Braddick and A. C. Sleigh (Springer-Verlag).

Rock, I. 1983. *The Logic of Perception.* MIT Press.

Sakata, H., H. Shibutani, and K. Kawano. 1980. Spatial properties of visual fixation neurons in posterior parietal association cortex of the monkey. *J. Neurophysiology* 43, no. 6: 1654–1672.

Schlag, J., M. Schlag-Rey, C. K. Peck, and J. P. Joseph. 1980. Visual responses of thalamic neurons depending on the direction of gaze and the position of targets in space. *Experimental Brain Research* 40: 170–184.

Smith, E. E., E. J. Shoben, and L. J. Rips. 1974. Structure and process in semantic memory: A featural model for semantic decisions. *Psychological Review* 81, no. 3: 214–241.

Sperber, R. D., C. McCauley, R. D. Ragain, and C. M. Weil. 1979. Semantic priming effects on picture and word processing. *Memory and Cognition* 7, no. 5: 339–345.

Swinney, D. A. 1982. The structure and time course of information interaction during speech comprehension: Lexical segmentation, access and interpretation. In *Perspectives on Mental Representation*, ed. J. Mehler, E. C. T. Walker, and M. Garrett (Erlbaum).

Tanenhaus, M. K., J. M. Leiman, and M. S. Seidenberg. 1979. Evidence for multiple stages in the processing of ambiguous words in syntactic contexts. *J. Verbal Learning and Verbal Behavior* 18: 427–440.

Tomko, D. L., N. M. Barbaro, and F. N. Ali. 1981. Effect of body tilt on receptive field orientation of simple visual cortical neurons in unanesthetized cats. *Experimental Brain Research* 43: 309–314.

Treisman, A. 1983. The role of attention in object perception. In *Physical and Biological Processing of Images,* ed. O. Braddick and A. C. Sleigh (Springer-Verlag).

Witkin, A. P., and J. M. Tenenbaum. 1983. On the role of structure in vison. In *Human and Machine Vision,* ed. J. Beck, B. Hope, and A. Rosenfeld (Academic).

Zeki, S. 1980. The representation of colours in the cerebral cortex. *Nature* 284: 412–418.

16

Cortical Connections and Parallel Processing: Structure and Function

Dana H. Ballard

Tremendous progress could be realized in the neurosciences through the introduction of information-processing models that would relate biological and behavioral data. Information-processing models (IPMs) have been successful in describing behavior at levels of abstraction useful to psychologists and workers in artificial intelligence, but have been much less successful in producing models that are directly useful to neuroscientists. One reason for this is that most IPMs are based on a conventional computer, and animal brains do not compute like a conventional computer. In the animal brain, comparatively slow (millisecond) neural computing elements with complex, parallel connections form a structure that is dramatically different from a high-speed (nanosecond), predominantly serial machine. Much of current research in the neurosciences is concerned with tracing out these connections and with discovering single-unit responses to complex stimuli. However, a crucial next step is to characterize neural function at the more abstract level that is related to behavior.

To characterize the endeavor it might help to consider a complementary approach: temporarily sidestepping the biological issues and studying the abstract computational problems that must be solved (Marr and Poggio 1976; Brady 1982; Marr 1982). The objective of this tack is to find useful abstract descriptions of the computations that are being performed without reducing them to anatomy. The level of formulation is in terms of symbolic constraints and algorithms for solving them. Subsequently, this class of models must be complemented by a description of how the brain implements the solutions to specific computational problems. This paper is aimed at this descriptive level. The implementation approach may be thought of as one of synthesis, and is logically at the boundary between biology and computer science. Neurobiological models describe the anatomy and physiology accurately while postponing the problem of computation. Computational models stress the abstract nature of the problems that must be solved, postponing the problem of implementation. In the implementational approach, one must choose a description of brain architecture that both describes how the abstract problems can be solved and is neurobiologically plausible.

One school of thought, termed *connectionist*, holds that the essential components of the abstract level can be described in terms of the synaptic contacts of networks of neurons. In other words, the functionality can be directly and usefully related to neural interconnection patterns. Early connectionist models (McCulloch and Pitts 1943; Hebb 1949; Rosenblatt 1958) were a step in this direction, but at the time those ideas were formed there was much less knowledge of the brain than there is now, and the abstract nature of computation was less well understood. The major attraction of connectionism is that it can stand the crucial test of timing. That is, given that entire behavioral responses can be realized in a few hundred milliseconds, connectionist models of neural units seem to be the only way to achieve these response times. Previous papers have suggested how a particular connectionist theory of the brain can be used to produce testable, detailed models of interesting behaviors (Feldman and Ballard 1982; Ballard 1984; Feldman 1981; Hinton et al. 1984). The purpose of this paper is to relate these ideas more closely to emergent anatomical and physiological knowledge of the cerebral cortex.

Overview

The principal hypothesis is that a major function of the cortex is to compute collections of invariants at different levels of abstraction.

An invariant is a description of a given situation in terms of a small number of parameters. For example, rigid motion can be described by six parameters: a rotation (three) about an instantaneous center (three). The usefulness of small-parameter descriptions that describe a large number of different situations pervades all aspects of perception and cognition. I suggest that the cortex has adopted representations and computational strategies that make the computation of invariants efficient.

Representing Possible Invariants

Any particular representation of information will have advantages and disadvantages. Yet neurons in different parts of the brain seem to represent information in very specific ways. One way to study these differences is through the single-cell recording technique (Eccles 1957) that allows re-

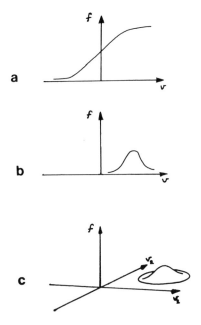

Figure 1
Different encodings as indicated by neural outputs. f = firing rate; v = stimulus value. (a)
Monotonic firing rate increases with scalar parameter indicative of a variable neuron. One-
and two-dimensional receptive fields indicative of value neurons. Variable neurons are
typically rapid-firing (500Hz), whereas cortical neurons are slow firing (50 Hz). Thus,
highly schematized plots in b and c are representative of the average of many trials—in
other words, the post-stimulus histogram.

cording of individual cells' responses to different stimuli. Let us compare
single-unit recordings from neurons functioning as basic parts of the ocular-
motor system (Robinson 1978) with those from cortical neurons in the
visual areas (Hubel and Wiesel 1962). Within the ocular-motor system,
neurons with linear outputs (figure 1a) are seen—that is, neurons whose
firing rate is proportional to a scalar parameter, such as the rate of eye
rotation. These neurons are part of the servo system controlling eye position and can be modeled as summation or integration devices. Their output
has two important features. First, a larger value for their output variable means more frequent pulses. Second, the variable output is one-
dimensional. In contrast, in the visual areas of cortex (indeed in all of the
cortex), most neurons seem to be using fundamentally different encodings
of their output (figures 1b, 1c). These neurons have multidimensional
receptive fields (RFs). (Traditionally, the receptive field of a neuron has

been defined with respect to a stimulus. This has the unfortunate effect of making it dependent on a particular experiment. In the present model, the receptive field is defined as the response to *all* the neurons' inputs, some of which may be feedback connections from neurons in more abstract cortical areas.)

If the input stimulus is within its receptive field, a neuron will fire; otherwise it is more or less quiescent. The degree of matching between the stimulus and the receptive field determines the firing rate. In physiological terms, the first kind of neuron uses *frequency coding* and the second kind of neuron uses *spatial (place) coding.* I have termed units using the latter kind of encoding *value units.* As first suggested by Barlow (1972), the value-unit way of representing information seems to be a property of most cortical cells. The characteristics are the representation of a portion of a complex stimulus that is signaled if the cell is firing.

Value units are a general way of representing different kinds of multidimensional variables and functions without requiring that each unit have a large bandwidth. The most optimistic estimate of discriminable signal range in a single neural output is about 1 : 1,000, and this is unsufficient to handle multidimensional variables. Value units overcome this limitation on neural output by breaking the ranges of a variable into intervals and representing each interval with a separate unit. These intervals can be organized in many different ways. One straightforward way is to represent a variable $\mathbf{v} = (v_1, \ldots, v_k)$ isotropically by allocating a unit for each of N^k discrete values. These values are the center of intervals of width $\Delta \mathbf{v} = (\Delta v_1, \ldots, \Delta v_k)$. The value k is the dimensionality of the variable. The term *parameter* will be used to denote a component of a variable.

Another way of thinking about the value/variable distinction is to compare the value-unit encoding with variable representations in conventional von Neumann computers. In a von Neumann machine, variables access only one value at any instant, and they acquire these values by assignment statements. For example, $x := 3; y := 4$ assigns values 3 and 4 to x and y, respectively. Since a sequential computer can access only one value of a variable at a time, the notion of unique values fro each variable at any instant is particularly appropriate. However, a parallel computer typically requires access to many values of a variable at the same time and thus requires a different encoding scheme. A value-unit representation such as an array of possible (x, y) values allows this parallel access. This difference is shown in figures 2a and 2b. Two other examples of value encodings are also shown in figure 2. Figure 2c shows a highly stylized representation of the orientation-sensitive cortical neurons found in striate cortex. In this

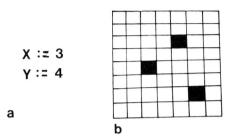

X := 3
Y := 4

a

b

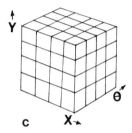

Y

c X→

θ

d

Figure 2
(a) Von Neumann encoding assigns a single value to a variable at any instant. (b) In constrast, value-unit encoding allows many values of the same variable to be accessed simultaneously. Two more examples illustrating the discreteness of value-unit encoding are shown by c and d. (c) Three-dimensional x-y-orientation units for striate neurons. In this scheme retinotopic coordinates and orientation are regarded as a three-dimensional space that is covered by the receptive fields of units. (This space is actually toroidal, owing to the periodicity of θ.) (d) Two-dimensional units for indicating directions in space. Directions can be described by coordinates on the unit sphere. The sphere can be tesselated (covered) with uniform intervals. The figure shows a triangular tesselation based on subdividing an icosahedron. If one imagines the figure as a helmet, then the units can indicate directions in space with respect to the head.

case the variable is three-dimensional, with $\mathbf{v} = (x, y, \theta)$. Each unit represents a specific value of (x_0, y_0, θ_0) and has an associated $(\Delta x, \Delta y, \Delta \theta)$ that may be loosely thought of as its receptive field. Figure 2d shows a value-unit representation for unit directions in three-dimensional space. In general, the intervals of neighboring value units will overlap.

An important advantage of the value-unit organization is that complex functions can be easily constructed. For example, suppose one neuron is sensitive to a red surround and a green center and another is sensitive to motion. In this hypothetical example, it is easy to see that, by combining these two neuronal inputs at a third, one could construct a neuron sensitive to moving, red-surround, green-center input. Similarly, one can combine responses to edge-sensitive and movement-sensitive neurons to construct more complex responses. This strategy can be used in a general way to construct arbitrary functions. Suppose one has such a function $f(x, y)$, that neurons are allotted for each interesting value of x, and that there is a similar set for the interesting y values. One can think of these different values as very similar to just-noticeable differences. Then these neurons can be used pairwise to construct the function as follows. The pairs of connections make synaptic connections with neurons representing appropriate values of f. It is assumed that both members of a pair of connections must be firing before the unit representing a specific value of f will fire. This type of input, termed a *conjunctive connection* (Feldman and Ballard 1982), could be realized by an appropriate spatio-temporal summation behavior of multiple synapses. The main point, however, is that with this table-lookup strategy arbitrary functions, such as $f(x, y) = e^{\sqrt{x}} \cdot \pi^{1/y}$, are easily represented.

The ability to represent multidimensional variables and functions is especially important in vision. At early levels of visual processing, the useful information about complicated stimuli is only implicit and is generally distributed over space. For example, in navigation the information needed to characterize one's trajectory stems from change measurements distributed over disparate parts of the retina. The value representation for cortical cells makes it possible to compute the requisite trajectory parameters by transforming the input through a succession of levels of abstraction, each level being represented by value units (Ballard and Kimball 1983). This organization solves the problem without directly interconnecting outputs from all combinations of disparate sensors. This strategy requires N^2 connections between N sensors. Such a solution may be realized by insects, owing to their smaller numbers of retinal and cortical cells (Olberg 1981a, b). However, for animals with huge numbers of retinal and

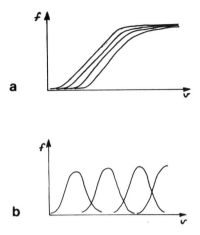

Figure 3
Firing rate f versus the value of a parameter v for neurons exhibiting different encodings.
(a) Ensemble of neurons that are variable-encoding exhibit monotonic behaviors.
(b) In contrast, value-encoded neurons exhibit response maxima that span the
measurement space.

cortical cells, an easier solution is to introduce intermediate levels of value
units.

The concept of the value unit is reminiscent of the idea of a "grandmother cell." Thus, it draws one of the principal criticisms of grandmother
cells: If the cell dies, the function is lost. However, it is possible to design
networks of value units that are impervious to such damage by distributing
the function among small groups of local units and allowing for the recruit-
ment (Feldman 1981) of new, previously unallocated units. Since these
notions are merely refinements of the useful idea of a value unit, I will keep
referring to units as if they were represented by single neurons.

How can one determine if value-unit encoding is being used? The basic
requirement, described in figures 1b and 1c, is elaborated in figure 3. To
determine value-unit encoding, the peak responses of the units must span
the useful range of measured values. The "useful range" depends on the
role of the variable, but may be deduced by various means. For example,
orientation value units should span the range $[0, 360°]$. Thus, figure 3a
shows a variable that is not value encoded, whereas figure 3b shows a
value-unit encoding of a variable. For our purposes, it is not necessary that
all the dimensions of a variable be value encoded. There are much stronger
predictions made by the value-unit encoding hypothesis, namely in the
interconnection patterns that would appear between different cortical areas.

The value-unit model is chosen as the simplest useful level of abstraction

Table 1
Neurons with the hypothesized different encodings have fundamentally different characteristics.

Value encoding	Variable encoding
Multidimensional representation	Single-dimensional representation
Receptive-field response with represented parameter	Monotonic response with represented parameter
Peak responses span parameter values	Peak responses may not span parameter values

of the cortical neuron. Shaw et al. (1982) proposed that about thirty neurons are usefully considered as forming a functional unit. Abeles (1982) considered several interesting firing properties that arise from analyzing detailed recordings of interesting simultaneously recorded units. One is that a neuron is far more likely to fire if its inputs are synchronized. Another very important idea is that neurons may be signaling probabilities (Hinton and Sejnowski 1983). The value-unit model is not incompatible with these more detailed models, and is the simplest description that can illustrate important computational properties.

The notion of the neuron as a functional unit dates from the very earliest anatomical studies (Golgi 1879; Cajal 1911). Other investigators have suggested that patches of dendrites might act as functional units (Shepherd et al. 1985). It could turn out that the value-unit model is extendable to dendritic trees considered as separate units. For purposes of explanation, however, I will stick to the level of abstraction that considers a neuron as a unit.

To summarize: Neural responses can be used in two qualitatively different ways, value encoding and variable encoding. The brain may have both value and variable neurons or may use combined strategies, but the gross organization of the cortex seems to exhibit value encoding. Table 1 shows the main points of difference. Conversions between these two kinds of representations are well within known synaptic properties. These two representations can be combined in a hybrid system, with the value neurons computing complex functions and the variable neurons computing dynamic control signals.

Computing Specific Invariants

To satisfy the criteria for a cortical model, it must be shown how value units can represent information, and also how to compute using this repre-

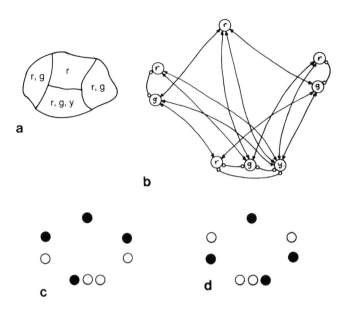

Figure 4

(a) A four-country map-coloring problem: Color the map with the colors shown (r = red, g = green, y = yellow) so that adjacent countries have different colors. (b) A value-unit representation of the map-coloring problem. A separate unit is allocated for each color of every country. Symmetric inhibitory connections are denoted by double-ended links terminating in small circles, symmetric excitatory links by double-ended links terminating in arrows. Other designs are possible. For example, one could use inhibitory connections between incompatible colors in neighboring countries. The particular design keeps inhibition local to individual countries. (c) A particular starting configuration where dark units are on and light units are off. (d) The correct solution achieved by iteration using the state-modification rule described in the text.

sentation. A strong argument for value units is the facility with which they support parallel computation. The reason for my emphasis on parallelism is that a growing body of psychological data suggests that many complex behavioral responses require only a few hundred milliseconds (Treisman and Gelade 1980). Parallel processing is indicated in these experiments, since the response time is independent of the number of tokens that must be processed. In addition to these experiments, an elementary analysis of the neural signal also suggests that sequential processing is unlikely.

To illustrate how value units can solve problems in parallel, I will describe the solution to a very specific problem. Consider the simple map in figure 4a, with four regions. The problem is to color the map so that no two adjacent countries have the same color. Each region may be colored with one of the colors shown. This problem is representative of a ubiquitous class of problems which can be posed as "Satisfy the largest set of compatible constraints" (Freuder 1978; Hummel and Zucker 1983; Prager 1980; Rosenfeld et al. 1976; Ullman 1979). When this problem is translated to value-unit notation, the color of each region is a separate value unit. If a particular color is compatible with the currently chosen value units representing neighboring colors, then that unit is likely to be chosen to represent its corresponding region's color. The constraints are represented as links between units. There are many different ways to do this. I choose to let connections between locally incompatible colors be inhibitory (lower confidences) and let connections between compatible colors be excitatory (raise confidences). These links are shown in figure 4b. For brevity, two symmetric links are drawn as a single double-ended link.

Now I shall describe how networks of value units compute. The ith unit can be thought of as having a small amount of information, $(s_i, \mathbf{w}_i)$, where s_i is the state and $\mathbf{w}_i = \{w_{i1}, \ldots, w_{in}\}$ is the synaptic weight vector. In the underlying computational model (Hopfield 1982), value units can be thought of as binary threshold units. Units start out in an initial state and converge to a stable final state. The state changes according to

$$s_i := 1 \quad \text{if } p_i \geq 0, \quad \text{else } s_i := 0,$$

where

$$p_i = \sum_k w_{ik} s_k.$$

This algorithm is only guaranteed to find local minima, but a feature of certain constraint-satisfaction problems is that a local minimum is sufficient for the task at hand. For example, if the map-coloring example is started in an arbitrary state, it will quickly converge to the state representing compatible colors, as shown in figure 4. In this case, the negative weights equal -2 and the positive weights equal 1.

Hinton and Sejnowski (1983) extended this algorithm, building on the concept of "simulated annealing" developed by Kirkpatrick et al. (1983). In this algorithm, the state is adjusted probabilistically according to

$$s_i := 1 \text{ with probability } P_i,$$

where

$$P_i = 1/(1 + e^{-p_i/T}).$$

In this updating rule the parameter T plays the role of "temperature" (analogous to its role in a Boltzmann distribution). The temperature is initially high, corresponding to equally probable state changes, and is gradually "cooled." The advantage of this algorithm is that it now finds a global minimum with a given probability. A drawback of the probabilistic version is that it may require too many iterations to be biologically plausible; however, the discovery of this algorithm is very recent, and ways may be found to overcome this problem. Also, although the algorithm formally requires symmetric weights, computer simulations have shown that it may be possible to relax this condition. Important details of this model are given in Kirkpatrick et al. 1983, Geman and Geman 1985, and Hinton et al. 1984. The second of these papers addresses convergence properties, and the last provides a learning algorithm. My extension, elaborated in later examples, uses nonsymmetric ternary weights (w_{ijk}) that model spatio-temporal summation (called here conjunctive connections).

The points behind the map-coloring problem are three. First, the problem is characteristic of other constraint-satisfaction problems in that empirical tests show that larger-scale versions do not require more time. Maps with more countries and colors can still be colored without any increase in processing time if the constraints are appropriately organized. This controversial statement about problem scaling is currently based on empirical tests. Kirkpatrick et al. argue that convergence is based on how "frustrating" (incompatible) the constants are; this point will be taken up below in the context of specific examples. The second point is that the constraints used are extremely general and can characterize a broad range of perceptual and cognitive situations (Hinton et al. 1984; Feldman 1982; Ballard and Hayes 1984). In particular, problems in visual gestalt recognition can be described as trying to satisfy an appropriately weighted collection of local constraints (Ballard et al. 1983; Feldman 1982). The third lesson of constraint satisfaction is that local constraints can imply a global solution.

There is a sense in which this problem can be thought of as an analogy to how more complicated problems are handled. If one interprets "map" as "cortical area," one sees how different local constraints might participate in a global computation. The requirement for a unique color for each region would be analogous to an inter-area cortical constraint, whereas the constraint between neighboring colors would correspond to a constraint between different cortical areas. However, it would obviously be a big mistake to think that this kind of computation is all that the cortex does. It is my view that a large class of problems crossing many domains (e.g., vision, motor control, portions of cognition) can be potentially solved in this fashion.

It is far from established that the cortex actually uses its signals in a way suggested by the constraint-satisfaction paradigm, although, as Terry Sejnowski suggests, the use of the post-stimulus histogram in data presentation implicitly appeals to an underlying statistical model. To go further, one might try to establish the role of a given neuron in a specific visual task and see if its firing rate increases or decreases markedly during the few-hundred-millisecond convergence period. With current techniques, this would be a very difficult experiment. Several experiments show that the response of cortical neurons is dependent on the task in which the animal is engaged (e.g. Shaw et al. 1983), but so far these are still not definitive in implicating the constraint-satisfaction paradigm. On the other hand, there is no evidence to rule out the constraint-satisfaction model, either. One problem is that very few testable alternative models have been proposed that meet the computational requirements. Holographic memory has been proposed, but this has the form of static memory and does not address the issue of problem solving.

A Review of Cortical Organization

The value-unit model has several implications for cortical organization, but in order to develop these implications it is first necessary to summarize several relevant cortical anatomical and physiological features. The summary represents an attempt to highlight important neurobiological features that are relevant to the proposed model. As such, it may deter neuroscientists from appreciating the abstract computational components of the model which are aided by but not vitally tied to the specific neurobiological associations. The other side of this is that committing the model to a particular anatomical substrate makes it easier to understand its salient features.

Cortical Columns: A Uniform Processing Architecture

To a coarse approximation, the cortex can be regarded as a two-dimensional sheet a few millimeters in thickness. Within this sheet the anatomy can be usefully thought of as organized into functional, overlapping columns about 800 μm in diameter (Mountcastle 1978, p. 21). Metaphorically, one can think of tightly packed interpenetrating cylinders stacked in axis-parallel fashion, each 0.3 mm in diameter and a few millimeters long. Szentagothai (1978a, b) has done extensive work that also shows elaborate anatomical similarities in structure of cortical columns from area to area, and many others have confirmed the columnar organization into interdigitated, repeated functional units (Goldman-Rakic and Schwartz 1982; Kaas et al. 1981; Lund 1981).

Superimposed on this organization is another organization dictated by the connections between the cortex and other parts of the brain. For this purpose, the sheet-like cortex may be thought of as approximately divided into three major layers. The uppermost layer (sublayers II and III) contains neurons that are connected to other neurons in different parts of the cortex. The middle layer (layer IV) receives input from other parts of the brain. The bottom layer (V and VI) contains neurons that handle cortical output to other parts of the brain.

Our main interest is in the connection patterns between different neuronal units in functionally different cortical areas. Recent experiments strongly suggest that the axonal arborization is an important vehicle by which the neuron expresses functional diversity. Three-dimensional reconstructions of striate neurons stained with HRP show that the axons exhibit striking geometric orientation preferences (Gilbert and Wiesel 1983), and a case in striate cortex where the axonal buttons from a neuron in layer IV remain exactly within an ocular dominance column has been reported (Blasdel et al. 1983). The important implication of the latter finding is that the connections are an important way to achieve functional diversity.

Functionally Different Cortical Areas

The two-dimensional, six-layer structure holds for almost all of the cortex, but at a lower level of detail the cortex can be differentiated into distinct areas. In fact, it has been known for a long time that the cortex itself can be divided into different cytoarchitectural regions (Brodmann 1909), with the different regions almost always having different functional characteristics. These functional characteristics have been determined through a variety of techniques, including anatomical track tracing, lesion studies, radioisotope labeling, and single-electrode recordings (Zeki 1978).

Figure 5 shows different areas of the owl monkey's cortex (predominantly visual areas and somatosensory areas). Other areas are in the process of being mapped. The visual areas are all *retinotopic*; that is, moving an electrode across the cortex in a visual area corresponds to traversing the visual field in a retinal coordinate frame. The different visual areas each exhibit geometric distortions of the visual field, as hinted at by the different midline locations shown on the figure. A helpful method of identifying such fields is to stain callosal fibers connecting the two hemispheres, since

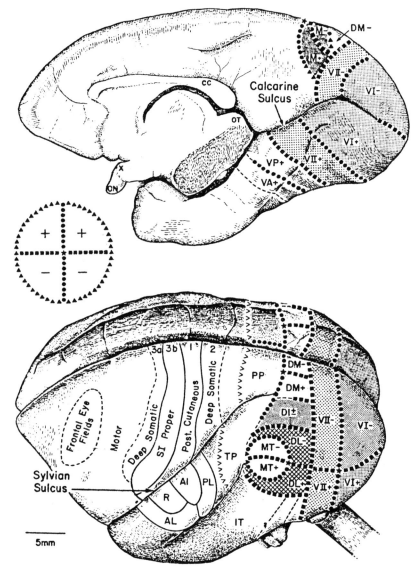

Figure 5
The representation of the distinct sensory domains in the cerebral cortex of the owl
monkey. Above: a ventromedial view of the right hemisphere. Below: a dorsolateral view.
DI: dorsointermediate visual area. DL: dorsolateral crescent visual area. DM: dorsomedial
visual area. IT: inferotemporal cortex. M: medial visual area. MT: middle temporal visual
area. PP: posterior parietal cortex. VA: ventral anterior visual area. VP: ventral posterior
visual area. AI: first auditory area. AL: anterolateral auditory area. CC: corpus callosum.
ON: optic nerve. OT: optic tectum. PL: posterolateral auditory areas. R: rostral auditory
area. From Allman et al. 1982.

companion visual areas are densely interconnected at the regions corresponding to the midline in the visual field (Van Essen et al. 1982).

The first visual area, V1, seems to represent primary visual parameters such as disparity, orientation, luminance, change, and color. Other areas seem to represent more abstract features. For example, MT neurons have been found that are sensitive to changes in physical motion.

The visual areas can be coarsely characterized as to whether they seem to be involved in stabilized vision or motion. For example, in the owl monkey, areas DL and DM (Allman et al. 1982), which have expanded foveal representations of the visual field, would seem to be carrying out computations important in stabilized vision. In contrast, MT and M, which are most responsive to moving random-dot patterns, would seem to be carrying out computations important for motion.

Areas adjacent to the visual areas generally represent very abstract parameters. However, the visually responsive neurons in superior temporal sulcus are responsive to nonretinotopic stimuli (Gross et al. 1982). For example, Sakata et al. (1980) have identified neurons responsive to full-field rotations in parietal cortex.

Abstraction Hierarchies

Different cortical areas seem to represent information at different levels of abstraction (Van Essen and Maunsell 1983). As an example, consider the relation between intensity changes and optic flow. Optic flow is a retinotopic projection of the three-dimensional velocity field. Early in the visual areas, neuron RFs are sensitive to some kind of motion; however, there is a distinction between motion as reflected in time-varying intensities and motion as represented by optic flow: Optic-flow neurons respond to changes in physical velocity changes but not to changes in illumination.

Movshon (1983) compared the response of neurons in V1 and MT in the macaque. Given a checkerboard stimulus, neurons in V1 responded optimally when the motion was perpendicular to the intensity gradients of the checkers. Some neurons in MT responded when the motion of the checkerboard was aligned with their preferred direction. Although the number of neurons tested in MT was small, the result hints that the representations that are arrived at by abstract mathematical analysis of the physical constraints may be directly implemented in the underlying neural structure. Furthermore, the neural responses are compatible with value-unit criteria (table 1).

Anatomical evidence that cortical areas may represent information at

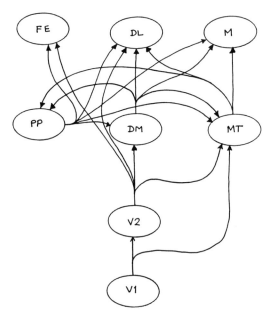

Figure 6
Organization of cortical areas of owl monkey into a functional hierarchy using Maunsell
and Van Essen's (1982) connection principles and data from Weller and Kaas (1982).
Arrows denote direction of hierarchy using either the feedforward or the feedback
principle.

different levels of abstraction comes from the consideration of cortico-
cortical connection patterns (Maunsell and Van Essen 1982). If area A is
more abstract than area B, it will receive different connections to its layer
IV and send connections to B's layers II, III, and V or II, III, and VI. Using
this result and the connection patterns for the owl monkey (Allman et al.
1982), one can construct the hierarchy shown in figure 6. This hierarchy
also can be partitioned into form (DL-DM) and motion (MT-M) channels,
following Maunsell and Van Essen's observations on the macaque. The
difference between form and motion is that form requires the processing of
distributed, spatial locations, whereas motion (in the case of a rigid body)
can be summarized as a few feature values such as rotation and translation.
Evidence for the form/feature distinction comes from a number of experiments (e.g., Mishkin et al. 1983) that have shown that macaques with
inferotemporal lesions perform poorly at feature-recognition tasks whereas
macaques with parietal lesions perform poorly at spatial-location tasks.
Much data exists to show that orderly abstraction hierarchies are also

present within an individual area. For example, Hubel and Wiesel (1962) and Hubel et al. (1978) have described simple, complex, and hypercomplex neurons in striate cortex, and other functional experiments imply that the most abstract neurons in an area reside in the upper layers (Movshon 1983; Pasternak et al. 1981).

Although the definitive experiments have not been done, preliminary evidence (Woolsey 1981) suggests that similar hierarchical organizations exist in motor and samatosensory areas.

Spatio-Temporal Channels

Another important feature of cortical structure is the retino-cortical pathways. The neurons in these pathways have markedly different spatio-temporal responses. (For a review, see Stone et al. 1979.) Neurons in these pathways can be broadly classified into three types: X cells, which have fine spatial resolution but coarse temporal resolution; Y cells, which have coarse spatial resolution and fine temporal resolution; and W cells, which have relatively coarse resolution in both space and time. The X-Y-W system is involved in two distinct spatio-temporal channels that are distinguished by different subcortical nuclei and by different cortical afferents. The most studied pathway is from the retina through the lateral geniculate to the striate cortex. In the cat, the X-Y-W systems have separate locales in both the LGN and the cortex, and this result seems to be true also for monkeys. The other pathway is from the retina to the superior colliculus, to the inferior pulvinar, and then to the cortex. Only the Y-W neurons seem to be involved in this pathway, and the cortical afferents terminate in most retinotopic areas (Weller and Kaas 1982). These two channels are summarized in figure 7.

The discussion in this section has focused on the cortex in order to describe findings that relate to connectionist models. The main points are these:

- The processing architecture is surprisingly uniform when the cortex is considered as a two-dimensional sheet of layered processing columns.

- The two-dimensional sheet is divided into different functional areas; that is, areas wherein single-unit recordings reveal different and characteristic responses.

- Emergent evidence suggests that much of the functional diversity is realized through axonal connection patterns.

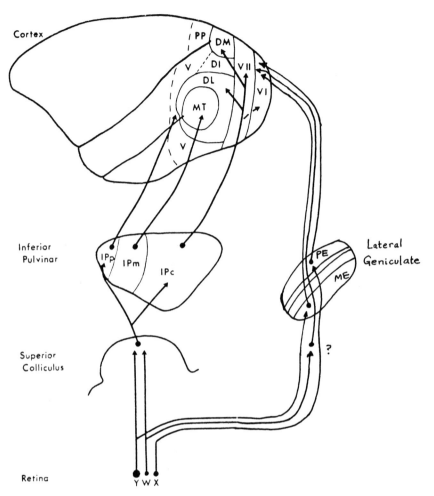

Figure 7
Spatio-temporal channels. The two principal pathways to cortex: (1) the tectopulvinar
relay system (*Y-W* only) and (2) the lateral geniculate relay system (*X-Y-W*). After Weller
and Kaas 1982.

• The different areas form a natural hierarchy, which is revealed through the layered patterns of efferent and afferent connections.

• The hierarchies can be thought of as further divided into channels. The principal channels are spatio-temporal channels and have direct anatomical correlates in terms of cell types.

How the Value-Unit Representation Constraints Cortical Organization

The value-unit model has huge consequences for cortical organization. This section shows how the value unit representation constrains the geometry of the cortical layout.

Relating Function to Cortical Topography in Striate Cortex

Let us first consider striate cortex. One of its main characteristics is an explicit representation of the visual environment. Marr (1978) and Barlow (1981) have articulated the notion of explicitness in cortical representations. An old puzzle was the huge ratio of cortical to retinal neurons, since in some sense the cortex cannot add to the information represented in the retina. Most data suggest that, although the cortex does not expand retinal information, it does make implicit information explicit. The visual field is mapped onto it retinotopically. The entire visual field is represented, but the central portion is magnified by having more cortical cells. Neurons in a certain area will respond only to inputs in a particular part of space, but within that cortical area several other parameters are represented. There are neurons sensitive to edge orientation (Hubel and Wiesel 1962), to scale or "spatial frequency" (De Valois 1977), to ocular dominance (Hubel and Wiesel 1962), and to other parameters for a particular part of visual space. Tootell et al. (1983) have shown that the representations of these different parameters occupy different but overlapping areas of cortical space. Since all values of this list of parameters may occur at a particular point in space (and its corresponding locale in the cortex), they must be represented somehow within that small cortical space. One way of doing this would be to have a neuron for discrete values of every parameter—e.g., each value for scale (spatial frequency), each value for orientation, and so on. To a first approximation, this seems to be the underlying representation. The major refinements are that neurons generally have multiparameter responses (e.g., a neuron that is sensitive to orientation will generally be sensitive to

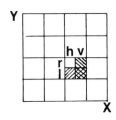

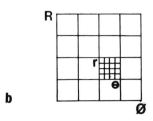

Figure 8
(a) Schematic of organization of striate cortex. Primary indices are X and Y; two of the secondary indices are ocular dominance and orientation. (b) Schematic organization of frontal eye fields (after Goldberg 1982). Primary indices (R, Φ) are for next eye movement; secondary indices (r, Θ) are for last eye movement.

certain values of velocity, as well as other parameters) and that neurons will have overlapping receptive fields.

Primary and Secondary Indices

The place-coded structure constrains the functional layout of striate cortex in ways that can be generalized. The problem is to represent multidimensional fundamental parameters in a two-dimensional architecture. This constraint usually means that two of the parameters can be regarded as the *primary indices*. Variations in these two parameters span the cortical area. In all the visual areas, the primary indices are retinal coordinates; the *secondary indices* are important visual parameters, such as orientation, colors, and motion. For each value of the primary indices, a complete set of secondary indices will represented. Figure 8a shows a schematic of some of the parameters of striate cortex in the macaque using secondary indices of edge orientation and ocular dominance. This basic organization has been found for many other cortical areas. For example, the body is represented four

Table 2

Area	Primary Indices	Secondary Indices
Macaque		
V1	space (retinal)	spatial frequency, color, orientation, ocular dominance
V2	space (retinal)	motion, disparity
V3	space (retinal)	
V3A	space (retinal)	
V4	space (retinal)	color
MT	space (retinal)	motion
FEF	Δ space (next eye movemt.)	Δ space (last eye movemt.)
1, 3b	body surface	cutaneous parameters
3a, 2	topological space	joint & muscle parameters
Cat		
17	space (retinal)	spatial frequency, ocular dominance, orientation
18	space (retinal)	motion
19	space (retinal)	

different times in Brodman's areas 1, 2, 3a, and 3b (Kaas et al. 1981). The primary indices are topographically related to the body surfaces, and the secondary indices are related to tactile and joint sensory parameters. Sensory areas have been found where the primary indices are not spatial (e.g., auditory cortex, olfactory cortex), but in general the correct nonspatial primary indices are difficult to deduce, since one must guess the correct parametrization. An area where the correct guesses may have been made is the frontal eyefields (M. Goldberg, personal communication, 1982), which govern eye movement. Here the primary indices seem to be the magnitude and the direction of the next eye movement, represented as a vector. Secondary indices that have been discovered are the last eye movement, also represented in terms of a radius, direction. Figure 8b schematizes this organization, and table 2 summarizes some current physiological findings in terms of the primary and secondary indices, drawing on data from Maunsell and Van Essen (1982), Tusa et al. (1979), Tusa and Palmer (1980), Burton and Robinson (1981), and Juliano et al. (1983).

Although the primary indices for the somatosensory areas are listed as body-topographic, this classification is becoming more tentative. Evidence presented by Burton and Robinson (1981) and Juliano et al. (1983) shows that the body parts are multiply represented. This may be due to the fact that body topography is a secondary index in these areas, and that there exists a primary index with a broader classification. One suggestion is that a body part is organized by broad kinds of tasks in which it participates. Thus, when a finger is used alone it might be in one locale, whereas when it is used with digits from the opposite hand it may be in another locale. (In both cases, however, it would be regarded as being within a task-indexed cortical area.)

Many neurons (e.g. frontal eyefield neurons) have large overlapping RFs, and this brings up an important point: The indices are defined by the parameter value that gives the maximum response. The neurons may have large RF widths that are related to their inputs and are, of course, totally unrelated to the width of their cortical columns.

The primary/secondary index dichotomy is meant to be useful in the interpretation of the possible function of cortical areas. An important refinement that this distinction does not address is the details of the packing of secondary indices. The models for striate cortex of Dow and Bauer (1983) and Cynader et al. (1983) address this issue directly, as does work by Tootell et al. (1983), Livingstone and Hubel (1984), Hubel and Wiesel (1963), and Singer (1981).

Space Limitations Require Different Functional Areas

A regular organization of neurons in the cortex, as in V1, is called here a *parameter net*. Its characteristics are that all values of a small set of parameters must be represented within a certain area. Why should these parameters be clustered in this fashion (Cowey 1981)? My answer is that, in any given area, a severe packing constraint follows from the fact that neurons have multimodal responses. Such responses are exemplified by orientation-sensitive neurons which will also respond to motion, spatial frequency, and other stimulus variations. A consequence of this property is that only about 5–15 scalar parameters can be represented in a given cortical area, because the number of units required grows exponentially with the number of parameters. If N is the number of just-noticeable differences in each scalar parameter and k is the dimensionality of the unit (the number of parameters), the total number of units required is N^k. Thus, this severe packing constraint is referred to as the N^k *problem*.

Overlapping the receptive fields can alleviate the N^k problem, but not to a significant extent. The main benefit of overlapping, multidimensional units is that, in an architecture where units are expensive and connections are relatively cheap, these units can allow for the representation of a given signal resolution with less units. Basically, one can intersect the RF of

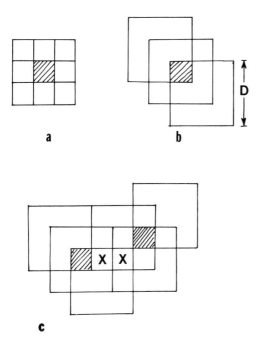

Figure 9
(a) Nonoverlapping encoding for a parameter space with $N = 3$ and $k = 2$. In general, total units required by this scheme is proportional to N^k. (b) A coarse coding of this space uses three arrays of units (one unit from each array shown), where each unit has a diameter $D = 3$ (defined in terms of the high-resolution units). The simultaneous firing of all three units denotes input in the area indicated. In general, the total units required by this scheme is N^k/D^{k-1}. (c) Developing the example in b further to show how closely spaced stimuli can lead to errors: Stimuli at the shaded positions produce two errors, denoted by Xs.

overlapping units through spatio-temporal summation (figure 9). Hinton (1981) has shown that the saving is a factor of $1/D^{k-1}$, where D is the diameter of the receptive field, in units of desired maximum resolution, and k is the dimension of the stimulus.

The encoding scheme that uses overlapping RFs has an accompanying disadvantage. It cannot signal closely spaced stimuli simultaneously without error (figure 9). Thus, the price paid for the encoding economy is some loss in parallelism.

It is informative to plot the number of units required as a function of N and k (figure 10). The different curves correspond to different values of D. These curves support the assertion that the dimensionality k that can be represented in any cortical region must be on the order of $5-15$, even

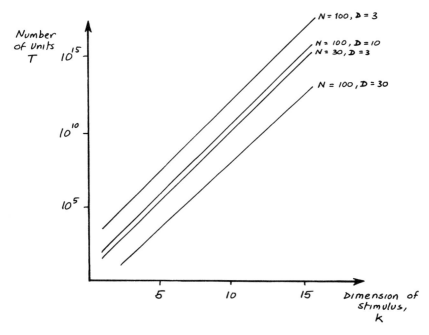

Figure 10
The fundamental restriction on the dimensionality of a cortical area. The graph shows the total number of units T required as a function of different values of k, N, and D, where $T = N^k/D^{k-1}$. Since the number of units in an area must be less than 10^{10}, the dimensionality of an area must be less than 15.

given the overlapping field strategy. Thus, a consequence of overlapping, explicit representations and the number of neurons available is a fundamental limitation on the number of parameters that can be represented in a given cortical area. If this is the case, then a natural consequence of having more parameters is to have more cortical areas. This may be one of the reasons for the several visual areas seen in cat and primate cortices. Extensive data from electrophysiological recordings reveal that neurons in the different visual areas have different responses. Figure 11 is a plot of data from Allman et al. 1982 for different cortical regions in the owl monkey. While all the visual areas have some neurons that respond to almost any given stimulus, certain areas have large portions of their neurons dedicated to particular subsets of visual parameters. These parameters are similar to parameters that have been shown to be computable by parallel algorithms: color, edge orientation, disparity, surface orientation, and optic flow (Brady 1982; Marr 1982; Ballard et al. 1983).

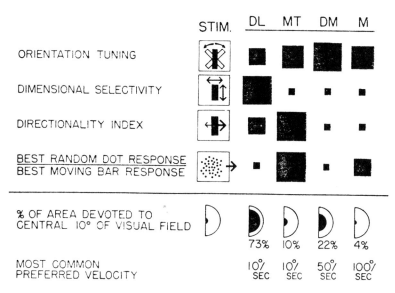

Figure 11

Functional specificity in visual areas DL, MT, DM, and M in the owl monkey. (Refer to figure 5 for the locus of these areas.) The strength of the functional attribute is indicated by the size of the black squares. From Allman et al. 1982.

Since low-dimensional spaces are an economical representation, one might wonder why minimal dimensions are not used. The answer is that low-dimensional spaces have special representational problems, termed "illusory conjunctions." These are described below.

Effects of Changing Indexing Schemes on Anatomical Connections

If different cortical areas use value units but with different parameters, it is natural to ask how they are interconnected. A major consequence of the value-unit hypothesis is that connections between the different areas should show up as distinctive patterns that can be revealed by current histochemical staining techniques. Basically, retrograde staining between areas with different primary indices should produce distinctive spot-like or band-like patterns. Furthermore, these patterns should be related to func-tional organization. Evidence for such bands has been demonstrated in retrograde HRP staining (Gilbert 1982; Montero 1981; Curcio and Harting 1978). To repeat the important point: Such patterns would arise from connections between areas with different primary indices. The different visual areas do not meet this condition, being indexed by space in every case. In fact, experiments by Montero (1981) on retinotopic areas in the cat strongly suggest that they are connected on a point-to-point basis.

To develop the argument for connections between areas where the primary index changes, we first consider an abstract example. Figure 12 shows a case of two representations that differ only in that the order of indices has been reversed. In figure 12a the primary indices are x and y; in figure 12b the primary indices are α and β. Now consider the connections from area B to area A. In particular, consider all connections that synapse in the shaded box in A. This box contains units that have all values of α and β and a particular value of x and y. Where are these corresponding units represented in area B? One quickly sees that the global pattern of area A must be repeated for every column of different vaues of α and β in B. Thus, retrograde staining from A to B would reveal these neurons as spots of stained cell bodies. Since the connections between the two areas are symmetrical, retrograde staining from B to A would reveal the same kind of pattern. An interesting feature of this organization is the insensitivity of the demonstration to the size of the site. Suppose, rather than a single cortical column, one considered several adjacent columns. Analysis shows that the spots in B would be larger but that the overall pattern would be unchanged.

Even when the indices change and are not α and β but instead $f(\alpha, \beta)$ and $g(\alpha, \beta)$, the same kind of patterns can occur. This analysis is derived from the connections between two different cortical areas. Consider the example of computing a global visual parameter with value units, say egomotion parameters, from a retinotopic map, such as optic flow. Figures 12c and 12d show representative connections for the subset of value units that have zero rotation. Thus, wherever the primary indices in the two areas are different, the connections between areas should form a characteristic pattern indicative of a one-to-many mapping. Thus, this model can explain the patchy areas of label in retrograde-staining experiments (Gilbert 1982; Goldman-Rakic and Schwartz 1982; Curcio and Harting 1978; Montero 1981).

To understand my intercortical connection hypothesis, it may help to compare it with the intracortical explanation advanced by Mitchison and Crick (1982) to explain Rockland and Lund's (1982) tree-shrew data. In the tree shrew, extracellular retrograde HRP transport from a striate-cortex injection site produced patchy labeling within the striate area. Mitchison and Crick hypothesized that the patchy labeling arises from the orientation of long axons that connect neurons of similar orientation selectivity. In my terminology, the primary indices do not change in this case, but the particular secondary index that is labeled happens to depend on parameter

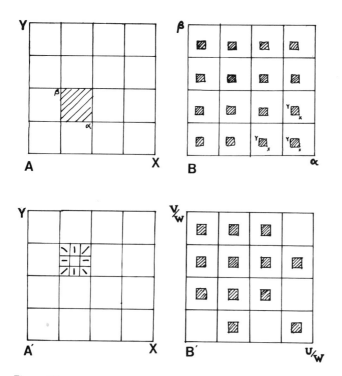

Figure 12

Two examples showing how connection patterns can change between retinotopic (A, A')
and nonretinotopic areas (B, B'). The upper two figures show how connection patterns
can change in a hypothetical situation where the primary and secondary indices are
interchanged in two different areas. In area A the primary indices are (X, Y) and the
secondary indices are (α, β), and in area B the primary indices are (α, β) and the secondary
indices are (X, Y). The shaded areas are examples of those that would be connected on a
point-to-point basis. The second example shows a subset of the connections in a situation
where the retinotopic area A' represents optic flow as indicated by direction vectors and
the nonretinotopic area represents rigid motion parameters for translation (U, V, W) and
rotation. The primary indices are assumed to be U/W, V/W. Shown next is a subset of
the connections from A' to B' that represent values of rotation equal to zero. The three
rotation parameters are not specified in the figure, but it is assumed that a rotation value
of zero is at the center of each of the areas with different primary indices. Both of these
examples are meant to be representative of the kinds of transformations that occur when
the primary indices of different areas are different. The patterns may not be as regular as
depicted here, but in general will be "point-to-many."

values in a specific geometric direction. In short, the tree-shrew data can be explained by connections between related parameters within the cortical area, but the same kinds of patterns could be produced as a consequence of changing indexing schemes in different cortical areas.

Developmental Constraints on Cortical Structure

The synopsis of the description of cortical representation of parameters was that the cortical areas were arranged in patches, using primary and secondary indices for groups of 5–15 parameters, and that connections between patches that had different primary indices should reveal characteristic spots or bands whereas connections between patches with the same primary indices would be one-to-one. That this organization should hold for the entire cortex has been argued by extrapolating current experimental evidence. These arguments become weaker as the representation becomes more abstract. That is, numerical or topological parameter organizations are naturally represented with certain primary indices in the cortex. In many computations one can imagine, connections are needed to nearby values (speaking numerically). Matters are greatly simplified in a representation where the nearby numerical quantity is also an anatomical neighbor. This advantage lessens as the parameters become more abstract. In dealing with sets, one might expect to be able to shuffle the order of neurons (while preserving connections) without result. However, these are not the only constraints on cortical organization.

Another source of constraints is developmental: The brain has to connect itself correctly in the first place. Experiments by Rakic (1974, 1981) and Goldman-Rakic and Schwartz (1982) have revealed an elegant pattern of cortical growth that produces interleaved connections between different areas. Interleaved connections may be achieved by the temporal phasing of growth (Rakic 1981). For example, connections from area A to cortical area B may initially be dense, but are spread apart by cortical growth. Another set of connections to B starting at a later time can use the first set of connections as guides to fit in between them in a uniform fashion. Thus, the parameters of secondary indices may be naturally placed at the ends of appropriately interleaved connections to areas that use them.

Summary

- The cortical architecture can be thought of as composed of functional areas, each representing a multidimensional parameter space.

• My hypothesis is that these parameters project onto the cortex in such a way that two dimensions are isomorphic to the cortical sheet and the rest are interleaved. The former are termed *primary indices* and the latter are termed *secondary indices.*

• Constraints on unit-value architecture suggest that only 5−15 parameters can be completely represented in any given cortical area.

• Savings in units can be achieved with overlapping RFs, but only with the sacrifice of parallel computing capability.

• Connections between cortical areas with different primary indices are primarily one-to-many.

• The value-unit concept is compatible with current ideas about cortical growth whereby connections from different regions are temporally sequenced.

Computing with Cortico-Cortical Connections

The introductory section described how value units can be used for a general class of computation. The map-coloring example faithfully represents the abstract nature of the computation but is removed from general perceptual and cognitive problems. This section closes this gap by discussing two examples, one from shape and one from motion perception.

The fundamental issue for value-unit encoding is the N^k problem. Given this limitation, how can one represent information in a way that captures sufficient diversity? The answer is that there are many different strategies for decomposing high-dimensional structures into networks of value units, each of low dimensionality. The most important of these strategies are hierarchies and subspaces.

Hierarchies split higher-dimensional spaces into more abstract and less abstract parts. As an example, consider some enumeration of tasks T (e.g. hammering, sawing) with objects O (e.g. nails, wood) to which the tasks are applied. Here the notion is that a task is a more abstract concept than the object of the task. One could have units for each combination (i.e., T × O), but a more economical decomposition is to have separate network for T and O with constraints between them.

Subspaces are a mathematical concept that logically includes the above example, but I (somewhat arbitrarily) use the term for decompositions at the same level of abstraction. The idea is simple: If a value-unit representation is infeasible for some dimension k (e.g. $N^k > 10^{10}$), then split the space into m subspaces, each of lesser dimensions $(k_1, \ldots, k_m)$, such that

$$\sum_{i=1}^{m} N^{k_i} \ll 10^{10}.$$

The first question that occurs is that of when the subspaces uniquely represent the original data. (This is very similar to the reconstruction-from-projections problem in computed tomography, except that now the units are either on or off.) Unfortunately, the answer depends on the number of high-dimensional units that would be on. If this number is n, then the number of subspaces of dimension $k' (= k_1 = k_2 = k_m)$ that are required to unambiguously represent the high-dimensional data has been shown to be bounded (Kemperman 1982):

$$1 + n((k \operatorname{div} m) - 1),$$

where div denotes integer division. This result requires the number of subspaces to grow as the complexity of the information grows. What this means is that, in general, some tradeoff will have to be made. The subspaces can be chosen to unambiguously represent a certain number of concepts; after that point, some ambiguity will be introduced into the representation. This ambiguity is dealt with in the next section. The remaining parts of this section illustrate specific solutions to the N^k problem that use hierarchies and subspace.

Since the following examples illustrate technical details of the value-unit approach, they may inadvertently overemphasize particular constraints in relation to competing parametrizations cast in terms of conventional computing models. Better constraints may be found; the main point that these examples illustrate is that, in order to be case in terms of the value-unit model, the constraints have to be expressed in terms of sets of relations, each involving only a small number of terms.

Shape Perception

One way of recognizing a familiar rigid shape is to relate visual features in a retinal coordinate frame to those of a stored prototype. The stored prototype is economically described with respect to an intrinsic frame which is related to some special features of the prototype itself (figures 13a, 13b). To relate the retinotopic data and the intrinsic data, a coordinate transformation between the two frames must be computed. By choosing the visual features appropriately, one can compute this coordinate transformation easily if the correspondence between a prototype feature and a

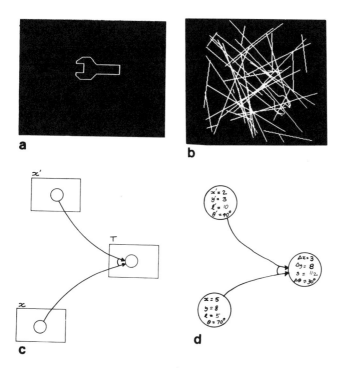

Figure 13
(a) Data for a "wrench" displayed as four-parameter (x location, y location, length, orientation) vectors. (b) Corresponding data for a simulated image. Here the wrench appears scaled, translated, and rotated together with other background vectors. (c) The principle of detecting a transformation via explicit transformation units. Each (x, x') pair of units is connected to a transformation unit. The unit that receives the most is selected as the appropriate transformation. (d) An example of a specific connection.

retinotopic feature is known. I have shown that the correct transformation can be computed even when this correspondence is not known in advance: all possible correspondences compute transformation values, and the correct value is selected as the consensus among the different values computed.

One very plausible use of cortico-cortical connections is for computing these kinds of coordinate transformations. The key to this computation is to represent possible transformation parameters as explicit value units (Ballard 1981; Hinton 1981). Once this is done, any transformation $x' = Tx$, where x' and x are data in two different coordinate frames and T is the transformation between them, can be captured as a relation between an explicit x' unit, an explicit transform unit, and an explicit x unit (Hinton

1981). Figure 13c shows conjunctive connections (described above) to a representative transform unit. Thus, a T unit will receive input only if both the $\mathbf{x}'$ unit and the $\mathbf{x}$ unit are on. To make this more specific, consider the domain of two-dimensional polygonal shapes such as that shown in figures 13a and 13b. Let each edge segment of the polygon $\mathbf{x}$ be described by four parameters: horizontal-position, vertical-position, length, and orientation. The components of the transformed polygon $\mathbf{x}'$ can be represented similarly. The transformation parameters T can also be represented by four components: change-in-horizontal-position, change-in-vertical-position, scale, and rotation. Let

$$\mathbf{x} = (x, y, l, \theta),$$

$$\mathbf{x}' = (x', y', l', \theta'),$$

and

$$T = (\Delta x, \Delta y, s, \Delta \theta). \text{ Then}$$

$$\Delta \theta = \theta - \theta',$$

$$s = l/l',$$

$$\Delta x = x - x's \cos \theta - y's \sin \theta,$$

and

$$\Delta y = y + x's \sin \theta - y's \cos \theta.$$

These relations can be used to determine connectivity patterns between three networks of four-dimensional value units. As an example of a particular connection, the unit $\mathbf{x}' = (2, 3, 10, 40°)$ and the unit $\mathbf{x} = (5, 8, 5, 70°)$ connect to the unit $T = (3, 8, \frac{1}{2}, 30°)$, as shown by figure 13b. Each pair of units that are on ($s(\mathbf{x}) = s(\mathbf{x}') = 1$) provides input for a transformation unit. If there is a subset of $(\mathbf{x}, \mathbf{x}')$ pairs that are related by the same transformation T, then that T unit will receive the most input.

This strategy was successfully used to recognize two-dimensional shapes (Ballard 1981). However, I was more interested in extending this result to three dimensions. In three dimensions, seven parameters describe the transformation: scale (one), rotation (three), and location (three). Simple calculations show that if there are M units, each of different $\mathbf{x}'$, $\mathbf{x}$, and T, there will be $3M^2$ total conjunctive connections and approximately M per unit. In the case where $M = N^k$ (where, as above, N is the number of just-noticeable differences and k is the dimension of the stimulus), the number of units can become prohibitively large. For the three-dimensional case, ($N = 100$, $k = 7$) would require 10^{14} units. Coarse coding can be used to reduce this number and will be especially effective for encoding T units since only one value will be present for most tasks. In general, however, additional economies must be sought.

One general strategy for dealing with high-dimensional parameters is to split them into subspaces (Ballard 1984; Ballard and Sabbah 1983; Hrechanyk and Ballard 1983). This is especially attractive in the case of transformations, since explicit algebraic relationships can be found between subdimensions, as shown by the earlier equations. This has recently been done for three-dimensional shapes (Ballard and Tanaka 1985), but I will stick with two-dimensional shapes in the present example because the graphic displays are more intuitive. In the two-dimensional example, four-dimensional $\mathbf{x}$, $\mathbf{x}'$, and T units can be split into nine subspaces, each of which contains only N^2 units. The image data are represented in terms of three groups of units position units, orientation and scale units, and coarse-resolution position-orientation-scale units. The last group is the group that was costly to represent under the earlier scheme, but in this case the resolution of these units is extremely coarse. This is possible since they work in conjunction with the other fine-resolution units. Model units are represented in the same way, with three groups of units like those that represent image data. These groups are similar to cells found in striate cortex. Simple cells are position sensitive, complex cells are orientation sensitive (and, unlike the units in our model, weakly position sensitive), and hypercomplex cells are coarsely sensitive to position and orientation. The transformation T is represented by three groups of units: scale-rotation units, rotated position units, and translation units. Figure 14 shows the relationship between these units. Note that only representative units are drawn. Each such unit is part of a group which collectively covers all values of the particular parameters.

This example reflects computational requirements more than the underlying biology; it is a sufficiency proof that the transform can be computed in parallel using only two-dimensional value units. Nonetheless, since the algebraic relationships are basic, it would not be surprising if they were exploited by the underlying biology. The "answer" is described by the most active rotation and scale unit (5 in figure 14) and the most active translation unit (9 in figure 14).

One drawback of the subspaces is that an image shape that matches correctly in each subspace but does not have the right location/orientation-scale correspondence would be indistinguishable from the correct shape. In other words, $(\uparrow \leftarrow)$ would match $(\leftarrow \uparrow)$. This is an example of a general

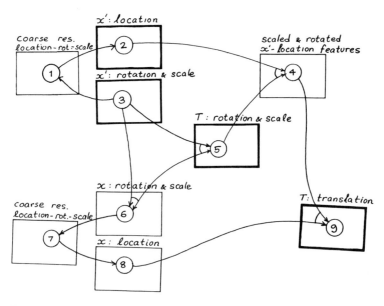

Figure 14
The decomposition of the four-parameter units into nine parameter spaces of two-parameter units. Only representative connections are shown. The boldface notation indicates the value units depicted in a computer simulation in figure 15.

phenomenon of errors in subspace correspondence known as the phenomenon of *illusory conjunctions* (Treisman and Gelade 1980). In my design I implemented constraints that loosely couple the two subspaces in order to reduce the amount of illusory rotation/scale conjunctions. However, this problem is probably solved by selective focus of attention. (Since this is a sequential mechanism, it is beyond the present scope.) Another helpful constraint is that of rotation/scale filtering, which gives more emphasis to length-orientation units that have an associated *on* transform unit and model unit.

Figure 15 shows several of the networks in the computer simulation after one parallel iteration. In this experiment the data of figures 13c and 13d were used as the model and the retinotopic input, respectively. The model is a caricature of a wrench that appears transformed in the simulated image, together with artificially generated noise vectors. Figures 15a and 15b show how the wrench looks in terms of the two subspaces (x': location) (x': rotation and scale), respectively. Figures 15c and 15d show that the network correctly computes the answer: single units in each of these spaces receive the most input.

Table 3
A table showing the different algebraic relations used to connect the units in figure 14.

Input	Output	Type*	Connection rule	Comment
$1:(X', Y', L', \Theta')$ $3:(l', \theta')$	$2:(x', y')$ $1:(X', Y', L', \Theta')$	A A	$x' = X', y' = Y'$ $L' = l', \Theta' = \theta'$	Loosely couples two subspaces
$2:(x', y'),\ 5:(s, \Delta\theta)$	$4:(x_r, y_r)$	M	$x_r = x's\cos\Delta\theta + y's\sin\Delta\theta$ $y_r = -x's\sin\Delta\theta + y's\cos\Delta\theta$	Rotate model
$4:(x_r, y_r),\ 8:(x, y)$	$9:(\Delta x, \Delta y)$	M	$(\Delta x, \Delta y) = (x_r - x, y_r - y)$	Translation matching
$3:(l', \theta'),\ 5:(s, \Delta\theta)$	$6:(l, \theta)$	M	$(l, \theta) = (sl', \Delta\theta + \theta')$	Rotation/scale filtering
$3:(l', \theta'),\ 6:(l, \theta)$	$5:(s, \Delta\theta)$	M	$(s, \Delta\theta) = (l/l', \theta - \theta')$	Rotation/scale matching
$6:(l, \theta)$	$7:(X, Y, L, \Theta)$	A	$l = L, \theta = \Theta$	Loosely couples two subspaces
$7:(X, Y, L, \Theta)$	$8:(x, y)$	A	$X = x, Y = y$	

*A = additive, connections summed $p_i = \sum w_{ij} s_j$; M = multiplicative, conjunctive connections $p_i = \sum w_{ijk} s_j s_k$.

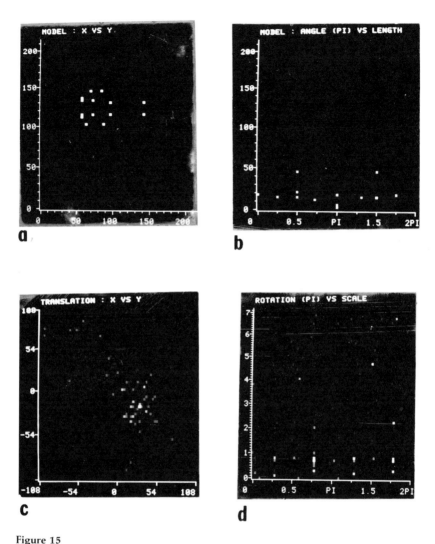

Figure 15

The results of a computer simulation, showing the parameter spaces outlined in figure 14. The input to a unit, p_i, is encoded as a gray level. The data shown in figures 13a and 13b were used as the prototype and the image, respectively. The objective is to find the correct transformation (scale, rotation) and (x translation, y translation) units that relate the prototype to a subset of the image data. The top two pictures show the subspace encoding technique using the prototype as an example. (a) Location units for figure 13a. (b) Rotation, length units for figure 13a. The bottom two pictures show the subspace encoding of the transformation space. (c) The correct *rotation-scale* unit receives the most input. (d) The correct *translation* unit receives the most input.

Shape recognition is only one of several problems that require the computation of coordinate transformations. Two other examples are sensory motor guidance (Sparks 1983) and stable perception. The solution for shape perception carries over directly to these other problems, although in each case there will be many other nontransformational issues. On stable perception, see Feldman 1982.

Motion Perception

Almost all computational approaches to vision adopt the use of hierarchies that represent parameters at increasing levels of abstraction. As mentioned above, there is considerable evidence that the cortical representations use similar hierarchies. These hierarchies were developed independently. The computational approach demands an explicit representation and algorithm to compute information necessary to do a specific task. The biological approach is aimed at explaining anatomical and physiological data from the cortical substrate. Yet despite this independence, the hierarchies reveal surprising correspondences. To be specific, consider the example of motion detection. Table 4 compares computational parameters with plausible biological areas. The biological areas were selected on the basis of single-neuron recording data and interconnection hierarchies (Maunsell and Van Essen 1982).

From the computational perspective, each of these levels solves a certain problem: They extract important parameters from the level below and represent them explicitly. The exact choice of representation between levels 1 and 2 is guided by the need to represent both spatial and spatial-

Table 4
Motion-perception hierarchy.

Level	Abstraction	Computational parameters	Plausible biological area
1	Image	Spatially distributed intensity levels	Rods, cones
2	Spatial and temporal change	Local intensity change due to movement, edges or lighting changes	LGN, V1, V2
3	Optic flow and derivatives	Physical velocities and spatial derivatives	MT (Allman et al. 1982; Movshon 1983)
4	Rigid motion	Parameters of rigid motion: rotation and translation	Posterior parietal (Sakata et al. 1980); superior temporal sulcus (Bruce et al. 1981)

frequency information (Sakitt and Barlow 1982) and the need to represent information at different scales (Poggio et al. 1982). Optic flow is the retinotopic velocity field induced by motion of the observer or objects in the world (Gibson 1950). Not all spatio-temporal change is due to movement; consider, e.g., changes in illumination strength. Thus, optic flow makes explicit the spatio-temporal change that arises from physical movement. The explicit representation of optic flow is an important step, but in order for motion stimuli to be used fully the information must be transformed into rigid-body parameters. In a value-unit model, optic-flow vectors turn on units representing global rotation and translation vectors. Information in this form can be used for recognition, eye movements, and navigation.

Are all these levels really necessary? From pure computational principles, it is possible to bypass levels and compute rigid-body motion parameters directly from image intensities; however, the value-unit representation scheme demands intermediate levels, because relations that are expressed in terms of many parameters involve too many connections. Like the number of units, the number of connections increases exponentially with the number of parameters. Thus, in value-unit representations the only scheme that is practical in terms of numbers of connections must use intermediate representational levels. Keeping the constraints simple by introducing hierarchies has another advantage: There is a better chance that abstract units can evolve naturally during a learning process by being fortuitously connected to highly correlated units representing less abstract information (H. B. Barlow, personal communication, 1983; von der Malsburg and Willshaw 1977; Hinton and Sejnowski 1983). Thus, in terms of normal spatio-temporal change, optic flow may be an invariant that is sufficiently probable to be learned by a Hebbian scheme (Hinton et al. 1984; Barto et al. 1982), whereas rigid motion parameters may be insufficiently correlated. On the other hand, the rigid motion parameters may be highly correlated in terms of optic flow. Once an abstract level has been learned, levels that are even more abstract can be learned.

Although the optic-flow computation is particularly elegant, similar constraints may be found for rigid-body motion parameters. Ballard and Kimball 1983 includes a formulation that uses temporal variations in the optic flow. In that implementation, rotation is found by assuming that three-dimensional velocity information is available from the time-varying image. Other parametric approaches to representing rigid-body motion have used the two-dimensional optic-flow image (Prazdny 1981; O'Rourke 1981; Ullman and Hildreth 1983). In particular situations, such as translatory motion, other interesting parameters can be computed directly from the optic flow (Lee and Reddish 1981; Hrechanyk and Ballard 1983). All these formulations can be translated into the value-unit formalism.

To see how the value-unit formalism can handle motion, let us start with the interconnections at the less abstract end of the hierarchy. Specifically, let us see how optic flow can be computed from spatio-temporal change. Computing the local velocity at a specific retinal location is done differently depending on whether or not the spatial image intensities are oriented. To consider the two different cases, suppose the image contains an edge. In this case, only velocity estimates perpendicular to the edge can be obtained (the well-known "aperture problem"). The other case is when the image contains relatively unoriented intensity patterns. If this image moves, the velocity can be detected by correlation in space and time. However, space-time correlation is costly to implement biologically. A computationally economical solution is to be content with the direction of motion and take advantage of motion blur. To do this, one can use oriented pattern detectors provided their integration times are sufficiently long. That is, motion blur produces a spatially oriented pattern which triggers the detector. These two strategies are depicted in figure 16. This slow

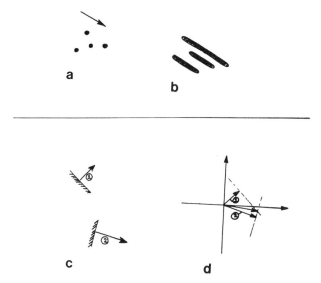

Figure 16
Two ways to measure optic flow. Top: (a) Moving high-frequency patterns indicate flow direction after (b) temporal blurring (Bandyopadhyay 1985b). Bottom: (c) Moving edges only indicate flow in the direction perpendicular to the edge. However, (d) two non-parallel edge measurements can be combined (Movshon 1983).

Table 5
Detector Summary.

Type of value unit	Integration time*	Spatial frequency	Oriented?
Edge	$\tau \ll V/D$	Low	Yes
Blur	$\tau \gg V/D$	High	Yes
Spot	$\tau \ll V/D$	Low	No

*τ = unit integration time; V = speed; D = diameter of spatial RF.

behavior contrasts with that of the edge detectors, which must have fast integration times. Slow integration times in the case of the edge detector will nullify its output.

In addition to velocity direction, velocity magnitude (speed) can be detected by linking pairs of spot detectors. The important point here is that speed can be detected with good accuracy given low spatial resolution. These three kinds of value units are described in table 5. The Edge, Blur, and Spot value units have strong similarities with neurons in the Y-X-W system of Stone et al. (1979), but these identifications must be considered very speculative at present.

Up to this point, the temporal response of the value units to the input has not been discussed. For most applications, simply thinking of the response as instantaneous is sufficient to illustrate important behavior. However, the motion example is a case where the temporal behavior of the unit is important. It is assumed here that for most cases the temporal response, expressed as an integration time τ, is very fast with respect to the stimulus (as before), but that in the special case of blur units it is more helpful to have the response time be slower than the stimulus. This allows the unit to respond to the blurred photometric pattern.

A circuit that uses these different kinds of value units to compute optic flow is shown in figure 17. All the units are spatially indexed (that is, repeated for different retinotopic locations); only the representative units necessary for the computation of one flow vector are shown. Units are on or off according to the model discussed above. Specifically, at each point, an edge (θ) unit is on if the input is a linear intensity discontinuity of the appropriate orientation angle; a blur (θ) unit is on if the input is moving past that location at the appropriate orientation angle (Bandyopadhyay 1985b). These are two different ways of signaling velocity direction. Speed is detected by combining coarsely tuned spot detectors from different spatial locations. Inputs are linked if spatio-temporal summation is required to turn the unit on. The notation δ means that the inputs must be different

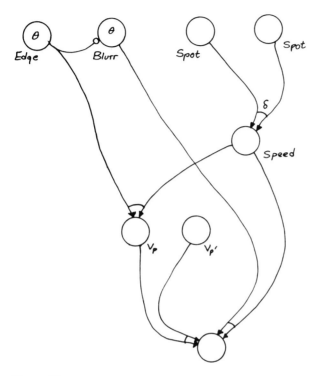

Figure 17

A circuit that implements the different optic-flow detection strategies described in the text. Oriented *Edge* units record the perpendicular direction of local motion. These can be combined with a measure of speed to estimate the velocity perpendicular to the edge, v_p. Two local estimates, v_p and v_p', can be combined to yield an optic-flow vector. A separate mechanism uses blur units that correctly measure velocity direction from temporally blurred images. These, when combined with a speed measurement, provide a separate estimate of optic flow.

by a fixed time delay δ. If the flow estimate is determined by an edge (θ) unit, additional computation is required to estimate the true flow vector, since the velocity estimate is only for the component perpendicular to the edge. One way of combining the information is to use two different estimates. The appropriate connection rule can be worked out simply from a graphical construction (Horn and Schunk 1981; Movshon 1983). Figure 17 shows how to combine two perpendicular components.

The value-unit approach can be also applied to the more abstract hierarchical levels (Ballard and Kimball 1983). One wants to characterize the gestalt of rigid-body motion; the solution is to define a parameter space of value units. Functional constraints determine the wiring between value units in the different representational spaces. If the parameter-space dimensionality requires an unrealistic number of units, the space is implemented as subspaces of interconnected units. Like the form-perception experiments, the motion experiments use rotational and translational subspaces.

In a value-unit experiment to detect rigid motion parameters, if depth and optic flow are available, a description of the motion can be created in terms of rigid-body parameters. It was assumed that related work in stereo (Marr and Poggio 1976) was successful, in addition to the optic-flow networks.

Given flow and depth, three-dimensional flow can be recovered. From 3D flow, use Newtonian kinematics:

$$v(X, Y, Z) = V_{\mathrm{T}} + \Omega x(X - X_c, Y - Y_c, Z - Z_c),$$

where $v(X, Y, Z)$ is the 3D velocity of a point in space, which may be expressed in terms of a rigid translational velocity V_{T} and a rotation ω about an origin (X_c, Y_c, Z_c). The summary of our method is as follows:

Step 1: For each pair of velocities $v(X1, Y1, Z1)$ and $v(X2, Y2, Z2)$, build a value-unit network to find dir(Ω) from dir($v(X1, Y1, Z1)$) $\times$ dir($v(X2, Y2, Z2)$).

Step 2: Build a value-unit network to find mag(Ω) and V_{T} from the above equation, assuming dir(Ω) is known.

In this description, dir and mag stand for direction and magnitude. Step 1 is actually an improvement over the originally proposed method (Ballard and Kimball 1983). The results of these experiments are shown in figure 18.

Different constraints than those of Ballard and Kimball (1983) are being tested (Prazdny 1981; O'Rourke 1981; Ullman and Hildreth 1983; Lee and Reddish 1981; Lawton 1983; Bandyopadhyay 1985a), but the usefulness of

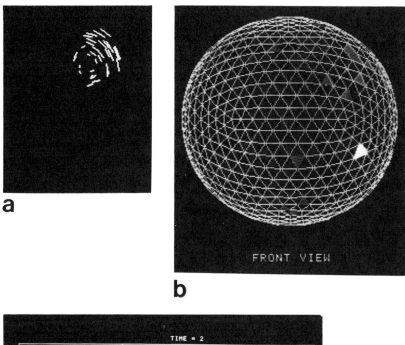

a

b

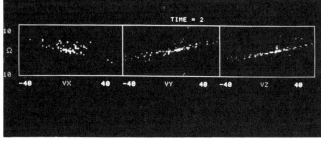

c

Figure 18

The next step in the hierarchy uses units to represent subspaces for global rotation and translation parameters. A global parameter is independent of retinotopic position and represents full-field stimuli. The figure shows a result of a computer experiment where three-dimensional velocity vectors provided input to rotation and translation subspaces of units as described in the text. (a) One frame of three-dimensional vectors. (b) A geodesic value-unit display representing possible rotation directions, showing that the correct rotation-direction unit receives the most input. (c) Three subspaces of units representing the magnitude of rotation combined with the three components of translational velocity. Although many units receive input, the three correct units receive much more input than the others.

the rigid motion parameters suggests that they will be likely to be represented cortically. Preliminary evidence for neurons sensitive to the appropriate full-field stimuli has been found in the superior temporal sulcus (Bruce et al. 1981) and in posterior parietal cortex (Sakata et al. 1980).

Though I have only sketched the principal features of a value-unit solution to motion representation, this level of discussion is sufficient to allow important conclusions. The most important of these concerns the meaning of the different cortical areas. The larger and larger receptive fields encountered as the anatomic hierarchy is progressed can be explained as a natural consequence of the more abstract parameters that are being represented. The most important point is that hierarchies of units represent visual information of a different nature, as implied by table 3.

Like the form-perception example, the motion example shows that physical constraints can be directly represented in terms of the cortico-cortical connections if the constraints involve only a small number of terms. If in fact the constraints used by the brain are multivariate and of high dimensionality, then the value-unit model is unrealistic.

Summary

• Important problems in visual perception can be readily expressed in connectionist models. Two examples are coordinate mappings and rigid body motion perception. The specific constraints used for each of these cases are constantly being refined, but I claim that the right constraints will still have value-unit implementations.

• The networks that solve these problems make extensive use of hierarchies and parameter subspaces. Both of these techniques help to keep the connection growth problem, introduced by the value-unit formalism, under control.

Associating Value Units in Different Modalities

The splitting of large parameter spaces into subspaces is a tremendously important strategy. It makes the value-unit model extensible to an arbitrary number of dimensions as long as they can be decoupled in some way. On the other hand, it is easy to see that the use of subspaces instead of the high-dimensional space can lead to problems. Consider figure 19, which represents a subspace of color units and a subspace of form units. The lower group of units differs from the upper in that the lower group are

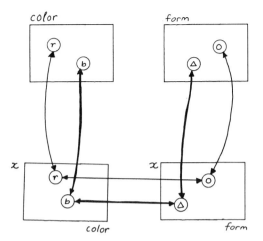

Figure 19
Using spatial units to couple despaced color and motion units. By selecting a specific modality, for example color, its corresponding spatially coincident feature may be found even if it is not directly coupled. In this case, non-spatially-indexed color units excite spatially indexed color units, which in turn are coupled to spatially indexed shape units. This preferentially excites the non-spatially-indexed shape units that correspond to the color. The enhanced links are shown in boldface.

retinotopically indexed whereas the upper group are not. For this reason the upper group are referred to as "despaced." Suppose the mechanisms of the preceding section (at a much coarser grain) are given a stimulus of a triangular blue object and a circular red object. If one considers the sub-spaces alone, as in figure 19, then the immediate problem is that the associations between the high-confidence units have been lost. A growing body of psychological evidence suggests that this is a ubiquitous problem in perception. During fast (~ 100 msec) tachistoscopic presentations of colored shapes, subjects will make submodality association errors (called *illusory conjunctions*), but given more time they can usually correct their mistakes (Treisman and Gelade 1980). The illusory-conjunction experiments suggest both that the separate groups of value units present a real difficulty and that, with additional processing time beyond a few hundred milliseconds, there is a solution to this difficulty. Furthermore, the psychological data suggest that the conjunctive mechanism is sequential. In experiments with displays of colored letters, subjects were asked questions of the form "Is there a red triangle?" In these experiments the processing time increased linearly with the number of visual tokens. However, if the question was "Is there a triangle?" the processing time was independent of the number of tokens. One value-unit solution to this problem, suggested by Feldman and Ballard (1982), uses spatial focus units to couple the different submodalities of color and form.

In accordance with the psychological data, this solution assumes that the overall computational behavior of the networks is *sequential* within the submodalities. That is, priming a despaced unit (say, "triangular") causes increased input to the appropriate spatial focus units, which then inhibit other spatial locations and help computations at the spatial focus locations. Thus, processing can be restricted to the appropriate spatial locus. This explanation captures only the gross features of Treisman's data: the fact of illusory conjunctions and sequential processing. Additional circuitry is necessary to simulate all the precise timing effects. Crick (1984) has suggested a neurobiological locus for this mechanism that implicates thalamic nuclei as well as cortical areas.

The ability to associate high-confidence value units provides a mechanism necessary for the isolation of a particular stimulus. This is especially important in the value-unit model for the following reason. Consider the example of picking up or looking at an object. Since it is postulated that all of the cortex is represented in value units, this control must be achieved through hard-wired connections from sensory to motor cortex. If the connections involve intermediate units, they are also value units. This means that if the stimulus is not isolated as a single, localized group of value units, the motor system will be compromised by receiving parallel inconsistent inputs. An example would be a frog snapping at the "average fly" produced by two concurrent moving spot stimuli (Didday 1976). Although this did occur in Didday's detailed simulation, it was rare; interestingly, he used network-like control structure to isolate a single stimulus.

Although for some situations it is sufficient to isolate a single stimulus, more complex situations require the ability to use two or more associations at the same time, or to remember previous associations. For these kinds of problems a number of solutions have been proposed: (a) shared links (Feldman 1982), (b) dedicated links (ibid.), (c) synchronously firing units (Abeles 1982; Crick 1984), and (d) fast, short-term synaptic weight changes (von der Malsburg 1981). Hinton and Sejnowski's (1983) weight-change formalism is also a candidate for (d), but it has been used to model long-term changes. This paper focuses on fast, short-term weight changes. A weight change is fast if it takes place in from 2 to 50 milliseconds. Such weight changes provide a passive memory for value-unit networks that avoids conjunctions between previous and ongoing computations.

The idea of fast, short-term synaptic weight changes has had a history of varying popularity. The novel addition to the idea proposed here is that the change in weights cannot be random or correlated with any repeated firings but instead must be more structured. The way I propose to do this is to use convergence states as a trigger for such modifications. The difficulty with an unstructured weight-modification scheme is that it may interfere with the base relaxation computations which require the weights to be kept constant. This requirement follows from the fact that, during the short convergence cycles of the relaxation, inappropriate units may temporarily have high confidence values. An example is the case of a local visual feature that turns out to be inconsistent with a more global context. A certain number of cycles are required to allow more global value units to "overrule" this local evidence (Sabbah 1981, 1982). If weights were allowed to change very quickly, then the local evidence would continue to predominate. Thus, the main point is that the weight modifications must not occur during short-term convergence, as the intermediate and final states may be different.

The other requirements are that the weight change be rapid relative to a few hundred milliseconds and that it be a state change that should persist for a substantial period (minutes) while other computations are carried out. The first requirement is strictly for performance; other computations which depend on the weight change are held up until it occurs. The second requirement characterizes the weight change as a system state change that should persist long enough to be useful in several other computations.

To illustrate the problem and solution further, a color-form example is developed. Consider again the case of four objects which are described by the different combinations of two shapes and two colors. A connectionist method of representation would allocate a unit for each of the objects (figure 20). Conjunctive connections can be used for each of the stimulus pairs. To change the weights, one can first use the focusing method described above to isolate an individual pairing, and only at that point increase the weights of all the active bindings and decrease the weights of all the inactive bindings. After this has been done, only the correct objects will be activated, even though all the combinations of features are active. (In this example, although the symbols on the units are the same for the purposes of discussion, the actual information will be different at each of the three levels. As in figure 19, the first two units represent retinotopically indexed information and despaced information, respectively. The third level has more coarsely coded information appropriate for object classes. For example, all canonical triangles at level 2 will map into the triangle category

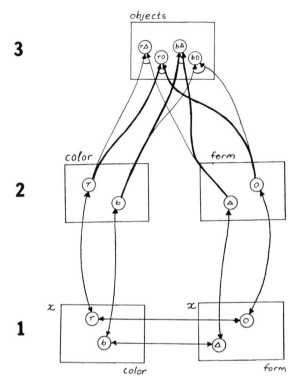

Figure 20

The basis for the crosstalk problem. The object network must be connected to handle feature cross-products and yet keep individual bindings distinct. Sequentially isolating the bindings allows the weights on the appropriate pairings to be changed to reflect the spatial correspondences. The changed weights are indicated by boldface links. The weights are reset when the bindings are no longer appropriate. The higher the level, the more abstract the encoding. Level 1 encodes retinotopic information. Level 2 encodes despaced object-centered information. Level 3 encodes categorial information.

node at level 3. If categories were not used at level 3, one would quickly run out of units.)

Special-purpose connection systems required to implement weight changes may reside in the hippocampus, but the evidence is also still very speculative. The hippocampus involves multimodal connections from almost all cortical areas. Furthermore, it is one of the few places where long-term synaptic potentiation has been observed. Also, interfering with the hippocampus impairs the ability to do tasks requiring the conversion of short-term associations to longer-term memories. A host of possibilities for a chemical mechanism are available, the most likely of which are calcium channels or peptides.

Summary

• The use of subspaces is ubiquitous and raises the difficult problem of how to associate units in different subspaces that are part of the same percept. Several connectionist mechanisms that solve this problem are under study. The possibilities emphasized in this paper are sequential focusing to isolate associations and fast synaptic weight changes to maintain associations.

• Fast synaptic weight changes are a passive form of memory that allows the same network to be used for additional computation. In active forms of memory, the separation of the remembered state from the current state is more difficult to control.

Conclusion

I have argued that the value-unit model is compelling in light of current neurological findings and computational studies. But what are the alternatives to value-unit connectionism? To address this question, let me briefly summarize the features of the value-unit design:

• It is a representation that allows parallel access to different values of a variable. This allows parallel computation within the observed 300-msec human responses.

• It is a representation that is independent of particular constraints. Although my examples came from vision, value units could be a lingua franca for the cortex that allows easy communication across different modalities. Value units also remove the distinction between symbolic and numerical data. Success in language modeling (McClelland and Rumelhart 1981) and the general features of somatosensory cortex (Woolsey 1981) suggest this ubiquity.

• It is compatible with a computational model that tries to minimize energy in satisfying constraints. This model, developed out of work by Hopfield, Kirkpatrick et al., Hinton and Sejnowski, and Geman and Geman, has the advantage that it divorces the representation from the computation, so that these two issues can be addressed separately.

• It is an encoding that emphasizes collections of small parameter descriptions. The decoupling of the vision problem into local constraints that can be represented in terms of low-dimensional variables has led to major advances (Maloney 1984; Pentland 1984). Thus, value units seem to be a representation that allows hard problems to be encoded into computationally tractable forms.

• Hierarchies of value-unit encodings are robust; networks still compute even when large portions are removed.

• Hierarchies of value-unit encodings can exhibit enormous diversity. One criticism that might be leveled is that 10^{11} neurons would not be sufficient to encode the necessary experiences. However, this is where hierarchies help. Crudely put, hierarchies of value units form a kind of "numeric" representation, with abstract units forming "higher-order bits" and less abstract units forming "lower-order bits" that can be composed. In a similar way, subspaces also expand the number of possibilities by allowing compositions. Thus, the number of objects representable would be (the number of object token units) × (the number of color units) × (the number of shape units) × (the number of motion units), etc.

• Hierarchies of value units that represent specific invariants that can be computed in parallel represent a straightforward answer to the Gestaltists: The things that naturally organize are just those that have explicit small-parameter descriptions.

Given these advantages, let us consider some alternatives. One alternative is a von Neumann-like design, but that would be too slow when built in neural circuitry. Parallel von Neumann computers are also infeasible, owing to the difficulty in satisfying the second property listed above. One of the big current problems with networks of von Neumann machines is the time taken in interpreting different message protocols.

A second alternative is variable encoding. Analog computers are designed on this principle, and there is no reason why differential equations could not be directly encoded in neural circuitry. Current models of the circuitry controlling eye movement are based on analog servomechanisms and have made several important predictions (Robinson 1978). The advantage of the analog encoding is that it is more compact than the value-unit encoding (but probably only by about a factor of 10^2, since the firing rate is extremely band-limited). Variable units have two important disadvantages: only one value of a variable can be accessed at a time, and the circuitry tends to be more delicate (i.e., adding or removing pieces affects performance unpredictably). Nonetheless, just as the thalamus uses some value encoding, the cortex could use some variable encoding. However, most single-cell electrophysiological recording data would rule out variable units.

One controversial aspect of the value-unit hypothesis is the encoding of values in a few units. This has become known as the "localist" hypothesis, as opposed to the "distributed" hypothesis, which suggests that encodings involve many hundreds of units or even more. The N^k argument sharpens this debate. Naturally, many hundreds of units will be involved in a percept; the crucial question is how small groups of parameters are handled. Keeping the number of units that represent a parameter vector small will facilitate parallel computations, since nearby values do not interfere, and may simplify the connection problem, since another network that requires the value need only connect to a few units. Besides these advantages, single-cell recording data seem to favor a localist encoding (certainly for the highly retinotopic areas, such as V1 and V2). I argue that, once the correct parameters are identified, locality will extend to other extrastriate areas as well.

What are the advantages of locality? In connectionist terms, to implement the useful relationships among sensory and motor parameters it is enormously useful to have value units that are similar in value be physically proximal. However, as the value units become increasingly abstract, the notion of value locality becomes more vague and the physical locality less imperative. Extremely abstract units may form a diffuse network that is scattered throughout the cortex and obeys no regular pattern. In this case the primary-secondary indexing concept may not be useful, but the concepts of value units and topological locality could still prove useful. Skimpy evidence comes from patients with lesions of the corpus callosum who exhibit very discrete functional losses (Dimond et al. 1977).

To conclude on a less technical note: For a long time, strictly computational models have not had significant interaction with basic studies in the neurosciences. However, new discoveries in both these areas are leading to a renaissance of attempts to bridge these disciplines. I hope that this paper will spark additional interest in interdisciplinary studies.

Acknowledgments

This paper was an outgrowth of a University of Rochester internal leave that allowed me to spend one year studying in the departments of anatomy and physiology with Paul Coleman. During that year many people helped initiate the effort that culminated in the paper. In particular, Paul critiqued many earlier drafts and the paper, and substantially improved the presentation. I thank Mike King, Joanne Albano, Dorothy Flood, Chris Block, Gloria Hoffman, Tanya Pasternak, and the Center for Visual Science seminar group, particularly Peter Lennie, Dave Williams, and Walt Makous. Also, Mike, Joanne, and Dorothy extensively reviewed earlier drafts, as did Francis Crick of the Salk Institute. In addition, on the computer science side, Jerry Feldman and Chris Brown provided helpful critique. I wish to acknowledge partial support from the National Science Foundation (grant MCS 820320) and the National Institutes of Health (grant HL21253). Finally, many thanks go to Peggy Meeker for preparing the numerous drafts of the manuscript.

References

Abeles, M. 1982. *Local Cortical Circuits: An Electrophysiological Study.* Springer-Verlag.

Allman, J. M., J. F. Baker, W. T. Newsome, and S. E. Petersen. 1982. Visual topography and function. In *Cortical Sensory Organization*, volume 2, ed. C. N. Woolsey (Humana).

Ballard, D. H. 1981. Generalizing the Hough transform to detect arbitrary shapes. *Pattern Recognition* 13, no. 2: 111−122.

Ballard, D. H. 1984. Parameter networks: Towards a theory of low-level vision. *Artificial Intelligence* 22: 235−267.

Ballard, D. H., and P. J. Hayes. 1984. Parallel logical inference. In Proceedings of the Cognitive Science Society Conference, Boulder.

Ballard, D. H., and O. A. Kimball. 1983. Rigid body motion from depth and optical flow. *Computer Graphics and Image Processing* 22: 95−115.

Ballard, D. H., and D. Sabbah. 1983. On shapes. *IEEE Transactions on Pattern Analysis and Machine Intelligence* 5: 653−660.

Ballard, D. H., and H. Tanaka. 1985. Frame-based form perception: Constraints, algorithms, implementation. Submitted to Ninth International Joint Conference on Artificial Intelligence, Los Angeles.

Ballard, D. H., G. E. Hinton, and T. J. Sejnowski. 1983. Parallel visual computation. *Nature* 306: 21–26.

Bandyopadhyay, A. 1985a. Constraints on the Computation of Rigid Motion Parameters from Retinal Displacements. Report TR 168, Computer Science Department, University of Rochester.

Bandyopadhyay, A. 1985b. Spatio-Temporal Blur Paths: A Representation for Image Motion. Submitted to Conference on Computer Vision and Pattern Recognition.

Barlow, H. B. 1972. Single units and sensation: A neuron doctrine for perceptual psychology? *Perception* 1: 371–394.

Barlow, H. B. 1981. Critical limiting factors in the design of the eye and visual cortex. *Proc. Roy. Soc. Lond.* B 212: 1–34.

Barto, A. G, R. S. Sutton, and C. W. Anderson. 1982. Adaptive Neuron-like Elements That Can Solve Difficult Learning Control Problems. COINS Technical Report TR 82-20, University of Massachusetts.

Blasdel, G. G., D. Fitzpatrick, and J. S. Lund. 1983. Organization and intracortical connectivity of layer IV in macaque striate cortex. In Proceedings of the Thirteenth Annual Meeting of the Society for Neuroscience, Boston.

Brady, M. 1982. Computational approaches to image understanding. *Computing Surveys* 14: 3–71.

Brodmann, K. 1909. *Vergleichende Lokalisationslehre der Grosshirnrinde in ihren Prinzipien dargestellt auf Grund des Zellenbaues.* J. A. Barth, Leipzig.

Bruce, C., R. Desimone, and C. G. Gross. 1981. Visual properties of neurons in a polysensory area in superior temporal sulcus of the macaque. *J. Neurophysiology* 46, no. 2: 369–384.

Burton, H., and C. J. Robinson. 1981. Organization of the S II parietal cortex: Multiple somatic sensory representations within and near the second somatic sensory area of cynomolgus monkeys. In *Cortical Sensory Organization*, volume 1: *Multiple Somatic Areas*, ed. C. N. Woolsey (Humana).

Cajal, S. Ramon y. 1911. *Histologie du Systeme Nerveux de l'Homme et des Vertebres.* Maloine, Paris.

Cowey, A. 1981. Why are there so many visual areas? In *The Organization of the Cerebral Cortex*, ed. F. O. Schmitt et al. (MIT Press).

Crick, F. 1984. The function of the thalamic reticular complex: The searchlight hypothesis. *Proc. Nat. Acad Sci.* 81: 4586–4590.

Curcio, C. A., and J. K. Harting. 1978. Organization of pulvinar afferents to area 18 in the squirrel monkey: Evidence for stripes. *Brain Research* 143: 155–161.

Cynader, M. S., J. Matsubara, and N. V. Swindale. 1983. Surface organization of functional and topographic maps in cat visual cortex. In Proceedings of the Thirteenth Annual Meeting of the Society for Neuroscience, Boston.

De Valois, K. K. 1977. *Vision Research* 17: 1057.

Didday, R. L. 1976. A model of visuomotor mechanisms in the frog optic tectum. *Math. Biosci.* 30: 169−180.

Dimond, S. J., R. E. Scammell, E. Y. M. Brouwers, and R. Weeks. 1977. Functions of the centre section (trunk) of the corpus callosum in man. *Brain* 100: 543−562.

Dow, B. M., and R. Bauer. 1983. Retinotopy and orientation columns in the monkey: A new model. In Proceedings of the Thirteenth Annual Meeting of the Society for Neuroscience, Boston.

Eccles, J. C. 1957. *The Physiology of Nerve Cells.* Johns Hopkins University Press.

Feldman, J. A. 1981. Memory and Change in Connection Networks. Report TR 96, Computer Science Department, University of Rochester.

Feldman, J. A. 1982. Four Frames Suffice: A Provisionary Model of Vision and Space. Report TR 99, Computer Science Department, University of Rochester.

Feldman, J. A., and D. H. Ballard. 1982. Connectionist models and their properties. *Cognitive Science* 6: 205−254.

Freuder, E. C. 1978. Synthesizing constraint expressions. *CACM* 21: 958−965.

Geman, S., and D. Geman. 1985. Stochastic relaxation, Gibbs distributions, and the Bayesian restoration of images. *IEEE Transactions on Pattern Analysis and Machine Intelligence* 6: 721−784.

Gibson, J. J. 1950. *The Perception of the Visual World.* Houghton Mifflin.

Gilbert, C. D. 1982. Presentation at Rochester Neuroscience Conference.

Gilbert, C. D., and T. N. Wiesel. 1983. Clustered intrinsic connections in cat visual cortex. *J. Neurosciences* 3: 1116−1133.

Goldman-Rakic, P. S., and M. L. Schwartz. 1982. Interdigitation of contralateral and ipsilateral columnar projections to frontal association cortex in primates. *Science* 216: 755−757.

Golgi, C. 1879. Di una nuova reasione apparentemente nera dell cellule nervose cerebrali ottenuta col bichloruro di mercurio. *Arch. Sci. Med.* 3: 1−7.

Gross, C. G., C. J. Bruce, R. Desimone, J. Fleming, and R. Gattass. 1982. Cortical visual areas of the temporal lobe: Three areas in the macaque. In *Cortical Sensory Organization*, volume 2, ed. C. N. Woolsey (Humana).

Hebb, D. O. 1949. *The Organization of Behavior.* Wiley.

Hinton, G. E. 1981. Shape representation in parallel systems. In Proceedings of the Seventh International Joint Conference on Artificial Intelligence, Vancouver.

Hinton, G. E., and T. J. Sejnowski. 1983. Optimal perceptual inference. In Proceedings of the IEEE Computer Vision and Pattern Recognition Conference, Washington, D.C.

Hinton, G. E., T. J. Sejnowski, and D. H. Ackley. 1984. Boltzmann Machines: Constraint Satisfaction Networks That Learn. Report TR CMU-CS-84-119, Computer Science Department, Carnegie-Mellon University.

Hopfield, J. J. 1982. Neural networks and physical systems with emergent collective computational abilities. *Proc. Nat. Acad. Sci.* 79: 2554–2558.

Horn, B. K. P., and B. G. Schunck. 1981. Determining optical flow. *Artificial Intelligence* 17, no. 1–3: 185–204.

Hrechanyk, L. M., and D. H. Ballard. 1983. Viewframes: A connectionist model of form perception. In Proceedings of the DARPA Image Understanding Workshop, Arlington, Va.

Hubel, D. H., and T. N. Wiesel. 1962. Receptive fields, binocular interaction and functional architecture in the cat's visual cortex. *J. Physiology* (London) 160: 106–154.

Hubel, D. H., and T. N. Wiesel. 1963. Shape and arrangement of columns in cat's striate cortex. *J. Physiology* (London) 165: 559–568.

Hubel, D. H., T. N. Wiesel, and M. P. Stryker. 1978. *J. Comp. Neurol.* 177: 361.

Hummel, R., and S. Zucker. 1983. On the foundations of relaxation labeling processes. *IEEE Transactions on Pattern Analysis and Machine Intelligence* 5: 267–287.

Juliano, S. L., O. Favorov, and B. L. Whitsel. 1983. Reproducibility of 2DG patterns in monkey SI and their relationship to single unit mapping data. In Proceedings of the Thirteenth Annual Meeting of the Society for Neuroscience, Boston.

Kaas, J. H., R. J. Nelson, M. Sur, and M. M. Merzenich. 1981. Organization of somatosensory cortex in primates. In *The Organization of the Cerebral Cortex*, ed. F. O. Schmitt et al. (MIT Press).

Kemperman, J. 1982. Recovering Multidimensional Punctate Data from Projections. Unpublished manuscript, Mathematics Department, University of Rochester.

Kirkpatrick, S., C. D. Gelatt, and M. P. Vecchi. 1983. Optimization by simulated annealing. *Science* 220: 671–680.

Lee, D. N., and P. E. Reddish. 1981. Plummeting gannets: A paradigm of ecological optics. *Nature* 293: 293–294.

Livingstone, M. S., and D. H. Hubel. 1984. Anatomy and physiology of a color system in the primary visual cortex. *J. Neurosciences* 4, no. 1: 305–356.

Lund, J. S. 1981. Intrinsic organization of the primate visual cortex, area 17, as seen in Golgi preparations. In *The Organization of the Cerebral Cortex*, ed. F. O. Schmitt et al. (MIT Press).

Maloney, L. 1984. Ph.D. dissertation, Stanford University.

Marr, D. 1978. Representing visual information. In *Computer Vision Systems*, ed. A. R. Hanson and E. M. Riseman (Academic).

Marr, D. 1982. *Vision*. Freeman.

Marr, D., and T. Poggio. 1976. From understanding computation to understanding neural circuitry. *Neuroscience Research Progr. Bull.* 15: 470–488.

Maunsell, J. H. R., and D. C. Van Essen. 1982. The Connections of the Middle Temporal Visual Area (MT) and Their Relationship to a Cortical Hierarchy in the Macaque Monkey.

McClelland, J. L., and D. E. Rumelhart. 1981. An interactive activation model of the effect of context in perception: Part 1. *Psychological Review* 85: 375–407.

McCulloch, W. S., and W. Pitts. 1943. A logical calculus of the ideas immanent in nervous activity. *Bull. Mathematical Biophysics* 5: 115–137.

Mishkin, M., L. G. Underleider, and K. A. Macko. 1983. Object vision and spatial vision: Two cortical pathways. *Trends in Neurosciences* 6: 414–417.

Mitchison, G., and F. Crick. 1982. Long axons within the striate cortex: Their distribution, orientation, and patterns of connection. *Proc. Nat. Acad. Sci.* 79: 3661–3665.

Montero, V. M. 1981. Topography of the cortico-cortical connections from the striate cortex in the cat. *Brain, Behav. Evol.* 18: 194–218.

Mountcastle, V. B. 1978. An organizing principle for cerebral function: The unit module and the distributed system. In *The Mindful Brain*, ed. G. M. Edelman and V. B. Mountcastle (MIT Press).

Movshon, J. A. 1983. Analysis of visual motion. In Proceedings of the Conference on Vision, Brain, and Cooperative Computation, University of Massachusetts, Amherst.

Olberg, R. M. 1981a. Object- and self-movement detectors in the ventral nerve cord of the dragonfly. *J. Comparative Physiology* 141: 327–334.

Olberg, R. M. 1981b. Parallel encoding of direction of wind, head, abdomen, and visual pattern movement by single interneurons in the dragonfly. *J. Comparative Physiology* 142: 27–41.

O'Rourke, J. 1981. Dynamically quantized spaces for focusing the Hough transform. In Proceedings of the Seventh International Joint Conference on Artificial Intelligence, Vancouver.

Pasternak, T., W. H. Merigan, and J. A. Movshon. 1981. Motion mechanisms in strobe-reared cats: Psychophysical and electrophysical measures. *Acta Psychologica* 48: 321–332.

Pentland, A. P. 1984. Shading into texture. In Proceedings of the National Conference on Artificial Intelligence, Austin, Texas.

Poggio, T., H. K. Nishihara, and K. R. K. Nielsen. 1982. Zero-crossings and Spatiotemporal Interpolation in Vision: Aliasing and Electrical Coupling between Sensors. AI Memo 675, Massachusetts Institute of Technology.

Prager, J. M. 1980. Extracting and labeling boundary segments in natural scenes. *IEEE Transactions on Pattern Analysis and Machine Intelligence* 2, no. 1: 16–27.

Prazdny, K. 1981. A simple method for recovining relative depth map in the case of a translating sensor. In Proceedings of the Seventh International Joint Conference on Artificial Intelligence, Vancouver.

Rakic, P. 1974. Intrinsic and extrinsic factors influencing the shape of neurons and their assembly into neuronal circuits. In *Frontiers in Neurology and Neuroscience Research*, ed. P. Seeman and G. M. Brown (University of Toronto Press).

Rakic, P. 1981. Developmental events leading to laminar and areal organization of the neocortex. In *The Organization of the Cerebral Cortex*, ed. F. O. Schmitt et al. (MIT Press).

Robinson, D. A. 1978. The functional behavior of the peripheral oculomotor apparatus: A review. In *Disorders of Ocular Motility: Neurophysiological and Clinical Aspects*, ed. G. Kommerell (J. F. Bergman, Munich).

Rockland, K. S., and J. S. Lund. 1982. Widespread periodic intrinsic connections in the tree shrew visual cortex. *Science* 215: 1532–1534.

Rosenblatt, F. 1958. The perceptron: A probabilistic model for information storage and organization in the brain. *Psychological Review* 65: 386–407.

Rosenfeld, A. R. A. Hummel, and S. W. Zucker. 1976. Scene labeling by relaxation operations. *IEEE Transactions SMC* 6: 420.

Sabbah, D. 1981. Design of a highly parallel visual recognition system. In Proceedings of the Seventh International Joint Conference on Artificial Intelligence, Vancouver.

Sabbah, D. 1982. A Connectionist Approach to Visual Recognition. Report TR 107, Computer Science Department, University of Rochester.

Sakata, H., H. Shibutani, and K. Kawano. 1980. Spatial properties of visual fixation neurons in posterior parietal association cortex of the monkey. *J. Neurophysiology* 43: 1654–1672.

Sakitt, B., and H. Barlow. 1982. A model for the economical encoding of the visual image in cerebral cortex. *Biological Cybernetics* 43: 97–108.

Shaw, G. L., E. Harth, and A. B. Scheibel. 1982. Cooperatively in brain function: Assemblies of approximately 30 neurons. *Experimental Neurology* 77: 324–358.

Shaw, G., P. Renaldi, and J. Pearson. 1983. *Experimental Neurology* 79: 293–298.

Shepherd, G. M., R. K. Brayton, J. P. Miller, I. Seger, J. Rinzel, and W. Rall. 1985. Signal enhancement in distal cortical dendrites by means of interactions between active dendritic spines. *Proc. Nat. Acad. Sci.* 82: 2192–2195.

Singer, W. 1981. Topographic organization of orientation columns in the cat visual cortex: A deoxyglucose study. *Experimental Brain Research* 44: 431–436.

Sparks, D. 1983. The role of the primate superior colliculus in sensorimotor integration. In Proceedings of the Conference on Vision, Brain, and Cooperative Computation, University of Massachusetts, Amherst. (See paper 2 in the present volume.)

Stone, J., B. Dreher, and A. Leventhal. 1979. Hierarchical and parallel mechanisms in the organization of the visual cortex. *Brain Research Reviews* 1: 345–394.

Szentagothai, J. 1978a. The local neuronal apparatus of the cerebral cortex. In *Cerebral Correlates of Conscious Experience*, ed. P. A. Buser and A. Roguel-Buser (North-Holland).

Szentagothai, J. 1978b. Specificity versus (quasi-) randomness in cortical connectivity. In Architectonics of the Cerebral Cortex, ed. M. A. B. Brazier and H. Peutsch (Raven).

Tootell, R. B. H., M. S. Silverman, R. L. De Valois, and G. H. Jacobs. 1983. Functional organization of the second cortical visual area (V2) in the primate. *Science* 220: 737–739.

Treisman, A. M., and G. Gelade. 1980. A feature-integration theory of attention. *Cognitive Psychology* 12: 97–136.

Tusa, R. J., and L. A. Palmer. 1980. Retinotopic organization of areas 20 and 21 in the cat. *J. Comparative Neurology* 193: 147–164.

Tusa, R. J., A. C. Rosenquist, and L. A. Palmer. 1979. Retinotopic organization of areas 18 and 19 in the cat. *J. Comparative Neurology* 185: 657–678.

Ullman, S. 1979. Relaxation and constrained optimization by local processes. *Computer Graphics and Image Processing* 10: 115–125.

Ullman, S., and E. Hildreth. 1983. The measurement of visual motion. In *Physical and Biological Processing of Images*, ed. O. J. Braddick and A. C. Sleigh (Springer-Verlag).

Van Essen, D. C., and J. H. R. Maunsell. 1983. Hierarchical organization and functional streams in the visual cortex. *Trends in Neurosciences* 6, no. 9: 370–375.

Van Essen, D. C., W. T. Newsome, and J. L. Bixby. 1982. The pattern of inter-hemispheric connections and its relationship to extrastriate visual areas in the macaque monkey. *J. Neuroscience* 2: 265–283.

von der Malsburg, C. 1981. Internal Report 81-2, Department of Neurobiology, Max Planck Institute for Biological Chemistry, Göttingen.

von der Malsburg, C., and D. J. Willshaw. 1977. How to label nerve cells so that they can interconnect in an ordered fashion. *Proc. Nat. Acad. Sci.* 74: 5176–5178.

Weller, R. E., and J. H. Kaas. 1982. Cortical and subcortical connections of the visual cortex in primates. In *Cortical Sensory Organization*, volume 2, ed. C. N. Woolsey (Humana).

Woolsey, C. N., ed. 1981. *Multiple Somatic Areas (Cortical Sensory Organization*, volume 1). Humana.

Zeki, S. M. 1978. Uniformity and diversity of structure and function in rhesus monkey prestriate visual cortex. *J. Physiology* 277: 273–290.

17

Visual-Cognitive Neuronal Networks

Arnold Trehub

For those of us perverse enough to want to understand the paramount physical basis of human achievement—that is, to understand the brain beyond metaphor, analogy, or abstract computability proof—the appropriate question now is this: How can the human brain *possibly* work? I stress the word *possibly* because of the apparent disparity between the power of current research tools in the neurosciences and the enormous challenge of the physical search space represented by the human brain. Yet if the problem of direct verification is currently beyond solution, it may nevertheless be possible to demonstrate both logically and empirically that a fully reduced and explicitly described neuronal model, within the proper constraints of neuroanatomy and neurophysiology, can be effective over a range of tasks normally included in the privileged domain of human cognitive performance. If such a model can be developed, tested, and judged competent, then at least one answer to the question posed above will have been found. If several significantly different reduction models are proposed for the solution of similar cognitive problems, then the scientific challenge of deciding among competing plausible theories can be addressed.

As a general principle, in the course of developing such models, the operating characteristics of the system must be commensurate with the ecological demands on the organism modeled. The frog that requires 5 minutes to decide if a moving object is prey or predator has already met its demise, and if analysis of a model of the frog visual system indicates a decision latency of that order the model cannot be viable. Similarly, a major constraint on any model purporting to account for human high-level visual-cognitive behavior is the requirement not only that objects and scenes in a perceived environment of particular ecological relevance be detected and classified accurately but also that the system have the ability, given the subsequent absence of that particular environment, to recall and actively reorganize significant elements of its internal representation as a basis for planning and future action. Thus, a model that cannot accommodate such recollection and reorganization or one that can do so only over an inordinate time period must be judged inadequate.

My aim in this paper is to provide an overview of a model neuronal system that, I believe, forms a credible physical foundation for understanding human visual-cognitive competence. The system has two key modules. One is a neuronal network for learning, pattern recognition, and imaging that is similar in its operation to an adaptive physical device called a *synaptic matrix* (Trehub 1967); the other is a network called a *retinoid*, which can assemble visual inputs from successive fixations on different parts of the frontal field into a coherent egocentric or allocentric spatial format and can reorganize internal representations of objects and scenes into new patterns for cognitive appraisal (Trehub 1977). The synaptic matrix, the retinoids, and various other hypothesized neuronal mechanisms interface to constitute an integrated brain model that can support high-level visual performance.

Tasks to be Performed

Listed below are some general tasks that may be taken as reasonable tests of a high-level visual-cognitive system. The initial model is a monocular version, and it is to be competent for visual tasks set in two-dimensional object space (Trehub 1977). As the model is elaborated to a binocular system with a capability for stereopsis, it should be able to perform in three-dimensional object space (Trehub 1978).

In a two-dimensional environment:

(1) Presented with an object or an arrangement of objects (a scene) on at least one occasion, the model must be able to recognize that object or scene on a later occasion despite substantial changes in object size, angular orientation, or position in space. This is the *semantic-learning requirement.*

(2) If an object or image has been learned, the model must be able to reconstruct an approximate image of that pattern when it is absent, and do so with substantial conservation of the information in the veridical stimulus structure.

(3) The model must be able to construct and learn new images by combining parts of objects and scenes recalled from its learned repertoire (memory).

(4) The model must be able to recognize learned patterns despite inputs that are substantially incomplete or degraded by noise.

(5) If the model is presented with a complex pattern composed by the superposition of previously learned patterns, it must be able to disambiguate the stimulus and sequentially recognize the constituent patterns.

(6) Given any arbitrary input pattern, the model must be able to respond with a series of recognition indicants and their associated images drawn from its learned repertoire, which are ordered in output according to some measure of pattern similarity with the arbitrary stimulus. This is the *gradient-of-association requirement*.

(7) The model must be able to learn substantial sequences of visual input and later accurately recall at least parts of the image content of selected sequences in correct temporal order. This is the *episodic-learning requirement*.

Neuronal Properties

The design of any dynamic model is critically dependent on the operating characteristics of the primitive elements that compose it. Since the present model is a neuronal system, the minimal assumed properties of the neurons that are postulated to be the basic building elements in the model must be specified clearly. All but one of the properties listed here are empirically well established (McClennan 1963; Horridge 1968; Shepherd 1974). The one assumed property that might not be accepted at the same level of confidence as the others is that of long-term synaptic modifiability (assumption 6 below). However, there is accumulating empirical evidence that this is more than just a tenable assumption (Møllgaard et al 1971; Bliss and Lømo 1973; Bliss and Gardner-Medwin 1973; Browning et al. 1979).

(1) There are two major classes of neurons: *excitatory neurons* and *inhibitory neurons*. Spike discharge along the axon of an excitatory neuron causes an excitatory postsynaptic potential (EPSP) in its contiguous target neuron(s), whereas similar discharge of an inhibitory neuron causes an inhibitory postsynatpic potential (IPSP) in its contiguous target neuron(s).

(2) When EPSPs and IPSPs occur concurrently on a common neuron, total EPSP is reduced as some monotonic function of total IPSP.

(3) Spatially and temporally distributed postsynaptic potentials (PSPs) are integrated in leaky fashion within the neuron.

(4) Whenever the integrated EPSP reaches a threshold level, the neuron discharges a spike output.

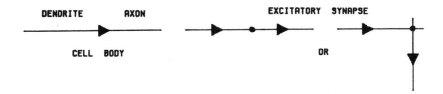

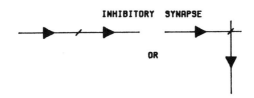

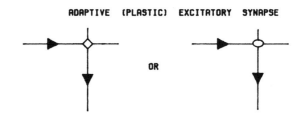

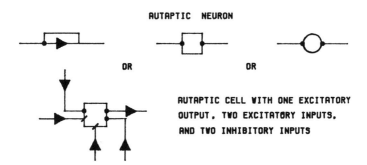

Figure 1
Standard symbols used for the neurons and synapses illustrated in this paper.

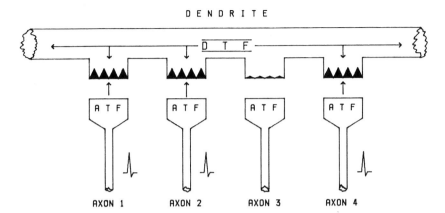

Figure 2
Synaptic junctions between four afferent axons and the dendrite of an adaptive neuron. Three axons have fired, and the postsynaptic cell has fired (indicated by the release of DTF to the coactive synapses). The darkened area at each postsynaptic receptor site indicates the magnitude of its local transfer weight (ϕ_i) after the reaction between ATF and DTF.

(5) Neuronal integration can be reset to its initial condition by sufficiently strong IPSP input to the cell.

(6) Some neurons have excitatory synapses which can be modified in graded fashion with respect to the magnitude of their contribution to the integrated EPSP of the associated cells (synaptic plasticity) given standard presynaptic input. The magnitude of any single synaptic contribution to the integrated EPSP of its associated cell, given standard presynaptic input, is called its *transfer weight* (ϕ).

(7) Some neurons receive excitatory synaptic input from recurrent collaterals of their own axons. Such cells are called *autaptic neurons* (Shepherd 1974).

In the networks to be described, standard symbols will be used to designates the various neurons and their processes. Figure 1 shows these symbols and their meanings.

Mechanism for Synaptic Plasticity

Synaptic junctions between several axons and a dendrite of an adaptive neuron are represented in figure 2. I postulate two active substances that contribute to the modification of the synaptic transfer weight ϕ: axon transfer factor (ATF) and dendrite transfer factor (DTF). A long-term increase in ϕ is assumed to occur only upon a reaction between ATF and DTF within the postsynaptic dendritic matter, and it is assumed that such a reaction can occur if and only if the presynaptic and postsynaptic neurons have fired in virtual coincidence. The latter assumption is consistent with the proposition, long held in psychology, that the organic correlates of two or more events must be contiguous if a direct association is to be formed between them (McGeoch 1942; Hebb 1949).

It is assumed that ATF is constantly renewed and available for release in axon terminals, whereas the limited store of DTF in the dendrites of adaptive neurons with multiple concurrent inputs is normally fully depleted in the initial reaction with infused ATF at each active synaptic site. Assume that after the postsynaptic reaction ATF has made a fixed contribution to the transfer weight (ϕ) of its local synapse, whereas DTF has made a ϕ contribution to each active synapse that is inversely proportional to the number of all concurrently active axonal inputs on the postsynaptic cell at the time the reaction took place.

Thus, after synaptic modification, we have

$$\phi_i = b + c + kN_{\alpha_{ij}}{}^{-1}, \tag{1}$$

where ϕ_i is the transfer weight of any particular synapse; b is the initial transfer weight of the unmodified synapse; c is the ATF contribution of the impinging coactive axonal contacts; $kN_{\alpha_{ij}}{}^{-1}$ is the proportional contribution of the DTF in the postsynaptic structure, taking account of the N coactive axons (α_{ij}) on the cell and the total store of DTF in the postsynaptic cell which is represented by the coefficient k; and it is assumed that $b < c \ll k$. This is our basic learning equation.

In equation 1, the assumed inverse relationship between the contribution of DTF at synaptic sites and the number of coactive axons is consistent with the finding that, when the number of parallel fibers in synapse with a Purkinje cell is experimentally reduced, the area of postsynaptic density at the fewer synapses increases proportionally (Hillman and Chen 1979).

An important qualifying assumption is the following. Equation 1 predicts the complete depletion of the total store of DTF (represented by the coefficient k) into the ATF-DTF reaction over all coactive synaptic sites. However, on physical grounds, there must be a real limit to the amount of DTF that can be utilized in the macromolecular change at each particular postsynaptic receptor region. Therefore, it must be assumed that complete depletion takes place only in those instances where the number of coactive axons (N) is sufficiently large relative to the total store of DTF (k). But in instances where N is very small relative to k, there should remain a residual store of DTF, which can contribute to synaptic changes on subsequent occasions. If $N = 1$ on the dendrite, a large store of DTF would remain in the postsynaptic cell after each instance of learning. It will be seen below that this situation occurs in the process of learning image patterns. The ratio of synaptically bound DTF to remaining free DTF can be characterized as an ogival function of the number of coactive afferent axons at the time of learning.

The Synaptic Matrix

Learning, recognition, and recall of visual images are accomplished by a neuronal mechanism called a *synaptic matrix* (figure 3). This self-organizing module uses the basic mechanism for synaptic plasticity outlined above to construct associative spatial filters in the brain.

In the simple example given, nine afferent inputs are assumed to be carrying information from a two-dimensional 3×3-cell retina. Thus, the lines α_{ij} sample a retinal space represented by $\alpha_{1,1}$ to $\alpha_{3,3}$. Each input line is in discrete point-to-point synapse with a second set of neurons called *mosaic cells* (M). The axon of each mosaic cell is in parallel adaptive synapse with all members of a set of cells in the detection matrix called *filter cells* (f). Each filter cell is in discrete synapse with an output cell called a *class cell* (Ω). The axon of each class cell bifurcates, sending a collateral back in adaptive synapse with the dendrites of the mosaic cells in the imaging matrix. Finally, an inhibitory neuron ($-$) receives as its input the axons of all class cells and sends its axon in parallel synapse to the dendrites (or cell bodies) of all class cells. This inhibitory neuron is called a *reset neuron*.

Each receptor cell on the retina connects to an afferent neuron labeled by the position of its associated receptor in the retinal array. Thus, each afferent neuron in figure 3 is designated α_{ij}, where ij represents the retino-topic coordinate of its associated retinal cell. It is assumed that center-surround inhibition and threshold properties of the retinal layer result in the extraction of a binary-valued contour transform of the light-intensity distribution caused by an image falling on the retina. Each afferent neuron discharges a spike (activity $= 1$) if an edge is detected at its associated retinal locus, or remains silent (activity $= 0$) if an edge is not detected at its retinal locus. This retinal contour transform composes the afferent excitation pattern on the mosaic-cell array. (Here and in the following presentation, the term *spike* or pulse indicates a train of axonal discharge producing an EPSP or an IPSP in the target cell. Since neurons fire when integrated EPSP

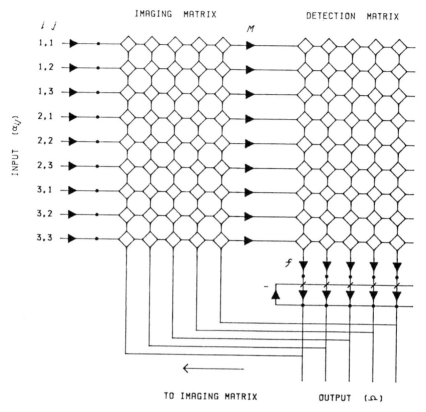

Figure 3

Schematic of a synaptic matrix. Afferent inputs from optic tract are designated α_{ij}. Mosaic cells are designated M. Filter cells are designated f. Class cell is designated Ω. Reset neuron (−) generates an inhibitory postsynaptic potential to reset all class cells when discharged. Given any arbitrary input, the class cell associated with the filter cell having the highest product-sum of active afferent axons (α_{ij}) and corresponding transfer weights (ϕ_{ij}) will fire first. Source: Trehub 1983. Copyright Lawrence Erlbaum Associates, Inc. Reproduced by permission.

rises to discharge threshold, it is clear that the latency of output in a cell will be inversely related to excitatory spike frequency at the input.)

The operation of the synaptic matrix at its early stage of development may now be summarized as follows. During some critical period in the maturation of a synaptic matrix, it is assumed that DTF is produced in each of the mosaic cells and the filter cells within the matrix, and that ATF is produced in the mosaic cells and the class cells. After production of the two synaptic factors, the transfer weights of the filter cells and the mosaic cells can be modified be environmental stimuli to the retina; the value of ϕ at each synapse changes according to equation 1.

In the naive matrix, before learning has occurred, all ϕ will be small and any visual pattern falling on the retina will result in relatively feeble, infrequent, and random firing of filter cells. However, any filter cell (say f_1) that happens to be fired by a retinal input pattern (say A) via the mosaic-cell array will undergo an increase in ϕ at those of its synapses that intersect the afferent firing pattern (A) in the detection matrix. Thereafter, since the cross-products of afferent stimulus units (α_{ij}) and synaptic transfer weights (ϕ_i) are integrated in each filter cell, whenever pattern A is presented, f_1 will fire at a higher frequency than other filter cells in the matrix because its rate of EPSP integration, given A, will be higher than that for any other filter cell not conditioned by the pattern A. Assuming uniform integration rates and spike thresholds in the following class cells, the class cell associated with f_1 will fire before any other Ω in the matrix output array, because its spike input rate will be higher than any other. Thus, spike frequency on labeled lines (class cells) is the effective code in this neuronal system. The first Ω_i to fire (in this case, Ω_1) then resets the integration levels in the entire class-cell array by discharging the inhibitory reset neuron (−), and the process recycles. In this fashion, any given visual pattern is identified by the particular class cell it discharges. Without resetting, all class cells in the matrix would continuously integrate EPSP and would reach their individual firing thresholds at random moments independent of the input pattern at the time.

Consider now the axon collateral from each class cell in figure 3 which courses back in adaptive synapse with the dendrites of all mosaic cells in the imaging matrix. If pattern A is presented, mosaic cells carrying the afferent pattern of A will be active, thus firing the appropriate filter cell (f_1) at the highest frequency in the detection matrix and, in turn, causing class cell Ω_1 to fire. The synaptic transfer weights of the Ω_1 collateral on mosaic cells that are not firing in the presence of pattern A remain unchanged, but its synapses with mosaic cells that are firing (as afferents carrying the input pattern A) are modified in accordance with the learning principle. Thus, synaptic-transfer weights are selectively increased for the M pattern A in the imaging matrix. Thereafter, assuming uniform discharge thresholds for mosaic cells, if Ω_1 is fired (addressed), either by its associated filter cell or by any other input, it will evoke the afferent firing pattern otherwise evoked on the mosaic-cell array only when visual pattern A is presented to the retina. In this way, by means of automatic yet selective synaptic weighting in the imaging matrix, the neuronal condition is established for retrieving, in the absence of retinal stimulation, an entire afferent pattern previously coded by a particular class cell. The capacity to recreate a specific afferent pattern on the mosaic-cell array in the absence of a corresponding retinal stimulus is one of the neuronal bases for imagination in this model.

Since only a single class-cell collateral is normally active at any given time on each mosaic-cell dendrite, the reduction of DTF stores is minimal. Thus, any given mosaic cell can participate in the adaptive construction of many different visual patterns in the imaging matrix.

Novelty Detection

It is probable that during the earliest years of human maturation most learning is passive and nonselective. This kind of learning is assumed to depend on a generalized high level of arousal (corticipetal discharge widely distributed by the reticular activating system), which lowers thresholds in the synaptic matrix so that filter cells are periodically fired and their transfer weights modified upon the presentation of visual stimuli to the alert child. In the more mature individual, however, it is unlikely that much learning occurs on such a vicarious basis. In the latter case, it is rather more likely that stimuli must be salient before threshold priming and subsequent changes in ϕ take place in the synaptic matrix. It is assumed that whatever is relevant to the needs of the individual and also novel (not previously learned) should be learned.

The issue of stimulus relevance requires a rather detailed exposition of motivational-perceptual mechanisms and is beyond the scope of the present discourse; however, stimulus novelty can be treated neatly within the present framework. Given a situation of relevance, by what physical process might the novelty of the visual input be determined? I propose that *classification time*, the time between the presentation of a stimulus and the firing of a class cell, is the basis for determining the novelty of the stimulus.

Figure 4 shows a neuronal mechanism for detecting novelty. At the presentation of an input in a context relevant to current motivation, a

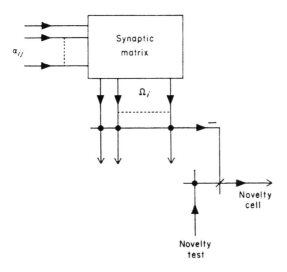

Figure 4
Schematic of novelty detector. Source: Trehub 1977. Copyright Academic Press (London) Ltd. Reproduced by permission.

novelty-test cell is discharged at a spike rate sufficient to fire its target novelty cell after the elapse of a standard period of time, during which the novelty cell is integrating EPSP from the novelty test cell. An inhibitory neuron (–), which serves to reset the novelty cell, receives its input from the axons of all Ω_i in the synaptic matrix. If the stimulus has been recognized (i.e., if a class cell discharges) within the criterion period, then the novelty cell will be reset before it reaches spike threshold and the stimulus will be treated as a familiar one. If an input pattern has not been learned, no Ω will fire within the criterion period, and the novelty cell (not having received a resetting input) will reach threshold and fire, signaling that the stimulus is novel. In the latter case, it is assumed that the firing of the novelty cell commands an increment of diffuse excitation to the synaptic matrix, thus lowering the thresholds of filter cells so that a previously unmodified f will fire and become tuned to the novel input in accordance with equation 1.

Retinal-Afferent Organization

For the proposed brain system to operate effectively as a high-level processor of events in visual space, it is essential that the retinotopic coordinates of the retinal receptor field be conserved through the afferent channels and in several of the neuronal networks for central processing. After exploring

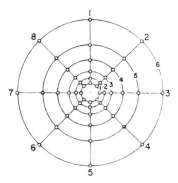

Figure 5
Ring-ray organization of retina. Open circles represent retinal receptors. Each receptor
and its afferent projection is identified by its coordinate in terms of the intersection of its
ith ring on its jth ray. Source: Trehub 1977. Copyright Academic Press (London) Ltd.
Reproduced by permission.

a number of different coordinate representations for retinotopic indexing, I
have found a *ring-ray* representation to be more useful and efficient than
any other I have considered. In this scheme, receptors in the retina and their
associated afferent projections are indexed with respect to the central
foveal axis in terms of their locations on imaginary concentric rings (i)
centering on the axis and imaginary rays (j) projecting from the axis and
intersecting all rings (figure 5). The rings are numbered from the smallest
($i = 1$) to the largest ($i = n_i$), and the rays are numbered in clockwise
sequence from the 12 o'clock position ($j = 1$) through one rotation to the
last position before 12 o'clock ($j = n_j$).

In the ring-ray arrangement of the model, it is assumed that the spacing
between concentric rings increases progressively as rings become larger.

Afferent-Field Aperture

The retinal organization described above easily lends itself to central-
nervous-system control of the effective aperature on the afferent field.
Figure 6 shows how inhibitory neurons can impinge on selected ring
groups of mosaic cells to constrict the diameter of the visual "window"
around the foveal axis. This mechanism allows dynamic masking or cropping
of images before they are conveyed to the synaptic matrix. It is assumed
that control of the afferent-field aperture plays an integral part in the
processes of focal attention and scene analysis.

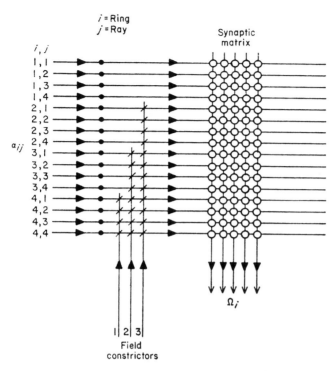

Figure 6

Controls for constricting effective visual field. Discharge of constrictor neuron 1 blocks input from ring 4 (outer ring); discharge of constrictor 3 blocks input from rings 4, 3, and 2, restricting input to ring 1, the innermost ring of receptors and afferents. Source: Trehub 1977. Copyright Academic Press (London) Ltd. Reproduced by permission.

Pattern Transformations

It is a remarkable characteristic of human perception that any complex visual pattern with a particular size and angular orientation at the time it is learned can later be recognized as the same pattern, despite wide variations in size and orientation. The neuronal network described below is capable of recognizing visual patterns that undergo such transformations.

Figure 7 shows a network in which the mosaic cells of a synaptic matrix similar in structure to that presented in figure 3 project in retinotopic order through two series-connected intermatrix neuronal layers onto a second detection matrix. The dendrite of each cell in the first intermatrix layer receives an excitatory input from each of two *decoupler cells*, one activated by an *initiate zoom* spike signal (command) and the other by an *initiate*

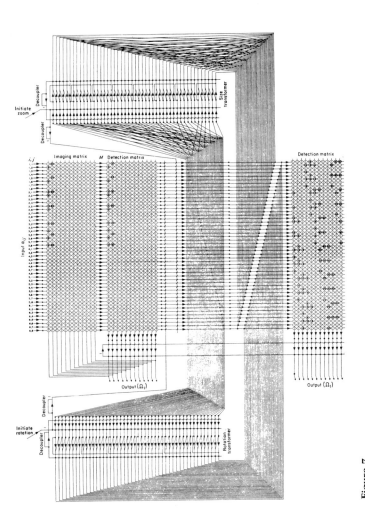

Figure 7

Schematic of synaptic matrix including neuronal circuits for transformation of size and angular orientation of input patterns. Values in detection matrix 1 represent synaptic transfer weights (ϕ) associated with the veridical input of two learned patterns ("T" and "Z"). Values in detection matrix 2 represent ϕ associated with all possible retinal sizes of the two patterns. Source: Trehub 1977. Copyright Academic Press (London) Ltd. Reproduced by permission.

rotation command. The axon of each cell in the first layer projects in excitatory synapse to its coordinate cell in the second intermatrix layer, and also sends off two excitatory collaterals: one to its retinotopically coordinate cell in the size transformer circuit and one to its coordinate cell in the rotation transformer circuit. The dendrite of each cell in the second layer receives, in addition to the input from its first-layer cell, excitatory inputs from its coordinate cells in the size transformer and the rotation transformer. Finally, the axon of each second-layer cell projects in adaptive synapse with all filter cells in the second detection matrix.

Size Transformer

One of the spatial-transformation circuits, shown at the top in figure 7, operates to expand or contract an initial activity pattern carried retinotopically over the mosaic cells. Inputs from the intermatrix cells representing the initial pattern do not activate the size transformer until the thresholds of neurons in the transformer array are lowered by a concurrent pulse from the initiate-zoom neuron. Under the latter condition, the pattern of discharge representing the current retinal image is evoked in the size transformer. At the same time, additional input to the transformer is blocked by the inhibitory output of two decoupler cells. One decoupler, activated immediately by input from the zoom-initiate cell, inhibits the first array of intermatrix neurons. The other decoupler, activated by the output of any cell(s) in the size transformer, inhibits the array of short interneurons linking the size transformer to the axons that have provided its retinotopically organized pattern of excitation. This pattern of excitation may be considered a prototypical image, which can then be neuronally re-represented in all possible size variations within the capacity of the size transformer.

The action of the size transformer can be likened to that of a zoom lens (hence "initiate zoom"). For a retina of 48 receptor cells (figure 7) organized into six rings and eight rays, the size transformer has a corresponding functional organization. Given any initial "real" input pattern (the prototype), the size transformer sends this pattern to the second array of intermatrix cells and thence to the second detection matrix. However, when any transformer cell on a given ring is fired, it in turn fires the cell that is in the next larger ring on its own ray (figure 6). Reversal of the direction of ring-to-ring excitation in an otherwise similar size transformer produces successive contraction in the projected size of any mosaic-cell pattern. Thus, the original pattern is successively enlarged or contracted by the appropriate retinotopic increment in a series of sequential projections onto the second detection matrix, where it can be learned and subsequently recognized in any size.

Rotation Transformer

The transformation circuit shown at the bottom of figure 7 operates to rotate any initial pattern of excitation carried retinotopically from the mosaic cells. As in the case of the size transformer, inputs from the inter-matrix neurons that represent a given pattern of stimulation do not activate the rotation transformer until the thresholds of neurons in the transformer array are lowered by a concurrent pulse from an enabling command neuron. In this case, the activating pulse is given by the initiate-rotation cell. When such a command is received, the pattern of discharge representing the current retinal image is evoked in the rotation transformer. At the same time, additional input to the transformer is blocked by the inhibitory output of two decoupler cells, as in the case of the size transformer. This "captured" pattern is the prototypical image, which can then be neuronally re-represented in all possible rotation variations within the capacity of the rotation transformer.

Given any "real" input pattern (the prototype), the rotation transformer projects this pattern of excitation to the second array of intermatrix cells and thence to the second detection matrix. When any transformer cell in a given ray is fired, it in turn fires the cell that is in the next clockwise ray in its own ring (figure 7). Thus, the initial pattern is successively rotated by the appropriate retinotopic increment in a series of sequential projections onto the second detection matrix, where it can be learned and recognized later under a range of angular transformations. Reversal of the direction of ray-to-ray excitation in an otherwise similar rotation transformer will account for counterclockwise rotation of any mosaic-cell pattern.

The neuronal circuits described above can accept a single visual pattern and re-afferent the same pattern through its full range of size and orientation transformations consistent with the structural constraints of the attached retina and transformer resolution. (See Pitts and McCulloch 1947 for an early treatment of pattern transformation.) Since the transforms are projected through a synaptic matrix, each can be learned by the filter cells in accordance with equation 1. Thus, the presentation of a single simulus can result in the learning of not only the given stimulus but also that stimulus in a variety of size and orientation manifestations. To avoid complications of interference between transformer outputs, it is assumed

that size and rotation transformers are in a relationship of reciprocal inhibition and that only one type of transformation is performed at any
given instant.

In order to recognize an object despite changes in size and orientation,
it is not necessary that filter cells be tuned to all possible combinations of
size and orientation. It is assumed that filter cells are normally tuned to a
wide range of size transformations of any given object, so that on any
fortuitous encounter the object will be recognized immediately despite
variations in retinal size. However, where the tradeoff of recognition time
for storage space in the brain is a reasonable one, filter cells might be
tuned to only a few orientation variants. If many retinal sizes of an object
are represented in the detection matrix, any veridical orientation later
encountered can be rotated internally until its re-afferented orientation
conforms to that of its appropriate size representation in the detection
matrix; at that point, the output of the appropriate filter cell will be
maximal and the object will be correctly identified.

Retinoids

Mechanisms that are primarily concerned with the reception, storage, transformation, classification, and retrieval of afferent stimulus patterns have
been described above. I now introduce a class of neuronal networks that
organize successive retinocentric afferent patterns into egocentric or allocentric representations of object space, reorganize object relationships to
construct heuristic representations of object space, construct new "objects,"
and model veridical and heuristic spatial relationships between the observing
system and the observed. These networks are called *retinoids* because, like
the retina, they represent visual space and project afferents to the mosaic-
cell array.

Short-Term Memory

The tuning of filter cells in the synaptic matrix by means of changes in ϕ
at their synaptic junctions is a mechanism of long-term memory. In contrast, retinoids serve as visual "scratch pads" with phasic and dynamic
content. The information stored is in the mode of short-term memory. The
mechanism of storage, in this case, is assumed to be a retinotopically
organized array of excitatory autaptic neurons. A neuron of this type has
at least one of its axon collaterals in recurrent excitatory synapse with
its own cell body or dendrite (Shepherd 1974). Normally, in order for

an active autaptic neuron to refire itself there must be other concurrent excitatory input to it. Thus, a sheet of autaptic neurons can represent in its sustained firing pattern any transitory organized input for as long as diffuse priming excitation is sustained. Remove the priming background input and the pattern on the retinoid is "erased."

Translation of Patterns on Retinoids

Shown in figure 8 is a retinoid of autaptic neurons joined by a grid structure of excitatory and inhibitory interneurons. Axon collaterals of *shift-control* neurons are in excitatory synapse with selected groups of interneurons. Operation of the translation retinoid proceeds as follows. Given a sufficient level of diffuse tonic excitation, any input from an afferent array to its homologous autaptic retinoid cells will evoke sustained firing of the retinoid targets. Thus, a mosaic-array stimulus pattern or input from any other source can induce a comparable retinoid pattern of spatially organized discharge. Each active autaptic neuron induces a subthreshold, priming excitatory postsynaptic potential (EPSP) in each of the eight contiguous interneurons capable of eliciting excitatory and inhibitory potentials (IPSP) in their targeted autaptic cells. If any primed interneuron receives an increment of excitation from one of the shift-control neurons, that interneuron will fire and send a spike input to its target cell. The rules are these: If an autaptic cell that is not discharging (off) receives an EPSP from an interneuron, it will fire (turn on). If an autaptic cell that is on receives an IPSP from an interneuron, it will turn off *unless* it receives simultaneously an EPSP from another interneuron, in which case it will remain on. If diffuse tonic excitation to the retinoid falls below a critical level, all cells in the retinoid will turn off.

If a standing pattern of excitation is evoked on a retinoid, the retinoid can then be temporarily isolated from additional confounding input by a decoupling mechanism similar to the size/rotation transformer decoupler described above, and its "captured" pattern can be spatially translated in any direction by appropriate pulses (spikes) from the shift-control command cells. For example, each pulse from the shift-right line will transfer standing activity from any active autaptic cell to the adjacent autaptic cell on its right and, at the same time, erase the activity in the previously active cell (on the left) unless that cell is also receiving transfered excitation from an active autaptic cell to its immediate left. Thus, successive command pulses from the shift-control cell will move the entire retinoid pattern to the right in successive increments of a single autaptic cell. The more rapid

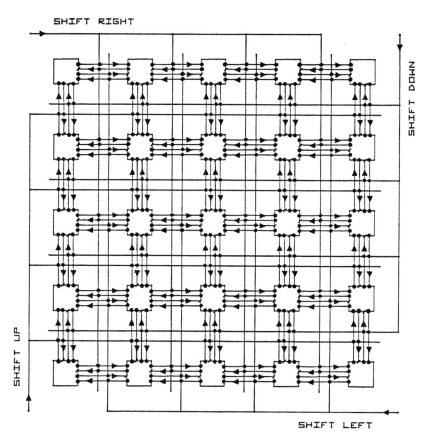

Figure 8

Translation retinoid. Large squares represent autaptic neurons serving short-term memory. Small filled triangles represent excitatory (terminating in a dot) and inhibitory (terminating in a slash) interneurons.

the pulses, the more rapidly will the pattern move; the longer the command pulse train is sustained, the greater will be the distance through which the pattern is moved. Appropriate pulse sequences of shift right/left, shift up/down can move the pattern of cell activity (Burt 1975) to any position on the retinoid surface.

With several translation retinoids in homologous projection, capable of coupling and decoupling with one another as well as with retina/mosaic-array inputs by the means described, it is clear that an extremely powerful mechanism exists for the organization and reorganization of spatial relationships among objects represented in retinoid space. This capability allows for complex scene construction and scene analysis, and it provides a dynamic physical substrate that might serve as a computational surface for motor operations in real (object) space.

Self-Locus

For an individual to engage in effective behavior in object space and to assess the personal consequences of various external states, he must have some internal representation of real and hypothetical spatial relationships between himself and other significant objects in veridical space. The self-locus retinoid, together with other retinoids, serves this purpose.

The self-locus retinoid may be thought of as a translation retinoid without afferent input but with the usual capability of point-to-point output projection to other retinoids (figure 9). The self-locus network is distinctive in that it maintains a uniquely coded "point" of autaptic discharge endogenously generated at the center of the retinotopic equivalent of the "normal" foveal projection (eyes and head centered on horizontal and vertical axes with respect to the body). Autaptic neurons representing the central self-point are constantly active, and neuronal activity replicating this point can be moved to any position on the surface of the retinoid by the usual shift-control commands. Such heuristic locations and excursion paths of the self-locus can be projected to other retinoids and can be combined with real and/or hypothetical objects and scenes represented on their surfaces to construct internal "maps" representing goal regions, obstacles, and direct and indirect paths to a goal. It is assumed that a replica of the self-locus sent to any selected region of retinoid space can serve as a reference marker so that the targeted pattern region represented on the retinoid can be translated to fall on the normal foveal axis (the source coordinate of the self-locus). Once it is in this position, the pattern can be projected back to the mosaic array to be recognized at maximum acuity in

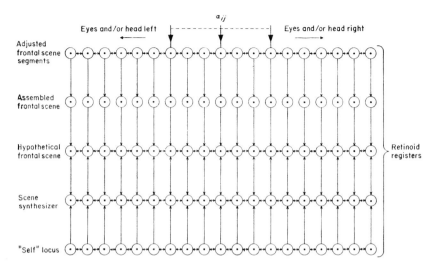

Figure 9
Flow schematic of stacked retinoid registers. Imagine a dimension of each retinoid array projecting orthogonally to the plane of the page in replicated autaptic cells. Source: Trehub 1977. Copyright Academic Press (London) Ltd. Reproduced by permission.

the synaptic matrix. This neuronal process makes it possible for a person to shift attention over different regions of visual space without corresponding eye movements (Posner 1980). Furthermore, neuronal discharge, projected by the self-locus at its current excursion site on the retinoid, can serve as a subthreshold priming excitor that facilitates response to afferent stimuli in its local region of visual space.

Scene Assembly

Given that the effective retinal receptive field is some small fraction of a larger object space and that human adaptive behavior requires knowledge of spatial relationships among relevant objects in the larger space, how can the visual system assemble and organize its partial inputs into a valid representation of an entire visual scene? Let us assume a complete frontal scene to be all discriminable objects within real space subtended by $180°$, with the vertex taken as the head in the normal frontal position. Since the receptive field for sharp foveal vision is only $2°-5°$ at the most, it follows that the eyes and/or the head must pivot to scan the whole frontal scene. Thus, a sequence of excitation patterns will be evoked on the foveal region of the retina, and these must be represented in the brain in some fashion to conserve their real spatial relationships (Didday and Arbib 1975).

Consider the top retinoid register in figure 9. This is a translation retinoid in which the shift-control neurons are modulated by eye and/or head position (and by motion detectors, which will not be discussed in this paper). Retinoid space is taken to be large enough to accomodate without overlap all the sequential retinal input patterns required to compose a complete representation of a frontal scene. It is assumed that the degree of pattern translation on the retinoid is directly proportional to the degree of eye and/or head shift from the normal "straight ahead" position. As each scene segment is registered and appropriately shifted, it is immediately transferred in its proper relative location to a second nontranslating retinoid and then erased on the first. In this fashion, a complete and homologously ordered representation of the frontal scene can be assembled on the second retinoid, and this information will provide the larger scene context for particular sensory inputs. For simplicity of illustration, an example of a 180° frontal scene assembly has been given; however, it is clear that similar mechanisms can assemble a 360° scene.

Hypothetical Scenes

The third retinoid in figure 9, labeled "hypothetical frontal scene," is a translation array that receives veridical information from the assembled frontal scene and endogenously fabricated patterns from the retinoid complex labeled "scene synthesizer." The scene synthesizer consists of two translation retinoids coupled as a functional unit. Thus, whereas the second retinoid in figure 9 (reading down) represents the current veridical scene, the third retinoid, by combining and spatially rearranging veridical, re-membered, and/or fabricated object representations, can create hypothetical frontal scenes, the properties of which can be tested according to the needs of the individual. If the properties of the hypothetical scene are judged as better than those of the veridical scene, and if the individual is capable of making the veridical scene conform to the hypothetical, he may change or reorganize his environment to this end.

Episodic Learning and Recall

The networks for processing objects and scenes in two-dimensional space provide the basis for a higher level of human visual-cognitive competence. Much if not most of our learning and memory is episodic in character, so sequences of experience are related and rendered meaningful by their temporal contiguity within particular time frames (Tulving 1972). The neuronal mechanism presented below serves to constrain and control a synaptic matrix to achieve episodic learning and recall in which temporal excursions of remembrance can be brought under motivational guidance (Trehub 1983).

Clock Ring

Figure 10 shows a neuronal network that can control the timing, registration, and location of episodic learning in a synaptic matrix, as well as the relative temporal locus and sequence of recalled (imaged) episodic experience (reminiscence). This mechanism depends on the short-term memory properties of autaptic neurons. The network consists of two rings of autaptic neurons, with each pair of autaptic cells within a ring linked by excitatory and inhibitory interneurons.

For each pair of autaptic cells in the inner (clock) ring, a clockwise direction around the ring can be established. Each autaptic cell innervates an excitatory interneuron, which innervates its clockwise autaptic neighbor. Conversely, each autaptic cell also innervates an inhibitory interneuron, which inputs to its counterclockwise autaptic neighbor. With this neuronal arrangement, if any particular autaptic cell becomes active (discharges), it will transfer its excitation (via the excitatory interneuron) to its clockwise neighbor, which will inhibit (turn off) its counterclockwise donor. Thus the circuit will sustain a constant sequential circulation of unitary autaptic-cell activity in a single direction (clockwise) around the neuronal ring. The circulation rate of cell activity, given fixed EPSP integration slopes and uniform thresholds for the neurons in the circuit, will depend on the level of diffuse excitation (arousal) within the network. The higher the level of arousal, the faster autaptic-cell activity will circulate (the clock will run faster); the lower the level of arousal, the slower autaptic-cell activity will circulate (the clock will run slower). We now have an explicit neuronal mechanism for temporal referencing and control. If the particular autaptic cell in the clock ring that happens to be active at a given moment should gate a frame in episodic learning, then the density of episodically learned experience would be directly proportional to the neuronal clock rate.

Recall Ring

Now consider the outer ring in figure 10 (the recall ring). Ignore for the moment the interneurons within the ring, and notice that each autaptic cell receives an excitatory input innervated by a paired clock cell at its own

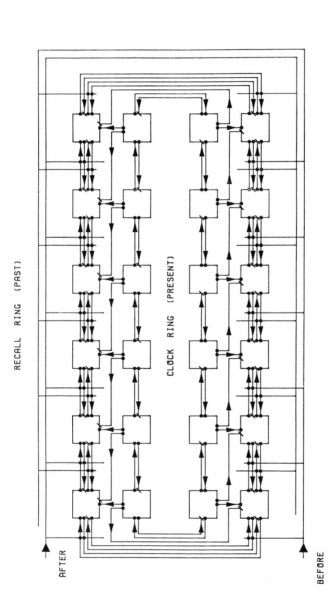

Figure 10

Schematic of neuronal clock and temporal priming circuit. Large squares represent autaptic cells which send priming excitatory pulses to synaptic matrix. Small triangles represent control neurons for clock rate and temporal direction (before, after). Inner ring of autaptic cells and interneurons composes clock circuit. Outer ring of autaptic cells and interneurons governs excursions of episodic recall. Source: Trehub 1983. Copyright Lawrence Erlbaum Associates, Inc. Reproduced by permission.

sequential position and an inhibitory input innervated by the clock cell clockwise to it. In the absence of any other input, this arrangement causes the autaptic cells in the outer ring to fire in synchrony with the inner neuronal clock. In addition, however, each pair of autaptic cells in the outer ring is linked by a counterbalanced set of excitatory and inhibitory inter-neurons. If we take a given autaptic cell in the outer ring as a spatial and temporal reference, a priming spike discharge (pulse) from the command neuron marked BEFORE will bias its local interneurons and transfer its activity to its counterclockwise autaptic neighbor (going back in time in the sense of an earlier autaptic state); a priming pulse from the command neuron marked AFTER will transfer autaptic-cell activity to its clockwise neighbor (going forward in time in the sense of a later autaptic state). The relative direction, rate, and distance of a temporal excursion will be deter-mined by which command neuron (BEFORE or AFTER) is discharged, its discharge rate, and the duration of its discharge. Notice the similarity between this control principle and that operating in the retinoid networks described above.

Network for Episodic Processing

Figure 11 shows a synaptic matrix that exhibits episodic learning and episodic recall. Aside from the fact that its activity is primed and controlled by the temporal neuronal circuit described above, it differs from the basic synaptic matrix only in the duration of changes in the synaptic transfer weights (ϕ) that constitute the physical substrate of learning. In this matrix, changes in ϕ related to episodic learning are assumed to decay over time and to approach an initial state. Although there is no generally accepted function to describe such decay, for the purpose of the simulation to be presented below I have arbitrarily chosen a long-term decay function in accordance with an empirically based proposal (Wickelgren 1974). Thus, for memory decay in episodic learning,

$$\phi_t = \phi_0(1 + \beta t)^{-\psi}, \tag{2}$$

where ϕ_0 is the synaptic transfer weight immediately after learning, t is the time elapsed since initial learning, β is a first decay-rate parameter, and ψ is a second decay-rate parameter.

In figure 11, each autaptic cell in the clock ring (PRESENT) sends an excitatory gating axon to a paired filter cell (f) in the detection matrix. Thus, at any given moment, only the filter cell that is primed by the

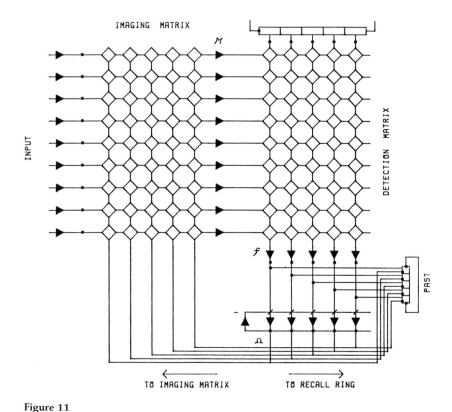

Figure 11
Schematic showing synaptic matrix for episodic learning and recall controlled by neuronal network illustrate in figure 10. Lozenges represent adaptive excitatory synapses. Rectangles at top represent autaptic cells in clock circuit (PRESENT). Squares at bottom right represent autaptic cells governing episodic recall (PAST). Each autaptic cell in the clock ring primes an associated filter cell (f) in the detection matrix. Each autaptic cell in the recall ring can discharge a class cell (Ω) which in turn evokes its related learned afferent pattern in the imaging matrix. The sequence of discharge in the clock ring is unidirectional (forward) in time. The sequence of discharge in the recall ring can vary in direction (forward or backward in "time"). Source: Trehub 1983. Copyright Lawrence Erlbaum Associates, Inc. Reproduced by permission.

neuronal clock can learn the current visual-afferent input. On this principle, learning is transferred over time sequentially and unidirectionally across the filter cells of the detection matrix, and the priming sequence is recycled as autaptic activity in the clock ring recycles. It is clear that for any given filter cell the changes in ϕ due to learning must decay to approach an initial state before the f cell is recycled in order to avoid a confounding of learned patterns.

Each autaptic cell in the recall ring (PAST) sends an excitatory axon to its paired class cell (Ω) in the detection matrix. In this way, sequences of class-cell discharge can be initiated and synchronously controlled by output from the recall ring. Since the discharge of any given class cell will evoke its associated (learned) afferent scene in the imaging matrix, sequences of Ω discharge will evoke (recall) sequences of learned visual experiences (images) in their original temporal order, going forward or backward in time from any arbitrary past reference scene in accordance with the controlling activity of the recall ring. This process constitutes episodic recall.

As the model has been described to this point, the initial temporal excursion for the recall of any particular past episode must recede sequentially over the recall ring locked to the currently active autaptic cell in the neuronal clock (PRESENT). In personal experience, the "leap" back to the beginning of a remembered episode rarely induces a complete sequential "playback" of intervening images (events) in reverse temporal order from present to past. Rather, the target event is usually retrieved first, and related episodic recollections are referred to earlier or later times with respect to the temporal locus of the target event. The proposed model can also perform in this fashion if the clock ring (PRESENT) is momentarily decoupled from the detection matrix (by a neuronal mechanism similar to that shown in figure 7) while a concurrent increase in diffuse excitation is applied to all filter cells in the synaptic matrix. Under this condition, any input pattern from the mosaic-cell array (M), whether exogenously or endogenously evoked, will maximally stimulate that filter cell having the highest sum of synaptic cross-products with the given pattern; its associated class cell (Ω) will fire first, and this Ω, through its axon collateral to its paired autaptic cell in the recall ring (see figure 11), will trigger episodic excursions from this point in the ring. In this way, sequential "playback" through intervening images from the present to a past target episode is eliminated, and recall will begin at a target point in "time" depending solely on the distribution of synaptic transfer weights (ϕ) within the synaptic matrix and the concurrent pattern of evocative excitation arriving from M.

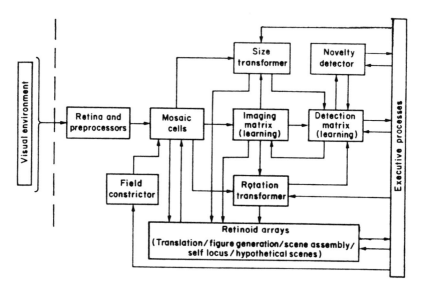

Figure 12
Block-flow diagram of visual-cognitive system. Source: Trehub 1977. Copyright Academic Press (London) Ltd. Reproduced by permission.

The Visual-Cognitive System

Figure 12 shows a block-flow diagram of an assembled visual-cognitive system. The neuronal mechanisms assumed within the labeled blocks have been described in detail above, with the exception of the "executive processes."

The overall input-output organization of the system follows from the function and the operating characteristics of each module. No attempt has been made to locate any specific module in a particular brain region. It should be possible, however, to assign rough likelihood values to particular neuroanatomical candidates, and one result of this enterprise might be to narrow the search space in direct investigations on the brain.

Simulations

Several aspects of the proposed model have been simulated on a digital computer. Examples from these simulations are presented below. (Whereas the preponderance of the computation in the simulated neuronal networks is performed in parallel, the machine simulation must carry out all operations in serial computation. Thus, response times that would be of the order of

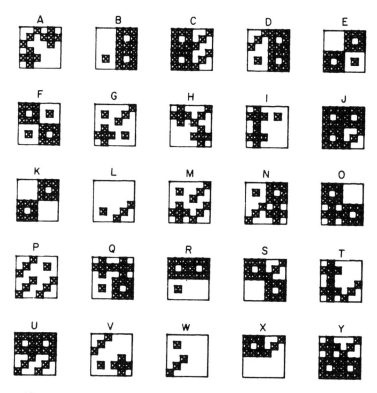

Figure 13
Scenes presented for learning and subsequent recall. Letters A—Y represent associated class
designations. Source: Trehub 1979. Copyright Academic Press (London) Ltd. Reproduced
by permission.

milliseconds in the neuronal system may take many minutes in computer
simulations.)

Pattern Learning and Associative Recall

A synaptic matrix receiving input from a 6 × 6-cell retina was simulated,
and two modes of associative sequential recall were examined (Trehub
1979). Stimuli consisted of 25 scenes (designated A through Y), each
composed of a combination drawn randomly from four objects or an empty
space and randomly assigned to each quadrant of the scene (see figure 13).
Filled regions designated points of stimulation to the retina and thence, in
retinotopic order, through the afferent channel to the coordinate mosaic
cells. Scenes were learned in accordance with equation 1 (arbitrarily: $b = 1$,

Input scene

```
          A B C D E F G H I J K L M N O P Q R S T U V W X Y
      ┌──────────────────────────────────────────────────────
    1 │ A B C D E F G H I J K L M N O P Q R S T U V W X Y
    2 │ G D X B K S M S T U E P G W R W F X F I R P P S H
    3 │ I N J N J Q I V G C J M L B B L B U X L J H N R I
    4 │ M Q T V N X T X M E N T T D D V D O H M X D L C S
    5 │ K D Y O G V A Y A K A W I V S M H J O G L N V H C
    6 │ E L M Q A O E Q Y R G V P E F U S D Q C O W G F T
    7 │ P S I S M H H W F C O U U A K J C O S Y Y C L I U M
    8 │ O U U R U Y L I H X O G C U Q T Y N C J P F M J Q
    9 │ T R P U C L C N X T C B Y H U G L B D P N S U I F
   10 │ J F G F O D Y G W Y R F E Q Y A V F V O D Q Y O O
   11 │ D K S L R U K T Q A B Q W R X F N A R Q S B T Y G
   12 │ R V E A B P P O O M Y D J O T D T Q B H E A A T J
   13 │ W E O P Y C H C J I M C O J A N I K U A B O K Q K
   14 │ V Y F Y D R N M F S D J K P C J U C J W F G E P W
   15 │ Q H K J W B J D R N W O H G N Y R E P F K Y Q G E
   16 │ N J L H T T V R S P I N D A I S A H T U W M D M B
   17 │ U M R K I I O B P G T S N Y K Q P I I X Q T C A X
   18 │ C A H E P J X U U D Q Y B L H X J T L S T U J D D
   19 │ B P A M Q M D J K L P I V M E I X V M V H R H V B
   20 │ Y G W H N U P E B X H U S M H W Y N R A X R N N
   21 │ X T Q G L A R W L F H A S F V O M P G E Y I F K V
   22 │ F W D X X W B L V Q S R Q C G R C G A K M C B E U
   23 │ L C N T S G S E N H V E X T L E G M K D I J O B A
   24 │ S X V C V K Q A D W L X F X P B K W E N V E X W L
   25 │ H I B I F E F K B V F K R I W K E L W B G K S L R
```

Associative recall hierarchy

Figure 14
Table showing hierarchical associative order of all scenes in response to each stimulus scene. Source: Trehub 1979. Copyright Academic Press (London) Ltd. Reproduced by permission.

$c = 2$, $k = 100$). The cross-products of active stimulus points (constituting the afferent scene) and synaptic transfer weights were summed for each scene against each of the 25 output classes (Ω_j) and ordered in terms of descending magnitude. This procedure yielded a table of associative rank, or hierarchy of recall, which is reflected in the relative latency of class-cell discharge (figure 14).

Sequences of associative recall are produced by inhibiting for the duration of the recall sequence each class cell immediately after it has fired and signaled the scene it has detected and classified. If an initial retinal pattern is maintained as a continuing stimulus to the mosaic cells while class cells are successively inhibited immediately after their activation, the sequence of associations is called a *stimulus-bound recall sequence*. If an initial pattern is not maintained as a stimulus, and subsequent excitation of mosaic cells is provided only by the brief class-cell collateral volleys back to the imaging matrix, the sequence of associations is called an *image-bound recall sequence*.

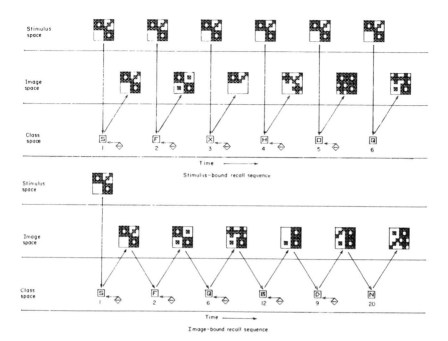

Figure 15
Example of two modes of recall in response to scene S. Numbers below class designa-
tions represent associative rank relative to S. Source: Trehub 1979. Copyright Academic
Press (London) Ltd. Reproduced by permission.

The two modes of recall initiated by the stimulus of scene S are compared in figure 15. In both modes, the first pattern class and image recalled
are those correctly matched to the initiating scene, as one would expect in
an accurate perceptual system. The second response of the network is also
the same for both modes; i.e., the class and image recalled are those
standing at rank order two in associative strength with scene S. This
outcome is also to be expected, since the image that generates the second
response (class F) in the image-bound sequence is identical to the external
scene in the stimulus-bound sequence (see figure 13). Thereafter, however,
the chain of association is quite different in the two modes.

Whereas the stimulus-bound sequence proceeds monotonically down
the associative hierarchy (orders 1, 2, 3, 4, 5, 6) with respect to the initial
scene, the image-bound sequence defies monotonicity and ranges widely
over the associative hierarchy of the initial scene (orders 1, 2, 6, 12, 9, 20).
Yet this latter sequence of associative recall, despite its random appearance,
is not due to random effects but is systematically determined by the
functional characteristics and learning history of the synaptic matrix.

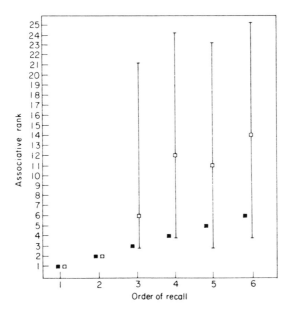

Figure 16
Median and range of associative rank of recalled scenes relative to initiating scenes
through six sequential recollections. Filled squares designate stimulus-bound recall. Open
squares designate image-bound recall. Source: Trehub 1979. Copyright Academic Press
(London) Ltd. Reproduced by permission.

The first six recollections of the synaptic matrix in response to each of
the 25 scenes were examined, and the median and range of associative
ranks were derived (figure 16). In the stimulus-bound recall mode, associative rank relative to the initial scene was always identical to the order of
recall. For the image-bound recall mode, however, after the second recall,
median associative rank deviated markedly from recall order and the range
of associations within the first six recollections spanned almost the entire
hierarchy. These data show that recall in a model brain mechanism that is
plausible within the constraints of neurophysiology and neuroanatomy can
exhibit characteristics of orderliness or looseness of association that appear
to conform with human associative behavior.

Pattern Recognition under Noisy Conditions

In this simulation, a microworld was constructed in which three motivated
characters moved about and interacted within an environment occupied
by a number of objects and natural features relevant to motivational struc-

tures installed in each of the characters. The microworld consisted of the following: David, Lisa, a dog named Wolf, David's house, Lisa's cottage, a restaurant, a pond, a pine-tree forest, and a rabbit. For purposes of the present topic, we will consider only the visual-cognitive aspects of the simulation.

The principal character was equipped with a synaptic matrix so that he was able not only to move among the objects in his "world," as the other characters could, but also to learn and later recognize the visual world about him. After David (the cognitive character) learned the individual elements of his world, the simulation program projected to his 21×21-cell "retina" all objects that happened to be within an arbitrary distance from him during the course of his activities, and he was programmed to make a "verbal" response appropriate to the objects he encountered. If two or more objects happened to be within "visual" distance, their patterns were superposed on the retina and the synaptic matrix had to disambiguate the complex image if the objects were to be correctly recognized. In addition to the problem of superposition, the program allowed the investigator to introduce controlled amounts of visual noise into the environment.

Figure 17, taken directly from the face of the CRT, shows a moment from the dynamic simulation in which David has encountered Lisa at the restaurant. The divided insert at the upper left of the CRT display shows the pattern of Lisa superposed on the pattern of the restaurant as it would appear to David's retina in a situation with no visual noise, and as it actually appeared, degraded by the introduction of 40 percent noise. It can be seen by David's verbal responses that, under this condition of pattern superposition and visual noise, he has correctly recognized both Lisa and the restaurant. Examination of records from extended periods of simulation indicate that, even with superposition of objects, errors in recognition are rarely made until the level of visual noise exceeds approximately 70 percent. In the initial learning situation, David was exposed to only one character or object at a time; thus, the ability of his synaptic matrix to disambiguate and properly recognize on a later occasion each superposed component of a pattern complex, degraded by substantial levels of visual noise, represents a powerful generalization of the original learned response.

Episodic Learning and Recall

The neuronal model for episodic learning and recall described above was simulated with added assumptions concerning the effects of arousal. Learning proceeded basically in accordance with equation 2, but with the initial

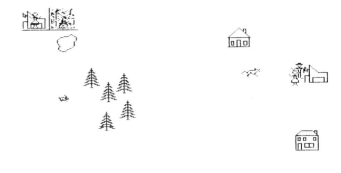

```
2(.4)LISA
2(.4)RESTAURANT
```

```
I HOPE THEY SERVE SEAFOOD CHOWDER TODAY.......
HI!..LISA!.....
```

Figure 17
One frame of the microworld simulation printed directly from the CRT display. David
has just encountered Lisa at the restaurant (far right). At the upper left of the display,
the divided graphic inset shows, on the left, the image of Lisa superposed on that of
the restaurant as it would appear to David if there were no visual noise. On the right of
the inset, is the same image degraded by 40 percent random visual noise, which is the
actual stimulus projected to David's retina. It can be seen from David's verbal responses
at the bottom of the CRT display that he has correctly identified both the restaurant and
Lisa despite superposition and substantial image degradation.

value of ϕ subject to modulation by the momentary level of randomly
fluctuating arousal. Thus, for each instance of learning,

$$\phi_0 = (b + c + kN_{\alpha_{ij}}^{-1})L, \tag{3}$$

where L is a normal random variable with $\bar{x} = 1.0$ and $\sigma = 0.2$ (arbitrarily
chosen) representing a randomly fluctuating arousal context in which learning occurs.

   Memory decay was determined by equation 2 with $\beta = 2.0$ and $\psi =$
0.5 (arbitrarily chosen). It was assumed that for any particular component
image in an episode to be recalled, the sum of ϕ_t values supporting
that image must exceed some concurrent threshold value. It was further
assumed that recall threshold would be an inverse function of arousal (L).
Thus,

$$\theta = L^{-1} + \gamma, \tag{4}$$

where θ is the recall threshold; L (the level of arousal) is a normal random variable with $\bar{x} = 1.0$ and $\sigma = 0.2$, modulating the recall threshold at each instance of recall; and γ is the base threshold level.

An appropriate repertoire of language was assumed to characterize component images in the episodic sequence. Figure 18 shows the set of primitive images and their associated language used in the computer simulation. The results of testing the neuronal network for episodic learning and recall are shown in figure 19. The complete episode was learned via input to a 6 × 6-cell retina over afferents to the mosaic-cell array. (See figure 11.) The complete initial episode is shown beside ELAPSED TIME 00. Tested recollections are shown at elapsed times corresponding to 1–14 days after the original experience. As time passes, failures of recall are observed to increase, although the occasional recovery of a forgotten detail is also seen (Trehub 1983).

Discussion

Perhaps the most succinct way to characterize the operation of the synaptic matrix alone is to think of it as an associative, spatial-stimulus comb filter with each of its multiple channels linked to a labeled output line. Its repertoire of pattern-differentiated parallel channels grows as it is exposed to new stimulus patterns relevant to the motivational structure of its host. This kind of perceptual mechanism is consistent with data suggesting that models of visual perception that operate in the spatial-stimulus domain will be more efficient than those based on processing in the spatial-frequency domain (Tieger and Ganz 1979).

Augmented by size and rotation transformers, and in concert with the retinoid system, the synaptic matrix can recognize objects despite changes in size, orientation, and position in space. If an output channel (class cell) is activated by a means other than its matched (learned) spatial pattern, that channel will generate its matched pattern of excitation in the mosaic-cell array of the network (image reconstruction). It has been demonstrated that the synaptic matrix can generalize on the basis of past learning, and that its performance is robust in noisy environments. It has also been shown that when tested with complex patterns composed by the superposition of previously learned patterns, the network can disambiguate the stimulus and recognize its constituents.

Evidence of the ability of the synaptic matrix to respond to an arbitrary input with an associatively ordered series of recognition indicants and images was obtained in the simulation of stimulus-bound sequential recall. It was also demonstrated that the system could respond associatively to its

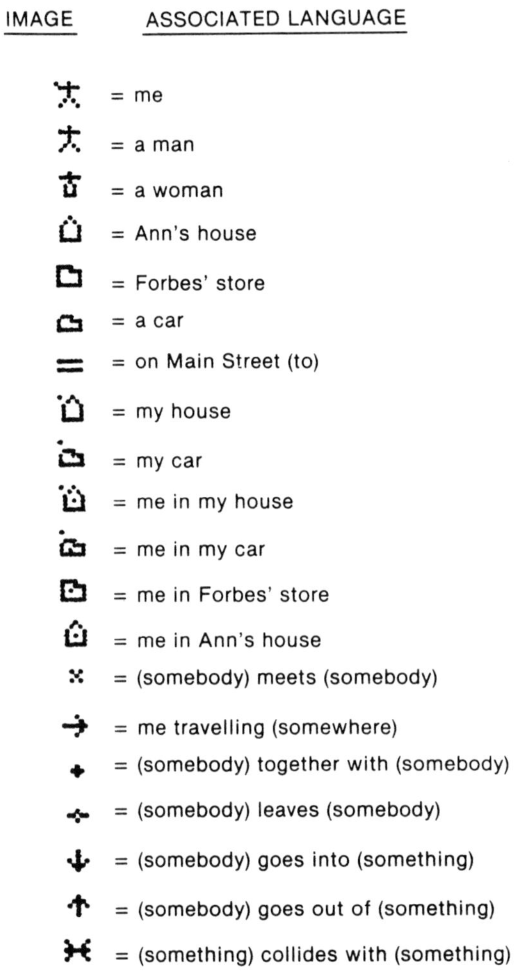

IMAGE   ASSOCIATED LANGUAGE

ᚼ.   = me

ᚼ.   = a man

ᚼ   = a woman

ᗟ   = Ann's house

◻   = Forbes' store

⌂   = a car

═   = on Main Street (to)

ᗟ̇   = my house

◻̇   = my car

ᗟ̈   = me in my house

◻̇   = me in my car

◻   = me in Forbes' store

ᗟ   = me in Ann's house

✕   = (somebody) meets (somebody)

⇥   = me travelling (somewhere)

✦   = (somebody) together with (somebody)

✦   = (somebody) leaves (somebody)

⬇   = (somebody) goes into (something)

⬆   = (somebody) goes out of (something)

⋈   = (something) collides with (something)

Figure 18
Primitive images and associated language. Source: Trehub 1983. Copyright Lawrence
Erlbaum Associates, Inc. Reproduced by permission.

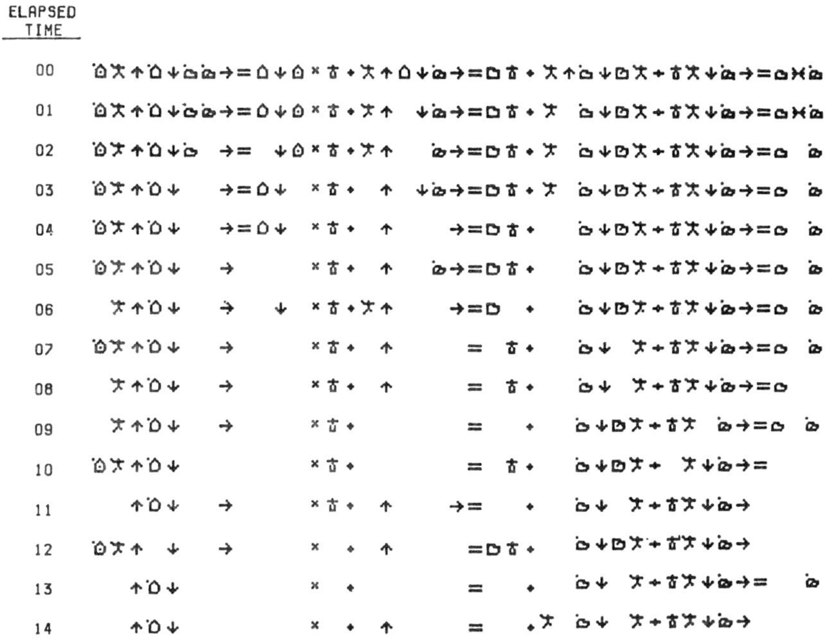

ELAPSED
TIME

| 00 |
| 01 |
| 02 |
| 03 |
| 04 |
| 05 |
| 06 |
| 07 |
| 08 |
| 09 |
| 10 |
| 11 |
| 12 |
| 13 |
| 14 |

Figure 19
Simulation test. Top row: the complete sequence of learned images in the original episode. Following rows: recalled episodic images at indicated elapsed times. Source: Trehub 1983. Copyright Lawrence Erlbaum Associates, Inc. Reproduced by permission.

own internally generated images. Given the reciprocal relationship between the synaptic matrix and the retinoid system, it is possible for the system to construct and learn new images by combining parts of objects and scenes recalled from its learned repertoire. When the temporal controls provided by the clock ring and the recall ring are integrated with the network, all of the semantic competence described above is augmented by comparable episodic competence. It seems fair to conclude that the cognitive tests outlined above have been met by the brain model detailed here. I have presented a neuronal network for stereopsis (Trehub 1978) and shown that it can resolve objects in depth; the details of its integration within the overall cognitive system remain to be worked out, however.

The retinoid networks have a number of properties similar to the "slide-box" metaphor (Arbib 1972) and suggest the detailed neuronal circuitry for its biological realization. An important capability of the retinoid system is the ability to inventively synthesize specialized patterns of autaptic-cell activity that can be transferred to long-term memory in the detection matrix for use as perceptual "tools." These guage-like tools (templates) can be used for quick and rough assessment of significant geometric properties in the visual environment (e.g., relative object size, distance, connectedness, straightness, angular relation). The synthesis of useful retinoid patterns that would be committed to long-term memory in the individual and shared cumulatively in the larger society would represent the evolutionary development of biological, intra-organismic tools in the same sense as the evolutionary development of material extra-organismic artifacts (Trehub 1977).

Attempts to relate the neuronal networks described in this paper to current theories of information processing in cognitive psychology reveal a close similarity between the present model and a number of aspects of Kosslyn's (1980) array theory. For example, Kosslyn's "surface array" corresponds to the mosaic-cell array in the synaptic matrix; his "deep representations" may be thought of as corresponding to the distribution of synaptic transfer weights on filter cells and mosaic cells; his "mind's eye" corresponds to the detection matrix. Kosslyn assumes four transformational operations, called "ZOOM," "PAN," "ROTATE," and "SCAN." The first three of these correspond to the activities of the size and rotation transformers in the present model, and "SCAN" is one of the operations of the retinoid system. Some independent empirical support for the neuronal model comes from the finding that these networks can account for all the experimental results that motivated the array theory (Pinker and Kosslyn 1983). Additional empirical support is provided by a large number of other studies involving visual perception and/or attention in which the results seem to be best explained by central processes of the kind realized by the networks detailed here. (See Shepard and Metzler 1971; Larsen and Bundesen 1978; McCloskey and Watkins 1978; Rayner et al. 1978; Shulman et al. 1979; Riggs and Day 1980; Posner 1980; Posner et al. 1980; Finke and Pinker 1983; Sparks and Jay, this volume.)

Granted that the brain mechanisms proposed are competent for the tasks described, what controls the command neurons in those functions where they are needed? In an earlier paper (Trehub 1977), I assigned overall coordination and control to a "black box" labeled "executive processes," with specified (but unreduced) properties. Regrettably, I must still invoke the executive processes. However, since the characteristics of the utility mechanisms to be coordinated and controlled have been detailed, progress is being made in the development of the total system control structure.

Here, design must address such issues as motivation, the sensing of internal states, and homeostatic set points.

Pinker and Kosslyn (1983) have raised several questions concerning possible capacity limitations in the present model. They suggest that the model implies a distinct cell for every shape that a person could learn over a lifetime. But this is not the case. What is required is that there exist at least one distinct filter and class cell for each prototypical pattern class and some of its transformations which might be particularly useful from an ecological point of view. Modifying descriptors learned by other neurons can be activated with the prototype as an output complex representing a unique pattern within a class. If humans learn to classify visual inputs into 1.0×10^5 distinct root categories, this would represent only a small fraction of the 4.0×10^6 filter cells and class cells which the brain can allocate without straining its neuronal resources (Trehub 1977). This issue of cell capacity has been discussed elsewhere in the context of a computational connectionist model of visual memory (Feldman 1981).

Another related question concerns the number of synapses that can be accommodated on the dendrite of a filter cell. If it were assumed that the number of axons from the mosaic-cell array to each filter cell corresponds to the number of principal cells in the lateral geniculate body (LGN), then one would expect approximately 6.0×10^5 synaptic contacts on the dendrite, since this is the estimated number of such cells in the LGN (Glezer 1968). This would appear to be more synapses than a single dendrite can support. However, inputs from only the foveal and the near parafoveal region of the retina (approximately $10°$ of visual angle) need be projected to the synaptic matrix. Furthermore, even this limited number of projections can be markedly reduced, without causing significant stimulus degradation, by sampling over the afferent inputs at an increasing interval as a function of retinal eccentricity. In addition, should a synaptic surface larger than that provided by a single cell be required, two or more cross-coupled filter cells converging on a common class cell would serve the purpose.

An explicit neuronal model for visual-cognitive processes has been described, and several aspects of its competence have been demonstrated in simulation tests. Work is continuing on the elaboration and extension of the present model. I believe that the goal of understanding the possible physical mechanisms of human cognition will be well served by parallel efforts to develop significantly different neuronal models at a level of detail that will make it possible to decide among competing theories on the basis of competence, biological plausiblity, and parsimony.

References

Arbib, M. A. 1972. *The Metaphorical Brain.* Wiley-Interscience.

Bliss, T. V. P., and A. R. Gardner-Medwin. 1973. Long-lasting potentiation of synaptic transmission in the dentate area of the unanesthetized rabbit following stimulation of the preforant pathway. *Journal of Physiology* 232: 357–374.

Bliss, T. V. P., and T. Lømo. 1973. Long-lasting potentiation of synaptic transmission in the dentate area of the anesthetized rabbit following stimulation of the preforant pathway. *Journal of Physiology* 232: 331–356.

Browning, M., T. Dunwiddie, W. Bennett, W. Gispen, and G. Lynch. 1979. Synaptic phosphoproteins: Specific changes after repetitive stimulation of the hippocampal slice. *Science* 203: 60–62.

Burt, P. J. 1975. Computer simulations of a dynamic visual perception model. *International Journal of Man-Machine Studies* 7: 529–546.

Didday, R. L., and M. A. Arbib. 1975. Eye movements and visual perception: A "two visual system" model. *International Journal of Man-Machine Studies* 7: 547–569.

Feldman, J. A. 1981. A connectionist model of visual memory. In *Parallel Models of Associative Memory*, ed. G. E. Hinton and J. A. Anderson (Erlbaum).

Finke, R. A., and S. Pinker. 1983. Directional scanning of remembered visual patterns. *Journal of Experimental Psychology: Learning, Memory, and Cognition* 9: 398–410.

Glezer, I. I. 1968. In *The Human Brain in Figures and Tables*, ed. S. M. Blinkov and I. I. Glezer (Basic Books).

Hebb, D. O. 1949. *The Organization of Behavior.* Wiley.

Hillman, D. E., and S. Chen. 1979. Determination of Postsynaptic Membrane Structure Is Intrinsic to the Purkinje Cell. Presented at Ninth Annual Meeting of Society for Neuroscience, Atlanta.

Horridge, G. A. 1968. *Interneurons.* Freeman.

Julesz, B. 1971. *Foundations of Cyclopean Perception.* University of Chicago Press.

Kosslyn, S. M. 1980. *Image and Mind.* Harvard University Press.

Larsen, A., and C. Bundesen. 1978. Size scaling in visual pattern recognition. *Journal of Experimental Psychology: Human Perception and Performance* 4: 1–20.

McClennan, H. 1963. *Synaptic Transmission.* Saunders.

McCloskey, M., and M. J. Watkins. 1978. The seeing-more-than-is-there phenomenon: Implications for the locus of iconic storage. *Journal of Experimental Psychology: Human Perception and Performance.* 4: 553–564.

McGeoch, J. A. 1942. *The Psychology of Human Learning.* Longmans, Green.

Møllgarrd, K., E. L. Bennett, M. R. Rosenzweig, and B. Lindner. 1971. Quantitative synaptic changes with differential experience in rat brain. *International Journal of Neuroscience* 2: 113–127.

Pinker, S., and S. M. Kosslyn. 1983. Theories of mental imagery. In *Imagery: Current Theory, Research, and Application,* ed. A. A. Sheikh (Wiley-Interscience).

Pitts, W., and W. S. McCulloch. 1947. How we know universals: The perception of auditory and visual forms. *Bulletin of Mathematical Biophysics* 9: 127–147.

Posner, M. I. 1980. Orienting of attention. *Quarterly Journal of Experimental Psychology* 32: 3–25.

Posner, M. I., C. R. R. Snyder, and B. J. Davidson. 1980. Attention and the detection of signals. *Journal of Experimental Psychology: General* 109: 160–174.

Rayner, K., G. W. McConkie, and S. Ehrlich. 1978. Eye movements and integrating information across fixations. *Journal of Experimental Psychology: Human Perception and Performance* 4: 529–544.

Riggs, L. A., and R. H. Day. 1980. Visual aftereffects derived from inspection of orthogonally moving patterns. *Science* 208: 416–418.

Shepard, R. N., and J. Metzler. 1971. Mental rotation of three-dimensional objects. *Science* 171: 701–703.

Shepherd, G. M. 1974. *The Synaptic Organization of the Brain.* Oxford University Press.

Shulman, G. L., R. W. Remington, and J. P. McLean. 1979. Moving attention through visual space. *Journal of Experimental Psychology: Human Perception and Performance* 5: 522–526.

Tieger, T., and L. Ganz. 1979. Recognition of faces in the presence of two-dimensional sinusoidal masks. *Perception and Psychophysics* 26: 163–167.

Trehub, A. 1967. Learning Machines and Methods. Patent 3,331,054. U.S. Patent Office, Washington, D.C.

Trehub, A. 1977. Neuronal models for cognitive processes: Networks for learning, perception and imagination. *Journal of Theoretical Biology* 65: 141–169.

Trehub, A. 1978. Neuronal model for stereoscopic vision. *Journal of Theoretical Biology* 71: 479–486.

Trehub, A. 1979. Associative sequential recall in a synaptic matrix. *Journal of Theoretical Biology* 81: 569–576.

Trehub, A. 1983. Neuronal model for episodic learning and temporal routing of memory. *Cognition and Brain Theory* 6: 483–497.

Tulving, E. 1972. Episodic and semantic memory. In *Organization of Memory*, ed. E. Tulving and W. Donaldson (Academic).

Wickelgren, W. A. 1974. Single-trace fragility theory of memory dynamics. *Memory and Cognition* 2: 775–780.

18

An Approach to Learning Control Surfaces by Connectionist Systems

Andrew G. Barto

Interest in neural-network approaches to computation is undergoing a revival. Numerous groups of researchers argue that networks of interacting neuronlike processing elements provide useful alternatives to conventional computational architectures and programming techniques. (See Ballard 1981; Feldman 1981; Hinton and Anderson 1981; Hinton and Sejnowski 1983; McClelland and Rumelhart 1981.) This use of massive parallelism is being called by some a *connectionist* paradigm. Not only have advances in microelectronics made the physical realization of massively parallel hardware a possibility, but advances in the understanding of certain types of problems suggest that the use of such hardware is necessary for real-time performance (especially in computer-vision systems).

Since they contain obvious parameters capable of being adjusted through experience (the connection weights), networks of neuronlike elements would seem to offer a promising avenue for the development of machine learning. Many efforts to construct self-organizing networks of neuronlike adaptive elements in the 1950s and the 1960s were predicated on this idea but failed to produce systems capable of more than simple forms of learning. Many current researchers in this area have purposefully avoided the question of learning and have instead concentrated on the representational and computational potential of networks.

My co-workers and I have explicitly focused on learning by means of the connectionist paradigm. We think that one reason for the lack of success of early research with adaptive networks is that the adaptive elements studied in the past were too simple. Most of the neuronlike adaptive elements that were studied can learn only if they are instructed by a knowledgeable "teacher" that can explicitly tell them how they should respond to their inputs. Although the environment of an adaptive network may be able to assess certain consequences of the collective activity of all the network elements, it cannot provide individualized instruction to the elements without knowing so much about the problem as to make learning unnecessary. In terms encountered in the artificial-intelligence literature (e.g. Cohen and Feigenbaum 1982), the network's internal mechanism is not very "transparent" to the "critic."

Other approaches to the problem of learning within adaptive networks rely on adaptive elements that require neither "teachers" nor "critics." These elements employ some form of unsupervised learning (or clustering) algorithm, often based on Hebb's (1949) hypothesis that repeated pairing of presynaptic and postsynaptic activity strengthens synaptic efficacy. Although clustering is likely to play an important role in sophisticated problem-solving systems, it does not by itself provide the necessary means for a system to improve performance in tasks determined by factors external to the system, such as the task of controlling a system having initially unknown dynamics. For these types of tasks, a learning system must not just cluster information but must form those clusters that are useful in terms of the system's interaction with its environment. Thus, it seems necessary to consider networks that learn under the influence of some sort of evaluative feedback, but this feedback cannot be so informative as to provide individualized instruction to each adaptive element.

The adaptive elements we have studied resemble more familiar neuron-like elements in that they implement simple input/output functions and communicate by means of excitatory and inhibitory signals rather than by symbolic messages. However, the algorithms used by the elements to adjust the parameters of their input/output functions are more complex than those generally considered. They use numerous auxiliary variables to implement short-term memory traces, reinforcement-comparison mechanisms, and reinforcement-anticipation mechanisms. They also use randomness as an essential part of their adaptive strategy. Since network components face environments (determined in part by the rest of the network) that do not present neatly structured problems, components must be opportunistic agents capable of improving performance in a wide range of conditions and under considerable uncertainty—an idea suggested by Klopf's (1972, 1982) concept of the "hedonistic neuron." Complex learning algorithms are required to adjust even simple input/output functions in unhelpful environments.

According to our view, the difficulty in obtaining deeper forms of learning by complex networks is chiefly due to the difficult "structural credit-assignment problem" that exists for complex networks. Somehow, evaluations of the behavior of the entire network must be apportioned correctly to the individual elements, and to the individual weights, that were responsible for that behavior. Rather than designing a centralized agent that knows enough about the network to correctly apportion credit, our approach, following Klopf's idea, is to endow each adaptive element with learning capabilities that are sophisticated enough to enable it to increase its own performance in the face of considerable uncertainty by using any information that is locally available. Uncertainty is present, since the influence of any single element on the evaluation of the overall network behavior will generally not be deterministic from that element's point of view.

Consequently, our research is not so much an attempt to show how very simple components can interact to solve problems as an attempt to show how components that are already capable of solving problems can interact cooperatively to solve more complex problems. In fact, the study of networks composed elements of this type involves many of the issues that arise in the study of the collective behavior of self-interested agents in the contexts of game theory, economics, and evolutionary biology.

In this paper I discuss this approach to learning, distinguish it from earlier adaptive network research, and attempt to outline its utility. For this latter purpose, I describe an approach to a kind of adaptive control that may play an essential role in many kinds of sensorimotor performance. Beginning with a characterization of control tasks, I develop the idea of a control surface determined jointly by the requirements of a control task and the abilities of an effector apparatus. A variety of means for representing control surfaces are discussed, including the use of networks of neuronlike elements. This discussion of control surfaces and their representations is largely tutorial, being well known by control theorists and roboticists, but within this context our approach to learning can be concretely described as a means for "filling in" partially specified control surfaces through experience. Several computer simulations of this kind of learning are described.

Control Surfaces

Aizerman et al. (1964) defined the general problem of automatic control as "the problem of assigning the input situation to one or another class, and [generating] the optimal response as a function of that class." The mapping or function that associates with each possible input situation the (optimal) action for that situation is often called by control theorists a *control surface* (Mendel 1970).

Part of the solution to a control problem involves pattern classification. Input situations must be separated into classes appropriate to the problem at hand. However, in addition to the classification of input patterns, the control system must generate the control action appropriate to each class. Consequently, the solution to a control problem requires not merely pattern classification but also the association of actions (which may themselves be complex patterns of signals) with input situations.

Moreover, the pattern-classification aspects of a control problem form a natural hierarchy. At the higher levels coarse and slowly varying control situations must be identified, whereas at lower levels the appropriate discriminations must be made between more detailed variations of the higher-level situations, forming parametrized families of those situations. At still lower levels, estimates of the instantaneous system state must be made. Consider, for example, a pilot controlling a plane. He must first recognize the overall control situation C: the type of plane and the configuration of the cockpit. This is a high-level pattern-classification problem. Then he must determine the response characteristics of the particular plane (determined in part by the mechanical properties of the plane and in part by the setup of the control devices in the cockpit). This is a parameter-identification problem. Finally, he must have a goal (e.g., the desired trajectory of the plane) and an estimate of the state of the plane (e.g., its position and momentum) to determine the appropriate control action to take at that time.

In short, recognition of the overall control situation C gives the pilot access to a parametrized family, f_p, of control surfaces, such that

$$a = f_p(g, s)$$

is the appropriate action to take toward goal g when the system of the class C is characterized by parameters p and is in state s. A control surface f_p is, then, more than just a stimulus/response map, since the input situations (g, s) for f_p need not consist solely of externally supplied (i.e., perceptual) signals, but may contain information from within the controlling system itself, providing, for example, state estimates for the controlled system and (goal) states of higher command centers.

Some control systems implement control surfaces that are completely specified from the start. A thermostat, for example, has a built-in control surface that causes it to turn the furnace on if a room is too cold and off if it is too hot. Here the goal g is the desired temperature, the state s is the actual temperature, and the action $f(g, s)$ determined by the control surface is

$$f(g, s) = \begin{cases} \textit{furnace on} & \text{if } g > s \\ \textit{furnace off} & \text{otherwise.} \end{cases}$$

These control decisions are wired-in "reflexes" of the thermostat.

Other types of control systems begin with partially specified control surfaces. Initially they may contain no information about which control actions are appropriate and operate randomly, or they may "know" exactly what to do in some situations but have no knowledge about what actions are appropriate in others, or they may initially implement control surfaces that specify actions for every input situation but only in an inaccurate or approximate way. If its performance is to improve, a control system with a partially specified control surface must contain mechanisms for filling in or refining its surface through its experience. Control systems capable of doing this are called *adaptive* or *learning* control systems.

To the best of our knowledge, the approach illustrated here does not closely correspond to the more orthodox approaches to adaptive or learning control. One reason for this is that our concern is ultimately with ill-defined systems that do not permit the degree of *a priori* knowledge that is commonly assumed in orthodox adaptive control. This should be borne in mind in reading the examples below. Although sufficient knowledge is readily available about these particular systems to allow the use of more orthodox methods, we have purposefully avoided using this knowledge.

Representing Control Surfaces

Computation and Table Lookup

Many methods can be used to represent a control surface, ranging from pure *computational* schemes (in which the function is specified by means of equations that can be evaluated by some calculating machinery) to pure *table-lookup* schemes (in which the values of the function for a large number of arguments are precomputed and stored in a table). In the first case a coded input situation acts as the data for a calculation (i.e., a computational procedure), whereas in the second case the coded input situation acts as a pointer to, or address of, the appropriate entry in a table that contains the specification of an appropriate action. Since table access can require varying degrees of computation, the computation/table-lookup distinction is not sharp. It is clearest when one restricts one's attention to conventional computing devices in which both mathematical computation and table addressing schemes are well-defined; it becomes less clear when one considers the unknown forms of computation and addressing that might occur in nervous systems (which may share some of the characteristics of the associative memory networks discussed below). I therefore refrain from

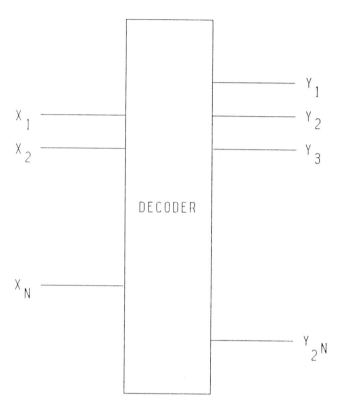

Figure 1
A binary decoder with N binary input channels and 2^N output channels. For each pattern
of ones and zeros presented as input, it selects a single corresponding output channel.

attempting precise definitions and instead contrast these methods in a
general way.

A major distinction between pure computation and pure table lookup is
the following: In pure computation an input situation is coded as a *pattern*
of activity over several pathways, each component of which provides one
of the arguments for the computation procedure; in pure table lookup an
input situation appears as activity on a *single* pathway leading to the
storage location that contains the appropriate action specification. Figure 1
shows this in terms of a decoder that accepts a pattern encoding of an input
situation and transforms it into activity on one of a large number of
pathways. I use the term *decoder* by analogy with the device used in
computer memory circuits to transform each memory address into a signal
on the wire connected to the physical storage cell having that address.

Although the decoding process is a kind of computation that accepts patterned input, it has a simple, general structure and takes little time to complete. By *computational method*, I mean a process that has a complex, specialized structure and requires a sequence of computational steps.

In the case of a pure table-lookup scheme, the control surface becomes a surface in the literal, spatial sense. The points of this surface correspond to the output pathways of the decoder. It has been tempting to view topographically organized neural layers as such explicit representations of control surfaces (Arbib 1972), particularly the optic tectum of the frog (Didday 1976). However, in general a control surface is a surface only in an abstract sense. The structure and the dimensionality of a control surface involved in motor control, for example, need have no direct relationship to the spatially organized structure of a neural array.

In addition to the obvious tradeoffs involving computation time and storage space, computational and table-lookup methods also differ in terms of how well they allow control-surface information to be altered or "re-mapped." For example, in the course of an animal's life, various characteristics of its motor-control surfaces must change. Some changes are required because of the alterations of the mass of body parts and the length of limbs that occur during growth. Other changes may be called for by the nature of specific actions, such as transporting objects of differing masses. In other words, various parameters of the control task must change. For a given control-surface representation, two types of parameters can be distinguished: explicit and implicit. Explicit parameters are those for which provision has already been made in the computational or storage structure. They can be viewed as input components that are distinguished only because they change infrequently or slowly. For example, symbols representing the link lengths and masses may appear explicitly in a system of equations specifying the control surface for a limb-movement task, and a corresponding computational mechanism may have explicit inputs for altering these values when "re-mapping" is required. Explicit parameters in a table-lookup method greatly enlarge the number of table entries. For example, to make link length explicit one would need to have a separate table for each admissible length. Since computational methods for representing control-surface knowledge generally do not require undue added complexity for explicit parameters, re-mapping for altered values of explicit parameters is generally easier for computational methods than it is for tabular schemes.

Implicit parameters, on the other hand, are those that determine the form of the control surface but do not appear as input components or as explicit parameters—for example, the fact that a limb has three links rather than two. Re-mapping for altered implicit parameters requires changing the algorithm used by a computational mechanism or changing the table entries in a tabular scheme. In either case, re-mapping involves adapting control-surface specification, or making a structural rather than a parametric alteration.

Computational and table-lookup methods for representing control-surface knowledge can be combined in various ways to obtain some of the advantages of each. For example, an indexed family of computational procedures may be used in which each procedure is suitable for a given region of the space of input situations. Each table entry specifies a computational procedure, or provides parameter values to a procedure, rather than a single action (Raibert 1977, 1978).

Pure table lookup becomes more computational when one considers *hierarchical* and *interpolating* tables. Hierarchical structures consist of tables that store parts of the addresses into other tables. Samuel (1959) used such hierarchical "signature tables" in his famous checker-playing program (further discussed in Page 1977), and Albus (1979) presented a structure in which the output from high-level tables together with environmental feedback determines entry points into lower-level tables. These methods can be helpful for reducing the exponential growth of storage requirements with increasing control-surface dimension.

Interpolating methods average neighboring table entries. If the control surface is reasonably smooth, this technique can help reduce storage requirements by permitting a coarse quantization of the control surface while retaining some degree of accuracy. Marr (1969) and Albus (1971) proposed that the granular layer of the cerebellum implements a "decoder" that is not restricted to activating a single address pathway (parallel fiber), and thus that the cerebellum, through the integrative action of the Purkinje cells, implements just this kind of interpolating table-lookup representation of motor-control knowledge.

Associative Memory Networks

An *associative memory network* is a mechanism for storing control information that combines aspects of computational and table-lookup methods. An associative memory network consists of a large number of neuronlike processing elements that compute in parallel. They are similar to tabular methods, except that information can be coded in terms of distributed patterns of activity rather than in terms of specific loci, and storage "locations" may exist only in an abstract sense. This ability to support *distributed representations* is one of the major reasons for the interest in those networks. This style of information storage provides built-in associational structure in which alterations of particular patterns are automatically generalized to other patterns according to their degree of similarity. Hinton (1981) argued that this kind of representation has certain advantages over conventional means of storing knowledge. Associative memory networks have been discussed by many researchers (see, e.g., Amari 1977a,b; Anderson et al. 1977; Kohonen 1977; Nakano 1972; Cooper 1974; Wigstrom 1973; Willshaw et al. 1969); a good overview of these structures, their applications, and their relation to neuroscience can be found in Hinton and Anderson 1981.

To make the nature of associative memory network storage concrete, I briefly describe one of the simplest examples, known as a "correlation matrix associative memory" (Kohonen 1977). Suppose $X = \{X^1, X^2, \ldots, X^k\}$ is a set of input situations, or "keys," where each X^i is a vector of, say, real numbers. If we wish to associate each key X^i with some scalar control action a_i, this can be accomplished by forming a vector

$$A = \sum_{i=1}^{n} a_i X^i.$$

Retrieval of the control action associated with a key, say X^j, is accomplished by taking the inner product of A and X^j:

$$\langle A, X^j \rangle = \sum_{i=1}^{n} a_i \langle X^i, X^j \rangle.$$

Perfect retrieval of information stored in the vector A requires only that the set of vectors X be an orthonormal set. One may regard the decoder used for pure table lookup (figure 1) as a generator of the orthonormal set of keys consisting of the standard unit basis vectors. One might therefore view the usual form of table lookup as a special case of this kind of associative memory. The unit vectors produced by the standard address decoder are orthonormal because there is no overlap of their localized nonzero values. However, vectors whose nonzero values overlap substantially, such as the vectors $(0.5, 0.5, -0.5, -0.5)$ and $(0.5, -0.5, 0.5, -0.5)$, can be orthonormal.

With such distributed but still orthonormal patterns used as "keys" for storage and recall, a memory system has properties not shared by conventional lookup tables. Each entry is distributed over many physical storage locations, and each location contains the superposition of many entries.

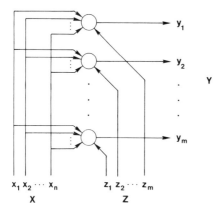

Figure 2
An associative memory network. The vector X is the input pattern or key; the vector Y is the output pattern. The lines labeled Z are used to instruct the network during the storage phase. Adapted from Sutton and Barto 1981 with permission of the authors. Copyright 1981 by the American Psychological Association.

This leads to a form of generalization not possible in conventional memory systems. If a pattern is presented to the system that was not one of the orthonormal keys used for storage, then information will be retrieved according to how similar (in the sense of the inner product) that pattern is to the keys that were used for storage. For a conventional memory system, on the other hand, providing an address that is similar to but distinct from the desired address can yield a completely unrelated output. Thus, one advantage of an associative memory network is that not all possible access keys have to be explicitly used in the storage process before they can be used for recall.

The term *associative memory network* is used to describe memory systems that use this superposition principle and distributed patterns as keys. Interpreting this summation as neural spatial summation leads to the view that neural networks can implement this kind of information storage, with "synaptic weights" storing information and afferent patterns acting as keys. Figure 2 shows an associative memory network, with key X, that implements a distributed lookup "table" that stores patterns Y instead of single numbers. The input lines labeled Z are used to instruct the network during the storage phase.

Associative memory networks play a dual role in terms of the present comparison of computational and tabular methods for implementing control surfaces. They are computational in that they require weighted sums to be formed, but they are also tabular schemes, although in a somewhat abstract sense. As computational schemes, they can provide high reaction speed by virtue of parallel computation. Viewed as abstract versions of tabular methods, associative memory networks provide automatic interpolation, or automatic generalization. If information can be coded in such a way that this form of interpolating provides correct generalization, the storage requirements can be much less than for explicit tabular methods.

Acquisition and Modification of Control-Surface Knowledge

Generality vs. Generalization

The various methods discussed above for representing control-surface knowledge have implications that affect the methods for acquiring and modifying that knowledge. Here, too, there is an important common-sense tradeoff that can be most clearly understood by contrasting pure computation and pure table lookup. This tradeoff is between the generality of the range of information that can be acquired, or of the degree of modification that can be accommodated, and the type of generalization that can be employed to reduce the amount of experience (and hence the amount of time) required for the acquisition or modification of knowledge. A pure tabular method has the potential for storing very detailed and complex control surfaces, since an arbitrary action specification can be stored at each table entry. It is limited only by the "grain" of the quantization used to divide the control surface into regions. The generality of a pure computational method, on the other hand, is limited by the form of the computational algorithm and its degree of parametrization. For example, if a learning process is restricted to adjusting the coefficients of a linear function of the control situation variables, then obviously only control surfaces that are linear in these variables can be formed.

The degree of constraint imposed on the set of potentially representable control surfaces by a given representational convention is directly related to the degree of generalization the convention provides. Since arbitrary entries can be stored in each location of a table, acquiring the correct contents of one table location (by means discussed below) does not constrain the contents of other locations. Therefore, a learning mechanism capable of utilizing the generality of a tabular storage medium must separately fill in each table location on the basis of knowledge acquired for the corresponding region of the control surface. Any generalization of such experience to other regions of the control surface is justified only on the basis of *a priori* restrictions on control-surface form. For example, an inter-polating tabular scheme that involves the averaging of neighboring table entries restricts the class of representable control surfaces to those that are smooth to a degree determined by the spread of the averaging function. Thus, the increase in learning speed obtained by removing the necessity to "visit" each control situation requires *a priori* constraints on control-surface form. By imposing considerable constraint on representable-control-surface form, and thus permitting considerable generalization, computational methods coupled with suitable learning algorithms can reduce the time required to acquire or "re-map" a control surface.

Any method that provides generalization can cause difficulties when that form of generalization is not correct in all circumstances. Instabilities may arise when experience in a given region A is incorrectly generalized to another region B and subsequent experience in B leads to correction of the erroneous generalization and consequent incorrect generalization back to region A. This can occur both in computational schemes and in tablular schemes that are based on too coarse a quantization of the control space. Solutions require alterations of the form of generalization through altera-tion of the intrinsic form of the computational algorithm or alteration of the control situation representation (e.g., adaptive refinement of the grain of quantization of the input space). These problems are quite difficult and have not yielded to any uniform solution method.

Associative Reinforcement Learning

One of the most important distinctions relevant to our approach to acquir-ing and re-mapping control surfaces by networks is the distinction between reinforcement learning and error-correction learning. This distinction can be most clearly made in terms of the quality of the information supplied to the learning system by its environment. This information may range from explicit specification of the actions that the system is required to perform to unreliable and infrequent assessments of certain distant consequences of the system's actions. In the first case the learning system need only remember what it is told, whereas in the second case the system must somehow discover what actions have consequences that lead to improved performance.

When there is a "teacher" in the environment that can tell the learning system exactly what action it should take for each input, then "learning" is easy. For a pure table lookup, this amounts to the rote storage of informa-tion, something that conventional computer memory systems accomplish very efficiently. For lookup tables implemented more abstractly as associative memory networks, the "learning" process under this high-quality information is also rote storage. For computational schemes, this type of rote storage is generally accomplished by means of some form of regression procedure designed to adjust the parameters of a computational algorithm in order to best produce the specified actions. Some of the more sophisticated schemes for the storage of information in associative memory networks are iterative linear regression algorithms (Duda and Hart 1973; Sutton and Barto 1981).

It is highly doubtful that this kind of teacher exists for many types of sensorimotor learning problems that animals routinely perform. Such a teacher would need to know, for example, how each motoneuron involved in the task should respond to each afferent volley, and would have to be able to provide these motoneurons with this information. For typical motor skills, even if learning were to take place only at higher motor levels, leaving lower-level synergies fixed, it is hard to imagine where such detailed information would come from. (There are, of course, many motor tasks for which instructional information of this quality is readily available. Reflexes provide a number of examples, the best studied of which is the adaptation of the gain of the vestibulo-ocular reflex in response to manipulations of visual or vestibular feedback [Ito 1982].)

A less knowledgeable teacher may know the correct actions for just some of the input situations. Under these circumstances, a rote storage method that provides some form of generalization may permit correct extrapolation of the teacher's knowledge to a broader class of situations. This type of learning problem has been extensively studied as "supervised learning pattern classification" (Duda and Hart 1973). The teacher provides the learning system with a set of input patterns and their correct classifications (e.g., a selection of exemplars and counterexemplars of each class), and the learning system must correctly classify these samples while extending, via its generalization capability, the classification of the samples to the set of all possible input patterns. In the context of a control problem, the input patterns correspond to patterns specifying control situations and the correct classifications correspond to the correct control actions. Many of these methods are iterative regression procedures that operate in real time as classified training samples arrive. Algorithms such as the one used by the adaline (adaptive linear element; Widrow and Hoff 1960) and the perceptron (Rosenblatt 1962) are examples of these methods. They can be regarded as *error-correction* methods that adjust parameters so as to reduce the discrepancy between how they respond and how their teachers instruct them to respond. Artificial-intelligence researchers study higher-level versions of this same type of problem as "learning from examples," "concept formation," or "inductive inference" (Cohen and Feigenbaum 1982). Although the capacity to generalize is important for both efficient learning and efficient information storage, we do not believe that all aspects of learning can be accounted for by mechanisms that require such explicit information, even if it is required for only a subset of the possible input situations.

More powerful learning capabilities result from the combination of information-storage methods with some form of problem-solving or "discovery" process. The problem-solving process determines what information needs to be stored in order that a given problem can be solved more efficiently in future encounters with it (or with a problem similar to it). The role of the "teacher" is played by the system's own problem-solving experience. What is needed for the implementation of this problem-solving component is a strategy variously called "blind variation and selective survival" (Campbell 1960), "trial-and-error search," or (more recently, by AI researchers) "generate and test." This type of process generates trials whose consequences are unforeseeable at the time they are generated. These trials are then evaluated and selected according to their consequences in furthering a given problem's solution. Trials need be "blind" only in the sense of not being based on *complete* knowledge of the outcome of a trial before it is generated. Any amount of knowledge present initially or acquired during the problem-solving process may be used to generate trials with high likelihood of improving problem-solving performance, but true discovery requires at least some initial doubt.

A *reinforcement-learning* system is a system employing this type of generation and selection process. The information from the environment rewards or punishes actions that were made but does not instruct the learning system as to what the correct actions would have been. The teaching information from the environment is a scalar evaluation or reinforcement signal rather than the more extensive teaching information required in error-correction learning. Reinforcement-learning systems are therefore able to improve their performance in environments that provide information that is of lower quality than required by error-correction systems. This is not to say that error correction plays no part in reinforcement learning. A reinforcement-learning system must internally determine estimates of error signals on the basis of some form of memory of its past actions and past performance. The point is that the learning system must do this for itself rather than rely on so helpful an environment.

One might also call reinforcement learning *selectional* and error-correction learning *instructional*. These terms have their origin in immunology, where a selectional theory of antibody formation is one in which specific antibodies are selected from an extensive existing repertoire of potential antibodies by the action of antigens, and antibodies so selected then proliferate. An instructional theory, on the other hand, holds that the structure of an antigen directly alters a molecule to make it an effective antibody; that is, the antigen acts as a kind of conformational template. This use of the term *selectional*, and its use to describe neural theories of learning (Edelman 1978), refer to selection from a repertoire of *simultaneously existing* candidates. However, the term *selectional* can equally describe processes in which the repertoire of candidates is generated *over time*. Selection from simultaneously existing candidates is undoubtedly an important mechanism of development and learning, but our research has focused on selectional mechanisms in which variety is generated over time.

Our research has focused on *associative* reinforcement learning in which the learning system receives *neutral input* (input that is not teaching or evaluative information) in addition to reinforcement input. The task is not just to discover an optimal action (as it is in studies of function-optimization algorithms) but also to discover an optimal mapping from input to output. Associative reinforcement learning has not received as much attention by cyberneticians and AI researchers as have pure search and error-correction learning. Yet, properly understood, associative reinforcement learning is an obvious way to improve the performance of a problem-solving system. Its essence is the "caching" of search results in an associative memory so that future search is converted into simple memory access. The importance of this process is appreciated by AI researchers (see, for example, Lenat et al. 1979), but its use in AI systems is not yet widespread.

Learning mechanisms combining information storage with problem-solving search are probably required for the solution of a large class of motor-learning and adaptation problems. Consider, for example, what would be required of a mechanism intended to learn the control surface for a trajectory-control task while receiving only instructive or evaluative information that can be determined from the visual inspection of performance trials, such as the instantaneous spatial error in "world" coordinates. What cannot be supplied is an instruction such as "Extend the duration of activation of motoneurons in group A and diminish the duration of activity of motoneurons in group B" (where A and B are subsets of the motoneurons involved). The controller must use a search process to discover, via a generate-and-test process, which of its actions have as consequences the

reduction of the spatial error of the movement. As these actions are discovered, they can be stored in association with a representation of the state
of the limb and the task command, so that eventually search will not be
required in order to execute the command. A system composed only of
error-correction components (such as perceptrons) cannot learn to correct
the spatial error unless some agency can supply individual error signals to
each component. In order to do this, that agency must already know what
patterns of component activity reduce the error; that is, it must already
know a great deal about the operation of the controller and about the task
faced.

Although it has been convenient to separate the information-storage
and problem-solving aspects of this type of learning in order to emphasize
these roles, it does not follow that these processes need to be carried out
by separate components or at separate times. In the following examples,
neuronlike elements perform both storage and problem-solving search.
Although space does not permit a thorough argument in favor of this
approach, I wish to suggest that the intimate combination of these capabilities at a low level in the functional hierarchy of a learning system is
important for effective learning of difficult tasks.

The Credit-Assignment Problem

Major problems need to be overcome if associative reinforcement learning
is to be useful in complex learning tasks. Foremost among these is the
credit-assignment problem (Minsky 1961). The credit-assignment problem for
reinforcement-learning systems is the problem of correctly assigning credit
or blame to each of the actions and internal decisions that contributed to
the overall evaluation received. This problem can become exceedingly
difficult as overall evaluations become more infrequent, making it less clear
which overt actions were responsible for changes in performance, or as the
learning system becomes more complex, making it less clear which internal
decisions were responsible. This suggests that it is useful to divide the
credit-assignment problem for complex learning systems into two subproblems: that of converting the overall evaluation for a sequence of steps
into an evaluation for each step and that of using the evaluation of each
step to assign credit to the internal processes of the learning system that
determined the action selected on that step. One can call the first sub-
problem the *temporal* credit-assignment problem and the second the *structural* credit-assignment problem.

The cause of either type of credit-assignment problem is initial uncertainty about the causal microstructure of the interacting system and environment. Unless one is willing to assume that sufficient *a priori* knowledge is built into the system or into an external teacher (as we are not), this uncertainty is unavoidable, and mechanisms must be devised that can reduce it over time. One approach that has been studied involves stochastic search algorithms that are capable of extracting specific types of statistical regularities from their interactions with random environments. These algorithms are related to those of the theory of stochastic learning automata (Narendra and Thathachar 1974). The concentration on associative reinforcement learning may be considered another prong in this attack on uncertainty. Neutral input can be used to divide a large problem into many subproblems in each of which the uncertainty is more manageable. A third aspect of our approach to uncertainty has been the development of an *adaptive critic* algorithm, in the form of a neuronlike element, that is capable of constructing from neutral environmental signals an evaluation function that is of higher quality than any available directly.

The adaptive critic, an extension of previous studies of classical conditioning (Sutton and Barto 1981; Barto and Sutton 1982), was influenced by Klopf's (1972) concept of "generalized reinforcement" at the level of single neuronlike elements. It turns out also to be closely related to a method used in the famous checkers-playing program developed by Samuel (1959). (If Samuel's "generalization learning" algorithm is simplified by removing from it features dependent on the domain of checkers and features determined by the limited computational resources available to Samuel, the resulting algorithm is a special case of the one implemented by our adaptive critic [Sutton 1984]). If particular stimuli are regularly followed by high reinforcement, then a good critic should assign credit to behavior occurring near the time of occurrence of those stimuli rather than to behavior occurring near the time of the high reinforcement. Credit should be assigned at the earlier time because that was when the critic was first informed that the high reinforcement was coming, and thus the most likely time of the action that caused it. Whereas *primary reinforcement* may be regarded as the credit delivered by externally supplied reinforcement, *secondary reinforcement* is credit delivered by stimuli that have acquired reinforcing properties through this kind of association with primary reinforcement. It is also possible for secondary reinforcers to be learned by association with previously established secondary reinforcers rather than only with primary reinforcers. Thus, secondary reinforcement can be "chained" backward in time. Secondary reinforcement mechanisms can help overcome the weakness of the "recency heuristic" in reinforcement learning. The adaptive-critic element described below creates secondary reinforcement that can be chained in this fashion. Minsky (1961) mentioned the addition of special devices to reinforcement-learning machines for this purpose, and temporal credit assignment was discussed extensively by Sutton (1984).

Examples of Control-Surface Acquisition

The examples that will be presented in this section illustrate many of the issues raised in the above discussion concerning control-surface representation and acquisition. The learning systems in these examples are networks of neuronlike adaptive elements that have been developed in order to explore issues in learning rather than as explicit neural models. These examples are based on a theory of associative search networks introduced in Barto, Sutton, and Brouwer 1981 and further developed in Barto and Sutton 1981, Barto, Anderson, and Sutton 1982, Barto, Sutton, and Anderson 1983, and Sutton 1984.

Acquisition of a Lookup Table

This first example illustrates a control surface represented as a lookup table and its acquisition under the influence of low-quality environmental feedback. (See Barto et al. 1983 for a complete discussion.) The control task is that of balancing a pole hinged to a movable cart (figure 3). The cart is free to move within the bounds of a one-dimensional track, and the pole is free to move only in the vertical plane of the cart and the track. The controller can apply a "left" or "right" force F of fixed magnitude to the cart at discrete time intervals. It is assumed that the equations of motion of the cart-pole system are not known by the controller and that there is no pre-existing controller that can act as a "teacher." The controller receives a vector at each time step giving the cart-pole system's state at that instant. If the pole falls or the cart hits the track boundary, the controller receives a failure signal, which is the only evaluative feedback provided by the environment. The controller must attempt to generate controlling forces in order to avoid the failure signal for as long as possible. It does this by constructing a control surface that assigns "left" or "right" to each controller input situation $(x, \dot{x}, \theta, \dot{\theta})$, where x is the position of the cart on the track, $\dot{x}$ is the cart's velocity, θ is the angle of the pole, and $\dot{\theta}$ is the angular velocity of the pole.

The sparsity and the nonspecific nature of the evaluative feedback creates a genuinely difficult temporal credit-assignment problem. The fail-

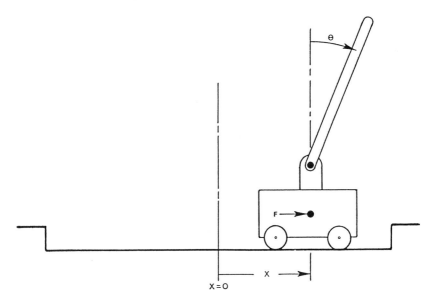

Figure 3
The cart-and-pole control problem. Reprinted from Barto et al. 1983 with permission of the authors. Copyright 1983 IEEE.

ure signal does not directly provide the controller with an indication of what it should have done and when it should have done it. Since the failure signal occurs only after a long sequence of individual control decisions, it is difficult to determine which decisions were responsible for the failure. There is neither a continuously available error signal nor a continuously available performance-evaluation signal, as is the case in more conventional formulations of pole balancing. For example, Widrow and Smith (1964) used a linear regression method, implemented by an adaline, to approximate the control law required for balancing the pole. In order to use this method, however, they had to supply the controller with a signed error signal at each time step, and the determination of this signal required external knowledge of the correct control decision for that time step. The problem we consider, on the other hand, requires the learning system to discover for itself which control decisions are correct, and, in so doing, to solve a difficult credit-assignment problem that is completely absent in the usual versions of this problem.

Much of the motivation for our solution to this problem came from the "Boxes" system developed by Michie and Chambers (1968a, b). In that system, the four-dimensional space of input situations is divided into dis-

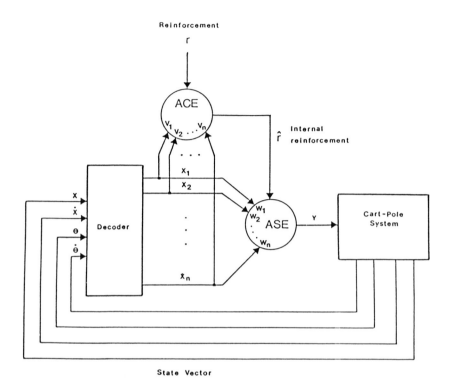

Figure 4
An adaptive network that learns to solve the cart-pole control problem. ASE: associative
search element. ACE: adaptive critic element. Reprinted from Barto et al. 1983 with
permission of the authors. Copyright 1983 IEEE.

joint regions ("boxes") by quantizing the four state variables. Three grades
of position, three of cart velocity, six of pole angle, and three of angle
velocity are distinguished. This yields $3 \times 3 \times 6 \times 3 = 162$ regions, corresponding to all the combinations of these grades. For example, one
region corresponds to a cart position between 0.8 and 2.4 meters *and* a
cart velocity between -0.5 and 0.5 meters per second *and* a pole angle
between $-1°$ and $1°$ *and* an angular velocity greater than $50°$ per second.
The problem, then, is one of filling in this lookup table of 162 entries with
the appropriate control actions. We followed Michie and Chambers in
choosing this state-space quantization to be refined enough to allow the
problem to be solved.

Our solution requires two adaptive elements, an associative search element (ASE) and an adaptive critic element (ACE), each having a "reinforcement" input for evaluative feedback and 162 other input pathways for
providing state information about the cart-pole system (figure 4). We

assume the existence of a decoder that implements the quantization of the controller's input space. It has 162 output pathways, only one of which is active at a time, that act as afferents to the adaptive elements. Each adaptive element will develop a "synaptic weight" associated with each of its input pathways. In the case of the ASE, these weights will be the entries in the control-surface table, with positive weights causing a positive output (control action "right") and negative weights causing negative output (control action "left"). In the case of the ACE, these weights will form another table specifying an internal evaluation function that greatly increases the speed of learning. The ACE receives primary reinforcement feedback r from the external environment and uses it to construct a table of internal or secondary reinforcement $\hat{r}$, which it supplies to the ASE. For the pole-balancing problem, we maintain the primary reinforcement r at zero until failure occurs, when we momentarily set it to -1.

The ASE operates as follows. Let $x_i(t)$, where $1 \leq i \leq 162$, denote the real-valued signal on the ith nonreinforcement input pathway at time t, let $y(t)$ denote the output at time t, and let $\hat{r}(t)$ denote the reinforcement value at time t. Reinforcement $\hat{r}$ will be provided by the ACE in such a way that positive values indicate improvement in performance and negative values indicate decrement in performance. Let $w_i(t)$ denote the value at time t of the weight associated with the ith nonreinforcement input pathway. The ASE's output is determined from its input vector $X(t) = (x_1(t), \ldots, x_n(t))$ as follows:

$$y(t) = f\left(\sum_{i=1}^{n} w_i(t)x_i(t) + \text{noise}(t) \right), \tag{1}$$

where $\text{noise}(t)$ is a normally distributed random variable with mean 0 and where f is the following threshold function:

$$f(x) = \begin{cases} +1 & \text{if } x \geq 0 \quad \text{(control action "right")} \\ -1 & \text{if } x < 0 \quad \text{(control action "left").} \end{cases}$$

According to equation 1, actions are emitted even in the absence of non-zero input signals. The element's output is determined by chance, with a probability biased by the weighted sum of the input signals. If that sum is zero, the control actions "left" and "right" are equally probable.

The weights w_i, $1 \leq i \leq 162$, change over (discrete) time as follows:

$$w_i(t + 1) = w_i(t) + \alpha \hat{r}(t)e_i(t), \tag{2}$$

where α is a positive constant determining the rate of change of w_i, $\hat{r}(t)$ is the real-valued internal reinforcement at time t, and $e_i(t)$ is the *eligibility* at time t of input pathway i. The eligibility of a pathway reflects the extent to which input activity on that pathway was paired with element output activity in the past. The eligibility of pathway i at time t is therefore a *trace* of the product $y(\tau)x_i(\tau)$ for times τ preceding t. For computational simplicity, we generate exponentially decaying eligibility traces e_i using the linear difference equation

$$e_i(t + 1) = \beta e_i(t) + (1 - \beta)y(t)x_i(t), \tag{3}$$

where β $(0 \leq \beta < 1)$ determines the trace decay rate. (Each "synapse" has its own local eligibility trace.)

The basic idea expressed by equations 2 and 3 is that a pathway's weight changes depending on the reinforcement received during periods of that pathway's eligibility. If the reinforcement indicates improved performance $(\hat{r}(t) > 0)$, then the weights of the eligible pathways are changed so as to make the element more likely to "do whatever it did" that made those pathways eligible and perhaps caused the improvement. If reinforcement indicates decreased performance $(\hat{r}(t) < 0)$, then the weights of the eligible pathways are changed to make the element more likely to do something else. The term *eligibility* and this weight-update scheme are derived from the theory of Klopf (1972, 1982), and have precursors in the work of Farley and Clark (1954), Minsky (1954), and others. The ASE implements the view of learning represented by Thorndike's (1911) "Law of Effect."

The ACE constructs a table of "predictions" or "expectations" of reinforcement whose entries are the weights associated with the ACE's input pathways. The ACE uses these predictions to determine an internal reinforcement signal as a function of cart-pole state, which it delivers to the ASE, thus permitting learning to occur throughout a pole-balancing trial rather than solely upon failure. The system effectively learns how "safe" or how "dangerous" are the cart-pole states. It punishes itself for moving from a state to a more dangerous state, and it rewards itself for moving from a state to a safer state. The learning process automatically stops when all externally supplied reinforcement is fully predicted by the ACE.

We implemented the ASE/ACE system shown in figure 4, and to provide a reference point for learning performance we implemented the Boxes system of Michie and Chambers (1968a,b). The cart-pole system was simulated by digital computer using a detailed mathematical model of the physical system. We simulated a series of runs of each learning system attempting to balance the pole. Each run consisted of a sequence of trials where each trial began with the cart-pole state $x = 0$, $\dot{x} = 0$, $\theta = 0$, and $\dot{\theta} = 0$, and ended with a failure signal. The learning systems were naive at

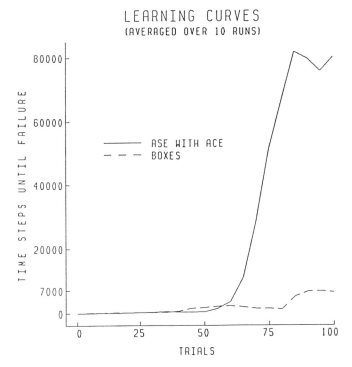

Figure 5

Network performance on the cart-pole task, averaged over ten runs, compared with performance of the Boxes algorithm. Each point represents a bin of five trials, giving average time until failure over the bin, averaged over ten runs. Reprinted from Barto et al. 1983 with permission of the authors. Copyright 1983 IEEE.

the start of each run, and different seeds were supplied to the pseudo-random number generator for each run. A run consisted of 100 trials unless the run's duration exceeded 500,000 time steps (approximately 2.8 hours of simulated real time), in which case the run was terminated.

Figure 5 shows the results of these simulations. The graphs are averages of performance over 10 runs. A single point is plotted for each bin of five trials, giving average time until failure over the bin. It is clear that both the Boxes system and the ASE/ACE system were able to improve their performance with experience. The ASE/ACE system showed dramatic improvement after about 50 trials as the ACE acquired the ability to provide internal evaluation in the absence of failure. Further details of these results are provided in Barto et al. 1983, and additional results are described in Sutton 1984.

These results show how a lookup table can be acquired from experience even when no knowledgeable teacher is available to specify its entries. It should be clear that such a learning system would be able to modify its existing tabular entries if various implicit parameters of the control tasks (for example, the mass of the cart, the length of the pole) were changed. Such an alteration would cause the system to receive reinforcement that would differ from the expected level for certain cart-pole states, thereby automatically reactivating the learning process for those states.

Acquiring a Computational Control Surface

The control surface acquired in the following example may be thought of as represented either by a simple computation or by an associative memory network, depending on what aspects of the representational scheme one emphasizes. In this example, a learning system faces a simple spatial learning task devised by Barto and Sutton (1981) as a simple illustration of the learning capabilities of a network of associative search elements.

Figure 6A shows the spatial environment of a simple "organism," which is represented by the asterisk. The tree in the center of the figure is the organism's target. It emits an "attractant odor" whose strength decays with

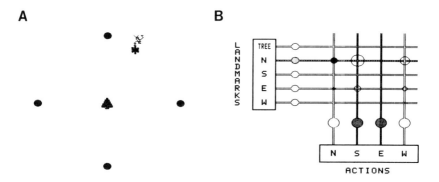

Figure 6
A: The spatial environment of a simple "organism," shown as an asterisk. The tree in the center is source of an "attractant odor"; the four disks represent landmarks which emit their own "odor" distributions, serving as cues to spatial location. B: The "organism's" "brain," a network of four adaptive elements controlling motions in the four cardinal directions. Connection weights between landmark inputs and action outputs are shown as circles centered on the intersections of input lines with adaptive element "dendrites." Positive weights appear as hollow circles, negative weights as shaded circles. Reprinted from Barto and Sutton 1981 with permission of the authors.

distance from the tree. Each of the landmarks at the cardinal points also emits a distinct "odor," decaying with distance, which does not act as an attractant (i.e., is neutral) but can serve as a cue to location in space. The organism's task in this environment is to approach the tree as efficiently as possible and remain in its vicinity. In order to do this, it acquires a control surface that tells the organism which way to go from every place in its environment. The inputs to this controller are the patterns of "odors" from the neutral landmarks, and actions determine movement in space. Once in possession of an adequate control surface, the organism can use it to move directly to the place where the attractant peak usually appeared, even in the complete absence of the attractant distribution. The organism is then able to "control" its spatial environment, in the sense of being able to drive it to a desired state.

The organism's "nervous system" is shown in figure 6B. The four adaptive elements control motions in the respective cardinal directions. Connection weights between input and output elements are shown as circles centered on the intersections of the input pathways with the element "dendrites." Positive weights appear as hollow circles, and negative weights appear as shaded circles. The size of a circle codes the weight's magnitude. The action commanded by the network is to move north if element 1 fires, south if element 2 fires, and so on. We implemented a kind of crossed inhibition to ensure that if (for example) the south and north elements were both active, the organism would take a step north if the north element were more activated than the south element, and vice versa. In the case where two nonopposing elements fire simultaneously, the appropriate compound move is made (e.g., northwest). It is assumed that each move is a fixed distance and is always completed in one time step. The control surface is to be stored as a matrix of weights connecting the neutral landmarks inputs with the action-generating elements.

The four adaptive elements form associations between places in space (signaled by vectors of landmark "odors") and actions leading up the attractant gradient. The weight associated with an input pathway from a given landmark to an element controlling movement in a particular direction increases if a step in that direction is taken in the presence of that landmark's signal and the resulting movement is up the attractant gradient. With sufficient experience, the organism learns to respond to the olfactory cues at each place with the action that is optimal for that place.

The problem of acquiring this control surface is similar to that of acquiring the pole-balancing control surface, and the adaptive elements used are very similar to the ASE discussed above. However, evaluative feedback is available directly from the environment immediately after every action in the form of an indication as to whether the chosen direction of movement was up the attractant gradient or down. Therefore, it is not necessary to use prolonged eligibility traces or an ACE. In particular, $\hat{r}(t)$ in equation 2 is equal to $z(t) - z(t-1)$, where $z(t)$ is the attractant level sensed by the organism at time t, and $e_i(t) = y(t-1)x_i(t-1)$ (which is the result of setting $\beta = 0$ in equation 3).

There is present in this problem, however, a simple form of the structural credit-assignment problem. Each particular move of the "organism" is caused by a pattern of activity of the adaptive elements, and the evaluative feedback rewards or punishes that entire pattern; it does not provide individualized information to each element. Yet, since each element tends to increase its own reinforcement even under the uncertainty caused by the activity of the other elements, it is able to determine what it should do by a kind of "statistical cooperativity." (This term was used by Farley and Clark [1954], who simulated a network of stochastic elements similar to the ASE described here.) This is a very simple illustration of how self-interested components can solve a structural credit-assignment problem, and we think that more complex problems will require extensions of this area.

Figure 7 illustrates the performance of this network. In this case, noise

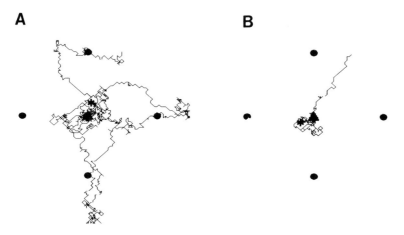

Figure 7
Example of network performance. A: The trail of an inexperienced "organism" in the presence of a noisy attractant distribution. B: The trail of the same "organism," replaced at its starting point after having undergone the experience shown in A. The network has learned how to climb the attractant gradient more efficiently. Reprinted from Barto and Sutton 1981 with permission of the authors.

has been added to the attractant level in order to make the hill-climbing task more difficult. Figure 7A shows the trail of an inexperienced organism that starts near the northern neutral landmark. It eventually remains in the vicinity of the tree. Figure 7B shows the trail produced by replacing the organism at its original starting point after it has undergone the experience shown in figure 7A. It now proceeds directly to the tree, clearly benefiting from its earlier experiences. Figure 8A shows the network after learning. Nonzero weights have appeared, so that, for example, proximity to the northern landmark causes a high probability of movement south because the "odor" of the northern landmark excites the element that causes movement south and inhibits the one that causes movement north. Figure 8B shows the results of learning as a vector field in which each vector shows the average direction that the organism will take on its first step from any place. The vector field is the organism's map of its environment. (It is never literally present in the environment.) The organism would follow this map even if the tree and its attractant distribution were to be removed (so long as the neutral landmarks remained). The organism has formed a control surface, so that on future encounters with a similar environment it need not perform trial-and-error search but will be able to use its control surface to directly find out in which direction it is best to move. The generalization capability of the present storage method is illustrated by the fact that the control surface is defined for places never before visited by the organism. Of course, the problem faced by the organism is simple enough that this

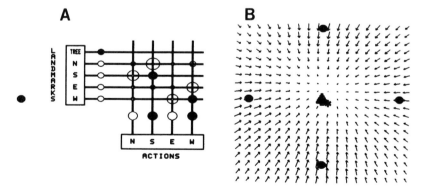

Figure 8
A: The network of figure 6B after learning, corresponding to the behavior shown in figure 7B. B: The results of learning shown as a vector field of the average directions that the "organism" would take on its first step from each position in the environment. Reprinted from Barto and Sutton 1981 with permission of the authors.

linear extrapolation turns out to be correct, but this clearly need not always be true.

Although this control surface specifies a direction of movement for each point in space, it is represented by just sixteen "synaptic" weights. It is not stored as a real physical surface; the vector field shown in figure 9 does not literally exist as a spatial map in the network. This network may be regarded as an example of an associative memory network where the role of the "key" is played by the afferent patterns of "odors" and the associated "recollections" are the actions that lead up the attractant distribution, although the learning process differs from the one usually studied for associative memory networks. (See above.)

A table-lookup approach to this problem would correspond to the presence of a separate landmark, with a corresponding input pathway to the network, in each small region of space. If each landmark's "odor" could be sensed only in its own region, then the landmark "odors" would correspond to table addresses. An interpolating tabular scheme would correspond to having a landmark for each small region but letting it have an "odor" distribution broader than its own region. (The storage scheme of the present example could be considered an interpolating lookup table with four entries.)

Remapping can occur in response to the alteration of an implicit parameter of the control problem. After the organism acquired the control surface shown in figure 8, the east and west landmarks were interchanged. Figure 9A shows the vector field resulting from evaluating the old control surface in this new environment. Starting from a place near the tree, the organism is "misled" by its sensory information and follows the vector field away from the tree (figure 9B1). Since the movement is down the attractant gradient, the learning rule alters the weights to the east and west output elements from the input labeled East (which now responds to the landmark to the west). This relearning results in the network of figure 9B2 and the vector field of figure 9B3. A similar excursion to the east modifies the weights to the east and west output elements from the input labeled West (which now responds to the landmark to the east) as shown in figures 9C1–C3. The system "rewrites" its control surface, thus erasing traces of previous learning. However, the associations from the north and south landmarks remain correct for the new environment and constrain movement to a band that is narrow in the north-south direction, thereby permitting the relearning of the new map to occur faster than the acquisition of the original map. Comparison of the incorrect vector field of figure 9A with the correct one of figure 9C3 shows that remapping has occurred in

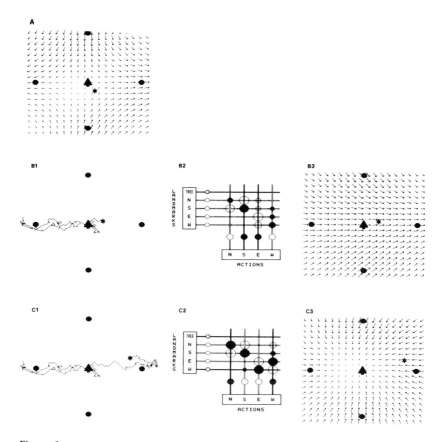

Figure 9

A: Vector field showing the behavior of the network of figure 8 in an environment in which the east and west landmarks have been exchanged. B1: Path of an organism "misled" in this altered environment. B2: The network after the experience shown in B1. B3: The corresponding vector field after the experience shown in B1. C1: Continuation of the path of B1, giving experience with the new east landmark. C2, C3: The network and vector fields, respectively, showing the control surface after the experience shown in C1; the organism has relearned its map of the environment. Reprinted from Barto and Sutton 1981 with permission of the authors.

regions of the space that were not visited in the east-west excursions. It is clear that remapping is easy because the generalization produced by the storage method is suitable. If the control surface had been represented by a lookup table, then each address would have to be visited for complete remapping. Transferring the remapped organism back to the original environment will result in the relearning of the original control surface after sufficient experience.

In the landmark-learning examples just described, no attempt was made to model the actual spatial behavior of any particular organism. It is, however, interesting to compare the behavior of our fictitious organism with that of actual organisms, and it may be an interesting topic for future research to attempt to develop realistic models of spatial learning behavior on the basis of similar principles. Of particular interest is the model presented by Cartwright and Collett (1982) for how honeybees use landmarks to guide their return to a food source. These authors also present vector field representations of their model's behavior.

From Landmark Learning to Motor Control

Although the control problems of the preceding examples are far less complicated than most motor-control problems routinely solved by animals, these examples can help us address, in a simple and concrete way, some of the issues that arise in realistic cases. In particular, the landmark-learning example provides an easily visualized setting for some concepts that may be useful in more difficult control tasks.

If one views the spatial position of the organism in the landmark-learning example as corresponding to the spatial position of a limb tip, then the attractant level sensed by the organism might correspond to an evaluation of positioning accuracy provided by a visual system overseeing the workspace. The "odors" of the four cardinal landmarks sensed by the organism might then correspond to proprioceptive signals giving the current position of the limb in some internal coordinate system. On this view, the system has to learn for each limb position what control actions reduce spatial error. Once this is learned, the system can position the limb accurately without the aid of vision. (Compare the ability of our simulated organism to approach the tree's location in the absence of the attractant distribution.) The remapping in response to interchanged east and west landmarks might be regarded as analogous to the adaptation that takes place after the surgical crossing of nerves innervating flexor and extensor muscles of the forearm and hand in monkeys (Brinkman et al. 1983).

Thus, although the landmark-learning problem has been presented in terms that suggest an actual spatial environment (e.g., odors, landmarks, etc.), many of the ideas illustrated carry over directly to more abstract "spaces," such as the state spaces of dynamical systems. Viewed in this more abstract light, a "landmark" (more specific, the "odor" distribution of a landmark) corresponds to response characteristics of a receptor. One could regard a joint receptor, for example, as an instance of a "proprioceptive landmark," in that an approach to a certain joint angle would increase the receptor's firing rate. More generally, such receptors are responsive to combinations of many dimensions, as are the landmarks in the landmark-learning task, rather than to just one. A specific combination of east-west and north-south positions defines the peak signal from one of these landmarks.

We have found the image of landmarks in state space having "odor" distributions of a variety of shapes to be useful for thinking about the character of information that may be required for the learning of control tasks involving dynamic limbs. A higher density of landmarks is required in regions of complex dynamic flow; their spread functions can be arranged in order to support a variety of forms of generalization; and one can consider mechanisms for the *creation* of appropriate landmarks by a system during its development and learning.

The landmark-learning example also illustrates an important point about what types of strategies may be necessary for learning to perform certain types of motor tasks. Unfortunately, the landmark-learning task is not sufficiently difficult to provide a vivid demonstration of this, since the coordinate system represented by the configuration of landmarks is not essentially different from the coordinate system in which the system's actions are defined. Thus, by simply watching the movement of the organism one would obtain enough information to provide an explicit error signal to each of the network's adaptive elements—for example, if it moved northeast but should have moved southeast, then the north and south elements were wrong and the east and west elements were correct. With this high-quality feedback (that is, a *vector* of individual element errors), simpler error-correction learning methods would suffice. However, although such an error vector could have been provided to the network for this task, we provided only a scalar evaluation of overall network performance (the attractant "odor"), and the network had to discover, via generate-and-test, which of its actions increased this evaluation.

In more difficult problems involving more complex coordinate systems, the observation of spatial movement may not yield enough information to provide the action-generating mechanism with this type of error vector. This would be true in a trajectory-control task, since it would not be obvious what component actions lead to reduced error. A learning mechanism having properties similar to the one illustrated by the landmark-learning problem would be necessary in order to discover what actions increase accuracy.

Many important aspects of limb control (higher-level planning, ballistic movements, and compliant motion, to mention only a few) have not been addressed here, but it is clear why the most widely studied learning methods are probably inadequate, by themselves, for many of the learning tasks that occur in the motor-control domain.

Discussion

Networks of neuronlike elements can implement control surfaces in a manner that combines aspects of computational and table-lookup representations. The associative character of networks using distributed representations of control situations provides a form of generalization that suggests the possibility of savings in storage resources and increases in the speed of acquisition and modification of control knowledge. On the other hand, if provided with a sufficiently refined encoding of input, such a network can act as a kind of lookup table. Although the examples presented here do not demonstrate the utility of networks for representing control surfaces for truly difficult control problems, they provide an idea of the type of learning capabilities that we think networks need if they are to form useful parts of adaptive motor control systems. Additionally, of course, we intend them to be suggestive about the types of mechanisms that the real neural networks implementing animal motor-control systems might employ.

A key problem, however, is that the utility of an associative network (in fact, of any representational medium) depends critically on the encoding of the control problem with which it starts. For the pole-balancing example, we initially provided a decoder with enough resolution to enable the network (in this case, just one element generating control signals and an adaptive critic element) to solve the problem. For the landmark-learning problem, we conveniently placed a sufficient number of landmarks in appropriate locations. Generally, however, the signals received by the elements generating control actions will be the result of extensive processing by other parts of the network. Since the input/output functions of individual network elements are relatively simple (although they need not be as simple as the linear threshold functions of the elements in our examples), the rest of the network must be capable of adaptively forming a set of features rich enough for a sufficiently accurate solution of the control problem.

Despite considerable effort, the promise of providing a means for this type of adaptive creation of useful features has not yet been convincingly fulfilled. (Creating new features is still a major problem for artificial learning systems, irrespective of the approach taken.) The well-known learning algorithms that work for training a single layer of adaptive elements cannot be extended easily to multilayer networks. One reason for this lack of success may be that researchers tend to think the problem is simpler than it really is. To move beyond simple single-layer adaptive networks, it is necessary for each network component to implement a fairly sophisticated learning algorithm.

An adaptive component that is deeply embedded within a network faces a learning problem that is difficult because of the high degree of uncertainty involved in evaluating its individual performance. As a network component, an adaptive element cannot be instructed how to behave by a "teacher" providing individualized desired responses or signed error signals. This is the Achilles' heel of supervised learning pattern classifiers as network components. Elements must be capable of learning under the guidance of reinforcement feedback that evaluates the consequences (which may be quite indirect) of component actions but does not specify these actions. Some results have been obtained that lend support to this approach to learning within networks (Barto et al. 1982; Anderson 1982).

One of the reasons that we originally developed the pole-balancing example was to evaluate the learning capabilities of individual adaptive elements in a task having many of the characteristics of the tasks faced by adaptive elements deeply embedded within complicated networks. We think that such tasks are at least as difficult as the pole-balancing task under the constraints described above.

Acknowledgments

This research was supported by the Air Force Office of Scientific Research and the Avionics Laboratory (Air Force Wright Aeronautical Laboratories) through contract F33615-80-C-1088. The author would like to thank R. S. Sutton and C. W. Anderson for collaborating in this research, M. Arbib and D. N. Spinelli for many helpful discussions, and S. Epstein for helping to write an earlier version of this paper.

References

Aizerman, M. A., E. M. Braverman, and L. I. Rozonoer. 1964. Theoretical foundations of the potential function method in pattern recognition learning. *Automation and Remote Control* 25: 821–837.

Albus, J. A. 1971. A theory of cerebellar function. *Mathematical Biosciences* 10: 25–61.

Albus, J. A. 1979. Mechanisms of planning and problem solving in the brain. *Mathematical Biosciences* 45: 247–293.

Amari, S. 1977a. A mathematical approach to neural systems. In *Systems Neuroscience*, ed. J. Metzler (Academic).

Amari, S. 1977b. Neural theory of association and concept-formation. *Biological Cybernetics* 26: 175–185.

Anderson, C. W. 1982. Feature Selection in a Reinforcement Learning System. Technical Report 82-12, Computer and Information Science Department, University of Massachusetts, Amherst.

Anderson, J. A., J. W. Silverman, S. A. Ritz, and R. S. Jones. 1977. Distinctive features, categorical perception, and probability learning: Some applications of a neural model. *Psychological Review* 85: 413–451.

Arbib, M. A. 1972. *The Metaphorical Brain: An Introduction to Cybernetics as Artificial Intelligence and Brain Theory.* Interscience.

Ballard, D. H. 1981. Parameter networks: Toward a theory of low-level vision. In Proceedings of the Seventh International Joint Conference on Artificial Intelligence, Vancouver.

Barto, A. G., and R. S. Sutton. 1981. Landmark learning: An illustration of associative search. *Biological Cybernetics* 42: 1–8.

Barto, A. G., and R. S. Sutton. 1982. Simulation of anticipatory responses in classical conditioning by a neuron-like adaptive element. *Behavioural Brain Research* 4: 221–235.

Barto, A. G., R. S. Sutton, and P. S. Brouwer. 1981. Associative search network: A reinforcement learning associative memory. *Biological Cybernetics* 40: 201–211.

Barto, A. G., C. W. Anderson, and R. S. Sutton. 1982. Synthesis of nonlinear control surfaces by a layered associative search network. *Biological Cybernetics* 43: 175–185.

Barto, A. G., R. S. Sutton, and C. W. Anderson. 1983. Neuron-like adaptive elements that can solve difficult learning control problems. *IEEE Transactions on Systems, Man, and Cybernetics* 13: 834–846.

Brinkman, C., R. Porter, and J. Norman. 1983. Plasticity of motor behavior in monkeys with crossed forelimb nerves. *Science* 220: 438–440.

Campbell, D. T. 1960. Blind variation and selective survival as a general strategy in knowledge-processes. In *Self-Organizing Systems*, ed. M. C. Yovitts and S. Camero (Pergamon).

Cartwright, B. A., and T. S. Collett. 1982. How honey bees use landmarks to guide their return to a food source. *Nature* 295, no. 5850: 560–564.

Cohen, P. R., and E. A. Feigenbaum, eds. 1982. *The Handbook of Artificial Intelligence*, volume 3. Kaufmann.

Cooper, L. N. 1974. A possible organization of animal memory and learning. In Proceedings of the Nobel Symposium on Collective Properties of Physical Systems.

Didday, R. L. 1976. A model of visuomotor mechanisms in the frog optic tectum. *Mathematical Biosciences* 30: 169–180.

Duda, R. O., and P. E. Hart. 1973. *Pattern Classification and Scene Analysis*. Wiley.

Edelman, G. M. 1978. Group selection and phasic reentrant signaling: A theory of higher brain function. In *The Mindful Brain: Cortical Organization and the Group-Selective Theory of Higher Brain Function*, ed. G. M. Edelman and V. B. Mountcastle (MIT Press).

Farley, B. G., and W. A. Clark. 1954. Simulation of self-organizing systems by digital computer. *IRE Transactions on Information Theory* PGIT-4: 76–84.

Feldman, J. A. 1981. A connectionist model of visual memory. In *Parallel Models of Associative Memory*, ed. G. Hinton and J. Anderson (Erlabum).

Hebb, D. O. 1949. *Organization of Behavior*. Wiley.

Hinton, G. E. 1981. Implementing semantic networks in parallel hardware. In *Parallel Models of Associative Memory*, ed. G. E. Hinton and J. A. Anderson (Erlbaum).

Hinton, G. E., and J. A. Anderson. 1981. *Parallel Models of Associative Memory*. Erlbaum.

Hinton, G. E., and T. J. Sejnowski. 1983. Analyzing cooperative computation. In Proceedings of the Fifth Annual Conference of the Cognitive Science Society, Rochester, N.Y.

Ito, M. 1982. Mechanisms of motor learning. In *Competition and Cooperation in Neural Nets*, ed. S. Amari and M. A. Arbib (Springer-Verlag).

Klopf, A. H. 1972. Brain Function and Adaptive Systems—A Heterostatic Theory. Air Force Cambridge Research Laboratories Research Report 72-0164. (A summary appears in the Proceedings of the International Conference on Systems, Man, and Cybernetics, Dallas, 1974.)

Klopf, A. H. 1982. *The Hedonistic Neuron: A Theory of Memory, Learning, and Intelligence*. Hemisphere.

Kohonen, T. 1977. *Associative Memory: A System Theoretic Approach*. Springer-Verlag.

Lenat, D. B., F. Hayes-Roth, and P. Klahr. 1979. Cognitive Economy. Working Paper 79-15, Stanford Heuristic Programming Project.

Marr, D. 1969. A theory of cerebellar cortex. *Journal of Physiology* 202: 437–470.

McClelland, J. L., and D. E. Rumelhart. 1981. An interactive model of context effects in letter perception: Part 1. An account of basic findings. *Psychological Review* 88: 275–407.

Mendel, J. M. 1970. Synthesis of quasi-optimal switching surfaces by means of training techniques. In *Adaptation, Learning, and Pattern Recognition Systems: Theory and Applications*, ed. J. M. Mendel and K. S. Fu (Academic).

Michie, D., and R. A. Chambers. 1968a. BOXES: An experiment in adaptive control. In *Machine Intelligence 2*, ed. E. Dale and D. Michie (Oliver and Boyd, Edinburgh).

Michie, D., and R. A. Chambers. 1968b. "Boxes" as a model of pattern-formation. In *Towards a Theoretical Biology: 1, Prolegomena* (Edinburgh University Press).

Minsky, M. L. 1954. Theory of Neural-Analog Reinforcement Systems and Its Application to the Brain-Model Program. Ph.D. dissertation, Princeton University.

Minsky, M. L. 1961. Steps toward artificial intelligence. *Proceedings of the IRE* 49: 8–30.

Nakano, K. 1972. Association—a model of associative memory. *IEEE Transactions on Systems, Man, and Cybernetics* 2: 380–388.

Narendra, K. S., and M. A. L. Thathachar. 1974. Learning automata—a survey. *IEEE Transactions on Systems, Man, and Cybernetics* 4: 323–334.

Page, C. V. 1977. Heuristics for signature table analysis as a pattern recognition technique. *IEEE Transactions on Systems, Man, and Cybernetics* 7, no. 2: 77–86.

Raibert, M. H. 1977. Analytical equations vs. table look-up for manipulation: A unifying concept. In Proceedings of the IEEE Conference on Decision and Control, New Orleans.

Raibert, M. H. 1978. A model for sensorimotor control and learning. *Biological Cybernetics* 29: 29–36.

Rosenblatt, F. 1962. *Principles of Neurodynamics*. Spartan.

Samuel, A. L. 1959. Some studies in machine learning using the game of checkers. *IBM Journal of Research and Development* 3: 210–229.

Sutton, R. S. 1984. Temporal Aspects of Credit Assignment in Reinforcement Learning. Ph.D. dissertation, University of Massachusetts.

Sutton, R. S., and A. G. Barto. 1981. Toward a modern theory of adaptive networks: Expectation and prediction. *Psychological Review* 88, no. 2: 135–171.

Thorndike, E. 1911. *Animal Intelligence*. Macmillan.

Widrow, B., and M. E. Hoff. 1960. Adaptive switching circuits. In WESCON Convention Record, Part IV.

Widrow, B., and F. W. Smith. 1964. Pattern-recognizing control systems. In *Computer and Information Sciences*, ed. J. T. Tow and R. H. Wilcox (Clever Hume Press).

Wigstrom, H. 1973. A neuron model with learning capability and its relation to mechanisms of association. *Kybernetik* 12: 204–215.

Willshaw, D. J., O. Buneman, and H. S. Longuet-Higgins. 1969. Non-holographic associative memory. *Nature* 222: 960–962.

19

Separating Figure from Ground with a Boltzmann Machine

Terrence J. Sejnowski and
Geoffrey E. Hinton

Many problems in visual processing can be formulated as searches: Given an image or a sequence of images, find the best interpretation from a large set of possible internal models. That humans are able to recognize three-dimensional objects in images within a few hundred milliseconds implies an effective search strategy. Mistakes, when they do occur, are usually confusions among similar objects. These fast, effortless, and generally reliable searches are carried out in parallel by a large number of neurons in the visual cortex. The architecture of visual cortex in primates has inspired parallel models of visual computation (Arbib 1975; Marr 1982; Feldman and Ballard 1982; Ballard et al. 1983).

In this paper we review a class of parallel visual algorithms that use relaxation to perform rapid best-fit searches and we examine some of the difficulties inherent in this search technique. In particular, we analyze the problem of separating figure from ground in an image and show how a parallel relaxation algorithm can be trapped in states that are locally optimal but globally incorrect. We introduce a general parallel search method, based on statistical mechanics, that overcomes this shortcoming and finds globally optimal solutions with a high probability (Kirkpatrick et al. 1983; Hinton and Sejnowski 1983). This approach is effective in small-scale simulations of parallel visual algorithms; its usefulness for large problems is still uncertain.

An intriguing aspect of the stochastic search procedure is that it depends on the presence of noise, which normally is considered a nuisance and which typically degrades the performance of a system. There is considerable evidence for a high degree of stochastic variability in the firing pattern of single neurons in visual cortex. This new approach raises the possibility that the noisiness of cortical neurons, rather than reflecting biological imprecision, may serve a useful purpose in improving parallel searches for optimal interpretations.

Computation of Binocular Disparity by Parallel Relaxation

Binocular depth perception, or stereopsis, has been intensively studied since Wheatstone invented the stereoscope in 1838. More recently it has been possible to study stereopsis free from other depth cues using the random-dot stereograms introduced by Julesz in 1964. Stereopsis is now known to be a difficult computational problem. Despite our much better understanding, no completely satisfactory computational solution exists, nor is there a consensus about how the problem is solved by the visual system (Mayhew and Frisby 1981; Mayhew 1983; Poggio and Poggio 1984).

Many of the issues that arise in studying stereopsis also apply to other computational problems in vision; in particular, parallel algorithms for stereopsis illustrate some of the generic difficulties of parallel visual algorithms (Ballard et al. 1983). The first step in seeing depth with two eyes is to establish matches between corresponding points on the two retinas. Matches are typically ambiguous, especially with random-dot stereograms where all local features are identical. One procedure for resolving ambiguities is to implement constraints on possible matches as excitatory and inhibitory links between processing units whose values represent depth (Sperling 1970; Julesz 1971; Dev 1975; Nelson 1975; Marr and Poggio 1976). The problem is then reduced to finding the matches that best satisfy all the local constraints.

In the Marr-Poggio (1976) algorithm for random-dot stereograms, each unit stands for a binary hypothesis about the correspondence of a particular pair of dots and therefore represents the existence of a patch of surface at a particular depth. There are exicitatory interactions between neighboring units with the same depth to ensure continuity of surfaces, and inhibitory interactions between units that represent different depths at the same image location to ensure that depth assignments are unique; if the sum of all the inputs to a unit from the two images and from local interactions is above threshold, the value of the unit is set to 1, and otherwise it is set to 0. Starting from all zeros, the units are iteratively updated: During the relaxation, various combinations of depth assignments are tried and the network eventually "locks" into a generally consistent solution in a way that resembles the human perceptual experience of fusing random-dot stereograms (Julesz 1971).

In general it is not possible to prove that this algorithm always converges to the correct depth assignments, partly because small clusters of units may form coalitions that are locally optimal but are not the globally best solution (Burt 1977; Marr et al. 1978). Another drawback of this relaxation method is the large number of iterations required to reach the final solution. If there are only nearest-neighbor interactions between units, then at least as many iterations are required as there are units across the image, since information must propagate between units one at a time and a global consensus must be reached by all the units. These problems can be minimized by the introduction of units with coarser spatial resolution (Rosenfeld and Vanderbrug 1977; Marr and Poggio 1979; Terzopoulos 1984).

Another computational problem that must be solved if only a sparse set of correct correspondences have been found is interpolating a smooth surface through the matched positions on the surface. Grimson (1981) has shown how this problem can be formulated as a variational principle in continuum mechanics by treating the surface as a thin plate. The problem is to minimize the energy of deformation of the surface constrained to pass through the matched positions. The discretized equations can be solved using a gradient-descent relaxation algorithm in which the energy is reduced at each step. As in the case of the correspondence problem, a parallel realization of the algorithm is possible with locally connected processing units. However, because in this problem the energy is a convex function possessing only a single optimum, the relaxation process always converges to the correct solution.

Special care must be taken with interpolation at locations where there are depth discontinuities. Decisions must be made either before or during the relaxation about where breaks should occur in the surface representation so that no attempt is subsequently made to interpolate smoothly across the breaks. One possibility is to monitor the local energy of deformation and "break" the thin plate if it exceeds some threshold (Terzopoulos 1984). However, once a break is made it is no longer possible to backtrack and correct for a wrong choice, so a globally optimal solution is no longer ensured. Discrete decisions must therefore be made together with the estimation of continuous variables. Similar problems occur in many other computations of intrinsic surface properties in early vision (Ballard et al. 1983).

Figure-Ground Separation

One of the simplest problems in visual perception where a discrete choice at a boundary affects subsequent processing is the organization of figure and ground in an image (Weisstein and Wong, this volume). The classic drawing that can be interpreted as either a vase or two faces (figure 1) gives

Figure 1
Rubin's (1915) demonstration of visual reversal of figure and ground. The form can be seen as a vase or as a pair of faces, but not both at the same time.

rise to two percepts depending on whether the figural part of the drawing is on the inside or the outside of the closed outline. Humans are remarkably good at performing the separation and can report within a few hundred milliseconds whether a small spot is inside or outside a briefly flashed closed outline (Ullman 1984). The discrimination probably requires two steps: a segmentation of the figure and the ground and a subsequent decision about whether the spot is located in the figure.

We briefly summarize here a simple parallel relaxation model of one type of process that occurs during figure-ground separation (Kienker et al. 1986; for previous work on scene segmentation using relaxation algorithms see Prager 1980, Zucker and Hummel 1979, and Danker and Rosenfeld 1981). The model is designed to mark the inside or the outside of a connected figure when given some lines that represent its edges and an "attentional spotlight" that provides a bias to either the inside or the outside. Examples of these two different types of input are shown in figure 3. The "bottom-up" input is not the raw image itself but is a highly processed version of the image containing the location and orientation of edges, as might be found in early visual cortex. The model must tolerate missing line segments, and it must be possible for changes in the "top-down" attentional spotlight to cause the same set of lines to be segmented differently.

There are two types of binary units in the model: figure units and edge units. Figure units correspond to small regions in the image. When a figure unit is on, its region is marked as being part of the current figure. To

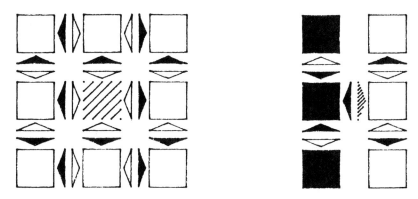

Figure 2
Summary of the weights betwen units in the figure-ground network. Because the pattern
of connectivity is isotropic, only the weights for a single figure unit (left) and a single
edge unit (right) are shown. The connections are represented not by conventional lines
but by the presence and shading of other units. A white (open) unit represents an
excitatory connection to that unit; a black (filled) unit represents an inhibitory connection
to that unit. For every connection indicated there is a reciprocal feedback connection
having the same weight; that is, all the connections are symmetric. Left: All the connections to a figure unit (cross-hatched square). The figure unit is connected to each of its
eight nearestneighbor figure units (squares) with weights of strength + 10. All the
connections between the central figure unit and the surrounding edge units (arrowheads)
can be deduced from the pattern (shown at right) for a single edge unit. Right: All the
connections to a single vertical edge unit (cross-hatched arrowhead). The edge unit is
connected to the figure unit toward which it is pointing with an excitatory weight of
+ 12 and to the figure unit it is pointing away from with an inhibitory weight of − 12. It
is also connected to laterally adjacent figure units with weights of either + 10 or − 10.
The two types of edge units, which point away from each other, are mutually inhibitory
with a weight of − 15. The diagram on the left shows the overall pattern of connectivity
between edge and figure units.

implement the constraint that figures tend to be connected, each figure
supports all eight neighboring figure units, as shown in figure 2. To implement the top-down constraint that the figure should have a particular
approximate scale and a particular approximate location, figure units receive top-down excitatory input from the attentional spotlight. An edge
unit is used to mark the presence and type of an edge. A line segment
between two regions can be interpreted in many ways. It could be the
bounding edge of a region to one side, or the bounding edge of a region
to the other side, or both if it is a crack. We ignore cracks, shadows, surface
markings, and edges where two non-coplanar three-dimensional surfaces
join, and allow only the two alternative bounding-edge possibilities. Between any two adjacent figure units there are two edge units corresponding

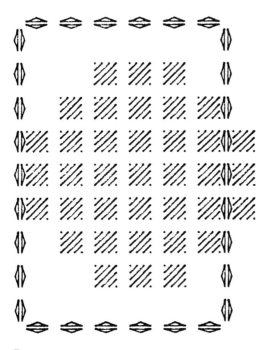

Figure 3

Two types of inputs to the figure-ground module: bottom-up inputs from the image to some of the edge units (arrowheads), which in this case form a 9×6 rectangle, and top-down attentional inputs to the figure units (cross-hatched squares). The strengths of the inputs to the figures units have a Gaussian distribution centered on the unit just to the right of the rectangle's center given by $15e^{-(d/2)^2}$, where d is the Euclidean distance of the unit from the center of attention. The figure units that are shown cross-hatched are those whose attentional input exceeds 1. Each figure unit has a threshold of 41, so the top-down input is not enough by itself to turn the figure units on. The edges composing the outline of the 9×6 rectangle have external inputs of 60, and all edge units have thresholds of 45. Thus, there was a strong bias for edge units composing the outline to be on; however, both types of edge units at each position of the outline received equal input.

to these two interpretations. Each of these supports one of the figure units and inhibits the other, and because cracks are not allowed the two edge units inhibit each other.

To implement the constraint that lines in the input require interpretation, each line segment provides equal excitatory input to the two relevant edge units. To implement the constraint that edges are implausible in places where there are no lines in the input, edge units have high thresholds that normally require excitatory input to overcome them. To implement the constraint that edges tend to be continuous, a figure unit supports the colinear neighbors of its bounding-edge units. This was found to work better than direct support between the colinear-edge units themselves, because it allows edge completion to occur around the figure region but not elsewhere.

The complete set of interactions of a figure unit and an edge unit are shown in figure 2. The precise strengths of the interactions were chosen by trial and error using a variety of outlines and were guided by the following two considerations:

• The region within the attentional spotlight should tend to be figure and the region outside should tend to be background.

• The discontinuity between figure and background should normally appear as a line in the image, and so there should be a penalty for "open frontier" where the figure region ends without there being a line in the image.

Whenever the spotlight of attention does not precisely align with the lines in the image, these two considerations are antagonistic and it therefore becomes necessary to perform a best-fit search.

One of the simplest updating algorithms consists of choosing a unit at random and summing the weighted inputs from all the active interacting units together with any external input. If this sum exceeds a fixed threshold, the unit adopts the 1 state; otherwise it adopts the 0 state. This algorithm quickly fills in the figure, but it often makes mistakes where figure units are incorrectly stabilized by edge units (as shown in figure 4). It can be made to perform reliably if the spotlight is strong; however, the performance then is very sensitive to the width of the spotlight, and this would require the top-down attentional input to already know the exact extent of the figure in the image. A more robust algorithm should be capable of good performance with a spotlight whose size and position do not already encode the exact size and position of the figure.

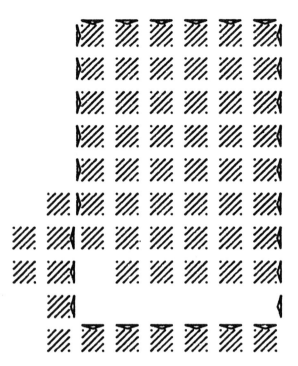

Figure 4
Final state of the figure-ground module using the gradient-descent update rule ($T = 0$). The simulation was started from a random starting state with approximately one out of ten units on. Each iteration consisted of 2,000 updates. For each update one of the 2,000 units was chosen at random, the weighted inputs from other active units were summed, and the binary threshold rule was applied to determine its new state. The system reached the steady-state configuration shown here after 28 iterations. The bottom line of figure units has been incorrectly stabilized outside the rectangle.

Analyzing Convergence

There is a useful analogy between binary networks of hypotheses that implement constraint-satisfaction problems (such as the figure-ground model introduced here) and models of interacting spins in physics. Our binary networks most closely resemble *spin glasses* (spin systems where both positive and negative interactions occur between spins). Because of competing interactions, spin glasses exhibit a phenomenon called *frustration* (Kirkpatrick 1977) in which conflicting constraints produce many local optima and degenerate ground states. One important difference, however, is that in spin glasses the spins interact randomly, whereas in binary networks that solve particular constraint-satisfaction problems the interactions are highly ordered.

The binary networks in the models of stereopsis and figure-ground separation previously discussed have the property that the connections (considered a matrix) are symmetric. A large class of constraint-satisfaction problems can be implemented with symmetric weights, including ones that require asymmetric constraints between hypotheses. For example, two hypotheses related by implication can be implemented by two units connected by symmetric weights and having different thresholds (Hinton and Sejnowski 1983). Symmetric connectivity has the significant advantage that optimization techniques and variational principles can be used to analyze the performance of the network (Hummel and Zucker 1983). In particular, Hopfield (1982) has shown that one can define an "energy" for a symmetric network of binary hypotheses that can be used to analyze its convergence. Each state is assigned an energy according to

$$E = -\frac{1}{2} \sum_{i \neq j} w_{ij} s_i s_j - \sum_i (\eta_i - \theta_i) s_i, \tag{1}$$

where s_i is the state of unit i, w_{ij} is the strength of connection between the units i and j, η_i is the input to unit i, and θ_i is the threshold of unit i. A simple asynchronous algorithm for finding the combination of hypotheses that has a local energy minimum is to choose asynchronously a unit at random and set its state to the one with the lowest energy. Because of the symmetric weights, this updating rule requires that the unit be set to 1 if the "energy gap"

$$\Delta E_i = \sum_j w_{ij} s_j + \eta_i - \theta_i \tag{2}$$

is positive, and to 0 otherwise. This is the familiar rule for binary threshold units that was used in describing the updating of units in the stereo algorithm and the figure-ground algorithm. Spin models for neural networks have been studied (Cragg and Temperley 1954; Little and Shaw 1975; Choi and Huberman 1984). However, the asynchronous updating rule we have used ensures convergence, whereas the synchronous updating rule in other models may produce oscillations and more complex dynamics. Synchronous models are more closely related to cellular automata (von Neumann 1966; Wolfram 1983).

In the case of the stereo algorithm, the search space is fairly well behaved (Nishihara 1984; Prazdny 1985; Szeliski and Hinton 1985). However, the global minimum in the figure-ground problem is shallower and the search space has many local minima within which to get trapped. Many problems in vision (such as grouping and line labeling) that require the global organization of discontinuities (Waltz 1975; Zucker and Hummel 1979; Zucker 1983) have energy landscapes similar to that of the figure-ground problem. In the next section we will introduce a general technique for finding good solutions to problems of this type.

The Metropolis Algorithm and Simulated Annealing

The problem of being trapped in local energy minima can be circumvented by altering the deterministic decision rule. A simple way to escape from a local minimum is to occasionally allow jumps to states of higher energy. An algorithm with this property was introduced by Metropolis et al. (1953) for the purpose of studying the average properties of thermodynamic systems (Binder 1978). This algorithm has recently been applied to problems of constraint satisfaction (Kirkpatrick et al. 1983; Hinton and Sejnowski 1983; Smolensky 1983; Geman and Geman 1984; Bienenstock 1985). Boltzmann machines (Fahlman et al. 1983) are networks of binary processors that use as their update rule a form of the Metropolis algorithm that is suitable for parallel computation: If the energy gap between the 1 and 0 states of a unit is ΔE_i, then—regardless of the previous state—set the unit to 1 with probability

$$p_i = (1 + e^{-\Delta E_i/T})^{-1}, \tag{3}$$

where T is a parameter that acts like temperature (figure 5). As T approaches zero, equation 3 approaches a step function: the deterministic update rule for binary threshold units already introduced.

Our analysis of Boltzmann machines is based on the statistical mechanics of physical systems (Schroedinger 1946). The probabilistic decision rule in equation 3 is the same as the equilibrium probability distribution for a

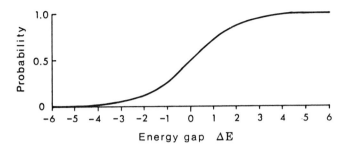

Figure 5
Probability for a unit to be on as a function of the energy gap ΔE plotted for $T = 1$ (equation 3). As the temperature decreases, the sigmoid approaches a step function; at $T = 0$ it becomes the decision rule for a binary threshold unit. As the temperature increases, the sigmoid becomes very broad and approaches a probability of 0.5 regardless of the energy gap. In this limit the effect of the weights between units becomes negligible in comparison with the thermal noise.

system with two energy states. A system of particles in contact with a heat bath at a given temperature will eventually reach thermal equilibrium, and the probabilities of finding the system in any global state will then obey a Boltzmann distribution. Similarly, a network of units obeying this decision rule will eventually reach a "thermal equilibrium" in which the relative probability of two global states of the network follows the Boltzmann distribution:

$$\frac{p_\alpha}{p_\beta} = e^{-(E_\alpha - E_\beta)/T}, \tag{4}$$

where p_α is the probability of being in the global state α and E_α is the energy of that state.

At low temperatures there is a strong bias in favor of states with low energy, but the time required to reach equilibrium may be long. At higher temperatures the bias is not so favorable but the equilibrium is reached sooner. This occurs because temperature enters as a scale factor for the energy difference in equation 4 and therefore scales the amount of discrimination between different energy states. The difficulty of breaking out of a local energy minimum depends on the heights and the degeneracies of saddle-shaped energy barriers separating them from other minima. At high temperatures these barriers are easily jumped, but lowering the temperature increases the time required to make the jump.

Kirkpatrick et al. (1983) introduced a way to find the global energy minimum using simulated annealing, a procedure derived by analogy from the annealing of solids. The system is started at a high temperature to reach equilibrium quickly, and the temperature is gradually reduced. As the temperature is lowered, the search space is explored, first at a coarse grain and then at successively finer grains. This search procedure is effective at solving some difficult combinatorial problems such as graph partitioning, and it performs well on a large class of problems (Johnson et al. 1986). However, simulated annealing is not a panacea; there are many problems where the search space is not suitably structured. For example, it does poorly at finding a very deep and narrow energy minimum, and it would do poorly at golf (Andrew Witkin, personal communication). It is therefore not at all clear whether simulated annealing would be useful in trying to satisfy multiple weak constraints such as those found in visual algorithms.

As a test case we have applied the Metropolis algorithm and simulated annealing to the parallel algorithm for separating figure from ground introduced above. (A more detailed account can be found in Kienker et al. 1986.) At high temperatures the figure and edge units make a structureless pattern (figure 6a). As the temperature is exponentially reduced, the figure units around the center of attention tend to remain on, and these on average support those edge units whose orientation is consistent with them (figure 6b). As the temperature is further reduced, local inconsistencies are resolved and the entire network "crystallizes" to the correct solution. In a series of 1,000 annealings from random starting configurations, every trial reached the correct solution, as is shown by figure 7. A single iteration consisted of 2,000 updates in which one of the 2,000 units in the problem was chosen at random. Similar results have been obtained for a variety of simple figures, including ones where the outline is incomplete. The performance of the algorithm on spirals using the same annealing schedule is very poor; however, with a much slower annealing schedule the algorithm reliably finds the correct solution. Humans also have great difficulty with spirals.

The model of figure-ground separation presented here is clearly much too simple to explain how the problem is solved in the human visual system. A more realistic model would need to take into account multiple levels of resolution (Terzopoulos 1984) and a greater range of orientations, and it would have to introduce distinctions between low-level edge labeling and higher-level attentional phenomena (Crick 1984). However, general features of more sophisticated models are probably reflected in this simple example. More complex representations in networks of locally interacting units may also benefit from stochastic parallel search as long as

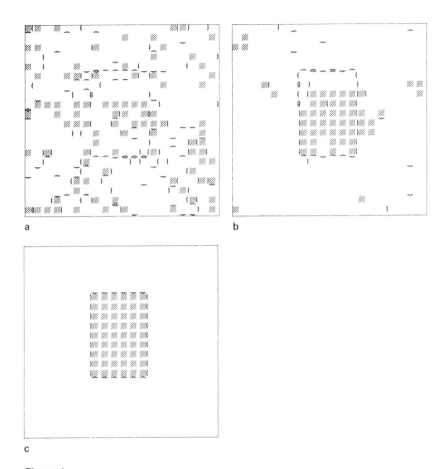

Figure 6
Simulated annealing applied to the figure-ground network shown at three temperatures—
(a) $T = 16.2$ after three iterations, (b) $T = 7.7$ after ten iterations, and (c) $T = 3.3$ after 28
iterations—using the probabilistic update rule of equation 3. The annealing schedule was
piecewise exponential: $T_i = p * T_{i-1}$, where $T_0 = 20$, $p = 0.9$ for $T_i > 4$, and $p = 0.99$ for
$T_i < 4$.

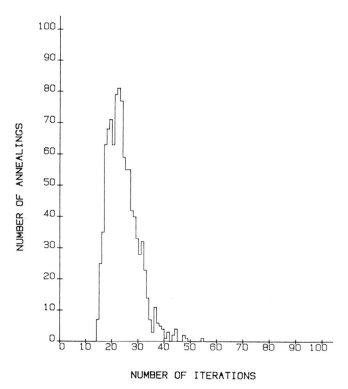

NUMBER OF ITERATIONS

Figure 7
Histogram of the number of simulated annealing trials that properly filled the inside of the rectangle as a function of the number of iterations required. The annealing schedule given in figure 6 was used in 1,000 trials, each starting from a different random state. The fastest solution took 14 iterations and the longest took 55 iterations; the median was 21 iterations.

the best-fit solutions can be expressed as the minima of a cost function. Geman and Geman (1984) have independently used a similar approach to the Bayesian restoration of images after degradation due to blurring, non-linear deformations, and noise.

The model of figure-ground separation used only information from the outlines of figures. Other cues, such as optical flow, may also provide information for separating figure from ground, which would require other modules. We can analyze the performance of several modules working together in parallel by simply adding together their cost functions. One of the consequences of this additivity is that different sources of evidence are weighed together linearly. It has been shown that several factors affecting the perception of depth in a rotating wire cube, including proximity luminance and perspective, are linearly additive (Dosher et al. 1985). This result is in agreement with our approach and suggests that linear additivity of evidence may be a general property of perceptual systems (Sperling et al. 1983).

Relationship between Boltzmann Machines and Neural Models

The energy gap for a binary unit has a role similar to that played by the membrane potential for a neuron; both are sums of the excitatory and inhibitory inputs, and both are used to determine the output state through a nonlinear transformation. However, a neuron produces action potentials (brief spikes that propagate down its axon) rather than a binary output. When the action potential reaches a synapse, the signal it produces in the postsynaptic neuron rises to a maximum and then decays with the time constant of the membrane (typically around 5 msec for neurons in cerebral cortex). The effect of a single spike on the postsynaptic cell body may be further broadened by electrotonic transmission down the dendrite to the spike-initiating zone near the cell body.

This suggests a neural interpretation for the binary pulses in a Boltzmann machine: If the average time between updates is identified with the average duration of a postsynaptic potential, then the binary pulse between updates can be considered an approximation to the postsynaptic potential. Although the shape of a single binary pulse differs significantly from a postsynaptic potential, the sum of a large number of pulses stochastically impinging on a processing unit is independent of the shape of the individual pulses. Thus, for networks having the large fan-ins typical of cerebral cortex (several thousand), the energy gap of a binary unit should behave like the membrane potential of a spike-producing neuron.

In addition to the nonlinear membrane currents in axons that produce action potentials, active membrane currents have also been found in the dendrites of some neurons that could support nonlinear processing (Perkel and Perkel 1985; Miller et al. 1985; Shepherd et al. 1985). This suggests that a single processing unit might be identified not with an entire neuron but with a patch of membrane. The interaction between two active membrane patches owing to electrotonic conduction on the same dendritic branch is approximately symmetrical and is always excitatory. With nonlinear interactions in dendrites, many more processing units are available; however, this advantage is partially offset by the limited topological connectivity of dendritic trees.

Noise in the Nervous System

How can the probabilistic decision rule in equation 3 be implemented by neurons? In particular, how can the temperature be controlled? The membrane potential of a neuron is graded; however, if it exceeds a fairly sharp threshold, an action potential is produced, and this potential is followed by a refractory period of several milliseconds during which another action potential cannot be elicited. If Gaussian noise is added to the membrane potential, then even if the total synaptic input is below threshold there is a finite probability that the membrane potential will reach threshold. The amplitude of the Gaussian noise will determine the width of the sigmoidal probability distribution for the neuron to fire during a short time interval, and it therefore plays the role of temperature in the model. Surprisingly, a cumulative Gaussian is a very good approximation to the required probability distribution (equation 3), never differing by more than 1 percent over the entire range of inputs.

Intracellular recordings in the central nervous system reveal stochastic variability in the membrane potentials of most neurons, which is due in part to fluctuations in the transmitter released by presynaptic terminals. Other sources of noise may also be present and could be controlled by cellular mechanisms (Verveen and Derksen 1968; Holden 1976). If some sources of noise in the central nervous system are gated or modulated, it should be possible to experimentally identify them. For example, the noise could be regularly cycled, and this would be apparent in the massed activity. Alternatively, noise may always be present at a low level and be increased irregularly whenever there is an identified need.

In the visual cortex of primates, single neurons respond to the same visual stimulus with different sequences of action potentials on each trial (Sejnowski 1981). In order to measure a repeatable response, spike trains are typically averaged over ten trials. The result, called the poststimulus time histogram, gives the probability for a spike to occur as a function of the time after the onset of the stimulus. However, this averaging procedure removes all information about the variance of the noise, so that there is no way to determine whether the noise varies systematically during the response to the stimulus or perhaps on a longer time scale while the stimulus is being attended. Such measurements of the noise variance over a range of time scales could provide evidence that this parameter has an active role in neural processing.

There are two ways to view the sigmoidal probability rule used to update units (figure 5). Over a short time interval, it represents the probability for a single unit to "fire"; over longer time intervals, in equilibrium, it represents the average "firing rate" of a unit. The average firing rate of a neuron is generally regarded as the primary neural code in the brain; however, it cannot be accurately measured over short time intervals, particularly during nonstationary conditions. The probability for a spike to occur can be defined for intervals as short as a few milliseconds and is routinely measured by ensemble-averaging spike trains, as in the post-stimulus time histogram. The probabilistic interpretation of spike firing as an information code may be of more general usefulness than the average firing rate.

Symmetry, Simultaneity, and Time Delays

In a Boltzmann machine all connections are symmetrical. It is very unlikely that this assumption is strictly true of neurons in cerebral cortex. However, if the constraints of a problem are inherently symmetrical and if the network on average approximates the required symmetrical connectivity, then random asymmetries in a large network will be reflected as an increase in the Gaussian noise in each unit, in effect raising the temperature (Hopfield 1982). Systematic asymmetries that would lead to oscillations in the network would invalidate the qualitatively important feature of settling to a stable state of equilibrium.

The decision rule used in the simulations presented here was asynchronous, and updates were instantaneous. In the brain, several connected neurons may spike simultaneously within an interval of a few milliseconds. The time required for the transmission of a spike down the axon to the nerve terminal, for the release of neurotransmitter, and for postsynaptic integration can delay the signal's arrival in the spike-initiating zone of the target neuron by several milliseconds. In some simulations both simultaneous updates and transmission delays were included, and these appear to increase the noise in the system, effectively increasing the temperature (Sejnowski et al. 1985; Venkatasubramanian and Hinton 1985). At low temperatures these effects are less pronounced because the rate of flipping is lower; thus, simultaneous decisions and time delays contribute noise that could mimic annealing even without an explicit temperature control (Francis Crick, private communication). Time delays are especially effective at introducing noise, and a delay of one iteration (2,000 updates in these simultations) starting from a random state and running at $T = 1$ was almost as effective as the standard exponential annealing.

Learning in Cerebral Cortex and Boltzmann Machines

The values of weights between units for the two examples of networks discussed in this paper were chosen as much by trial and error as by plan. It would be desirable to have an automated procedure for incorporating the constraints from a given task domain in the weights. The evolution of cerebral cortex is closely linked to the ability of mammals to learn from experience and adapt to their environments; this adaptability may be the consequence of rules for modifying the strengths of cortical synapses.

A single weight between two units can be considered a "microscopic" variable in comparison with the "macroscopic" performance of the network. In general it is not possible in a network of nonlinear processing units to predict how changing a single weight will affect the overall performance. However, in a Boltzmann machine that has relaxed to equilibrium the weights between units and the probabilities of their global states are related by the Boltzmann distribution given in equation 4. Because each weight contributes independently to the energy, each weight also contributes independently in determining the relative probabilities of global states (Hinton and Sejnowski 1983). This simple probabilistic relationship makes possible a simple "microscopic" learning rule that automatically improves the "macroscopic" performance. The learning rule is similar to but different from the Hebb learning rule and has been successfully demonstrated for several small problems (Ackley et al. 1985; Hinton et al. 1984; Sejnowski et al. 1986).

Unlike the bulk of the brain, which is composed of many morphologically different nuclei, the cerebral cortex is relatively uniform in structure. Different areas of cerebral cortex (e.g. visual cortex, auditory cortex, and somatosensory cortex) are specialized for processing information from different sensory modalities, and other areas are specialized for motor functions; however, all these cortical areas are similar in anatomical organization, and they are more similar in cytoarchitecture to one another than to any other part of the brain.

The similarity between different areas of cerebral cortex suggests that massively parallel searches may also be performed in other cortical areas. Many problems in speech recognition, associative retrieval of information, and motor control can be formulated as searches. However, there is a serious obstacle that appears to prevent symmetric modules from modeling sequential information processing: At thermal equilibrium there can be no consistent sequences of states. It is tempting to use asymmetrical weights to produce sequences, but this would be incompatible with the central idea of performing searches by settling to equilibrium.

An alternative that we are exploring is sequential settlings in a hierarchy of asymmetrically connected modules. The result of each search could be considered a single step in a strictly serial process, with each search setting up boundary conditions for the next. An attractive possibility for speeding up sequential settlings is to cascade partial settlings so that an approximate solution for one module could be used to start the search for the next one up the line (McClelland 1979). Although there are some similarities between the organization of cerebral cortex and parallel stochastic search in Boltzmann machines, more experience with larger problems and a wider range of applications are needed before the general usefulness of this approach can be properly assessed (Fahlman et al. 1983).

Acknowledgment

This research was supported by grants from the System Development Foundation and a grant from the National Science Foundation (BNS-8351331) to T.J.S. We especially thank Paul Kienker, Lee Schumacher, and Tony Yang for their assistance with the simulations.

References

Ackley, D. H., G. E. Hinton, and T. J. Sejnowski. 1985. A learning algorithm for Boltzmann Machines. *Cognitive Sciences* 9: 147–169.

Arbib, M. A. 1975. Artificial intelligence and brain theory: Unities and diversities. *Annals of Biomedical Engineering* 3: 238–274.

Ballard, D. H., G. E. Hinton, and T. J. Sejnowski. 1983. Parallel visual computation. *Nature* 306: 21–26.

Bienenstock, E. 1985. Dynamics of central nervous system. In *Proceedings of the Workshop on Dynamics of Macrosystems*, ed. J. P. Aubin and K. Sigmund (Springer-Verlag).

Binder, K. 1978. *The Monte Carlo Method in Statistical Physics.* Springer-Verlag.

Burt, P. J. 1977. A procedure for evaluating cooperative models for stereopsis. *Brain Theory Newsletter* 3: 31–34.

Choi, M. Y., and B. A. Huberman. 1984. Digital simulation of magnetic systems. *Physical Review* B 29: 2796–2798.

Cragg, B. G., and H. N. V. Temperley. 1954. The organization of neurones: A cooperative analogy. *EEG and Clinical Neurophysiology* 6: 85–92.

Crick, F. H. C. 1984. The function of the thalamic reticular complex: The search-light hypothesis. *Proceedings of the National Academy of Sciences* 81: 4586–4590.

Danker, A. J., and A. Rosenfeld. 1981. Blob detection by relaxation. *IEEE Transactions on Pattern Analysis and Machine Intelligence* 3: 79–92.

Dev, P. 1975. Perception of depth surfaces in random-dot stereograms: A neural model. *International Journal of Man-Machine Studies* 7: 511–528.

Dosher, B. A., G. Sperling, and S. Wurst. 1985. Tradeoffs between stereopsis and proximity luminance covariance as determinants of perceived 3-D structure. *Vision Research* (in press).

Fahlman, S. E., G. E. Hinton, and T. J. Sejnowski. 1983. Massively parallel architectures for AI: NETL, THISTLE, and Boltzmann machines. In Proceedings of the National Conference on Artificial Intelligence, Washington D.C.

Feldman, J. A., and D. H. Ballard, 1982. Connectionist models and their properties. *Cognitive Science* 6: 205–254.

Geman, S., and D. Geman. 1984. Stochastic relaxation, Gibbs distributions, and the Bayesian restoration of images. *IEEE Transactions on Pattern Analysis and Machine Intelligence* 6: 721–741.

Grimson, W. E. L. 1981. *From Images to Surfaces.* MIT Press.

Hinton, G. E., and T. J. Sejnowski. 1983. Optimal perceptual inference. In Proceedings of the IEEE Computer Society Conference on Computer Vision and Pattern Recognition, Washington, D.C.

Hinton, G. E., T. J. Sejnowski, and D. Ackley. 1984. Boltzmann Machines: Constraint-Satisfaction Networks That Learn. Carnegie-Mellon Computer Science Technical Report CMU-CS-84-119.

Holden, A. V. 1976. *Models of the Stochastic Activity of Neurones* (Lecture Notes in Biomathematics 12). Springer-Verlag.

Hopfield, J. J. 1982. Neural networks and physical systems with emergent collective computational abilities. *Proceedings of the National Academy of Sciences* 79: 2554–2558.

Hummel, R. A., and S.W. Zucker. 1983. On the foundations of relaxation labeling processes. *IEEE Transactions on Pattern Analysis and Machine Intelligence* 5: 267–287.

Johnson, D. S., C. R. Aragon, L. A. McGeoch, and C. Schevon. 1986. Optimization by simulated annealing: and experimental evaluation. In preparation.

Julesz, B. 1971. *Foundations of Cyclopean Perception.* University of Chicago Press.

Kienker, P. K., T. J. Sejnowski, G. E. Hinton, and L. E. Schumacher. 1986. Separating figure from ground with a parallel network. *Perception* (in press).

Kirkpatrick, S. 1977. Frustration and ground-state degeneracy in spin glasses. *Physical Review* B 16: 4630–4641.

Kirkpatrick, S., D. D. Gelatt, and M. P. Vecchi. 1983. Optimization by simulated annealing. *Science* 220: 671–680.

Little, W. A., and G. L. Shaw. 1975. A statistical theory of short and long term memory. *Behav. Biol.* 14: 115–133.

Marr, D. 1982. *Vision.* Freeman.

Marr, D., and T. Poggio. 1976. Cooperative computation of stereo disparity. *Science* 194: 283–287.

Marr, D., and T. Poggio. 1979. A computational theory of human stereo vision. *Proc. Roy. Soc. Lond.* B 204: 301–328.

Marr, D., G. Palm, and T. Poggio. 1978. Analysis of a cooperative stereo algorithm. *Biological Cybernetics* 28: 223–239.

Mayhew, J. 1983. Stereopsis. In *Physical and Biological Processing of Images,* ed. O. J. Braddick and A. C. Sleigh (Springer-Verlag).

Mayhew, J. F. W., and J. P. Frisby. 1981. Psychological and computational studies towards a theory of human stereopsis. *Artificial Intelligence* 17: 349–385.

McClelland, J. 1979. On the time relations of mental processes: An examination of systems of processes in cascade. *Psychological Review* 86: 287–330.

Metropolis, N., A. Rosenbluth, M. Rosenbluth, A. Teller, and E. Teller. 1953. Equation of state calculations by fast computing machines. *J. Chem. Phys.* 21: 1987–1092.

Miller, J., W. Rall, and J. Rinzel. 1985. Synaptic amplification by active membrane in dendritic spines. *Brain Research* 325: 325–330.

Nelson, J. I. 1975. Globality and stereoscopic fusion in binocular vision. *J. Theor. Biol.* 49: 1–88.

Nishihara, H. K. 1984. PRISM: A Practical Real-Time Imaging Stereo Matcher. Memo 780, Artificial Intelligence Laboratory, Massachusetts Institute of Technology.

Perkel, D. H., and D. J. Perkel. 1985. Dendritic spines: Role of active membrane in modulating synaptic efficacy. *Brain Research* 325: 331–335.

Poggio, G. F., and T. Poggio. 1984. The analysis of stereopsis. *Ann. Rev. Neurosci.* 7: 379–412.

Prager, J. M. 1980. Extracting and labeling boundary segments in natural scenes. *IEEE Transactions on Pattern Analysis and Machine Intelligence* 2: 16–27.

Prazdny, K. 1985. Detection of binocular disparities. *Biological Cybernetics* 52: 387–395.

Rosenfeld, A., and G. J. Vanderbrug. 1977. *IEEE Transactions on Systems, Man, and Cybernetics* 7: 104–107.

Rubin, E. 1915. *Synoplevede Figurer.*

Schroedinger, E. 1946. *Statistical Thermodynamics.* Cambridge University Press.

Sejnowski, T. J. 1981. Skeleton filters in the brain. In *Parallel Models of Associative Memory,* ed. G. E. Hinton and J. A. Anderson (Erlbaum).

Sejnowski, T. J., P. K. Kienker, and G. E. Hinton. 1986. Learning symmetry groups with hidden units: Beyond the perceptron. *Physica* D (in press).

Shepherd, G. M., R. K. Brayton, J. P. Miller, I. Segev, J. Rinzel, and W. Rall. 1985. Signal enhancement in distal cortical dendrites by means of interactions between active dendritic spines. *Proc. Nat. Acad. Sci.* 82: 2192–2195.

Smolensky, P. 1983. Schema selection and stochastic inference in modular environments. In Proceedings of the National Conference on Artificial Intelligence, Washington, D.C.

Sperling, G. 1970. Binocular vision: A physical and neural theory. *J. Amer. Psych.* 83: 461–534.

Sperling, G., M. Pavel, Y. Cohen, M. S. Landy, and B. Schwartz. 1983. Image processing in perception and cognition. In *Physical and Biological Processing of Images,* ed. O. J. Braddick and A. C. Sleigh (Springer-Verlag).

Szeliski, R., and G. E. Hinton. 1985. In Proceedings of the IEEE Computer Society Conference on Computer Vision and Pattern Recognition.

Terzopoulos, D. 1984. Multiresolution Computation of Visible-Surface Representations. Ph.D. thesis, Massachusetts Institute of Technology.

Ullman, S. 1984. Visual routines. *Cognition* 18: 97–159.

Venkatasubramanian, V., and G. E. Hinton. 1985. On the Effects of Communication Time Delays in Boltzmann Machines. Unpublished.

Verveen, A. A., and H. E. Derksen. 1968. Fluctuation phenomenon in nerve membranes. *Proceedings of the IEEE* 56: 906–916.

von Neumann, J. 1966. *Theory of Self-Reproducing Automata,* ed. A. W. Burks (University of Illinois).

Waltz, D. 1975. Understanding line drawings of scenes with shadows. In *The Psychology of Computer Vision,* ed. P. H. Winston (McGraw-Hill).

Wolfram, S. 1983. Statistical mechanics of cellular automata. *Rev. Mod. Phys.* 55: 601–644.

Zucker, S. 1983. Computational and psychological experiments in grouping: Early orientation selection. In *Human and Machine Vision,* ed. J. Beck et al. (Academic).

Zucker, S. W., and R. A. Hummel. 1979. Toward a low-level description of dot clusters: Labeling edge, interior, and noise points. *Computer Graphics and Image Processing* 9: 213–233.

Contributors

Michael A. Arbib
University of Southern California

Dana H. Ballard
University of Rochester

Andrew G. Barto
University of Massachusetts, Amherst

Michael Brady
Oxford University

David Burr
University of Western Australia

Peter J. Burt
Radio Corporation of America
Princeton

Jerome A. Feldman
University of Rochester

Allen R. Hanson
University of Massachusetts, Amherst

Geoffrey E. Hinton
University of California, San Diego

Donald H. House
Williams College

Thea Iberall
Center for AI
Hartford

Martha Jay

Daryl Lawton
Advanced Decision Systems
Mountain View, California

Damian Lyons
Philips Laboratories
Briarcliff Manor, New York

Kenneth J. Overton
GE Corporate Research and Development
    Center
Schenectady

Joachim Rieger
Queen Mary College
London

Edward M. Riseman
University of Massachusetts, Amherst

David A. Robinson
Johns Hopkins Medical School

John Ross
University of Western Australia

Terrence J. Sejnowski
Johns Hopkins University

David L. Sparks
University of Alabama Medical Center
Birmingham

D. Nico Spinelli
University of Massachusetts, Amherst

Martha Steenstrup
Bolt, Beranek, & Newman, Inc.
Cambridge, Massachusetts

Arnold Trehub

John K. Tsotsos
University of Toronto

Naomi Weisstein

Eva Wong
University of Denver

Alan Yuille
Harvard University

Steven W. Zucker
McGill University

Index